Fear Not!
Is There Anything Too Hard For God?

*Trusting His Heart When
You Can't Trace His Hand*

Margaret Roberts Davis, PhD
Co-authored by the Holy Spirit

ASPECT Books
www.ASPECTBooks.com

World rights reserved. This book or any portion thereof may not be copied or
reproduced in any form or manner whatever, except as provided by law,
without the written permission of the publisher, except by a reviewer
who may quote brief passages in a review.

This book is sold with the understanding that the publisher is not engaged
in giving spiritual, legal, medical, or other professional advice.
If authoritative advice is needed, the reader should
seek the counsel of a competent professional

Copyright © 2011 Aspect Books
ISBN-13: 978-1-57258-712-0 (Paperback)
ISBN-13: 978-1-57258-713-7 (Ebook)
Library of Congress Control Number: 2011936837

Published by

ASPECT Books
www.ASPECTBooks.com

All scripture quotations, unless otherwise indicated, are taken from the King James Version Bible.

Scripture quotations marked AKJV are from the American King James Version. Used by permission.

Scripture quotations marked AMP are taken from the Amplified Bible, Copyright © 1954, 1958, 1962, 1964, 1965, 1987 by The Lockman Foundation. Used by permission.

Scripture quotations marked ASV are taken from the American Standard Version, Thomas Nelson and Sons, 1901. Public domain in the United States.

Scripture quotations marked BBE are from The Bible in Basic English, C.K. Ogden, Cambridge University Press, 1965. Public domain in the United States.

Scripture quotations marked Clear Word are taken from the The Clear Word. Texts credited to Clear Word are from The Clear Word, copyright © 1994 by Jack J. Blanco.

Scripture quotations marked (CEV) are from the Contemporary English Version Copyright © 1991, 1992, 1995 American Bible Society, Used by permission.

Scripture quotations marked (CEB) are from the Common English Bible. (c) Copyright 2011 by the Common English Bible. All rights reserved. Used by permission. (www.CommonEnglishBible.com).

Scripture quotations marked ESV are taken from The Holy Bible, English Standard Version® (ESV®), copyright © 2001 by Crossway, a publishing ministry of Good News Publishers. Used by permission. All rights reserved.

Scripture quotations marked GNB are taken from the Good News Bible © 1994 published by the Bible Societies/HarperCollins Publishers Ltd UK, Good News Bible © American Bible Society 1966, 1971, 1976, 1992. Used with permission.

Scripture quotations marked GSB are taken from the Geneva Study Bible. The 1599 Geneva Study Bible is in the public domain and may be freely used and distributed.

Scripture quotations marked GWT are taken from God's Word. GOD'S WORD is a copyrighted work of God's Word to the Nations. Quotations are used by permission. Copyright 1995 by God's Word to the Nations. All rights reserved.

Scripture quotations marked ISV are taken from the Holy Bible: International Standard Version®. Copyright © 1996-2008 by The ISV Foundation. ALL RIGHTS RESERVED INTERNATIONALLY. Used by permission.

Scripture quotations marked The Message are taken from THE MESSAGE. Copyright © by Eugene H. Peterson 1993, 1994, 1995, 1996, 2000, 2001, 2002. Used by permission of NavPress Publishing Group.

Scripture quotations marked NAB are taken from the New American Bible with Revised New Testament and Revised Psalms © 1991, 1986, 1970 Confraternity of Christian Doctrine, Washington, D.C. and are used by permission of the copyright owner. All Rights Reserved. No part of the New American Bible may be reproduced in any form without permission in writing from the copyright owner.

Scripture quotations marked NASB are taken from the New American Standard Bible®, Copyright © 1960, 1962, 1968, 1971, 1972, 1973, 1975, 1977, 1995 by The Lockman Foundation. Used by permission.

Scripture quotations marked "NCV™" are taken from the New Century Version®. Copyright © 2005 by Thomas Nelson, Inc. Used by permission. All rights reserved.

Scripture quotations marked NET are taken from NET Bible. Scripture quoted by permission. Quotations designated (NET) are from the NET Bible® copyright ©1996-2006 by Biblical Studies Press, L.L.C. http://bible.org All rights reserved

Scripture quotations marked NIV are taken from the Holy Bible, New International Version®, NIV®. Copyright ©1973, 1978, 1984 by Biblica, Inc.™ Used by permission of Zondervan. All rights reserved worldwide.

Scripture quotations marked "NKJV™" are taken from the New King James Version®. Copyright © 1982 by Thomas Nelson, Inc. Used by permission. All rights reserved.

Scripture quotations marked NLT are taken from the Holy Bible, New Living Translation, copyright © 1996, 2004, 2007 by Tyndale House Foundation. Used by permission of Tyndale House Publishers, Inc., Carol Stream, Illinois 60188. All rights reserved.

Scripture quotations marked NRSV are taken from New Revised Standard Version Bible, copyright 1989, Division of Christian Education of the National Council of the Churches of Christ in the United States of America. Used by permission. All rights reserved.

Scripture quotations marked TLB are taken from The Living Bible, copyright © 1971 by Tyndale House Publishers, Wheaton, Ill. Used by permission.

Scripture quotations marked TNIV are taken from the Holy Bible, Today's New International Version®. Copyright © 2001, 2005 by Biblica®. Used by permission of Biblica®. All rights reserved worldwide.

Scripture quotations marked WEB are from the World English Bible, Rainbow Missions, Inc. Public domain in the United States.

Scripture quotations marked YLT are from Young's Literal Translation, Robert Young, 1898. Public domain in the United States.

Dedication

To my mother, Anna Roberts, who, by precept and example, taught me to love the Lord.
To my grandson, Noah Sterling, a miracle, whose healing is a gift from God.
To my friend Edna O'Connor whose faith, courage, and spiritedness inspired me.

January 1

New Year's Resolution: Claiming the Source of My Peace

Now may the Lord of peace Himself give you peace always in every way. 2 Thess. 3:16, NKJV.

The alarm clock sounded at 5:30 a.m., awakening me to a hushed, peaceful morning in my bedroom sanctuary. This quiet hour allows me the time to reflect and converse with God. Briefly, I am ushered into His presence, surrounded with serenity. But at 6:30 a.m. the morning news jolts me back to reality with the images of war, violence, calamities, economic woes, and evil human predators.

In this spiraling out-of-control world, we cannot avoid evil people or their wicked actions and dreadful events. The Bible verifies it. We shall have tribulation (John 16:33), and tumultuous events will occur (Matt. 24:6) until Jesus returns and ushers in everlasting peace (John 14:27). But the Bible assures us that, "when the storm has swept by, the wicked are gone, but the righteous stand firm forever" (Prov. 10:25, NIV). And whoever heeds God's Word will dwell safely without fear of evil (Prov. 1:33). Thus, my present and everlasting peace depends on my choices (1 Tim. 6:11, 12).

Therefore, I am determined to say no to wickedness and to pursue righteousness. The wicked rebel against the light and stray from its paths (Job 24:13). Thus, I resolve to have clean hands and a pure heart (Ps. 24:4, 5).

I am determined to say no to ungodliness and seek godliness. The ungodly have not "crucified the flesh with its passions and desires" (Gal. 5:24, NIV). Godliness is having the mind of Christ (Phil. 2:5). Thus, I resolve to have the mind of Christ and to love the Lord with all my heart, soul, mind, and strength and to love my neighbor as myself (Luke 10:27).

I am determined to say no to distrust and bolster my faith in the Word. Thus, I resolve that, since God is my salvation, I will not be afraid. He is my strength and song (Isa. 12:2).

I am determined to say no to dropping out of the race for eternity and endure until my time on earth ends or until Jesus returns. Thus, I resolve to set the Lord always before me. Because He is at my right hand, I will not be shaken or moved (Ps. 16:8).

I am determined to say no to discord, coarseness, and fits of rage and to demonstrate the character of Christ. Thus, I resolve to put on a heart of compassion, kindness, love, humility, gentleness, and patience, and to forgive my neighbor as God forgives me (Col. 3:12, 13).

I resolve to follow Jesus wherever He leads. Will you?

January 2

Deliverance From Fear

I sought the LORD, and he heard me, and delivered me from all my fears. Ps. 34:4.

Fear is a long-lived monster. It has afflicted humanity since Adam and Eve disobeyed God's Word and ate fruit from the forbidden tree. When "the LORD God called to the man, 'Where are you?' He answered, "'I heard your voice in the garden, and I was afraid because I was naked; so I hid" (Gen. 3:9, 10). Fear is "an ancient and universal emotion," a sensation of danger of impending dread, and it can result from sin—Adam's fear emanated from the sin of disobedience.

As is typical today, and as was evident with Adam's response, fear usually begins with some type of stressful internal or external stimuli and culminates in the release of chemicals that produce shallow, quick breathing, a racing heart, and energized muscles that prepare our bodies to fight or flight. Walter Cannon, a Harvard physiologist, discovered this response and proved that it is a part of our genetic makeup and is necessary to keep us from harm and danger. Dizziness, headaches, insomnia, and exhaustion among other physical problems accompany intense fear. And along with the physical symptoms are agitated states of mind like anxiety, terror, horror, and panic or even nightmares.

Adam knew that a negative consequence would follow his disobedience—he feared it and ran from God. We can only imagine what horrors assailed Adam's mind as he waited for the repercussions. Obviously, he worried profusely about the "You shall surely die" warning given by God in the Garden of Eden. And doubtless, Adam's fear spanned the continuum from dread to terror as he waited for God's return to the Garden.

The Greek define "fear" three ways. *Eulabeia* is a reverential respect, evoking feelings of awe as in "fear God and give glory to Him" (Rev. 14:7). *Phobeo*, from which the English word "phobia" is derived, means a fear that causes one to be shocked or amazed. When the angel appeared to Joseph in a dream after Mary had conceived by the Holy Spirit, he was told, "Do not be afraid to take Mary as your wife" (Matt. 1:40, NASB). And, *deilia* means to be timid or a coward: "For God hath not given us the spirit of fear; but of power, and of love" (2 Tim. 1:7).

Adam experienced the latter. And the very One he needed in this ordeal, he purposely avoided because of this fear. Clearly, disobedience opened Adam up for Satan to control his mind and instill a spirit of fear. But God can deliver us from all our fears and replace them with a spirit of power, love, and a disciplined mind.

To banish fear from settling in, draw closer to God, trust His Word, and gather strength from His presence. Claim the unfailing Word of God that says, "The LORD is my light and my salvation; whom shall I fear? the LORD is the strength of my life; of whom shall I be afraid?" (Ps. 27:1).

January 3

The Battle is the Lord's

Thus says the LORD to you, Do not fear or be dismayed because of this great multitude, for the battle is not yours but God's. 2 Chron. 20:15, NASB.

Satan is a smooth operator. From our earliest history, he began his efforts to deceive humanity. After inciting rebellion in heaven and being expelled, he determined to connect with humanity to fight against God's government. Adam and Eve were perfectly happy under the law of God, but Satan wanted to ruin their happiness. He worked hard to cause the first couple to sin and fall from grace. Diabolically, he planned to separate them from God and take control of the earth as his territory, standing in total defiance of His Creator.[1]

The battle between good and evil has raged on earth for more than 6,000 years, but, paradoxically, Jesus won the battle thousands of years ago. Satan's plan against Adam and Eve trumped on only one critical point. He won the battle to tempt Adam and Eve to sin, but he lost the war to Jesus at the cross, fulfilling the prophecy that his head would be crushed. Meanwhile he is in a frenzy to inflict as many fatal wounds on humanity as possible before he takes his last breath (Gen. 3:16).

But Satan is powerless to overpower us without our permission. The Bible says, "Submit yourselves, then, to God. Resist the devil, and he will flee from you. Come near to God and he will come near to you" (James 4:7, 8). But the power to resist is conditional—it comes from obedience to the laws and commandments of God and from complete submission to His will. If we are unable to forgive offenses, if we sin willfully, or if we harbor thoughts of revenge and hatred, Satan establishes residence in our minds and takes control, blocking our resistance.

Yes, "the battle is not yours but God's." However, the Lord will not defend us if we commit treason against His kingdom while in the enemy's camp by submitting to Satan's will. In so doing, we become traitors to the kingdom of God. Unless we are loyal, vigilant soldiers in His army, fully clothed with His armor, He will not fight our battles. So, "be strong in the Lord, and in the power of his might. Put on the whole armour of God, that ye may be able to stand against the wiles of the devil" (Eph. 6:10).

Why foolishly cling to the losing side when the battle is already won? Put on the belt of truth as a reminder that Jesus is the way, the truth, and the life; slip on the breastplate of righteousness, grateful that Jesus covers us with His virtue; step into shoes of peace, prepared to take the gospel message to others; brandish the shield of faith and trust that God will never abandon us; secure the helmet of salvation, which is our guarantee of deliverance in Jesus Christ; and clutch the sword of the spirit, which is the Word of God. Then you will be victorious over that scheming, crafty devil.

January 4

God Is Always With Us

Do not be afraid, for I am with you; I will bless you. Gen. 26:24, NIV.

A benevolent, unselfish shāh, who showed kindness toward his people, once ruled the land of Persia. One day he disguised himself as a poor man and visited the public baths, journeying to the cellar where the bathwaters were heated in the furnace and sitting down beside the man who stoked the fires. The shāh befriended the lonely man and even ate the same simple food. Daily the ruler visited the poor man who became attached to the shāh.

One day the shāh revealed his true identity, expecting the man to seek something of monetary value from him. Instead, the poor man looked long into his leader's face, and with love and wonder in his voice, he said, "You left your palace and your glory to sit with me in this dark place, to eat my coarse food, and to care about what happens to me. On others you may bestow rich gifts, but to me you have given yourself!"[2]

Likewise, God emptied heaven for us and gave of Himself in the person of His Son, Jesus. Obviously, after that precious, unparallel investment, nothing can remove His love from us (Rom. 8:35). "He who resided in Heaven, co-equal and co-eternal with the Father and the Spirit, willingly descended into our world. He breathed our air, felt our pain, knew our sorrows, and died for our sins. He didn't come to frighten us, but to show us the way to warmth and safety."[3]

Immanuel, translated "God with us," holds manifold blessings for His anointed (Isa 7:14). The eternal, immortal God has been with us since Creation, but when He divested Himself of His divinity, packed up and moved to earth as a baby physically living among us, He partook of the troubles inherent in a sinful world. Having lived in the trenches with us, He both sympathizes with our weaknesses and identifies with our trials and temptations, for He was tempted in all things as we are (Heb. 4:15). In the trenches, we daily walk in the valley of darkness, death, and troubles, the Lord's spiritual presence is always near to comfort us and allay our fears (Ps. 23:4).

As Jesus' sojourn on earth came to a close, He promised His disciples that He would send a Substitute who could be everywhere at once (John 16:7). And He did. David asks, "Where can I go from your Spirit? Where can I flee from your presence?" (Ps. 139:7, NIV). That is how all-pervasive He is (Ps. 139:7).

When we submit to His Lordship, the Holy Spirit burrows deep inside our hearts as a living reminder of His abiding presence. "'Am I only a God nearby,' declares the LORD, 'and not a God far away? Who can hide in secret places so that I cannot see them?' declares the LORD. 'Do not I fill heaven and earth?' declares the LORD" (Jer. 23:23, 24, NIV).

When it appears that our world is spinning out of control, it is comforting to know that He who is a prayer away and who came where we are is a divine source of peace.

January 5

Complete in Christ Jesus

Peace be with you, do not be afraid. Your God ... has given you treasure in your sacks. Gen. 43:23, NKJV.

Oil tycoon John D. Rockefeller, the first American worth more than a billion dollars, was once asked how much wealth he needed to be happy. He responded, "Another million dollars." Unaware that neither money, nor fame nor power brings peace or happiness, he speaks foolishness. Apparently, then he had not yet sought the peace that comes from a loving, intimate relationship with Jesus whose birth prompted the angels to exclaim "Peace and good tidings on earth." Carnal happiness, as Rockefeller describes, is based on external circumstances that bring a momentary feeling that easily slips away.

In contrast, the Beatitudes point to a treasure trove of lasting joy. "Happy the poor in spirit — because theirs is the reign of the heavens. Happy the mourning — because they shall be comforted. Happy the meek — because they shall inherit the land. Happy those hungering and thirsting for righteousness — because they shall be filled. Happy the kind — because they shall find kindness. Happy the clean in heart — because they shall see God. Happy the peacemakers — because they shall be called Sons of God. Happy those persecuted for righteousness' sake — because theirs is the reign of the heavens. Happy are ye whenever they may reproach you, and may persecute, and may say any evil thing against you falsely for my sake — rejoice ye and be glad, because your reward [is] great in the heavens, for thus did they persecute the prophets who were before you" (Matt 5:3-12, YLT).

How complete we are in Jesus, who promises to supply all our needs, is a measure of happiness. Completeness stems from a spiritual union between Jesus, through His Spirit and the believer comparable to the oneness between Jesus and His Father or the ideal union between husband and wife. Jesus says, "I and My father are one" (John 10:30). Separate Beings, they are one in purpose, will, and nature. Trust, love, obedience, and the mutual exclusion of others highlight intimate relationships that define completeness.

Wholly complete in Jesus, we find peace even in suffering and troubles. At times, the trials are sizzling hot and the waters are at flood level; sometimes we are disappointing or disappointed. At times, we cry and grieve and complain, but nothing can keep us permanently down if we trust Jesus for the reason and the relief. Trusting in ourselves or our circumstances or another finite being, we become anxious and fearful. So step out of the way and prayerfully allow God to handle the uncertainties of life and the problems that wreck your peace. Remember, the "mind of sinful man governed by the flesh is death, but the mind governed by the Spirit is life and peace" (Rom. 8:6 NIV).

Genuine happiness and peace, then, are the treasures in our sack when we are complete in Jesus.

January 6

God Inhabits Praise

You will not have to fight this battle ... stand firm and see the deliverance the LORD will give you.... Do not be afraid; do not be discouraged. 2 Chron. 20:17.

Jennifer LaMountain tells of a little boy who sang regularly to his unborn sister. But complications arose during her birth, leaving the baby critically ill. Her brother begged to visit the baby, but the doctors cautioned the parents not to bring him to the neonatal intensive care unit. However, the day the doctors gave up hope, the parents determined to let her little brother visit. They marched him in dressed in scrubs, and he proceeded to sing, "You are my Sunshine," the tune he had sung while she was in the womb. The baby rallied at the familiar voice, and doctors released her the next day.

Songs of praise and worship are powerful weapons and have been used successfully to uplift, comfort, or defeat the enemies of God's children. It has been said that music soothes depression and faith rebounds with songs of praise and worship. Likewise, evil thoughts flee with songs of praise and worship, as evidenced by Saul's peace after David sang and played the harp (1 Sam. 16:23). Words of praise and worship are tantamount to a rousing sermon, touching the core of our being and raising our focus to heavenly things. Words and songs of praise and worship encourage us, inspire us, comfort us, strengthen us, motivate us.

Godly men appointed by King Jehoshaphat sang, "Give thanks to the LORD, for his love endures forever," while marching at the head of the army after they had prayed and fasted. As they sang praises, the Lord ambushed and defeated their enemies—the Ammonites, Moabites, and Meunites—who had confidently invaded Judah. Confused by unseen forces, these allies annihilated each other without Israel breaking a sweat (2 Chron. 20:20-23)!

Paul and Silas not only found comfort in singing songs of worship and praise, but also their worship so impressed their jailer that he accepted Jesus as his Savior. Stripped and beaten savagely and thrown in prison, "at midnight Paul and Silas prayed, and sang praises unto God: and the prisoners heard them" (Acts 16:25, NIV). Their singing preceded an earthquake, causing all the prison doors to open and loosen their chains. Frightened for his life, the jailer almost committed suicide which Paul and Silas prevented. Then he fell trembling before them and asked, "Sirs, what must I do to be saved" (verse 30).

Martin Luther wrote, "Music is a fair and lovely gift of God ... Music drives away the devil and makes people happy ... Next after theology I give to music the highest place and the greatest honor.... We know that to the devils music is distasteful and insufferable. My heart bubbles up and overflows in response to music, which has so often refreshed me."[4] God truly does inhabit our praise. When walking in shadows and doubt, lift your voice in songs of praise and feel the hand of God brush away the spider webs of darkness. Your spirits will be boosted as your focus returns to Him.

January 7

He Canceled Our Sin Debt

Fear ye not; stand still and see the salvation of the LORD. Ex.14:13.

Tetelestai is a contemporary musical presented by the Cleveland Performing Arts Ministries that portrays the week in Jesus' life culminating in His death on the cross. "It is finished," Jesus' final words before He died, are translated from the Greek word *tetelestai,* which also means paid in full. In ancient Israel debtors were given a certificate of debt by their debtors. When the debt was paid in full, the debtor wrote *tetelestai* across the top of the document and nailed it above the threshold of his door, proving that he fully met his obligation.

Tetelestai is one of the most glorious phrases humanity will ever hear. *Tetelestai*—our salvation is secured. *Tetelestai*—our sin debt is paid in full by the sinless Son of God. When we were dead in our transgressions, He made us alive together with Him, having forgiven all our transgressions, having canceled the certificate of debt which was hostile to us, and removed it. It was nailed above the cross, signaling that He fully satisfied the debt (Col. 2:13, 14).

Salvation is a precious gift. We cannot earn it or buy it, but we are blessed recipients of God's amazing grace. "For it is by grace you have been saved through faith … ; it is the gift of God—not of works" (Eph. 2:.8, 9 NIV). The penalty for sin had to be met since God's Word says that the wages of sin is death and that the remission of sins demands the shedding of blood (Rom. 3:23, 6:23; Heb. 9:22). Because God loves us so much, He provided a Substitute to satisfy every aspect of His requirements. Jesus, the sacrificial offering, shed His blood and bore our sins even while we as sinners rejected and dishonored Him.

Satan darkens the mind and lulls the unwary into a sense of safety, even when their eternal good is at stake. He lies to keep them in bondage as slaves to sin by blinding their minds "so that they cannot see the light of the gospel" (2 Cor. 4:4). Failing to read and study the Word and walking independent of the Holy Spirit leaves us vulnerable to Satan's deceptions. Simply believing that we are good people is not enough to warrant eternal life—salvation requires a life change and a commitment to obedience.

The greatest mistake in life is to neglect salvation because this life is over in a few decades or less, but eternity is limitless. Why die when Jesus has already died for us? There is a word for people who would do that—foolish—for fools despise wisdom and instruction (Prov. 1:7) and will die disinherited and subject to God's wrath.

Jesus is the way to salvation, the bridge of righteousness spread across the snares placed before us by Satan. He is the truth, the Word made flesh. And the truth frees us from bondage to sin. He is the life—God so loved us that He sacrificed Jesus, His only Son, who endured humiliation, pain, and rejection so we can share His inheritance. What incomparable love! Jesus saves to the utmost.

January 8

Tested By God, Never Tempted

Do not fear, for God has come to test you, that the fear of him may be before you, that you may not sin. Ex. 20:20, ESV.

Several women studying the book of Malachi were interested in what the following statement meant regarding the ways of God: "He shall sit as a refiner and purifier of silver" (Mal. 3:3). One of the women found a silversmith who allowed her to observe him at work. As she watched, he held a piece of silver close to the fire and explained that in refining silver one needed to hold the silver in the middle of the fire where the flames are hottest to burn away all the impurities but must keep his eyes fixed to the silver. For if the silver is unattended even a moment too long in the flames, it is destroyed. The woman asked, "How do you know when the silver is fully refined?" He answered, "When I see my image in it."[5]

Testing and tempting are fundamentally different. Satan tempts us, not God. "Let no one say when he is tempted, 'I am being tempted by God'; for God cannot be tempted by evil, and He Himself does not tempt anyone" (James 1:13, NASB). Satan is that ancient serpent responsible for successfully tempting our first parents and leading the whole world astray (Rev. 12:9). Tempting us to do evil, to doubt, or to despair is the way Satan frames and fills in his days. Day and night, night and day, he and/or his co-demons stalk us at every turn in an attempt to steal our joy and our eternal salvation. That is why we are warned to stay vigilant through prayer and to stay aware of his tactics through the Word (1 Peter 5:8).

Love moves God to test us. Psalm 11:5 states, "The LORD trieth the righteous" for several reasons. For one, it builds our patience and our faith—two essentials for our survival in this fallen world (James 1:2, 3). And the stretching of our faith expands our spiritual growth. God also tests us to purify us and to open our eyes to our spiritual frailties as His eyes pierce to the marrow of the bone. This testing is compared to the refiner's fire that removes dross from silver. Job 23:10 says, "He knoweth the way that I take: when he hath tried me, I shall come forth as gold." Painful, but necessary, testing is crucial to the success of our spiritual transformation. Without the tests we cannot pinpoint the character flaws and work to overhaul them.

Turning dross-covered silver into pure and valuable silver calls for lava-hot temperatures to cleanse the ingrained impurities. Likewise, the character purification process calls for extreme heat in the form of suffering to melt down the "old man" and remold us into the image of Jesus. Melting and molding are agonizing and lengthy processes that God uses at times to gauge the substance of our faith. "So when your faith remains strong through many trials, it will bring you much praise and glory and honor on the day when Jesus Christ is revealed to the whole world" (1 Peter 1:7, NLT).

Those who pass the tests are blessed with untold graduation gifts, including a crown of life placed on their heads by King Jesus (James 1:12).

January 9

Do Not Miss Out on Heaven

Seek the LORD while He may be found; call on Him while He is near. Isa. 55:6, NKJV.

Vivian told her sister a dream many years ago that troubled Vivian for a moment but clung unshakably to her sister's mind. In her dream Vivian approached the front of her family church where she saw several family members ascending slowly to heaven with Jesus. Quickly, running toward the ascending group, Vivian jumped up as high as she could several times in a futile attempt to clutch somebody or something to rise with them. Each time she jumped, she missed and fell back to the ground. With agony of spirit, she watched them disappear in the clouds—she was left behind.

God mercifully gave Vivian a vivid picture of her dark future if she does not seek Him while He can be found. Lamentably, years later she is still spiritually blind, for Satan has done a thorough work on her as on all unbelievers. The "god of this world hath blinded the minds of them which believe not" (2 Cor. 4:4). The bliss of eternal life, an abundant life on earth, and the love of Jesus hold no weight. The Holy Spirit does not dwell in the heart of unbelievers; therefore, things of the Spirit are foolishness to them. Spiritual things are not understood because they can only be comprehended through spiritual eyes (1 Cor. 2:14). Thus, Satan easily dupes unbelievers by closing their eyes to the truth of salvation and by cushioning the awful impact of rejecting God.

Jesus reaches down from heaven through His servants, His Word, and the Holy Spirit, earnestly pleading with His wayward children to turn to Him before the day of no return. "Declares the Sovereign LORD, I take no pleasure in the death of the wicked, but rather that they turn from their ways and live. Turn! Turn from your evil ways! Why will you die…?" (Eze. 33:11, NIV). He begs all unbelievers to accept the free gift of salvation and the packages that frame the gift. These packages contain a bright future, a peaceful present, and a refuge in the time of trouble. Contrast that with the darkness of a future with Satan who himself has a fiery end coming (Rev. 20:10).

Seeking God is one of the wisest things we will ever do. He promises that "those that seek me early shall find me" (Prov. 8:17). Backsliders, unbelievers, and half-hearted Christians, seek Him today. Confess and forsake your sins; ask Him to be the Lord of your life. Seek Him through His Word. Then, start your day with inspired Words of comfort, guidance and reproof to guide you along the narrow path of righteousness. Seek Him daily through prayer, anywhere and anytime, He is waiting and listening.

"Seek the LORD and His strength, seek His face continually" (1 Chron. 16:11)! The world as we know it will end upon Jesus' return (Matt.16:27). No one knows the day or hour, not even the angels in heaven—only the Father (Matt. 24:36). Moreover, God said, "My Spirit will not contend with man forever" (Gen. 6:3, NIV). What on earth are you waiting for? Do not hang back another second in the grip of the evil one who hates you. Call on the Lord, submit to Him, and beat the devil at his game.

January 10

God Cannot Lie

Only do not rebel against the LORD, nor fear the people of the land, for they are our bread; their protection has departed from them, and the LORD is with us. Do not fear them. Num. 14:9, NKJV.

We make a marked distinction between a little white lie and a lie or black lie. The phrase "white lie" was first introduced in 1741. An article in *The Gentleman's Magazine* stated, "A certain Lady of the highest Quality ... makes a judicious Distinction between *a white Lie and a black Lie*. A white Lie is That which is not intended to injure any Body in his Fortune, Interest, or Reputation but only to gratify a garrulous Disposition and the Itch of amusing People by telling Them wonderful Stories." A white lie, albeit a lie, is uttered without a malicious intent unlike a black lie which is intended to harm or cover-up. But, "White lies [soon] introduce others of a darker complexion."[6]

White or black, lying is condemned by God, the Creator whose essence is truth, thus God does not lie. Conversely, Satan is a liar and the father of lies. Hence, when we doubt God's Word, we infer that He, who is truth, is a liar and accept lies as truth from the father of lies. The Bible tells us that unbelief is sin (John 16:9) and proceeds from an evil heart (Heb. 3:12) and a hard heart (Mark 16:14); if we do not believe, we call God a liar (1 John 5:10) and deny His power (Ps. 78:19, 20).

God *does* not lie. "God is not a man, that He should lie, nor a son of man, that He should repent. Has He said, and will He not do it? Or has He spoken, and will He not make it good?" (Num. 23:19, NASB). He personifies the highest form of goodness—an aggressive goodness aimed at His treasured possessions. This goodness overflows His Being. Merciful and gracious, His heart of compassion reaches out, willing His children to trust Him enough to enter His rest. We will not enter His rest without believing His promises, which are as faithful as He.

Obviously, God *cannot* lie (Titus 1:1, 2). Humanity may speak lies with flattering lips or great words with a heart full of deceit, uttering promises that are impossible to keep, but "the words of the LORD are pure words: as silver tried in a furnace of earth, purified seven times" (Ps. 12:6). And God's Word is preserved forevermore with no possibility of change, for Jesus promised, "Heaven and earth shall pass away, but my words shall not pass away" (Matt. 24:35). They are truly carved in stone.

Clearly it is *impossible* for God to lie (Heb. 6:18). Thus, when God promises that our enemies are unable to harm His anointed, believe Him. Look not at your circumstances with fear and give credence to the father of lies. Do not believe his false report and rebel against God in your unbelief. Look upon your circumstances with eyes of faith and be reminded that the LORD is your protection, and success is assured. Let your mantra be "God said it. I believe it. That settles it!" And fear not.

January 11

Cause and Effect

The LORD has taken away your punishment, he has turned back your enemy. The LORD ... is with you; never again will you fear any harm. Zeph. 3:15, NIV.

Newton's third law of physics states that for every action, there is an equal and opposite reaction—"The size of the forces on the first object equals the size of the force on the second object. The direction of the force on the first object is opposite to the direction of the force on the second object. Forces always come in pairs - equal and opposite action-reaction force pairs."[7] Imagine, the size of the force of a tiny bug that hits the windshield of a tractor-trailer truck equals the size of the force of the truck!

This law is equal to cause and effect, where an action or event will produce a certain response to the action in the form of another event. For example, sinful natures result in sinning people. "People do not come into this world good and then get a sinful nature upon their first willful sin.... Rather, we come into the world with a sin nature and all of our sins are a *result* of having that sin nature. We act according to our natures."[8]

Our first earthly parents assumed the nature of Satan—a liar, thief, and murderer—when they rebelled against God (Rom. 5:12). From henceforth, their tainted DNA pollutes the gene pool of all subsequent generations. We not only possess sinful natures at birth, but also at conception (Ps. 51:5). Our natures are as sinful as our natural hearts are inherently deceitful, contaminated and incurable (Jer. 17:9). Draped in our aberrant nature and attached to carnal desires, we are Satan's slaves.

By sacrificing His life, Jesus drafted a spiritual Emancipation Proclamation and signed it with His blood to address the plight of those bound by sin and bowed down by guilt. Similar to the mandate signed by Lincoln to free literal slaves in the South, Jesus grants freedom to spiritual slaves from sin. He proclaimed, "The Spirit of the Lord GOD is upon me, because the LORD has anointed me to bring good news to the afflicted; He has sent me to bind up the brokenhearted, to proclaim liberty to captives and freedom to prisoners" (Isa. 61:1, NASB).

His death brings life as "Salvation is found in no one else, for there is no other name under heaven given to men by which we must be saved" (Acts 4:12, NIV). Holy and sinless, Jesus fully paid our sin debt. And everyone who hears the Word and believes in the Father who sent Jesus "has everlasting life, and shall not come into judgment, but has passed from death to life" (John 5:24, NKJV). And through baptism, we shed the outward mantle of sin (Acts 2:38). The act of baptism, by total immersion, symbolizes Jesus' death, burial, and resurrection and also symbolizes our spiritual death and rebirth.

Although our DNA is contaminated by sin, our hearts can be purged of sin, sanitized by Jesus' blood and covered in His righteousness, removing the threat of eternal punishment. That is divine cause and effect.

January 12

Let Go and Let God

And the LORD said ..., Fear him not: for I have delivered him into thy hand, and all his people, and his land. Num. 21:34.

Let go and let God is a short pithy phrase with a tall silhouette and immeasurable impact. When the quicksand generated by unwise choices and disobedience is sucking us under, let go and let God. When the suffering is so overwhelming that it takes our breath away, let go and let God. When wrong habits and evil companions wreck our dreams and our finances, let go and let God. And when worry and fear are constant companions, let go and let God. Let go of handling it independently, and surrender fully to the God who loves you. He will deliver you.

Our enemies—sometimes human and sometimes circumstances, poverty, sickness, death and fear, among others—are everywhere. These enemies are bigger and more powerful than we. Incredibly, we expend energy and emotions trying to manage them, ignoring God's promise to deliver them into our hands. As Christians we mouth the words that God is in control, but our actions speak volumes louder. At times, we hand over our enemies to Him, but we snatch all or part of them back. Because we are unable or unwilling to let God take full control, we evolve into quivering, depressed messes.

Typically, we worry about things we cannot change. Faith and trust plead with us to let go and let God, but doubt grips us around the heart. Upon accepting Jesus as our Lord and Savior, we commit to let Him take control over our life. Far in advance of our existence, God sketched and planned the outline for our lives, brightly colored with a future and a hope (Jer. 29:11). He promises that the steps of a righteous person are ordered by Him who makes no mistakes (Ps. 37:23). In ordering our steps, He personally guides us through, not around, our problems and setbacks. Going through them profits our faith and the outcome benefits us.

To let go and let God is placing absolute trust in Him. "Trust indicates a depth and a sense of assurance that is based on strong but not logically-conclusive evidence, or based on the character, ability, or truth shown by someone or something … Trust makes for a sense of being safe or of being free of fear, enough so your focus can be on other matters because that matter is taken care of. It becomes easier to simply *enjoy* life."[9] Without trust, full surrender is impossible.

The wisest man on earth counseled us to trust in the Lord with all our heart, to denounce our own defective understanding, to acknowledge God as Lord and Savior, and to let Him direct our paths (Prov. 3:5). Jeremiah, to whom God spoke directly, advised us to not depend on ourselves because "it is not in man that walketh to direct his steps" (Jer. 10:23). Finite and shortsighted, we are not capable or competent enough to go in the right direction. When we relinquish control and wait patiently, we will find rest in Him. Let go and let God perfectly fight all our battles (Ps. 37:7).

January 13

Encouraging Words

Do not fear him, for I [the Lord] have delivered him and his people and his land into your hand. Deut. 3:2, NASB.

A group of frogs were traveling through the woods and two fell into a deep pit. The other frogs gathered and observed the deep pit and advised the two fallen frogs that escape was hopeless. Ignoring the comments, the fallen frogs tried valiantly to climb out. But the counseling friends pressured them to succumb to their fate. Finally, one of the fallen frogs internalized the counsel, fell down and died. The surviving frog jumped even harder and finally escaped. The frog friends asked him if he had heard them. He explained that he was deaf and thought they were encouraging him.

Encouraging words are words of life whereas a destructive word can tear down the vulnerable as well as the strong. Be careful to uplift. Even in the midst of what must have been his greatest disappointment, Moses, whom God banned from entering Canaan because he disobediently struck the rock at Meribah, encouraged Joshua to fear not the enemy and instead claim God as his sword and shield. God had told him to speak to the rock to bring forth water, but the Israelites had severed the nerve of Moses' last shred of patience with their complaining and murmuring, moving him to strike the rock and speak words that misrepresented his power.

Told by God that he would die before entering the Promised Land, Moses meekly and uncomplainingly transferred to Joshua the responsibility of leading the large community of "stiff-necked" people into a land without a welcome mat. In fact, the Israelites had to seize the Promised Land because God requires us to do our faith walk before He fights for us. So put your faith where your fear is.

Joshua was surely intimidated by the responsibility ahead of him after experiencing the anger, ingratitude, and unconverted hearts of the majority of Israelites. But Moses encouraged him by reciting God's past faithfulness and protection. He reminded Joshua how God had delivered a previous king into their hands stating, "you shall do to him just as you did to Sihon king of the Amorites, who dwelt at Heshbon" (Deut 3:2). The many times and many ways God has delivered us in the past is assurance of future victories.

There is power of life and death in the tongue. An encouraging word to one who is down is uplifting, whisking away shadows and ushering in the sun. The Bible says to encourage one another, build each other up, and apply the Golden Rule (1 Thess. 5:1; Matt. 7:12). It is easy to speak words that harm, wound, and provoke to anger or with an evil intent, but the "mouth of a righteous man is a well of life" (Prov. 10:11).

Speak life to those who cross your path as you would have them speak to you, for words can be powerful tools for good. And strive to be that Christ-like person whose words bring comfort, instruction, and improvement.

January 14

If God be for You

Today you are going into battle against your enemies. Do not be fainthearted or afraid; do not be terrified or give way to panic before them. Deut. 20:3, NIV.

"Pure mathematics is, in its way, the poetry of logical ideas," wrote Albert Einstein, a genius in physics. But divine math turns this notion on its head. From our perspective, divine mathematics is totally illogical in that by dividing you get more, not less. Jesus' disciples discovered this when Jesus divided the fish and loaves (Matt. 15:36-38). Divine math achieves what our human experience tells us is impossible as the widow of Zarephath discovered when she gave her last trace of flour and oil to Elijah (1 Kings 17:14-16).

No matter how small the minority of God's people, the mathematical impact is supernaturally one-sided when God is for us. Divine math is a great equalizer, for God plus you equal a majority. For instance, the Israelites were vastly outnumbered by the Midianites, but they triumphed, not by might, nor by power, but by God's Spirit (Zech. 4:6). God demonstrated divine math once again by whittling down Gideon's 32,000-member army to 300 soldiers to wage a victorious battle against a Midianite army of 135,000. Gideon's battle against the Midianites is a powerful example of the might of God and God alone as opposed to the might of human numbers (Judges 7).

Gideon trusted in God's math after being assured by a prophetic dream whose interpretation was given to an enemy soldier. When Gideon heard the telling of the dream and its interpretation, he worshiped God and then encouraged the troops. Returning to the camp before the battle began, he commanded, "Arise, for the LORD has delivered the camp of Midian into your hand" (Judges 7:15, NKJV). God is compassionate and merciful, ever cognizant of our weak, human frame. Since Gideon was a peaceable thresher of wheat and not a soldier, God bolstered his faith. Gideon, encouraged that God had already won the battle, went forth courageously with his fear in check and his faith swathed in peace and security.

With God as an ally, even better, with God as Captain of our lives, we have nothing to fear. Paul reminds us, "If God is for us, who can be against us?" (Rom. 8:31, NIV). Creator and sustainer of all things, and so great in power and authority even the wind and seas obey Him. A big God, He towers above all animate and inanimate creation, all tangible and intangible things (Mark 4:41). In power and authority, everything must obediently submit to His will. Thus, He commands—not suggests, hints, or recommends—that His elect not fear or tremble or be terrified of their enemies. His hand is on the pulse of our lives, day and night, controlling and directing events that end ultimately in our favor. Job writes "I know that you can do all things, and that no purpose of yours can be thwarted" (Job 42:2, ESV).

Ever vigilant, if He is for us, nothing and nobody can touch us without His consent, and nothing can defeat His purpose for our lives.

January 15

The Presence of the LORD

Be strong and of good courage, do not fear nor be afraid of them; for the LORD your God, He is the One who goes with you. He will not leave you nor forsake you. Deut. 31:6, NKJV.

Faith and fear are staunch enemies, vigorously in opposition on the battlefield within our minds. When fear conquers faith, fear masters us. Even as we walk in the presence of the Lord, the enemy manages to assail us with this very potent weapon. Why, some of God's greatest leaders had moments of great fear even after God revealed Himself and His power through them and to them! Elijah, after his great faith yielded mind-boggling miracles, became terrified of Queen Jezebel who promised to kill him as he had killed her priests. He fled and hid in a cave. Even, Peter and the other disciples, who walked with Jesus for years and witnessed His authority, ran in fright when the rabble came to arrest Him.

Fear is an absence of courage and a lack of trust in God's ability to provide and protect. That fear does not come from God, for He promises, "For God hath not given us the spirit of fear; but of power" (2 Tim. 1:7). Since fear is a negative emotion that provokes distrust in God, logically, the spirit of fear comes from the evil one. But we render Satan powerless when we resist his lies (James 4:7). Furthermore, God is peeved at our fear of mortal man in the face of His unlimited and unmatched power: "Who *are* you that you should be afraid of a man *who* will die ... And you forget the LORD your Maker, Who stretched out the heavens and laid the foundations of the earth (Isa. 51:12, 13, NKJV).

When Jesus Christ ascended to heaven, He promised to send the Holy Spirit in His stead to work unimpeded by time or space. With our permission, the Holy Spirit takes up residence inside of us as God pledges: "I will put my Spirit within you and cause you to walk in My statutes" (Eze. 36:27, NKJV). Heaven and earth cannot contain Him, but because of His irrepressible love for us, He condescended to dwell in this wicked, violent, chaotic world by living in our hearts. At all times with us, the Holy Spirit is our internal compass, always pointing us to Christ and always pointing us to the path of righteousness. Rhetorically, David asked, "Where can I go from Your Spirit? Or where can I flee from Your presence?" (Ps. 139:7, NKJV). We breathe the very air of His presence through the indwelling of the Spirit.

God is omnipresent. Meister Eckhart wrote, "Man goes far away or near but God never goes far-off; he is always standing close at hand, and even if he cannot stay within he goes no further than the door." Acts 17:27 tells us that God is "not far from each of us" (NKJV). And Revelation 3:20 reveals that God stands patiently at the door of our hearts waiting for entrance.

We can choose to believe the truth that He will never leave us or forsake us—as revealed by God who cannot lie—and find peace, or we can choose to believe the lies promulgated by Satan, the father of lies, and remain fearful. Did you choose yet?

January 16

Resilience - Bending Not Breaking

So do not throw away your confidence; it will be richly rewarded. You need to persevere so that when you have done the will of God, you will receive what he has promised. Heb. 10:35, 36, NIV.

Bamboo trees are a marvel of resilience. Adaptable, they survive in temperature extremes from frigid to tropical. Considered stronger than oak, the bamboo's durability is incomparable among the hardwoods—it sways and bends but does not break even in hurricane-strength wind. The stronger the wind the lower it bends, but when the wind subsides, the bamboo tree straightens to its full height again. No matter how brutal the conditions, the small, hollow, seemingly fragile bamboo tree takes the punches on the chin, shakes them off, and returns to the struggle more determined.

We need the resilience of the bamboo tree. Life throws us curveballs at times—unexpected events that take us off guard and are capable of devastating us. They are pitched our way in the form of unfairness, fear, tragedy, persecution, loss, and a myriad other forms. We can choose to break under the pressure or bounce back as the bamboo tree does, strengthened to face another day. In God there is supernatural help to stand up under any affliction. "Let us therefore come boldly to the throne of grace, that we may obtain mercy and find grace to help in time of need" (Heb. 4:16, NKJV).

It takes courage, resolve, and trust in the power of God to withstand and overcome the curveballs. As long as life lasts, we will face them. Remember, however, that the Lord "who works all things according to the counsel of His will" controls the pitcher and his rogue balls (Eph. 1:11). With our desire to live happy, uneventful lives and with our limited understanding of the workings of God's will, we may be taken aback by these fearsome, backbreaking happenings. But the Lord promises, "You do not realize now what I am doing, but later you will understand" (John 13:7, NIV).

Curveballs do not a defeat make. Just remember, tomorrow is another day, and God never gives us more than we can bear. Trust in His proven faithfulness and sovereignty. Temptations and trials come, but God never overburdens us for He bundles them to perfectly fit our endurance, provides a perfect solution and a new opportunity to grow spiritually (1 Cor. 13:10). "There will be another inning, another game, another chance, and 'how' you handle the curve balls is really up to you. You can lose your confidence, your spirit, your love of the game or, you can take your stance at home plate, swing like you have never swung before and know you have a chance at hitting that ball far out into the outfield or the stands."[10]

Hope, the hallmark of a resilient person, gives us the courage to move forward. And those who are walking in obedience drink from the reservoir of hope in God. He promises that the dark times will become light, and those who trust Him and His promises can rest in that hope. The resilient person's hopeful refrain is, "I am still confident of this: I will see the goodness of the LORD in the land of the living" (Ps. 27:13, NIV).

January 17

The Lord's Standard

When the enemy shall come in like a flood, the Spirit of the LORD shall lift up a standard against him. Isa. 59:19.

Excluding floods caused by hurricanes, the Great Flood of 1889 is branded the deadliest flood in the history of the United States. It destroyed Johnstown, Pennsylvania, piling up a death toll of 2,200 people when a horrific storm dropped six to ten inches of rain in twenty-four hours. Swollen with rain, the otherwise docile water in creeks and streams became powerful enough to rip up trees and telegraph poles. Before daybreak the Conemaugh River, which runs through Johnstown, flooded its banks after the South Fork Dam gave way. Twenty million tons (4.8 billion gallons) of rushing water and debris, moving at 40 miles per hour, pulverized the town.

Similar to the Great Flood, the enemy delights in pulverizing our faith and water logging our hope, overwhelming us with difficulties and temptations to drown our spirits. He bombards us with lies that unleash a torrent of sin and woe on unsuspecting victims. Once he weakens our resolve, he drops a deluge of doubt in our minds about the promises of God that flood us with untold anxiety and fear. Inundated by the vicious storms of loss, pain, and depression, his captives' lives are splintered.

But Satan can only hold captive those who "have forsaken me the fountain of living waters, and hewed them out cisterns, broken cisterns, that can hold no water" (Jer. 2:13). Those refusing to drink of the Living Water, the water without cost, are led by Satan to drink water contaminated by parasites, viruses, protozoa, and bacteria-sin. Immersed in sin that appears harmless, his prisoners are stricken by what appeared attractive but, ultimately, proved to be destructive and debilitating.

But Jesus quiets the storms and leads us beside still waters, waters pure enough to quench our thirst for truth. His perfect peace stills the storms raging all around us. Such peace is gained by focusing on Him and trusting Him implicitly (Isa. 26:3). Trust His promises. When you go through deep waters, He will be with you. When you go through rivers of difficulty, you will not drown. When you walk through the fire of oppression, you will not be burned up; the flames will not consume you. For He is the Lord, your God, your Savior (Isa. 43:2, 3).

Moreover, for those who call Him their God and seek Him earnestly—whose soul thirsts for Him; whose soul yearns for Him in a dry and weary land where there is no water—He will lift up a standard against the enemy (Isa. 63:1). Following His clearly marked standard or banner lifted high above all others, you are guaranteed victory in the battle for your life. When Satan sends a flood of fear and anxiety, Jesus will part the waters and let you walk on the dry land of His peace and safety. Although you will get battles-scars in the fray, you will emerge triumphant. God offers invincible protection and victory for He is Jehovah Nissi, the Lord our banner.

January 18

Profiles of Courage

Fear not, nor be dismayed, be strong and of good courage: for thus will the LORD do to all your enemies against whom you fight. Joshua 10:25.

The Profile in Courage Award, the most prestigious award conferred on civil servants, highlights the "conscientious and courageous acts" performed by civil servants. It rewards and honors elected officials who stand up for right even at the peril of their positions. "In whatever arena of life one may meet the challenge of courage, whatever may be the sacrifices he faces if he follows his conscience—the loss of his friends, his fortune, his contentment, even the esteem of his fellow men—each man must decide for himself the course he will follow."[11]

The first recipient of the award was Carl Elliott, a former Alabama Congressman who co-authored the National Defense Education Act of 1958. This act provided low-interest loans so persons of any race or economic status could earn a college education. He chose right over convenience, but his courageous stand in segregated Alabama cost him his seat in Congress, and he ended up impoverished. Samuel Johnson said, "Courage is reckoned the greatest of all virtues; because, unless a man has that virtue, he has no security for preserving any other."

Courage characterizes a faithful Christian struggling against demonic forces. We are told up front that we will have troubles, and we do; that as heirs of God and co-heirs with Christ we will share in His glory and share in His sufferings, and we do; that the whole creation has been groaning as in childbirth up to the present time, and it is (John 16:33; Rom. 8:17, 22). Still, we keep following Jesus. Christians are not sadistic; we do not enjoy pain and suffering. But like Jesus we learn obedience through our suffering (Heb. 5:8).

It took courage for John the Baptist to stand firm in the face of affliction and suffering. Jesus noted his faithfulness: "Among them that are born of women there hath not risen a greater than John the Baptist" (Matt. 11:11). John fulfilled his exalted mission to herald the coming of Jesus and call Jews to repentance and reformation. Courageous to the end, he did not shrink in the face of power, particularly as he voiced Herod's adultery for which he was beheaded.

Take hold of the power from above. Be courageous; stand firm in the Lord; fight the good fight; and finish the course in spite of the suffering. For the faithful, the future holds a "crown of righteousness, which the Lord, the righteous judge, will award to me on that Day ... to all who have loved his appearing" (2 Tim. 4:7, 8, ESV). Suffering is short-lived compared to eternity. After we have suffered for a little while, God will perfect, confirm, strengthen, and establish us (1 Peter 5:10). Also, suffering is God's way of maturing His people spiritually. It keeps our knees bent in prayer, strengthens our walk, and humbles us.

January 19

Tough Love

I am the LORD your God; fear not the gods of the Amorites, in whose land ye dwell: but ye have not obeyed my voice. Judges 6:10.

"Tough love" is a phrase that came into vogue in the 1980s after David and Phyllis York set down tactics to deal with a wayward teenage daughter. Generally, tough love avoids enabling bad behavior by making excuses and requires accepting the consequences of one's actions. However, God practiced tough love centuries before the Yorks. He instructed Moses to vocalize His tough love to the Israelites. Before they entered the Promised Land, He gave them remedial lessons on obedience and blessings and the penalty for disobedience (Deut. 11:26-32).

The blessings for obedience were tremendous—they would ascend above all nations and their lives and livelihoods would be hedged in with prosperity and peace. Also, they would be established as a favored holy people, bringing glory to the nation and to Him. Their enemies would fear them because of their distinction as children of the Most High God, and they stood to be deemed superior to all other nations under the sun—always the head and never the tail (Deut. 28).

Soon, Israel apostatized again, and God used their pagan enemies as instruments of judgment against them. The Midianites invaded their land, causing them to live in dens and caves and scurry around in the dark like rats. They planted and marauding nations took their harvest. Desperate, the Israelites cried to God for a deliverer, but He sent them a prophet to remind them that they were reaping what they had sown after fornicating with other gods and turning their backs on Him.

But He is a merciful, longsuffering God who loves His wayward children with a strong, abiding love. After permitting their uncultivated and ignorant western Midianite enemies to conquer, enslave, and humiliate them for seven years, He raised up a deliverer. But not before they learned lessons in humility and obedience through a restriction of their freedom and a stab at their pride. The Midianites were empowered to triumph not because God wanted to destroy Israel but because He wanted to bring them to a place of repentance and peace with Him.

Sorrow is a master teacher. Robert Browning Hamilton described it poetically: "I walked a mile with Pleasure, She chattered all the way; But left me none the wiser, For all she had to say. I walked a mile with Sorrow And ne'er a Word said she; But oh, the things I learned from her When Sorrow walked with me!"[12] God loves us so much that sometimes He exercises painful and tough love. The trials that bring sorrow are harsh and agonizing, but they are necessary for our spiritual growth. Similar to earthly children, now adults, who were disciplined by loving parents, God's children will one day thank Him profusely for the lessons that sorrow taught.

January 20

Face to Face With God

The LORD said ...Peace .... fear not: thou shalt not die. Judges 6:23.

"When Gideon realized that it was the angel of the LORD, he exclaimed, 'Ah, Sovereign LORD! I have seen the angel of the LORD face to face!'" (Judges 6:22, NIV). Angels regularly minister between heaven and earth but generally behind a veil of invisibility. Thus, when Gideon encountered a visible angel, he was slow to realize it. The angel touched his staff to the meat on the altar and to the unleavened bread. Fire sprang from the rock and consumed the food; then the angel vanished. Once Gideon realized he was an angel of the Lord, he cowered in fear for his life (verses 21-23).

Patriarchs and prophets had a healthy fear of seeing God face to face. When Moses asked to see God's glory, God replied, "You cannot see my face, for no one may see me and live" (Ex. 33:20). Other men of God had reactions just as dramatic as Gideon's when they encountered God. Simeon denounced his life after he held the baby Jesus (Luke 2:29). Isaiah was convicted of his sinfulness when he saw a vision of the Most High God sitting on His throne (Isa. 6:5). And John, who sheltered and loved Mary after Jesus' death and was a close companion for three years, fell prostrate after seeing God in His shekinah glory.

But the Bible promises that the pure in heart shall see God and live (Matt. 5:8). Purity defines things that are clean or spotless or uncontaminated. God is looking for genuine Christians with clean hearts to populate the new earth, for He is emphatic that nothing impure will enter the kingdom of God (Rev. 21:27). Those whose purity is surface deep, who have a form of godliness but have not yielded to the cleansing power of the Holy Ghost, will be rejected (2 Tim. 3:5). Only to bona fide Christians who strive to live holy lives through the power from above will heaven be open.

Jesus cautions us to "be careful not to do your 'acts of righteousness' before men, to be seen by them. If you do, you will have no reward from your Father in heaven" (Matt. 6:1, NIV). For example, the Pharisees exhibited behavior in opposition to Jesus' requirements. He condemned them soundly for their impure hearts—their hypocrisy. Annoyed at their pretense, Jesus compared them to "whitewashed tombs, which look beautiful on the outside but on the inside are full of dead men's bones and everything unclean" (Matt. 23:27).

The purity that permits a face-to-face encounter with Jesus is not a shallow, outward show of religiosity, but a wholesomeness that permeates our entire being and transforms our characters to the similitude of Jesus' character. St. Augustine wrote, "Only he who has shrugged off human praise and in his life is concerned just to please God, who searches our conscience, has a simple, that is, pure, heart."

Living a life of obedience pleases God and ushers the pure in heart into His presence. If we continue to wrestle with Him until the heart is purified, one day we shall see Him face to face and know Him as we are known (1 Cor. 13:12).

January 21

Breaking the Chains of Sin

Hide thy face from my sins, and blot out all mine iniquities. Ps. 51:9.

Did you know that a two-ton elephant held by tiny ropes around its ankles has no idea that it can easily walk away? Tie a baby elephant to a tree or stake with a chain that is strong enough to hold him, and he will tug and pull vigorously to break loose from the restraint. As he grows larger and the restraint still holds, he pulls and tugs less vigorously until he no longer tries to escape. An adult, and strong enough to easily break the chain, he is still convinced that he cannot escape. Thus, a small rope can keep him captive because his mind is imprisoned.

Satan, the master swindler who deceives the whole world, imprisons our minds just as readily to hold us captives of sin (Rev 12:9). Described as cunning, he deceived Eve once she engaged in conversation and immediately cast doubt on the truth of God's word—truth taught firsthand from God. Satan masterfully blinded her mind by slightly bending the truth, tainted her thought processes, and she tumbled headlong into sin (Gen. 3). To win the souls of humanity and relegate them to a dark reality now and eternal darkness in the future, Satan uses any underhanded means at his disposal. For he is fighting a ferocious battle to take as many as possible to hell with him.

Without internalizing spiritual truth, we are all captives because only the truth breaks the chains of sin and sets us free (John 8:32). Jesus, in every way human, proved during the forty days of fasting He not only met the challenge but prevailed. Weak, thirsty, and hungry, Jesus held Satan at bay with three simple words: "It is written." Satan tempted Him on appetite, wealth and power, and worldly adoration and recognition—lusts and pride—things that ring the death knell for a right relationship with God.

But for those who have a right relationship with God, he is a defeated foe who has no power over us unless we yield to him. He may hook chains of sin around our ankles, but we have a master key called the Word of God. When Jesus announced at the cross, "It is finished," he received authority over the enemy of sin, fear, and death (Matt. 28:18). Through the Word and His Spirit, He opens eyes blinded by Satan's deceptions. As well, He thoroughly briefed Satan that if we defy his advances, he must flee.

Sin has no more authority over those who are in Christ, for He cleanses us so thoroughly that sinning is distasteful. It loses its power to enslave us to the lusts and pride that we were beholden to before our conversion. But the sin nature has not completely vanished, and we will fall periodically despite the progress made. But, when we sin, we have an Advocate who pleads our case. Then, if we remain obedient, He goes that extra mile and hides His face from all our sins and blots out all iniquities so that our record in heaven is sparkling clean.

Confound Satan with the mindset that by God's grace "you can chain me, you can torture me, you can even destroy this body, but you will never imprison my mind."[13]

January 22

Be Kind to One Another

"Don't be afraid," David said to him, " for I will surely show you kindness for the sake of your father Jonathan. I will restore to you all the land that belonged to your grandfather Saul, and you will always eat at my table." 2 Sam. 9:7, NIV.

Ruthless power many times stems from insecurity and fear. For instance, Athaliah, wife of King Joram of Israel and daughter of Ahaz and the infamous Jezebel, in counsel with Joram, ruthlessly ordered the murder of her husband's six brothers, fearing that they may overthrow the throne. On the other hand, the powerful King David showed that "wherever there is a human being, there is an opportunity for a kindness."[14] To a potential threat to his crown, He extended a hand of mercy, not a death sentence. Mephibosheth, the son of David's best friend Jonathan and King Saul's grandson, initially became fearful, but gained confidence at David's assurance.

David's tender concern for Mephibosheth is an example of God's grace. Mephibosheth had absolutely nothing to offer, making him a perfect candidate for grace. The Hebrew word for kindness, *chesed,* means "loving-kindness, mercy, and steadfast love." It is most often used of God in His dealings with us, and it points to the blessed one-sided nature of His love. He loves us not because we are lovely or because we have something to offer but because it is His nature to love. God *is* love.

In addition, David's grace is also a pattern for us in serving and ministering to others. Like David, love should move us to seek out our enemies and bless them; to seek the poor, weak, lame, and hidden to bless them; to bless others when they don't deserve it, and bless them more than they deserve; to bless others for the sake of someone else; and to show the kindness of God to others. Anybody who professes to love the Lord will put on a heart of "compassion, kindness, humility, gentleness and patience" to both the kind and the unkind (Col. 3:12, NIV).

Forgiveness is also a manifestation of kindness, that fifth fruit of the Spirit. David's liberality to Mephibosheth highlights Paul's instructions to the Ephesians about kindness and forgiveness. "And be kind to one another, tenderhearted, forgiving one another, even as God in Christ forgave you" (Eph. 4:32, NKJV). This is a sure safeguard against giving Satan authority in our lives. According to E. M. Bounds, "The readiest way to keep Satan out is to keep the spirit of forgiveness in. The devil is never deeper in hell, nor farther removed from us than when we can pray 'Father forgive them; they know not what they do.'"[15]

Mark Twain wrote that kindness is "seen" by the blind and "heard" by the deaf. Kindness is an expression of love, an emotion and attitude that identifies an authentic Christian. God exemplified this love through Jesus who loves the just and unjust alike. "But I say, love your enemies! Pray for those who persecute you! In that way, you will be acting as true children of your Father in heaven. For he gives his sunlight to both the evil and the good, and he sends rain on the just and the unjust alike" (Matt. 5:44, 45, NLT).

January 23

Noble Character

Now don't worry about a thing, my daughter. I will do what is necessary, for everyone in town knows you are a virtuous woman. Ruth 3:11, NLT.

A nineteenth-century building at the Hermitage in Dunkeld, Scotland, called Ossian's Hall of Mirrors contains a small room overlooking a waterfall. The walls and ceiling are covered with mirrors, reflecting the waterfall and giving the illusion that the water "sometimes runs upwards, contrary to the direction of gravity, and sometimes in a horizontal stream over the head."[16] Although, unreal and deceptive, the illusion pleasantly surprises tourists who visit the building, which was created as a shrine to the blind poet Ossian.

Reputation is many times an illusion, for man cannot see the heart. For years Tiger Woods had a stellar reputation as a squeaky clean athlete with strong family values who was sought after by advertisers to promote their products. But he shattered that illusion when his hidden life of sex addiction was exposed for the world to see. The principle "You may fool all the people some of the time, you can even fool some of the people all the time, but you cannot fool all the people all the time" corresponds with the illusion of reputation.

Reputation and character differ vastly. Reputation is what people around us see while character is our reality—what God sees. William Hersey Davis wrote, "Reputation is what men say about you on your tombstone; Character is what angels say about you before the throne of God." A noble character—having high moral qualities—is highly esteemed by God. Christians must make every effort to supplement faith with moral character, a Christ-like character identified by love (2 Peter 1:5). When we follow the Word and walk as Jesus walked in holiness and truth, we are building noble characters, the only earthly possession we will take to heaven.

Abigail, the wife of the very wealthy Nabal, possessed a noble character. And God used her to prevent the future king of Israel from rashly shedding blood for personal reasons. Nabal's refusal to give provisions to David, even after David protected his men and flocks, sent David into a murderous rage. He vowed to kill all of the men in Nabal's house by the next morning. Abigail interceded by delivering abundant provisions to David on bended knees and begging him to not make a decision that would negatively affect his future as king (1 Sam. 25:2-25).

David, grateful for her kind heart and her wisdom, blessed her for her advice and blessed the Lord God who sent her (1 Sam. 25:32, 33). The Bible says, "Bad company corrupts good character" (1 Cor. 15:33, NIV). But by God's grace, Abigail maintained her noble character despite living in wedlock with a selfish fool. Upon learning of his close call with death, Nabal suffered a stroke and died ten days later. David married the widowed Abigail, making her his future queen and recognizing her worth—the hidden person of the heart with the enduring quality of a gentle and quiet spirit (1 Peter 3:3, 4).

January 24

The Mind of Christ

And Elijah said to her, "Do not fear; go and do as you have said, but make me a small cake from it first, and bring it to me; and afterward make some for yourself and your son. 1 Kings 17:13, NKJV.

I was born with a heart condition called mitral valve prolapse, a condition affecting a small percentage of the population. Mitral valve prolapse causes the flaps of the mitral valve to fall back into the left atrium during the heart's contraction. This distorts the tissues of the valve, making them abnormal and stretchy, which causes the valve to leak. Thus, the leaky valve makes the left side of the heart pump more vigorously, which physically enlarges the left side.

Contrariwise, a *spiritually* enlarged heart is a blessing. The widow of Zarephath possessed a spiritually enlarged heart, a heart for service and strong faith. Although a Gentile, she allowed the Holy Spirit to teach her the mind of Christ. Paul counsels us to "let this mind be in you which was also in Christ Jesus" (Phil. 2:5, NKJV). Jesus poured out His earthly life, reputation, and peace as a drink offering for the benefit of others without consideration of His own well-being. He loved and lived to serve.

Having the mind of Christ embraces several things, particularly humility. In John 13:15, Jesus washed His disciples' feet and told them, "I have given you an example, that you should do as I have done to you" (NKJV). This is a lesson in foot washing on one level, but on another deeper level, He taught the principle of humility and the generosity of a humble spirit. Here was the majesty of heaven, the Son of God stooping low to wash the dusty, dirty feet of sinful man, thus making Himself nothing and taking on the attitude of a servant.

Sacrifice is another telltale sign of one having the mind of Christ. When Elijah asked the widow of Zarephath to relinquish her last morsel of flour and oil to make a bread cake for Elijah, she readily did so even though she and her child would starve. By faith she emulated Jesus who did not please himself but pleased *his* neighbor for *his* good. He sacrificed Himself for all people, and as it is written, "The reproaches of those who reproached You fell on Me" (Rom. 15:3, NKJV).

As well, obedience is a hallmark when we have the mind of Christ, and it carries both blessings and short-term affliction. The widow chose to be obedient, performing an act that might have caused her death. Nevertheless, she was greatly blessed with an inexhaustible pantry and a son snatched from death (1 Kings 17). But Jesus, the definitive example, went to the cross as a human sacrifice, foregoing His well-being and ultimately His life for us, slaves to sin. In human form, "he humbled himself by becoming obedient to the point of death, even death on a cross" (Phil. 2:8, ESV) and descended to an earthly hell to obediently do the will of His heavenly Father (John 6:38).

Jesus promised that those who have His mind will make their home with Him and His Father in heaven (John 14:23, 24). Can there be any higher blessing?

January 25

Taste the Lord's Flavor

O taste and see that the LORD is good: blessed is the man that trusteth in him. Ps. 34:8.

Without taste buds all food would taste the same. How boring! Thankfully, the average person has approximately 10,000 taste buds on the tongue and on the sides and roof of the mouth to taste sweet, salty, bitter, and sour. These taste buds, called papillae, are located in and around the tongue bumps and contain extremely sensitive microvilli or microscopic hairs that transmit messages to the brain about the different tastes.

It is through tasting and ingesting that we savor the flavors of the food we eat. Using a culinary analogy, David challenges us to experience God is the same way. He implies that intellectual knowledge and hearsay are insufficient to experience the incredible flavors of God. Doubtless, it is impossible to taste Him and not savor His goodness. Talk to Him, call on Him, sense His presence, and embrace His promises. Take refuge in Him; trust Him; claim His help. When we do, He saves us and delivers us from ourselves and evil, notwithstanding that we may be battered in the process (Ps. 37:40).

Jesus is the Living Bread delivered from heaven. His flesh is the nourishing "constant gift of spiritual strength."[17] Eat it and you will live forever. That is the flavor of salvation. Unless you eat His flesh and drink His blood, you will have no life in you, neither the abundant earthly life nor eternity. Just as Jesus lives because of the Father, so also will those who ingest the Living Bread, the Word, live because of Him who will raise them up on the last day (John 6:51-58). That is the flavor of life eternal.

He is the vine and we are the branches, and abiding in Him, we bear lush fruit. Through the Vine flow uninterrupted nutrients to sustain the life of the branch. The only stipulation is that the branch must stay connected (John 15:5). Abiding in Him, "we have our redemption through his blood, the forgiveness of our trespasses, according to the riches of his grace" (Eph. 1:7, ASV). He proffers manifold grace-saving grace, sanctifying grace, redemptive grace, and natural grace. That is the flavor of grace.

Confidently rest on His promises, believe in Him when life appears impossible, and trust Him even in the midst of painful trials. "Faith is the soul's taste; they who test the Lord by their confidence always find him good, and they become themselves blessed."[18] That is the flavor of faith.

Sample His forgiveness. Upon confessing, He forgives our sins and cleanses us from all wickedness (1 John 1:9). Savor His grace, for it is by grace that we have been saved through faith, which is a gift from God (Eph. 2:8). Relish His mercy, for those who trust in Him shall be surrounded by mercy (Ps. 32:10). Enjoy His faithfulness, for He is a kind God, abounding in love and faithfulness (Ps. 86:15). And taste His love, for He loves us with an everlasting love and draws us with lovingkindness (Jer. 31:3). God is very tasty!

January 26

Key to Prosperity

Then you will prosper, if you are careful to observe the statutes and the ordinances which the LORD commanded Moses concerning Israel. Be strong and courageous, do not fear nor be dismayed. 1 Chron. 22:13, NASB.

Today prosperity gospel is the new gospel, and many televangelists allege to have the prosperity key. They preach a gospel of health and wealth—a message that assures obedient Christians who give sacrificially to their coffers in tithe and offerings will reap untold financial, physical, and spiritual blessings. However, the main focus is on financial blessings. But this simplistic depiction of one and all reaping huge financial blessings seems to contradict Jesus who said, "You will always have the poor among you" (Matt. 26:11, NLT).

Prosperity gospel sets people up for a great fall into discouragement and disbelief. No matter how generously we give of our time, talents, and treasure, Christians still suffer financial, emotional, or physical setbacks at times (John 16:33). This one-sided philosophy reduces God to a Santa Claus or a vending machine. But He is not a "Vending Machine God: put in faith and out pops blessings – money, homes, cars, beautiful spouses, clever kids, good neighbors, big churches, and plush vacations. For the prosperity gospel, humans are The Happiness Machine: receive the blessings, rely on the promises, act on the commandments and you can put on a happy face – a big one. Every day, from the moment you get up to the closing of your eyes, happiness is the aim of life. In the prosperity gospel, God is there for us; we are here for God to bless."[19]

We populate a world awash in a great controversy between good and evil, and Christians wear red bull's-eyes on their backs. When Satan cannot convince us to follow him, he hurls huge rocks of difficulties and setbacks, shoots arrows of pain and suffering with a sure aim, and bombards our mind with doubt and anxiety. Each committed Christian has suffered under satanic attacks even while holding true to the Word of God and faithfully giving of their time, talent, and treasure. God allows these difficulties for our own spiritual good even while He desires us to prosper (3 John 1:2).

Prosperity is not merely tangible material gain but also intangible blessings such as internal peace, spiritual courage, protection, increased desire for God, holiness, and emotional and physical healings. Because the kingdom of God is concerned with righteousness, joy, and peace, things pleasing to Him, Jesus focuses on us prospering spiritually, not necessarily materially, as we travel the narrow path to heaven. (Rom. 14:17, 18). A bank account full of money, fame, and a truckload of possessions cause angst to the person who loses out on eternal life because of them (Matt. 6:33).

Obedience and complete surrender to Him guarantees soul prosperity and salvation plus eternal life, glory, and riches in the earth made new. That is true prosperity gospel.

January 27

Payment in Kind

He repays people according to their deeds. Job 34:11, NLT.

In Islamic criminal jurisprudence, Qisas law, with a basis in the laws God gave to Moses for the newly emancipated Israelites, requires retaliation. Moses wrote, "But if there is serious injury, you are to take life for life, eye for eye, tooth for tooth, hand for hand, foot for foot, burn for burn, wound for wound, bruise for bruise" (Ex. 21:23-25, NIV). Recently, based on the law of Qisas, a Pakistani judge ruled that the ears and noses of two defendants be cut off as equivalent punishment for cutting off the nose and ears of a woman who spurned one defendant's marriage proposal. With Qisas law, the victim and/or the victim's family who have the power to modify the sentence, are to be satisfied that the punishment fits the crime.

Payment in kind is a prerogative of God, Creator of heaven and earth. He is the only Being who can foster a perfect balance between justice and mercy, for it is impossible for God to be unfair or imbalanced. "All his ways are justice: A God of faithfulness and without iniquity, just and right is he" (Deut. 32:4, ASV). Justice requires that fair treatment and recompense, in accord with the law or societal standards, be sustained. It appears, however, that many injustices to God's people are slow to be addressed, but not forever. Although God is longsuffering, He will not acquit the wicked (Nahum 1:3).

Micah asked rhetorically, "Who is a God like You, who pardons iniquity and passes over the rebellious act of the remnant of His possession? He does not retain His anger forever, Because He delights in unchanging love" (Micah 7:18, NASB). God is longsuffering with sin and sinners, but one day He will destroy sin and repay those sinners who remain loyal agents of Satan for their rebellion and their evil deeds. God will "avenge his own elect, which cry day and night unto him, though he bear long with them? I tell you that he will avenge them speedily" (Luke 18:7, 8).

On that day God will weigh actions and motives in the scales of justice and reward each of us accordingly. Here, where the prince of darkness reigns in many hearts, the scales of justice are vastly off balance, leaning heavily to one side. Evil, freely holding sway, accuses and batters God's people. But when God implements His retributive justice, the scales of justice will swing back to the center. For He will ensure that punishment is wielded in proportion to the deeds (Deut. 32:35). And His redeemed, whose prayers for justice inundate Him, will be satisfied (Rev. 6:10).

The converted Christian, walking as Jesus walked, need not harbor anxiety or fear in the coming judgment, for we will be hidden in the day of God's anger (Zeph. 2:3). Although we deserve to die, Jesus conquered death for us. Thus we receive what He deserves—eternal life; and He received what we deserve—death. Now, by the power of the indwelling Holy Spirit, "sin shall not have dominion over you: for ye are not under law, but under grace" (Rom. 6:14). Despite the slow wheels of justice, continue to sow seeds of righteousness so that your in-kind payment is an indestructible crown.

January 28

Remedy for Affluenza

Watch out! Be on your guard against all kinds of greed; a man's life does not consist in the abundance of his possessions. Luke 12:15, NIV.

Monkey trappers in North Africa catch their prey by filling gourds with grain and chaining them to a tree. Each gourd has a hole just large enough for the gullible monkey to stick its open hand through. When a monkey discovers the grain, it reaches in and grabs a handful. But the hole is too small for it to withdraw its closed, bulging fist. Since the monkey is too greedy to open its hand and release the food, it is taken captive.[20]

Similarly, fallen human beings are selfish, greedy and, materialistic (Ps. 58:3). Money is a god for many and much evil stems from their love of it. People, resolute to enrich themselves at any cost, fall into traps that plunge them into ruin and eternal destruction (1 Tim. 6:9, 10). The Bible is rift with spiritual and physical carcasses of covetous, greedy persons such as Ananias and Sapphira. Following the lead of genuine philanthropists, they sold a piece of property and pledged the proceeds to the church. However, they conspired to keep a portion for themselves. Peter asked, "Ananias, why has Satan filled your heart to lie to the Holy Spirit …?" (Acts 5:3, ESV). Alas, they died in their sin.

In these last days, many Christians are self-absorbed in materialism to the peril of their own souls as well. Materialism is a desire for wealth and material possessions with *little interest in ethical or spiritual matters.* Similar to Ananias and Sapphira, many who are eager for money wander from the faith. Jesus warned His people centuries ago against pledging allegiances to the idol of materialism as sixteen of His thirty-eight parables "deal with money, possessions, their use, and their relationship to us."[21]

Wealth and prosperity are not inherently wrong, for God wants us to prosper. But when achieving things becomes a preoccupation, we tread on shaky ground. Mark calls our attention to the "deceitfulness of riches" that can choke off our faith. "Now these are the ones sown among thorns; *they are* the ones who hear the word, and the cares of this world, *the deceitfulness of riches*, and the desires for other things *entering in choke the word, and it becomes unfruitful*" (Mark 4:18, 19, NKJV).

Christians friends, be wary of affluenza, a term coined by Joshua Harris to describe the "disease of greed with a selfish, materialistic mindset that is the ultimate aim of life." "There is something perverse about more than enough. When we have more, it is never enough. It is always somewhere out there, just out of reach. The more we acquire, the more elusive enough becomes."[22] If not prevented, affluenza will spread its toxicity throughout our spiritual bodies and poison our entire system, making us unfit for heaven. Its tentacles stretch to destroy our finances, freedom, and reputations.

The antidote for affluenza, however, can be found in a daily injection of the inspired Word, a transfusion of the Holy Spirit, and an unceasing consultation with God in prayer. Love God supremely, and make Him, not your possessions, Lord and Master of your life.

January 29

The Gift of Unanswered Prayer

Hagar, what's wrong? Do not be afraid! God has heard the boy crying as he lies there. Gen. 21:17, 18, NLT.

An unknown Confederate soldier prayed, "I asked God for strength that I might achieve. I was made weak that I might learn humbly to obey. I asked for health that I might do greater things. I was given infirmity that I might do better things. I asked for riches that I might be happy. I was given poverty that I might be wise. I asked for power that I might have the praise of men. I was given weakness that I might feel the need of God. I asked for all things that I might enjoy life. I was given life that I might enjoy all things. I got nothing that I asked for, but everything I hoped for."

Prayer is a navigational gift to commune with God, not a vehicle to truck in our wants. Consider the greediness of a lab rat being administered cocaine whenever it pressed a bar. Soon nothing else mattered to it but pressing the bar, not food, not drinks, nothing. "God in his wisdom knows that if prayer were just asking him for what we want and 'puff', we immediately get it, most of us in our sinful imperfection would become like our poor little rat friend, banging away like crazy at heaven's gate for more and more of what we want with little attention to who God is, what we really need and our responsibility to our family and others."[23]

Earthbound, corporeal, and finite, we cannot know what is best for us. Only God does. Thus, when our prayers and pleas to Him appear to evaporate into thin air, we dare not sink into despair. Rejoice, and thank God for unanswered prayers, for these are invaluable gifts. Love withholds much of what we plead for. And if we could see the whole picture of our lives as God does, we would nod in approval at HIs wisdom for "some of God's greatest gifts are unanswered prayers."[24]

In our shortsightedness, it is difficult to grasp that unanswered prayer "protects us from ourselves. If all our prayers were answered, we would only abuse the power. We would use prayer to change the world to our liking, and it would become hell on earth. Like spoiled children with too many toys and too much money, we would only grab for more. We would pray for victory at the expense of others; we would be intoxicated by power. We would hurt other people and exalt ourselves."[25]

God hears and answers every prayer (Matt 7:7, 8). Anticipate that some answers may be contrary to our wishes, but they are always in our best interest. Even so, He abundantly answers 'yes' to our petitions for salvation, forgiveness, sanctification, power to love, and strength to stand (John 14:13). Leave your petitions in His divine hand, and hold on. If you trust Him and His love for you when your prayers are not answered as you desire and when you desire, you *will* find peace.

Whatever His response, trust His love, His divine wisdom and His infallibility, for He cannot, will not, and never makes a mistake.

January 30

Shepherd and Overseer of Our Souls

Yea, though I walk through the valley of the shadow of death, I will fear no evil: for thou art with me; thy rod and thy staff they comfort me. Ps. 23:4.

The shepherd owns two apparatuses, the rod and the staff, to protect and guide his sheep. The rod is comparable to a walking stick or cane, used for utilitarian purposes. By bashing them in the head or poking their bodies, the shepherd uses the rod to keep wild animals at bay. The staff, however, is a longer stick with a crook at the top to curve around the neck of wayward or lost sheep to lead them back to the fold.

In our own sheep-like power, we are no match for the morass of troubles and trials that combine to make our world a valley of death. But the rod and the staff symbolize peace, protection, and provision. They promise relief from fear of the evil one, the uncertain road we travel on the Christian journey and protection from evil. No one except our Shepherd can provide such a horn of plenty, for He can make a way out of no way and provide for every spiritual and physical need "according to his riches in glory by Christ Jesus" (Phil. 4:19).

We live in the shadow of death and destruction and desperately need a Shepherd to guide us through the darkness. Without intervention and to our eternal damage, we stray into trouble of our own making or into danger from outside forces that trap us. All of us as sheep have gone astray, but graciously, the Godhead instituted a plan to shield us from the penalty of our straying (Isa. 53:6). Jesus agreed to be sin for us; thus, He became the "Shepherd and Bishop [or Overseer] of your souls" (1 Peter 2:25). If we repent and confess our sins, Jesus covers our filthy rags of stained virtue with the spotless white robe of His righteousness.

The Shepherd protects His flock by night and wards off evil (John 10:2, 3). He is Jehovah-Shammah, an ever present help in time of trouble, for our "help cometh from the LORD, which made heaven and earth" (Ps. 121:1, 2). And God promises to protect us from high waters and the fires of hell, for He is the Lord, our God, the Holy One of Israel, our Savior (Isa. 43:2, 3).

And He leads us to "springs of living water" that forever quench our thirst, fulfilling the promise that those who spiritually hunger and thirst after righteousness will be filled (Rev. 7:17). And He restores our soul. The Bread of Life, He nourishes us with the Word and all who partake shall live forever (John 6:51). As Jehovah–Jireh, our provider, He guarantees that our bread and water are sure as the wealth of the earth is His (1 Cor. 10:26).

For every valley, situation, and temptation that besets us, the Shepherd has a plan. So fear no evil—the Good Shepherd never slumbers or sleeps, and His watchful eyes rove over the earth ever vigilant to protect and abundantly provide for His sheep.

January 31

God is our Shield

The Word of the LORD came to Abram in a vision, saying, "Do not be afraid, Abram. I am your shield, your exceedingly great reward. Gen. 15:1, NKJV

"I was shocked," recalled Elizabeth Eckford on the day school opened. "I had thought the National Guard would protect all students, but when I approached the corner, they either closed ranks or crossed rifles to bar me." She, along with eight other African American students, attempted to enter Little Rock Central High School in 1957 but were prevented. Known as the Little Rock Nine, these students unsuccessfully tried to enter the school weeks later. A day later the politically courageous President Dwight Eisenhower sent soldiers into a racist city in a racist society armed with rifles to provide protection for these nine black students.

Like Abraham, the Little Rock Nine left the safety and comfort of home to venture into a cruel and unforgiving world. Unable to navigate the hate of the white majority on their own strength, the students placed hope in their government. Thankfully, the army troops surrounding them somewhat alleviated their fear of physical harm. How much better that God promises to always be a shield to those who put their trust in Him! (Prov. 30:5).

Abraham walked away from Ur on faith. When God called him to go to an unidentified, foreign country, his abiding trust led him to obey. Meekly, Abraham left his ancestral land to voyage to an unknown destination following an invisible God (Gen. 15:1). By faith, he willingly relinquished his past, readily accepting his call to sacrifice, service, and salvation. Afterward, he poised to give up his future by sacrificing Isaac at the Lord's command (Gen. 22:2). His was a dynamic faith credited as righteousness.

Pitfalls and problems surround those who accept God's call, and difficulties plague us on the journey. But God is faithful to perform all that He promises (Gen. 15:5, 6). God told Abraham, "Now look toward the heavens, and count the stars, if you are able to count them … So shall your descendents be" (Gen. 15:5, NASB) and "in you all the families of the earth shall be blessed" (Gen. 12:3, ESV). Countless descendants from Ishmael and from Isaac, miraculously born of parents long past childbearing age, became Abraham's earthly reward. Through Isaac he established Judaism and Christianity, and through Ishmael the Islamic prophet and the Muslim faith. And Jesus, also a descendant of Abraham, immeasurably blessed and continues to bless earth's inhabitants.

As well, God honored His pledge to be a shield for Abraham. He terrorized Abimelech through a dream, forcing him to release Abraham's wife Sarah whom he kidnapped (Gen. 20). He brought victory to Abraham and his men when they attacked the king of Elam who had kidnapped his nephew Lot (Gen. 14). And God shielded Abraham from poverty, drought, and harm during his long journey from Ur through Canaan and Egypt. "His way *is* perfect; the word of the LORD is proven; He *is* a shield to all who trust in Him" (Ps. 18:30, NKJV).

February 1

Building Faith

In God, whose word I praise, in God I trust; I will not be afraid. What can mortal man do to me? Ps. 56:4, NIV.

"Faith is the confidence that what we hope for will actually happen; it gives us assurance about things we cannot see" (Heb. 11:1, NLT). Faith has its basis in something or someone proven to be trustworthy. For David that was God. He experienced God's protection when he was a lad tending his father's sheep and God delivered him from a lion and a bear. Thus, he believed that God would deliver him out of the hand of the Philistine giant Goliath after he sought permission from King Saul to challenge him (1 Sam. 17:34-37). David prevailed against Goliath, and years later Samuel anointed him king, but God permitted the future king to endure numerous trials to teach him invaluable lessons in humility and faith and to test his endurance.

Tests in school measure the breadth of the knowledge learned in a particular subject. Thus, we may be very weak in an area, but until tested, we remain ignorant of that fact. This principle applies to those who profess to love the Lord. Our Master Teacher knows our weaknesses and enlightens us. He allows the suffering, but eventually, He "will himself restore you and make you strong, firm and steadfast" (1 Peter 5:10, NIV).

Obviously no one is thrilled to endure trials. God warns that we may have "to suffer grief in all kinds of trials. These have come so that your faith—of greater worth than gold, which perishes even though refined by fire—may be proved genuine and may result in praise, glory and honor when Jesus Christ is revealed" (1 Peter 1:6, 7, NIV). David spent years running for his life, living in caves and in the desert to escape from the wrath of King Saul who wanted to kill him. Living like a homeless vagabond seems degrading for an anointed future king, but God had a plan for his life.

Paul tells us: "No discipline seems pleasant at the time, but painful. Later on, however, it produces a harvest of righteousness and peace for those who have been trained by it" (Heb. 12:11, NIV). Mostly because of his transgressions, David suffered through the loss of his first wife, the death of his firstborn son with Bathsheba, the rape and societal shame of his daughter Tamar at the hand of his son Amnon, the ambush and murder of Amnon by David's firstborn and favorite son, Absalom, the five years of banishment of Absalom, the attempted coup by his son Absalom who declared himself king and attempted to seize the throne and kill his father, and the death of Absalom in the ensuring battle (2 Sam. 13).

Though David endured countless trials, he steadfastly cultivated a desire to be a man after God's own heart. After the fiery trials subsided, David himself exhorted, "It is *good* for me that I have been afflicted; that I might learn thy statutes" (Ps 119:71). He agonized in prayer in trying times; he praised God in the midst of his trials; and he put his full faith in the God who confirmed countless times that He is trustworthy. Every setback drew him closer to God, for every setback is a set-up for God's power.

February 2

God's Sufficiency

If God be for us, who can be against us? Rom. 8:31.

Walt Whitman wrote, "Many a good man I have seen go under." But with God on our side, going under is not an option. With us and for us, the Lord is our helper, enabling us to eventually look in triumph on our enemies (Ps. 118:7). As He guided His chosen people from Egypt to Canaan, He crushed their enemies, defeating some supernaturally through praise, shouting, marching, hornets, and angels. "A consciousness of our powerlessness should cast us upon Him who has all power.... God's sovereignty... reveals His sufficiency and shows us our insufficiency."[26]

If God is for you, He can free you from the most powerful ruler on earth. David said, "I was in trouble, so I called to the Lord. The Lord answered me and set me free" (Ps. 118:5, NCV). Likewise, during that long period of bondage in Egypt, the Israelites cried out to God. He "heard their groaning, and God remembered his covenant with Abraham, with Isaac, and with Jacob," and He raised up Moses to lead them out (Ex. 2:24).

If God is for you, He can exorcise powerful demons and transform the medium from a raving maniac to full sanity. During His sojourn on earth, Jesus traveled to the region of the Gergesenes and encountered a man possessed of a multitude of devils for a long time. He lived in the tombs and ran around naked and bleeding from self-inflicted wounds. The power of the demons promptly broke any type of restraint put on him for the safety of the community. After Jesus encountered this frenzied demoniac, the townspeople found him "from whom the demons had gone out, sitting at Jesus' feet, dressed and in his right mind" (Luke 8:35, NIV).

If God is for you, He can change a stony heart to flesh and transform a murderous zealot into "a preacher, and an apostle ... a teacher of the Gentiles" (1 Tim. 2:7). The fledgling church at Jerusalem had a powerful and persistent enemy, the zealous Pharisee Saul of Tarsus. When Stephen condemned the Sanhedrin, many Jews stoned him to death. "And Saul was there, giving approval to his death" (Acts 8:1, NIV). Then Saul systematically worked to destroy the church. "Going from house to house, he dragged off men and women and put them in prison" (verse 3) And, "Saul ... still breathing out murderous threats against the Lord's disciples" obtained arrest warrants for Christians at the synagogues in Damascus" (Acts 9:1, NIV). But He encountered God.

Surely, God is for the righteous. By His authority, Jesus delivered the human race from the penalty of death, assumed our sins, and provides life everlasting. In the unchanging Word of God, the penalty for sin is death. When Adam sinned, sin entered into the world, and death became the lot of humanity, for all have sinned (Rom. 5:12). We needed a sinless substitute to die in our stead, and God provided that Substitute, made Him our advocate, and accepted His blood as an atonement for our sins (1 John 2:1-3) Thus, the righteous are very wise to keep God on their side!

February 3

Peace Unshaken

God is our refuge and strength, a very present help in trouble. Therefore will not we fear, though the earth be removed, and though the mountains be carried into the midst of the sea. Ps. 46:1, 2.

On December 26, 2004, the Sumatra-Andaman earthquake, with a magnitude of 9.2, struck at approximately 7:00 a.m. on a Sunday morning about 100 miles off the western coast of Indonesia's Sumatra Island. It reigns as the third largest earthquake ever recorded on a seismograph but had the longest duration of faulting ever observed, between 8.3 and 10 minutes. Powerful enough to vibrate the entire planet as much as 0.4 inches, it triggered other earthquakes as far away as Alaska.[27] As well, this earthquake activated a tsunami whose waves can stretch as long as 60 miles with the next wave as far as one hour apart. Fast and powerful, these waves can cross an ocean at speeds comparable to a jetliner.[28]

The Sumatra-Andaman earthquake and resulting tsunami are examples of Jesus' prediction centuries ago of the astounding effects of natural calamities on the environment and in the lives of humanity. Jesus forecast that the seas and waves would be roaring, fitly describing hurricanes, cyclones, and tsunamis. Also, He predicted these events would cause many people to suffer heart problems from the great fear caused by these subsequent and escalating disasters. Distress among the nations is prevalent. The news abounds with conflicts and tensions across the planet and all the brilliant human minds have no solution (Luke 21:25-26).

But fear not, God is our refuge—a safe place. "Let the righteous rejoice in the LORD and take refuge in him" (Ps. 64:10, NIV). Still, the fear that accompanies the realization of Jesus' predictions will not abate without fostering a trusting relationship with Him, because His peace is a far distance from the intentionally disobedient. It is in righteousness that we find strength and help. And the Word coaches us to sprint away from evil, high jump over the troubles, and land safely in Jesus' capable hands.

Jesus promises that His strength is our strength. And we can do all things that are within His will through His strength (Phil. 4:13). Power to keep standing in adverse circumstances is readily available from the ultimate Source; we just need to ask for it. With faith in the Word and hope in the promise of salvation, nothing should destroy our peace or shake our confidence for long. Peace accompanies the belief that God is steadfast, faithful, vigilant, and a very present help in time of trouble.

God alone is our rock and our salvation. He is our fortress, therefore, not one of His anointed need be shaken (Ps. 62:6). Diligently seek Him, lean confidently on His broad shoulders, and cling to His strong right arm. It is then that you will be able to ride out the tempests in peace.

February 4

Wisdom Listens

But whoso hearkeneth unto me shall dwell safely, and shall be quiet from fear of evil. Prov. 1:33.

"Knowledge speaks, but wisdom listens," states an old Jewish proverb. Wisdom and knowledge are parts of a continuum. Where knowledge relates to the acquisition of facts and skills from our life experiences and from our formal and informal education, wisdom is the application of those facts and skills. "Wisdom reflects the values and criteria that we apply to our knowledge. Its essence is discernment." With wisdom we can discern right from wrong, choose the helpful from the harmful, and extract truth from error.[29]

"A wise *man* will hear, and will increase learning; and a man of understanding shall attain unto wise counsel" (Prov. 1:5). Listening goes beyond the use of our ears. It requires obedience, action, and choices, and it leads to learning. "You may be good. You may even be better than everyone else. But without a coach you will never be as good as you could be."[30] In the realm of an abundant earthly life and a joyous eternal life, that Coach is Jesus. And wise counsel comes from the Word of God, which is "a lamp unto my feet, and a light unto my path" (Ps. 119:105). This counsel is embedded in our daily Bible study and prayer and the workings of the Holy Spirit.

The opposite of wisdom is foolishness. And people who despise wisdom and instruction are fools in God's eye (Prov. 1:7). "Hear now this, O foolish people, and without understanding; which have eyes, and see not; which have ears, and hear not" (Jer. 5:21). These are the people who read the Word and listen to its explication but do not allow it to permeate their hearts and minds to change them to mirror Jesus' character. Fools reject the parts that do not fit within their agendas and continue to follow their own counsel. Take heed; the way of a fool is right in his own eyes and leads to death. However, a wise man listens to advice (Prov. 12:15).

Proverbs 4:6, 7 states, "Do not forsake wisdom, and she will protect you; love her, and she will watch over you. Wisdom is supreme; therefore get wisdom. Though it cost all you have, get understanding" (NIV). The Bible is an accurate guide covering every aspect of our existence. In this useful and inspired Book, God has deposited sound advice on how to live healthy, both mentally and physically, and how to live godly lives. The Bible points out God's purpose for our lives and the way to salvation. It reveals the past and predicts the future—where God's people have been and where they are finally going after this great controversy between good and evil has ended.

Nothing will stand the test of time like the wise counsel offered by the God who supremely loves us. This counsel will stand forever and will continue to ennoble us. Listening to wise counsel and receiving sound instruction will ensure that wisdom exudes from our very pores. Know also that wisdom is sweet to your soul; if you find it, you will experience an everlasting future of inestimable value (Prov. 24:14).

February 5

The LORD, My Confidence

Do not be afraid of sudden terror, nor of trouble from the wicked when it comes; For the LORD will be your confidence, and will keep your foot from being caught. Prov. 3:25, 26, NKJV.

On the eighth day after Noah and his family entered the ark, dark ominous clouds formed, thunder boomed, lightning flashed, and huge raindrops fell. The fountains of the deep oceans and seas surged up, and the windows of heaven opened. Rain cascaded from the sky in sheets and rivers overflowed. "Jets of water burst from the earth with indescribable force, throwing massive rocks hundreds of feet into the air."[31] This new phenomena, rain falling from the heavens, must have exacted sheer terror in the hearts of Noah's neighbors who had mocked him for 120 years.

Noah experienced the terror and ruin of the wicked in a forty-day deluge of rain a few generations after God had created Adam and Eve (Gen. 6). Mocked and scorned, Noah's faith in God assured his safety and peace. "By faith Noah, when warned about things not yet seen, in holy fear built an ark to save his family. By his faith he condemned the world and became heir of the righteousness that comes by faith" (Heb. 11:7, NIV).

God revealed to Noah His purpose and directed him to build the ark while preaching of the pending Flood. Anyone who believed his message and wished to avoid the destruction was invited to repent, reform their behavior, and find safety in the ark. Noah's childlike faith in God shielded him and his family from the destruction experienced by the rest of the world in the Flood. He labored many years to build that enormous ark without knowledge of the span of time required to build it or the span between building it and the rain. Despite all that uncertainty, "…Noah did; according to all that God commanded him" (Gen. 6:22, NKJV).

Through his great faith and obedience, Noah found grace in the eyes of God. Living in the midst of a wicked and corrupt people, he was a breath of fresh air in God nostrils. The Bible affirms that "Noah was a just man, perfect in his generations. Noah walked with God" (Gen 6:9, NKJV). And Hosea clarifies what defines a walk with God. The wise understand righteous things and the prudent know that the ways of the Lord are righteousness. Therefore, the righteous who seek and do the will of the Lord are walking with Him (Hosea 14:9).

Do not lose your confidence for "it will be richly rewarded" (Heb. 10:35, NIV). Noah surely needed confidence while he labored under a cloud of uncertainty. When doubts emerged, he affirmed God as his confidence and found joy in His love and support. "When I said, 'My foot is slipping,' your love, O LORD, supported me. When anxiety was great within me, your consolation brought joy to my soul (Ps. 94:18, 19, NIV). Severely tested as we all are, Noah remained assured, resting on the sure promises of God, his confidence.

February 6

God Loves Sinners

Say to him, 'Be careful, keep calm and don't be afraid. Do not lose heart because of these two smoldering stubs of firewood.' Isa. 7:4, NIV.

"For my sake, deal gently with young Absalom," said King David even after Absalom wrenched the kingdom away from David with plans to assassinate him, his children, and his wives (2 Sam. 18:5, NLT). Before the temporary coup, Absalom hired a hit man to murder his brother Amnon. Painfully, David had banished him but greatly yearned for him. While banished, Absalom furtively stole the allegiances of Israel from David in anticipation of becoming king. After the coup, he openly slept with David's concubines, dishonoring his father's home, but when the news arrived that Absalom had died in battle, David's grief was inconsolable. Notwithstanding that his son had been a selfish, vain, conniving murderer, liar, and incestuous traitor, David had loved him with an abiding love.

David's love for his son is a striking illustration of how God loves His rebellious children. Even as we break all His commandments, reject His many offers of mercy and grace, and embrace demonic powers, He loves us "with an everlasting love" (Jer. 31:3). Ahab was an idolater and a rebellious child of God who "did more to provoke the LORD God of Israel to anger than all the kings of Israel that were before him" (1 Kings 16:33), but Ahab had God's assurance that He would defeat the kings of Syria and Ephraim who were "smoldering stubs of firewood" (Isa. 7:4, NIV).

Still, the courage of Ahab and his people "were shaken, as the trees of the forest are shaken by the wind" (Isa. 7:2, NIV). Their sins drove a wedge between them and their God, reducing their faith to sawdust. Frightful, guilty, and anxious, wicked King Ahab and the nation of Judah were ready to flee at the shaking of a leaf (Lev. 26:36). The gods formed by their own hands offered no peace, no security, and no protection. Foolishly they had made their only source of peace, the omnipotent, omniscient God of the universe, their enemy. But God loved them, pleaded with them, and protected them until they filled to overflowing the cup of His indignation.

"God judgeth the righteous, and God is angry with the wicked every day" (Ps. 7:11). Sin is so opposed to His will that our wicked actions infuriate Him. As with any father, He gets angry but that does not reduce the love. He counsels His children, points us to the way of righteousness, protects us, and supplies all our needs. Yet many accept the gifts but reject the Giver. To add insult to injury, we give our allegiance to the very things that steal our safety and peace while our Father mournfully watches us self-destruct. He agonizes over our rebellion but is helpless since He cannot force His will on us. He laments, "How can I give you up, Ephraim? … My heart churns within Me; My sympathy is stirred" (Hosea 11:8, NKJV).

Does God love sinners? Of course! He proved it by giving the ultimate Gift to release sin slaves. "God demonstrates His own love toward us, in that while we were still sinners, Christ died for us" (Rom. 5:8, NKJV).

February 7

Our Present Troubles

You will laugh at destruction and famine, and need not fear the beasts of the earth. Job 5:22, NIV.

Robel, a former Islamic leader in Ethiopia, converted to Christianity pursuant to a dream in which Jesus appeared to him. Leaders dismissed him from his mosque when he began to ask questions about Jesus. After he converted, Islamic militants destroyed his home and property and gravely stabbed his son. Further intimidation included militants threatening him and his family while brandishing spears. A year after the militants stabbed his son, they returned and burned his house a second time, causing Robel to flee without his family. Missing his family and longing to be close to protect them, he persevered by clinging to his faith.

Unable to deter Robel by violence, the militants used another tried and proven tactic to entice his return to Islam—monetary gain. They promised him a trip to Saudi Arabia for Islamic training and wealth upon his return to Ethiopia. Nevertheless, Robel chose to serve the risen Savior and shunned those treasures, which moths and rust destroy and where thieves break in and steal (Matt. 6:20). He preferred "poverty and to sleep in trees - with the freedom to choose his own faith still intact. According to Voice of the Martyrs, Robel said: 'People always seek the money and the wealth of the earth, but what I seek is from God.'"[32]

Counting the great cost in human terms to live for Christ, including suffering and possibly death, Robel remained faithful. The fear of violence and riches failed to dictate his loyalty, for he placed his trust in God who has authority over fear. He will keep those who trust in Him in perfect peace—the highest level of peace (Isa. 26:3). As is Robel, we are urged to doggedly seek God, place our troubles before Him, and patiently wait for deliverance. In God, the helpless have hope that one day injustice will shut its gaping mouth. In fact, God promises that on that day we will laugh at the efforts of evil men and at violence or any hardship, loss, or struggle.

The darkest hour is always just before deliverance. When Moses asked Pharaoh to release the Israelites, Pharaoh made their burden ten times harder by demanding they produce a full quota of bricks without providing them straw, and whipping the overseers because they could not fulfill this impossibility. The people became discouraged and Moses complained, "O Lord, why have you brought trouble upon this people?"(Ex. 5:22, NIV). But in His time God stretched out His hand against the enemy, showed them who was boss, and Pharaoh released His children.

Trials are as necessary to the Christian's faith building and endurance as weights are to a weight lifter. They change us from spiritually scrawny to spiritually powerful. So please be patient and look beyond the trials. "For our present troubles are [comparably] small and won't last very long. Yet they produce for us a glory that vastly outweighs them and will last forever" (2 Cor. 4:17, NLT). Then, we will laugh heartily.

February 8

A Settled Spirit

Surely he shall not be moved for ever: the righteous shall be in everlasting remembrance. He shall not be afraid of evil tidings: his heart is fixed, trusting in the LORD. Ps. 112:6, 7.

Former President Theodore Roosevelt wrote, "It is not the critic who counts: not the man who points out how the strong man stumbles or where the doer of deeds could have done better. The credit belongs to the man who is actually in the arena, whose face is marred by dust and sweat and blood, who strives valiantly, who errs and comes short again and again … who knows the great enthusiasms, the great devotions, who spends himself in a worthy cause; who, at the best, knows … achievement, and who, at the worst, if he fails, at least he fails while daring greatly, so that his place shall never be with those cold and timid souls who knew neither victory nor defeat."[33]

Michelangelo modeled such persistence and immovability. He accepted a challenge to paint the ceiling of the Sistine Chapel although he considered painting inferior to his avowed profession as a sculptor. For four years he lay on his back on a catwalk to paint 12,000 square feet of a sixty-seven-foot-high ceiling. He fell from a scaffolding three years after he began painting the ceiling, leaving him severely injured and bedridden with broken bones and lacerations. Thus, this accident abruptly interrupted and seemingly ended his passion.

Previous to his assuming the task, a controversy arose regarding commissioning Michelangelo, and detractors criticized the pope for selecting him. Michelangelo, difficult to deal with, deviated from the directions to paint only the twelve apostles, making the painting lag a year behind schedule and over budget. Under pressure from outside sources, the College of Cardinals, fearing he was unable to complete the project in his condition, met over the matter while Michelangelo recuperated.

Painting the ceiling was, itself, an ordeal, but the fall rendered Michelangelo weaker and wearier. Heat gathered at the top of the dome, causing the space to be nearly intolerable. His eyesight was compromised by the dripping paint as he lay on his back. Nevertheless, when he heard that the future of this undertaking was in jeopardy, Michelangelo devised a plan that personified persistence. He relied upon his aides to fashion a canvas body sling and hoist him up the scaffolding to the top of the dome. There he finished painting the ceiling of the venerated Sistine Chapel, fulfilling his commission and recuperating simultaneously.[34]

Like Michelangelo's resolve, the Christian's heart should be fixed and not disintegrate in defeat or dissolve into self-pity in the face of evil or difficult circumstances. That inner resolve emanates from obedience and explicit faith in Jesus. For we are not victims; we are more than conquerors in Him (Rom. 8:37). The spiritual conflict is won by the power of the Holy Spirit, and as super conquerors, our faith grows wider, our love grows broader, our joy grows deeper, and our walk grows closer.

February 9

Peace, the Absence of Fear

His [the righteous] heart is established and steady, he will not be afraid while he waits to see his desire established upon his adversaries. Ps. 112:8, AMP.

Growing up, I lived in an end house next to the woods where the trees thrived without benefit of chemical sprays to keep the insects at bay. A majority of the trees were wild cherry trees, home to the worm-like larval stage of butterflies. In the spring when the larvae had matured enough to eat through their ethereal dwellings, they would wiggle and inch determinately toward our home. Thousands of these larvae in different stages of growth would cover our home as if it were new paint. My older sister Shirley was deathly afraid of these caterpillars. With movable screens in our windows, we found that some of them crawled into our bedrooms. Screaming hysterically, she would gyrate and batter her body unmercifully to dislodge those that had crawled on or near her.

Fear, using the word as an acronym, suggests "False Evidence Appearing Real." Over the years, Shirley's mind had made these precursors to gorgeous butterflies her worst nightmare. These uncertified, false thoughts had crafted feelings of panic, dread, and terror that she believed and acted upon. Caterpillars never harmed her in any way—they are tiny crawling creatures without fangs or teeth or any other means of harming their adversaries. Even a picture of a caterpillar on a container of weed killer sent her into spasms of fear. Regrettably she cannot articulate this irrational fear that spilled over into all worms, for it controls her otherwise sound reasoning.

Causing anxiety and terror, fear is the absence of peace. Paul wrote, "The mind of sinful man is death, but the mind controlled by the Spirit is life and peace" (Rom. 8:6, NIV). The world's peace is sometimes precipitated by oppression and violence, but it is always uncertain and short-lived. After World War I, nations created the League of Nations to prevent another world war. All nations were to defer to this international organization to work toward a safer world. But the objective failed. History records the carnage of World War II and subsequent wars, evidence that world peace is sporadic and transitory. No matter how we try, world peace remains elusive. But spiritual peace thrives when we follow after the things that make for peace (Rom. 14:9).

Peace comes from Jesus, the Prince of Peace (Isa. 9:6). When we follow in His footsteps, obedient as He was obedient, submitting to His Father's will as He submitted, and trusting in the heavenly Father as He did, inner peace flourishes. Before Jesus ascended to heaven, He promised, "Peace I leave with you…. Let not your heart be troubled, neither let it be afraid" (John 14:27).

Like Isaiah, Paul declares Jesus Himself is our peace, bringing peace in various ways. Inner peace comes pursuant to submission, acceptance, and faith. Peace comes by reconciling ourselves with the Father who transmits His peace through Him to us. By acquiring the mind of Christ, we make peace with one another and allow Him to handle the adversaries who work to steal our joy.

February 10

Calming a Fearful Heart

Say to those who are fearful-hearted, "Be strong, do not fear! Behold, your God will come with vengeance ... He will come and save you. Isa. 35:4, NKJV.

Two thousand and eight will go down in infamy as the year of the systemic financial crisis. Nouriel Roubini blogged, "The rising risk of a systemic financial meltdown: the twelve steps to financial disaster." He detailed how the housing market collapse would lead to huge losses for the financial system, particularly in securing loans. Also, he warned that a national bank might go bust and that, as trouble deepened, investment banks and hedge funds might collapse. Even Roubini was taken aback at how quickly this scenario unfolded. The investment bank Bear Stearns failed. The pace and scale of the disaster accelerated and, as Roubini predicted, it destroyed the banking sector, Freddie and Fannie collapsed, stock markets tanked, and the economy entered a recession.[35]

As a result of the financial meltdown, some of the wealthy became so fearful that they lost hope. The German billionaire Adolf Merckle, who bought up large sums of speculative Volkswagen stock, committed suicide when he lost hundreds of millions of Euros. The financial global crisis engulfed his large wealth and status, and he could not face the horror of financial ruin. And Jed Horowitz wrote of how one financial advisor, watching his client's portfolios spiral down, killed himself. One statement in his suicide note clarified his reasoning: "Since you are reading this, I have just taken my life. It was necessary because the alternatives were totally unpalatable."[36]

Fearful hearts are created by uncertainty in the future, circumstances, and other people. And uncertainty also produces disquiet and insomnia. Opposite the feelings of uncertainty is assurance, which springs from belief in God's unfailing grace and in His character. Complete assurance says confidently, "God said it. I believe it, and that is the end of it," and it conquers fear. Assurance is believing the myriad promises in God's Word, promises extolling His unmatched love and protection of comfort and peace in times of trouble. These promises are a universal remedy for fear.

The Word provides the process for reducing and dismantling fear—hand your problems to God in the spirit of thanksgiving. "And the peace of God, which transcends all understanding, will guard your hearts and minds in Christ Jesus" (Phil. 4:6, 7, NIV). The handing over part is a struggle. Sometimes we grip our problems tightly while praying for peace. Other times we readily hand them over, then snatch them back. Only when we relinquish our problems totally to the waiting, outstretched hand of God and trust Him to decide the outcome, are fearful hearts calmed.

"Casting the whole of your care [all your anxieties, all your worries, all your concerns, once and for all] on Him, for He cares for you affectionately and cares about you watchfully" (1 Peter 5:7, AMP). Then, watch your fears dissolve.

February 11

Holding Our Hand

For I, the LORD your God, will hold your right hand, saying to you, 'Fear not, I will help you.' Isa. 41:13, NKJV.

The right hand is believed to be noble in some cultures, and certain core traditions are built around that belief. For instance, Indians of the Hindu faith have a fundamental rule that when dining the right hand is only used to receive food while the left hand is banned since it is perceived to be unclean. Arabs of the Islamic culture use the right hand to perform respectful tasks like eating, entering the mosque and receiving things. "It is mustahabb [a form of worship] to start on the right or use the right hand" when executing noble and hygienic pursuits. The left hand is used for exiting the mosque and bathroom and taking off ones clothes, among other things, while the right hand is considered more noble and honored and never used to handle or remove impurities.[37]

God's right hand symbolizes omnipotence, significance, and authority—He is divinely capable. The hand of God created and sustains the universe and calms the wind and the waves. And, imperceptibly, God's right hand turns our unregenerate hearts 180 degrees from carnal to righteous. Salvation, an offshoot of His lovingkindness, flows through His right hand for those who trust in Him (Ps. 17:7). When we call, He answers from heaven with the "saving strength of His right hand" (Ps. 20:6, NASB). Furthermore, He promises to uphold us with My righteous right hand" (Isa. 41:10, NKJV).

When God holds *our* right hand, comfort and peace ensue. He either grips our hand tightly or smothers them both in His hands as afflictions ravage our mind and body. The psalmist counsels us to set the Lord always before us: "because he is at my right hand, I shall not be moved" (Ps. 16:8). Turmoil and unease permeate our changing world, but God can be relied on to breathe peace in our little corner, peace so thick and potent that our hearts can rest on it. In addition, holding our hands is a sure sign of the love and compassion He so freely lavishes on His anointed. No matter how bad we are, no matter if we abandon Him, no matter our offenses, God loves us with an everlasting love.

The hand that holds our hand is a helping hand, a beneficent hand, a hand of refuge and strength, a miracle-working hand. The hand that holds our hand is a faithful hand, a forgiving hand, a hand of blessings and love. This hand holds us so securely that "No one can snatch them away from me [the Father's hand]" (John 10:28, NLT). The hand of God is a big hand, big enough to hold and keep the whole world. It is an authoritative hand, a hand that guides and controls the world and all that is in it. And it is an omnipotent hand, unlimited and eternal, for with Him all things are possible.

"The strong right arm of the LORD has done glorious things! The strong right arm of the LORD is raised in triumph. The strong right arm of the LORD has done glorious things! (Ps. 118:14-16, NLT). Trust that strong right arm that moves the hand of God.

February 12

Help in Time of Trouble

"Do not be afraid, O worm Jacob, O little Israel, for I myself will help you," declares the LORD, your Redeemer, the Holy One of Israel. Isa. 41:14, NIV.

To make a cocoon, the tiny little silkworm spins the silk used for clothing and other things. Silkworm larvae are the offspring of moths who lay eggs on the leaves of mulberry trees that hatch by the sun's warmth. Microscopically small, the larvae take months to grow large enough to spin silk. Then, two little jellylike threads are secreted from both the left and right sides of its head, hardening as they make contact with the air. As the worm moves its head back and forth, the two threads interlock until a cocoon of silk threads meshed into a mass like parchment paper is built. The larvae grow to maturity inside the cocoon. But if they are harvested for silk, the mature moths are not allowed to eat their way out of the cocoon, which is the raw silk.[38]

Although silk worms produce a luxurious and sought-after product, a worm denotes death, decay, and irrelevance in the story of Job. "And though after my skin worms destroy this body, yet in my flesh shall I see God" (Job 19:26). "They [the wicked] shall lie down alike in the dust, and the worms shall cover them" (Job 21:26). "The womb shall forget him; the worm shall feed sweetly on him; he shall be no more remembered; and wickedness shall be broken as a tree" (Job 24:20). "How much less man, that is a worm? and the son of man, which is a worm?" (Job 25:6).

Also, a worm signifies weakness and vulnerability as Isaiah depicted Israel—a nation that had fallen from its glory and were now despised, disparaged, conquered, and fearful of their enemies. But because they are precious in the sight of their Redeemer, He hears their fervent pleas for help and promises their powerful enemies will suffer defeat. The survivors will scamper back home, disgraced by the beating inflicted by the insignificant nation of Israel (Isa. 41:11). To alleviate their fear and ours, Isaiah points to God's omnipotence. "Lift up your eyes on high and see: who has created these? He who brings out their host by number, calling them all by name, by the greatness of his might, and because he is strong in power not one is missing" (Isa. 40:26, ESV).

All of us can recount feelings of insignificance, sorrow, and despair as we journey through our trials. Even Jesus, enduring awful suffering, is compared to a worm, "Yet, I am a worm and not a man. I am scorned by humanity and despised by people" (Ps. 22:6, GWT). But despite His suffering, despite the derision directed at him, Jesus clung to the cross and triumphed. Likewise, all of God's children will not only bear a cross but must also cling to it and hang on until our change comes.

Circumstances appear hopeless at times, but we have to hold on. Hold on when our enemies persecute us without cause. Hold on when the way is dark and cloudy. Hold on when every avenue of escape is blocked. God "has not despised nor abhorred the affliction of the afflicted; Nor has He hidden His face from Him; But when He cried to Him, He heard" (Ps. 22:24, NKJV). He is the supreme source of help when troubles arise.

February 13

Redeemed By His Blood

Fear not, for I have redeemed you; I have called you by your name; You are Mine! Isa. 43:1, NKJV.

Netta, speeding to get to work on time, ran through a red light, and the police stopped her and issued her a speeding ticket. Arraigned and found guilty, Netta was fined $2,000 and three points. She pleaded with the judge to reduce the fine, but the judge, a stickler for following the letter of the law, adamantly refused. With remorse Netta withdrew money from the bank to pay the fine, only to find out that the judge had already paid it. Although the judge would not and could not change the law, he mercifully conceived a way to both satisfy the law and rescue Netta, his child.

Likewise, but beyond comparison, Jesus redeemed us by paying the penalty required for sin. *Because we were bought with a price, we belong to God.* To fully compensate for our sins, He sacrificed His life as a ransom. God unconditionally accepts Jesus as the perfect substitute for every human being since Adam until the end of time (Rom. 3:23-25). Without redemption our disobedience would keep us forever at the mercy of sin with its awful and fatal consequences. And sin clutches us in bondage, preventing the desire to escape. Having a sinful nature, our thoughts and emotions are corrupted and our hearts are exceedingly wicked (Jer. 17:9). But Jesus broke the chains that hold us captives to sin and spiritual death (1 Cor. 6: 20).

God established His justice and mercy through His self-sacrificing plan of salvation, which was birthed before the creation of this world (1 Peter 1:20). *Hence, we belong to God through His grace.* God not only opens a way of redemption for us but also offers it as a free gift, clothing us with the garments of salvation and covering us with the robes of righteousness (Isa. 61:10). With our redemption and as we surrender to the will of God, we become His adopted children, destined to receive the full rights of legitimate heirs (Gal. 4:5). "In love he predestined us to be adopted as his sons through Jesus Christ, in accordance with his pleasure and will" (Eph. 1:4, 5, NIV).

While teaching and preaching on earth, Jesus demonstrated how to live a godly life as a prelude to eternal life, and He requires us to follow His example of love and self-sacrifice. He returned to heaven at the end of His earthly ministry and sent the Holy Spirit as a Comforter and Guide. With the indwelling of the Holy Spirit, we can achieve victory over sin as did Jesus. Moreover, we belong to God because He chose us to be saved "through the sanctifying work of the Spirit and through belief in the truth" (2 Thess. 2:13, NIV).

Astonishingly, we are deserving of obliteration but are offered the gift of salvation—a gift weighty with untold blessings. He calls each person to accept His proffer of grace, but many foolishly refuse. How privileged are we, who obediently accept His grace, to belong to God whose love is unfathomable!

February 14

The Glorious Homegoing

Fear not, for I am with you; I will bring your descendants from the east, And gather you from the west; I will say to the north, 'Give them up!' And to the south, 'Do not keep them back!' Bring My sons from afar, And My daughters from the ends of the earth— Everyone who is called by My name. Isa. 43:5-7, NKJV.

Defiance of God brought Jacob to plunder, Israel to the robbers, and the nation to homelessness (Isa. 42:24). Eventually the progeny of Abraham were dispersed among almost every nation on earth. Moses predicted this scattering as a result of their disobedience that brought severe sickness and prolonged disasters and uprooted them from the Promised Land and scattered them among the nations. After the dispersion, anxiety and longing for home gnawed at them and dread shadowed them as they languished in fear (Deut. 28:64-66).

Even so, He consoled Israel with the promise of bringing them home from captivity. This promise extends to spiritual Israel as well. Who is spiritual Israel? "Therefore, the promise comes by faith, so that it may be by grace and may be guaranteed to all Abraham's offspring—not only to those who are of the law but also to those who are of the faith of Abraham. He is the father of us all" (Rom. 4:16, NIV). "Understand, then, that those who believe are children of Abraham.... So those who have faith are blessed along with Abraham, the man of faith" (Gal. 3:7-9, NIV). "If you belong to Christ, then you are Abraham's seed, and heirs according to the promise" (verse 29).

Jewish believers who claim Jesus as the Messiah are the remnant of Israel, and Gentiles who accept the gospel are counted as the children of Abraham. These Christian believers became inheritors of the covenant promises given to Abraham, Isaac, and Israel.[39] God created both literal and spiritual Israel for His glory, for us to glorify Him by the lives we live. And we who glorify Him through appreciation, adoration, affection, and subjection will experience that glorious homegoing.

One day the "Israel of God [will] stand listening, with their eyes fixed upward,"[40] watching Jesus descend from the sky accompanied by a retinue of countless angels. Theirs will be among the names of the redeemed, both living and dead, whom He gathers from the four corners of the earth. "And it shall be said in that day, Lo, this is our God; we have waited for him, and he will save us: this is the LORD; we have waited for him, we will be glad and rejoice in his salvation" (Isa. 25:9).

"Soon there appears in the east a small black cloud, about half the size of a man's hand. It is the cloud which surrounds the Saviour and which seems in the distance to be shrouded in darkness. The people of God know this to be the sign of the Son of man. In solemn silence they gaze upon it as it draws nearer the earth, becoming lighter and more glorious, until it is a great white cloud, its base a glory like consuming fire, and above it the rainbow of the covenant. Jesus rides forth as a mighty conqueror."[41] Truly, it will be a glorious homegoing!

February 15

Whom God Has Chosen

He who made you, who formed you in the womb, and who will help you: Do not be afraid, O Jacob, my servant, Jeshurun, whom I have chosen. Isa. 44:2, NIV.

In the poem "Chosen Vessel" several containers made out of priceless materials vie for the Master to use them in His work of salvation. Gold claimed he could outshine the rest while Silver bragged of his graceful lines and exquisite carvings. The Master passed those two by and encountered Brass who felt his shiny exterior would be the best for men to view while Crystal believed her transparency would clearly show the contents of the vessel. Passed by also, Wood, polished and carved proudly, felt his use would be better for fruit than for bread. Finally, the Master encountered Clay:

"Empty and broken it helplessly lay.
No hope had the vessel that the Master might choose,
To cleanse, and to make whole, to fill and to use.

"Ah! This is the vessel I've been hoping to find.
I will mend and use it and make it all Mine....

"Then gently He lifted the vessel of clay,
Mended and cleansed it and filled it that day.
Spoke to it kindly. There's work you must do,
Just pour out to others as I pour into you."[42]

We do not choose God. It is impossible to liberate ourselves from the prison of sin without the power of God working in us to "will and to do of his good pleasure" (Phil. 2:13). First comes the knock on the door of our hearts; then we opt to invite Him in or remain unchanged by our disobedience (Rev. 3:20). Jesus said, "You did not choose me, *but I chose you* and appointed you to go and bear fruit—fruit that will last" (John 15:16, NIV). Without the saving grace of God and the tugs on our conscience by the Holy Spirit, our hearts remain depraved. Shackled, we are powerless to break free. But, "where the Spirit of the Lord is, there is liberty" (2 Cor. 3:17).

Like the empty and broken clay vessel, once chosen we are obliged to humbly submit to the Master's leading. "For the LORD takes delight in his people; he crowns the humble with salvation" (Ps. 149:4, NIV). Filled with His grace and armed with every resource to fulfill His plan for our lives, we bear lasting fruit and become His disciples. We are commanded to "love one another, even as I have loved you, that you also love one another. By this all men will know that you are My disciples" (John 13:34, 35, NASB).

God reshapes the chosen in His image, and then pours His love and compassion into us with the expectation that we will then pour His love and compassion out to the world.

February 16

No More Shame

Fear not; you will no longer live in shame. Don't be afraid; there is no more disgrace for you. Isa. 54:4, NLT.

"Give me a child or I shall die," begged Rachel. She lived in ancient times when they considered barrenness both a curse from God and a disgrace. Rachel, the sister of Leah and the second wife of Jacob, was barren and felt like an abject failure. Yearning for children so frantically, she persuaded Jacob to sleep with her servant and bartered with Leah to sleep with Jacob for mandrake leaves, a "remedy" for infertility. After Leah bore Jacob six sons, God opened Rachel's womb, and she bore him two sons. One was Joseph who saved the lives of His family during the famine in Canaan.

The Bible mentions several barren women. Rebekah, the wife of Isaac, the child conceived by Sarah and Abraham, was barren for twenty years, and dutifully, Isaac prayed for her all those years. Finally, she became pregnant with twins. One of these twins was Jacob from whose loins came the twelve tribes of Israel. Also, Manoah's wife, who was faithful to God, was barren. In her senior years an angel informed her that she would conceive and bear a son. Seemingly so insignificant that she is not mentioned by name in the Bible, God called her to bear and raise Samson as a judge and liberator of Israel from the Philistines (Judges 13). Likewise, Elizabeth, the cousin of Mary, the mother of Jesus, was barren. But in her old age she gave birth to John the Baptist.

So, too, was Sarah, Abraham's wife. Before the Lord opened her womb at age ninety, she became so desperate to have a child that she orchestrated nights of passion between her husband and her Egyptian handmaiden, Hagar. Sarah succeeded in getting her pregnant, but did not enjoy motherhood because of Hagar's impertinence. Miraculously, God poured life into her ninety-year-old womb and Isaac, the child of promise was born.

Similarly, Hannah, one of the two wives of Elkanah, was infertile while his other wife, Peninnah, bore him many children. Hannah was bitterly disappointed by her perceived failure. And to make matters worse, Peninnah made cruel remarks about Hannah's infertility. But Hannah entered into a covenant with God to return the child to Him if she conceived. By God's grace, she conceived and bore Samuel. After weaning him, she delivered him to the temple to live with Eli, the priest, where Samuel became a faithful prophet.

Few people in that culture considered barrenness an opportunity to glorify God. They considered it a shameful existence and a punishment for disobedience. Mosaic Law promised that faithfulness guaranteed blessings above all people, and fruitfulness, for no human or animal female would be barren (Deut. 7:14). Nevertheless, God used barrenness, in some instances, not to punish but to glorify Himself. Eventually, these women conceived, shamed no more, and gave birth to sons whom God used to fulfill His will. Trust him in your circumstances, for n*othing is too hard for God.*

February 17

Fair Weather Faith

But do not fear ... For behold, I will save you from afar, and your offspring from the land of their captivity; Jacob shall return, have rest and be at ease; No one shall make him afraid. Jer. 46:27, NKJV.

According to John Wesley's journal entry, he and his brother Charles were sailing back to England from America when a vicious storm hit. A huge wave engulfed the ship at one point, and the ship tossed and rolled from gale force winds, terrorizing many of the passengers. The English passengers screamed in terror at the prospect of dying in this storm, but the Moravian Christians calmly sang despite the terrifying waves and wind. Their demeanor highlighted their strong faith and the lack of faith of others. Noticeably, they had an inner peace that sustained them through the storm.

Approaching the Moravians after the storm had abated, John asked them if they had been afraid. They said no, and after a brief discussion John realized that their trust in God was bigger and wider than his. Should the ship sink, they feared not because they trusted that God would never forsake them. If they perished, they accepted His will completely, demonstrating the peace that passes understanding. John Wesley, founder of Methodism along with his brother, wrote, "I went to America, to convert the Indians; but oh! who shall convert me? Who, what is he that will deliver me from this evil heart of mischief? I have a fair summer religion. I can talk well; nay, and believe myself, while no danger is near; but let death look me in the face, and my spirit is troubled. Nor can I say, 'To die is gain!' I have a sin of fear, that when I've spun my last thread, I shall perish on the shore!"[43]

Wesley labeled his fear "sin" for fear is a doubt of God's Word—the Word that was made flesh and dwelt among us, the Word that is truth. Doubt announces that God is a liar when He says He cannot lie and that He is unable to fulfill His promises when He says that all things are possible with Him. Doubt says that God is uncaring and aloof when He says He loves us with an everlasting love.

But the Word says, "Do not be anxious about anything, but in everything, by prayer and petition, with thanksgiving, present your requests to God. And the peace of God, which transcends all understanding, will guard your hearts and your minds in Christ Jesus" (Phil. 4:6, 7, NIV). It begins and ends with gratitude, trust, and faith. Digging through His Word and following the clear directives, we unearth the sweet peace that the carnal mind cannot comprehend.

And this peace cannot be shattered by outward circumstances because it is based on an inward conviction of God's unfailing Word. It is the peace that allowed the Moravians to sing and praise when all appearances conveyed that the ship would sink. It is the serenity that comes when we fully trust God to handle our adversities, for those who trust Him find peace (Ps. 5:11).

February 18

Call on the Lord

You drew near on the day I called on You, And said, "Do not fear!" Lam. 3:57, NKJV.

"Seven days without prayer makes one weak" announced a church bulletin. How true and how tragic! Prayer is like a vitamin for our soul—it brings vitality to our relationship with God. Nevertheless, too many of us fail to use the power of prayer readily at our disposal. God wants to hear from us; He wants us to call on Him on "all occasions with all kinds of prayers and requests" (Eph. 6:18, NIV). To call on God intimates a prayer.

Calling on God is an essential component of the Christian life. And our spiritual strength is in direct proportion to our prayer life. For example, a *Newsweek* survey reported that 64 percent of adults said they pray every day; 10 percent several times a week; 4 percent once or twice a month; 2 percent a few times a year; 6 percent seldom; and 8 percent never. Thirty percent of those surveyed admitted to having a sporadic or non-existent prayer life. Is there any wonder that many people feel hopeless and helpless in a society marked by violence, disease, natural and manmade calamities, corruption, and lies?

Prayer is power. But as with the power inherent in electricity, it is useless unless we flip the switch. However, unlike electrical energy, prayer is free, welcomed, and so much more potent. God beseeches us to "Call to me and I will answer you and tell you great and unsearchable things you do not know" (Jer. 33:3, NIV). He promises that when we call, He will answer. God uses our petitions to forge a friendship that results in a secure personal relationship with Him and informs us that He no longer calls the righteous servants, but friends. He wants us to love, trust, and confide in Him, for that's what friends do (John 15:15).

Often, when we begin our prayer life, we use trite phrases and learned repetitions. But as the relationship grows, as we learn to walk with God. As we learn to trust Him and love Him, our prayers change. No longer concerned with impressing Him or hiding our weaknesses, we become comfortable in His presence. Freely, we are now able to share our concerns, shower Him with praise, thank Him for the mighty things He does, ask for forgiveness, and intercede for others. Like Abraham, we become His friend through regular communication and obedience. For, if we turn away our ear from hearing the law, even our prayers are an abomination.

A great poet wrote: "Speak to Him, thou, for He hears, and Spirit with spirit can meet -- Closer is He than breathing, and nearer than hands and feet."[44] The poet intimates that God cannot overlook our prayers because He is too close to miss them and he echoes Jeremiah who wrote: "I called upon thy name, O Jehovah ... hide not thine ear at my breathing, at my cry" (Lam. 3:55, 56, ASV). Prayer like breathing is a requisite for life. Without the air moving in and out of our lungs interminably, our physical bodies die. Correspondingly, without our prayers ascending to the throne of God unceasingly, our spiritual life expires. Call on God; He is listening.

February 19

Because of Your Words

Do not fear, Daniel, for from the first day that you set your heart to understand, and to humble yourself before your God, your words were heard; and I have come because of your words. Dan. 10:12, NKJV.

Angels are ministering spirits who work with God to protect, direct, and serve humanity. One, dispatched to minister to Daniel, gently touched his shoulder. He was on a special mission from heaven to assure Daniel that God is an active force for good in the lives of His saints. Faithful, obedient, and persistent, Daniel fasted and prayed for three weeks without a peep from heaven for an explanation of a vision that greatly troubled him. Contrary to appearances, all the while he was praying and fasting, God listened and worked to answer his earnest prayer in the affirmative.

Daniel did not receive an instant answer to his prayer but had to wait—a very tough place to be, especially when needs are urgent. Through Daniel God gave us a glimpse of how He works behind the scenes to address our petitions even when it appears that He is not listening. Because God's thoughts are not our thoughts, neither are His ways our ways, we may fail to understand why He does not instantly answer our pressing concerns. He works within the realm of infinite space and timelessness while we are earthbound and time controlled. Time and space do not manage God as they do us. With eternity in mind, He works out our circumstances for the larger good and His glorification, not necessarily for our immediate gratification or fleeting happiness.

God's vision is so much bigger than our meager circumstances. Even His peripheral vision extends from beginning to end, end to beginning, and bends around corners whereas our view is limited to here and now and barely a few feet ahead. The length of our days is approximately seventy years, full of trouble and sorrow, quickly pass, and we die. Conversely, a thousand years in God's sight are like a day (Ps. 90:4, 10). So, at times, we fret, denounce God, rant, rave, and sink into despair when we feel He is not listening or is unconcerned while our lives are falling apart.

Yet, God is never inactive where the righteous are concerned, and He moves heaven and earth to timely and precisely provide all the needs of those who wait on him. "For from of old no one has heard nor perceived by the ear, nor has the eye seen a God besides You, Who works and shows Himself active on behalf of him who [earnestly] waits for Him" (Isa. 64:4, AMP). How do we earnestly wait on God? Follow Daniel's example, pray and trust that He will provide according to His perfect will and timing. And, it is a peaceful wait if we accept that our Father God knows best.

Like Daniel, be faithful and continue to pray and trust even when deliverance is slow. Patiently waiting on God is a humbling exercise that builds our faith muscles and shows confident assurance in His wisdom and timing. While waiting, find peace in the psalmists' words, "I have never seen the righteous forsaken" for "the LORD loves the just and will not forsake his faithful ones" (Ps. 37:25, 28, NIV).

February 20

Great Things He Has Done

Fear not, O land; be glad and rejoice: for the LORD will do great things. Joel 2:21.

"And then the dispossessed were drawn west—from Kansas, Oklahoma, Texas, New Mexico; from Nevada and Arkansas, families, tribes, dusted out, tractored out. Car-loads, caravans, homeless and hungry; twenty thousand and fifty thousand and a hundred thousand and two hundred thousand. They streamed over the mountains, hungry and restless—restless as ants, scurrying to find work to do—to lift, to push, to pick, to cut—anything, any burden to bear, for food. The kids are hungry. We got no place to live. Like ants scurrying for work, for food, and most of all for land."[45]

Vividly described is the devastation of a severe drought combined with the overuse of the land that crippled thousands of families—four hundred thousand individuals—to flee the Great Plains. Using the prairie grasses for animal feed further depleted the natural protection from prairie winds endemic to the Midwest. These winds blew away the topsoil, and the lack of rain turned the ground into dust. Dust storms plagued the land and its inhabitants, causing respiratory problems that led to death.

God has a preventive remedy for drought and other calamities that occur in the land and in our hearts. The Bible says, "If my people, which are called by my name, shall humble themselves, and pray, and seek my face, and turn from their wicked ways; then will I hear from heaven, and will forgive their sin, and will heal their land" (2 Chron. 7:14). He is an unchanging God and His Word holds true forever.

Drought appears in the land because of a lack of rain and in our spiritual life because of a shortage of Jesus. Without that spiritual rain, we live purposeless, empty lives devoid of peace now and speed toward a future of death and destruction. But look unto Jesus who said, "Anyone who drinks the water I give will never thirst—not ever. The water I give will be an artesian spring within, gushing fountains of endless life" (John 4:13-14, *The Message*). Drink deeply, for His water prevents droughts in our lives.

But we all need a periodic revival to remain right with God. We need to use that preventive remedy for drought-filled lives. Such a personal revival requires humility and prayer to relinquish our will to the will of God so He can increase as Lord while we decrease. It is only then that God can do great things in us, through us, and for us. He is waiting to fulfill even the largest and most comprehensive of our needs. He says, "I *am* the LORD your God ... Open your mouth wide, and I will fill it" (Ps. 81:10, NKJV).

Parallel with our obedience or repentance and reformation is God's promise to provide abundantly with an unbelievably loaded benefit package full enough so that we are more than satisfied. Count the benefits—He forgives sins, heals diseases, redeems our lives, crowns us with love and compassion, satisfies our desires with good things, and works righteousness and justice for the oppressed (Ps. 103:3-6).

February 21

Beloved of God

And said, O man greatly beloved, fear not: peace be unto thee, be strong, yea, be strong. Dan. 10:19.

What a great honor! An angel speeds from heaven to share the news that the Sovereign God of heaven, the Creator of heaven and earth, the invisible, immortal, and invincible God not only hears but also is answering your prayer. And, the wonder of it all, He calls you greatly beloved! The term "beloved" is a term of endearment that conveys close intimacy, huge respect, and great love for a special person.

How did Daniel earn that signal honor, the beloved of God? One, he was disciplined in his undertakings. A pagan nation conquered his homeland, Judah, in 605 BC because of their disobedience. In the midst of paganism, the youthful Daniel refused to break the strict dietary laws given by God to Moses on Mount Sinai. Also, he studied rigorously, and by the grace of God, he excelled in all of his undertakings (Dan. 1:1-7).

Besides, Daniel had both a tremendous faith in God and an unswerving prayer life. As an adult, in the face of a royal decree to the contrary, he continued to pray to God three times a day. Even though exposure meant certain death that did not hinder him. Jealous of Daniel, his enemies immediately carried the news to Nebuchadnezzar who was compelled to carry out a death sentence despite his respect for Daniel. Nonetheless, Daniel remained faithful to God even as he was pitched into a den of ravenous lions (Dan. 6:4-27).

In addition, Daniel remained humble. The Bible says he turned to God and pleaded in the posture and attitude of humility to return home. He prostrated himself before God, entreating Him through prayer and petition, in fasting and in sackcloth and ashes. Daniel confessed his sins, admitting that he and his fellow Judeans were covered in shame and scorned by their bondage to pagan nations. Humbly he admitted that it was their rebellion, defiance, and transgressions that had caused their bondage (Dan. 9:3-11).

Furthermore, Daniel patiently interceded for his countrymen, praying not simply for his own return but for an entire nation of displaced Jews. He reminded God of how He had brought His chosen nation out of Egypt with a mighty hand, and he begged His mercy for them. "O Lord, in keeping with all your righteous acts, turn away your anger and your wrath from Jerusalem, your city, your holy hill." Even though Daniel knew from reading the book of Jeremiah that their captivity would be turned after seventy years, he fervently prayed, taking nothing for granted (Dan. 9:15-19, NIV).

Without a doubt, Daniel exhibited the characteristics of a godly person—faithful, prayerful, humble, patient, disciplined, loving, and well versed in God's Word. He pleased God who is no respecter of persons. Therefore, each of us is God's beloved when we live such an exemplary life of righteousness.

February 22

The Reality of Rebirth

Be not afraid, O wild animals, for the open pastures are becoming green. The trees are bearing their fruit; the fig tree and the vine yield their riches. Joel 2:22, NIV.

Elizabeth is a gardener who knows that an annual plant lives for only one year while a biennial plant lives for a cycle of two years. And an herbaceous perennial has a natural life cycle of more than two years. Herbaceous describes a plant that dies back and appears dead but resurrects the following year. These plants have soft, succulent stems as opposed to the brown, woody stems of other plants. With the sunshine and rain that identifies spring, these plants regain their vigor, sprout, and grow.

Symbolically and physically, spring ushers in light after darkness and life after death. Spring is a reminder of God creating the earth and its vegetation. "Then God said, 'Let the land produce vegetation: seed-bearing plants and trees on the land that bear fruit with seed in it, according to their various kinds'" (Gen. 1:11). Notwithstanding the brutal cold and frigid winds of winter, herbaceous plants, with their God-placed internal clock, revive to unremittingly dazzle us with their beauty.

Spring is also an object lesson in the Christian life. While death is a precursor of new life in spring and in the lives of born-again Christians, spring's revival is symbolic of the work of the Holy Spirit. Before we answer the knock on the door of our hearts, we are dead in our sins (Rev. 3:20). Our souls and hearts are housed in hard, woody, sin-laden containers. But upon confessing our sins and accepting Jesus as our Lord and Savior, the Holy Spirit shines the warmth of Jesus' forgiveness and morality into our heart, turning it succulent. The love of Jesus drives away the frigid winds and brutal cold of the winter of our lives where sin once reigned (Eze. 36:26).

Symbolically, we buried our old sinful lives through the God-ordained ritual of baptism so "just as Christ was raised from the dead by the glory of the Father, we too might walk in newness of life" (Rom. 6:4, ESV). Before we relinquished control of our lives, we were brown and woody inside, but salvation in Him gives us newness of life, a new start, regeneration. Spring emerges; sin loses its power; depression and darkness are driven away to be replaced by love and unselfishness. We receive a brand-new life in Him.

A gift from God, spring's unending cycle is a witness to the reality of rebirth. Born in sin and shaped in iniquity, we must be born again if we want to see the kingdom of God (John 3:3-7). After Adam and Eve sinned, every person born from their lineage inherited a sinful nature. "For just as through the disobedience of the one man the many were made sinners, so also through the obedience of the one man the many will be made righteous" (Rom. 5:19, NIV). Jesus came into the world to appease God's wrath against unrepentant sinners. He justifies us by delivering us from sin's penalty, sanctifies us by delivering us from sin's power, and glorifies us by delivering us from sin's presence. That is the reality of rebirth!

February 23

The Blessings of Intercessory Prayer

So will I save you, and you will be a blessing. Do not be afraid. Zech. 8:13, NIV.

"There is a place where thou canst touch the eyes, of blinded men to instant perfect sight; There is a place where thou canst say, 'Arise!' To dying captives, bound in chains of night … There is a place where Heaven's resistant power, Responsive moves to thine insistent plea; There is a place—a silent, holy hour, Where God Himself descends and works for thee. Where is that secret place? Dost thou ask where? O soul! It is the secret place of prayer."[46]

Prayer is a very potent weapon against the powers of darkness and against sickness, death, and want. Prayer has snatched individuals from death, closed lions' mouths, stopped the sun in its track, carved a highway through deep waters, and turned the clouds into lead, averting rain for three years. And at our disposal is an assortment of prayers to fit every need. Paul encourages us to, "Pray at all times (on every occasion, in every season) in the Spirit, with all [manner of] prayer and entreaty. To that end keep alert and watch with strong purpose and perseverance, interceding in behalf of all the saints (God's consecrated people)" (Eph. 6:18, AMP).

Out of this assortment of prayers is intercessory prayer, which is, in fact, a Christian obligation. Samuel said, "As for me, far be it from me that I should sin against the LORD by failing to pray for you. And I will teach you the way that is good and right" (1 Sam. 12:23, NIV). Many of us are blessed by intercessory prayer without even knowing we are the object of such love. Moses interceded for the Israelites after God threatened to consume them because of their wickedness. And Abraham pleaded, "Turn from Your fierce anger, relent and do not bring disaster on your people" (Ex. 32:12, NIV) And the "LORD relented and did not bring on his people the disaster he had threatened" (verse 14).

God specifically asked Job to intercede on behalf of the friends whose lack of support aggrieved Job as well as God. "My wrath is aroused against you and your two friends, for you have not spoken of Me *what is* right, as My servant Job *has.* Now therefore, take for yourselves seven bulls and seven rams, go to My servant Job, and offer up for yourselves a burnt offering; and My servant Job shall pray for you. For I will accept him, lest I deal with you *according to your* folly; because you have not spoken of Me *what is* right, as My servant Job *has*" (Job 42:7, 8, NKJV). Job prayed; God relented.

Like the sweet smell of incense that fills the room with its aroma, the fragrance of intercessory prayer floats back and envelopes the sender. "I commend intercessory prayer, because it opens man's soul, gives a healthy play to his sympathies, constrains him to feel that he is not everybody, and that this wide world and this great universe were not after all made that he might be its petty lord, that everything might bend to his will, and all creatures crouch at his feet."[47] Bless others and in so doing bless yourself through, committed intercessory prayer.

February 24

Power of the Holy Ghost

Joseph, son of David, do not be afraid to take Mary as your wife; for the Child who has been conceived in her is of the Holy Spirit. Matt. 1:20, NASB.

    The Holy Trinity is composed of God the Father, God the Son, and God the Holy Ghost, also called the Holy Spirit. Even so, there is one God. John expounds on the mystery of the Holy Trinity: "For there are three that bear record in heaven, the Father, the Word, and the Holy Ghost: and these three are one" (1 John 5:7). Peter told Ananias that Satan had so filled his heart that he had lied to the Holy Spirit. Then he said, "You have not lied to men but to God" (Acts 5:4, NKJV). As a member of the Godhead and the living Spirit of God, the Holy Ghost is all powerful.

    To earthbound, finite humans, He exhibits miraculous power by transcending or working contrary to the natural physical laws by which we are bound. For instance, He surpassed natural conception and supernaturally created an embryo in a virgin's womb without medical intervention. The angel's pronouncement of the conception and birth of a Son puzzled Mary who was a virgin. His answer bears witness to the omnipotence of the Holy Ghost. "The Holy Spirit will come upon you, and the power of the Most High will overshadow you. So the holy one to be born will be called the Son of God" (Luke 1:35, NIV).

    Omnipotence is an exclusive prerogative of God and is evident in "each of the three persons of the glorious Trinity. The Father has power: for at his word the heavens were made, and by his strength all things continue, and through him they fulfill their destiny. The Son has power: for like his Father, he is the Creator of all things; 'Without him nothing was made that has been made' [John 1:3], and 'in him all things hold together' [Colossians 1:17]. And the Holy Spirit has power."[48] Creating life is a mere thought for the Holy Spirit as is resurrecting the dead. He reduced Jesus from God to an embryo to start life as an infant. Fully human, Jesus suffered all the needs and limitations of humans and died so we might live. And the Holy Spirit raised Him from the dead.

    Similarly, the Holy Spirit's power is evident in the lives of Christians. Only He can transform an unregenerate sinner with a "heart [that] is deceitful above all things, and desperately wicked" to live a godly life (Jer. 17:9). Given permission, the Spirit will gently prod and mold even a serial murderer, hard-core addict, or brazen adulterer into an obedient and faithful candidate for heaven. Established bad habits, unregenerate hearts, and addictions are powerful and extremely hard to break, but they are no match for Holy Ghost power. Every stubborn habit, every evil inclination bows down and shatters at His presence. And His power is accessible.

    God the Father will give the Holy Spirit to those who ask, for He is not willing that anyone should perish (Luke 11:13; 2 Peter 3:9). Love provides this incomparable gift of the Holy Spirit who is the "great sanitizer" whose authority and power cleanses us from sin and perfects our characters for heavenly citizenship.

February 25

Finding Favor with God

But the angel said to her, "Do not be afraid, Mary, for you have found favor with God." Luke 1:30, NIV.

Favor is an indulgent privilege or friendly regard or approval shown to one by a superior.[49] And favor is comparable to God's grace, which is "a manifestation, an appropriation and an application of mercy." Grace, a byproduct of mercy, is an outgrowth of love. When Justice demands death, Mercy says, "Grace, I need you to apply yourself to this case." And Grace, who is at Mercy's disposal, does just that.[50]

Mary found such favor with God that He chose her as the earthly vessel to bear the Messiah. As He promises, God's favor cascades over such an humble, willing servant as she. Mary, understanding her inimitable mission, gratefully rejoiced and praised God. "My soul glorifies the Lord and my spirit rejoices in God my Savior, for he has been mindful of the humble state of his servant. From now on all generations will call me blessed" (Luke 1:46-48, NIV). Immediately obedient, Mary exhibited a quiet but firm faith as she became central to a supernatural, unprecedented event.

Likewise, Jesus (Luke 2:52), Samuel (1 Sam. 2:26), Joseph (Gen. 39:21), and David (Acts 7:46) found favor in God's eyes. But God is no respecter of persons. In Him is not found any trace of partiality (Acts 10:34, 35). God offers each of us mercy, grace, forgiveness, and the promise of eternal life. Therefore, we all begin at the same starting point. How is it then that some end up finding favor in God's eyes and others do not?

Psalm 5:12 provides the explanation. "Surely, O LORD, you bless the righteous; you surround them with your favor as with a shield" (NIV). He favors those who exhibit mercy and truth, for through the Word made flesh, iniquity is purged (Prov. 16:6). And the purging of iniquity opens the floodgates of heaven so that those who humbly yield their will to Him receive not simply ordinary blessings but a super abundance of good things and goodwill as well as special treatment. Sometimes, that preferential treatment includes discipline and trials, but "in his favour is life," for weeping may last for a season but eternal joy arrives thereafter (Ps. 30:5).

Moreover, His offer of grace and mercy and His love for sinners is a tangible sign of His favor, for we deserve nothing but death. Even when we rebuff Him and choose to serve the enemy, He courts us to offer us parity with His sinless Son. The riches of God's grace and favor fill our spiritual coffers to overflowing, and anyone who fails to secure this wealth of blessings will one day suffer the keenest pangs of agony and regret.

Thankfully, the indulgent privilege of His favor remains available for the modern Mary, David, Samuel, and Joseph. God gives grace and glory, and He will not withhold any good thing from the upright (Ps. 84:11).

February 26

Peace in the Midst of Turmoil

Be anxious for nothing, but in everything by prayer and supplication, with thanksgiving, let your requests be made known to God; and the peace of God, which surpasses all understanding, will guard your hearts and minds through Christ Jesus. Phil. 4:6, ,7 NKJV.

A billionaire business tycoon promoted an art competition, offering fame and fortune to the artist who best portrayed peace. Many artists entered the contest and turned in varied renderings of the concept of peace. By the deadline, artists had submitted pastoral scenes with sunshine, flowering trees, green grass, and a peaceful sky; undersea vistas with the bluest, calmest water housing schools of small fish darting playfully in and out of underwater caves; flowers in every hue and shape, kissed by the sun and flowing up a hillside with birds soaring slowly overhead; and paintings of mothers singing lullabies to their yawning babies.

Mildly disappointed at the predictability of the submissions, the tycoon became agitated at one painting seemingly presenting the antithesis of peace. This artist, a bedraggled young woman whose eyes spoke volumes of her meager existence, submitted a depiction of a raging, violent storm. Surprisingly, as the tycoon looked closely at the painting, he began to smile. Her painting won the competition.

She painted a vicious tornado at sea. The frantic waves violently crashed against the rocks on the shore. In the distance high above the shadowy waves that snarled menacingly, the purple and orange sky kept watch. A tornadic waterspout formed and its tip crammed into the bulging clouds while the bottom twisted and turned upon the water with great agitation. Lightning flashed and thunder cracked in the sky as the gusty wind filched the vegetation off the trees near the shoreline.

But sheltered in a tiny crevice in the rocks high above the waves sat a peregrine falcon with a small dark head covering her chicks with her wings. In the midst of that deafening storm, the mother bird slept peacefully. Jesus offers us that kind of peace. He lamented when Jerusalem continued to reject Him: "How often I wanted to gather your children together, as a hen gathers her chicks under her wings, but you were not willing!" (Matt. 23:37, NKJV). David, longing for that peace, supplicated, "hide me under the shadow of thy wings" (Ps. 17:8).

The peace of God that passes understanding is spiritually discerned. By faith we believe that God is everywhere at once and all powerful, that His ears are tuned to our pleas and His eyes rove protectively over this earth where the apple of His eye dwells (Ex. 3:7; 2 Chron. 16:9; Zech. 2:8). Precious and dear to Him are His saints. Clearly He did not rescue us from the bondage of sin through the agonizing death of His Son to abandon us. So, we can rest safely in the arms of Him who promises to carry our burdens and alleviate our fears. Trust Him to handle your burdens, and peace will envelop your mind despite the storms.

February 27

You Shall Be Safe

Stay with me; do not fear. For he who seeks my life seeks your life, but with me you shall be safe. 1 Sam. 22:23, NKJV.

Massacre is an indiscriminate and cruel act. To savagely kill scores of innocent people typifies man's heartlessness and speaks to the suspension of reason. Possessed of demons, King Saul ordered Doeg the Edomite to massacre eighty-five priests of Nob in addition to the men, women, children, cattle, and livestock. Abiathar, one of the priests, escaped and fled to David who was himself fleeing from the wrath of Saul. David assured Abiathar that he would be safe with him (1 Sam. 22:19, 20).

But this inhumanity is not without consequences. God promises to deliver the obedient and righteous from fear, but He leaves the wicked to their vices and the attendant results, one of which is fear. In effect, the wicked often times harbor genuine fear. "As for those of you who are left, I will make their hearts so fearful in the lands of their enemies that the sound of a windblown leaf will put them to flight" (Lev. 26:36, NIV).

Saul descended from humbleness and confidence as an obedient follower of the most High God into fearfulness and wickedness subsequent to defying God's will. This defiance caused his sons to be disinherited upon the Lord's rejection of him as king. Saul's insolence opened the door for the evil spirits to shadow him, rendering him unbalanced and depressed. He continued to spiral downward into lawlessness and barbaric cruelty. Anxiety and fear of the future prompted him to consult a medium, a capital offense in ancient Israel and an abomination to God.

Although the underdog when he promised to protect Abiathar, David kept his promise for the umbrella of God's favor fully covered David and, by association, extended to Abiathar. After David became king, he appointed Abiathar high priest (1 Kings 2:26) and his companion and counselor (1 Chron. 15:11, 27:34). David's kindness to Abiathar reaped important benefits for himself as well. For instance, when David escaped from Jerusalem in the wake of the coup by his son Absalom, he requested Abiathar and the prophet Zadok to remain with the Ark and continue their priestly duties while spying for him. This spying yielded valuable intelligence that contributed to David's survival and triumph over Absalom.

Compliant to God's will and trusting in His protection, David saved himself and his followers. God promises that if we keep His commandments, we will abide in His love, His joy will remain in us, and our joy will be full (John 15:11, 12). The joy Jesus offers is not fleeting happiness but the peace of knowing that God is near, that His love is secure and deep as He holds our eternal future in His hand, that He has prepared a place for us and is coming back for us, and that He is our advocate and friend. Accordingly, with Him we are safe.

February 28

How Valuable We Are!

But even the very hairs of your head are all numbered. Fear not therefore: ye are of more value than many sparrows. Luke 12:7.

"Icons" is the name of one of the MasterCard "priceless" ads. Included are icons like the Jolly Green Giant, Charlie the Tuna, the Vlastic Pickle Stork, the Pillsbury Doughboy, and others sitting around a table. The narrator states, "broccoli: $1.79; tuna: $3.59; and crescent rolls: $2.39. Getting everyone together for dinner—priceless." A faceless narrator closes with, "There are some things money can't buy."[51] The term "priceless" is tossed around quite loosely. But the meaning of the word is fulfilled to the maximum in the value God places in us.

God's long-suffering is an indication of the value He places on our souls. His mercy is packaged in His patience. "The Lord is not slack concerning his promise, as some men count slackness; but is longsuffering to us-ward, not willing that any should perish, but that all should come to repentance" (2 Peter 3:9). For 120 years while Noah preached about the end of days, God showed forbearance to the wicked antediluvians. Throughout earth's history, He has been patient with His wayward children, not wanting anyone to perish (2 Peter 3:9).

Our value also is evidenced by His love. Jesus says, "Greater love hath no man than this, that a man lay down his life for his friends" (John 15:13). Jesus, fulfilling the will of our heavenly Father, died for us while we were entrenched and deliberate sinners. While we held Him in contempt, while we embraced other gods and rejected Him, Jesus died for us. While we trampled upon His holy precepts, while we, without a hint of gratitude, consumed His bounties, while we committed egregious sins and executed wicked injustices, Jesus died for us.

That God created us for His glory and made us fearfully and wonderfully in His own image again highlights our value (Ps. 139:14). We are his handiwork, recreated in Jesus to do good works (Eph. 2:10). Although we are born with a sinful nature, He sees our potential, recognizing that with spiritual growth we will rightly reflect His character. And He has prepared exquisite dwelling places in heaven for us to coexist alongside Him and the entire sinless heavenly host. Even more amazingly, He adopts us as His children, clearing the way for us to share in the inheritance of His Son Jesus.

"Just as every drawing by Picasso has tremendous value because Picasso made it, so we as God's unique creations have unimaginable, intrinsic worth."[52] Never, never underestimate your worth in the eyes of our heavenly Father! We are His priceless masterpieces, created and sustained by His own hand, comforted and guided by the Holy Spirit, trained in righteousness by His Word, brought into His presence through prayer, and saved and sanctified by His Son Jesus. What more can He do or say or be to show how important we are to Him? We are truly His valued possessions.

February 29

Divine Intervener

Then all the people of the region of the Gerasenes asked Jesus to leave them, because they were overcome with fear. So he got into the boat and left. Luke 8:37, NIV.

In Milton's *Paradise Lost*, Mammon is personified as a fallen angel living in hell who looks down and not up—Mammon does not focus on celestial and eternal things. For "even in Heaven his looks and thoughts Were always downward bent" as he coveted the streets of gold. Once on earth, he influenced mankind to ransack the wealth in the earth even if it meant crushing those who opposed this wickedness.[53] A false god, he is worshipped by hordes of people who give him power in exchange for riches.

Mammon, an Aramaic word defined as "riches," has connotations of greed and deceit. Covetousness generates greed which generates deceit which generates corruption all of which are strewn along that broad path that leads to destruction. Covetousness, the desire to get wealth or fame or things at any cost, compels people to step on an iceberg of wrongdoing that floats toward present and eternal destruction. God is opposed to it evidenced in the Commandments and throughout the Bible. In fact, He warns us to "Watch out! Be on your guard against all kinds of greed; a man's life does not consist in the abundance of his possessions" (see Luke 12:14).

Sadly, the love of economic gain motivated the people from the country of the Gerasenes to reject and dismiss the Majesty of heaven after Jesus exorcised demons from two men. The exorcised demons then possessed a herd of swine that ran over a cliff and drowned in the sea. Previously, the demon-possessed men had terrorized the coastline, threatening the well-being of all passersby. The pig herders witnessed the miraculous transformation of men who once were demoniac but now sat peacefully and reverently at the feet of Jesus. Still, they demanded that Jesus leave the country because His intervention had dipped into their profits.

Talk about bad choices! They chose tangible financial profits over the eternal benefits of Jesus' grace. Through the craving for riches "some have been led astray and have wandered from the faith and pierced themselves through with many acute [mental] pangs" (1 Tim. 6:10, AMP). The love of God and the love of money are mutually exclusive since they cannot simultaneously exist. Additionally, they are collectively exhaustive. For, one will most certainly dominate until it overpowers the other.

We gain tremendously if we welcome the divine Intervener into our hearts and allow Him free reign in all areas and in all ways. This is effortless when we love Him absolutely. "Hear, O Israel, the Lord our God, the Lord is one. Love the Lord your God with all your heart and with all your soul and with all your mind and with all your strength" (Mark 12:28-30, NIV). This all-compassing love for Him will reap lasting benefits including untold wealth and happiness in the kingdom of God.

March 1

Obey God at Any Cost

And fear not them which kill the body, but are not able to kill the soul: but rather fear him which is able to destroy both soul and body in hell. Matt. 10:28.

John Huss, a Bohemian reformer living in the fifteenth century, is a well-known martyr who determinately accepted death rather than recant his religious principles. Huss, influenced by the writings of an earlier martyr, John Wycliffe, also became an enemy of the papacy by proclaiming that the scriptures were the supreme authority and Christ stood as the head of the church during the time the pope claimed supremacy.

Huss was called before a council and judged to be a heretic. The cardinal of Cambray advised him to confess the errors in his articles; swear that he would not teach, hold, or maintain these articles; and openly recant. Huss replied, "I am ready to submit myself to the information of the council; but this I most humbly require and desire you all, even for his sake which is the God of us all, that I be not compelled or forced to do the thing which my conscience doth … strive against, or the which I cannot do without danger of eternal damnation."[54]

Recant his written religious beliefs and silence his conscience or die—those were his choices. He chose death at the hand of men rather than eternal death. At the stake Huss said, "In the truth of the Gospel which I have written, taught, and preached, I die willingly and joyfully today."[55] With the flames, fed by his own books, flaring up to consume him, Huss calmly sang a hymn. Dying a martyr's death, he recognized that our sojourn on earth is temporary and uncertain for "man that is born of a woman is of few days and full of trouble" (Job 14:1).

Huss, like other martyrs, died because he "fear[ed] Him who is able to destroy both soul and body in hell" (Matt. 10:28, NKJV). God is the only Being who has power over our soul's salvation. Because God is our Creator, Redeemer, and Lord, it goes without saying that we should esteem Him unconditionally. Yet Scripture resounds with texts that warn, admonish, and counsel us to fear God who made heaven and earth, to respect and obey Him at any cost. Among them, Psalm 76:7 is emphatic that "You [God] alone are to be feared" (NIV). And Acts 5:29 advises us to obey Him rather than man when man's requirements conflict with the Word.

Furthermore, Jesus gives those who fear Him a wonderful promise: "Whosoever therefore shall confess me before men, him will I confess also before my Father which is in heaven" (Matt. 10:32). We confess Him by acknowledging that He is the Son of the living God and by our walking in righteousness as He walks through the "washing of regeneration, and renewal of the Holy Spirit" (Titus 3:5). We confess Him when no circumstance, no person, or no sin is allowed to move Him out of the center of our lives. Sometimes obedience is difficult, scary, or inconvenient, but continue to confess Him and render respect to whom respect is due and honor to whom honor is due, for obedience is the greatest respect and the greatest honor.

March 2

Encountering Jesus

Fear not ye: for I know that ye seek Jesus, which was crucified. Matt 28:5.

A Salvation Army commercial titled "Amazing Grace" uses the hymn of the same title as its base. "Amazing grace, how sweet the sound that saved a crack head, drug addict, alcoholic, meth freak, a wretch like me. I once was homeless, broken, sad, just lost. But now I am sober, happy, I'm found, was blind but now I see. Everyday shattered lives are restored thanks to the goods you donate to the Salvation Army."[56]

Really?!? I contend that the Master life-changer and restorer of shattered lives is Jesus. The Bible declares, "Therefore if any man be in Christ, he is a new creature: old things are passed away; behold, all things are become new" (2 Cor. 5:17). After we truly encounter Him, our lives are amazingly transformed from selfish, uninhibited sinners to Christ-like, heaven bound saints who love Jesus above all.

The Holy Spirit empowers us and alters our thought processes. No longer to be feared, a burning stake and hungry lions lose their power. Death and torture are temporary setbacks. Love for self is no longer paramount. We bury self and willingly sacrifice our time, means, and talent for our neighbors and pray for our enemies. Jesus asks us to deny self and endure hardships, and we do (Matt. 16:24, 25).

Jeffrey Dahmer, a notorious serial killer, is reported to have murdered seventeen young men and teenage boys and cannibalized some of them. While in prison, Dahmer allegedly accepted Jesus as His Savior, allowing guards to baptize him in the prison whirlpool. That Dahmer may be a heavenly citizen one day is difficult for some to accept. But Jesus died for and is powerful enough to convert the most egregious sinner.

Jesus hung on the cross between two convicted criminals who cursed and reviled Him along with the Jewish rabble at the foot of the cross. One of the criminals, however, accepted Jesus as His Lord and Savior. Pursuant to Jesus' traversing the area speaking as never a man had spoken before, the criminal encountered Him (John 7:46). Unconsciously, he stored Jesus' life-giving words in his heart, and on the cross, convicted that this was the Messiah, the converted thief asked Him to remember him when He comes into His kingdom.

Moreover, our inner heart change is confirmed by our outward actions. George Frederick Müller, a well-known missionary who cared for the poor and orphans, emerged in his early teens as an incorrigible thief and liar who drank and gambled. Years later, he encountered Jesus who transformed him into an evangelist with a desire to minister to orphans. Altered by the power of the Holy Spirit, he refused a fixed salary and sold all his worldly possessions, trusting God for his sustenance. Encountering Jesus, he generously gave to God and man.

March 3

The Compassion of Jesus

So the women hurried away from the tomb, afraid yet filled with joy, and ran to tell his disciples. Suddenly Jesus met them.... Jesus said to them, "Do not be afraid. Go and tell my brothers to go to Galilee; there they will see me." Matt. 28:8-10, NIV.

Our Daily Bread shared the story of a little boy determined to buy a puppy from a farmer, and he chose a puppy with a crippled leg. Gamely, the farmer tried to alert the boy to the limitations of a lame puppy, prompting the little boy to pull up his pant leg and point to his braces. He told the farmer of his struggle to walk and, cuddling the puppy in his arms, vowed to give the puppy lots of similar love and help. This is compassion.

Compassion is the deep awareness of the suffering of another coupled with the wish to relieve it and comprises two different levels. First, we sympathize at another person's suffering; then, we take action to relieve that suffering. Jesus suffered the ultimate sacrifice by giving His life as a substitute and surety for our sins. Nevertheless, He realized the women who came to embalm His body would be terrified at the violent earthquake caused by the angel who opened the tomb at His resurrection and whose countenance shone as lightning. First, the angel assured them. Then they met Jesus who calmly *reassured* them.

Women in the ancient near East were treated as second-class citizens. According to Josephus, a first century Jewish historian, Jewish law described women as inferior in all matters.[57] But, Jesus, culminating the most important mission of all time on earth and poised to return to the glories of heaven, took the time to reassure these societal second-class citizens not once but twice. And then He commissioned them to spread the gospel.

His compassion encased other societal outcasts as well. A leper knelt before Jesus believing He could heal him. "Filled with compassion, Jesus reached out his hand and touched the man. 'I am willing,' he said. 'Be clean!' Immediately the leprosy left him and he was cured" (Mark 1:40-42, NIV). Jesus could have healed the leper without touching Him. But He knew the lonely, vilified leper had known only condemnation and censure since he had been declared unclean, never the comfort of human touch. People looked at him with fear and loathing, but Jesus looked at him with compassion. His touch and healing validated the leper as valuable.

God's compassion is not confined to the physical human condition but to our eternal spiritual welfare as well. Love engenders compassion, and Jesus deeply loves us. Love prompted Him to prepare a plan of salvation before Adam and Eve sinned, to institute it at the moment they sinned, and to finish it on the cross. "Because of the LORD's great love we are not consumed, for his compassions never fail. They are new every morning; great is your faithfulness" (Lam. 3:22, 23, NIV). What a blessing to encounter Jesus and partake of His compassion!

March 4

Resurrection Power

When Jesus therefore had received the vinegar, he said, It is finished: and he bowed his head, and gave up the ghost. John 19:30.

"It is finished" rang from the parched lips of the outwardly defeated crucified man of Galilee. It resounded from earth to heaven to hell. All heaven knew it was the triumphant last expression of a conqueror who vanquished His enemy. The enemy cringed in eternal defeat. To His earthly family, friends, and disciples, this cry brought hopelessness. "With the death of Christ the hopes of His disciples perished. They looked upon His closed eyelids and drooping head, His hair matted with blood, His pierced hands and feet, and their anguish was indescribable…. They saw only the cross and its bleeding Victim. The future seemed dark with despair."[58]

"It is finished" signified that the plan of salvation had reached its culmination. Jesus became the sacrificial Lamb who took away the sins of the world. Through Adam's disobedience, we all are sinners and deserve to die. But God gave us the gift of eternal life through the death of His beloved Son, Jesus, the second Adam (Rom. 3:23, 5:18, 6:23). Isaiah tells us that our iniquities separate us from a holy God and our sins cause Him to turn away, rendering fruitless our prayers and pleas (Isa. 59:2). But Jesus' death appeased the wrath of an angry God, induced our reconciliation with Him, and redeemed us through His own shed blood.

As important as His death is, His resurrection is equally as central. It is the archetype of all subsequent resurrections, and it guarantees that we, too, have that option. He promises that "because I live, you also will live" (John 14:19, NIV). His resurrection, the resurrection of the first fruits who arose at His resurrection, and the resurrection of Lazarus and others who had died and were restored to life by His Word prove His divinity, that He is the Son of God with the power to revive the dead.

We are spiritually anew to a living hope through the resurrection of Jesus (1 Peter 1:3). "Just as Christ was raised from the dead by the glory of the Father, we too might walk in newness of life" (Rom. 6:4, ESV). His resurrection assures us of the new birth revealed to Nicodemus, a spiritual renewal made possible by obedience and trust in a living Savior (John 3:1-15). Spiritually renewed, we become new creatures as we discard the old carnal natures (2 Cor. 5:17). Jesus' resurrection and subsequent return to heaven allow Him to mediate and advocate for His people. And because He is exalted and worthy, Jesus offers His blood for our forgiveness and grace, perking up God's ears who hears and answers in the affirmative (Heb. 7:25).

"It is finished" was certainly not a cry of defeat but a cry of an unimaginable victory by an incredible Champion for the salvation of a fallen human race. This cry cemented our rescue; deflected the wages of sin from us to the broad, sacrificial shoulders of our Savior, Jesus Christ (1 John 2:1); and allowed us to walk victoriously in His footsteps. Thank God for resurrection power through Jesus!

March 5

Mysteries of God

Fear not, Zacharias: for thy prayer is heard; and thy wife Elisabeth shall bear thee a son, and thou shalt call his name John. Luke 1:13.

Both Elizabeth and Zechariah, parents of John the Baptist, came from a long line of priests through the lineage of Aaron, the brother of Moses. Jewish law held that only males from Aaron's linage could serve as priests in Solomon's temple. After Aaron died, his two sons Eleazar and Ithamar served. And their descendants were split into divisions for ministering appointments in the temple. Zechariah came from the order of Abijah, the eighth of twenty-four orders (1 Chron. 24:1-5).

While Zechariah burned incense in the temple of the Lord and the worshippers prayed outside, an angel stood at the altar of incense (Luke 1:8-11). The angel terrified Zechariah but thoughtfully calmed his fears and notified him that God had heard his fervent, prayers for an offspring. At the time the angel appeared, the couple was childless. Elizabeth was barren and past the childbearing age, for Zechariah described him and his wife as well along in age, prompting him to question the angel doubtfully, "How can I be sure of this?" (verse 18)

Zechariah, blameless and upright, looked at the natural world and its limitations and doubted the word of God. Maybe he was so overwhelmed at the thought that this longing might become a reality after years of passionate prayer that he overlooked the Source. Like His character, God's Word contains mysteries that cannot be understood by humans. "To minds the strongest and most highly cultured, as well as to the weakest and most ignorant, that holy Being must remain clothed in mystery."[59]

Many doubt or reject particular doctrines because they cannot entirely understand God's Word, ways, or power. Consider God! Scientists have estimated there are a billion trillion stars in the universe and God calls each of them by name (Ps. 147:4). David tells us "Your eyes saw me when I was only a fetus. Every day [of my life] was recorded in your book before one of them had taken place" (Ps. 139:16, GWT). How presumptuous of us to measure our knowledge with that of the sovereign God! How haughty of us to suppose we are entitled to discern every nuance of His Word! Impossible! Ludicrous! His thoughts and ways are light years beyond our meager comprehension (Isa. 55:9).

Although some of His ways remain a mystery to us and "clouds and darkness are round about him: righteousness and judgment are the habitation of his throne" (Ps. 97:2). The Bible provides all we need, and faith assures us of things unseen. Martin Luther King Jr. said, "Faith is taking the first step when you don't see the whole staircase." And faith, which pleases God, sustains us in our belief that one day all mysteries will be cleared up and we will have perfect, complete knowledge (1 Cor. 13:9, 10). That we learn of the mystery which is Christ in us and the hope of glory should be sufficient for now until we know as God knows us.

March 6

Child of the King

But when the fullness of time had come, God sent forth his Son ... to redeem those ... under the law, so that we might receive adoption as sons. Gal. 4:4, 5, ESV.

During the French Revolution, the populace beheaded King Louis XVI and his queen, Marie Antoinette. Six years old and terrified, the prince watched his father's execution. The frenzied crowd, still blood thirsty after the public execution of his parents, lobbied for a similar outcome for him. As the prince stood as heir to the throne, the crowd, intensely and murderously disillusioned toward royalty, demanded he be executed.

"Suddenly from out of the crowd came another cry: 'Don't kill him. You'll only send his soul to heaven. That's too good for royalty. I say, turn him over to Meg, the old witch. She'll teach him to steal, to lie, he'll roam the streets as a tramp, and when he dies, his soul will go to hell. That's what royalty deserves!'" Appeased, the mob turned the lad over to old Meg. "This vile woman of the back alleys began to teach him bad words. But history tells us that every time this wicked woman prompted the prince to be profane, he would stubbornly stamp his little feet, clench his fist and declare, 'I will not say it. I will not say those words. I was born to be a king, and I won't talk that way!'"[60]

Showing evidence of Christ-like behavior, the young child of the king denounced wickedness. That is the standard for a child of the King of kings, made possible because Jesus descended to earth, leaving the unimaginable glory of heaven to accomplish the will of God. God promised a Messiah after the first couple disobeyed, ushering in a kingdom of evil, and Jesus fulfilled that promise (Gen. 3:15). Heralding Jesus' birth, the angel brought the greatest news ever. His birth, life, and death brought glad tidings of great joy for this perverse world because He came to bear "the sin of many, and interceded for the transgressors" (Isa. 53:12, NASB).

All who accept Jesus as Redeemer and Savior "to them He gave the right to become children of God, to those who believe in His name" (John 1:12, NKJV). Both the right and authority to become His child—to be adopted as sons—belong only to those who are born again and living righteously (John 3:5). It is faith that launches and obedience that preserves our status as God's children (Gal. 3:26).

What benefits and blessing are given to the children of the King! God supplies all our needs, disciplines us to strengthen us and return us to the right path, forgives our sins, and loves us unconditionally. He comforts, heals, and protects us and brings inner peace here on earth even in the midst of turbulence. One glorious day He will usher in eternal world peace and a kingdom of righteousness where love and unselfishness reign. Truly, He is "like a father to his children, tender and compassionate to those who fear him. For he knows how weak we are; he remembers we are only dust" (Ps. 103:13, 14, NLT). All these blessings are an outcome of the glad tidings of Jesus' life, birth, and death. Thank God for Jesus who facilitated our adoption!

March 7

Catcher of Men and Women

Jesus said to Simon, "Don't be afraid; from now on you will catch men." Luke 5:10, NIV.

David Ramos was born in Cuba and raised with few material goods. Upon finishing the sixth grade at age sixteen, he was snatched from school by officials who conscripted him into the Cuban army. As a Christian Ramos' commander persecuted him to force him to denounce his beliefs and turn his back on God. For three years his persecutors subjected him to hard labor, denied him food, and dumped him in solitary confinement among other harsh maltreatment. But he did not waiver. He chose to suffer afflictions rather than sin (Heb. 11:25).

However, Ramos was commissioned by God and spiritually enabled to become a catcher of men. After he was discharged from the army, a bus accident seriously injured him, requiring an arduous healing process, but God opened a door for him and his family to come to America. Settling initially in a Cuban refugee camp, Ramos led many lost souls to Jesus.[61] As he evangelized, he fanned into flames the smoldering gift that God had given him (2 Tim 1:6). The more he mined the Word, the more he prayed for the salvation of others, the closer became his relationship with God.

An effective catcher of men and women must first follow Jesus in word and deed adhering to His superior model of evangelizing. "The Saviour mingled with men as one who desired their good. He showed His sympathy for them, ministered to their needs, and won their confidence. Then He bade them, 'Follow Me.'"[62] Gospel tracts and Bible texts mean little to a person who is suffering in mind and body. But a tender touch, a word of comfort, and fulfilled needs break down barriers and enable the catcher to strike a chord that resounds all the way to a person's soul.

Soul winning has a domino effect. "One soul won to Christ will flash heaven's light all around him, penetrating the moral darkness and saving other souls."[63] When his brothers wrenched Joseph from family and homeland, he resolved to follow God's word and live a pious life. His godly witness to the pagan Egyptians bore much fruit as they respected and acknowledged God. Pharaoh asked his officials, "Can we find anyone like this man, one in whom is the spirit of God?" (Gen. 41:38).

The call to be catchers of people is a part of the Great Commission to lead lost souls who are groping blindly in darkness from pending death to life in Jesus. It requires obedience, sacrifice, and faith to answer and to proceed. For instance, Peter and his brother left families, jobs, and inheritance to follow Jesus. When called, *without questioning* "they left their father Zebedee in the boat with the hired men and followed him" (Mark 1:20, NIV).

Notwithstanding that the call opened them to a drastic life change, they straightaway answered the summons. And even in the midst of poverty, adversity, and uncertainty, they remained steadfast even unto death. He expects no less from us.

March 8

Belief Feeds on Faith

But when Jesus heard it, he answered him, saying, Fear not: believe only, and she shall be made whole. Luke 8:50.

A college professor prided himself on proving that Christians are the hapless victims of a hoax. Each semester during the first class he singled out the Christians and strived to humiliate them because of their faith. One semester he asked if God was the creator of the universe. A Christian young man answered in the positive, prompting the professor to respond, "If God made everything, then God made evil, and if we can only create from within ourselves, then God is evil." Stymied, the student did not respond, leaving the professor to gloat over his triumph. A second young man received permission to ask questions. First, he asked if there is such a thing as cold. The professor responded in the affirmative, sarcastically asking him if he had ever been cold. But the student disagreed with his answer, informing him, "Actually, sir, cold does not exist. What we consider to be cold is really only the absence of heat. Absolute zero is when there is absolutely no heat, but cold does not really exist." His answer silenced the professor.[64]

Mortal human beings will never have all the answers about God and the universe, but He gives us sufficient evidence to believe in His existence. The vast expanse of galaxies, the laws of physics and nature, and the wonders of the human body all testify to a powerful, loving Creator (Ps. 19:1). And Jesus is proof positive of the nature of God (John 1:1). What "may be known about God is plain to them, because God has made it plain to them. For since the creation of the world God's invisible qualities—his eternal power and divine nature—have been clearly seen, being understood from what has been made, so that men are without excuse" (Rom. 1:19, 20, NIV).

Imagine the mortal created ones wanting parity with the immortal self-existing Creator! It is arrogance and irreverence to believe that frail humans can and should have perfect knowledge akin to the Creator who spoke things into existence. We cannot comprehend His ways. "Everything is uncovered and laid bare before the eyes of him to whom we must give account" (Heb. 4:13, NIV). Now we see only "puzzling reflections in a mirror" and faith should keep us content with that (1 Cor. 13:12, NLT).

Truly, faith is an effective eraser for unbelief and is a gift from God, which the professor shunned (Eph 2:8). It is an abiding trust that God is in control and is intentional about our salvation—so intentional that He would rather die than abandon us. And faith comes from hearing the Word of God and allowing the word to dwell in us (Rom. 10:17; Col. 3:15). However, "If you refuse to believe until every shadow of uncertainty and every possibility of doubt is removed you will never believe. The doubt that demands perfect knowledge will never yield to faith. Faith rests upon evidence, not demonstration."[65] God will never erase all opportunities for doubt. For it is through faith that we please Him and are richly rewarded.

March 9

The Kingdom is Promised

Fear not, little flock; for it is your Father's good pleasure to give you the kingdom. Luke 12:32.

Written more than seventy years ago, the following reflects our present economic reality: "In such a spirit on my part and on yours we face our common difficulties. They concern, thank God, only material things. Values have shrunken to fantastic levels; taxes have risen; our ability to pay has fallen; government of all kinds is faced by serious curtailment of income; the means of exchange are frozen in the currents of trade; the withered leaves of industrial enterprise lie on every side; farmers find no markets for their produce; the savings of many years in thousands of families are gone."[66]

FDR, the president of the United States from 1933 to 1945, gave thanks that the problems the country faced during his terms in office were only material. And with this speech, he pointed to the encouraging side of the economic downturn. "Nature still offers her bounty and human efforts have multiplied it. Plenty is at our doorstep."[67] As the leader of the free world, he had an insider's look at the solution to the problem.

Likewise Jesus tells His "little flock" not to harbor fear of the economy or anything else. The phrase "little flock" intimates that He is a Shepherd who is proficient and prepared to provide for His dependent sheep. He recognizes that many are so worried or preoccupied with filling our storehouses for the lean years or to live lavishly now that we neglect our salvation. However, we are reminded how splendidly He arrays the flowers and dresses the grass both of which are particularly short-lived. "How much more will God do for you, you people of weak faith! Don't chase after what you will eat and what you will drink. Stop worrying. All the nations of the world long for these things. Your Father knows that you need them" (Luke 12:28-30, CEB).

"'The time promised by God has come at last!' he announced. 'The Kingdom of God is near! Repent of your sins and believe the Good News!'" (Mark 1:15, NLT) of the gospel. Seeking His kingdom first—making it primary and supreme in our lives—we get a two-for-one deal. For He promises to attach to our strong desire for and pursuit of righteousness sufficient provision to take care of all our needs if not our wants sometimes even before we even ask. It pleases God to freely and liberally give us the kingdom as it is not incumbent upon us to earn it for ourselves. For God withholds nothing good from his children.

Jesus' arrival on earth ushered in the kingdom of God, which is a present reality. He established His rule and authority—His kingdom—when He crushed the head of the serpent through His death and resurrection. After Jesus' ascension to heaven, He sent the Holy Spirit to comfort us, guide us, and prepare us for the literal future kingdom to be manifested when Jesus returns to reap His harvest of souls (John 16:13). Until He returns, the kingdom nestles inside of us in the form of the Holy Spirit. So let us single-mindedly pursue righteousness until we reside in the literal kingdom promised by God.

March 10

The Great I AM

Jesus spake unto them, saying, Be of good cheer; it is I; be not afraid. Matt. 14:27.

"It is I." The letter "I" is an insignificant, unadorned letter with none of the curves or spikes of a "g" or a "w," for example. But when it announces the Majesty of heaven, it is the most powerful, most regal, and most significant letter ever seen or written by man. Jesus claims His rank as deity—the great I AM—throughout Scripture. As deity He has the power to forgive and save sinners among other things. "Therefore I said to you that you will die in your sins; for unless you believe that *I am He*, you will die in your sins" (John 8:24, NASB). Our salvation hinged on His victory over death as He declared, "*I am* the resurrection, and the life*" (John 11:25).

"I am Who I AM." The many names of God highlight His nature, His character, and His relationship to His people. Commissioned by God to lead the Israelites living in bondage to freedom, Moses wanted to know who he should tell them sent him. The self-existent One, God said to Moses, "I AM THAT I AM" (Ex. 3:14). He "is the fullness of Being and of every perfection, without origin and without end. All creatures receive all that they are and have from him. But he alone is his very being, and he is of himself everything that he is."[68]

"I AM God." There is only one God—the only living God. "For even if there are so-called gods, whether in heaven or on earth (as indeed there are many 'gods' and many 'lords'), yet for us there is but one God, the Father, from whom all things came and for whom we live; and there is but one Lord, Jesus Christ, through whom all things came and through whom we live" (1 Cor. 8:5, 6, NIV). *El Elyon* means "The Most High God," and the name stresses God's strength, sovereignty, and supremacy.[69] Not anything can tower above the great I AM, for His power and position cannot be overruled!

"I AM God Almighty" (Gen. 35:11). As well, to Abram He said: "I am the Almighty God; walk before me, and be thou perfect" (Gen. 17:1). "El-Shaddai means God Almighty. El points to the power of God Himself. Shaddai seems to be derived from another word meaning breast, which implies that Shaddai signifies one who nourishes, supplies, and satisfies. It is God as El who helps, but it is God as Shaddai who abundantly blesses with all manner of blessings."[70]

I AM a provider God. Jehovah-jireh as Moses called God after he had witnessed that the Lord sees our needs and provides (Gen. 22:14). Supernaturally perceptive, God discerns and prepares for our needs far in advance of our asking, and without fail he delivers them on time and on target (Luke 12:30). The exact thing we need, many times to our amazement, is what He provides.

The great I AM is everything we will ever need on earth. And He is everything we could want, beyond our wildest imagination, in the coming Kingdom.

March 11

The King is Coming

Fear not, daughter of Zion; behold, your king is coming, sitting on a donkey's colt! John 12:15, ESV.

The Davidic Covenant is one of five in the Bible that God made with the literal nation of Israel. In it, He established David's throne evermore. Speaking through the prophet Nathan, He said, "Your house and your kingdom will endure forever before me; your throne will be established forever" (2 Sam. 7:16, NIV). The tribes of Israel, descendants of Abraham's grandson Jacob, became a literal kingdom under the rule of King David. And through David God established a dynasty of kings over Israel. Christ Himself, as "the Son of David," inherited David's throne (Matt. 1:1; Luke 1:32).[71]

During His mock trial after Pilate asked if He were a king, Jesus affirmed, "You are right in saying I am a king. In fact, for this reason I was born, and for this I came into the world" (John 18:37, NIV). However, His kingdom is a far cry from lavish earthly kingdoms. Born poor, raised humbly, unassuming, not comely, Jesus literally walked from place to place healing, comforting, and releasing lost souls from bondage. He preached the gospel, trained disciples, died by crucifixion, was resurrected, and ascended to heaven.

His disciples wanted His rule to duplicate that of earthly potentates, while the Pharisees and Sadducees wanted a kingdom where they could enforce stringent rules based on their interpretation of the Mosaic Law. And, they wanted a Messiah, their King, to hold lawbreakers accountable not change the laws (Matt. 5:18). As well, the common folk wanted Jesus to vanquish the Romans and liberate them from their rule (John 12:13). All carnal-minded, they were all disappointed.

Nonetheless when He returns, no longer seated on a donkey's colt but with breathtaking pomp and circumstance, He will descend as King Jesus, a mighty conqueror, wrapped in flaming fire. "Ten thousand times ten thousand, and thousands of thousands (Rev. 5:11) of adoring angels compose His entourage (Rev. 19:11-14). The heavens will shine brighter than the light of a sub-tropical summer sun with God's glory that is reflected onto His angelic host.

"No human pen can portray the scene; no mortal mind is adequate to conceive its splendor. 'His glory covered the heavens, and the earth was full of His praise. And His brightness was as the light' (Habakkuk 3:3, 4). As the living cloud comes still nearer, every eye beholds the Prince of life. No crown of thorns now mars that sacred head; but a diadem of glory rests on His holy brow. His countenance outshines the dazzling brightness of the noonday sun. 'And He hath on His vesture and on His thigh a name written, *King of kings, and Lord of lords*" (Rev. 19:16).[72]

Are you ready for His rapidly approaching appearing?

March 12

Like Ripples in the Water

And said, 'Do not be afraid, Paul. You must stand trial before Caesar; and God has graciously given you the lives of all who sail with you. Acts 27:24, NIV.

Ripples in a body of water occur when an object heavier than water is dropped in. The water, pushed below the surface by the weight, is raised up by its natural buoyancy. Since this buoyancy is greater than the weight of the water, the depressed water quickly returns to the surface. Once it reaches its original level at the top, the water stops rising and falls back in place. This process of oscillation causes the waves to move out in a circular fashion, thus creating ripples.

Righteousness also has a ripple effect. God's umbrella of grace covers those who recognize Him as their sovereign Lord and Savior, those who are ambivalent, and even those who are openly rebellious, especially when associates of the faithful. The apostle Paul's presence on the ship sailing to Rome saved the crew and passengers because of his faithfulness (Acts 27:23, 24). To plant a gospel seed in their hearts, God allowed the pagan jailers and crew to experience His sheltering grace.

And God saved Rahab's entire family because of *her* faith in Him. Rahab, a citizen of Jericho, hid the Israelite spies and aided their escape. The spies, sent by Joshua whom God appointed leader of Israel after Moses died, promised her protection if she assisted them. Although a Canaanite Gentile, a woman, and a harlot, Rahab had more faith than many of the Israelites who witnessed God's many miracles. She heard of the living God and His power and trusted that He would save her and her family from the pending carnage in Jericho (Joshua 2).

Likewise, Noah's righteousness saved his family. Generations after the Fall, the population increased and grew so wicked that God regretted He had created them and resolved to destroy them. However, blameless, faithful Noah walked with God and found favor in His eyes. He told Noah to build an ark pledging, "I will establish my covenant with you, and you will enter the ark—*you and your sons and your wife and your sons' wives* with you" (Gen. 6:18).

Similarly, it was because of God's promise to David that He did not eject Solomon from the throne after his fall into idolatry. Solomon began his rule humbly and obediently, but as the years passed, he married many foreign wives, contrary to God's commands, who turned his heart away from Him. Solomon sanctioned the idolatry of his wives and even practiced idolatry himself. Angry, God pledged to wrench the kingdom away. But He delayed doing so while Solomon was alive "because you have done this, and have not kept My covenant and My statutes, which I have commanded you, I will surely tear the kingdom away from you and give it to your servant. Nevertheless I will not do it in your days, for the sake of your father David; I will tear it out of the hand of your son" (1 Kings 11:11, 12, NKJV).

Our virtue, combined with prayer, has a similar ripple effect on the salvation of friends and family. In fact, God says that the fervent prayers of the righteous produce results.

March 13

I Trust in Thee

So we can confidently say, "The Lord is my helper; I will not fear; what can man do to me?" Heb. 13:6, ESV.

Adele taped Hebrews 13:6 on her computer at work. As she struggled in the midst of a crucible, a severe and long-term ordeal, this verse became a lifeline. She endured unfair and unwarranted persecution by a vindictive supervisor whose selfishness was palpable and blatant. Relished by her, the text was an essential reminder of God's protection as man seeks to triumph over His beloved.

Although the trial seemed interminable and appearances whispered she would lose her job and professional reputation, God turned events in her favor at the moment she became incapable of another second of maltreatment. The persecution stopped immediately, for God worked things out in an incredibly effective way. He faithfully fulfilled His Word: "let all those that put their trust in you rejoice: let them ever shout for joy, because you defend them: let them also that love your name be joyful in you" (Ps. 5:11, AKJV).

Today, Adele thanks God for the lessons learned through that awful, protracted experience. Intellectually, she knew that God was her helper and that she should be anxious for nothing; nonetheless, her faith was weak. But the day came when at the end of her rope, she cried out to God in sheer agony and despair. He heard her cries and immediately extinguished the fire that He had never left unattended. Watching attentively to ensure that only the dross burned, God's intent to reveal the pure gold of her character inched forward.

The Lord *is* her helper. He did not allow one speck of skin to burn, one strand of hair to singe, or one wisp of smoke to enter her lungs. God walked with Adele every step of the way, even when the persecution appeared to continue far beyond her perceived endurance. In hindsight, He stretched her faith and stamina. Although hot and very uncomfortable, His furnace is as secure as a mother's womb. The burning is crucial to prepare us for the kingdom of heaven. Obviously, He tempered the persecution, curtailing the enemy's viciousness. Consider Job; then imagine what the enemy would have done to him without Jesus' watchful eye and His intervention.

Confidently, Adele can say, "O my God, I trust in thee" (Ps. 25:2). Truly, she knows both intellectually and believes in her heart that God accompanies her in the midst of the fire, that God's Word is faithful and true. Plus, she knows and believes that even when He is silent He is intently scrutinizing her happenings, and that right on time, He will come to the rescue. Plus, she knows and believes that even the burning of the inferior metal from her character is a love tap that will lead to peace, joy, and love eternally with her Savior. Adele prays diligently that when the next trial comes, and it will, she will echo Job who affirmed, "though He slay me, yet will I trust in him" (Job 13:15).

March 14

Circle of Eternity

And when I saw Him, I fell at His feet as dead. But He laid His right hand on me, saying to me, "Do not be afraid; I am the First and the Last." Rev. 1:17, NKJV.

Apples of Gold jewelry advertises the unity wedding band as two halves coming together in eternal union. Once it is crafted by the jeweler, it has no beginning and no end, no first and no last. The wedding band began its history with the ancient Egyptians along the Nile River. They fashioned the papyrus that grew on the riverbanks into braided rings and bracelets using the circular shape that symbolizes eternity. Today, tradition still holds that the wedding band, in the shape of a circle, connects the parties together until their end.

Our triune God not only symbolizes eternity, but He *is* eternity. He points out, "I am Alpha and the Omega, the beginning and the end, the first and the last" (Rev. 22:13). Infinite without end or beginning, He is the great Deity, supreme above all else. "Before the mountains were born or You brought forth the Earth and the world, from everlasting to everlasting You are God" (Ps. 90:2; see also Isa. 44:6). God, the self-existing great I AM, is complete, endless, and total in Himself.

"There is none other than God. God is the giver and the receiver. God is all actions, and thus non-active; all motions, thus unmoved. God is the secret of the universe, the jewel of enlightenment, The Self of all selves, the Heart of all hearts, the Mind of all minds. And God may be thought of as three in one: Creator, Sustainer and Destroyer. But being all these He is none. The Absolute God cannot be categorised; nothing exists which He is not. He is dark and light, infinitely mysterious and simply beautiful. He is the Alpha and the Omega, the beginning and the end. Thus He is the complete circle, beginningless and endless."[73]

For the thirsty, He is the circle of deliverance—the beginning and end—for He gives freely of the "fountain of the water of life" (Rev. 21:6). Those with parched throats need God's grace to satiate their desire for the Living Water. Thus, He promises that all who thirst for righteousness shall be filled. Grace provides salvation, for by grace, Jesus' death and resurrection conquered sin and death (Matt. 5:16). Furthermore, grace's goal is to prepare us for heaven by fostering a heart change and a life change. Through submission and obedience, Jesus' character is stamped onto us, thereby, guaranteeing a perpetual new beginning—a circle of eternity (John 3:16).

The basis of all things, the beginning of all things, the source of all things good and perfect, God will soon bring the righteous to full circle. He created Adam and Eve perfect in health, beauty, wisdom, and righteousness, and then He gave them the tree of life to live a perfect life forever. They lived in Paradise, a perfect location, and talked with God face to face until sin interrupted. But one bright morning Eden will be restored, and we will again live in the perfect, heavenly circle of eternity with our Creator.

March 15

What You Do in the Dark

Therefore do not fear them. For there is nothing covered that will not be revealed, and hidden that will not be known. Matt. 10:26, NKJV.

Owner of a New York penthouse, yachts in Florida and the Mediterranean, and a mansion in the Hamptons, Bernard Madoff lived the life of the rich and famous. And he claimed to be forthright in business dealings. His Web site held: "Clients know that Bernard Madoff has a personal interest in maintaining the unblemished record of value, fair-dealing, and high ethical standards that has always been the firm's hallmark."[74] But his Ponzi "rob-Peter-to-pay-Paul" scheme disintegrated, exposing Madoff's secret life. No, the prosperity of the wicked will not endure (Job 20:21).

Before his Ponzi scheme, Madoff chaired the NASDEQ where he championed greater transparency. So, when the SEC obtained proof of Madoff's fraud, they dismissed the whistleblower's charges because of Madoff's "alleged" honesty. But the word "alleged" is not in God's vocabulary. All our deeds are transparent to Him—the heavens will expose the guilty (Job 20:27). Our ways are in His full view, and He examines all our paths (Prov. 5:21, 22). Not only does He see our deeds, He also knows our motives and invites us to serve Him in truth with all our heart (1 Sam. 12:24).

Malevolently bilking investors out of billions of dollars, their life savings and future financial support, Madoff lined his pockets and amassed a huge personal fortune. But, under arrest, he, in fact, confessed to the FBI that he was broke and that this scheme was doomed. To the federal prosecutors, Madoff admitted that his investment practice was one big lie. Thus, while Madoff lived extravagantly, he existed in apprehension of detection because he wisely perceived that such schemes are far from invincible.

Prior to his exposure, he appeared confident and in control, but cords of sin held him fast, and his secret spawned fear and anxiety. Fear of detection affects us emotionally for "the triumphing of the wicked is short, and the joy of the hypocrite but for a moment?" (Job 20:5, GWT). The Bible also says, "In the midst of his plenty, distress will overtake him; the full force of misery will come upon him" (Job 20:22, NLT). And the dread of exposure turns the deception into bitter gall, for "he will spit out the riches he swallowed; God will make his stomach vomit them up" (Job 20:15, NIV). Lamentably, Madoff was unwise in the ways of God. For the "fear of the LORD leads to life: There one rests content, untouched by trouble" (Prov. 19:23, NIV).

God is always straight with His people and has clearly revealed His omniscience. The Bible states, "Neither is there any creature that is not manifest in his sight: but all things are naked and opened unto the eyes of him" (Heb. 4:13). So isn't it foolish to endeavor to hide our awful deeds and our base motives when they are as clear as glass to God? Hiding from Him works to our detriment and to our eternal ruin. Confess those hidden sins. God seeks to help us, to strengthen us where we are weak, and to lift us up when we fall (2 Chron. 16:9).

March 16

Temporarily Asleep

Jesus told the synagogue ruler, "Don't be afraid; just believe." Mark 5:36, NIV.

"My daughter is dying, save her!" was likely the plea of Jairus, a local synagogue ruler who sought Jesus to heal his daughter. For he had stayed abreast of the miracles that Jesus had performed throughout the countryside. Finding Jesus, Jairus kneeled, acknowledging faith in His power and His ministry of compassion. On the way to his home, he and Jesus encountered Jairus' servants who informed him that the little girl had died, remarking, "Why bother the teacher any more?" (Mark 5:35, NIV). Moved by Jairus' faith, Jesus encouraged him to keep hope alive despite the news.

Before Jesus raised the little girl from the dead, His ministry had consisted of healing the sick, forgiving sins, exorcising demons, and breaking timeworn but spiritually stultifying traditions. That may be the reason the servants dismissed Him so quickly. After the girl's resurrection, Jesus proclaimed to the world that Death had its marching orders, a military term used by superior officers giving instructions for troops to depart—an authoritative order to leave. Death is thusly commanded, and Jesus saluted His authority over Death by raising Lazarus' rotting four-day old corpse from the tomb.

Jesus counseled Jairus not to fear death, just believe. That same assurance is ours if we trust His Word, for He is the resurrection and the life and all who believe in Him will not die (John 11:25). In other words, Death is no match for omnipotence. It is an interloper, an enemy that will be destroyed (1 Cor. 15:26). John prophesied Death's demise as well as the painful emotions elicited by it, noting, "God shall wipe away all tears from their eyes; and there shall be no more death, neither sorrow, nor crying, neither shall there be any more pain: for the former things are passed away" (Rev. 21:4).

Without Jesus' death and resurrection, Christianity would be an empty form. Paul says, "If Christ has not been raised, our preaching is useless and so is your faith." Moreover, he declares, "If Christ has not been raised; your faith is futile; you are still in your sins. Then those also who have fallen sleep in Christ are lost. If only for this life we have hope in Christ, we are to be pitied more than all men." Finally, Paul, to whom God appeared and conversed, confidently acclaims, "But Christ has indeed been raised from the dead, the firstfruits of those who have fallen asleep" (1 Cor. 15:20, NIV).

The Bible, recognizing death's transience, describes death as sleep at least fifty times. For Christians, death is not a mystery, neither is it permanent. It is a position of stasis, a defeated enemy with temporary authority over us in our sinful state. Jesus' sacrifice took away its victory and its sting (1 Cor. 15:55). After succumbing to the temporary authority of death, we rest in an unconscious state until, at the first resurrection, Christ summons His faithful saints forth from the grave (John 11:11; 1 Thess. 4:16). Should we fall asleep one hour or a thousand years before He returns, as time is suspended for the temporarily asleep in death, we will see Jesus in all His glory seemingly only a split second later.

March 17

Sleep Like a Baby

When you lie down, you will not be afraid; when you lie down, your sleep will be sweet. Prov. 3:24, NIV.

"'What's this?' Carl asked. 'It's your stuff,' the man explained. 'It's your stuff back. Even the money in your wallet.… We picked on you because you were old, and we knew we could do it. But every time we came and did something to you, instead of yelling and fighting back, you tried to give us a drink. You didn't hate us for hating you. You kept showing love against our hate.' He stopped for a moment. 'I couldn't sleep after we stole your stuff, so here it is back.'"[75]

Guilt is a sleep stealer for "an anxious heart weighs a man down" (Prov. 12:25). Guilt and sin are brothers, sin being the firstborn, the corrupter. Countless times our evil deeds or rogue motives produce guilt couched in anxiety and fear, which creates sleeplessness. Physically, a lack of sleep causes fatigue, mental grogginess, and prevents the body from recharging and healing itself. "'We don't take sleep seriously enough,' says Michael J. Sateia, MD … 'It's essential to life. If you disrupt the sleep cycle, you could face grave health repercussions throughout your body.'"[76]

The young man who assaulted and harassed Carl mislaid that sweet sleep that attends a settled mind and a clear conscience. For "the wicked are like the troubled sea, when it cannot rest, whose waters cast up mire and dirt. There is no peace … to the wicked" (Isa. 57:20, 21). Like the troubled sea, they are edgy and restive and their minds are robbed of peace. We have the promise of peace with God through Jesus Christ (Rom. 5:1, 12:18), but first we must be at peace with one another.

Hence, finding peace may entail making restitution to persons we harmed and/or offended. Although making restitution obliges humility and honesty, it frees the restorer. The young criminal, finally using sound wisdom and discretion, recognized the value of making amends. Until he offered penance to Carl for his criminal behavior, tranquility eluded him. Pursuant to his changed heart, he attained freedom from the guilt, fear, and anxiety that escorted him to bed, alienating him from Sleep. But restitution assuaged his guilty conscience, brought inner tranquility, and helped bridge the chasm between him and God. Sleep gently cuddled him yet again.

By his conscience, by the pricks of the Holy Spirit, the young man's spirit of repentance, confession, and subsequent act of compensating Carl became motivated. The Holy Spirit turned Carl's inner compass toward heaven; his thoughts changed, his actions changed, his motives changed, and his focus changed. But very importantly, repentance and restitution brought him relief.

Be careful to eliminate sin in your life for sin causes fear that contributes to other types of emotional distress. And, "If possible, so far as it depends on you, be at peace with all men" (Rom. 12:18, NASB).

March 18

The Voices of God

Jesus came and touched them, saying, "Rise and have no fear." Matt. 17:7, ESV.

On a walk home from school, a little girl encountered a very scary electrical storm escorted by thunder and bolts of lightning. Her mother, afraid her daughter may be struck by lightning and frightened of the storm, drove to meet the child. But her actions took the mother aback, for the daughter walked steadily through the storm, and at each flash of lightning, stopped, looked up, and smiled. As soon as the girl got into the car, her mother asked why she was smiling. Addressing her mother's inquiry, the child answered, "I'm smiling, because God just keeps taking pictures of me."[77]

Unlike the little girl, the Israelites, upon hearing the thunder and the noise of the trumpets and seeing the lightning and the mountain smoking as God spoke the Ten Commandments, implored Moses to intercede. Shaking with fear, they backed away from the voice of God, preferring Moses and not God in the communication department. (Ex. 20:18, 19). Moses assured them that God's wrath was not about to descend. But to discourage sin, God demonstrated His awesome power to instill in them a healthy fear of His sovereignty and majesty.

During the transfiguration, when Moses and Elijah appeared to encourage Jesus, Peter impetuously advocated permanent shelters for them to remain and rule on earth. Then, God spoke from a cloud that enveloped them saying, "This is my Son, whom I love; with him I am well pleased. Listen to him!" (Matt. 17:5, NIV). Terrified like the Israelites, the disciples, including the impetuous, brash Peter, fell prostrate. Although no thunder and lightning accompanied God's command, His voice still frightened the men.

When God first spoke to the young Samuel, he did not cower in fear. Four times God called Samuel and thrice Samuel thought Eli had called him. As yet, he did not know God's voice. It was not until Eli instructed him to answer that Samuel realized that God had called him. The fourth time God called Samuel answered, "Speak LORD, your servant hears" (1 Sam. 3:9, ESV). God gently shared the predictions regarding Israel and alerted Samuel to his calling as a prophet. It was necessary for God to instruct Samuel personally since Eli, called to be priest and mentor of the younger priests, had fallen short of his duty, particularly with his sons (1 Sam. 3:1-10).

Moreover, after Jezebel's promise to kill Elijah spooked him, he scampered away in fear and hid in a cave. The Lord passed by and a strong wind tore into the mountains and broke the rocks in pieces, but the Lord was not in the wind. Neither was He in the earthquake, nor the fire. Finally, Elijah heard a still, small voice that prompted him to leave the cave to listen to God's directions (1 Kings 19:11-15).

Sometimes God uses radical means to get our attention. At other times He approaches quietly to engage with us. But always, His sheep hear His voice and follow Him (John 10:27). If we remain in His presence where there is fullness of joy, we should hear His voice not in fear but in gladness (Ps. 16:11).

March 19

Joy Comes in the Morning

Do not fear what you are about to suffer. Rev. 2:10, ESV.

Pupa is the non-feeding, externally inactive life stage between the larva and the adult emperor moth that lives in a cocoon. To emerge from its cocoon, the adult must roughly gnaw its way out of the tough shell-like cocoon with the use of a sharp hook on its forewing after regurgitating a fluid to soften the hard cocoon. If this process is short-circuited, it inhibits the development of the moth.

A story is told of a man who did just that. Watching a moth struggle to exit from its natural shelter, he attempted to assist it by snipping off the hard end of the cocoon. The moth effortlessly slithered out, but it was physically deformed. It spent the rest of its life crawling around, unable to fly with a swollen body and shriveled wings. Inadvertently the man hamstrung the moth. "The restricting cocoon and the struggle required for the moth to get through the tiny opening were God's way of forcing fluid from the body of the moth into its wings so that it would be ready for flight once it achieved its freedom from the cocoon.... By depriving the moth of struggle, he deprived the moth of health."[78]

It is a given that we will suffer in this world. "Many are the afflictions of the righteous: but the LORD delivereth him out of them all" (Ps. 34:19). God offers us His presence, His comfort, His deliverance, and His peace, but He does not promise us an exemption from suffering. On the contrary, these blessings are provided to counter the despair and hopelessness that would consume us without His intervention.

God knows our nature, and He will not cripple us by removing painful situations. Without struggles and suffering we could not recognize our great need of Him. "Even though on the outside it often looks like things are falling apart on us, on the inside, where God is making new life, not a day goes by without his unfolding grace" (2 Cor. 4:16, *The Message*). If He allows us to be faith couch potatoes, we would lack the will and strength to persist in the battle where the enemy is invisible, clever, and more potent than we in our own strength. So, God allows situations and events to buffer us to the point of anguish at times, but He expects us to rise from our couches, do all that is humanly possible, and then exercise faith in Him to bring conclusion to the matter.

God's discipline pains us and Him, for like any loving father, He wants to fold us in His arms and block the source of our hurt. But because of our bent toward evil, He cannot do so. However, He mercifully tempers our suffering, shortens it, and promises that one day He will wipe away everything that generates suffering. If we are faithful to the end, He will give us the crown of life, and Jesus Himself will restore us and make us strong, firm, and steadfast (Rev. 2:10; 1 Peter 5:10).

Joy *will* come on that one-in-a-lifetime morning that will never end, a morning that will end sin and suffering and usher us into the physical presence of God.

March 20

Suffering for Right Doing

But even if you should suffer for what is right, you are blessed. "Do not fear what they fear; do not be frightened." 1 Peter 3:14, NIV.

Admiral Gaspard de Coligny, the military and political leader of the French Calvinist Protestants or Huguenots said, "I see clearly that which they seek, and I am ready steadfastly to suffer that death which I have never feared and which for a long time past I have pictured to myself. I consider myself happy in feeling the approach of death and in being ready to die in God, by whose grace I hope for the life everlasting."[79]

Coligny was assassinated during the French Wars of Religion on the first day of The St. Bartholomew Massacres. Catherine de' Medici, the mother of King Charles IX with his sanction, is credited with plotting and carrying out his murder. After a retinue of abuses against his dead body, a Roman Catholic mob decapitated and sent his head to Rome. They grossly mutilated his body, threw it into a stable, then dragged it through the streets to the bank of the Seine.[80]

Persecution because of one's faith, though sometimes physically and emotionally agonizing, has its spiritual reward. Coligny, whose crime was being a Protestant, died with his faith intact and his eyes on Jesus. God says, "Blessed are you when people insult you, persecute you and falsely say all kinds of evil against you because of me. Rejoice and be glad, because great is your reward in heaven, for in the same way they persecuted the prophets who were before you" (Matt. 5:11, 12, NIV).

Suffering is inevitable for the Christ follower—Jesus suffered and counsels us to accept our cross and follow Him (Matt.16:24, 25). "Suffering … is the badge of true discipleship. The disciple is not above his master.… If we refuse to take up our cross and submit to suffering and rejection at the hands of men, we forfeit our fellowship with Christ and have ceased to follow Him. But if we lose our lives in his service and carry our cross, we shall find our lives again in the fellowship of the cross with Christ."[81]

Persecution of God's people has produced awful carnage throughout history, but the persecutors do not go unpunished. Charles IX was undone by the St. Bartholomew's Massacre. Emotionally and physically fragile from his youth, he became a semi-invalid and died at the age of twenty-four—his body and mind weakened to the point of his becoming delusional and bedridden. Battered by his conscience, he had mood swings "from coarse boasting about the extremity of the Massacre, to claims that the screams of the murdered Huguenots kept ringing in his ears."[82]

Because Satan hates Jesus, he hates His followers and will use anything or anybody to force us to denounce our allegiance. But God promises both to ride out the storm beside us and to provide a great reward in heaven if we persevere. Through Jesus' tribulation, He proved and we learn that, although unwelcomed and painful, suffering produces fruit that is crucial to our future happiness.

March 21

Why Worry?

Can all your worries add a single moment to your life? And if worry can't accomplish a little thing like that, what's the use of worrying over bigger things? Luke 12:25, 26, NLT.

Erma Bombeck described the fears of a first grader on the first day of school: "My name is Donald, and I don't know anything! I have new underwear, a new sweater, a loose tooth, and I didn't sleep well last night; I worried. What if the school bus jerks after I get on, and I lose my balance and my pants rip and everyone laughs? What if a bell rings and a man yells, 'Where do you belong?' and I don't know? What if the thermos lid on my soup is on too tight, and when I try to open it, it breaks? What if I splash water on my name tag and my name disappears, and no one will know who I am? What if they send us out to play, and all the swings are taken?"[83]

Worry emotionally disjointed him. Imagine how insufferably long his first day of school was! And many Christians are equally disjointed and disabled by *merimnan*, which is Greek for "useless worry." Mark Twain wrote, "I am an old man and have known a great many troubles, but most of them never happened." Dale Carnegie's assessment of his worries illustrates Twain's statement. Forty percent of the things he worried about were calamities out of his control. Thirty percent embraced past decisions, twelve percent involved his health, and ten percent regarded the welfare of his kids. Amazingly, only *eight percent* of his worries involved things that he could control.[84]

Jesus yearns to carry our burdens. But our distrust, evidenced by unnecessary worry, diminishes Him to the likes of human deadbeat dads who intentionally and selfishly evade an obligation owed their children. As sinful as we are, God loves us with the same degree of love He has for His Son. Jesus said, "I in them and you in me. May they be brought to complete unity to let the world know that you sent me and have loved them even as you have loved me" (John 17:23, NIV). He desires to give us every good and perfect gift. "Or what man is there of you, whom if his son ask bread, will he give him a stone? Or if he ask a fish, will he give him a serpent? If ye then, being evil, know how to give good gifts unto your children, how much more shall your Father which is in heaven give good things to them that ask him?" (Matt. 7:9-11). Clearly, He is perfectly capable of supplying all our needs (Phil. 4:19).

"Worry never robs tomorrow of its sorrow, it only saps today of its joy," remarks Leo Buscaglia.[85] Exactly in line with Jesus' counsel, Buscaglia frames the futility and downside of worry. We ruin our present peace by focusing on a future maybe. Worrying does not change the problem, but it does change the worrier, causing both physical problems and emotional distress. Call a halt to worrying about tomorrow; we have enough to deal with today (Matt. 6:34). Seek the Lord and trust His promise of deliverance from all our fears (Ps. 34:4). And pray for His peace to fill every nook and corner of your mind, peace that crowds out fear and worry.

March 22

Vengeance Belongs to God

Joseph said unto them, Fear not: for am I in the place of God? Gen. 50:19.

"Man Held in Revenge Killing, D.C. Police Say: Father Allegedly Retaliated for Slayings of Son and His Mother" blared a headline in the *Washington Post*. Three weeks after a suspect allegedly killed his four-year-old son and the child's mother, the father purportedly took revenge on the suspected killer whom the police found shot to death. They suspected the alleged murderer but did not have enough evidence to charge him with the crime. Studies conclude that about 20 percent of homicides nationally are revenge murders, and in 2005, of the 16,692 murders in the U.S., 3,300 of them were revenge killings.[86]

Joseph's brothers were so certain that he would avenge their maltreatment after their father, Jacob, died that they bowed and begged him to relent. But Joseph was beyond that and assured them that vengeance belongs to God who, perfect in wisdom and knowledge, is the sole authority to settle up with wrongdoers (Deut. 32:35).

Revenge permeates our culture as surely as it did theirs. Popular movies demonstrate its allure. When the offended protagonist retaliates against his antagonist, the audience erupts in cheers and soaring high fives. As well, revenge is a popular theme in music, books, and through the actions of famous and prominent people. The message, loud and clear in our society but contrary to God's law, is that revenge rules!

"Beloved, never avenge yourselves, but leave it to the wrath of God, for it is written, 'Vengeance is mine; I will repay'" (Rom. 12:19, ESV). God alone can read the motives of the heart and measure justice accordingly. Revenge is not the fruit of a Christian—the desire for revenge resides in an unregenerate heart controlled by hate and selfishness. And carnal man's obsession for revenge is deep-rooted and very compelling. It is "a primitive, destructive, and violent response to anger, injury, or humiliation."[87]

"See that no one pays back evil for evil, but always try to do good to each other and to everyone else" (1 Thess. 5:15, NLT). To allow God to do His perfect work in us, bitterness, rage, and anger, brawling and slander and malice must be checked and replaced with forgiveness (Eph. 4:31, 32). Christ-like love forgives insults and injuries, erases bitterness, and quells resentment. The injured psyche may sting a while or the physical injury may take time to heal, but God still asks us to step back and give Him room to handle the perpetrator. That kind of forgiveness is not easy but with God all things are possible, and He will empower all who ask to love their offenders through Him.

"Do not seek revenge or bear a grudge against a fellow Israelite, but love your neighbor as yourself. I am the LORD" (Lev. 19:18, NLT). This is sage advice. Our world would be a mass of chaos and bloodshed if each of us took it upon ourselves to avenge wrongs. Rise above the evil in the hearts of your offenders. God will pay back trouble to those who trouble us, and we retain our claim to heaven (2 Thess. 1:6).

March 23

Reassurance

No, don't be afraid. I will continue to take care of you and your children. So he reassured them by speaking kindly to them. Gen. 50:21, NLT.

Realizing his family had no food, a man took his old shotgun and three bullets and went hunting. He shot at a rabbit and a squirrel, but he missed both of them. As he readied his gun to kill a wild turkey with his last bullet, a voice said, "Pray first, aim high and stay focused." Before he could shoot, he spied a deer and aimed at it, but as a rattlesnake crawled between his feet, he lowered the gun to shoot it. Again, the voice said, "Pray, aim high and stay focused." After some internal struggle, the man listened, prayed, aimed high, and shot the wild turkey. The bullet penetrated the turkey, ricocheted off a tree, and killed the deer. Then the handle snapped off the gun, hit the snake in the head, and killed it. Lastly, the impact knocked the man into a pond. When he recovered and stood up, fish were in all his pockets.[88]

"For who among men knows the thoughts of a man except the man's spirit within him?" (1 Cor. 2:11, NIV). That blessed voice of conscience, the voice of the Holy Spirit, is a ready and faithful guide to those who are right with God. Dwelling in our bodily temples, He speaks to us in our thoughts, through the Holy Word, and through others bringing peace of mind. The reassurance and comfort provided by the Spirit is worth more than gold in our confused and changing world. He reassures us that God offers us a "new birth into a living hope through the resurrection of Jesus Christ from the dead, and into an inheritance that can never perish, spoil or fade" (1 Peter 1:3, 4, NIV). This inheritance is reserved in heaven for the faithful until Jesus' second coming.

In this reassurance is God's promise to provide for His children, for "they that seek the LORD shall not want any good thing" (Ps. 34:10). This promise is comprehensive, contains no exceptions, no room for hedging, and is directed at those who love Him supremely, those who seek Him. With our restricted, imperfect vision, we see one avenue to a solution to our problems and needs. But in God's storehouse is a thousand plus supernatural ways to provide. Where we see a closed door, He sees an opportunity both to glorify Himself and to provide spiritual and physical necessities. No way is too dark, no door closed so tight that God cannot find a way to provide.

Look at how He provided for Esther, Mordecai, and the Jews when evil promised to destroy them; for Joseph when sibling rivalry proved callous and unrequited lust cast him in prison; for Abraham when he left home for an unknown destination; for David confronting a menacing giant soldier; for Jacob when Laban purposed to deceive and impoverish him; for the woman caught in adultery; and for you and me in a world of chaos and uncertainty.

Jehovah-jireh, our Provider, *will* supply all our needs (Phil. 4:19). And be reassured that those who seek Him want for no good thing, for the righteous will never be forsaken.

March 24

Lift Up Those Limp Hands

"Do not fear, O Zion; do not let your hands hang limp. Zeph. 3:16, NIV.

An old, useless donkey fell into an abandoned well, and unable to get out, she brayed pitifully for help. The farmer heard and sympathized, but decided she was no longer functional, reasoning it would take more time and money than she was worth to retrieve her. Hence, the farmer solicited his neighbors to help him toss dirt into the well to bury the donkey and the well in one fell swoop. The hard dirt plopped loudly as it landed on the donkey's back, terrorizing her. Predictably, after the initial flurry of activity to escape failed, she nearly sank into despair. But a thought wound its way past the fear and lodged in her brain. "Shake the dirt off and step on it." Soon, she rose higher and higher by shaking off the dirt and standing on it until she stepped to freedom.[89]

Disappointment and adversity are used by the enemy to bring us to the brink of despair. And despair amounts to the loss of all hope if we focus on the problem and not the Problem Solver. Moreover, if we choose to focus only on the problem, we are choosing defeat. But opting to focus on the big God we serve and trusting in His providences, we are able to shake off the despair and escape the enemy's plot to control us. Hope in God's providences shows a determination not to go limp in defeat. It shows a desire to lift up our shaking hands to our Refuge and Strength, and like the old donkey, shake off the fear and step up to Jesus. Use the Word of God to cheer up and the power of God to chin up.

The world we live in produces fear—fear of national calamity; fear of violence; fear of nuclear weapons; fear of divorce; fear of unemployment; fear of depleted portfolios; fear of illness and death mortify us. But we are powerless to control most of the things we fear. So straighten up that back, lift up that head, and bring those limp hands up to catch hold of His outstretched hand. Why do you continue carrying burdens that bow your back and render your hands limp when God's all-powerful hands are yearning to relieve you? Cast your burdens on Him for He cares for you (1 Peter 5:7).

Do not let your hands hang limp. Fold those hands in a posture of prayer and ask God to increase your faith. Inquire how to release your burdens and permit Him to carry them however and wherever He desires. Invite Him to help you put on the whole armor of God to fortify yourself against the attacks of the enemy. Beseech Him to erase all doubt in your mind about His love for you and how to abide in Him so He can abide in you.

If you truly love Him, implore Him to help you remember and believe this promise when fear arises, "'Because he loves me,' says the LORD, 'I will rescue him; I will protect him, for he acknowledges my name. He will call upon me, and I will answer him; I will be with him in trouble; I will deliver him and honor him … and show him my salvation" (Ps. 91:13-16, NIV). Then lift those hands in praise and victory over fear.

March 25

Love Covers a Multitude of Sins

You will not fear the terror of night ... nor the pestilence that stalks in the darkness, nor the plague that destroys at midday. Ps. 91:5, 6, NIV.

Plague and pestilence—the words themselves elicit fear. Black Death and the Great Mortality are names for a bacterial infection originating in the blood of rodents that decimated the population in the fourteenth century. Fleas feasted on the host rodent's blood and then transmitted the bacteria to humans, and sometimes the rats themselves transmitted the bacteria. In the Middle Ages, this plague reportedly killed between 75 to 200 million people worldwide. "Having no defense and no understanding of the cause of the pestilence, the men, women and children caught in its onslaught were bewildered, panicked, and finally devastated."[90]

A plague is toxic, virulent, and destructive as hate. And hate like a plague poisons the system and, unless checked, destroys the carrier. Hate is strong and almost always demands some negative action of the host, often compelling the host to execute horrible, destructive deeds. Hate is a desire to devastate people, places, and things based on revenge, intolerance, fear, and jealousy—it is the antithesis of love. It has plagued humanity from Creation as Cain, beset by hate, struck down his own brother in cold blood (Gen. 4:8). The first murder and the first fratricide in our history evolved from jealousy, which twisted into hate.

Live long enough and you will experience what hate and fear can do to individuals and to societies. Mull over the six million Jews who died in the Holocaust. Reflect on the two million Vietnamese who died at the hands of the Khmer Rouge. And consider how hate and fear propelled the Rwandan Genocide, the mass murder of an estimated 800,000 to 100,000,000 Tutsis by the Hutus in the small East African nation of Rwanda.

The antidote is love. The solution is love. God is love. Through the washing of rebirth and the renewal by the Holy Spirit, the goodness of God will control our old unregenerate natures. With a heart of love, the times of foolishness, disobedience, and bondage to all kinds of wicked passions and pleasures are past. The times of malice toward each other and hating and being hated by others are past (Titus 3:3-5). On the other hand, the times of forgiveness, compassion, and love are are our present, for Jesus counsels us to love our enemies, bless those who curse us, and pray for those who harm and persecute us (Luke 6:27, 28).

In the natural, it is well-nigh impossible to love our enemies for our sinful nature prompts us to retaliate; thus, loving those who are not lovely comes directly from our Supreme source of power. Plug in daily. For only through the power of prayer are we able to love those who kill our sons and daughters, rape and murder our sisters, persecute us unfairly, burn down our homes and steal our property, and look and act differently than we do. That heart change is the wonderful mystery of godliness.

March 26

Total Confidence and Full Surrender

Though a mighty army surrounds me, my heart will not be afraid. Even if I am attacked, I will remain confident. Ps. 27:3, NLT.

Overly conscientious, Sally would dissolve into misery over the smallest setback or failure. Sally's grandfather took her for a drive after a heavy snowstorm and said, "Notice those elms; the branches are so badly broken that the trees may die. But just look at those pines and evergreens. They are completely undamaged by the storm…. An elm holds its branches rigid. As it becomes weighted down, eventually its limbs break. But when an evergreen is loaded, it simply relaxes, lowers its branches, and lets the burden slip away. And so it remains unharmed."[91]

Sally, like many Christians, needs a confidence booster—Jesus who is faithful, authentic, and able. How many ways do we depend on Jesus to keep us confident? To echo Elizabeth Barrett Browning, "Let me count the ways!" We depend on Him for salvation and are assured of eternal joy. "He who has the Son has life; he who does not have the Son of God does not have life" (1 John 5:12, NKJV). And desiring all men and women to be saved (1 Tim. 2:4), He not only became the sacrificial Lamb but also commissioned angels, humans, and the Holy Spirit to work toward that end.

Depend on Him for comfort and strength in times of difficulties and loss. Paul said, we shall have tribulation (Rom. 8:35). And embodying his own words, the Jews flogged him on five different occasions, administering forty stripes save one. He was beat three times with rods, stoned once, shipwrecked three times, spent a night and a day in the deep, and often traveled by foot. He was in danger on the high seas and in peril of robbers, his countrymen, and the Gentiles. He struggled with weariness and toil, sleeplessness, hunger and thirst, cold and nakedness, among other things (2 Cor. 11:23-28). Still, he accepted his circumstances and remained faithful based on confidence in His Savior (Phil 4:10).

When we depend on God alone, we do not depend solely on that paycheck to pay the rent. Nor do we depend on the doctors to heal us. We lose our job, we hold God to His word to supply all our needs. We get sick, we trust the Great Physician. Don't despair over the struggles and trials; they strengthen us, for faith building is like surgery. Pain inevitably accompanies surgery, but the positive end results are generally improbable without the pain. When we have done all we can do, then it is time to surrender.

Surrender to Jesus; relax and give him the heavy load. Do we manage our own lives, or do we allow our Creator to do so? When we call Him Lord and Master, we acknowledge that He is in full control of our lives and circumstances. Full surrender requires us to make a conscious choice. Trusting only in God, realizing that He can do anything, realizing that He did not save us to leave us at the worst times of our lives, we can confidently exclaim, "I will never be shaken" (Ps. 62:2, NIV). That's confidence!

March 27

The Reproach of Others

Listen to Me, you who know righteousness ... in whose heart is My law: Do not fear the reproach of men, nor be afraid of their insults. Isa. 51:7, NKJV.

"One 'zinger' will erase twenty acts of kindness," wrote the authors of *We Can Work it Out*, a marriage self-help book. They discovered that the couples who weathered the marriage storm and avoided divorce hurled less insults and putdowns at each other than those who split up. As the years passed, those who eventually divorced launched five times as much blame, disapproval, and criticisms than those who stayed married. Clifford Notarius concluded, "Hostile putdowns act as cancerous cells that, if unchecked, erode the relationship over time."[92]

Can you imagine the reproach that Adam and Eve must have endured from each other after they sinned? Before the Fall they enjoyed a type of emotional and physical utopia without fear or difficult trials. But their disobedience propelled them into a world of drudgery, fear, and anxiety. After the Fall natural enmity existed between the sexes that still exists today. Imagine Jesus, their marriage therapist, counseling, "Get rid of all bitterness, rage and anger, brawling and slander, along with every form of malice. Be kind and compassionate to one another, forgiving each other, just as in Christ God forgave you" (Eph. 4:31, 32, NIV). Because, "if you keep on biting and devouring each other, watch out or you will be destroyed by each other" (Gal. 5:15, NIV).

But for God's grace all would remain condemned to death; thus, we are commanded to be introspective not condemnatory—to take the beam out of our own eyes. "Don't pick on people, jump on their failures, criticize their faults— unless, of course, you want the same treatment. That critical spirit has a way of boomeranging. It's easy to see a smudge on your neighbor's face and be oblivious to the ugly sneer on your own.... Wipe that ugly sneer off your own face, and you might be fit to offer a washcloth to your neighbor (Matt. 7:1-5, MSG).

Reproach or criticism is self-glorification at the expense of another. And, self-glorification and pride are cronies that settled in the bosom of Satan, ushering in his downfall. However, suffering the reproach of evil men and women is preferable over their praise, particularly in spiritual matters, for the world is out of step with the ways of God and His requirements. Jesus admonishes us to, "Beware of these teachers of religious law! For they like to parade in flowing robes and love to receive respectful greetings as they walk in the marketplaces. And how they love the seats of honor in synagogues and the head table at banquets" (Luke 20:46, NLT). Any Christian who seeks the praise and approval of the world is of the world and does not walk as Jesus' walks.

God will reprove those who reproach His people in the spirit of hate. "Pay no attention to insults, and when mocked don't let it get you down. Those insults and mockeries are moth-eaten, from brains that are termite-ridden, But my setting-things-right lasts, my salvation goes on and on and on" (Isa. 51:7, 8, MSG). Let God handle it.

March 28

When God Testifies Against You

Then I will come to you and judge you. I will be quick to testify against those who take part in evil magic, adultery, and lying under oath, those who cheat workers of their pay and who cheat widows and orphans, those who are unfair to foreigners, and those who do not respect me. Mal. 3:5, NCV.

Eyewitness accounts of crimes are often not trustworthy. Researchers state, "Memory is imperfect … because we often do not see things accurately in the first place. But even if we take in a reasonably accurate picture of some experience, it does not necessarily stay perfectly intact in memory.… The memory traces can actually undergo distortion. With the passage of time, with proper motivation, with the introduction of special kinds of interfering facts, the memory traces seem sometimes to change or become transformed."[93]

In the Bible God required that a court of law should hear at least two witnesses before a person is convicted of sin (Deut. 19:15). He instituted this fail-safe method being cognizant of man's propensity to bear false witness against his neighbor. Nevertheless, God's memory is perfect and trustworthy, and He promises to be a swift witness against the immoral, oppressors of the poor and needy, liars, and swindlers. God's law is the standard of witnessing against the unrighteous; it is the mirror that reflects our impiety.

Sorcerers and idolaters beware! He promises to testify against those who take part in the occult and witchcraft and who place other gods before Him. Our mainstream society is awash with movies, television shows, celebrities, and statesmen who are entertained by and trust in spiritualism. This is an abomination and affront to God who singularly is omniscient. "And when they say to you, 'Seek those who are mediums and wizards, who whisper and mutter,' *should not a people seek their God? Should they seek the dead on behalf of the living?*" (Isa. 8:19, NKJV).

Adulterers, liars, swindlers, and oppressors beware! God promises to testify against you as well. Any form of immorality that violates the two principles on which God's law is based—love your God with all your heart and your neighbor as yourself—will be held up to the light of the law and will be found wanting. When we become indifferent to God, when we fail to build a close personal relationship with Him, and when our godliness is superficial, the love for our fellow humans waxes cold as well. This lack of love manifests itself in corrupt, fraudulent actions against our neighbors and a disregard of God.

The portion of wrath reserved for the wicked is the "fiery lake of burning sulfur. This is the second death" (Rev 21:8, NIV). God promises "to call heaven and earth to witness against you this day, that you will soon utterly perish" (Deut. 4:26, NKJV), but He yearns to relent and save His wayward children who turn from their wickedness and accept His offer of salvation and grace. Those who fear God—the righteous—have no fear of the judgment for His salvation is near those who fear him (Ps. 85:9).

March 29

The Beginning of Wisdom

Afterward he said within himself, 'Though I do not fear God nor regard man.' Luke 18:4, NKJV.

An eagle perched on a block of ice just above Niagara Falls where the swift current propelled the ice and its occupant to the edge of the waterfall. In vain, other eagles and animals cried out a warning about the danger before him. "'I have great and powerful wings,' he boasted. 'I can fly from my perch at any time. I can handle it.'" Abruptly, the rush of water pushed the slab of ice over the waterfall. The confident eagle spread his powerful wings to fly over the precipice, discovering too late that his claws had frozen to the ice.[94]

Fearlessness is a benefit for parachute jumpers and race car drivers. But when it envelops recklessness, it is unwise in any occupation or avocation. Recklessness prompts us to disregard and, therefore, have no fear of the living God. To fear Him is to hold Him in reverent awe, to acknowledge His power and majesty, and to obey His law. All of nature reveals God's power and dominion, and acknowledging His omnipotence, we are obliged to fear Him. The angels fear Him: "In the council of the holy ones God is greatly feared" (Ps. 89:7, NIV). Pointing to His power of creation and authority over it, He asks His created beings a rhetorical question, "Should you not fear me?… Should you not tremble in my presence?" (Jer. 5:22, NIV).

Fools show contempt for God and His Word. "The fear of the LORD is the beginning of knowledge: but fools despise wisdom and instruction" (Prov. 1:7). Achan is a paradigm of the fool who fancied trinkets and stuff more than eternal life. He well knew that coveting is a sin that leads to further offenses, but he confessed, "When I saw among the spoils a goodly Babylonish garment, and two hundred shekels of silver, and a wedge of gold … I coveted them, and took them" (Joshua 7:21). Envisage losing your soul over things—a large gold nugget, a bag of silver, and an expensive garment.

As with the eagle whose arrogance and recklessness carried him over the precipice to disaster, so goes a person who disregards God and His Word. The psalmist describes the human version of that eagle. "There is no fear of God before his eyes. For in his own eyes he flatters himself too much to detect or hate his sin" (Ps. 36:1, 2, NIV). God is long-suffering with His wicked, wayward children, but the day will come when He will close probation and the intractable wicked will be lost forever.

Heed His counsel! Listen to His pleas! Learn to fear Him for the fear of the Lord is a fountain of life, snatching us from the snares of death (Prov. 14:27). "If you accept my words and store up my commands within you, turning your ear to wisdom and applying your heart to understanding, and if you call out for insight and cry aloud for understanding, and if you look for it as for silver and search for it as for hidden treasure, then you will understand the fear of the LORD and find the knowledge of God. For the LORD gives wisdom, and … knowledge and understanding" (Prov. 2:1-6, NIV).

March 30

Courageous and God Fearing

After a very hard delivery, the midwife finally exclaimed, "Don't be afraid—you have another son!" Gen. 35:17, NLT.

Midwives are revered and celebrated among the Ga people in Ghana, West Africa. At Christmas time they are showered with gifts pursuant to a legend about Anna the Midwife who assisted in the birth of Jesus. In the United States there are approximately 7,000 certified nurse-midwives who assist in the delivery of 200,000 births annually, primarily in hospitals. They work singly or in groups of midwives, have practices with physicians and HMOs, work in rural and urban areas, and assist private and public clients. These certified nurse-midwives work in tandem with an obstetrician in the event of complications.

The king of Egypt ordered Shiphrah and Puah, two Hebrew midwives, to perform infanticide—an unthinkable act. Specifically, he commanded them to kill the living, breathing male Israelite infants upon delivery. Exercising civil disobedience, they balked at Pharaoh's dictate and safely delivered and preserved the babies (Ex. 1:15-17). Courageous beyond measure, the midwives refused to obey a direct order from the highest human authority. This order, however, superseded God's sixth commandment not to kill, and these God-fearing women opted to obey God rather than man despite the consequences (Acts 5:29).

Their obedience not only caused the Israelites to continue to multiply and grow more powerful, but Shiphrah and Puah each reaped a personal benefit—a highly revered benefit in their era. The Bible says that God was "good to the midwives" (Ex. 1:20, NASB). The Egyptian king accepted their word at the failure to execute his command. Obviously God placed a shield of protection around them.

Obedience is a key element in a loving relationship with God, and Jesus blazed the path to obedience. He learned obedience by His sufferings, and through His obedience, we have access to life eternal (Heb. 5:8, 9). Our Savior denied His own will and followed the will of His Father who sent Him (John 6:38). Can we do any less? Our obedience points to our respect for and faith in God's direction for our lives and affairs. It speaks to our gratitude for His beneficence, to our awe of His power.

Fear is a four-letter word for obedience when applied to God as Shiphrah's and Puah's fear/reverence for God dictated their obedience. And God's salvation is near those who fear Him (Ps. 85:9). "Who are those who fear the LORD? He will show them the path they should choose. They will live in prosperity, and their children will inherit the land. The LORD is a friend to those who fear him. He teaches them his covenant" (Ps. 25:12-14, NLT).

March 31

God Is No Respecter of Persons

Jael went out to meet Sisera and said to him, "Come, my lord, come right in. Don't be afraid." So he entered her tent, and she put a covering over him. Judges 4:18, NIV.

God is a God of variety, mixture, and multiplicity. Nature demonstrates His variety; humanity highlights His multiplicity and mixture. With His human creation, God is an impartial judge; He offers salvation to everyone—He is "no respecter of persons" (Acts 10:34). Clearly the Bible supports that point. "You are all sons of God through faith in Christ Jesus, for all of you who were baptized into Christ have clothed yourselves with Christ. There is neither Jew nor Greek, slave nor free, male nor female, for you are all one in Christ Jesus. If you belong to Christ, then you are Abraham's seed, and heirs according to the promise" (Gal. 3:26-29, NIV).

Throughout the Bible God shows His respect for and compassion toward woman, even in societies where women were degraded and objectified. Deborah and Jael are examples of God using women respectively as a judge and a warrior in a patriarchal society. After Israel had entered the Promised Land, they shed their role of victim and became warriors and conquerors. But because of their disobedience, God, at times, withheld His protection, allowing them to be subjugated, and this time to Jabin. Skillfully, God used these two women like bookends in the conquest of Jabin, King of Hazar.

After decades of hearing their cries for deliverance, God spoke to Deborah, His appointed prophet and judge of Israel. Deborah issued the summons to Barak to commence the battle, "Go, take with you ten thousand men … and lead the way to Mount Tabor" (Judges 4:6, NIV). And Jael, God's appointed warrior, ended the battle by killing the captain of the opposing army. "Jael, Herber's wife, picked up a tent peg and a hammer and … drove the peg through his temple into the ground, and he died" (verse 21).

Ironically, Barak feared instigating the battle against Jabin without Deborah. This speaks to the respect she commanded as a judge and to her faithful relationship with God as a prophet. Barak showed a weak, insubstantial faith in God. Because he trusted that God called him through her and knew her relationship with God, he reasoned that victory was a given with her in the battle. But Deborah warned, "the honor will not be yours, for the LORD will hand Sisera over to a woman" (Judges 4:9, NIV). As predicted, God deposited Barak's blessing into the lap of Jael who did not hesitate to do battle alone.

God used Deborah and Jael because of their unwavering faith and their willing obedience. Deborah sang, "Most blessed of women be Jael … most blessed of tent-dwelling women" (Judges 5:24, NIV). And, as judge and prophet, Deborah brought forty years of peace to Israel. Very importantly, under her leadership and counsel the people returned to a right relationship with God. Surely, He uses any willing, humble servant.

April 1

Attempered by Mercy

"Do not fear, for you have borne a son." But she did not answer, nor did she regard it. Then she named the child Ichabod, saying, "The glory has departed from Israel!" because the ark of God had been captured. 1 Sam. 4:20, 21, NKJV.

The ark of God, the ark of the covenant, the ark of the Lord, and the ark of the testimony all refer to the same sacred container crafted by ancient Israelite artisans using a God-inspired blueprint. The ark safeguards the two tables of stones on which God inscribed the Ten Commandments, Aaron's rod that blossomed, and a jar of manna (Heb. 9:4). Joseph Parker writes, "Law is at the center of the Ark and the lid is the mercy…. Law is coming up from the center and comes through the lid of the covering of mercy. It is so to speak, attempered or it would come like a sword or a fire or a judgment terrible in righteousness."[95]

God's law is inseparable from His character—He is the same yesterday, today, and forever. Thus, the law of God is immutable and irrevocable; it is carved in stone and written in the hearts of man. He declares, "And *there is* no God else beside me; a just God and a Saviour; *there is* none beside me" (Isa. 45:21). A just God executes justice; however, pure rigid justice mandates a penalty for lawbreakers, and spiritual transgressors rate capital punishment. That is the law (Rom. 6:23). Although He is long-suffering, merciful, and forgiving, He will not clear the guilty (Ex. 34:7). So without mercy, the guilty stands accused and condemned to death.

But thank God, He is both a just God and affluent in mercy, which attempers the law. Transgression of the law separated us from God and cast us into eternal darkness. Bankrupt with nothing to offer, no claim to forgiveness, and captives of sin, we were doomed. Mercifully, God allowed His only Son to pay our sin-debt in full. And thanks to the nail-scarred hands of Jesus, and through our consent and faithfulness, those crimson sins are history.

"But God—so rich is He in His mercy! Because of and in order to satisfy the great and wonderful and intense love with which He loved us, Even when we were dead (slain) by [our own] shortcomings and trespasses, He made us alive together in fellowship and in union with Christ; [He gave us the very life of Christ Himself, the same new life with which He quickened Him, for] it is by grace (His favor and mercy which you did not deserve) that you are saved (delivered from judgment and made partakers of Christ's salvation)" (Eph. 2:4-6, AMP).

East is the polar opposite of west. Travel east ad infinitum and west will remain an impossible destination. Sinful though we are, God removed our transgressions from our record so far away that they are irrecoverable, for His mercy is great toward those who fear Him (Ps. 103:11, 12). We are forgiven, enlightened, and empowered to live godly lives because God permitted mercy and grace to intersect. And His great mercy allows us to be born again to a living hope through the resurrection of Jesus.

April 2

Wine Is a Mocker, Strong Drink Is Raging

Mark ye now when Amnon's heart is merry with wine, and when I say unto you, Smite Amnon; then kill him, fear not: have not I commanded you? be courageous, and be valiant. 2 Sam. 13:28.

Amnon was easily subdued while under the influence of a fermented beverage. The use and abuse of alcohol—wine, beer, distilled liquor—wreaks havoc physically, emotionally, and psychologically and all of society suffers. The National Institute on Drug Abuse, the National Institute on Alcohol Abuse and Alcoholism, and the National Institutes of Health estimate that the economic cost of alcohol abuse is $148 billion a year. And approximately 75,000 people die annually from the use and abuse of alcohol in the U.S alone, which often causes deadly and chronic physical damage.

Alcohol is also a health menace. "Psychologically and emotionally [alcohol] can lead to brain degeneration, severe depression, insomnia, and even suicide. It causes social problems for the individual and those around him because alcoholics often get in trouble with the law, end up in debt, destroy their interpersonal relationships, can't hold down a job or finish their education."[96]

According to MADD, approximately 12,998 people were killed in alcohol-impaired driving crashes in 2007; someone is killed every 50 minutes on average; in alcohol-related crashes, on average, one person is injured almost every minute, totaling more than half a million people. It doesn't matter the alcoholic drink of choice; it is all intoxicating. As a standard, 12 ounces of beer, 5 ounces of wine, or 1.5 ounces of 72-proof distilled spirits all contain about .54 ounces of alcohol.[97]

Proponents of alcoholic beverages, even as sacrament offerings, promulgate the "one wine theory." Taken to its logical conclusion, the one wine theory offers that Jesus partook of and condones the use of intoxicating beverages that destroy lives, homes, finances, and tatters the very fabric of society. But Jesus is sinless, pure, and holy and is currently in heaven interacting with a holy and perfect God. The Bible unequivocally states, "Nothing impure will ever enter it [heaven]" (Rev. 21:27, NIV).

The Bible embraces a "two wine theory"—fermented grape juice and pure juice from the grape. Proverbs 20:1 and 21:17 and Habakkuk 2:15 clearly warn us of the perils of intoxicating beverages. Based on the woes that alcoholic beverages cause for individuals and society, I conclude that Jesus provided only pure grape juice at the wedding at Cana and only drank pure juice (John 2:1-10). Otherwise, we accuse Jesus of partaking of and condoning sinful, destructive activities. Our Savior wants us to prosper and be in health just as our soul prospers (3 John 1:2). Wisdom, then, offers that it is impossible for the Holy Spirit, who resides in us, to guide us if our minds are clouded and numbed by even moderate drinking of intoxicating beverages. Come let us reason together.

April 3

Obey Your Leaders

And Gedaliah sware to them, and to their men, and said unto them, Fear not to be the servants of the Chaldees: dwell in the land, and serve the king of Babylon; and it shall be well with you. 2 Kings 25:24.

Jeremiah said it more graphically: "Bow your neck under the yoke of the king of Babylon; serve him and his people, and you will live" (Jer. 27:12, NIV). God permitted the Babylonians to subjugate the Judeans to highlight the sinfulness of sin and His people's need of repentance and reformation. Gedaliah submitted to the Babylonians, who appointed him governor, and he encouraged others to submit. But former Judean high officials murdered him because he obeyed God and the Babylonian leaders.

"To obey God in some things, and not in others shows an unsound heart. Childlike obedience moves toward every command of God."[98] He requires our allegiance to civil authorities, knowing our tendency for self-rule and self-centeredness. Since their power and authority issue from God, submission to earthly authorities is indirectly submission to Him (Rom. 13:1-4). Paul expands on that counsel. "They keep watch over you as men who must give an account" (Heb. 13:17, NIV). God holds them accountable for the maltreatment we receive at their hands after submitting to their rule.

God structured organized government to achieve order, safety, and efficiency. When He established the nation of Israel, He gave Moses explicit instructions for an effective operation. "God personally gave them (through Moses) the finest governmental and legal system any nation ever had (Deuteronomy 4:5-8) … In fact, it is amazing that this Mosaic legal code has since served effectively as the basic legal code for all the greatest nations in modern history."[99]

Titus also reiterates the theme, "Remind the believers to submit to the government and its officers. They should be obedient, always ready to do what is good" (Titus 3:1, NLT). But Acts 5:29 adds a caveat—obey God rather than man. Thus, we are not required to obey immoral laws that require us to disregard the plain "thus saith the Lord." Following the Great Commission as Jesus commanded, the apostles ran headlong into the brick wall of the Jewish ruling class who said, "'We gave you strict orders not to teach in this name … Yet you have filled Jerusalem with your teaching…' Peter and the other apostles replied: 'We must obey God rather than men!'" (Acts 5:28, 29, NIV).

Likewise, two Hebrew midwives refused to obey Pharaoh's order to kill all Hebrew newborn boys (Ex. 1:15-17); Daniel refused to pray to the heathen king (Dan. 6); and the three Hebrew boys rebuffed his law requiring idol worship (Dan. 3). All were rewarded by God for their stand. He protected them from the civil penalties for disobedience against immoral rules. Obey your leaders, but God is our supreme and final authority.

April 4

Transparent Secret Sins

Speaking lies in hypocrisy; having their conscience seared with a hot iron. I Tim. 4:2.

    Ted Haggard, a popular televangelist, allegedly engaged in a secret sin that he condemned in others. That makes him a hypocrite. His alleged partner in sin outed him when he learned that Haggard spoke against same-sex marriages while engaging in homosexual sex. Jesus described hypocrisy as the "leaven of the Pharisees" (Luke 12:1). The word hypocrite derives from the Greek word *hupokrisis* meaning stage acting. The Pharisees, along with the Sadducees, were the powerful, wealthy, and influential Jewish ruling class who made a production of their charitable giving, wowed audiences by praying loudly in the street corners and in the synagogue, and showcased fasting with pious facial expressions (Matt 6:1-8).

    Jesus told His disciples, "Be sure to guard against the dishonest teaching of the Pharisees! It is their way of fooling people. Everything that is hidden will be found out, and every secret will be known. Whatever you say in the dark will be heard when it is day. Whatever you whisper in a closed room will be shouted from the housetops" (Luke 12:2, 3, CEV).

    For some, their secret sins will not be revealed until they stand before the judgment bar of God. For Ted Haggard, his secret sins were revealed at the zenith of his ministry. But as surely as the sun rises and sets each day, "the LORD … will bring out darkest secrets to light and will reveal our private motives" (1 Cor. 4:5, NLT).

    It is the Holy Spirit who convicts us of wrongdoing, reproves the world of sin, and guides us along the path of righteousness. Grieving the Holy Spirit by disregarding His gentle pricks with willful sin leads to blaspheming Him, and "who blasphemes against the Holy Spirit never has forgiveness, but is subject to eternal condemnation" (Mark 3:29, NKJV). To protect us from evil and eternal death, God gave us consciences with sensitive nerve endings. Using the analogy of a cauterizing iron, Paul explains we can sear our consciences by living as lying hypocrites (1 Tim. 4:2). And cauterization creates a worthless conscience deadened to evil and guilt.

    André Gide posits, "The true hypocrite is the one who ceases to perceive his deception, the one who lies with sincerity." Thus, hypocrites, who are spiritually bankrupt but professing godliness, conceal their sins and deny their guilt to the risk of their soul. This sin is highly condemned by Jesus, and He described the perpetrators as "whited sepulchers," "blind guides," "fools," and "brood of vipers," among other things. Sin separates us from God, the source of all light, and lands us in darkness where Satan reigns.

    However, upon confessing our sins God will both forgive us and cleanse us from all unrighteousness, for He loves all sinners (John 1:9). Genuine repentance, a turning away from sin where trouble lurks, and a turning toward God where manifold blessings reside, opens the door to forgiveness and acceptance once again.

April 5

Closer Than a Brother

"Don't be afraid," he said. "My father Saul will not lay a hand on you. You will be king over Israel, and I will be second to you." 1 Sam. 23:17, NIV.

Pee Wee Reese, a southern white man, and baseball great Jackie Robinson, the first black player in the baseball major league, were Brooklyn Dodgers teammates who became close friends in 1940s racist America. After spring training in Robinson's first year, a group of players from the South circulated a petition to boycott him. Reese, the captain of the team, refused to sign, which effectively ended the petition drive. Pee Wee Reese continually showed himself to be a friend who sticks closer than a brother (Prov. 18:24). Witnessing a particularly violent eruption of racist heckling against Robinson in Cincinnati, Reese walked onto the field and put his hand on Robinson's shoulder, a powerful expression of solidarity. Said Robinson, "Pee Wee kind of sensed the sort of hopeless, dead feeling in me and came over and stood beside me."[100]

From the earliest time to the present, God has wrapped the gift of friendship in human packages for our benefit. Jonathan, son of the king who determined to kill David, strengthened David's hand in God in spite of peril to his life (1 Sam. 23:16). Jonathan and David's friendship was instantaneous and solidly sealed with a pledge. "After David had finished talking with Saul, he met Jonathan, the king's son. There was an immediate bond between them, for Jonathan loved David.... And Jonathan made a solemn pact with David" (1 Sam. 18:1-3, NLT).

God's favor showed in His loving care over the future king of Israel. "In his heart a man plans his course, but the LORD determines his steps" (Prov. 16:9, NIV). God touched the heart and mind of Jonathan to become David's close ally, unveiling part of His plan to preserve David's well-being after his days of glory screeched to a halt with Saul. Insane with jealousy over David's courage and fame, Saul relentlessly and maliciously persecuted him. "When Saul realized that the LORD was with David and that his daughter Michal loved David, Saul became still more afraid of him, and he remained his enemy the rest of his days" (1 Sam. 18:28, 29, NIV). Saul's attempted murder of David and his own son were tools to dispose of David. Still, Jonathan remained steadfast.

"Many are the plans in a man's heart, but it is the LORD's purpose that prevails" (Prov. 19:21, NIV). No matter how minuscule nothing happens outside of God's control. Before David and Jonathan were "glints in their father's eyes," God had handpicked Jonathan to walk in friendship with David. Prince Jonathan served in Saul's inner circle and kept his pulse on the paranoia, moods, and plots against David for God had divinely ordained his intervention to preserve David until he mounted the throne (1 Sam. 20:2).

Providentially, Jonathan remained humble enough to renounce his claim to the kingdom pursuant to Saul's death because he knew God had anointed David king over Israel. Closer than a brother, Jonathan remained David's strong shoulder and confidant through the sunshine and the rain. Isn't God amazing?

April 6

Confession Is Good for the Soul

Therefore do not fear them. For there is nothing covered that will not be revealed, and hidden that will not be known. Matt. 10:26, NKJV.

Ffyona Campbell earned a place in the Guinness Book of Records by walking around the world. However, pregnant during one leg of her record-breaking feat, she accepted rides from her support truck. The lie that she walked the entire route ate at her soul prompting her to take drugs to assuage her guilt. "I couldn't continue with the lie," she says. "I had a choice between another hit of smack, or something else. I was doomed. I was going to die, that was the alternative. I thought I could get away with it. I couldn't get away with it. I couldn't carry on living it."[101]

Satan can and does use concealed sins to debilitate us and drive us to hopelessness and despair. But God has the remedy. Confess your sins and He is faithful and just to forgive them and to cleanse you from all unrighteousness (1 John 1:9). Mercifully He forgives and graciously He mends. The lie Ffyona concealed and the accompanying guilt took her to the brink of self-destruction. As she learned, self-condemnation is the most vicious pain a mind can handle. But confession put her back on track; it was good for her soul.

Sins that have not been confessed are like the pus generated when a splinter is embedded under the fingernail. Left untreated, the splinter festers, becomes inflamed, and pus engulfs it, causing the finger to throb and ache. Permanent damage to the fingernail may occur unless the splinter is removed, which itself is very painful. Once the splinter is extracted, however, the inflammation clears up, the pus dries up, and the pain ends. Sin, like pus, invades and damages our psyche. But confession dries up the pus that causes the soul to throb and ache.

R. Cody Smith gives several reasons why confession is good for the soul: no longer hidden but given life as we speak them, our sins became real and we see how they stink up God's nostrils; confessing and standing up to our sins, we take off the mask of deception and reveal who we are; and we discover that we are not alone—that others struggle with the same issues.[103] Nonetheless, the premier reason is to restore the breach in our relationship with God so we can walk in the light of His presence and claim His forgiveness. For he "who covers his sins will not prosper, but whoever confesses and forsakes them will have mercy" (Prov. 28:13, NKJV).

Secrecy is an effective tool to persist in sinning, to remain in denial, and to display a façade of piousness. Conversely, confession is painful, reveals our weaknesses, and exposes our wretchedness. But who feels like confessing when it reveals the maggots eating the dead tissue of our righteousness? Confessing *is* therapeutic for it makes us right with God and heals our brokenness (James 5:16). As the Word proclaims, the narrow, moral way is by far the best way although not the easiest.

April 7

The Light of Love

There is no fear in love. But perfect love drives out fear, because fear has to do with punishment. The one who fears is not made perfect in love. 1 John 4:18, NIV.

"Don't do it! Don't do it! Don't do it!" This was the earnest advice given us by a nurse after the resident emergency room doctor advised Carla, whose water had broken, to abort her 21-week-old fetus because survival and quality of life were very slim at this stage. He was cold and clinical and determined to make a quick end of Carla's "problem." But the entire time he spoke, the nurse standing behind him and monitoring Carla's vital signs vigorously and consistently shook her head no. After the doctor had left the room, she advised Carla to ignore his advice and informed her of her two micro-preemie nephews who were now healthy adults. She offered comfort, hope, prayer, and regularly visited the baby in the intensive care unit. Incredibly, her given name is Love!

With Carla's situation, Love offered perfect love. Her prayers and compassion while she held Carla's hand and convinced her not to cry brought crucial calm to this precarious situation. Love worked to alleviate Carla's fear and provided the compassionate care lacking in the doctor. Clearly, the emotions of love and fear are colleagues in strength but opponents in effect. Love is complete; fear is deficient. Love, where nurtured, reproves fear. Fear, where allowed, immobilizes love. Fear shines the light on self. Love shines its light outward. Love encompasses the fruit of the Spirit. Fear is negatively grounded in selfishness, pride, hate, lust, offense, guilt, and insecurity.

Perfect love is obedient. Jesus said, "For I came down from heaven, not to do mine own will, but the will of him that sent me" (John 6:38). In so doing, He removed the penalty of sin from us. Perfect love promotes a strong inclination in the recipients to respond to this remarkable free gift of salvation by offering Him our enduring and unshakable obedience. Obedience to His will casts out fear and ushers in faith.

Perfect love is also sacrificial as Jesus demonstrated. He loved so perfectly that He gave to His own detriment (Gal. 2:20). The Ancient of Days, the King Eternal, the Great I AM descended to earth and took the form of a lowly man in a decaying human body, which was battered and extinguished for us. The Son of man did not come to be served, but to serve, and to use His life as a ransom (Mark 10:45). For us, He denounced His dignity and covered His sovereignty. For us, Jesus became a servant and taught that a true master is a servant (Phil. 2:7).

He who was adored and worshipped by sinless angels, He who lived in majesty and dazzling grandeur, He who is one with the triune God willingly relinquished all for us. For thirty-three years, Jesus lived in poverty, sacrificing His own well-being to provide us with a future of magnificent luxury and peace. Though rich, for our sakes He became poor. Why? Because His privation on earth permits us to be co-heirs of the kingdom of God with the King of kings (Rom. 8:17). Can love be anymore perfect?

April 8

A King's Ransom

Surely God is my salvation; I will trust and not be afraid. Isa. 12:2, NIV.

Charles Lindbergh made the first solo, nonstop flight from New York to Paris across the Atlantic Ocean in the *Spirit of St. Louis* in 1927, flying nearly 3,600 miles in 34 hours. World famous, Lindbergh experienced a personal tragedy when an intruder kidnapped his toddler son, his namesake, from a second-story bedroom. The man left a ransom note, and Lindbergh paid the price demanded for the baby's life. However, the kidnapper breached the agreement and murdered the baby.

Likewise, Jesus handsomely paid the price, but He paid the ultimate price, which was demanded for our release from the wages of sin. God accepted this ransom and released us from Satan's grasp. Jesus suffered and carried our pains and disfigurements, all the things wrong with us. God heaped all our sins, everything we've done wrong, on Jesus. Our sins ripped and tore and crushed Him. He took the punishment that made us whole. But through his bruises we can heal (Isa. 53:4, 5). No other could fulfill the requirement (1 Tim. 2:5, 6).

It was no ordinary payoff. Jesus paid a King's ransom—a substitutional atonement for our freedom. With the great treasure of His own life and comfort, He reconciled us to God by bridging the gaping abyss of sin with His own lifeless body. "Atonement is, properly, an arrangement by which the literal infliction of the penalty due to sin may be avoided; it is something which may be substituted in the place of punishment.... The atonement is the governmental provision for the forgiveness of sins, providing man meets the conditions of repentance and faith towards our LORD Jesus Christ."[103]

What is man that God is concerned with him, so concerned that He sacrificed His own Son for us? The object of unfathomable love! Jesus veiled His glory, dressed in human garb and let death conquer Him for a season. But contrary to what the devil expected, His death became a victory, not a defeat. Jesus' sacrifice broke Satan's chokehold on the grave that he had reserved for us, and it freed all those who fear death (Heb. 2:8). The ransom note that Jesus paid redeemed us not only from the power of the grave and eternal death but will also destroy death and the grave forevermore (Hosea 13:14).

Moreover, His death rescued us from the bondage to and punishment for sin. Proverbs 5:22 explains that the evil deeds of a wicked man ensnare him, the cords of his sin hold him fast. And unconfessed sin brings with it the unchangeable promise of physical destruction by a Holy God whom we will stand before in judgment (Matt. 25:46). But Jesus became the propitiation for our sins through His shed blood, allowing God to dismiss the sins we previously committed (Rom. 3:25). Clearly, we have no power to disentangle ourselves from the power of sin. Only the sinless Redeemer can and did accomplish that. Our strength and song, the Lord God has become our salvation. What an unfathomable gift!

April 9

Acknowledging God

"Because they love me," says the LORD, "I will rescue them; I will protect them, for they acknowledge my name." Ps. 91:14, TNIV.

Paul rightly accused Elymas, a magician, as one who led people astray. Paul said, "You son of the devil, you enemy of all righteousness, full of all deceit and villainy, will you not stop making crooked the straight paths of the LORD?" (Acts 13:10, ESV). Paul's accusation came after Elymas attempted to prevent Sergius Paulus, a Roman proconsul from hearing the gospel.

God promises if we trust and acknowledge Him He will make our paths straight (Prov. 3:5-6). Acknowledging Him means answering that knock on the door of our hearts and clearing out the cobwebs of sins, transgressions, and iniquities. The straight path embodies repentance of sin and obedience to God's Word. It represents turning away from the former lusts and denying evil inclinations and desires and appreciating that we can do nothing without Him and that all things are possible with Him. It means we no longer have the spirit of fear, but we have power and discipline through the Holy Spirit.

But when we disregard God's sovereignty and follow the paths warped, twisted, and curved by Satan, God yields. Incapable of forcing us to love Him He reluctantly turns His back, abandoning us to a depraved mind that fosters evil and lawlessness. "Since they didn't bother to acknowledge God, God quit bothering them and let them run loose. And then all hell broke loose: rampant evil, grabbing and grasping, vicious backstabbing. They made life hell on earth with their envy, wanton killing, bickering, and cheating. Look at them: mean-spirited, venomous, fork-tongued God-bashers.… They keep inventing new ways of wrecking lives" (Rom. 1:28-32, MSG).

Elymas represents the barriers to virtue that regularly challenge us. He characterizes things that cause us to harbor "a sinful, unbelieving heart that turns away from the living God" (Heb. 3:12, NIV). But like Sergius, we are empowered to resist such hindrances. Sergius rejected Elymas' attempt to prevent his hearing the Word, proving that Satan cannot coil the straight paths without our consent. The Holy Spirit who is within us and aids us in our walk on the straight paths is more powerful than Satan who lives in the world (Eze. 36:27; 1 John 4:4).

The upright walk safely, but "those who follow crooked paths will slip and fall" (Prov. 10:9, NLT). There is no light and, therefore, no guidance along the crooked path where sin and temptation lurk. Stay away from those paths, for without our wholehearted devotion to God, the promise of protection and deliverance will fail. Acknowledge the Lord, press on to recognize Him, and walk in the light of righteousness. And one day "every valley shall be filled, and every mountain and hill shall be brought low; and the crooked shall be made straight, and the rough ways shall be made smooth" as we see the fulfillment of the salvation of the Lord (Luke 3:5, 6).

April 10

Our Modern Idols

Like a scarecrow in a melon patch, their idols cannot speak: they must be carried because they cannot walk. Do not fear them; they can do no harm nor can they do any good. Jer. 10:5, NIV.

Scarecrow, one of the characters in the classic movie *The Wizard of Oz,* revealingly shares with Dorothy that he does not have a brain. The brain is the control center of our existence, for we are "fearfully *and* wonderfully made" (Ps. 139:14). The mastermind of God created the human brain, a complex organ that "allows us to think, move, feel, see, hear, taste, and smell. It also controls our body, receives information, analyzes information, and stores information (our memories)."[104]

In contrast, a lifeless scarecrow, like an idol, is fashioned by the hands of a mortal human being. Idol worship is an abomination to the Creator God; those who worship them "became as detestable as that which they loved" (Hosea 9:10, NASB). He ardently commanded that His created beings put no other gods before Him or make an idol in the form of anything in heaven or on earth or in the waters, for He is a jealous God (Ex. 20:3-5).

We dare not condemn the Israelites who worshipped idol gods and smugly shake our heads at their pigheaded disobedience. We, too, worship idols. They are anything and everything that we love more than God. "We're much more sophisticated, carving out images in the securities exchange, bowing down to the idolness of retirement, gazing into the peep-stone of tomorrow's worry, kowtowing to the swelling pride of education, seeking the increasing status of self in one's field, or basking, if only for the night in the deity of drugs, with the goddess of sex, under the deceptive fetish of coveting or mesmerized by the graven image in the mirror."[105]

God is Lord and Master over the universe, high and lifted up above creation. Holiness incarnate, His glory consumes and His majesty is measureless. Praise, glory, honor, worship, and obedience are due Him and Him alone. "Jehovah your God, he is God of gods, and Lord of lords" (Deut. 10:17, ASV). He declares, "I am the LORD, that is My name; I will not give My glory to another, Nor My praise to graven images" (Isa. 42:8, NASB). By two means we belong to Him. He created us; therefore, we belong to Him, and He redeemed us, so we are His. His jealousy, then, is warranted. "His jealousy does not grow out of insecurity, anxiety, frustration, covetousness, pride, or spite, as ours usually does. It is the natural and necessary by-product of His absolute sovereignty and infinite holiness."[106]

God requires and deserves the highest tribute in line with His elevated status as Lord of lords. It grieves Him when His created beings, who are the object of His love, reject Him. "A son honors his father, and a servant his master. If then I am a father, where is my honor? And if I am a master, where is my fear?" (Mal. 1:6, ESV). It behooves us to remove all the gods from our life and put God first, to reverence and worship Him only.

April 11

God Will Not Budge

For I am persuaded, that neither death, nor life, nor angels, nor principalities, nor powers, nor things present, nor things to come, nor height, nor depth, nor any other creature, shall be able to separate us from the love of God, which is in Christ Jesus our Lord. Rom. 8:38, 39.

The "most powerful words ever written" describe the powerful message in Romans 8, verses 38-39. "Their sound is able to grasp human souls in desperate situations. In my own experience they have proved to be stronger than the sound of exploding shells, of weeping at open graves, of the sighs of the sick, of the moaning of the dying. They are stronger than the self-accusation of those who are in despair about themselves and they prevail over the permanent whisper of anxiety in the depth of our being."[107]

Paul wrote these verses using a literary device called merism, which is prevalent in biblical literature. Merism is a listing of opposite parts that stand for a whole. He organizes these opposites in twosomes, entering at one extreme and exiting at the opposite. This device screams that the two opposites cover the totality of a thing and by implication everything in between. Romans 8:38, 39 underscore that nothing in heaven or on earth or in the waters, whether visible or invisible, whether tangible or intangible, can block the love of God. Nothing, nada, zero, zilch!

Neither heights nor depths nor death nor life can disengage God's love. God the Father and the Son have dominion and power over life and death. "The LORD brings death and makes alive; he brings down to the grave and raises up" (1 Sam. 2:6, NIV). He further declares, "There is no god besides me. I put to death and I bring to life, I have wounded and I will heal, and no one can deliver out of my hand" (Deut. 32:39, 40, NIV). God is matchless in power and strength.

Likewise, neither angels or demons or anything in the spiritual realm can detach us from God's love. "Christ knew that the enemy would come to every human being, to take advantage of hereditary weakness, and by his false insinuations to ensnare all whose trust is not in God. And by passing over the ground which man must travel, our Lord has prepared the way for us to overcome. It is not His will that we should be placed at a disadvantage in the conflict with Satan. He would not have us intimidated and discouraged by the assaults of the serpent."[108] Satan is conquered, and Jesus gives us sufficient grace and power to resist him (James 4:7; John 16:33).

Lastly, neither the present nor the future, nor any powers can disconnect His love. Jesus willingly died to fulfill the punishment for *our* sins even though He knew an unnumbered quantity of His children would reject Him. Still, we are engraved on the palms of His powerful, loving hands for His love transcends rejection (Isa. 49:16). Resting in His arms, we can count on His power, His mercy, His providence, His forgiveness, and His grace no matter how intimidating the situation. Since He loves us that much and will not budge in His love and His commitment, what is there to fear?

April 12

God, Our Champion

What shall we then say to these things? If God be for us, who can be against us? He that spared not his own Son, but delivered him up for us all, how shall he not with him also freely give us all things? Rom. 8:31, 32.

Samuel refers to Goliath as the Philistine champion in the build-up to Goliath and David's historic battle (1 Sam. 17:23). "David and Goliath engage in a contest of champions, a form of battle known almost exclusively from the Greek epic tradition."[109] Confident, Goliath challenged the Israelites to proffer their champion to fight him, knowing that in this battle of champions the loser and his nation would become subjects of the victor. The Israelites became distraught at Goliath's taunts and threats that continued twice a day for forty days. Even more so, they were demoralized and terrified by this bold, gigantic Philistine because of a feeble faith in God.

The Philistines were certain that Goliath could defeat any foe based on his valor, size, and experience, and they designated him their champion. But David toppled the nine-foot giant, arrayed in huge glistening armor, with one smooth stone slung from his low-tech slingshot. With Goliath hung the arms of flesh, but with David stood the Lord God. When the Philistines saw David kill their hero, they tucked their tails between their legs and fled while hotly pursued and slaughtered by the invigorated Israelites. God's pledges to His obedient children are faithful and true. He promises that He will cause our enemies to be defeated and that when they pursue us from one direction, they will flee in seven directions (Deut. 28:7). The defeat of the Philistines testifies to that.

God *is* for us, so who can defeat us? He is the indomitable champion who guards His faithful ones. Through His great power, we eventually prevail over our enemies (1 Sam. 2:9). Thankfully, He is our defense in the midst of the battle of our lives as we fight enemies both physical and spiritual, both visible and invisible, both temporary and lifelong. He is our strength in whom we trust, our rock to hide behind, our fortress with secure ironclad doors, and our deliverer who rescues us from danger. He is our buckler surrounding and protecting us with defensive armor, the horn of our salvation, our power and strength, and our high tower to spot the enemy's approach. With God leading our regiment, we are unconquerable (Ps. 18:1-3).

God is also the indomitable champion who rescues us from the condemnation of sin (Rom. 8:1). In the criminal justice system, prosecutors bring charges against alleged criminals, and if the charges are proven, they are condemned to a punishment that fits the crime. Under the government of God, criminals as well as law-abiding citizens are under the condemnation of death from birth. But those in Jesus are absolved of the death sentence. He covers our sins with the white robe of His righteousness and provides mercy and grace abundantly each time we falter, fail, and fall on that straight and narrow path. Fear not, for He is the ardent defender of those who love Him.

April 13

The Light of the World

The LORD is my light and my salvation; whom shall I fear? the LORD is the strength of my life; of whom shall I be afraid? Ps. 27:1.

    Light comes from the sun which fuels life on earth. It provides the entirety of the light and energy that plants, animals, and humans need for existence. And the heat and energy generated by the sun provides warmth and physical benefits as well. Green plants absorb carbon dioxide from the atmosphere and use the energy from the sunlight to change water and carbon dioxide gas into food and oxygen. Plants so yearn for the benefits of sunlight that they bend toward it when in the shadows.

    Also, light symbolizes truth, goodness, and life, attributes of Jesus who is the spiritual sunlight of the world. He promises, "He who follows Me will not be walking in the dark, but will have the Light which is Life" (John 8:12, AMP). He illuminates the way to our heavenly home. Like sunshine, Jesus beams above the dark clouds that inevitably darken our paths. No matter how dire our circumstances, no matter how painful the trials, His light shines the light of compassion on our pain, the light of peace on our inner turmoil, and the light of love to reassure us. "You were once darkness, but now you are light in the Lord. Live as children of light" (Eph. 5:8, NIV).

    Water, like sunlight is also absolutely essential for physical and spiritual life. In Him who absorbs the carbon dioxide of our sins and emits oxygenated living waters are both life eternal and a bountiful earthly life. For the water He gives will turn into a spring inside welling up into eternal life (John 4:14). Water deprivation causes discomfort and fosters death in a few days. Similarly, rejecting His offer of spiritual water is a death knell to the soul when the water He offers forever quenches thirst.

    When life leaves us parched and dehydrated, seemingly without relief, Jesus, alone, hydrates our dried out souls. But, first, toss out that bucket of dirty, stagnant water polluted with presumptuous sins, transgressions, and iniquities, and extend it to collect the living water. "The Spirit and the bride say, "Come!" And let him who hears say, "'Come!' Whoever is thirsty, let him come; and whoever wishes, let him take the free gift of the water of life" (Rev. 22:17, NIV). Those who quench their thirst with unholy and unhealthy things will not find relief, for deep inside is an unquenchable thirst for Him that only He can satisfy.

    The water of life, like the light of the world, is a gift offered by a tender, devoted God. Liberally, He offers it to everyone and even pleads continually for the thirsty to accept this bounty (Rev. 21:6). Included in this gift are treasures approximating liberty from the iron grip of sin and its aftermath—treasures such as peace of mind, freedom from fear, protection from enemies, the comfort of His presence, strength for the battle, and guidance through the minefields of the enemy. But the most beautiful part of the present is the gift wrap of eternal life, eternal peace, and eternal happiness. Oh, the joy that is ours to stand in the light of the presence of God drinking the living waters! Live as children of light (Eph. 5:8).

April 14

Jesus Triumphant

The LORD is with me; I will not be afraid. What can man do to me? The LORD is with me; he is my helper. I will look in triumph on my enemies. Ps. 118:6, 7, NIV.

The Romans created a signal honor called the "triumph" for commanders who scored a decisive battle for the republic. If the opponents were Romans or slaves, the commander was not eligible for the honor. Having conquered a formidable opponent from a foreign land during a critical, victorious battle and riding in a luxurious chariot, the commander would lead a spectacular processional within the city gates with his booty—both human and material parading after him. The "triumph" celebration resembled a high feast day and established the commander's solid reputation forever.

However, Jesus' entry into Jerusalem seemed piteous compared to the spectacle of the Roman triumph. As Zechariah predicted, He entered riding on a lowly animal. "Behold, thy King cometh unto thee: he is just, and having salvation; lowly, and riding upon an ass" (Zech. 9:9). Jews, who craved a temporal king to defeat their Romans captors, placed coats on the ground, waved palm branches, and shouted in victory as Jesus passed by. But unlike the Romans His triumph is everlasting not temporal.

Thus, Jesus ended His days of preaching, healing, and exorcising demons and began the journey toward crucifixion. Keenly aware of His mission, He acknowledged that the cross preceded the crown. Mentally striding past the humiliation, pain, and rejection, Jesus skidded to a halt before His rightful booty—you and me. Surrendering to the temporary supremacy of the Jews by dying, He disarmed the powers and made a public spectacle of them by triumphing over them at the cross (Col. 2:14, 15).

Living a sinless life and submitting to the will of His Father were key to His triumph over Satan and the legions of evil doers at the cross. "Could one sin have been found in Christ, had He in one particular yielded to Satan to escape the terrible torture, the enemy of God and man would have triumphed. Christ bowed His head and died, but He held fast His faith and His submission to God."[110] The Word exclaims His victory: "Now is come salvation, and strength, and the kingdom of our God, and the power of his Christ: for the accuser of our brethren is cast down, which accused them before our God day and night" (Rev. 12:10).

Like a colossal magnet in the sky, He draws the righteous up above the fray of vindictive enemies and the uncertainties of life and deposits us in a safe place, a place of victory. What can man do to God's anointed? God is "before all things, and by him all things consist. And he … is the beginning, the firstborn from the dead; that in all things he might have the preeminence (Col. 1:17, 18). By His divinity and victory He has supremacy over all things, particularly finite, dependent human beings. God speaks and things are created. How awesome is that? What visible created being can match Someone who is matchless?

April 15

Rock of Ages

Do not tremble, do not be afraid.... You are my witnesses. Is there any God besides me? No, there is no other Rock; I know not one. Isa. 44:8, NIV.

There is nothing more durable, stable, or timeless than a rock. The most famous rock in the world is the Rock of Gibraltar located at the south of Spain on the Iberian Peninsula. Standing 1,398 feet above sea level, it underwent at least fourteen sieges but withstood each one. "Solid as the Rock of Gibraltar" is a popular phrase in the English language depicting something secure, something that will not go amiss or be defeated. Rock of Ages, also implying stability, is used to depict the strength and dependability of Jesus.

"Heretics have been heard in absent moments whispering over 'Rock of Ages,' as if they clung to it when they had let slip all things beside. Great statesmen have been known to turn it into Latin, as if to perpetuate its fame."[111] Written by an Englishman named Augustus Montague Toplady, "Rock of Ages" is a classic hymn which begins, "Rock of ages cleft for me." Cleft, a past tense and past participle of cleave, means to split apart. Thus, Toplady implores the rock to open so he can hide in it, but he is not referring to an ordinary rock but to Jesus, the Rock of Ages.

David also acknowledges God's durability and protection. "The LORD is my rock" (Ps. 18:2). "And who is a rock, except our God?" (Ps. 18:31, ESV). A rock is substantial and enduring, and it provides shelter and safety as well as a cool lifesaving shade from the hot sun. When we run to the Rock of Ages—the Lord, our Rock—we find shelter from the hot sun of adversity, worries, and fears. The Rock cools the parched throat of sorrow, loss, and death. And hiding behind the Rock of Ages, the weary find respite after dodging the enemy's arrows.

Jesus Himself uses the analogy of the rock's stability in the parable of the wise and foolish builders. "Therefore whoever hears these sayings of Mine, and does them, I will liken him to a wise man who built his house on the rock: and the rain descended, the floods came, and the winds blew and beat on that house; and it did not fall, for it was founded on the rock. But everyone who hears these sayings of Mine, and does not do them, will be like a foolish man who built his house on the sand: and the rain descended, the floods came, and the winds blew and beat on that house; and it fell. And great was its fall" (Matt. 7:24-27, NKJV).

The wise person hears the Word and lives it. God's Word is the only solid foundation on the quicksand of life in a collapsing world. On the other hand, defiance of the Word is akin to a catapult that propels us onto the loose, wet, sandy soil from which escape is difficult. Anyone whose sins are sucking them downward toward the grasping, eager arms of hell should call on Jesus in humility and contriteness. Then step up onto the Rock and trust in the Lord, for in Him you have an everlasting rock.

April 16

Engraved on His Palms

Can a mother forget the baby at her breast and have no compassion on the child she has borne? Though she may forget, I will not forget you! See, I have engraved you on the palms of my hands; your walls are ever before me. Isa. 49:15, 16, NIV.

Sally Field won an Oscar for the movie *Places in the Heart* in 1984. As she accepted the award, she exclaimed, "I wanted more than anything to have your respect. The first time I didn't feel it, but this time I feel it and I can't deny the fact you like me. Right now, you really *like* me!" Apparently, members of the Academy of Motion Picture Arts and Sciences liked her acting enough to award her the Oscar. Like suggests finding something or someone pleasant or attractive, to enjoy or have a preference for, or to be pleased with in a moderate degree.

Like is good but does not rise to the height and breadth of love, however. For love knows no boundaries. It is patient and kind without envy, pride, or boastfulness. It is unselfish, kind, and even-tempered; does not keep record of others' wrongdoings nor does it take pleasure in doing evil. Love rejoices in the truth, always protects, always trusts, always hopes, and always perseveres. Love never fails (1 Cor. 13:4-8). Incredulously, love even lays down its life for a sinful enemy. For, when we were powerless to extricate ourselves from sin, Christ died for the ungodly. Most of us shrink from the idea of dying for a godly man let alone a reprobate. But God's love for sinners sacrificed Jesus to redeem us from sin and its wages (Rom. 5:6-8).

Both symbolically and tangibly, our names are engraved on the palms of God's hands, demonstrating His unwavering love for us. Symbolically, engraved palms represent the permanency of His love. Hands are always in motion, symbolizing that we are constantly in His thoughts, mind, and vision. He will never forget us, forsake us, or leave us comfortless. Tangibly, the nail scars in His hands are proof positive of His love for us. "Jesus will present His hands with the marks of His crucifixion. The marks of this cruelty He will ever bear. Every print of the nails will tell the story of man's wonderful redemption and the dear price by which it was purchased."[112]

Love so fierce, so intense, and so incomparable held His trembling hands firmly to the cross where He suffered, bled, and died. That strong right hand that holds the worlds in place, that pasted the sun in the sky, and that hung all the countless galaxies in space remained immobilized by His love. Those everlasting arms, lacerated and painfully stretched, suppressed the use of supernatural power to extricate Himself from the brutality of the cross because of love for us.

Soon, the Lord God will come with strong hands, and His arms shall rule for Him, and His reward is with Him (Isa. 40:10). To become a curse for us and to demonstrate His great love for us, He declined to remove those all-powerful arms and hands from the barbarity of crucifixion. Our Lord's amazing love moved Him to be disfigured, and He will carry those scars throughout eternity for you and me!

April 17

He Will Sustain You

Even to your old age and gray hairs I am he, who will sustain you. I have made you and I will carry you; I will sustain you and I will rescue you. Isa. 46:4, NIV.

My dear little grandson, Noah, was born three months too soon, coming into this world by Caesarean section at 24-weeks gestation. He weighed one pound eleven ounces at birth, and one day later he dropped down to one pound eight ounces. Oh, the torturous, traumatic subsistence such micro-preemies experience while struggling for survival in the neonatal intensive care unit! My daughter, son-in-law, and I watched helplessly as he was pricked and stuck and endured blood transfusions, positional breathing tubes, and feeding tubes, among other medical torments relied on for healing. Over and over Noah flat-lined, went limp, turned blue, and required resuscitation. Through our agony of spirit at his heart-wrenching suffering and the daily uncertainty of his existence, we learned to cast our cares on God. We learned to trust in Jesus.

As He promised, God sustained us while Noah suffered what no newborn baby should ever endure. God sustained us as Carla's postpartum depression heightened as she watched her precious firstborn suffer and struggle for his life. He sustained us when the admitting doctor persistently urged her to abort the unborn baby because he would suffer too many developmental and health problems to live a productive life. He sustained us as we spent 109 days straight visiting him at the hospital, praying for him, willing him to fight, and yearning for his complete healing. He sustained us when we brought him home hooked up to an oxygen tank that had to be monitored day and night, 24/7. He sustained us when his heart and/or breathing monitors would sound alarms over and over throughout the day and night. *He sustained us*.

Cast your cares on the Lord. Not only will He sustain you, He will never let the righteous fall (Ps. 55:22). We threw, no hurled, every problem we encountered, every emotional pain, every bit of suffering that Noah endured, every uncertainty, every doubt, and every worry at the Lord daily. He adeptly caught all of our cares in His strong right hand. God's grace abounded, and He provided sweet healing for Noah. He changed our despair to hope, turned our heartbreak to joy, and filled our hearts with peace and happiness as Noah grew and developed into a healthy, happy, inquisitive little toddler.

Cast all of your cares on the Lord because He cares for us (1 Peter 5:7). Because giving Him our burdens is so beneficial to us, He commands that we do so. His arms are big enough to simultaneously handle all the cares and all the burdens of all the people living on this earth. Carrying our own burdens will sabotage us emotionally and physically, and attempting to resolve our problems and issues in our own strength, we fall into Satan's trap. Because while we distractedly struggle in vain to fix things outside of our control, Satan attacks with discouragement, hopelessness, and despair. Resist Satan's tricks. Do not fear when testing comes—take God at His word, trust His providence and wisdom. He *will* sustain you.

April 18

Ordered By the LORD

The steps of a good man are ordered by the LORD, and He delights in his way. Though he fall, he shall not be utterly cast down; For the LORD upholds him with His hand. Ps. 37:23, NKJV.

Soren, a Danish philosopher, wrote, "Above all do not lose your desire to walk. Every day I walk myself into a state of well being and walk away from every illness. I have walked myself into my best thoughts and I know of no thought so burdensome that one cannot walk away from it. But by sitting still, and the more one sits still, the closer one comes to feeling ill ... if one keeps on walking everything will be alright."[113] He rightly associates walking with physical health and well-being and immobility with ill health.

Similarly, walking with God promotes spiritual health and physical well-being for the steps of a good person are ordered by the Lord. Psalm 37 describes the good person as one who trusts in the Lord, revels in doing good deeds, and is submissive to her Lord. Plus, this righteous, patient, self-controlled one heeds the leading of the Spirit (verse 4-7). And God delights in a righteous person, delights in reigning in her sanctified heart and guiding her from here to eternity (Ps. 48:14).

Acknowledge God in all that you do, and He will order your steps (Prov. 3:6). This ordering embraces instructing us in the driving school of morality and providing Holy Ghost combustion power to defeat sin. When He detects hidden stop signs, treacherous potholes, hazardous dead ends, and dangerous crossings in our walk of faith, He is ordering our steps. Moreover, He points our attention to the billboards that emblazon Jesus and Him crucified and provides roadmaps, GPS systems, and MapQuest directions to guide us onto the highway to heaven. And He nudges us onto the narrow road where the broad and the narrow way diverge (Ps. 32:8).

To order our steps, He first establishes our footsteps in the Word. Scripture is a surefire, safe haven for our lives as it makes us wise for salvation through faith in Christ Jesus (2 Tim. 3:15). Very importantly we are directed to let the Word of Christ richly dwell within us to provide a barrier against sin. Hence, iniquity no longer has dominion over us, and Satan's deceptions are exposed, diminishing their effect.

God made provision through the Power who lives in our hearts to enable us to keep His precepts and walk in obedience. "Moral problems are only solved by obedience... Intellectually things can be worked out, but morally the solution is only reached by obedience. One step in obedience ... will take us into the center of God's will for us."[114] Not just a cursory reading of the Word but meditating on it, pondering it, making it a focal point leads to the obedience that is pleasing to God. "A simple man believes anything, but a prudent man gives thought to his steps" (Prov. 14:15, NIV).

When we allow God to order our steps, we become good persons in whom He delights. And even when we stumble and fall He continues to sustain us.

April 19

A Glorious Future

"For I know the plans I have for you," declares the LORD, "... plans to give you hope and a future." Jer. 29:11, NIV.

A missionary came home to America to retire after working in Africa for years. He spent many years in labor for the Lord, depriving himself and his family of comforts that many take for granted. With no retirement funds and in ill-health, he felt discouraged and afraid. To make matters worse, he sailed on the same ship as the president of the United States where cheering crowds, a military band, a red carpet, and the media welcomed the president home. The missionary slipped off the ship unnoticed. Feeling self-pity and resentment, he began complaining to God in prayer. Then God gently reminded him, "But my child, you're not home yet."[115]

Tired of this wicked, uncertain world as was this missionary—I long for a better place as I am sure you do. Thankfully, the Word is very explicit that the world as we know it will end; that a new world order will be ushered in after the gospel is preached to the entire world (Matt. 24:14). Jesus said that He is coming quickly, and He cautions us to hold fast to our morality so that we may receive our promised crown (Rev. 3:11). The mansions are waiting, and at His personal return, He will rescue us from this temporary home called earth to live in heaven with Him (John 14:3; Heb. 11:16).

The redeemed, those who follow the Word and are faithful until the end, will amass from every corner of the globe (Luke 13:29) and "will be caught up together ... in the clouds to meet the Lord in the air. And so we will be with the Lord forever" (1 Thess. 4:17, NIV). His coming will shatter all things that steal our peace and joy unspeakable will inform our lives forevermore (Rev. 21:4). Thus, the route to our heavenly home starts and ends with Jesus who said: "I am the way, the truth, and the life: no man cometh unto the Father, but by me" (John 14:6). His blood cleanses us from sin, redeems us, and prepares us for heaven (1 John 1:7).

Under this new world order, the deaf will hear, the lame will walk, the mute will talk, and the blind will see. Furthermore, negative words like exhausted, fear, and depression will vanish from our vocabulary (Isa. 35:5, 6; 40:31). And wicked, violent people will cease spreading the toxic poison of sin for they will be destroyed (Rev. 21:8). In heaven life will be unimaginably peaceful, for fear will disappear in the presence of Jesus. In His presence there is fullness of joy and pleasures evermore (Ps. 16:11). He offers "beauty for ashes" and "the oil of joy for mourning" (Isa. 61:3).

Are you among the redeemed? Waiting for your glorious prospect? Do not fear the future! Remember, the difference between those who love the world and those who love Christ is unmistakably plain. While the world is earnestly seeking to secure earthly treasures, God's people show by their earnest, watching, waiting position that they are transformed and that their home is not in this world, but that they are seeking a better country—a heavenly home.[116]

April 20

Return to God

I have blotted out, like a thick cloud, your transgressions, and like a cloud, your sins. Return to Me, for I have redeemed you. Isa. 44:22, NKJV.

The wind causes clouds, which are formed by moisture in the air reaching dew point, to move across the sky. Thin and delicate cirrus clouds hover high in the sky at heights between 25,000 and 40,000 feet. When pushed along by the jet stream, cirrus clouds move at a clip upwards of 150 miles per hour. As well, high-level contrail clouds are formed when aircraft engines emit water vapors into the air that freeze and form ice crystals, which create condensation trails called contrails.

Our Creator formed these clouds and all things in the heavens, earth, and sea, and the totality of His creation provides insight and knowledge of His omnipotence. "The heavens declare the glory of God, and the skies announce what his hands have made. Day after day they tell the story; night after night they tell it again. They have no speech or words; they have no voice to be heard. But their message goes out through all the world; their words go everywhere on earth" (Ps. 19:1-4, NCV). Wordlessly but vigorously, creation shouts the truth about His love, faithfulness, and power.

His power to save is equally as magnificent. Although backsliders crucify Jesus anew and subject Him to public disgrace, Jesus pleads with those whom He already redeemed to return to Him. Using a simile, God, speaking through Isaiah, promises to sweep away offenses like the wind blows away clouds. And if wind can move clouds across the sky at 150 miles per hour imagine how quickly and thoroughly God can forgive those offenses! If angels can move like a flash of lighting from heaven to earth, how fast can God, who created all beings and things, forgive those sins?

Only divinity has the power to forgive sins. God in human form, unwanted in the region of the Gadarenes, arrived in a town where friends presented a paralytic on a mat for healing (Matt. 9:1-8). Seeing the strong faith of the friends, Jesus said to the paralytic, "Take heart, son; your sins are forgiven" (verse 6). The man got up from his mat and walked. The scribes murmured that He was blaspheming, but Jesus read their thoughts and queried them to tell Him the difference between healing a man paralyzed from birth and forgiving sin. Both acts require the power only possessed by God.

When backsliders first believe in the Lord Jesus Christ, He detaches their sins from them as far as the east is from the west, and casts them into the depths of the sea (Ps.103:12; Micah 7:19). But they walked away, and He wants them back. Backsliders, seek Him while He may be found, call Him while He is near. Do not wait, for tomorrow is not promised. Forsake the broad path; seek the narrow way; return to the Lord who will abundantly pardon your sins (Isa. 55:6, 7). "As I live, declares the Lord GOD, I have no pleasure in the death of the wicked, but that the wicked turn from his way and live.... For why will you die?" (Eze. 33:11, ESV). Bring a contrite heart and a humble spirit and bank on His promise to "return unto you" as soon as you return to Him.

April 21

Nothing Is too Hard for God

I am the LORD, the God of all flesh: is there any thing too hard for me? Jer. 32:27.

"A woman was asked by a co-worker, 'What is it like to be a Christian?' The coworker replied, 'It is like being a pumpkin.' God picks you from the patch, brings you in, and washes all the dirt off of you. Then He cuts off the top and scoops out all the yucky stuff. He removes the seeds of doubt, hate, greed. Then He carves you a new smiling face and puts His light inside of you to shine for all the world to see."[117]

Impossible does not exist for divinity. "The things which are impossible with men are possible with God" (Luke 18:27). There is no sinner too hard core for God to change. Raised a Christian, Adoniram Judson became an atheist after attending college where he met an atheist named Ernest who became his mentor and fueled the fire of atheism in his heart. But God directed Adoniram to a hotel room where he heard an atheist's dying laments, and suddenly the thought of death brought tremendous fear to him. To his dismay, the next morning Adoniram discovered that the dying man was Ernest. Thus, he changed the course of his life and became a missionary.

"With God nothing shall be impossible" (Luke 1:37). There is no circumstance too hard for God to alleviate. Cheri Peters, a recovering drug addict, author, and founder of *True Step Ministries*, is a flesh-and-blood, bona fide miracle. Raised in a drug-infested environment by addicted parents, she became a homeless heroin addict. Cheri, abused, illiterate, unwanted, and unloved, lived on the streets for ten years beginning at age twelve. At age twenty-three and weary of her miserable existence, she intended to commit suicide but encountered Jesus' love. This encounter reversed her life, turning her into an ambassador for Christ where she labors to set addicts free and rescue children from prostitution.

"Is any thing too hard for the LORD?" (Gen.18:14). There is no prayer too hard for God to answer. Ahab was a wicked, disobedient king of Israel who married Jezebel, a daughter of the king of Sidon who instituted the worship of the false gods Baal and Asherah. The Israelites embraced these idols and shunned the living God. But the time arrived for the Israelites to choose between God and the idols. So Elijah set up a scenario that would amplify their faith in God—he prayed for a drought. With the same power of prayer that we possess, Elijah prayed fervently that it might not rain, and for three years and six months rain ceased. Then he prayed again, the rain resumed, and the earth became fruitful again (James 5:17, 18).

There is no road too crooked for God to straighten, no depression too deep that He can't lift, no situation that He can't resolve, no marriage that He can't sustain, no pain that he can't relieve, no sin that He can't forgive. "Ah, Lord God!... Nothing is too hard for you" (Jer. 32:17, NIV).

April 22

A Jolt of Divine Discipline

Do not fear, O Jacob my servant, for I am with you ... Though I completely destroy all the nations among which I scatter you, I will not completely destroy you. I will discipline you but only with justice. Jer. 46:28, NIV.

Harry Emerson Fosdick wrote, "No horse gets anywhere until he is harnessed. No stream or gas drives anything until it is confined. No Niagara is ever turned into light and power until it is tunneled. No life ever grows great until it is focused, dedicated, disciplined." Discipline, then, is a catalyst to bring out the best in us. Out of love and concern for our eternal good, God uses this tool to mold us into the similitude of Jesus.

God's wrath and His discipline are poles apart as His wrath is reserved for those who forever reject Jesus (John 3:36). And it is revealed from heaven against all the wickedness of men who suppress the plain truth (Rom. 1:19). Wrath is meted out to impenitent, wicked, immovable people who reject pleas to repent and offers of mercy. Contrariwise, discipline is a message of love. Jesus says, "My son, do not despise the LORD's discipline and do not resent his rebuke, because the LORD disciplines those he loves" (Prov. 3:11, 12, NIV). And it works! David admitted that before he was afflicted he went astray (Ps.119:67).

As she was about to administer punishment to me, my mother used to say, "This hurts me more than you." Not understanding her reasoning, I grumbled about her logic. But with the passing of time, I thank my mother for teaching me through the medium of discipline. "No discipline seems pleasant at the time, but painful" (Heb. 12:11, NIV). Likewise, the Lord's discipline is a measure of His tender concern for His children's present and future. God disciplines those whom He loves to jolt us back to the narrow path from which we continue to drift (Heb. 12:4). That jolt includes hardships, tests, fears, sorrows, and losses to draw us closer to Him and away from the precipice of eternal failure. For obedience deflects God's wrath at the judgment, allowing us to cross over from death to life (John. 5:24).

Divine discipline is an absolute requirement for growth, development, and emotional release. King David lamented that his bones wasted away and he groaned all day because of his unconfessed sins. To jolt David into humbling himself, confessing and repenting, God placed His hand heavy upon him, bombarding him with troubles and fear. But once David confessed, God forgave him and relieved him of "the guilt of his sin." David's struggle brought both emotional relief and increased trust (Ps. 32:3-6).

How blessed we are when God disciplines us! Discipline produces a harvest of peace and righteousness for those who learn the lessons taught (Heb. 12:11). When we positively respond to discipline, we increase our faith, mature spiritually, and learn to persevere in the face of hardship and suffering. In addition and thankfully, we become partakers of the divine nature, shed the label of illegitimacy, and become holy children of God (James 1:2-4; Heb. 12:8, 10).

April 23

Satan Is Doomed

The God of peace will soon crush Satan under your feet. Rom. 16:20, ESV.

God uttered a statement to Satan, disguised as a serpent in the Garden of Eden, which may be the greatest understatement of all times. After Adam and Eve rebelled against God, He pronounced judgment. To Satan He stated, "And I will put enmity between you and the woman, and between your offspring and hers; he will crush your head, and you will strike his heel" (Gen. 3:15, NIV). He placed a hatred of sin in the hearts of His followers that induced enmity against Satan.

The understatement is contained in the phrase "and you shall bruise him on the heel." Jesus is the "You," and His death and crucifixion are the bruising part. He predicted that Satan would wound Him to death but would lose the war. And agents of Satan, including priests, scribes, Sadducees, Pharisees, and His kinsmen, physically beat and emotionally abused Jesus. The Roman soldiers and the mob, incited by the leaders of Israel, battered His face and body such that "his appearance was so disfigured beyond that of any man and his form marred beyond human likeness" (Isa. 52:14, NIV).

Imagine what it means to be "disfigured beyond that of any man." Then, imagine how heavy blows transformed Jesus' face into a bloody mass of purplish-blue flesh swollen and damaged. Imagine His crushed and broken nose beaten crooked causing the cartilage and bone to shift out of place from the repeated trauma. As well, imagine how the accompanying swelling and clotted blood limited His airflow causing him to heave with the effort to breath. Finally, envision also how His eyes were swollen shut from a battering vicious enough to damage the tissues and how blood forced into the tissues blackened His eyes. To add shame and insult to injury, some of His tormenters sadistically plucked out His beard, leaving bloody bald spots, while others spit in His face until rank, phlegm-laden spittle ran down His cheeks (Isa. 50:6).

Scourging is an additional torture that preceded Jesus' crucifixion. Twice in the hours before the crucifixion, soldiers whipped Jesus until they literally ripped his back to shreds. To scourge Him, they used short, heavy whips fashioned with leather strips and small pieces of metal and bone attached to the tips. These tips gouged His flesh, producing excruciating pain and weakness throughout His already tortured body.

Too, crucifixion is as barbarous an act as any human being can inflict on another. They placed Jesus' tattered back on a hard, splintery wooden crossbeam and nailed His wrists through the median nerve with 7-inch spikes, causing red hot pain to radiate over His upper torso. Similarly, they spiked His feet, one crossed over the other, to the cross through His ankles, causing excruciating pain in His lower torso.

Although "bruised," Jesus lives. He lives! He "destroy[ed] the works of the devil" and promises to cast him to the ground where He will be crushed under our feet one day (1 John 3:8; Eze. 28:12-17). Thus, Satan, who is already defeated and doomed, cannot control you without your permission. Resist him; he is doomed!

April 24

Now or Later

It is written: "As I live, says the LORD, Every knee will bow to Me, And every tongue shall confess to God." Rom. 14:11, NJKV.

Mocking the Savior of the world, a whole cohort of Roman soldiers replaced His clothing with a scarlet robe, twisted together a crown of thorns, jammed it on His head, and put a reed in His right hand. In jest, they kneeled down before Him and said sarcastically, "Hail, King of the Jews!" Afterwards, they spit on him and hit Him on the head with the reed. Then they stripped Him of the robe, dressed Him in His own clothes, and led Him, like a lamb to slaughter, to His crucifixion (Matt. 27:28-31).

Bowing the head or body or kneeling is generally a sign of reverence, submission, or shame. The Romans, however, bowed to show contempt for the "King of the Jews." And throughout the ordeal of sham trials and the events leading to His crucifixion, Jesus endured mocking, scorn, and disrespect. Inside the Roman soldiers' headquarters, Jesus was mocked. As well, the religious leaders accused Him of blasphemy and mocked Him who called Himself the Son of God. On the road to Golgotha, Jews and others hissed in derision, shook their heads, and wagged their fingers at Jesus in contempt of Him. The thieves who hung on His left and right side mocked Him who was literally and figuratively suspended between heaven and earth. And Jesus silently endured.

But after Jesus' victory over sin and death, God highly exalted Him and gave Him a name above every name (Heb. 1:2, 3). And at that name every knee should bow in a posture of reverence and submission to God in the person of Jesus. A special resurrection will take place for those who vigorously opposed the gospel and those instrumental in Jesus' torture and death unless they repented and reformed before closing their eyes in death. "Behold, he cometh with clouds; and every eye shall see him, and *they also which pierced him*" (Rev. 1:7).

Imagine the horror of those on whom the spotlight of truth shines on the day of judgment. "Those who derided His claim to be the Son of God are speechless now. There is the haughty Herod who jeered at His royal title and bade the mocking soldiers crown Him king.… The men who smote and spit upon the Prince of life now turn from His piercing gaze and seek to flee from the overpowering glory of His presence. Those who drove the nails through His hands and feet, the soldier who pierced His side, behold these marks with terror and remorse. With awful distinctness do priests and rulers recall the events of Calvary. With shuddering horror they remember how, wagging their heads in satanic exultation, they exclaimed: 'He saved others; Himself He cannot save.'"[118]

Have you bowed your knee to God in adoration and submission? If not, Jesus is still waiting for you. "I have called, and ye refused; I have stretched out my hand, and no man regarded; But ye have set at nought all my counsel, and would none of my reproof" (Prov. 1:24, 25). Bow your knee to Him now and live, or you *will* bow later when all hope for salvation is lost.

April 25

He Brings His Reward With Him

He who is unjust, let him be unjust still; he who is filthy, let him be filthy still; he who is righteous, let him be righteous still; he who is holy, let him be holy still. And behold, I am coming quickly, and My reward is with Me, to give to everyone according to his work. Rev. 22:11, 12, NKJV.

"You lent a hand to a fallen one; life in love was given. You saved a soul when hope was gone and helped him on toward heaven and, so for that help you offered there, you'll have a reward sometime-somewhere."[119] Everyone appreciates a reward, thus, our society capitalizes on a reward system to motivate positive behavior. Law enforcement offers monetary rewards for information leading to the capture of a criminal; many school systems institute reward systems for high academic achievement; and corporations offer bonuses to reward personnel productivity.

God, too, has a reward system, and He promises to bring a reward to each holy and righteous person alive or dead at His Second Coming. His reward is given to "everyone according to what he has done" (Rev. 22:12, NIV). With any reward system, there is a price to pay to earn the blessings—blessings that the filthy and unjust will be denied because they have walked in darkness and rejected God's offers of forgiveness and mercy. The unholy refuse to "lay aside all filthiness and overflow of wickedness, and receive with meekness the implanted word, which is able to save your souls" (James 1:21, NKJV). Waiting to get right with God until He returns for His redeemed is too late.

Noah preached 120 years for the salvation of his brethren, but when the angel closed the door, mercy ceased and the filthy and unjust remained so. Likewise, there will come a day when all offers of mercy will cease, when all unconfessed sins will remain unforgiven, and when the final harvest of souls will be reaped. "Another angel came out of the temple in heaven, and he too had a sharp sickle ... called in a loud voice to him who had the sharp sickle, 'Take your sharp sickle and gather the clusters of grapes from the earth's vine, because its grapes are ripe.' The angel swung his sickle on the earth, gathered its grapes and threw them into the great winepress of God's wrath" (Rev. 14:17-19, NIV).

Although, the righteous pay a dear price for following Jesus while on earth, that price pales in comparison to the rewards He has waiting in heaven. His "chosen have been educated and disciplined in the school of trial. They walked in narrow paths on earth; they were purified in the furnace of affliction. For Jesus' sake they endured opposition, hatred, calumny. They followed Him through conflicts sore; they endured self-denial and experienced bitter disappointments. By their own painful experience they learned the evil of sin, its power, its guilt, its woe; and they look upon it with abhorrence.... Having been partakers of Christ's sufferings, they are fitted to be partakers with Him of His glory."[120]

A righteous few make up the remnant of God. They have the stamp of His character in their hearts and follow closely His commandments—an assurance of eternal rewards.

April 26

A Mighty Refuge for the Oppressed

The LORD is a refuge for the oppressed, a stronghold in times of trouble. Those who know your name will trust in you, for you, LORD, have never forsaken those who seek you. Ps. 9:9, 10, NIV.

San Jose State University held an annual Tunnel of Oppression exhibit for a few days in the spring of 2007 to impress on students what oppression looks and feels like. Along the hallway leading into the tunnel were images of a swastika and a crossed-out Star of David, as well as racial slurs and other indignities. The theme conveys oppression equals prejudice plus power. The Tunnel of Oppression demonstrated that oppression occurs when the powerful wield tyrannical authority over the powerless.

Oppression is offensive to God. "Woe to those who make unjust laws, to those who issue oppressive decrees, to deprive the poor of their rights and withhold justice from the oppressed of my people" (Isa. 10:1, 2, NIV). When Pharaoh oppressed the Israelites for centuries and the "Israelites groaned in their slavery and cried out ... their cry for help ... went up to God [who] heard their groaning" and God sent a message by His servant Moses, "Let my people go" (Ex. 2:23, 24; 5:1, NIV). The stubborn Pharaoh felt the potent sting of God's wrath as he continued in his evil oppression.

God called Amos, a shepherd and a fruit picker, to prophecy to Israel when their apostasy reached to heaven, moving Him to pronounce judgment upon them—"I will crush you as a cart crushes when loaded with grain" (Amos 2:13, NIV). For one, their oppression and disregard for the powerless disgusted God. "They sell the righteous for silver, and the needy for a pair of sandals. They trample on the heads of the poor as upon the dust of the ground and deny justice to the oppressed" (Amos 2:6, 7, NIV). Similarly, Jeremiah said, "Cut down the trees and build siege ramps against Jerusalem. This city must be punished; it is filled with oppression" (Jer. 6:6, NIV).

God denounced Jehoiakim son of Josiah king of Judah because His eyes and his heart were "set only on dishonest gain, on shedding innocent blood and on oppression and extortion" (Jer. 22:17, NIV). This so offended God He cursed him, sending word through Jeremiah that Jehoiakim's burial would be like that of a donkey. His body would be tossed outside the gates of Jerusalem and left there to rot. God said, "I will hurl you and the mother who gave you birth into another country, where neither of you was born, and there you both will die" (Jer. 22:26, NIV).

Do not fear the impenitent oppressor for they are under God's judgment. But the oppressed have His deep regard. To live the redeemed life and to claim our inheritance, we are obliged to imitate Jesus by living the Golden Rule—do unto others as you would have them do unto you. Thus, we are obliged to act justly and love mercy and walk humbly with our God (Micah 6:8) and to "dispense true justice and practice kindness and compassion each to his brother" (Zech. 7:9, NASB). Such will reap the kingdom of heaven.

April 27

Joy in My Heart

The Lord is my strength and shield. I trust him with all my heart. He helps me, and my heart is filled with joy. I burst out in songs of thanksgiving. Ps. 28:7, NLT.

The Old Faithful geyser in Yellowstone National Park propels hot spring water and steam to heights reaching 185 feet. "Near the surface of a geyser, there are one or more constrictions. Expanding steam bubbles generated from the rising hot water build up behind these constrictions, squeezing through the narrow passageways and forcing the water above to overflow from the geyser. The release of water at the surface prompts a sudden decline in pressure of the hotter waters at great depth, triggering a violent chain reaction of tremendous steam explosions in which the volume of rising, now boiling water expands 1,500 times or more and bursts into the sky."[121]

The actions of Old Faithful parallel the elation that rose up and overflowed in King David when he considered God. Springs of joy welled up inside of him until they burst forth into a crescendo of praise. David's joy required not some advantage or favorable circumstance or some desired material benefit. The joy that moved him to erupt was the warm glow of peace from trust in God and perceiving that He was his everything. David endured great trials, great loss, and great suffering, but the joy of the Lord remained his strength (Neh. 8:10).

When David needed protection, which was frequent, he found shelter with God. "You are my hiding place; You shall preserve me from trouble; You shall surround me with songs of deliverance" (Ps. 32:7, NKJV). When weak, weary, and aimless, he relied on God and found strength and direction. "It is God who arms me with strength and makes my way perfect" (Ps. 18:32). And, when harassed and hindered, David trusted God to give him rest. "I go to bed and sleep in peace, because, Lord, only you keep me safe" (Ps. 4:8, NCV). Joyful that all his needs were supplied, he exclaimed, "Who *is* mighty like You, O LORD?" (Ps. 89:8, NKJV).

But above all, David could not contain his joy when he calculated the, magnanimous gift of eternal life. "You will show me the path of life; in Your presence *is* fullness of joy; at Your right hand *are* pleasures forevermore" (Ps. 16:11, NKJV). When David fell off that path, God showered him with droplets of blessings dubbed trials to redeem him. The trials brought misery, and in his misery David earnestly sought God (Hosea 5:15; 7:13).

That the Paschal lamb foreshadowed the Lamb of God and His blood that takes away the sins of the world was well-known to David. The Paschal Lamb was "a shadow of the things that were to come; the reality, however, is found in Christ" (Col. 2:17, NIV). And Jesus guarantees the inestimable gift of eternal life to all who believe on Him. Sheer joy at the thought of salvation rose in David's heart until he burst out in songs of praise. "The LORD lives! Praise be to my Rock! Exalted be God my Savior" (Ps. 18:46, NIV).

April 28

God Inhabits Our Praise

Why then be downcast? Why be discouraged and sad? Hope in God! I shall yet praise Him again. Yes, I shall again praise Him for His help. Ps. 42:5, TLB.

Corrie Ten Boom and her sister Betsie refused to be discouraged even while prisoners in Ravensbruck, a horrific concentration camp in Germany. They endured hunger, beatings, deprivation, and hard labor, but found reasons to praise God. Incredibly, they praised Him for fleas! One day Betsie ecstatically told Corrie that she had overheard the guards discuss boycotting their bunkrooms because of a flea infestation. What a praiseworthy blessing for they hid a banned Bible in their bunkroom which if discovered warranted a punishable offense![122]

When the rain falls and the shadows descend on our lives, we tend to become weak and joyless and have difficulty framing praises. But praise God anyhow through both the sunshine and rain for it honors Him. Be encouraged to "offer the sacrifice of praise to God continually, that is, the fruit of our lips giving thanks to his name" (Heb. 13:15), for God inhabits the praise of His people (Ps. 22:3). He actually sits on the throne of our praise that ushers us into His presence. And praise shifts Him from the outskirts to the center of our lives, humbles us, and elevates Him to His rightful place as Lord God Almighty.

Indeed, praise measures our faith especially when the way is dark. All of us have experienced tribulation and a silent, seemingly inactive God—times when our prayers appear to hit a lead dome rather than the ear of God (John 16:33). But praise him anyhow. Faith says, don't focus on how big your problems are; focus on how big your God is! It is a measure of our faith when we can confidently exclaim, "I will bless the LORD at all times: his praise shall continually be in my mouth" (Ps. 34:1).

Moreover, praise works like an elevator; it lifts us high enough to see God's majesty, recognize and appreciate His authority, and feel His comforting presence. Consider King David who entered into God's presence through paying tribute to God. He exclaimed, I will "enter His gates with thanksgiving, And into His Courts with praise" (Ps. 100:4, NKJV). Sadly, many forget all the benefits and blessings and leave praise at the door of happy times. Should they believe that He is literally everything we need, praise will regularly be on their lips. At praise for God in speech or in song, negativity is subdued and the enemy, who fosters the spirit of fear, depression, and sadness, flees like a coward along with his negative spirits.

Moreover, our praise is a hallmark of our salvation. As we draw closer and closer to Him and see Him in all His fullness, we praise His goodness, mercy, and grace nonstop. Those who love Him, praise Him. Those who honor Him, praise Him. Those who fear Him, praise Him. "It's the praising life that honors me. As soon as you set your foot on the Way, I'll show you my salvation" (Ps. 50:23, MSG).

April 29

Strengthened in the Word

When I pray, You answer me, and encourage me by giving me the strength I need. Ps. 138:3, TLB.

"Hold fast the truths we bought you, through flood and flame and sword; use well your open Bible, the LIVING WORD OF GOD."[123] The Word is our defense and shield. The everlasting gospel, it is immortalized in the Bible, inspired by God, discerned by the Holy Spirit, and personified in Jesus' character. The truth that defines the Word cuts through the lies and distortions of the enemy and the vain imaginations that he inserts into our mind. When false prophets "prophesy not unto us right things, speak unto us smooth things, [and] prophesy deceits," the Word reveals their deceptions (Isa. 30:10).

The entire Bible is a love letter to fallen humanity, revealing the depths of God's love and the lengths He will go to stitch the severed seams in our relationship ripped apart by sin. Look no further than the cross to divulge this astounding love. In our state as helpless sinners, God sent His only Son to die for us, and His blood restored our standing in God's eyes and saved us from His wrath. Jesus' sacrifice turned us from enemies of God to His special friends (Rom. 5:6-11). His unconditional love continues unabated even as we hold him in contempt and worship the enemy. And despite our spiritual warts and ignorance of His beneficence, His love persists.

Moreover, the inspired Word of God is our how-to-live manual. It is our stairway to heaven—a path to salvation that twists and turns as it goes higher and higher. Situated along this path are rough surfaces of exposed rocks of temptation and crevices of sin that threaten to wreck our progress. But as a lamp to our feet and a light unto our path, the Word counsels, exhorts, and commands, offering guidance for every circumstance on the narrow way. David posed this rhetorical question, "How can a young man keep his way pure?" And he answered it thusly, "By living according to your word" (Ps. 119:9, NIV). So when we lock the Word in our hearts and live accordingly, we gain footing on that narrow path.

Power, miracle-working power radiates from the Word of God. "Is not my word like as a fire? saith the LORD; and like a hammer that breaketh the rock in pieces?" (Jer. 23:29). Like fire, His Word consumes and purifies, and like a hammer it breaks down the enemies strongholds in the lives of His people and provides strength for the journey. His Word created the heavens and the earth and all life therein; expels demons, awakens the dead, and changes depraved sinners into sanctified saints.

The Word promises to strengthen us if we are committed to study it diligently and trust its Author (Phil. 4:13). Then it builds faith, stifles fear, and fortifies the mind against sin (Rom. 16:25).

April 30

The Power of God

O Sovereign LORD! You made the heavens and earth by your strong hand and powerful arm. Nothing is too hard for you! Jer. 32:17, NLT.

Scientists estimate that there are hundreds of billions of galaxies in the universe, each containing 100 to 1,000 billion stars. According to NASA, the Hubble telescope "observed a tiny patch of sky (one-tenth the diameter of the moon) for one million seconds (11.6 days) and found approximately 10,000 galaxies, of all sizes, shapes, and colors." The Milky Way galaxy alone, where earth is located, has hundreds of billions of stars. Oh the power of the glory of the heavens! "By the word of the LORD were the heavens made; and all the host of them by the breath of his mouth" (Ps. 33:6). When I consider your heavens, the work of your fingers, I am utterly amazed (Ps. 6:3)!

The entire universe of human beings are dependent upon God's power for every breath of air taken—between 12 and 70 breaths per minute depending on individual needs. Paul told the men of Athens that their present and continued existence depended on God. "In him we live, and move, and have our being" (Acts 17:28). Similarly, Daniel, explaining to King Belshazzar the meaning of the handwriting on the wall, admonished him for not honoring the God who holds his very breath in His hands (Dan. 5:23).

Even after the universe and humans were created, "His energy is still exerted in upholding the objects of His creation. It is not because the mechanism that was once set in motion continues to act by its own inherent energy that the pulse beats and breath follows breath; but every breath, every pulsation of the heart, is an evidence of the all-pervading care of Him."[124]

God can and does take away the stony heart and give us a heart of flesh (Eze. 36:26). It takes miraculous power, divine power, to regenerate a cold, lifeless heart bent on sin and rebellion into a warm, supple heart characterized by love. It takes the power of God to end a young man's twenty-eight year pornography addiction and free him to become a pastor,[125] to turn an avowed atheist who dabbled in the occult into a Christian whose voice is heard today in such works as the *Chronicles of Narnia*,[126] to turn the five-time married woman living in adultery into a convert spreading the gospel of Jesus Christ to her fellow Samaritans (John 4:39-42).

God's offer of and desire to use His power to save us spiritually is itself a miracle of love. What is humanity that He is mindful of us? That the sovereign God seeks to have a relationship with us! That He seeks us while we are lost in sin willfully turning our backs on Him! That He seeks us while we are still fervently clutching the evil prince of this world! Yes, He sees our loathsome, filthy selves, yet He pursues us, peering beyond what we are to what we can become through His power. O LORD, our Lord, how majestic is your name in all the earth (Ps. 8:1)! Nothing is too hard for You!

May 1

Showers of Blessings

You can be sure that the more we undergo sufferings for Christ, the more He will shower us with His comfort and encouragement. 2 Cor. 1:5, TLB.

The Amazon rainforest is an amazing blessing to humanity. The world's largest rainforest, covering 2.5 million miles, Amazonia receives about nine feet of rain every year during the rainy season, catapulting the water level in large areas of the rainforest to 30 to 40 feet. Leftover water drains into the Amazon River, which daily discharges enough freshwater into the Atlantic to supply the needs of New York City for nine years. The rain promotes a vast foliage canopy that creates approximately twenty percent of our oxygen, giving it the moniker "the Lungs of the Earth." And rainforest plants are used to cure fatal and debilitating diseases.

As He showers the Amazon rainforest with life-sustaining, life-giving rain, God continually showers us with blessings that fall in due season. His Word blesses us beyond measure. "Give ear, O heavens, and I will speak; And hear, O earth, the words of my mouth. Let my teaching drop as the rain, My speech distill as the dew, As raindrops on the tender herb, And as showers on the grass (Deut. 32:1-2, NKJV). Throughout the doctrines in the Old and New Testament lay the principles of God's amazing grace—grace that supplies all good and perfect gifts to the wise. These gifts make the difference between life and death, between hope and hopelessness, and between peace and fear.

"Blessed *be* the God and Father of our Lord Jesus Christ, who has blessed us with every spiritual blessing in the heavenly *places* in Christ" (Eph. 1:3, NKJV). What greater blessing can sinful man receive than to be made acceptable to God though Jesus. Entangled in the widespread net of sin, we deserve a penalty of death. But Jesus assumed our guilt and bore the penalty in our stead. This justified us in the sight of God and freed us from the wages of sin since Jesus' righteousness is credited to our account by faith and accepted by God. Now, "There is therefore now no condemnation to those who are in Christ Jesus" (Rom. 8:1, NKJV).

Can you imagine never being tired or sick, never worrying about bills or uncertainty? Have you ever imagined life without selfish, evil people, without trouble or disaster or death? What about endless bliss, splendor, and peace? These are the blessings of eternal life. Jesus promises all "who listen to my message and believe in God who sent me have eternal life. They will never be condemned for their sins, but they have already passed from death into life" (John 5:24, NLT).

"I will cause showers to come down in their season; there shall be showers of blessing" (Eze. 34:26, NKJV). In seasons of distress, doubt, or loss, God will shower the faithful with peace. Whatever the issue, He will strengthen us to equal or surpass the challenge, for the greater the suffering, the more abundant the blessings.

May 2

Our Covenant With God

For I am with you ... This is what I covenanted with you when you came out of Egypt. And my Spirit remains among you. Do not fear. Haggai 2:4, 5, NIV.

Covenants vary depending on the culture. People in Timor, located in the Malay Archipelago, participate in a blood brotherhood covenant where they swear eternal friendship. The parties cut their arms and bleed into a bamboo container that holds gin and wine. Then they take a sword and a spear from a sacred room and retire to a secluded spot to plant a fig tree. Hanging the bamboo container on the fig tree, they pledge to each other with a mixture of the blood-alcohol mixture. Lastly, they swear that if either of the contracting parties reneges, may blood issue from his mouth, ears, and nose as it does from the bamboo container that they puncture. The fig tree, stained with their blood, stands as a perpetual monument to their covenant.[127]

A covenant is an agreement recognized and protected by law to do or keep from doing a specified thing; it is a solemn compact between parties. God entered into five covenants with finite man beginning with Noah and ending with Jesus. With Noah, He covenanted to never again destroy the earth by a flood (Gen. 9:15) Later, He covenanted with Abraham to bless his descendants and designated them His chosen people (Gen. 12:1-5). In the Mosaic covenant between God and Israel, God said, "If you obey me fully and keep my covenant, then out of all nations you will be my treasured possession" (Ex. 19:5, NIV). And He established a throne forevermore for David's descendants in the Davidic covenant (2 Sam. 7:16).

When His unfaithful daughter Israel wandered, God entered into a new and final covenant with spiritual Israel, including all nations and Jews and Gentiles. "Behold, the days are coming, says the LORD, when I will make a new covenant with the house of Israel and with the house of Judah—not according to the covenant that I made with their fathers in the day that I took them by the hand to lead them out of the land of Egypt, My covenant which they broke ... says the Lord" (Jer. 31:31, 32, NKJV). With this covenant God puts His law in our minds and writes the laws in our hearts through the indwelling of the Spirit. This is the covenant of grace.

And Jesus is the fulfillment of that covenant of grace. Said God, "I will preserve You and give You As a covenant to the people, To restore the earth, To cause them to inherit the desolate heritages; ... To those who *are* in darkness, 'Show yourselves'" (Isa. 49:8, 9, NKJV). Central to this covenant, Jesus reconciles God and humanity by restoring us to a right relationship with God. Jesus is the bridge over troubled waters, the only Mediator between God and man who stands in the gap for sinners. There He exposed Himself to torture and death to protect us from the consequences of sin.

God's promises are sure and fail proof, but we have been known to fail Him. However, if we fulfill the requirement of obedience, we are assured of the plans He has to give us hope and a future.

May 3

God Delights in You

The LORD your God ... He will take great delight in you. Zeph. 3:17, NIV.

Savvy corporations such as Zappos, an online shoe merchant, have mastered the technique of customer delight and counsel their call center representatives to delight the customers. "Delighted customers are those where you anticipate their needs; provide solutions to them before they ask; and where you are observing to see if new and/or additional expectations are about ready to be required." The goal is to create such a 'wow' experience that the customer will never forget.[128]

God does not simply love His chosen people, He delights in us—a deeper than ordinary love. God's joyful pleasure in those who live sanctified lives is evident by His words, His deeds, and His solicitous concern for us. Because He delights in those striving for perfection, God bristles at the thought of our defeat by the forces of evil. "He rescued me from my powerful enemy ... the LORD was my support. He brought me out into a spacious place; he rescued me because he delighted in me" (Ps. 18:17-19, NIV). It takes faith to accede handling our problems to God; it takes prayer to apprise Him of our needs; and it takes intimacy with Him to distinguish who He is and why He desires to intervene in the lives of His children. God delights in us because we delight in Him; because we recognize His supremacy and astounding love.

The plan of salvation is evidence of the delight He takes in us for "He is mighty to save. He will take great delight in you" (Zeph. 3:17). If angels rejoice over even one sinner who repents, imagine the joy flooding the heart of God over lost sheep returning to the fold. Without His plan to save wayward sinners, not one human could ever see Him face to face for "we love him, because he first loved us" (1 John 4:19). While we were hopelessly sinning, headed for a bleak future, a dark grave, and a fiery end, He stepped in and "put his love on the line for us by offering his Son in sacrificial death while we were of no use whatever to him" (Rom. 5:8, MSG).

Not satisfied to wind us up spiritually and allow us to spin aimlessly around in circles, He devised ways to keep us pointed heavenward. "If the LORD delights in a man's way, he makes his steps firm; though he stumble, he will not fall, for the LORD upholds him with his hand" (Ps. 37:23, 24, NIV). Through discipline He catches our attention using tough tactics to extricate us from sin. "Is not Ephraim my dear son, the child in whom I delight? Though I often speak against him, I still remember him. Therefore my heart yearns for him; I have great compassion for him" (Jer. 31:20, NIV).

The wonder of it all! A pure and holy God finds delight in His piteous, fallen creatures! But He says, "I do what's right and set things right and fair, and delight in those who do the same things" (Jer. 9:24, MSG). He delights in our praise and in our appreciation for His manifold blessings and in "those who fear him, in those who hope in his steadfast love" (Ps. 147:11, ESV). Aren't you encouraged that you mean so much to Him, that you are the apple of His eye, that He delights in you?

May 4

Lie Down in Contentment

The remnant of Israel shall not do iniquity, nor speak lies… for they shall feed and lie down, and none shall make them afraid. Zeph. 3:13.

Connie Culp, America's first full face transplant recipient, became severely disfigured after her husband shot her in the face with a shotgun. News reports revealed that her cheekbones, nose, mouth, and an eye were destroyed by the blast that buried countless bone splinters and shotgun pellets in her face, requiring the assistance of a tracheotomy to breathe. To refashion as much face as possible, doctors used bones from her rib cage and leg and skin from her thighs in a series of thirty operations.

The violence that caused Connie's injury and in myriad other forms is rampant in our land. There is violence in nature, violence in the church, violence among families, among our leaders, in society, and among nations. To keep safe, we buy home alarms and car alarms, flood lights and flashlights, handguns and pepper spray, rent security guards and bodyguards, and put 911 on our speed dial. But to no avail. According to the FBI Uniform Crime Reporting Program statistics, in 2009, 500 out of every 10,000 people living in the United States were victims of a violent crime.

Jesus' sheep are spread out across this violent earth, but He promises, "I will tend them in a good pasture…. There they will lie down in good grazing land, and there they will feed in a rich pasture on the mountains of Israel" (Eze. 34:14, NIV). In that good pasture, signifying life after death, life in the literal presence of God is perfect peace. Neither violence or strife nor evil or harm nor enmity between men will dare show its face there (Isa. 60:18; 65:25). Moreover, enmity between nature and man will turn to affection. The nursing child will play by the hole of the cobra, and the weaned child will put his hand on the viper's den. There, the wolf will dwell with the lamb, and the leopard will lie down with the young goat. Moreover, the calf, the young lion, and the yearling will rest together, and a child will lead them (Isa. 11:6-8).

God promises, "My people shall dwell in a peaceable habitation, and in sure dwellings, and in quiet resting places" (Isa. 32:18). When sin is eliminated, along with those who cling tenaciously to sin despite God's best efforts to transfer their allegiance to Him, justice and righteousness will hold sway. Because the work of righteousness is peace and its offspring is quietness and assurance forever, life pivots and becomes an oasis of nonviolence that rises to the level of perfect tranquility. The redeemed now fully assimilate the character of Jesus, and all live out the principles of the kingdom in perfect harmony.

So "do not be afraid, little flock, for it is your Father's good pleasure to give you the kingdom" (Luke 12:32) where you can eat and lie down in peace after God turns this violent land into an oasis of peace inhabited by peacemakers and the Prince of Peace.

May 5

The Apple of God's Eye

For he that toucheth you toucheth the apple of his eye. Zech. 2:8.

The complexity of the eye is astounding. Even Charles Darwin admitted that the eye confounded his theory of evolution. He wrote, "To this day the eye makes me shudder."[129] "To suppose," he admitted, "that the eye with all its inimitable contrivances ... could have been formed by natural selection, seems, I freely confess, absurd in the highest degree."[130]

The human eye is "a perfect and interrelated system of about 40 individual subsystems, including the retina, pupil, iris, cornea, lens and optic nerve.... About 130 million of the cells [in the retina] look like rods and handle the black and white vision. The other seven million are cone shaped and allow us to see in color. The retina cells receive light impressions, which are translated to electric pulses and sent to the brain via the optic nerve.... [where] the visual cortex interprets the pulses to color, contrast, depth, etc., which allows us to see 'pictures' of our world. Incredibly, the eye, optic nerve and visual cortex are totally separate and distinct subsystems. Yet, together, they capture, deliver and interpret up to 1.5 million pulse messages a milli-second!"[131]

The phrase "apple of the eye" refers to the vital apple-shaped pupil, the clear part that allows light to enter. Figuratively, the eye is the lamp of the body (Matt. 6:22). Upon accepting Jesus as Lord and Savior, we throw open the drapes and admit the Light of the world to dispel the darkness. Those who embrace the Light are the apple of His eye, indicating how He cherishes the faithful ones. The Lord's people are the lot of His inheritance, His portion, and His love for us is everlasting (Deut. 32:9; Jer. 31:3). Living as homeless captives of sin, God found the Israelites in the desert of Egypt, led them out with a strong right hand, and instructed them in the ways of righteousness (Deut. 32:10). Even after they rebelled against God, the Israelites remained the apple of His eye and He labored mightily to save them.

No matter how many times we fail God or crucify Him anew by falling short, we remain His treasured possessions, infinitely valuable as long as we are making progress on the ancient paths where the good ways are. Even when we self-inflict an assessment of insignificance and worthlessness on ourselves, our value does not diminish in the eyes of God. His passionate love continually sets us in the center of His attention.

Fiercely protective, God is "like an eagle that stirs up its nest and hovers over its young, and that spreads its wings to catch them and carries them on its pinions" (Deut. 32:11, NIV). Humble Christians are akin to the newborn eaglets whose legs are too weak to hold their weight and whose eyes are partially closed. Helplessly dependent, we are shielded and nurtured by God who cares for His own, guarding us as the apple of His eye. My plea is "keep me as the apple of the eye, hide me under the shadow of thy wings" (Ps. 17:8). Do you concur?

May 6

Taming the Tongue

And you, son of man, do not be afraid of them or their words... Do not be afraid of what they say or terrified by them. Eze. 2:6, NIV.

The horsefly or gadfly begins life in the mud at the base of stagnant water. There it moves and eats but can rise no higher than its mud bassinet for a period of time. Once an adult, it flies away to seek food from the blood of domestic animals. To feed, the gadfly painfully pierces the hide of the animal, cuts in a "scissor like fashion," and then sucks the blood. It uses six different parts of its mouth that feel like razors to obtain the blood. Agonizingly, its mouth wounds the animal like a weapon.

"Sticks and stones may break my bones, but words will never hurt me" is a popular saying. But words, biblically called 'tongue,' when used in an ungodly manner create wounds that last longer and hurt worst than weapons. A deceitful tongue is so powerful that it crushes the spirit (Prov. 15:4). "The tongue also is a fire, a world of evil among the parts of the body. It corrupts the whole person, sets the whole course of his life on fire, and is itself set on fire by hell" (James 3:6, NIV).

Our words, like wildfire, can destructively consume everything in its path. For example, a series of wildfires sweeping across California in 2007 forced more than 500,000 people to evacuate their homes of which 1,700 were destroyed, consumed 500,000 acres of land, killed nine people, and injured eighty-five others. One was started by drought, another by downed power lines, another by an overturned truck, another was deliberately set, and still another by a child playing with matches. Each fire, started by a spark, became a raging, out-of-control wildfire.

Hastily spoken words are traps that also ensnare the speaker (Prov. 6:2). Despite the damage we do to our neighbor, whom we are commanded to love, we damage ourselves eternally. There are no secrets in heaven, and our irresponsible words will soon witness against us. "But I say to you that for every idle word men may speak, they will give account of it in the day of judgment. For by your words you will be justified, and by your words you will be condemned" (Matt. 12:36, 37, NKJV).

God designed the tongue to be used prudently, an instrument for good. A timely word brings joy (Prov. 15:23), commends knowledge (Prov. 15:2), heals (Prov. 12:18), and sweetens the soul (Prov. 16:24). But using the power tendered by the Holy Spirit, we must diligently strive to tame the tongue. "I will guard my ways that I may not sin with my tongue; I will guard my mouth as with a muzzle" (Ps. 39:1, NASB). Negative speech including gossip, cursing, lies, deceit, boasting, and backbiting rise to the level of sin. And detestable words that reveal the hate in our hearts break the very spirit of the sixth commandment to not kill (Matt. 5:21).

To tame the tongue, think on true, noble, righteous, and pure things and those things will reach your lips, revealing your reformed heart.

May 7

Fruit of Righteousness

The fruit of righteousness will be peace; the effect of righteousness will be quietness and confidence forever. Isa. 32:17, NIV.

At the judgment God will judge us by our fruit—our conduct and character. "Prayer governs conduct and conduct makes character. Conduct, is what we do; character, is what we are. Conduct is the outward life. Character is the life unseen, hidden within, yet evidenced by that which *is* seen. Conduct is external, seen from without; character is internal -- operating within. In the economy of grace conduct is the offspring of character. Character is the state of the heart, conduct its outward expression. Character is the root of the tree, conduct, the fruit it bears."[132]

In nature each type of seed reproduces unique fruit. But the seed has no inherent power in itself, for God hard wired a germinating principle in the heart of each seed (Gen. 1:29). "Every seed grows, every plant develops, by the power of God."[133] Even with that innate principle, unplanted seeds are useless and impotent. Planting requires labor and commitment on man's part and connection with the supernatural power that provides sun, soil, and rain for nourishment. Similarly, character building requires our effort and the supernatural power of God's Spirit who implants a seed of desire within us to bear fruit so that we do not remain as barren trees swaying in the wind.

Likewise with character building, we must tap into the Vine or wither spiritually. Jesus said, "I am the Vine, you are the branches. When you're joined with me and I with you, the relation intimate and organic, the harvest is sure to be abundant. Separated, you can't produce a thing. Anyone who separates from me is deadwood, gathered up and thrown on the bonfire" (John 15:5-7, MSG). Christians who bear no fruit—those who regress, backslide, and tread water spiritually—Jesus promises to hacksaw to a nub and throw in the fire on His return.

God, whose righteousness is everlasting, requires those who bear His Son's name to do good works, to display righteous conduct, and to assimilate the character of Jesus (Matt. 5:16). With this requisite, He provides the power to achieve uprightness in conduct and character. Truly, we are incapable of righteous conduct without the power of God working within us, for our so-called righteousness is smelly and stained like discarded menstrual rags (Isa. 64:6). So, to move us along the continuum of virtue, God prunes vigorously to remove the deadwood that prevents new growth.

And no matter how scarce the fruit, He promises to prune the fruitful branches until they are fruit-laden (John 15:2). This pruning is very uncomfortable and intermittent throughout our Christian lives, but so beneficial to our fruit-bearing. So strive to be filled with the knowledge of His will in all wisdom and spiritual understanding to walk worthy of the Lord, fully pleasing *Him*, being fruitful in every good work, and increasing in the knowledge of God (Col. 1:9, 10). Therein lies our quietness and confidence forever.

May 8

The God of Multiple Second Chances

Just as I determined to punish you when your fathers provoked Me to wrath ... and I would not relent, so again in these days I am determined to do good to Jerusalem and to the house of Judah. Do not fear. Zech. 8:14, 15, NKJV.

There is something very encouraging and comforting about second chances. They reaffirm the good in human nature. For instance, Roy Riegels nearly lost the game for the University of California in the first half of the 1929 Rose Bowl. He recovered a fumble against Georgia Tech and, disconcerted, ran 65 yards the wrong way. Except for a tackle by a member of his own team, he would have scored a touchdown for Georgia Tech. Embarrassed and distraught, Riegels sat on the bench at half time and cried like a baby, certain that Coach Nibs Price would never allow him to play in the second half. But the coach gave him a second chance. And spurred on by his second chance, Riegels played his hardest, including blocking a Georgia Tech punt.

Second chances also illustrate the great mercy and astounding grace of a holy God. As long as there is life in us and as often as we humbly repent, God willingly forgives us. *But forgiveness is just the beginning.* Next, He stretches this forgiveness exponentially by completely erasing the sins. Paul wrote, "Repent therefore, and turn to God so that your sins may be wiped out" (Acts 3:19, NRSV). As far as the east is from the west is the distance He puts between sinners and their sins (Ps. 103:12). Then, He imputes Jesus' virtue to us through faith to shield our blemishes from His eyes (Rom. 4:22-24).

Not only does God provide us with multiple second chances, He also expects that we grant our neighbors the same mercy. The biblical measure of forgiveness is boundless. When Peter asked Jesus how often he should forgive those who sinned against him, Jesus held that seven times was miserly. His standard of forgiveness is seventy times seven (Matt. 18:21, 22). But after forgiving 490 times, we do not have the right to be hard-hearted. Jesus' response instructs us to follow His example and forgive as He forgives and as often as He forgives (Mark 11:25, 26). Furthermore, providing second chances and forgiving our debtors is beneficial both to our spiritual and mental health. When we refuse to forgive, the person who offends us holds us captive. Thoughts of the offender and the offense spontaneously invade our mind day and night to pilfer our peace. It is certainly not easy to go against the grain of our nature that cries out for vengeance, but we have a source of supernatural power to plug into that softens our hearts against revenge.

Unlike sinners, we are not free to love only those who treat us well. Jesus expects us to be merciful to the unlovely, just as our Father also is merciful to us (Luke 6:36). Thus, the wise will utilize the power of the Holy Spirit to wipe anger, bitterness, and resentment out of the heart and, like Jesus, be the Christian of multiple second chances.

May 9

Weapons Lose Their Power

No weapon formed against you shall prosper.. Isa. 54:17, NKJV.

At a charity boxing event to assist firemen and police who survived the 9/11 attacks on the World Trade Center in New York City, James Butler threw a sucker punch at Richard Grant. Both were light heavyweight boxers contending for a win at this event. Butler, after losing the bout, removed his gloves and went across the ring to Grant, supposedly to congratulate him. Instead, he hit Grant with a brutal right hook to the jaw, dislocating his jaw and gashing his tongue so viciously that it required twenty-six stitches.

The term "sucker punch" is slang for a standard street fighting technique where the antagonist punches another person with malicious intent at close range without warning and usually without provocation. Sucker punches come as a total surprise and are difficult, well-nigh impossible, to block. In boxing a sucker punch is illegal; thus, Butler was convicted of aggravated assault and served time at Riker's Island.

Like Grant, Merlene's supervisor sucker punched her with the news in October that he wanted her to leave her position by the end of the year. Six months earlier he had been openly antagonistic against her, but he seemed to abandon his attack. Merlene ducked under the radar screen, so she thought, but his evil intent to replace her took a more subtle approach. He hit her on the blind side of belief that anybody can change and worked behind the scenes to fulfill his desire. However, his weapon hit Merlene's spiritual vest, stunned her, bruised her ribs, and then fell impotently to the ground.

God allowed the trial but tempered the full impact of the weapon. After two years of his on-again, off-again unwarranted persecution, Merlene finally learned to entrust the problem to God. She actually felt a twinge of guilt at how she shoved the problem in His hand and walked away. Mind you, in a few months she would either be without a job or have such reduced pay that she could not remain financially solvent. Merlene praised God anyhow. A short time later, God miraculously turned the situation around, removed her from his direct supervision into a lesser position where she could keep her full salary and have more autonomy and less stress.

The traps were set; the weapons were aimed at her heart and head, but they were adroitly deflected by faith and the power of prayer. Likewise, God deflected the fury of the hungry lions who licked their chops when Daniel was thrown into their lair, the heat of a lava-hot furnace when the three Hebrew boys would not bend their knee to an idol, and the world-conquering power of the Assyrians who threatened to annihilate Hezekiah and the Judeans but lost 185,000 of their own. God clearly stated to Hezekiah, "Because you have prayed to Me ..." (Isa. 37:21).

Except for the power of prayer and the accompanying faith that lifts the hand of God, such weapons would prosper. Prayer and faith are potent weapons against the weapons formed against us. Stay prayerful!

May 10

God's Watchful Eyes

Wherever you go, I will watch over you, then later I will bring you back to this land. I won't leave you--I will do all I have promised. Gen. 28:15, CEV.

Unlike any human being, the comic hero Superman is endowed with super optical powers among others. He has X-ray and telescopic vision that penetrate all substances except lead no matter how far away; microscopic vision sharp enough to peer through the galaxy and focus on a single particle of dust; heat vision for concentrated heat to burn through any substance except lead; infrared vision and radar vision to see far beyond the visible spectrum of human sight; and photographic vision to speed read books and recall each word. Gotham City citizens feel safe with Superman around. Still, kryptonite renders useless all of his super powers.

Not so with God. His supernatural optical vision and other powers are perfect. So acute is His vision that, although seated on high and peering down, He never misses a grimace of pain or sorrow; a wandering, lost soul; gray and rainy days in the life of His saints; or a hand clapped in praise. His eyes scan the earth to strengthen those who love Him (2 Chron. 16:9). Be it resolved, God keeps close watch over the redeemed. "Truly the eye of the LORD is on those who fear him, on those who hope in his steadfast love" (Ps. 33:18, NRSV). In addition, Psalm 34:18 states, "The LORD is close to the brokenhearted and saves those who are crushed in spirit" (NLT).

God keen eyesight does not simply see the things man sees. His vision penetrates straight to the heart of the matter. When God dispatched Samuel to anoint Saul's successor, God gave Him sound advice. "Don't be impressed by his appearance or his height…. God does not view things the way men do. People look on the outward appearance, but the Lord looks at the heart" (1 Sam 16:7, NET). Quickly, He discerns the faithful from the hypocrite.

It is reassuring to know that He who watches over us will never slumber or avert His eyes. Every aspect of our lives is carefully observed by our devoted heavenly Father who safeguards us from dangers seen and unseen. Not only does He preserve us from all evil but He also preserves our soul from hell. Why else would the psalmist ask rhetorically, "I will lift up mine eyes unto the hills, from whence cometh my help." His ecstatic answer, "My help cometh from the LORD" (Ps. 121:1).

"The eyes of the LORD are in every place, keeping watch on the evil and the good" (Prov. 15:3, ESV). The watchful eye of God symbolizes His pervasive presence in and over the lives of those who love Him. That He never slumbers or sleeps highlights that His eyes are never averted from His people as He is in constant motion working not only to redeem and save us but also to protect and comfort us. And God promises "but I will not forget you" indicating the degree to which we are in His thoughts. Nothing hinders His protective care where His treasured possessions are concerned.

May 11

Power Vacuum

Pilate demanded. "Don't you realize that I have the power to release you or crucify you?" Then Jesus said, "You would have no power over me at all unless it were given to you from above. John 19:10, 11, NLT.

Very arid parts of Australia are home to the world's most deadly snake, the Inland Taipan. When it strikes venom is pumped from its oral gland by powerful jaw muscles into hollow fangs. With one attack it produces enough venom to kill thousands of mice or a hundred people! Its venom is more potent than ten rattlesnakes and almost eight hundred times more powerful than the cobra. Alas, its lethal venom does not kill instantaneously but brings excruciating pain, nausea, convulsions, respiratory failure, paralysis, and coma before death mercifully occurs.[134] What an apt analogy of how Satan would attack and kill God's people without His intervention!

Venom denotes the painful attacks on God's people by agents of Satan in our homes, on our jobs, in public, and even in church. Many of these attacks are unfair, unprovoked, and unnecessary but they occur over and over to our chagrin. Some attacks are short-lived but many last for months and years. Still none is allowed to destroy God's people. For God parcels out limited power to Satan and his agents to assist in our character building but not our destruction (1 Peter 1:6, 7).

Consider Job. After God gave Satan complete freedom and authority to wreak havoc on Job's possessions and his health, he did not hesitate to spew toxic venom at Job. In quick succession, the Sabeans stole Job's oxen and donkeys and killed his servants; fire from heaven burned up the sheep and their attendants; Chaldeans stole his camels and killed their attendants; and a desert wind blew his son's house down on him and his nine siblings and killed them (Job 1).

But God drew the line at Satan taking Job's life (Job 2:6), and he did not have the power to override God's will—this clearly confirms that God and God alone is sovereign. Satan only had the power that came from above. But without the protection that God promises and delivers, Satan's attacks, as toxic and destructive as the Inland Taipan's venom, would annihilate us instantly or mete out unrelenting, excruciating pain or bring a merciless slow, agonizing death.

Power vacuums exist in Satan and all other creation unless God supplies the power. Isn't it comforting to know that God has total power and control over nature, humanity, and the spirit world and that Satan and his evil agents are only allocated limited power to assist God's perfect will in our lives? Isn't it reassuring to know that we can trust Him to do what is best for us in the eternal perspective? Fear not!

When the venom is spewed in your direction through hollow fangs of hate, sprint toward that shield called Jesus; duck into the bunker of faith and clutch the antidote of peace that obeying God provides.

May 12

Come Hell or High Water

The angel of the LORD encampeth round about them that fear him, and delivereth them. Ps. 34:7.

The New York Post Office Building opened in 1914 with an inscription carved into the building by William M. Kendall from the architectural firm that designed the building. It reads, "Neither snow nor rain not heat nor does gloom of night stay these couriers from the swift completion of their appointed rounds." This statement has long been wrongly attributed as the motto of the United States Post Office. Nevertheless, the inscription contains a solemn pledge that nothing will impede the mail carrier from delivering the mail on time and intact.

As well, God promises to station angels around His people, and neither hell nor high water will hinder angels from delivering God's children from evil and danger. Spirit beings and servants of God, angels are directed to protect His obedient disciples. "For He shall give His angels charge over you, to keep you in all your ways. In their hands they shall bear you up, lest you dash your foot against a stone" (Ps. 91:11, 12, NKJV). Angels, although invisible, are tirelessly involved in our daily existence as a physical and spiritual safeguard against Satan's agents.

God rules over all creation, and angels, who are created beings, are equipped with certain attributes to uplift and protect His ransomed. Some angels "excel in strength, that do his commandments, hearkening unto the voice of his word" (Ps. 103:20, 21). And innumerable angels work between heaven and earth to minister according to God's will. "As the host of heaven cannot be numbered, neither the sand of the sea measured" (Jer. 33:22). Assigned at birth, your guardian angel is always on task.

Angels are vigilant for God's beloved. He dispatched an angel to nullify the effects of fire for three faithful Hebrews. Ordered to bow down before an idol, Shadrach, Meshach, and Abednego refused, telling the king, "we will not serve your gods" (Dan. 3:18, NIV). Angry, the king ordered them thrown into a roaring inferno. Suddenly, he exclaimed, "I see four men walking around in the fire, unbound and unharmed, and the fourth looks like a son of the gods" (verse 25).

Thousands of years later, an angel protected me from what appeared to be a fatal automobile accident. I entered an intersection as the traffic light turned green, but a young man sped through a red light full throttle toward my side of the car. Suddenly my steering wheel turned, moving my car enough to avoid the oncoming speeding car. The steering wheel turned with such supernatural force that I could not budge it until the accident was averted. My guardian angel's action prevented the collision.

As promised, an angel encamps around us and delivers us. Until the end of time, angels will work on the behalf of those who love Him. For God has commanded His angels to guard the godly in all ways until our probation on earth ends.

May 13

Do Not Be Troubled

Let not your heart be troubled; you believe in God, believe also in Me. In My Father's house are many mansions ... I go to prepare a place for you.... I will come again and ... where I am, there you may be also. John 14:1-3, NKJV.

Max Lucado personifies Doubt and labels him a nosy neighbor, an unwanted visitor, and an obnoxious guest. "He will pester you, irritate you, and criticize your judgment. His aim is not to convince you but to confuse you. He doesn't offer solutions, he only raises questions."[135] Doubt or to lack confidence in something or someone is the number one troubler of God's elect. We doubt or are skeptical about or disbelieve God who cannot lie. How offensive is that to the One who supplies our every need and, unequivocally, proved to heaven and earth that He loves us intensely?

According to Jesus, the key to thrusting doubt, the father of fear, out of your life forever is to "Trust in God; trust also in me" (John 14:1, NLT). God's character and nature, the attributes which are inherently Him, should engender complete trust. He self-exists and self-sustains and has existed from everlasting to everlasting without beginning or end (Ps. 90:2). He alone is Master and Sovereign ruler of heaven and earth, holding unlimited authority over the literal and spiritual powers of life and death. "God does what he wants with the powers of heaven and the people on earth. No one can stop his powerful hand or question what he does" (Dan. 4:35, NCV).

God is omniscient, omnipotent, and omnipresent. 'Omni' is the Latin root meaning "in all ways," "in all places," or "applying to all things." God knows all things at once, and hears and answers billions of prayers offered simultaneously. His knowledge is prescient, unbounded, and infinite—He knows the end and the middle from the beginning. "He telleth the number of the stars; he calleth them all by their names. Great is our Lord, and of great power: his understanding is infinite" (Ps. 147:4, 5).

His power and presence are limitless, knowing no bounds. "Through him all things were made; without him nothing was made that has been made" (John 1:2, 3, NIV). And His unbounded presence puts Him in every place at the same time. David wrote, "Where can I go from your Spirit? Where can I flee from your presence? If I go up to the heavens, you are there; if I make my bed in the depths, you are there" (Ps. 139:7, 8, NIV).

God is the answer to all the problems and concerns in our world. Big enough, wise enough, powerful enough, and ubiquitous enough to handle our affairs is our God. "He can satisfy all your needs, and He can do it instantaneously. He supplies strength for the weak and He's available for the tempted and the tried. He sympathizes and He sees. He guards and He guides. He heals the sick. He cleansed the leper. He forgives sinners and He discharges debtors. He delivers the captives. He defends the feeble. He blesses the young. He regards the aged. He rewards the diligent. He beautifies the meek.... You can trust Him!"[136] So loosen that furrowed brow; there is no God like Jehovah!

May 14

The Lord Is Good

Oh, how great is Your goodness, which You have laid up for those who fear You, which You have prepared for those who trust in You. Ps. 31:19, NKJV.

Summum bonum, Latin for the highest good, can only be ascribed to God who is the perfect good, therefore the highest good. God is the source of everything good and wonderful, and every good thing and every perfect gift (James 1:17). "He is so omnipotent, that even out of nothing, that is out of what is absolutely non-existent, He is able to make good things both great and small, both celestial and terrestrial, both spiritual and corporeal."[137]

Many of us take God's goodness, patience, and forgiveness for granted, not fully comprehending that His goodness leads to repentance (Rom. 2:4, 5). Even in a world ruled by the prince of evil and populated by people born with sinful natures, God is able to produce repentant, compliant disciples. This conversion process begins upon our concession that we have a sin problem. With that concession we give God permission to begin His good work in us, to will and do His good pleasure.

"For the LORD is good and his love endures forever; his faithfulness continues through all generations" (Ps. 100:5, NIV). God *is* good, which is evidenced by His beneficence and patience in dealing with His erring children. We reject His Son, accuse Him, and blaspheme Him; we neglect Him, harm ourselves, and make alliances with the enemy; and we grieve both Him and the Holy Spirit. Still He provides abundantly. Knowing we will cause Him anguish, He faithfully awakens us each morning to give an added opportunity to make peace with Him.

"All that emanates from God—His decrees, His creation, His laws, His providences—cannot be otherwise than good."[138] Yes, He is a God of good deeds, but His goodness goes immeasurably beyond that. Good is not simply a descriptor for God; good is His nature, His essence, His makeup. Good is His personality, His temperament. He is goodness incarnate, and He sets the standard for His followers. "'Why do you call me good?' Jesus answered. 'No one is good—except God alone'" (Luke 18:19, NIV).

"O give praise to the Lord, for he is good: for his mercy is unchanging for ever" (Ps. 107:1, BBE). Lovingkindness is "the Divine Love condescending to His creatures, more especially to sinners, in unmerited kindness."[1239] He comforts and delivers us when we fall into self-made traps, forgives us for the most egregious deeds, and directs us to the path of righteousness. His mercy is unwavering. He protects us from our enemies, and He provided a Substitute to suffer the death we deserve.

His praise should continually be on our lips for truly the goodness of the Lord fills the earth, smothering us with benefits and blessings.

May 15

Working Together For Our Good

And we know that all things work together for good to them that love God, to them who are the called according to his purpose. Rom. 8:28.

A king in Africa had a close friend who found good in every situation. On a hunting expedition, the friend badly prepared one of the guns, causing it to blow off the king's thumb. The friend stated, "This is good!" But the king, unable to see the good, sent his friend to jail. Later, superstitious cannibals captured the king, noticed his missing thumb, and released him. The king visited his friend and admitted it was good that his thumb was blown off and regretted sending him to jail. The friend replied, "This is good.... If I had not been in jail, I would have been with you."[140]

The promise that all things work together for our good serves as a security blanket for confused and hurting people in a chaotic, dangerous, and fearful world. It conveys the comforting message that the world and the future are in God's mighty hands, and that if we humble ourselves, He will lift us above our problems and resolve them advantageously (1 Peter 5:6, 7). Received in faith, this promise calms fears even in the midst of the evil and uncertainty pervasive in our present life. For God can transform any bleak situation into a blessing. Patience and faith, however, are needed to wait on His faultless timing.

Tragedies are commonplace and test our faith to the utmost. In the fabric of earthly existence, we will not always see the good when terrible things happen. When tormentors nailed Messiah to the cross, His followers could not make sense of this turn of events. They despaired. "With the death of Christ the hopes of His disciples perished.... The future seemed dark with despair. Their faith in Jesus had perished."[141] But soon they learned that Jesus' death, a part of the master plan, shaped an eternal benefit for them and the future descendants of Adam.

When the good is not evident, cover your eyes of flesh with the eyeglasses of faith. One day, "all that has perplexed us in the providences of God will in the world to come be made plain. The things hard to be understood will then find explanation. The mysteries of grace will unfold before us. Where our finite minds discovered only confusion and broken promises, we shall see the most perfect and beautiful harmony. We shall know that infinite love ordered the experiences that seemed most trying. As we realize the tender care of Him who makes all things work together for our good, we shall rejoice with joy unspeakable and full of glory."[142]

Paul assures us that, because God is trustworthy, all the painful parts of the puzzles of life will one day fit perfectly in place. We will no longer see the disjointed pieces but an amazing unfolding. Remember, God holds and controls the things that destroy our peace and those that give us peace. His master plan is too multifaceted for our finite minds to comprehend. While we may not yet understand the *why* of our trials and burdens, let us reflect on the *who* and trust Him who loves us immeasurably to work them out for our ultimate good.

May 16

Do Not Fret

Do not fret because of evil men or be envious of those who do wrong; for like the grass they will soon wither… soon die away. Ps. 37:1, 2, NIV.

In Greek mythology a strikingly handsome young man named Narcissus lived in the forest. Deeply loved by others, He did not love in return. Upon spurning a nymph named Echo, she punished him and made him fall in love with himself. When Narcissus happened upon a clear pool that showed his enviable beauty, he became so enamored of himself that he could not turn away from the reflection. Hour after hour, day after day, his only goal in life, until he died, remained to look at himself.

Narcissism in clinical terms is an inordinate fascination with oneself, excessive self-love, and vanity. Derivatives of the word—narcissistic and narcissist—highlight negative personality traits like vanity, conceit, egotism, and selfishness. A narcissist with high levels of narcissism possesses a personality disorder whereby he or she overvalues his or her talents and abilities, coupled with an undue need for praise and approval. Clearly, low self-esteem is at the heart of narcissism and narcissists. How Ian knows intimately the narcissistic personality disorder! He questioned how God, who controls events, permitted him to endure back-to-back painful encounters from two people with the same emotional defect. One he encountered in a long-term relationship and the other as an employee. Thankfully, one relationship reached its finale at the genesis of the other, for God knows how much we can bear (1 Cor. 10:13). But as time passed, Ian realized that the Master Teacher led him to interrelate with these two pathologically selfish individuals to teach him to trust in Him.

His supervisor, the latter unprincipled, hyper-vigilant narcissist, possessed a markedly higher degree of narcissism. Her selfishness was so striking it appeared she lacked a conscience. And her self-esteem was such that she needed constant affirmation. Therefore, when someone innocently and unintentionally wounded her fragile self-esteem, to their chagrin, her vindictiveness erupted. With the power of her position, she stunned her victims both with harsh criticism and a resolve to destroy their careers by any underhanded means possible. She engendered fear in the hearts of her victims. But God is in control of even the most powerful adversary (Ps. 21:1).

On the surface, it appears as if these two high-achieving individuals are immune from the trials and pain that they caused Ian and others. However, from experience, Ian knows they are miserable because their fruit reveals they have no intimate relationship with God (Matt. 7:16). In the name of love, our job is to pray for their salvation. Although God loves the sinner, there are limits to His long-suffering, and His "spirit shall not always strive with man" (Gen. 6:3). Their triumph is short-lived as grass in the noonday sun, but their inglorious end is everlasting. Should they fail to make their peace with Him, they will wither like grass unlike the meek victims who will inherit the land and enjoy great peace (Ps. 37: 2, 11).

May 17

Loaded With Benefits

Blessed be the Lord, Who daily loads us with benefits, the God of our salvation! Ps. 68:19, NKJV.

A friend asked R. C. Chapman, a devout Christian, how he was feeling. "I'm burdened this morning!" he said. But his cheerful countenance contradicted his words. So the puzzled questioner exclaimed, "Are you really burdened, Mr. Chapman?" "Yes, but it's a wonderful burden—it's an overabundance of blessings for which I cannot find enough time or words to express my gratitude!"[143]

There *should* be no limit to our gratitude. Still, at times selfish human nature controls. Cheerfully we extol God when our gardens bloom with fragrant flowers and our world is full of sunshine. But when the stink weeds and thorns take over and the gray skies drop rain, we dissolve into self-pity, anger, and depression. It pays to remember that God is merciful, faithful, and compassionate in all ways and at all times. The psalmist declares that the abundance of His mercy and faithfulness is such that it fills up earth and reaches to the heavens (Ps. 36:5). Moreover, His great mercies are renewed daily to prevent our being consumed by evil and want (Lam. 3:22, 23).

Even in the midst of trials, His blessings are abundant. God "sends sometimes his choicest mercies to us in black-edged envelopes. The very brightest gems of heaven come to us, and we know them not."[144] We do not know them because we view our circumstances with jaded eyes of flesh not the spiritual eyes of faith. We allow fear to control. So, "Let us fix our eyes on Jesus, the author and perfecter of our faith, who for the joy set before him endured the cross, scorning its shame, and sat down at the right hand of the throne of God. Consider him who endured such opposition from sinful men, so that you will not grow weary and lose heart" (Heb. 12:2, 3, NIV).

Indeed, the greatest benefit we receive is Jesus, the Lord of our salvation, who stands in the gap for us. He willingly bore our grief and carried our sorrows. He was wounded for our transgressions and bruised for our iniquities, and His punishment brought us peace (Isa. 53:5). Jesus "saved [us] from the tyranny of the world, saved [us] to the prosperity of the Kingdom of God." He healed our sickness and disease and healed us to wellness in body, soul, and spirit. We are delivered from hell and destruction, but delivered to the freedom of the Holy Spirit, to the liberty of receiving the love, forgiveness, faith, truth, and hope that only Jesus can deliver to us.[145]

Daily, those benefits and blessings overflow our cup and spill over the edge of the saucer as His bountiful showers of love satisfy both physical and spiritual needs now and evermore. What more could we want or need? God forgives iniquities and heals all our diseases; redeems us, crowns us with lovingkindness and tender mercies; and satisfies our mouths with good things (Ps. 103:1, 2), and provides protection and security. Truly, we are loaded, no, overloaded with benefits.

May 18

God is God Alone

Woe to those who go down to Egypt for help ... But who do not look to the Holy One of Israel, nor seek the LORD! Isa. 31:1, NKJV.

A man encountered his neighbor carrying a large, heavy appliance-sized box on his back. He stopped his pickup truck and offered him a ride. The neighbor climbed into the truck bed, but peering in his rearview mirror, the driver was taken aback to see the box resting on his neighbor's back. When he asked why, the neighbor said he wanted to bear some of the heavy load to preserve the truck's engine.

Similarly foolish are our attempts to help God. Look at Ahaz king of Judah who sought military alliances with both Assyria and Egypt, two pagan nations who had rejected God. Fearful of the power of ruthless nations who threatened to invade and conquer his kingdom, Ahaz ignored a directive from the prophet Isaiah to trust God to crush these enemies (Isa. 7:8). And even after Egypt demurred, Ahaz contacted Assyria pleading, "I am your servant and your son. Come up and save me from the hand of the king of Syria and from the hand of the king of Israel, who rise up against me" (2 Kings 16:7, NKJV).

Absolute power belongs to God and God alone (Ps. 62:11). He created everything and should He will to resolve a situation, He resolves it, period. Isaiah writes, "You are the God, you alone, of all the kingdoms of the earth; you have made heaven and earth" (Isa. 37:16, ESV). And God announces, "I am the LORD, who makes all things, who stretches out the heavens all alone, who spreads abroad the earth by Myself" (Isa. 44:24, NKJV). And, "I have made the earth, and created man on it. I—My hands—stretched out the heavens, And all their host I have commanded" (Isa. 45:12, NKJV).

Why then would Ahaz rely on horses and horsemen because they appear strong and trust in chariots because they are many (Isa. 31:1)? Fear! Fear of what he could see, and a lack of faith in the promises of God moved him to seek protection from hands of flesh while ignoring the extended right hand of God. Ahaz, whose degenerate life put an ocean of distance between him and God, no longer believed. Desperate and vainly, he sought refuge with limited human kings who had no power apart from God (John 19:11). To God, "All the peoples of the earth are regarded as nothing. He does as he pleases with the powers of heaven and the peoples of the earth. No one can hold back his hand or say to him: 'What have you done'? (Dan. 4:35).

Seeking to master problems in our own power or trusting humans to resolve them places us in contempt of the Lord who deserves and commands our reverence. Man and nations are finite, weak, and unreliable, and even the most sincere human being cannot be trusted because our very existence is precarious. Sickness, financial decline, death, and other unforeseen circumstance make us unreliable. To allay fears, for peace's sake, shun Egypt and seek and trust God, who is wise, capable, and infinite and who shields those who trust Him (Prov. 30:5).

May 19

The Promise of a Long Life

My son, do not forget my law ... keep my commands; for length of days and long life and peace they will add to you. Prov. 3:1, 2, NKJV.

Finding humor in the aging process, one senior lady told her friend that old people are worth a fortune. They have SILVER in their hair, GOLD in their teeth, STONES in their kidneys, LEAD in their feet, and GAS in their stomachs. She admitted that since they last met, a few changes had occurred, and she was seeing several gentlemen every day: "As soon as I wake up, Will Power helps me get out of bed. Then Charlie Horse comes along ... When he leaves Arthur Ritus shows up and stays the rest of the day.... After such a busy day I'm really tired and glad to go to bed with Ben Gay."[146]

Notwithstanding the levity in longevity, disobedience on the part of our first parents brought us to the point of deteriorating systems and diseased cells in our bodies and minds. And our own disobedience further destroys our health, shortens our lifespan, and spawns fear. "To many of the afflicted ones who received healing, Christ said, 'Sin no more, lest a worse thing come unto thee' (John 5:14). Thus He taught that disease is the result of violating God's laws, both natural and spiritual. "The great misery in the world would not exist had men from the beginning lived in harmony with the Creator's plan."[147]

Car manufacturers provide manuals for car maintenance. Incredibly, some car owners preserve their cars but neglect the personal health principles prescribed by God. Above all things His desire for His people is that we prosper financially and spiritually and be in good physical health (3 John 1:2). He created our bodies; of course He knows how each part works and what keeps them fine-tuned. Too, He provides a manual, the Bible, with a health message to preserve physical, emotional, and spiritual health.

The Bible says, "Therefore, whether you eat or drink, or whatever you do, do all to the glory of God" (1 Cor. 10:31, NKJV). Reeking, poisonous tobacco smoke, a source of lung cancer, and mind-altering narcotics cannot and do not bring glory to God. And not only does intoxicating alcohol destroy the liver and the kidneys but it also causes nervous disorders and damages the memory. The Bible asks rhetorically, "Who has woe? Who has sorrow? Who has strife? Who has complaints? Who has needless bruises? Who has bloodshot eyes? Those who linger over wine, who go to sample bowls of mixed wine" (Prov. 23:29, 30, NIV).

Obviously sexual immorality produces diseases and actions that ravage, kill, and destroy feelings of self-worth. Our body is the temple of the Holy Ghost, which indwells in our hearts and is bought by Jesus with the price of His life. Glorify God in the body and in the spirit, both of which belong to Him (1 Cor. 6:19, 20), and obey the clear Word of God that provides a comprehensive health message. Following His laws, we are authorized to embrace the gift of health for long life, length of days, and peace. In so doing, He is able to fulfill His promise to "take sickness away from the midst of thee" (Ex. 23:25).

May 20

Angels Watch Over Us

Fear not: for they that be with us are more than they that be with them. 2 Kings 6:16.

Charlene left work late one night and walked down a dark road having missed the bus. While in the middle of the road, she spied a tall, brutish man lounging in a nearby doorway. Sensing danger, she prayed for protection, fearing his intent gaze as she passed, but he did not approach her. The next day a newspaper reported a young lady's murder in that same area. Charlene saw a picture of the murderer—the man in the alley. He confessed that he wanted to approach Charlene but feared the two very large men walking on each side of her. Amazed, Charlene had not seen her protectors, for her angels were only visible to the attacker.

Angels are demonstrably powerful. Threatened by an immense, potent Assyrian army, King Hezekiah prayed for God's protection. Hezekiah acknowledged his powerlessness and recommitted his kingdom to God, and God rewarded his faith: "The LORD says, 'I will rescue those who love me. I will protect those who trust in my name" (Ps. 91:14, NLT). God sent one angel who annihilated 185,000 men in the Assyrian camp. The next morning dead bodies were strewn everywhere (Isa. 37).

The Bible says, "Do not forget to entertain strangers, for by so doing some people have entertained angels without knowing it" (Heb. 13:2, NIV). Lot graciously extended hospitality to three men—angels—who rescued him and his family. The nephew of Abraham, who had earlier entertained the same three men, Lot was unaware that his whole world was about to explode in a fiery conflagration. But angels were dispatched by God to rescue him. They urged Lot to take his wife and daughters quickly out of the city to escape the judgment descending on Sodom and Gomorrah. Incredibly, he hesitated, but the angels seized his and his family's hands and guided them outside the city with a warning to flee (Gen. 19:15-17).

"For he will command his angels concerning you to guard you in all your ways" (Ps. 91:11, NIV). After his attack against the young Hebrew boys failed, Nebuchadnezzar blessed God "who ... sent his angel and delivered his servants, who trusted in him" (Dan. 3:28, ESV). Faithful to God, they refused to worship an idol and received a sentence of death by burning in a roaring furnace. The regular temperature was not severe enough for their disobedience; thus, the king ordered the furnace heated seven times hotter. The young men were bound and thrown into a furnace so hot that it instantly cremated their executors. Stunned, the king swore he saw an additional man in the furnace walking around with the unbound and unharmed young men (Dan. 3:8-28).

God appoints each person a guardian angel to stand watch over us in a world that is a staging ground for demons (Matt. 18:10). And it is comforting to know that God has twice as many angels as Satan has demons and is unmatched in power (Rev. 12:4).

May 21

Deliverance from Fear

For God has not given us the spirit of fear; but of power, and of love, and of a sound mind. 2 Tim. 1:7.

The vehicle of disobedience crashes through a wall into Meg's mind, providing a breach for Satan to crush this impenitent sinner with guilt, doubt, and unbelief. Bleeding and dazed, her walls crumble easily through neglect of eternal things, and she yields to his lies. Having no footing in spiritual things, she lets fear insert its evil self unlike the redeemed who are grounded in God's promises: "When I am afraid, I will trust in you. In God, whose word I praise, in God I trust; I will not be afraid (Ps. 56:3, 4, NIV).

"The wise man in the storm prays to God, not for safety from danger, but for deliverance from fear."[148] Fear is endemic in our society as confirmed by 500 people responding to a survey who listed 7,000 things that made them fearful. It is debilitating, self-defeating, and destructive, and fear and its companion, depression, thrive in calamities, violence, economic woes, selfishness, and confusion. Fear is also a shackle twisted in all shapes and sizes that emotionally constrains us. Children fear darkness and monsters under the bed, and birds fear cats. Citizens fear a bad economy, war, and poverty, and recovering alcoholics fear alcohol.

"Fear is a thief; a disgusting con man cheating us out of our rights and duping us into letting him steal from us. Fear is a weakling acting like a bully, humiliating us. It is low life asking us to strip ourselves of our Christ-bought freedom and dignity. It holds a toy gun to our head and for no rational reason we let it order us around. Fear is a malicious prankster hoping we will be terrorized by a cardboard cutout. Fear is a dirty, pesky fly getting in our face, annoying us. It is a filthy liar falsely accusing us, and we not only meekly sit there listening to the slanderous putdowns, we stupidly accept the garbage as truth. The appropriate response is to rise up in anger and refuse to let fear rob, cheat and bluff us any longer."[149]

This negative emotion is a spirit and, although invisible, is sensed and experienced. Mercifully, we have the peace of God through Jesus before whom spirits flee for He is the absolute ruler over demons, a supreme authority over any spirit. Although Satan and his harmful spirits are already defeated, he continues to utilize them to harass and defeat God's people. But keep in mind, "there are two great forces at work in the world today: the *unlimited power* of God and *the limited power* of Satan."[150]

Despite circumstances that promote fear, there is freedom in God who supplies a Christ-centered person an arsenal of peace, power, and a sound and disciplined mind. Even in the worst tragedy, in the midst of oppression and in the face of death, God delivers those who "were all their lifetime subject to bondage" (Heb. 2:15). Although we amass battle scars in the confrontation with the forces of evil, fear is conquered by handing the anxiety off to the Lord in prayer and trust that the Lord Who delivers us from all our fears will show Himself (Ps. 34:4).

May 22

Do Not Grow Weary

And let us not grow weary of doing good, for in due season we will reap, if we do not give up. Gal. 6:9, ESV.

A very critical man had a patient wife who tried very hard to please him, but she regularly failed. His criticism peaked at breakfast. If she presented scrambled eggs, he wanted poached; if she poached them, he wanted scrambled. One morning after surveying her options all night, the wife poached one egg and scrambled the other. Confident she resolved the problem, his wife eagerly waited for the response. He pushed the plate away and snarled, "Can't you do anything right, woman? You've scrambled the wrong one!"[151]

How can generosity thrive in the face of such selfishness? How do we forgive in the face of continued abuse? How do you love your enemy when the attacks are vicious and unrelenting? How do you keep from reaching the end of your rope when adversaries set the opposite end on fire? How can we not grow weary in doing good when our efforts seem fruitless? It is difficult but certainly achievable. For God gives power to the weak and to the powerless He increases strength (Isa. 40:29).

Human nature is such that we grow weary easily. Most drivers remember the thrill at earning a driver's license and the prospect of driving. But driving soon grows routine as do most things we purchase or pursue. Similarly, as life becomes a long round of stress, worry, and duty, Christians sometimes grow weary in fruit production and ministry, for even the most dedicated believer experiences periodic burnout. But we are never left alone to face our limitations. "Commit your way to the LORD, Trust also in Him, and He will do it" (Ps. 37:5, NASB).

In addition, look unto Jesus, the perfect example. Although He grew physically, emotionally, and spiritually weary, He persevered. Three times He pled with His Father to unload the burden of the cross from His shoulders, but He submitted nevertheless (Mark 14:36). Also, He agonized emotionally via torture by Satan who harassed him with the idea that He would never bridge the expanse that sin placed between Him and His Father (Matt. 27:46). "Despised and rejected by men; a man of sorrows, and acquainted with grief," He persisted in trusting God and holding on (Isa. 53:3). Now, He continually reaps a bountiful harvest of souls.

Prayer remained Jesus' primary resource, and He counsels that "they ought always to pray and not lose heart" (Luke 18:1, ESV). Check out your prayer life, bolster your hope, and recalibrate your focus for each may need ratcheting up to ward off weariness and burnout. The promise stands. "Those who hope in the LORD will renew their strength. They will soar on wings like eagles; they will run and not grow weary, they will walk and not be faint" (Isa. 40:31, NIV). Weary, yes, but hold on tenaciously, persevere in God's strength and reap your harvest.

May 23

God Will Never Abandon You

My father and mother walked out and left me, but God took me in. Ps. 27:10, MSG.

Along with four siblings, Stacey Mendolia endured abandonment by her mother who loved heroin more than her children. Social Services placed Stacey, who never knew her father, in an orphanage. Unable to find the love and stability she craved, she followed in her mother's footsteps and became a drug addict. "Marijuana, heroin and crack cocaine kept her company after she was raped, after she gave up her first child for adoption at 15, after she watched her sister die of AIDS."[152]

Stacey can attest that abandonment by someone you love, especially a mother, produces some of the keenest pain imaginable. And studies prove that a mother's love is critical to the proper development of a growing child. A "mother's love and nurturing even directly impacts the biological development of the child's brain and central nervous system" concluded researchers. "In effect, mother and child are 'hard-wired' for mutual love." Researchers compare the brain of a child to a stencil waiting for the imprint of love and affection. One study showed that hugs and kisses during the developmental period assist neurons to properly grow and connect.[153]

God inserted an IV line of nurturing, unselfish love into the veins of a mother, sank it deep and stretched it wide. Still, some mothers abandon their children. But God promises that even if that mother, whom He created to love her child unconditionally, walks away, you will never walk alone. Fully human, Jesus desired intimacy but knew His disciples would abandon Him at His lowest moment. He said, "Yet I am not alone, because the Father is with me" (John 16:32). Too, Paul suffered persecution because of the gospel, and when everyone deserted him at his first trial, he noted, "But the Lord stood at my side and gave me strength" (2 Tim. 4:16, 17, NIV).

Abundant proof of God's abiding presence resides in His Word. "You're all I want in heaven! You're all I want on earth! When my skin sags and my bones get brittle, GOD is rock-firm and faithful. Look! Those who left you are falling apart! Deserters, they'll never be heard from again. But I'm in the very presence of GOD—oh, how refreshing it is! I've made Lord GOD my home. GOD, I'm telling the world what you do!" (Ps. 78:25-28, MSG). It is in abiding with Him that we can bask in His aura. "Surely the righteous will give thanks to Your name; The upright will dwell in Your presence" (Ps. 140:13, NASB).

We are never alone. "For the LORD your God is a merciful God, he will not abandon you" (Deut. 4:31, NLT). It is impossible for God to forsake the objects of His love. The fierce love He holds for us supersedes that of a thousand parents' love. Rhetorically, God poses a question. "Can a mother forget the baby at her breast and have no compassion on the child she has borne?" Then He offers the answer. "Though she may forget, I will not forget you" (Isa. 49:15)! He is supernaturally faithful and ever present.

May 24

God to the Rescue

The righteous person faces many troubles, but the LORD comes to the rescue each time. Ps. 34:19, NLT.

St. Bernard dogs have helped save lives since the early eighteenth century when monks used them to rescue people trapped in the snow along the St. Bernard Pass, a treacherous route through the Alps between Italy and Switzerland. These dogs use their massive chests to shovel the snow aside, and they have an incredible sense of smell, allowing them to locate people buried deep in the snow. "Over a span of nearly 200 years, about 2,000 people, from lost children to Napoleon's soldiers, were rescued because of the heroic dogs' uncanny sense of direction and resistance to cold."[154]

Who will rescue me? That is a refrain mournfully resonating throughout our sin-laden world. I confessed my sins, but I continue to do sinful things; who will rescue me? I have lost my job and my mortgage is going into foreclosure. My marriage is on the rocks. My children are experimenting with drugs and their tomorrow hangs in the balance. I have been diagnosed with cancer. I am overwhelmed by emotional pain, depressed and alone. Who will rescue me? Who? David, himself, constantly seeking deliverance, reached high and secured the lifeline. "I waited patiently for the LORD; he turned to me and heard my cry. He lifted me out of the slimy pit, out of the mud and mire; he set my feet on a rock and gave me a firm place to stand" (Ps. 40:1, 2, NIV).

Who will rescue us from the spiritual blunders we continually make even when committed to God? Paul, wrestling with sin, concedes, "Wretched man that I am! Who will rescue me from this body of death?" (Rom. 7:24, NRS). "For if I know the law but still can't keep it, and if the power of sin within me keeps sabotaging my best intentions, I obviously need help! I realize that I don't have what it takes. I can will it, but I can't do it. I decide to do good, but I don't really do it; I decide not to do bad, but then I do it anyway" (Rom. 7:17-20, MSG).

Knowing intimately who God is and having experienced His amazing love, Paul bursts with joy, confident that the answer is in Him. "Thanks be to God through Jesus Christ our Lord!" (Rom. 7:25, ESV). "Therefore there is now no condemnation for those who are in Christ Jesus. For the law of the Spirit of life in Christ Jesus has set you free from the law of sin and of death" (Rom. 8:1, 2, NASB).

How wise is the little boy who prayed, "God please take care of yourself because if anything happens to you we're in a world of trouble!" Apart from Him, we are totally helpless, but He is "the rock of my strength, and my refuge, is in God" (Ps. 62:7). Unlike the legendary St. Bernard who brings a keg of spirits to warm the near frozen victim of the cold and snow, God brings salvation and glory and is a very present help in times of trouble.

May 25

Momentary Affliction

For our light affliction, which is but for a moment, worketh for us a far more exceeding and eternal weight of glory. 2 Cor. 4:17.

"From the cradle to the coffin, affliction and sorrow are the appointed lot of man. He comes into the world with a wailing cry, and he often leaves it with an agonizing groan! Well is this earth called 'a valley of tears,' for it is wet with them in infancy, youth, manhood, and old age."[155] Affliction is a scary word. To be afflicted is to be in pain, to be distressed, to have grief and misery. Affliction connotes sickness, persecution, loss, and calamity; thus, the phrase "light or slight momentary affliction" appears to dismiss the enormity of our suffering.

But how is the betrayal and desertion by a cheating husband whose wife is a stay-at-home mom with three preschool children a light affliction? How is the slow, agonizing death from burns, shrapnel, and nails to persons injured in suicide bombings a light affliction? How is systematic, excruciating torture after an unjustifiable arrest and incarceration of a disciple of God or birthing a stillborn baby a light affliction?

Because God said so! His Word is faithful and true. And by faith, we trust the character of God and the Word of God. As mortals, we see things from a limited, one-dimensional perspective while God sees things in their totality with an unobstructed, panoramic, multidimensional view. We are not eligible, qualified, or equipped to understand the eternal weight of glory for soon sight and hearing will be dumbfounded at heaven's glories. Even the most brilliantly inventive mind cannot imagine the splendor of our future eternal existence (1 Cor. 2:9). After shedding this corrupt earthly tent and dwelling in eternity, we will be pleasantly surprised to find that heaven is worth the outlay of obedience and loyalty to God's will (2 Cor. 5:4).

Our afflictions, lasting at most a few decades, *are* light in the face of timelessness. Humans only have a miniscule slice of time created by God out of our foreign concept of timelessness. The time allotted for us to build character and faith, although sufficient, is like a drop of water in a vast ocean filled with countless trillions of drops. In fact, James compares our short time on earth as a wisp of smoke that vanishes quickly (James 4:14). This slice of time is fraught with hardship and pain for the sake of our salvation, but those who are faithful under trial are promised a crown of life (James 1:12).

No, our light afflictions cannot compare with the eternal weight of glory, so fear not today's or tomorrow's difficulties. Physical injuries do heal; emotional pain does subside as healing obeys God (Luke 4:23). Death has already been conquered by Jesus through His crucifixion and death, and one day He will fit us for new bodies that are incorruptible and immune from illness, disease, pain, and death (Heb. 2:14, 15; 1 Cor. 15:53). And in glory, we receive our incorruptible, fadeless inheritance, never threatened by temptation or sin again (Rev. 21:4; 1 Peter 1:4). Then, see how vastly far the reward outweighs the afflictions!

May 26

Battlefield of the Mind

Do not be afraid of the king of Babylon ... do not be afraid of him... for I am with you to save you and deliver you. Jer. 42:11, NASB.

God reassured the Israelites who stood in fear of the ruthless Babylonian army with the same reassurance He extends to us. But we are in the midst of *spiritual* combat and contending with battle fatigue also known as shell-shocked and Post-Traumatic Stress Disorder. These are military terms that describe the emotional toll that combat inflicts on the human psyche typified by irritability, apprehension, and depression. Unlike the literal Babylonian armies, the combatants in this spiritual warfare consist of demons and Christians and the battlefield is in our minds.

In any battle, the best defense is a good offense. Know your enemy's tactics and his strategic plan because ignorance defeats us. There is no hope of winning unless the combatants are disciplined and vigilant at all stages of the battle, for we are fighting invisible powers of evil. The Bible compares Satan, the wily, psychopath leading the forces, to a starving, stalking beast who spends his time and intellect searching to consume us (1 Peter 5:8). Those who will not exercise authority over him (1 Peter 5:9), those who are unaware of his deceptions, (2 Cor. 2:11), and those who are not armed with the whole armor of God will be ripped apart (Eph. 6:11).

Satan's chief weapon in this battle is the subtle deception of doubt and lies. John says he was a murderer from the beginning, and lies are his native language, for he is a liar and the father of lies (John 8:44); a thief, a terrorist, and a murderer (John 10:10). He cloaks his deception behind a veil of invisibility to take control over our minds, the center of our thoughts and emotions. Then he influences our belief that the lies, doubts, and evil thoughts originated with us. His victory lies in controlling our thoughts.

Do not be fooled! Satan and his demons do not simply glide around like disembodied, invisible ghosts. They hunt for a place to live and establish strongholds—very lethal weapons. *Topov*, Greek for stronghold, is a military word for fortress or an impenetrable shelter. The key that unlocks our defenses and allows him to gain entry and control our thoughts is willful sin. Once the door is open, he builds a stronghold and easily coerces self-destructive, violent, and immoral actions and thoughts until we retake control.

But the faithful, obedient Christian need not fear this enemy activity. We are commanded not to give place to the devil and are given authority over his tactics (Eph. 4:27). "For the weapons of our warfare are mighty in God for pulling down strongholds, casting down arguments and every high thing that exalts itself against the knowledge of God, bringing every thought into captivity to the obedience of Christ" (2 Cor. 10:4, 5, NKJV). Satan will flee when he encounters a sanctified heart where the formidable Holy Ghost resides.

May 27

Jesus Our Refuge

You have been my stronghold and a refuge in the day of my distress. Ps. 59:16, NASB.

Manslaughter, a 1930s movie, depicts the story of a rich socialite who accidentally hits a man with her automobile and kills him. She is arrested and prosecuted by a district attorney who must work for survival. Offended by the class difference in society, he gains a conviction and is satisfied when the judge sentences her to a ten-year term. American courts protect citizens such as the socialite until proven guilty; therefore, we do not need cities of refuge as did the Israelites in biblical days. These cities of refuge protected people who had committed manslaughter in their "eye for an eye" society.

Because Israel lacked the innocent-until-proven-guilty protection offered to us today, God established this merciful way to deal with persons who accidentally killed another. He intended that these cities of refuge framing the Jordan River would prevent the killer from receiving the same fate as that of a cold-blooded murderer. The killer could flee to one of the six cities for protection from the relative who would invariably avenge the death until given due process and an opportunity to be heard (Deut. 19:12; Num. 35:12).

As the cities of refuge were to the Israelites temporarily, Jesus is to us forever. Our surety, Jesus is our guarantee of salvation, our refuge. He is our shelter and protection from both physical and spiritual danger. Physically, He promises to be a shield all around us (Ps. 3:3). Spiritually, as our Redeemer, he shed His "own blood provided for the transgressors of God's law a sure retreat, into which they may flee for safety from the second death. No power can take out of His hands the souls that go to Him for pardon."[156]

Sin and death are synonymous in God's Word. Without divine help, Adam's progeny, the entire race of humans, stood eternally doomed. But Jesus loved us too much to accept that end for us. Thus, the Godhead devised a plan in the counsels of heaven for Jesus to be our substitute (Rom. 5:8). Only the sinless Son of God possessed the efficacy to be sin for us, and He redeemed us from the curse of the law by being a curse for us (Gal. 3:13). He assumed the sins of the world from the time sin entered our planet until it is forever eradicated!

The supreme Liberator, Jesus rescues us from powerful, vicious foes. In the day of our disaster, He protects His own. Look how He stood up for the disciples when the Jewish mob came to arrest Him. "I told you that I am he," Jesus answered. "If you are looking for me, then let these men go." This happened so that the words he had spoken would be fulfilled: "I have not lost one of those you gave me" (John 18:8, 9). Similar to the protection found in the cities of refuge, protection for the righteous who run to Him in faith is found in Jesus. Should we delay, the enemy will overtake us. Should weariness or trials impede our flight, we risk missing the deadline. Flee posthaste toward the "refuge to lay hold upon the hope set before us" (Heb. 6:18).

May 28

Sarah's Daughters

You are her [Sarah's] daughters if you do what is right and do not give way to fear. 1 Peter 3:6, NIV.

Lookism is discrimination based on appearance. This discrimination can be measured in the workplace when the more physically attractive of equally qualified and credentialed workers are hired and/or promoted. In our society, physical appearance matters. For instance, upwards of 80 percent of American women are unsatisfied with their physical appearance.[157] In 2007 American women spent $7 billion on cosmetic products and $5.3 billion more on revamping surgical procedures. "Good looks have what social scientists call the halo effect ... Because someone is attractive, we assign other positive attributes to him or her that have nothing to do with looks."[158]

Sarah's daughters do not base their worth on outward beauty that will fade, but rather they put stock in the unfading beauty of a gentle and quiet spirit (1 Peter 3:6, 7). Society puts pressure on all of us to measure up to the world's standard of beauty, and many are compelled to wear makeup, jewelry, and fashionable clothes. But these only doll up the surface. *Star*, *Us*, and *People* magazines divulge that some breathtakingly beautiful stars' actions confirm that beauty is skin deep.

In God's eyes beauty is as beauty does. He examines actions and deeds and settles for nothing less than an inner radiance in His children. After He commissioned Samuel to find a king to succeed Saul, God rebuked him, "Do not consider his appearance or his height, for I have rejected him.... Man looks at the outward appearance, but the LORD looks at the heart" (1 Sam. 16:7, NIV). The heart is where godliness resides. Cosmetics are applied and removed daily. But godliness—resembling God in character—is the work of a lifetime (2 Tim. 3:5).

The world may adore us and deify us for our outer beauty, but God sees the warts and blemishes on our characters. Mercifully, He directs and empowers His people to be nonconformists, to be transformed by the renewal of our mind and to do what is good, acceptable, and perfect in His sight (Rom. 12:2). Everything connected with that old way of life, which is completely rotten, must be discarded. Then put on "a God-fashioned life, a life renewed from the inside and working itself into your conduct as God accurately reproduces his character in you" (Eph. 4:24, MSG).

To change our carnal mindset to the mind of Christ, where love, unselfishness, and humility reside, born-again Christians must cooperate with the Holy Spirit. "For as many as are led by the Spirit of God, they are the sons of God" (Rom. 8:14). The power to live godly lives is accessible, and as we plug into the transforming power of the Spirit, inner beauty is generated and radiates throughout our actions, words, and deeds. This beauty is fade proof, ageless, and brings a bountiful reward. Real beauty, the kind that will take us to eternity is what identifies Sarah's daughters who stand for right without fear of consequences.

May 29

Jesus Appeased God's Wrath

And the kings of the earth, the great men, the rich men, the commanders, the mighty men, every slave and every free man, hid themselves in the caves and in the rocks of the mountains, and said to the mountains and rocks, 'Fall on us and hide us from the face of Him who sits on the throne and from the wrath of the Lamb!'" Rev. 6:15, 16, NKJV.

Aristotle wrote, "Anybody can become angry—that is easy, but to be angry with the right person and to the right degree and at the right time and for the right purpose, and in the right way—that is not within everybody's power and is not easy." Even angry with sinners, only God is guaranteed to execute justice evenhandedly. Every evil motive and deed both secret and open, witnessed by God, are to be punished appropriately (Matt. 6:18). After the saints have been a 1,000 years in heaven reviewing the records, John saw the resurrected dead standing before the throne of God being judged according to their deeds (Rev. 20:12, 13).

God intends to avenge His character, His law, and His saints on the day of Jesus' return (Jer. 9:9; Luke 18:7), for His word is carved in stone and is as unchangeable as His character. Had he been able to retract the mandate that the wages of sin is death, Jesus would not have drunk the cup of God's wrath by dying to satisfy the law (Rom. 6:23). Although He is slow to anger, loving, forgiving, merciful, and gracious, God will punish those who consistently rebel against His law of love (Ex. 34:6, 7).

God says, "Have nothing to do with the fruitless deeds of darkness" (Eph. 5:11, NIV). However, that person who persists in fruitless deeds of darkness will kindle a fire in God's anger, which will destroy them root and branch. "Cursed is the man who trusts in man, and makes flesh his strength, whose heart departs from the LORD" (Jer. 17:5, NKJV). Blinded by Satan, who hardens hearts, unrepentant sinners as well as unconverted Christians bring the curse of death on themselves. Amazingly, they nonchalantly sit on death row after sadistically signing and sealing their own death warrant.

But in His great mercy and immeasurable love for even the most egregious sinner, God forgives sins and provides all that is needed to subdue our rebellious spirits. The parable of the prodigal son demonstrates His readiness to pardon and restore. When the rebellious son came to himself and returned home, aspiring only to live the life of a servant, his father directed the servants to dress him in the best apparel and prepare a feast. The father rejoiced that his son, once dead in his sins, lived again; that the son once lost was now found (Luke 15:11-22).

Do not fear God's wrath, for He is good, a refuge in times of trouble. He cares for those who trust in him (Nahum 1:7). As soon as the wicked forsake their ways and the unrighteous their thoughts and return to the Lord, He has mercy on them and will abundantly pardon them (Isa. 55:7). Jesus appeased God's wrath once and forever; why should anybody die? While our probation lasts, God offers the greatest gift ever given—the gift of eternal life. Let our actions show we wholeheartedly accept the gift.

May 30

The Gateway to Life

But the gateway to life is very narrow and the road is difficult, and only a few ever find it. Matt. 7:14, NLT.

In the allegory *Pilgrim's Progress*, Christian begins a convoluted and sometimes tortuous journey from the City of Destruction—earth—to the Celestial City—heaven. Christian's journey is more difficult because he is carrying a heavy burden on his back called sin that is revealed to him by the good Book. Mercifully, at the Wicket Gate he encounters the cross where his burden is removed. In between the City of Destruction and the Celestial City, Christian encounters life- deep muddy holes, mountains, monsters, erroneous advice, and temptations along the way. The journey to salvation is not easy, however. Only those who faithfully follow the narrow path make it.

The narrow way is delineated clearly enough that anyone can discover it. And if we single-mindedly follow the directions leading to the Celestial City, it is impossible to get lost. That is a promise from the heart of God. Isaiah writes that a highway and a road shall be there called the "Highway of Holiness." Anybody who walks the road shall not go astray (Isa. 35:8, NKJV). God loves us and wants all of us to live with Him in the earth made new. But because of His deep love, He cannot compel our love; thus, He grants us a free will. And He sets before us the way of life and the way of death and asks us to choose whom we will serve (Jer. 21:8; Joshua 24:15).

The journey begins and ends at the narrow gate, not the wide gate. Because the wider the gate and the easier the way, the closer we move to total destruction. In fact, the narrow gate is not as popular and much more difficult—many enter through the broad gate but very few enter the narrow one (Matt. 7:13, 14). Jesus is that gate, and He makes it abundantly clear that He is the one and only route to heaven. "I am the way, the truth, and the life. No one comes to the Father except through Me" (John 14:6). To come through Jesus, we must walk, even as He walked (1 John 2:6).

The way *is* hard; it is narrow, and it is bumpy. In the movie *All About Eve*, a drama about scheming and sabotage in the movie industry, Bette Davis stated, "Fasten your seatbelts. It's going to be a bumpy night." This is a suitable analogy for a journey that is rife with unexpected potholes, fissures, sink holes, and rough uneven surfaces. Although we cannot avoid the bumpy, narrow way, we are assured that Jesus, our seatbelt and navigator on this journey, will provide a safe ride toward eternal day.

Fellow Christians, beware; destruction is lying in wait on the broad path. At the judgment many people who walked the broad road to destruction while doing good deeds will question God's judgment and point to all their good works. But God will answer, "I never knew you; depart from Me, you who practice lawlessness!" (Matt 7:23, NKJV). Be careful; examine yourself, walk in faith, and acquire the character of Jesus who points away from destruction and points to a realm of peace (2 Cor. 13:5).

May 31

A Time to Laugh

You shall laugh at destruction and famine, and you shall not be afraid of the beasts of the earth. Job 5:22, NKJV.

An enduring adage states that "laughter is the best medicine," making it the cheapest, most accessible medicine ever. Scientific studies show that laughter is a mood enhancer in that a good laugh releases endorphins, is a natural pain reducer; boosts the immune system by decreasing stress hormones and increasing immunity; and improves the blood flow, which benefits the heart. Laughter can also fix awkward moments and lighten burdens. "A merry heart maketh a cheerful countenance" (Prov. 15:13). Truly, laughter is a gift from a God.

But laughter in the mouth of God is sometimes derisive. Laughing at destruction and famine, He looms over all adversities and adversaries that share this world with His elect. What appears distressing and insurmountable to us is laughable to God. How dare any created being or tool of darkness audaciously amble up to His elect without His permission! In fact, any evil plan to destroy His chosen is useless, for the Lord, laughs scornfully, making fun of the foolish and "rebukes them, terrifying them with his fierce fury" (Ps. 2:5, NLT).

Pathetic weakness is the lot of the so-called earthly powerful. Satan uses his limited power over natural events and human agents to control and ravage God's people through fear. But he and his workers are surely not a match for the all-powerful God. Although these evildoers make life miserable for the anointed, God protects us from harm no matter how often trouble strikes. And in times of war and famine, He provides safety. However, should He allow Satan to touch us, it is designed as discipline for eternal reasons. Remember, God may allow injuries, but he bandages and heals our wounds with His own loving hands (Job 5:17-21).

God also laughs derisively after His extended hand of mercy is rebuffed repeatedly and when His counsel is deliberately disregarded. He turns His back on them and angrily laments, "You completely ignored me and refused to listen; you rejected my advice and paid no attention when I warned you. So when you are struck by some terrible disaster, or when trouble and distress surround you like a whirlwind, I will laugh and make fun. You will ask for my help, but I won't listen; you will search, but you won't find me" (Prov. 1:24-28, CEV).

This is not easy for a loving God who takes no pleasure in the destruction of the wicked, His rebellious children. Thus, His mocking laughter is a cover-up for the profound, intense pain He feels at the loss of so many of them. He laughs to keep from crying. So, counsel unsaved friends and family to heed His heart-wrenching plea to "Turn! Turn from your evil ways! Why will you die?" (Eze. 33:11, NIV).

June 1

The Laughter of Skepticism

Then Sarah denied, saying, I laughed not; for she was afraid. Gen. 18:15.

Sarah's skepticism overshadowed her faith at a promise by God that is impossible to fulfill in a natural way. Sarah, who abandoned family and comfort for an unknown destination with her husband, Abraham, so doubted God's word that she laughed to herself thinking, "After I am worn out and my master is old, will I now have this pleasure?" (Gen. 18:12, NIV). And Abraham, who was called by God, exhibited incredibly strong faith in Him and later readied to sacrifice his son based on God's instructions, also doubted that God could create a son in a barren womb.

Faith, doubt, and unbelief are lines on a scale. "Faith is acceptance before the fact; doubt is acceptance after the fact."[160] Unbelief is a failure to accept. Abraham and Sarah's doubt merged from disappointment and uncertainty, which produced a temporary lack of faith in God's sure word. Neither could imagine that the ninety-year-old Sarah could conceive a child by the ninety-nine-year-old Abraham, so their skepticism played out in laughter (Gen. 17:17). For too many years they longed desperately for an heir, so they chose to suspend belief to avoid further heartache.

Like Sarah and Abraham, many begin to doubt when strong desires and God's promises do not engage in our time frame. Moreover, this couple lived in a culture where honor and respect were tied with the number of children in the home. Year after year while they were still in the childbearing stage, they yearned for children, but Sarah remained barren and Abraham remained childless. Keenly disappointed that his dream of a son would never materialize, the younger Abram cried, "O Sovereign LORD, what good are all your blessings when I don't even have a son?" (Gen. 15:2, NLT).

Even as God's words echoed in their ears, "You will have a son of your own who will be your heir," they remained skeptical (Gen. 15:4, NLT). Now senior citizens, they ended their wait and assisted God with disastrous consequences by conspiring to exploit Hagar as the mother of Abraham's promise. They soon learned that when we attempt to help God, who is perfectly capable of managing alone, we create chaos.

God is pained by our skepticism. When Peter walked on the water for a short period then faltered and sank, Jesus said, "You of little faith, why did you doubt?" (Matt. 14:31, NASB). Even so, Jesus rescued him. Clearly He understands and sympathizes with our weaknesses and continues to bless us. But we *do* face the inevitable consequences of the actions birthed by doubt.

Wait peacefully on God! "God can do anything ... far more than you could ever imagine or guess or request in your wildest dreams!" (Eph. 3:20, MSG). But His promises are fulfilled in His perfect time and are a product of His perfect wisdom evidenced by the execution of His promise to Abraham. When both were nonagenarians, with Abraham teetering on the brink of his one hundredth year, Sarah conceived Isaac.

June 2

When the Tables Turn

Now that their father was dead, Joseph's brothers became fearful. "Now Joseph will show his anger and pay us back for all the wrong we did to him." Gen. 50:15, NLT.

There is a maxim my neighborhood elders used to urge upon the youth, "Be careful who you step on going up the ladder, you may need them to help you back down." The sage advice condemned our haughtiness when we achieved or received something of greater value in our eyes than others. They cautioned us to remember that fortunes do change, sometimes unexpectedly, and the lesser becomes master over the greater in various ways. Their bottom line required us to treat others like we want to be treated.

Potiphar's wife is a prime illustration of this maxim. Mrs. Potiphar falsely accused Joseph of attempted rape after he determinately rebuffed her advances and thwarted her plans to "lie" with him (Gen. 39:8-15). After her accusation, Potiphar stripped Joseph of the position as overseer of his entire estate and sent him to prison. Ultimately, her exalted status as wife of one of pharaoh's top officials turned, and the the Hebrew slave became her master. For pharaoh appointed Joseph prime minister.

Did fear settle in the pit of her stomach after she learned of Joseph's promotion as vice pharaoh? Did the smug satisfaction at exacting revenge on a lowly, powerless slave who dared disobey her change to anxiety and a fear of retribution? Human nature says yes, for her power decreased and his increased. She, like Joseph's brothers, clearly understood Egyptian law and the power of an absolute monarchy.

There were no checks and balances to the pharaoh's power, and by decree his power became Joseph's power. "You shall be in charge of my palace, and all my people are to submit to your orders. Only with respect to the throne will I be greater than you" (Gen. 41:40, NIV). The tables had turned; now she and his brothers' lives were in Joseph's hands. Anxiously, they waited for the judgment, terrified of the penalty because fear follows evil. To the sinful, God promises that He will fill their hearts with fear and the sound of a leaf that is blown by the wind will scare them away (Lev. 26:36).

Wrote Lord Acton, "Power tends to corrupt and absolute power corrupts absolutely. Great men are almost always bad men."[161] Joseph's persecutors believed thusly and panicked (Prov. 23:7). Because Mrs. Potiphar and his brothers wielded their power from selfish, uncaring hearts, they ascribed the same evil to Joseph. But Joseph allowed the transforming power of the Holy Spirit to cleanse him of sin and teach him to forgive as the Spirit brought Joseph's thoughts and deeds in line with His. Joseph's character became evident after refusing to sleep with Mrs. Potiphar. He said, "How could I do such a wicked thing and sin against God?" (Gen. 39:9). Goodness and mercy punctuated his deeds as it should ours.

"Do not say, 'I'll pay you back for this wrong!' Wait for the LORD, and he will deliver you" (Prov. 20:22, NIV). God will turn the tables.

June 3

By Any Means Necessary

As Pharaoh approached, the Israelites looked up, and there were the Egyptians, marching after them. They were terrified and cried out to the LORD. Ex. 14:10, NIV.

In the bright light of the desert sun, the Israelites experienced a terrifying darkness brought on by unbelief and unconfessed sins. Physically, they marched victoriously out of Egypt, but spiritually and emotionally, they were tightly caught in her vise. God delivered them, but they remained in bondage. In spite of all the miracles God performed to release Pharaoh's grip on them, they lacked trust in Him. Knowing they needed the darkness expelled and their faith strengthened, God positioned them on a meandering path to the Promised Land.

To them, God seemed distant even while actively in their midst. Enslaved in Egypt, they walked with a stiff-neck through what mystics call a dark night of the soul—"a lengthy and profound absence of light and hope. In the dark night you feel profoundly alone."[162] Martin Huber, a twentieth-century Jewish philosopher, calls that deep and fearful darkness the absence of the presence of God. "You are experiencing bleak desperation, you are in searing agony, the darkness is all around, and it is wholly real. That which you call God is absent. But, this absent one is yet known as the one who can be present; this absent one is yet known as the one who will be present."[163]

Packing this darkness into their baggage, they left Egypt along with their little red wagons full of corrupt habits and idolatrous mindsets. They felt spiritually deserted as they turned away from God, who is always present, a gentleman who will not intrude. When we empty our lives of God, we become famished and succumb to spiritual starvation that ushers in feelings of hollowness and hopelessness. Then we fill that emptiness with temporary, poisonous feasts of sin that destroy our lives. But Jesus is the Bread of Life, and it takes munching on that bread to overcome the emptiness of soul when we operate outside of God's will.

God used the roundabout trek though the desert to increase their faith and to teach them His precepts and laws. Through hunger, thirst, setbacks, tragedies, pain, and suffering, they learned trust and obedience. Sometimes God takes us on a circuitous route through highways of pain and byways of drought to prepare our hearts and minds to be like Jesus. Incredibly, if the Israelites had traveled the direct route from Egypt to Canaan, the 200 miles could have been covered in approximately one month. Even so, it took forty years and countless thousands of miles for God to expel the darkness and produce a generation worthy to enter the Promised Land.

God can and does change the dark night of our soul into the dawn of sweet peace. Fear nothing. Call on Him as did the terrorized Israelites. Didn't He promise to "rescue [us] from hidden traps, shield [us] from deadly hazards. His huge outstretched arms protect [us]— under them [we're] perfectly safe; his arms fend off all harm" (Ps. 91:3-6, MSG). Call on Him; He will save us by any means necessary.

June 4

The Enemies of God

I will send My terror ahead of you, and throw into confusion all the people among whom you come, and I will make all your enemies turn their backs to you. Ex. 23:27, NASB.

The phrase "mad as a March hare" derives from the behavior of hares during their mating season. They engage in "boxing matches" where the doe, while standing upright, fends off would-be suitors by striking them with her paws. The males are rebuffed if they miss the part of one day that she has her oestral cycle and is sexually receptive. Notwithstanding the nonlethal boxing matches and frustrated bucks, hares have many natural enemies like hawks, coyotes, bobcats, foxes, and snakes.

God, too, has enemies. But because God is love and all-powerful, you have to question the sanity of anybody who provokes Him to enmity. I propose that they are as mad as a March hare to challenge Him. And when enemies do battle with His elect, they also do battle with Him for our enemies are God's enemies. To defeat some of our enemies, he uses the supernatural weapon of terror. Moses says, "Terror and dread fall upon them; by the greatness of Your arm they are motionless as stone" (Ex. 15:16, NASB). And "the LORD will grant that the enemies who rise up against you will be defeated … They will come at you from one direction but flee from you in seven" (Deut. 28:7, NIV).

After the Fall, mankind became a natural enemy of the Godhead, becoming stubborn, presumptuous sinners—Satan's allies. The enemies of God freely indulge in the following: "sexual immorality, impurity and debauchery; idolatry and witchcraft; hatred, discord, jealousy, fits of rage, selfish ambition, dissensions, factions" (Gal. 5:19, 20, NIV). They thumb their noses at Him, disrespectful of His majesty and fearless of His power.

Humanity inherited the nature of their father the devil and has no natural desire to be friends of God. "The sinful mind is hostile to God. It does not submit to God's law, nor can it do so. Those controlled by the sinful nature cannot please God" (Rom. 8:7, 8, NIV). So out of His incredible love for us, God put enmity between Satan and the woman to reconcile us to Him, using Jesus to bridge that cavernous gulf of separation (Gen. 3:15)."For if, when we were God's enemies, we were reconciled to him through the death of his Son, how much more, having been reconciled, shall we be saved through his life! Not only is this so, but we also rejoice in God through our Lord Jesus Christ, through whom we have now received reconciliation" (Rom. 5:10, 11, NIV).

This reconciliation liberates us from slavery to sin and from blindly following the will of Satan. It gives us freedom to be friends of God and the authority to be His sons and daughters. Accepting Jesus, our will is in synch with His will. Now we make every effort to please Him. Now we willingly submit to the law of God. Thus He is able to save us to the uttermost. What a friend we have in Jesus!

June 5

A Tearless Society

And God will wipe away every tear from their eyes. Rev. 7:17, RSV.

Basal, reflex, and emotional are a variety of tears with different purposes. Basal tears provide consistent lubrication to prevent our eyes from becoming dry while reflex tears are triggered by irritants such as smoke and dust and prevent them from harming the sensitive cornea. These tears also soothe the discomfort caused by irritants. And unique to humans are emotional tears that act in union with the endocrine system to release hormones to form tears when stimulated by distress.

God created emotional tears as a blessing to humans who live in a sinful world, and scientists uncovered the benefits of tears aside from the emotional release they provide. In a study, "Volunteers were led to cry first from watching sad movies, and then from freshly cut onions. The researchers found that the tears from the movies, called emotional tears, contained far more toxic biological byproducts. Weeping, they concluded, is an excretory process which removes toxic substances that normally build up during emotional stress."[164]

Sickness, sorrow, and death, much of which comes from our own disobedience, produce tears. David cried, "My eyes shed streams of tears because your law is not kept" (Ps. 119:136, NRSV). Still, much anguish occurs because Satan, the prince of this world, works to steal, kill, and destroy. Nevertheless, death and sorrow are all-inclusive—all are destined to feel sorrow, and all are destined to feel death's sting. Job laments, "Man that is born of a woman is of few days and full of trouble" (Job 14:1).

But one day God will dry up all tears. With the end to sin and its effects and the end of Satan and his demons, God will accomplish the promise to wipe the tears from the eyes of the redeemed (Rev 20:10). Death, which is already defeated by the crucifixion and resurrection of Jesus, will be swallowed up in victory. Born-again Christians are presently waiting for the victory parade to be celebrated in heaven on V-day.

God won't literally dab our tears with tissues and comfort us as we cry, but He will remove forever the reason for our tears. Shame and guilt will be abolished. Death and mourning will cease. Pain and anguish will be history. Christians will no longer be persecuted, maligned, and ridiculed. Sickness, disease, and physical defects will be eradicated. "Then the eyes of the blind shall be opened, and the ears of the deaf shall be unstopped. Then the lame man shall leap as an hart, and the tongue of the dumb shall sing" (Isa. 35:5, 6).

The old order of rebellion and decay will pass away, and perfection will hold preeminence as love fills the earth. "And the ransomed of the LORD will return and come with joyful shouting to Zion, with everlasting joy upon their heads. They will find gladness and joy, and sorrow and sighing will flee away" (Isa. 35:10, NASB). What a glorious, tearless future for the ransomed of God!

June 6

Lift Up the Downcast Soul

Why are you downcast, O my soul? Why so disturbed within me? Put your hope in God, for I will yet praise him, my Savior and my God. Ps. 43:5, NIV.

Cast down is an old English term describing a sheep that is flat on its back unable to stand. On occasion this happens to sheep whose wool becomes heavy with rain. Sometimes, finding a soft patch of grass with a little hollow depression, sheep will lie down and relax, but should the sheep stretch or move and can no longer touch the ground with its feet, it rolls over in panic. It ends up stationary on its back, desperately flailing the air with its feet in a helpless struggle to rise. "After a few hours on their backs, gas begins to collect in their stomachs, the stomach hardens, the air passage is cut off, and the sheep will eventually suffocate."[165] Also, in this position the blood flow to its limbs is dangerously impeded.

Vulnerability defines a cast down sheep. It is vulnerable to predators, its own circulatory and digestive systems, and to the elements. Tender, patient care is required to restore a cast down sheep. The shepherd gently lifts the sheep to its feet and balances it between his legs until the sheep regains its balance, allowing the blood to flow freely. Several tries and failures ensue before the sheep is strong enough to stand alone. Throughout this laborious process, the shepherd consoles his sheep with his familiar voice and presence.

"What a picture of what God wants to do for us! When we are on our backs, flailing because of guilt, grief, or grudges, our loving Shepherd reassures us with His grace, lifts us up, and holds us until we've gained our spiritual equilibrium."[166] When your soul is downcast, when you feel dejected and worried about things past, things present, or things future, look through spiritual eyes and see the hovering presence of the Shepherd gathering you close to His heart in restoration (Isa 40:11).

In the midst of coping with his despondency, the psalmist lifted his eyes heavenward and praised the Lord from whom came his hope. Likewise, Job praised God when his entire world mysteriously imploded. He cried, "The LORD gave, and the LORD hath taken away; blessed be the name of the Lord" (Job 1:21). Similarly Habakkuk declared that even if the fig tree does not blossom and no fruit is on the vine and though the fields produce no food and no sheep are in the fields, he will continue to praise the Lord (Hab. 3:17, 18).

These men of mature faith knew as did David that praise fortifies the downcast soul and that in spite of setbacks and suffering we are abundantly blessed. David sang, "Praise Yahweh, my soul! All that is within me, praise his holy name!… and don't forget all his benefits; who forgives all your sins; who heals all your diseases; who redeems your life from destruction; who crowns you with loving kindness and tender mercies; who satisfies your desire with good things, so that your youth is renewed like the eagle's" (Ps. 103:1-5, WEB). Like a hydraulic lift, praise and trust elevate a downcast soul.

June 7

Sin Produces Fear

Abimelech rose early in the morning, called all his servants, and told all these things in their hearing; and the men were very much afraid. Gen. 20:8, NKJV.

In his dramatic play a "Miserly Knight," Russian poet A. S. Pushkin describes conscience as a "sharp clawed animal, which scrapes the heart ... an uninvited guest, annoying discourser." Obviously, he is describing a susceptible but guilty conscience, one that steals our peace of mind. A healthy conscience or our inner voice assails us unexpectedly and spontaneously without any cognizant effort when we act contrary to right. To our benefit, a vigorous conscience is capable of refining our actions unless we willfully disregard it into total silence.

Rebellion against what is right will summon that very unsettling, uncomfortable feeling as our conscience converses with us. For instance, David, whom King Saul pursued to murder, got an opportunity to revenge himself. To relieve his bladder, Saul walked into a cave where David was hiding. Stealthily, David cut off a corner of Saul's robe. "Afterward, David was conscience-stricken ... He said to his men, 'The LORD forbid that I should do such a thing to my master, the LORD's anointed, or lift my hand against him; for he is the anointed of the LORD" (1 Sam. 24:5, 6, NIV).

Likewise "in great fear and distress Jacob divided the people who were with him into two groups, and the flocks and herds and camels as well" when he discovered that Esau, the brother he had conned years earlier, trailed him (Gen. 32:7, NIV). Raised in a God-fearing home and taught obedience, Jacob suffered the agony of a guilty conscience followed by fear of the consequences. In a quest to steal Esau's heritage, his lies and deception left him with a very troubled mind.

Now consider Moses who fled Egypt after taking the law in his own hands and committing murder. The man who witnessed the murder said, "Are you going to kill me as you killed that Egyptian yesterday?" Then Moses fearfully thought, "Everyone knows what I did," and he fled from Egypt in a panic (Ex. 2:14, NLT). Maintaining a settled mind depends on being right with God who provides peace of mind. "When a man's ways are pleasing to the LORD, he maketh even his enemies to be at peace with him" (Prov. 16:7).

"I was afraid," Adam explained when God found him hiding in the garden after eating the forbidden fruit (Gen. 3:10). To be sure, the requirements of God's law are written on our hearts as our conscience bears witness, and when we sin against God's law, our thoughts accuse us (Rom. 2:15). Thus, immorality produces fear, guilt, and remorse. Unless seared, a conscience is a faultless moral authority wired in us to govern our actions. So, the closer our walk with the Savior the clearer and more peaceful is our conscience.

June 8

Feed the Right Wolf

He that overcometh shall inherit all things; and I will be his God, and he shall be my son. Rev. 21:7.

One evening an old Cherokee told his grandson about a battle that rages in the heart of people. "'My son, the battle is between two 'wolves' inside us all. One is Evil. It is anger, envy, jealousy, sorrow, regret, greed, arrogance, self pity, guilt, resentment, inferiority, lies, false pride, superiority, and ego. The other is Good. It is joy, peace, love, hope, serenity, humility, kindness, benevolence, empathy, generosity, truth, compassion and faith.' The grandson thought about it for a minute and then asked his grandfather, 'Which wolf wins?'" The old Cherokee replied, "The one you feed."[167]

We are cautioned against loving the world and its allures, for it is impossible to love the world and God concurrently (1 John 2:5). The evil wolf raging inside of us is fueled by friendship to the world, and worldliness is evidenced by sinful behavior. Hostile toward God and contemptuous of all righteousness, the worldly embrace values contrary to the law of God and violate His commandments. Ungrateful for the blessings received from a gracious God, this bad wolf, fed by carnal Christians and blatant sinners alike, is God's enemy (James 4:4).

From Adam until now, all have gratified the cravings of a sinful nature. Spiritually destitute, the worldly-minded are blinded and deceived by the prince of darkness and are citizens of a topsy-turvy, sin-directed world (Eph. 2:2). They hate good and love evil, call evil good and good evil, put darkness for light and light for darkness, and put bitter for sweet and sweet for bitter (Micah 3:1, 2; Isa. 5:20). Those who are worldly are so deceived that they are unaware of their slavery to sin and to that evil wolf that holds them captive, for feeding bad habits ingrains them and makes them second nature.

The choice of which wolf to feed belongs to each person. Jesus stands at the door of our heart and knocks looking for an invitation to deposit His Spirit. Once the choice is made to feed the right wolf, all heaven reaches down to assist in the spiritual regeneration of the once-captive sinner. The evil wolf is defeated with the desire to change allegiances and to cooperate with the Holy Spirit who works to produce a change. The Spirit yearns to resuscitate those dead in trespasses and recreate them into the image of Jesus by transforming the mind (Rom. 12:2).

Feed the good wolf. Fill him up with the fruits of the spirit, envelop him with prayer, read to him the words of life, and walk with him on the narrow path. Being faithful, thusly, we become overcomers positioned to inherit all things reserved in heaven. Overcomers will inherit peace and prosperity; we will "inherit the land and dwell in it forever" (Ps. 37:29, NIV); and we will be "heirs of God and co-heirs with Christ" (Rom. 8:17, NIV). Overcomers are ensured of their inheritance; it is set in stone if only the good wolf is fed.

June 9

His Strength Is Made Perfect

He gives power to the weak and strength to the powerless. Isa. 40:29, NLT.

"Where God is, a spider's web is as a stone wall. Where God is not, a stone wall is as a spider's web." These words were written by a soldier who, facing defeat by the enemy, scattered with his company. Soon the frightened solder, tired and alone, hid in a cave and prayed fervently for God's protection. Rising from his knees, he saw a spider weaving a delicate web across the mouth of the cave. By the time the enemy soldiers had reached the hiding place, the web completely covered the mouth of the cave. The soldiers left without searching the cave, reasoning that no one could have entered since the web was undisturbed.

God's wisdom and power are astounding. To fulfill His purposes, He can control events with one instrument then reverse the results using the same instrument. When Zechariah doubted His word, God struck him dumb. The angel said, "But now … you will be silent and unable to speak until the child is born" (Luke 1:20, NLT). In contrast, God gave a voiceless donkey speech. Balaam, attempting to curse the Israelites for gain contrary to the express word of God, "received a rebuke for his own transgression, for a mute donkey, speaking with a voice of a man, restrained the madness of the prophet" (2 Peter 2:16).

God miraculously used a big fish to capture His wayward prophet's attention when Jonah refused to preach deliverance to the Ninevites. So, "the LORD appointed a great fish to swallow Jonah, and Jonah was in the stomach of the fish three days and three nights" (Jonah 1:17, NASB). On another occasion He used fish to show compassion and love to thousands of tired and hungry followers. "He … took the five loaves, and the two fishes … he blessed, and brake, and gave the loaves to *his* disciples … And they that had eaten were about five thousand men, beside women and children" (Matt. 14:19-21).

Likewise, God used the wind to fashion a road at the bottom of the sea for the Israelites to escape the Egyptians who followed in hot pursuit. "Then Moses stretched out his hand over the sea, and all that night the LORD drove the sea back with a strong east wind and turned it into dry land" (Ex. 14:21, NIV). The waters divided, and the Israelites walked on dry ground. But using a gale force wind, he redirected Jonah, a recalcitrant prophet who tried to flee to Tarshish when directed to go to Nineveh. "Then the LORD sent a great wind on the sea, and such a violent storm arose that the ship threatened to break up," moving the sailors to throw him overboard (Jonah 1:4, NIV).

Standing in front of the furnace of affliction there is plenty of anxiety. But we serve a God who does not know impossible. He created the world out of nothing, and making a way out of no way is His specialty. Our anxiety, then, is a needless exercise that saps our strength and shines a light on the quality of our faith. Trust His promises to "gives power to the faint, and to him who has no might he increases strength" (Isa. 40:29, ESV).

June 10

He Welcomes Sinners

And him that cometh to me I will in no wise cast out. John 6:37.

Caiaphas, the high priest, joined "the chief priests and the elders of the people" who "took counsel against Jesus to put him to death" (Matt. 27:1). Still, Jesus offered salvation to them. And while suffering intensely on the cross, Jesus solicited His Father to forgive the Jews, the Romans, and every person born in sin. If God forgave deicide, the cold-blooded, premeditated murder of His Son, He will forgive any sin. Love and compassion for His lost world fills God's heart. Knowing our frame, God desires to rescue us as spiritual dullness leaves us clueless to the full extent of our actions (Luke 23:34).

There is no sin too monstrous for God to forgive—rape, prostitution, torture, mass murder, kidnapping, adultery, child molesting, theft, devil worship, and witchcraft. You name it, someone committed it, and Jesus forgave it for God is "not willing that any should perish, but that all should come to repentance" (2 Peter 3:9). So if and when a willful sinner asks for forgiveness, He will in no wise cast her out. But should we reject His invitation to come into the kingdom of light, then we are accepting Satan's invitation to remain in ignorance, fear, and hopelessness.

Self-righteous hypocrites accused Jesus, and rightly so, of receiving sinners, but sinners are Jesus' specialty. He welcomes those with little faith and faint trust, those who feel too useless to be saved. Jesus welcomes the serial sinner, the atheist, and the troublers of God's people. We come feeling empty and hollow like a walking corpse. "We come by prayer, and that prayer broken; with confession, and that confession faulty; with praise, and that praise far short of His merits, but yet He received us. We come diseased, polluted, worn out, and worthless; but He does not cast us out."[168] And He dips the penitent sinner in His blood to cleanse them from all iniquities.

But where is the *impenitent* sinner cast? By spiritual default they are cast out into the kingdom of darkness, in the dark realm where Satan reigns as prince. The parable of the wedding feast shows that those without a wedding garment will be bound hand and foot and thrown into the "outer darkness, [where] there shall be weeping and gnashing of teeth" (Matt. 22:11-13). The wedding garment is the imputed righteousness of Jesus freely given to forgiven and faithful Christians. But the guests without a wedding garment are not repentant, neither have they received forgiveness nor cleansing of iniquities. Hearts far from God, they exhibit a form of godliness without the transforming power of the Holy Spirit.

But accept His invitation to abide in the kingdom of light and you ***will*** abide in the kingdom of light. And to all who come to Him with a contrite and humble spirit, God holds with an iron grip and never lets go.

June 11

More Than Enough

I do not trust in my bow, my sword does not bring victory; but you give us victory over our enemies, you put our adversaries to shame. Ps. 44:6, 7, NIV.

"Now Satan stood up against Israel, and moved David to number Israel" (1 Chron. 21:1, NKJV). David commissioned a seemingly innocuous census to number the fighting men of the nation, but this act brought down the wrath of God. A plague raged through Israel consuming 70,000 men. Pride in his pre-eminence over the nations motivated David's flagrant sin against God. This census taking denied God His rightful place as the true King of Israel; it conveyed that David's victories resulted from a large army and his wise leadership. It failed to acknowledge that the arm of flesh is totally powerless unless linked with the strong right hand of God (Ex. 6:1).

Self-importance denies that God weaves and charts the minutest fibers in the fabric of our spiritual and physical lives. Arrogant, we become the great I am—I am smarter, wiser, powerful; I am the greatest; I am controlling my own life and destiny. We deny the active involvement of God, the only great I AM in whom we live and move and have our being (Acts 17:28). Without God allotting us power to move our limbs, power to think, and power to breath, we would be useless, lifeless stick figures.

To depend on our own strength, wisdom, and weaponry in spiritual battles is as smart as taking a straw gun into a war where the enemy uses M60 machine guns. Trusting in manmade solutions or self-made solutions, depending on what we see and a lack of faith brings quick, decisive, and utter defeat in any battle. For only God gives victory over our enemies. Battles are the norm for the Christian—battles with the evil one who hates us because we snatched our allegiance from him and gave it to Jesus. Satan is a dedicated, tireless purveyor of anxiety and trouble for God's people, and he forces us to battle temptations and our own sinful natures. Major distractions consume our energy unless, by faith, we hand them to Jesus and leave them there.

David's pride opened a stronghold—"an argument or high thing that exalts itself against the knowledge of God" (2 Cor. 10:5)—that allowed Satan's temptations to prevail over the Word of God. Joab, the army commander, counseled David not to allow this "ambitious pride" to cause him to sin against God. Not until Joab's army completed the census did David bring his thoughts into captivity and admit his folly. God forgave him, but punishment resulted because David and the nation's pride needed to be checked. Faced with a choice of punishments, David pled, "Please let me fall into the hand of the LORD, for His mercies are great" (2 Sam 24:14, NKJV).

Following are valuable lessons to carry in our spiritual luggage. "No king [is] saved by the multitude of an host: a mighty man is not delivered by much strength. A horse is a vain thing for safety: neither shall he deliver any by his great strength" (Ps. 33:16, 17). How much better it is to put trust in the Lord rather than in man (Ps. 118:8)! Truly, our only hope is in the Lord who brings victory. He is more than enough!

June 12

The Gift of Godly Fear

Fear the LORD, you his saints, for those who fear him lack nothing. Ps. 34:9, NIV.

Open a new deck of playing cards and the first person in the lineup of characters is the jester with such aliases as fool, wearer of the motley, trickster, buffoon, and jack-pudding. During the Middle Ages, a court jester worked as a licensed fool, receiving compensation for acting the fool. But a licensed fool stands in contrast to a natural fool who is deficient in judgment and understanding. "The wicked, in the haughtiness of his countenance, does not seek Him. All his thoughts are, 'There is no God'" (Ps. 10:4, NASB).

Basing right and wrong on *his* feelings and *his* imperfect wisdom, a fool is his own worst enemy, for the essence of self-deception is to look inward for wisdom. "Those who trust their own insight are foolish, but anyone who walks in wisdom is safe" (Prov. 28:26, NLT). "What does the LORD your God ask of you but to fear … God, to walk in all his ways, to love him, to serve the LORD your God with all your heart and with all your soul, and to observe the LORD's commands and decrees" (Deut. 10:12, 13).

We can, however, fear God but in the wrong spirit. A very important distinction exists between servile and filial fear. Filial fear is that humble, reverent respect due to a parent from a child while servile fear is a cringing for fear of a hard master or a fear of punishment rather than remorse for sins committed. King Saul feared God after being deposed for repeated disobedience, which culminated in a refusal to destroy the Amalekites (1 Sam. 15:30). But, "It was not sorrow for sin, but fear of its penalty, that actuated the king of Israel as he entreated Samuel, 'I pray thee, pardon my sin, and turn again with me, that I may worship the Lord.'"[169] Conversely, Abraham passed his test of faith. Upon God's command, he laid his only son on an altar to sacrifice him, complying with a request that is a parent's worst nightmare because he feared and trusted God (Gen. 22:12).

Filial fear is selfless and self-decreasing and emanates from intense affection for the God of grace and mercy. He is so special and so deserving that offending Him causes pain and remorse and pleasing Him is a paramount ambition. At the core, filial fear springs from fickle human love, responding to the amazing concept of the unconditional love of God for fallen beings. When we develop a healthy fear of God through an intimate relationship with Him, we move across the spectrum from foolishness to wisdom.

The world's wisdom is foolishness in the eyes of God, "for it is written, 'He catches the wise with their own trickery'" (1 Cor. 3:19, ISV). For instance, evolutionists deny God. But when we regard that the DNA in our cells is similar to a complex computer program and "within the tiny space in every cell in your body, this code is three billion letters long," evolution is folly. An attempt to read that code day and night at "three letters per second would take thirty-one years."[170] Does not God, who can create and sustain such complexity in bodies so wonderfully made, deserve our reverence, our filial fear?

June 13

Forgiveness and Cleansing

If we confess our sins, he is faithful and just to forgive us our sins, and to cleanse us from all unrighteousness. 1 John 1:9.

In the comedy *Liar, Liar,* Jim Carrey's character is Fletcher Reede who has a bona fide gift of gab and whose lies come as regularly and easily as breathing. As a lawyer his ability to convincingly lie exponentially has advanced his career. His lies do not end at promoting his career, however. The divorced father of Max, he lies to his son, breaking promise after promise. Blowing out the candles at his fifth birthday, Max wishes his dad would stop lying for 24 hours. And his wish comes true to the utter chagrin of Fletcher whose world is fragmented by the force of this alien concept of truthfulness.

Honesty is a sign of righteousness (Prov. 12:17). Thus, "you shall not bear false witness against your neighbor" (Ex. 20:16, ESV). Lying is a sin so hateful to God that He included it in the Ten Commandments that were written with His own finger on tablets of stone and stored in the ark of the covenant. We, however, categorize sins, rebuking some and tolerating others. While murder is an outrage, lying is accepted, and we minimize the impact of lying by categorizing some lies as little and white and use euphemisms like exaggeration to avoid calling it what it is—a sin.

God hates "a false witness who breathes out lies, and one who sows discord among brothers" (Prov. 6:19, ESV). The toxicity of lies brings untold pain, stigmatization, and at times irreparable damage personally and professionally to innocent persons. Clearly, the bold, blatant lies of my friend Nan's supervisor, who is a habitual liar in the manner of Fletcher Reede, tarnished Nan's professional reputation by labeling her a slacker. Thankfully for Nan, her supervisor's reputation in the workplace condemns him.

Based on research, the typical human being tells a lie on average every eight minutes. And researchers labeled former President Richard Nixon the biggest liar on record after telling 837 lies in a single day. Unless converted, we assume the posture of Satan for whom lying is essential. "He was a murderer from the beginning, and has nothing to do with the truth, because there is no truth in him … for he is a liar and the father of lies" (John 8:44, ESV). Lies come by omission or commission, by exaggeration or fabrication. But God will punish liars who fail to repent and reform. "A false witness will not go unpunished, and he who breathes out lies will perish" (Prov. 19:9, ESV).

Still, God knows our weaknesses and works through His Spirit to reform our tendency to lie. Once we surrender this sinful habit to the Holy Spirit, our strength is combined with the purifying power of His and transformation takes root. And as long as we are striving and making progress, God's mercy and grace will continue to abound. Then, slowly but surely lying and all sin become a nasty taste in our mouths as we imitate the character of Jesus.

June 14

Recovering Sin Addicts

For I will restore health to you, and I will heal you of your wounds, said the LORD. Jer. 30:17, AKJV.

David was nineteen when he first injected crystal meth into his blood stream. Addicted, he lived to stay high without considering the consequences to his health or his victims. While serving time in prison before conquering his habit, "he got a tattoo of a laughing devil to hide track marks on his right arm and a crying Jesus on this left arm. They serve to remind him that meth brings instant joy but suffering later." Still, David is troubled by a recurring nightmare where he is using meth and has no plans to discontinue its use. [171]

Addicts are habitual drug users who are powerless to curb the need for mind-altering chemicals notwithstanding the negative outcomes. Also, they will steal, kill, or die to get their fix, and they will destroy their lives, their parents' or their children's lives to fulfill an uncontrollable compulsory need for the drug of choice or the drug of convenience. Interestingly, substance abusers have many parallels with sinners who are also unable to extricate themselves from sin and its negative circumstances.

Many addicts are running from emotional hurt and feelings of unworthiness; thus, they use drugs to palliate the pain. But in a vicious cycle, each successive "hit" requires a higher dosage to duplicate the previous high. Successful rehabilitation is required to break the cycle. Similarly, sin is the substance of choice for sinners since we are all born with sin-addicted personalities, and without help, we cannot beat the habit (Rom. 8:7). For recalcitrant sinners, wise advice and counsel are useless, personal experiences of loved ones or friends are disregarded, and past painful circumstances are ignored. They choose slavery to their sin-addiction and "live as enemies of the cross of Christ" (Phil. 3:18, NLT).

Like the recovering addict, penitent sinners also are in recovery by God's grace. We are commanded not to allow sin to reign in our mortal body so overpowering that we are compelled to its evil desires (Rom. 6:12). Mercifully, when God gives us a command, He provides the means to fulfill the same. Although, sin is still in our DNA, we have the power through the indwelling of the Holy Spirit to control our tendencies. Obedience to the Word of God frees us from our sin-addiction and allows us to become slaves of righteousness (Rom. 6:17, 18).

Sin, like drugs, alters our thoughts and our allegiances. We embrace evil and shun good; we clutch the father of lies and the architect of destruction and reject Jesus who seeks to protect us, save us, and give us a future. And we turn our faces toward the kingdom of darkness and turn our backs to the kingdom of light. No doubt we need healing, and the Lord declares that He is the one who heals (Ex. 15:26). He is Jehovah-Rapha who takes the sting out of our trials and suffering with His presence, and who supernaturally rearranges our DNA so that sin is abhorrent and, therefore, shunned. Fill every corner of every need with Jesus and remain steadfast in recovery.

June 15

God's Purchased Possessions

He will remove the disgrace of his people from all the earth. The Lord has spoken. Isa. 25:8 GWT

A very powerful king not only invited an old hermit to his kingdom but also flattered him. Smugly, the king told the hermit he envied his piety and humility at being satisfied with a pauper's existence. Likewise, the hermit complimented the king for being content with even less than the hermit. The king took offense and wanted an explanation since he owned the entire country. The hermit answered, "I have the music of the celestial spheres, I have the rivers and mountains of the whole world, I have the moon and the sun, because I have God in my soul. Your Majesty, on the other hand, has only this kingdom"—an earthly kingdom that only lasts a few years.[172]

But the kingdom that God promises Jesus, "the throne of his father David" is everlasting; "there shall be no end" (Luke 1:32, 33). This kingdom begins as a spiritual kingdom and continues forever as a literal kingdom where Jesus will reign as King of kings. Inhabiting a human form, Jesus apprised His followers, "My kingdom is not of this world" (John 18:36). But His followers were slow to accept His refusal to conquer the Romans with supernatural power and reign on an earthly throne. Also, they were slow to grasp why He remained content with poverty, powerlessness, and submission.

Jesus' kingdom is the total opposite of worldly kingdoms. Currently, it is a kingdom where Jesus reigns in our hearts; a kingdom that promotes love for both our neighbors and our enemies. It is a kingdom that seeks the captives and then sets them free. In this kingdom, the subjects are not beaten down, exploited, and destroyed, but lifted up, encouraged, and saved. Jesus, battered, tortured, and shamed by His enemies, illustrates nonviolence and forgiveness of injustice and abuse. And His followers, who are strangers on earth and here temporarily, are required to follow His lead.

God's people, ill-content to remain in this kingdom of evil and considered misfits, make sinners uneasy. Moreover, some exhibitions of humility and love generate hatred. On the other hand, slaves of demonic forces and blinded to real wisdom—the fear of God—contented citizens of this world appear wise in their own eyes. But soon His kingdom will come. And "when the Son of Man comes in his glory, and all the angels with him, he will sit on his throne in heavenly glory" and will separate His people from the company of the disobedient who persist in ungodliness (Matt. 25:31).

Finally, Jesus shall be King and reign over all the earth (Zech. 14:9). No longer will His purchased possessions be subjected to ridicule and persecution. No longer will hate, sin, and death exist. The ransomed will give Him "the glory due to his name; Worship the LORD in the beauty of holiness" (Ps. 29:2, NKJV). All humanity will bow down before Him month after month and from Sabbath to Sabbath (Isa. 66:23). And God Himself will be with them and be their God (Rev. 21:3).

June 16

Blessings Follow Compassion

He that giveth unto the poor shall not lack: but he that hideth his eyes shall have many a curse. Prov. 28:27.

In earlier times, a little boy entered an ice cream parlor to purchase a sundae. He asked a busy waitress the cost, and she replied, "Fifty cents." He pulled his stash of coins out of his pocket, studied them carefully, and then asked, "How much is a plain dish of ice cream?" Her impatience showing, the waitress retorted curtly, "Thirty-five cents," and he ordered the plain ice cream. After he paid his bill and left, the waitress found a fifteen-cent tip. With tears welling in her eyes, she realized he had sacrificed the sundae and settled for plain ice cream to leave such a generous tip.[173]

It is not enough to be generous; it is not enough to write a check for income tax purposes, or in response to pressure, but it is God-blessed to give with an open hand in the spirit of love. "Give generously to him and do so without a grudging heart; then because of this the LORD your God will bless you in all your work and in everything you put your hand to. There will always be poor people in the land" (Deut. 15:10, 11, NIV). This blessing transfers from generation to generation and is characterized by the life and work of George Mueller. God showered his consummate faith and loyalty with manifold blessings.

A nineteenth-century preacher and philanthropist born in Prussia, Mueller became a naturalized British subject. He labored intensely for the poor and helpless in England for more than sixty years, building five orphanages that housed 2,000 orphans. When impressed to build the orphanages, his purse held less than a dollar but his heart held a million dollars worth of faith. He prayed rather than solicit donations to build and manage the orphanages, and God orchestrated his receipt of more than seven million dollars in aid. Daily and miraculously, God supplied all their basic needs.

Giving is an act of worship to God who has given generously and unselfishly to a world full of people who deserve nothing less than death. To acknowledge Him and show thankfulness for all that we receive from His bountiful hand, we are compelled to give. If we love Him with all our heart, then generosity will flow for our heart is where our treasure is also. "Give to the LORD, O families of the peoples, Give to the LORD glory and strength. Give to the LORD the glory due His name; Bring an offering, and come before Him. Oh, worship the LORD in the beauty of holiness! (1 Chron. 16:28, 29, NKJV).

Because of His promises, we can worry less about the times we live in and the economic downturn we are experiencing. God can do much with nothing but faith as he did for George Mueller. We reap a blessing by helping the poor where we meet Jesus through them. For when we are kind to the poor, we lend to the Lord, "and he will reward him for what he has done" (Prov. 19:17, NIV)—for blessings follow compassion.

June 17

When Words Are Not Enough

Be strong and of good courage, and do it: fear not, nor be dismayed: for the LORD God… will be with thee; he will not fail thee, nor forsake thee. 1 Chron. 28:20.

His yearning grew intense and the passion reached fever pitch for him to build the sanctuary of God to house the ark and the holy vessels, but God disappointed King David. He denied him the privilege of building His temple because David had shed too much blood on the earth (1 Chron. 22:8). I can imagine that the blood of Uriah, the soldier whom David killed to claim his wife, cried loudly to God. Notwithstanding the keen disappointment, David encouraged and supported his son in the construction of the Temple.

They spared no expense to build this house of God. Four hundred and eighty years after the people of Israel came out of the land of Egypt, Solomon began to build the ninety feet long, thirty feet wide, and forty-five feet high Temple and completed it seven years later (1 Kings 10:18-20). Young and inexperienced, Solomon probably recoiled privately at the thought of superintending the construction of such a sacred and magnificent structure. Truly, this task would intimidate the most experienced builder.

However, David did not merely pat him on the back, offer words of encouragement, and walk away. He supplied incalculable support in the form of gold and silver, sound advice, and materials as well as loyal, experienced workmen. Guided by the Holy Spirit, David also meticulously drew up the blueprint for the Temple. Additionally, He commissioned the aliens and the leaders of Israel to assist.

Sometimes, we are required to offer more than words, more than prayer. Consider the Good Samaritan on a mission that probably included a deadline. He did not merely pray for the wounded traveler and leave him on the roadside. He stopped and assisted him, possibly exposing himself to assault by the same robbers who had attacked the wounded man. Not satisfied with that, he delivered him to an inn and paid for his room and board. Jesus said to His disciples, "Go, and do thou likewise" (Luke 10:37).

Henry Drummond's sage words "there is no happiness in having or in getting, but only in giving" is a truism with a counterpoint to God's words "it is better to give than to receive." A wise traveler found a precious stone near a mountain but gave it to another who discovered it when the traveler opened her bag to give him food. He took the stone and rejoiced at this fortune that offered lifelong security, but he returned it a few days later. " 'I've been thinking,' he said, 'I know how valuable the stone is, but I give it back in the hope that you can give me something even more precious. Give me what you have within you that enabled you to give me the stone.' "[174]

The love of God and the mind of Christ motivated her to be sacrificially kind. We, too, are admonished to go and do likewise to friend and foe alike.

June 18

Hated Without Cause

Marvel not, my brethren, if the world hate you. 1 John 3:13.

Frank J. Loesch, chair of the Chicago Crime Commission, popularized the phrase "public enemy" during the 1930s to label and condemn thugs like Al Capone. Later, the FBI, under the leadership of J. Edgar Hoover, used the term to describe infamous criminal fugitives like Bonnie and Clyde. On the list of public enemies, public enemy number 1 figured as the most dangerous to society and the vilest of the vile. When Jesus walked the earth, Jewish leaders ranked Him public enemy number 1, putting Him in the same league as the base and dangerous bank robber, Al Capone.

The Jewish religious leaders hated Jesus even though His ministry consisted of healing the sick, seeking and saving lost souls, exorcising demons, and showing compassion to the poor, weak, and marginal populace. Meek and lowly, His life and work exemplified unselfishness and love. But these leaders hated Him so intensely they plotted to execute Him for the capital offense of blasphemy and because "it was expedient for one man to die on behalf of the people" (John 18:14, NASB).

The Sanhedrin, or ruling council, composed of Pharisees, scribes, and wealthy Sadducees, demanded that the Jews follow the letter of the law, but their souls were empty of forgiveness and love. Proudly self-important, they showed intolerance and disdain of the lower class and a lack of compassion for the sick and diseased. On the other hand, Jesus' sinless witness stood in sharp contrast to the hypocrisy of the hard-hearted, unbelieving Jews. And His exemplary life silently pointed out their defects. At other times, He frankly rebuked them out of concern for their salvation, but they could not handle the truth.

Rather than accept their reality and Jesus' power to transform, they worked to discredit and silence Him. Hate and selfishness rallied, and those associated with the gospel truth became a target of their malice. Despite the consequences, Jesus warned His disciples to tell the truth even if it killed them, to avoid popularity contests, and to firmly stand on principle. "There's trouble ahead when you live only for the approval of others, saying what flatters them, doing what indulges them. Popularity contests are not truth contests—look how many scoundrel preachers were approved by your ancestors! Your task is to be true, not popular" (Luke 6:26, MSG).

This is a caution and encouragement to all Jesus' followers who are hated by loyalists to the prince of this world. "If the world hates you, keep in mind that it hated me first. If you belonged to the world, it would love you as its own. As it is, you do not belong to the world, but I have chosen you out of the world. That is why the world hates you" (John 15:18, 19, NIV). The current price of hate is costly, and the redeemed, the converted, the obedient, the unselfish, the faithful will suffer for a season. But isn't it wonderful to be chosen and in such good company and God until this earthly dystopia changes into our heavenly utopia?

June 19

Captain of My Salvation

For it became him ... in bringing many sons unto glory, to make the captain of their salvation perfect through sufferings. Heb. 2:10.

It is ironic that a ship called the "Good Ship Jesus" was involved in the most abhorrent inhumanity to man—the African slave trade. King Henry VIII purchased the "Jesus of Lubeck" that years later fell into disrepair. During her reign, Queen Elizabeth loaned the ship to Sir John Hawkins, credited with beginning the slave trade in Britain, and permitted him to carry slaves from Africa to America. Initially, the queen's consent only covered Africans traveling to America on their own free will, but that changed once the practice of selling them reaped enormous economic gain for her.

Thank God, Jesus is our Captain on the ship of salvation. What a magnificent Captain He makes! Ship captains are qualified to take the helm of a wide range of ship types from cruise ships to tugboats and deliver them safely to port. And Jesus is imminently qualified to deliver all humanity—the most benign citizen to the raving maniac, the introvert to the extrovert, the young to the old—safely to their heavenly port. His life, given as a ransom for many, guarantees that deliverance (Mark 10:45).

Too, a ship captain is commissioned to control the vessel's operations and keep meticulous logs regarding the ship's course, speed, and weather conditions. Captain Jesus commands the waves and weather conditions that propel or halt the ship of life. Pursuant to Jonah's disobedience, He "hurled a great wind on the sea and there was a great storm on the sea so that the ship was about to break up" (Jonah 1:4, NASB). And "he commandeth even the winds and water, and they obey him" (Luke 8:25).

Superb communication and problem-solving skills and the wherewithal to respond to crisis situations are also hallmarks of a great captain. Jesus' communication runs the gamut from impressions on the heart and mind to a still small voice to booming thunder. And His ear is always open to hear the prayers of His saints. Thus, He invites us to call on Him when in need (Ps. 10:17; Heb. 4:16). When we fall as broken driftwood floating on the choppy waters of life, the hand that created and holds up the vast universe reaches down to pluck us to safety.

If Jesus is the Captain of your salvation, the hand that holds your future is at the helm, so allow Him to turn your rudder in the direction He chooses. He may purposely head into a dark cloud at times to dim your view of the world's preoccupations. Or He might head into a storm with waves that beat at the bow and threaten to overwhelm the ship, but trust Him. When the gale winds blow and tatter the mast, he is able to hold it fast with the strong rope of His protection (John 16:33). Intermittently, He steers the ship into the calm of a peaceful, safe harbor until you are shipshape enough to resume the journey. Trust Jesus, your Captain, for He is navigating you toward a waterway called "Godliness," the waterway which leads to eternal salvation.

June 20

Strong Enough to Be Meek

Seek righteousness, seek humility. Perhaps you will be hidden in the day of the LORD's anger. Zeph. 2:3, NASB.

Taming a wild horse is a dangerous exercise. Weighing a ton or more, a wild horse does not welcome the human touch. Recoiling violently at an attempt to tame it, the horse rises up on its hind legs and slams its front hooves down in an attempt to crush its antagonist. Whinnying, snorting, and grunting madly, it viciously kicks out its hind legs, breaking limbs or posts or whatever is in its path. Then it gallops in circles, bucking and heaving in an exhibition of its displeasure and its high-spiritedness. Taming does not make the horse weak, but his still-intact spiritedness and strength is harnessed for a useful purpose.

One word for meek in the Greek language is *prautes*, which describes a controlled power. Greeks used *prautes* "to describe a soothing wind, a healing medicine, and a colt ... broken" and harnessed. Power defines each because "a wind can become a storm, too much medicine can kill and a horse can break loose."[175] Thus, a meek or humble person is not a wimp or a pushover as many suppose, but a spirited person who wields self-control allied with a strong faith and a determined obedience.

Described as the meekest man on earth, Moses did not fit the derogative label of being a wimp (Num. 12:3). Tough enough to lead hundreds of thousands of obstinate people across a desert for forty years, Moses earned respect as an uncompromising, godly leader. He talked to God, served as judge, rebuked the people, and executed wrongdoers. More than once his anger erupted. The newly emancipated Israelites worship of a golden calf moved him to smash the Ten Commandment tablet against a rock, pulverize it, and compel them to drink it in their water.

Meekness is a two-pronged attitude pointing horizontally to humility before God and pointing vertically toward tenderness to our neighbors. Toward God, the meek recognize His preeminence and their irrelevance, His power and their inability, His authority and their submission. Toward his neighbors, the meek possess a gentle and quiet spirit that controls the carnal spirit of petulance and temper. They hold a generosity of spirit that manages the carnal spirit of selfishness. Without fail, the meek repay good for evil and seek the good even in the spiteful and mean-spirited.

Biblical meekness describes a person with a strong will to submit to the will of God and is validated by Jesus who described Himself as "meek and lowly in heart" (Matt. 11:29). Jesus beckons us to come to Him, the master Teacher and prime example, and learn from Him because our prideful hearts struggle against being meek. "The meek will he guide in judgment: and the meek will he teach his way" (Ps. 25:8, 9). When vilified and terrorized by the people He came to rescue and save, He turned the other cheek and beseeched His Father to forgive His trespassers in their ignorance. Lowly in heart, He came not to extol Himself but to commend His Father by the life He lived.

June 21

Rescued From the Jaws of Death

The LORD protects those of childlike faith; I was facing death, and he saved me. Ps. 116:6, NLT.

Mike Brick, an engineer, created the phrase "Jaws of Life" after rescuers noted that tools used to extract people from wrecked cars saved them from the jaws of death. A trademark of Hurst Performance Inc., these hydraulic tools extract victims trapped in crashed vehicles with doors or windows that are jammed shut. The rescue tools used are cutters, spreaders, and rams and are safer, quieter, and more efficient than the circular saws and crowbars formerly used.

Jesus is humanity's Jaws of Life, extracting us from the waiting, gaping jaws of death propped open by Satan. He has a trademark on the tools that trap humanity into eternal darkness, including tools of pleasure, discouragement, and disbelief. And he uses all kinds of lures to draw us close enough to clamp shut and trap the unwary inside those deadly jaws. Friendship with the world is an excellent lure that puts a wall of separation between God and His children. And once separated from the arms of safety, we are unable to resist Satan's subterfuges and are doomed.

Creeping compromise by association with the world ensnares the righteous. If Satan cannot persuade us to dive into big, bold sins, he uses this strategy to masterfully bring a gradual spiritual decline. Donald Grey Barnhouse shared how musicians found that errand boys in certain parts of London all whistled off key as they scurried around. They figured out that the Westminster bells were out of tune, and the boys unconsciously mimicked the bell's pitch. Thus, we imitate the people with whom we associate and sponge ideas from the materials we read and the programs we see or hear so indiscernibly that we barely notice.

Clearly the world does not and cannot subject itself to the law of God (Rom. 8:7). Thus, friendship with the world results in hostility to God and makes us His enemy (James 4:4). "Our only safety is to recognize the clever camouflages of the enemy. A thousand disguised death traps have been planted all around us. Almost imperceptibly our thinking has been affected by what we see and hear. Spiritual convictions have softened and disappeared altogether. The fine sensitivity to sin has been blunted by incessant exposure to the apparent innocent influences of our baited society."[176]

God's people cannot dabble in the world and not expect to be lured by its tempting attractions. Earthly temptations are like fool's gold—they glitter and shine but when appraised they turn out to be worthless. To shake off the cloud of compromise that Satan uses to blind us to the clear dictates of the Word, we need to stand firm on "it is written" as Jesus did and trust His promises. He will intercede and ensure the temptation is not beyond our endurance and will point out the trapdoor so we can make our exit. For He longs to rescue us from the jaws of death.

June 22

Stand Firm

By standing firm you will gain life. Luke 21:19, NIV.

In the 1946 movie *Gilda*, an Argentinean prosecutor arrests Johnny Farrell, the right-hand man of a crooked casino owner and puts him in protective custody. Obregon, the prosecutor, determines to keep Johnny in custody until he provides the information he seeks. "I can out wait you, Mr. Farrell. You see, I have the law on my side. It's a very comfortable feeling. It's something you ought to try sometime," said Obregon.

Obregon, standing under the authority of the law, remained convinced that if he stood firm and waited, eventually right would triumph over wrong. Biblically, standing firm means to put away sin, avoid evil, and remain faithful to that commitment. And standing firm in virtue allows interactions with God without shame or fear of the coming judgment (Job 11:14, 15). But we need a firm foundation to keep from toppling.

The cornerstone of that foundation is Jesus who anchors us to the spiritual ground and distributes the weight of our burdens over Himself. Those who submit to Him and obey His laws are comparable to one who builds a house on a rock foundation where nothing can shake it off its base. But those who hear the Word and ignore it are like those who build a house on a sandy foundation. When the floods come, the house collapses and washes out to sea (Luke 6:47-49).

The builders on the firm foundation are wise. "Behold, I am laying in Zion a stone, a tested stone, a costly cornerstone for the foundation, firmly placed. He who believes in it will not be disturbed" (Isa. 28:16, NASB). With Jesus as the solid Rock of our foundation, winds of strife howl and incessant waves of temptations batter against our spiritual resolve but to no avail. We lay a firm spiritual foundation by confronting our sinful tendencies and outright rejecting sin as the Holy Spirit settles in. Then we erect twin pillars of faith and obedience through prayer and the study of His Word.

However, while we are building that house of righteousness, Satan is watching intently, plotting and exerting toxic energy to topple it. Jesus cautions us to stay focused for "If you think you are standing firm you had better be careful that you do not fall" (1 Cor. 10:12, GNT). Through lies like "once saved always saved," Satan means to topple us, but the Word says, "By this gospel you are saved, *if* you hold firmly to the word I preached to you. Otherwise, you have believed in vain" (1 Cor. 15:2, NIV). Anyone who says, "I know him," but do not keep His commandments until He returns or until death is a liar and the truth is not in him" (1 John 2:4).

Stand firm with the belt of truth buckled around your waist, with the breastplate of righteousness in place, and with your feet fitted with the readiness that comes from the gospel of peace. Satanic and "worldly influences, like the waves of the sea, beat against the followers of Christ to sweep them away from the true principles of His meekness and grace; but we are to stand as firm as a rock to principle."[177] Stand firm.

June 23

He Will Deliver Us

He will call upon me, and I will answer him; I will be with him in trouble, I will deliver him and honor him. Ps. 91:15, NIV.

Essie, a lone shipwreck survivor, found refuge on a small, uninhabited island and prayed daily for God to deliver her. After some time had passed and silence from God, she decided to build a shack for her possessions and for shelter from the rain and sun. Returning one day from foraging for food on the island, she found the shelter fully engulfed in flames and choking black smoke filled the air. Discouraged, she thought angrily, "How could God do this to me." Falling into a fitful sleep, she awakened upon the ship's approach, realizing the smoke had guided the rescuers to her.

Many times we are not delivered in a way we expect. A faithful Christian whose husband is diagnosed with a fatal disease fasts and prays for his recovery, but he suffers agonizingly and then dies. A home of a tithe-paying Christian is to be repossessed, moving the congregation to offer up prayers. Still, she loses her home. A father of three preschoolers who loses his job and his pension becomes despondent. His God-fearing wife prays, yet, he murders the entire family and commits suicide.

Didn't God say if we call on Him He will answer? Didn't He promise to deliver us from trouble? Didn't He say, "Because he loves me … I will rescue him; I will protect him, for he acknowledges my name" (Ps. 91:14, NIV)? Where was God when these faithful Christians called on Him as trouble barged in? Where He always is—standing beside them—for God never leaves the presence of His anointed (Ps. 139:7)! We, however, may not understand His methods or timing, for His ways are higher than our ways, and His thoughts higher than our thoughts (Isa. 55:9).

God is in control of all things, and sometimes He delivers us in unforgettable ways as He delivered the faithful Hebrew boys. Sentenced to be burned alive and wise enough to understand and trust His ways, they responded, "If we are thrown into the blazing furnace, *the* God we serve is able to save us from it, and he will rescue us from your hand, O king. But even *if he does not*, we want you to know … that we will not serve your gods or worship the image of gold" (Dan. 3:17, 18, NIV).

Oftentimes, however, He allows the difficulties to teach valuable lessons. Lessons of humility, of trust in His providences, of faith in His Word, of perseverance, and of dependence on Him are invaluable, but painful. Like a broken piece of clay needs pounding and grinding before it can be restored, we must endure the painful process or remain broken. But we will be delivered, if not now, later, and maybe not until His Second Coming. We *will* be delivered.

Be assured His Word is certain (2 Tim. 3:16, 17). When you believe that God delivers as He promises, and when you accept His method as well as the timing of the delivery, fear is replaced with incredible peace.

June 24

Protection from the Evil One

But the Lord is faithful, and He will strengthen and protect you from the evil one. 2 Thess. 3:3, NASB.

Cliff Pickover compiled a list of the most evil people in history, giving points to those who relished the pain and terror they inflicted. Number two on his list is Vlad the Impaler, his nickname. A prince in Romania, Vlad used impalement, a cruel, gruesome, perverted torture as his favorite means of executing those who ignored his trade laws. Sometimes executors inserted the semi-dull, oiled impaling stake through the buttocks and slowly forced it into the body by horses attached to the victim's legs until the stake exited through their mouth. He also tortured by skinning, boiling, roasting, hacking, burying alive, and nailing his enemies. Incredibly, at times he witnessed the suffering while feasting among the corpses.[178]

Vlad ruled as a spawn of Satan who casually destroyed life. He produced amplified evil as fruit and exhibited morally objectionable behavior. This inhumanity supports a seared conscience, a quenching of the Holy Spirit, and defenseless bowing to the powers of darkness. Malevolent, his attitude and behavior promoted cruelty in the highest degree, sanctioned and cooperated with inhumanity to man, and fostered an excessive abuse of power.

We are surrounded by the evil one and his demons, for God expelled untold thousands of angels from heaven with Satan, and they are swirling around earth doing his bidding. "The whole world lies in the power of the evil one" (1 John 5:19, ESV). Satan is the "god of this world" who blinds the eyes of the perishing and the "prince of the power of the air" who works in the sons of disobedience (2 Cor. 4:4; Eph. 2:2). But Jesus made it clear that even if he is the ruler of this world, Satan is powerless over Him.

Without divine intervention, we are helpless pawns in the hands of the devil who stays on the offensive, seeking whom he can devour (1 Peter 5:8). But fear not, God promises to protect us and to release us from slavery to his evil will. Jesus has full authority over the powers of darkness and forces them to flee when we resist them. "For with authority and power he commands the unclean spirits, and they come out" (Luke 4:36, ESV).

The Bible says, "Anyone born of God does not continue to sin; the one who was born of God keeps him safe, and the evil one cannot harm him" (1 John 5:18, NIV). Through the authority of love, we are delivered from the power of darkness and are transported into the kingdom of Jesus, and through Jesus, we have redemption and forgiveness (Col. 1:12-14). With our deliverance comes the power to withstand the evil one since Jesus disarmed the powers of darkness and triumphed over them at the cross (Col. 2:15). And because the Holy Spirit who resides in us is greater than Satan who is in the world, we are strengthened and protected from the evil one (1 John 4:4).

June 25

Making Peace With God

Or let him take hold of My strength, that he may make peace with Me; and he shall make peace with Me. Isa. 27:5, NKJV.

Sin is like a vigorous, toxic shield that not only blocks but also bats away the peace of God. To illustrate, one anonymous young lady explains how her increasingly immoral and rebellious ways left her despondent. "I tried smoking and drinking to appear cool to my peers. I became sexually active at a very young age, and that brought more despair, guilt and heartache.… I experimented with the Ouija Board, read horoscopes, and watched many horror movies which left scars of fear in my life for years to come. My interest in dark music grew and I often had thoughts of suicide."[179]

No God, no peace! *Shalom* is the Hebrew word for peace, embracing completeness and soundness. The Greek word for peace, *eirene*, signifies the sound relationships between God and man established through the gospel.[180] As with a virus, sin invades and corrupts or prevents a relationship with the Peacemaker, resulting in emptiness, anxiety, and guilt. Without a relationship with God, the angst that haunts the wicked will not abate. The "wicked are like the troubled sea, when it cannot rest, whose waters cast up mire and dirt. There is no peace … to the wicked" (Isa. 57:20, 21).

Know God, know peace! Clearly, to conquer our inner turmoil and capture peace, we must endeavor for a right relationship with God. "Those who obey God's commandments remain in fellowship with him, and he with them. And we know he lives in us because the Spirit he gave us lives in us" (1 John 3:24, NLT). Can't you see a broad smile on God's face each time one of His children pursues an intimate relationship, a loving friendship with Him? Shalom characterizes a covenant relationship with God—meaning we do our part, God does His. Giving our hearts to Jesus, He justifies us through faith, and we experience peace with God through Jesus (Rom. 5:1).

To know Him is to love and trust Him. Know this, He is sovereign, His strong right hand *covers* all, and His outstretched arm *controls* all. Not even a dust mite escapes His purview. Know that the forces of evil and negative spirits wither at His commands, that He loves us supremely and watches over us intently. And that the amazing love He holds for mankind gave His only Son to be a curse and sin for us even while we flirted with Satan. Know that the stretching and growing of our faith is painful, but concern for our spiritual well-being keeps Him from relenting. And know that He has made provision for our peace—a peace that is innate in a relationship with Him.

To take hold of God's strength means to let go of control over our lives. Without faith that He is Who He says He is and will do what He says He will do, we signal fear to appear even though the Word provides adequate proof of His character. To make peace with God, permit Him to be Lord, submit to His will. Jesus already mended the broken fences of our relationship with God through His death. Thus, for peace to sweeten your existence, diligently stay within the gates of His love.

June 26

Famine Relief

In famine, he'll keep you from starving, in war, from being gutted by the sword. You'll be protected from vicious gossip and live fearless through any catastrophe. Job 5:20, 21, MSG.

A famine is an acute shortage or insufficiency. The Great Leap Forward famine, occurring between 1959 and 1962 in China, has the distinction of being the greatest famine in history. It reportedly led to the deaths of 20 to 43 million people through disease and starvation. Sadly, human error led to this catastrophe. China's leader, Mao Zedong, determined that China would surpass Britain in producing steel and other products within a short period of time. They neglected agriculture in this rush for industrialization, diminished grain reserves, and ushered in the famine.

We seldom, if ever, connect the word famine with God's Word. But the Bible says the days will come when the earth will experience a unique famine. "I will send a famine in the land, not a famine of bread, nor a thirst for water, but of hearing the words of the LORD" (Amos 8:11). People will urgently seek the Word but to no avail. Hearing, in this instance, goes beyond the perception of sound to the act of listening. And listening requires attention and concentration which leads to learning.

In 1996 the British *TIMES* newspaper noted "the Bible is the best-selling book every year," and it is readily available. Statistics from 1993 show that 92 percent of households in America own at least one copy of the Bible,[181] but only 37 percent read the Bible at least once a week.[182] By their own neglect, many have ushered in a famine; thus when God allows Satan's delusions, they will believe his lies (2 Thess. 2:11).

There is no shortage of the Word, just our own insufficiency in reading and digesting it for ourselves. The Bread of Life is sent by God to prevent spiritual malnourishment. Still, many rely on their pastors once or twice weekly to read the Word for them. However, Jesus pointed out that many false prophets will come in the last days and deceive the multitudes; thus, He cautions us to beware of those who tickle our ears with smooth words to cover the hard truths of the gospel (Matt. 7:15; 24:11).

Our salvation is too important to rely on fallible humans to read and interpret the Bible for us. Love and respect them, but take every spokesperson for God with a grain of salt. Study and call on the Holy Spirit to provide an understanding of God's Word. "The Spirit searches all things, even the deep things of God. For who among men knows the thoughts of a man except the man's spirit within him? In the same way *no one knows the thoughts of God except the Spirit of God*" (1 Cor. 2:10, 11, NIV).

John Locke wrote, "The Bible is one of the greatest blessings bestowed by God on the children of men. It has God for its author; salvation for its end, and truth without any mixture for its matter. It is all pure." And it brings famine relief.

June 27

A Trusted Deliverer and Refuge

The LORD is my rock, and my fortress, and my deliverer; my God, my strength, in whom I will trust. Ps. 18:2.

During an early morning walk in my neighborhood, I encountered a red fox speeding behind a tiny gray squirrel. The little squirrel, with desperation in his gait, darted up an incline and scampered across the road directly in front of me. The fox almost gained a savory breakfast, accelerating close enough to chomp down on the squirrel's tail. Just in time, the squirrel darted up a tree and hid in a small crevice in the tree trunk, instinctively knowing that the crevice would provide refuge. Although the fox worked to retrieve the squirrel from the crevice, he left unsuccessful.

Foxes are crafty and predatory animals, predatory like Herod the Great who stalked and murdered innocent babies in his quest to kill Baby Jesus whom he viewed as a threat to his throne. Foxes can be cruel, similar to the Jews who stalked Jesus to silence Him, and destructive, as Herodias, Herod Antipas' wife who pursued John the Baptist and beheaded him because John broadcast her immorality. Jesus labeled Herod a fox, indicating his weak and sneaky character, after some dishonest Pharisees warned Jesus to flee from Herod's sword. Fearlessly, Jesus dismissed the threat and asserted that He had a mission to fulfill (Luke 13:31, 32).

Indicating His homelessness, Jesus explained to a scribe who wanted to follow Him that foxes have holes and birds have nests but He had nowhere to lay His head (Matt 8:19, 20). In love with you and me, He left His heavenly estate, as well as His earthly home, to be a refuge and elevate us above the world. "Even when we were dead (slain) by [our own] shortcomings and trespasses, He made us alive together in fellowship and in union with Christ.... And He raised us up together with Him and made us sit down together [giving us joint seating with Him] in the heavenly sphere ... in Christ Jesus" (Eph. 2:5, 6, AMP).

Jesus' implacable grief over the rejection of His offer of refuge to Jerusalem shows how strong is His desire to rescue and harbor His people. He audibly wept and lamented how they had killed the prophets sent to guide them into righteousness, and "how often I have longed to gather your children together, as a hen gathers her chicks under her wings, but you were not willing!" (Luke 13:34, NIV). They possessed a proud, self-righteous spirit that moved them to look to self for salvation and not to the Author and Finisher of their faith.

Taking refuge in Jesus and trusting Him, we will be delivered. When crafty human foxes stalk you on the job, in public, or at home to sabotage your peace, run to Jesus. When vicious gossip threatens to ruin your reputation, seek His outstretched arms; when the lies surrounding you are so loud that you can barely hear the voice of truth in your own ears, embrace Jesus. And when the breath of the evil one is hot on the back of your neck, call on Jesus. He is a trusted deliverer and a sure refuge.

June 28

Hope Overflowing

May the God of your hope so fill you with all joy and peace in believing ... that by the power of the Holy Spirit you may abound and be overflowing. Rom. 15:13, NIV.

Niagara Falls, one of the most famous waterfalls in the world, is comprised of three individual waterfalls: the American Falls, Bridal Veil Falls or Luna Falls, both in America, and Horseshoe Falls in Canada. The water from the falls originates from four of the five Great Lakes. Every second in excess of 3,000 tons of water flow over the falls, dropping at 32 feet per second and hitting the bottom with 280 tons of force on the America side and over 2,500 tons of force on the Canadian side. And the force is powerful enough to generate over 4 million kilowatts of electricity.

But there is no power like the Holy Ghost. After His resurrection, Jesus asked His Father to send His followers a mysterious power called the Holy Spirit, a Comforter and guide (John 14:16). Since the Godhead is comprised of God the Father, God the Son, and God the Holy Spirit—three Persons but one in purpose—all the powers of God are the powers of the Holy Spirit. He functions as the presence of God who resides inside converted believers and tugs on the hearts of unbelievers to convict them to accept Jesus as their Lord and Savior. Importantly, He embodies a transforming power that enables us to fulfill God's requirements and to reflect the image of Jesus.

With the power that is within us we are fitted to overcome worldly cravings and tendencies that bring guilt and dampen hope. Dying to self is a daily struggle, for godliness is contrary to our nature. But this necessary death is wholly possible with diligent prayer and total submission to the Holy Spirit's direction. He erects trellises in our hearts and hangs on them the fruit of love, joy, peace, patience, kindness, goodness, faithfulness, gentleness, and self-control (Gal. 5:22, 23). The indwelling Spirit also superintends the cultivation of His fruit, thus enabling a solid victory over self.

Like a spark of fire, the Holy Spirit ignites our godly engines and keeps them running. But like any fire, this power can be quenched or grieved by our resistance to the truth, by accepting error, and by living immorally in contravention of the Word of God (Eph. 4:30; 1 Thess. 5:19). Always vigilant, the Holy Spirit pricks the conscience when we stray from the path of righteousness. But when the pricks are ignored and the believer willfully follows his own base desires, the Holy Spirit vacates the premises taking His fruit with Him. He is loathe to linger in the hearts of traitors who transfer their allegiance to the enemy.

Hope, overflowing as the waters that flow over Niagara Falls, is ours through the Holy Spirit. This hope is tapped into a Source that will never run dry. Through Him we have the present hope of living a holy life. The blessings of redemption, God's enduring presence, forgiveness, and the hope of immortality are only a drop in the ocean of blessings that overflow in the life of the saved. "For in hope we were saved ... if we hope for what we do not see, we wait with endurance" (Rom. 8:24, 25).

June 29

A Specialist in the Impossible

Do not put your trust in princes, nor in a son of man, in whom there is no help.... Happy is he who has the God of Jacob for his help. Ps. 146:3-5, NKJV.

A congregation built a small church on land donated by a member and used the entire lot except for the mountain it backed up against. Just before the church's scheduled opening, an inspector notified them of the parking lot's inadequacy. Without doubling the size of the lot, the church could not open. Unworried, the pastor called for members with "mountain-moving faith" to pray with him. Prayer moved God's hand, because the next day a construction foreman asked to haul dirt from the mountain to use as fill dirt. And he promised to pave all exposed areas after removing the it. The foreman's intervention expanded the lot and the church opened on schedule.[183]

The pastor exhibited faith great enough to be honored by God and of the kind described by Jesus when His disciples failed to exorcise demons from a boy. They queried Jesus and "He said to them, 'Because of the littleness of your faith; for ... if you have faith the size of a mustard seed, you will say to this mountain, 'Move from here to there,' and it will move; and nothing will be impossible for you" (Matt. 17:20, NASB). Interestingly, a mustard seed is one of nature's tiniest seeds, but it produces a huge plant. Likewise, a small act of faith produces extraordinary results.

Faith shouts, "There is nothing too hard for God." How foolish of us, then, to distrust the Creator and trust the creature! Not only is it foolish, it is also offensive to God when we rely on weak human beings with the effect of lost blessings. To rely on man is to depart from the Lord for "cursed is he man who trusts in man and makes flesh his strength" (Jer. 17:5, ESV). God will not shoot arrows down on the head of persons with misguided trust, but their actions usher in doubt, fear, worry, guilt, and a plethora of other negative emotions and negative outcomes.

Conversely, those who trust and hope in the Lord are blessed. Jeremiah compares them to trees planted by the waters whose roots are close to the river. When droughts of trials mar the landscape, fear and anxiety are thoroughly quenched (Jer. 17:6). The cross of setbacks and painful circumstances will inevitably nail the faithful, but down the hill a resurrection moment is guaranteed. Burdens are lifted as we hold on to the outstretched hand of Jesus and as we trust His love and His mountain-moving power.

Our God is a specialist in the impossible. Are you losing sleep over things that seem to have no possible solution, over seemingly lost causes? Said the psalmist, "When I am afraid, I will trust in you" (Ps. 56:3, NIV). In faith, call on God and relinquish the situation, habit, or person—the burdens. Relinquish them to the supreme Burden Bearer as readily as you relinquish surgery to surgeons and toothaches to dentists. He who resolves burdens in jaw-dropping ways has a mighty arm: strong is His hand, high is His right hand that makes the impossible possible (Ps. 89:13).

June 30

God's Unfailing Love

Let the morning bring me word of your unfailing love, for I have put my trust in you. Show me the way I should go, for to you I lift up my soul. Ps. 143:8, NIV.

Since 1977, Team Hoyt participated in more than 1,000 athletic events including triathlons, marathons, and duathlons consisting of running and cycling. Once they biked 3,735 miles across the U.S. in 45 days. Incredibly, the team consists of a quadriplegic mute son with cerebral palsy and an aging father who pushes the son in specially-crafted vehicles. And Dick regularly drives long hours to Rick's apartment to bathe, feed, and dress him in preparation for his day. "No challenge is too tough, no obstacle too high, provided they face it together."[184] Dick Hoyt's love for Rick is exceptionally reliable.

But, God *is* love. What a succinct and simple statement, but an ocean of ink cannot describe adequately the force, depth, and meaning of those words. Love is not something God gives or offers; it is who He is. Therefore, under no circumstance is it possible for Him to fail to love. His love, accompanied by every good and wonderful gift, is trustworthy, dependable, and constant—unfailing. *Chehsehd,* Hebrew for unfailing love, is pregnant with grace, mercy, favor, charity, and lovingkindness.

Furthermore, His abiding love cannot be moved. "Though the mountains be shaken and the hills be removed, yet my unfailing love for you will not be shaken … says the LORD, who has compassion on you" (Isa. 54:10, NIV). Even when Adam and Eve put their trust in the devil's word over God's and ate the forbidden fruit, He showed lovingkindness in the face of their weakness by providing animal skins to cover their nakedness and a plan of salvation to cover their sinfulness. His love never faltered.

Equally to all, God offers His constant love. "How priceless is your unfailing love! Both high and low among men find refuge in the shadow of your wings" (Ps. 36:7, NIV). And salvation, couched in that love, is available to all, by the grace of God, Jesus tasted death for all men (Heb. 2:9). When the Samaritan woman encountered Jesus at the well, she sat amazed that He would talk to her, for Jews had no dealings with Samaritans. During the conversation, she voiced her belief that the Messiah would come to answer her questions, which prompted Jesus' answer: "I am he; you don't have to wait any longer or look any further" (John 4:25, MSG).

Graciously, His unflagging love encircles those who rely on Him. "Many are the woes of the wicked, but the LORD's unfailing love surrounds the man who trusts in him" (Ps. 32:10, NIV). This love wraps around us like a magnetic field, shields us from the penalty of sin, and bars against the destructive force of Satan's weapons of fear, discouragement, and difficulties. Trusting in His unfailing love, we flourish like an olive tree in the house of God where we drink in the love that strengthens us to fight against our own inclinations, as well as the enemy's deceptions, and win.

July 1

Trouble Won't Last Always

Though I am surrounded by troubles, you will protect me from the anger of my enemies ... and the power of your right hand saves me. Ps. 138:7, NLT.

Brenda surrounded herself with troubles, fears, and distresses so numerous that they formed a mountainous pile. Regularly she climbed onto the pile to catalog and resolve them but failed. One day she fell off the huge pile and violently hit the ground holding shattered peace, hopes, and dreams. When well-meaning friends voiced concern, she revealed not her source of discontent and pain, so they moved on. But one lady asked, "Can I help?" "Not unless you can change the past," Brenda responded. "I can't change the past ...but God can change the world and he cares."[185]

Like Brenda, Christians face a mountain of troubles because Satan does not easily relinquish his former slaves. We can choose to worry about the solutions to these troubles or we can do all that is humanly possible and then trust God to bring resolution. Not one finite human being can conclude what tomorrow will bring; however, we can by faith temper needless stress that worry brings. Since God commands us to "be joyful in hope, patient in trouble, and persistent in prayer" we are empowered by His Spirit to do so (Rom. 12:12, ISV).

Jesus also cautions us to repress our anxiety about tomorrow's problems; it is more than enough to wade through the troubles today brings. Projecting on tomorrow equates to assuming a burden beyond our strength, for God promises sufficient strength for today only (Matt. 6:34). When we worry about what *might* happen tomorrow, we speed past His mercies and sabotage our peace. God faithfully renews His mercies not days in advance, but daily. "*Through* the LORD's mercies we are not consumed, Because His compassions fail not. *They are* new every morning; Great *is* Your faithfulness" (Lam. 3:22, 23, NKJV). He sufficiently strengthens us to wade into tomorrow's troubles when tomorrow dawns.

Peace and salvation are nestled in the trust we find in Him. Knowing that God provides for our future before we even think of it should anchor us even in the midst of deep, troubled waters. We may have to swim against the current of evil or struggle against the undercurrents of doubt that threaten to suck us under. But Jesus' lifejacket full of promises and His supreme authority provide buoyancy enough to keep our heads above the waters of worry and distress. Let us strive to live in "day-tight compartments" and let tomorrow fade from view.

Expect that you will not live a trouble-free life until satanic forces are eradicated: "Man that is born of a woman is of few days and full of trouble" (Job 14:1). Expect that God may not deliver you before the trials. But do expect that He will never forsake you. And anticipate increased faith pursuant to each difficulty overcome, and that He will walk beside you, lessen the intensity and duration of the trials and strengthen you every step of the way. And know and believe that troubles won't last always.

July 2

Grateful for the Thorns

They that sow in tears shall reap in joy. Ps. 126:5.

Christians have always suffered for their faith. Caesar Nero, an unbalanced and vulgar reprobate who committed incest with his mother and homosexual and heterosexual rape, is distinguished as the first emperor to persecute Christians. Diabolical, he murdered his own mother and sister and made the hated sect of Christians fair game. He crucified them, sewed them up in animal skins for wild animals to rip apart, and tied them to mad bulls that dragged them through the streets. "Nero enjoyed dipping the Christians in wax, and impaling them on poles around his palace, he would then set them on fire, and yell: 'Now you truly are the light of the world.'"[186]

The Christian life, consisting of both agony and ecstasy, is comparable to a rose with fragrant petals wrapped in spiny, sharp thorns. We experience inner joy and contentment, but living a godly life in Christ Jesus brings persecution (2 Tim. 3:12). Peter tells us we should not be surprised at painful trials, for they are an integral part of the journey. We must suffer because suffering builds character. After sharing in Jesus' agony and at the revealing of His glory, we will experience ecstasy beginning on the day of His appearing (1 Peter 4:12).

The earthly garden where Christians sow is hard, rocky, drought-stricken, and laden with weeds. Cultivation requires a daily struggle. We struggle to overcome the drought of peace as our enemies flourish in evil deeds. We struggle to penetrate the hard, rocky soil of reluctance by friends and family to accept the gospel truth of salvation. We struggle with the thorns of sin as we strain against human nature to imitate the character of Jesus. And we struggle in the midst of the sickness, disease, decay, and death that accompany our earthly existence.

But the hard work and bitter tears of sowing *will* reap a bountiful harvest and joyful laughter. Success is guaranteed because the master gardener superintends. His method of cultivation breaks up the fallow ground of gospel indifference by our loved ones and brings fruit. Consider Manasseh, king of Judah, who committed idolatry, sacrificed his sons and practiced witchcraft. But when God removed His protection and the Assyrians dominated the nation, Manasseh humbled himself as affliction turned his heart to God (2 Chron. 33).

When praying for the salvation of loved ones, pray also for the strength to comfort them in their afflictions and not to remove the afflictions. Sometimes it takes extreme measures to get the attention of the disobedient. But it is better to sow in tears and reap in joy—the way to heaven is scattered with thorns that assign value to the rose petals. Pray, "Teach me the glory of the cross I bear, teach me the value of my thorns. Show me that I have climbed to Thee by the path of pain. Show me that my tears have made my rainbow."[187]

July 3

He Hears Our Desperate Pleas

Listen to my cry, for I am in desperate need; rescue me from those who pursue me, for they are too strong for me. Ps. 142:6, NIV.

Eight-year-old Tessa heard her mother whisper in utter desperation that only a miracle could save her little brother who suffered from a brain tumor. They had exhausted their finances and could not afford surgery. So, Tessa took her savings to the pharmacist who busily talked to his brother. Getting his attention, she told him her brother was really sick and she wanted to buy a miracle with her savings of $1.11. The pharmacist shrugged, but his brother said, "Well, what a coincidence … A dollar and eleven cents - the exact price of a miracle for little brothers." A neurosurgeon, his brother successfully operated on Tessa's brother.[188]

Desperate like Tessa's mother, the woman with the issue of blood sought a solution. She had used up all human options and now yearned for a miracle. For twelve long years she had hemorrhaged from abnormal uterine bleeding, spending her life savings on doctors. Still, her condition worsened. In fact, the medical treatments caused her great suffering (Mark 5:25, 26). Physically growing weak and anemic from the chronic loss of blood, she emotionally endured the stigma of a social outcast. Jewish laws prescribed a woman with a menstrual period unclean for seven days—anyone who touched her as well as anything she sat or lay on remained unclean until evening (Lev. 15:19-23).

However, desperation can be a valuable emotion. Having nearly abandoned all hope, the desperate cannot see a human end to problems. Only at this point do many reach out and touch Jesus. Having witnessed Jesus' healing miracles, she believed in His healing power. In desperation she called out to Him by touching His garment. "Immediately her bleeding stopped and she felt in her body that she was freed from her suffering" (Mark 5:29, NIV). He heard her call, subdued the enemy, and eliminated her desperate need.

The Holy Spirit uses the state of desperation to reach the unreachable who have exhausted their search for healing in all the wrong places. In their search they forage in the bottom of a bottle or the illegal fluids in needles or in unhealthy relationships or crime and mayhem. Many finally reach rock bottom, a place where there is nowhere else to go but up. Then and only then do they unclench the fist that tightened in desperation at the futility of their lives and grasp the hand waiting to rescue them.

When it appears that God is not listening, do not despair. He dare not always give us what we want when we want it because then we need nothing, not even Him. Thus, desperation is a great motivator that obliges us to turn away from ourselves and reach out to the mighty El Shaddai. In humility and faith, call on Him anytime, anywhere, and for any need, and wait for His answer. He is listening.

July 4

Without Fear of Evil

But all who listen to me will live in peace, untroubled by fear of harm. Prov. 1:33, NLT.

"Then Samuel took a flask of oil and poured it on Saul's head and kissed him, saying, 'Has not the LORD anointed you leader over his inheritance?'" (1 Sam. 10:1). Pouring oil over the head of the first king of Israel symbolized the anointing of the Holy Spirit to comfort and guide. He said, "The Spirit of the LORD will come upon you in power ... and you will be changed into a different person. God is with you" (verses 6, 7).

As long as Saul remained obedient, God guaranteed his security and peace. Led by the Holy Spirit in godliness, Saul commanded the respect of the Israelites with courage and authority after his people wept over a threat by the Ammonites. "When Saul heard their words, the Spirit of God came upon him in power, and he burned with anger" (1 Sam. 11:6, NLT). And by the power of God, his army mightily defeated the Ammonites (1 Sam. 11).

But Saul turned a corner on His peace and the well-being of the nations through disobedience. After Samuel anointed him king, he instructed, "Go down to Gilgal ahead of me. I will join you there to sacrifice burnt offerings and peace offerings. You must wait seven days until I arrive and give you further instructions" (1 Sam. 10:8, NLT). Impatient and distressed over the gathering Philistine army, Saul, trusting in himself, sacrificed a burnt offering, which was a sacred duty performed only by priests. This act sounded the death knell of a dynasty through Saul's lineage. But God mercifully gave Him another test of obedience.

Apparently, the pride, power, and prestige of his kingly stature provided a stronghold for Satan who changed Saul from a Spirit-filled man to an arrogant, disobedient reprobate. In defiance of God, Saul spared the Amalekite king and confiscated his livestock. Again, Samuel challenged him, and Saul proved his escalating ungodliness by lying and blaming his actions on his soldiers (1 Sam. 15). Thus, his defiance estranged him from God who rejected him and snatched away the kingdom. Now his peace was utterly shattered.

God's Spirit departed from Saul, leaving a void quickly filled by evil spirits. The Bible counsels to "grieve not the holy Spirit of God with whom you were sealed for the day of redemption" (Eph. 4:30). But Saul's defiance snuffed out every flame of Holy Ghost fire that had illuminated his soul and left dead, cold ashes of ungodliness. And fear accompanies an empty soul.

"Oh that you had paid attention to my commandments! Then your peace would have been like a river, and your righteousness like the waves of the sea" (Isa. 48:18, ESV). There is no peace apart from obedience to God, apart from a relationship with God, and apart from the favor of God. Peace is a trade-off between God and man—we give Him our allegiance and He ensures inner peace now and incredible heavenly peace later.

July 5

Turn to Jesus

"Do not be afraid ... "You have done all this evil; yet do not turn away from the LORD, but serve the LORD with all your heart." 1 Sam. 12:20, NIV.

"Human beings, like plants, grow in the soil of acceptance, not in the atmosphere of rejection."[189] The Israelites rejected Samuel's sons as their prophets, rejected God as their King, and cried out for an earthly king (1 Sam. 8:5). Samuel keenly felt this rebuff. But God said, "It is not you they have rejected, but they have rejected me as their king" (verse 7). Even so, in mercy God had Samuel warn them of the perils of serving a human king. Still they persisted in turning away from God (verse 19).

Who do we have to turn to when we turn away from God? When many of the other disciples left Jesus' service, Jesus asked if the twelve disciples wanted to leave as well. Simon Peter answered, "Lord, to whom shall we go? You have the words of eternal life" (John 6:68, NKJV). And, he is right. Satan lays trap after trap to ensnare us. But when the blast of the terrible one is as a storm against the wall, God will be to His people a refuge from the storm (Isa. 25:4).

God is our refuge, but Satan has perfected a proven system of turning us away from Him. When we harbor any sin, Satan gains a foothold in our lives. Once he penetrates the barrier erected by righteousness, he tempts us to greater sin, persuades us that things are hopeless, and we land in the valley of defeat. Should we buy into his lies, we abandon Jesus, our safety net. But thankfully, He never abandons *us*. A simple prayer for forgiveness will reinstall Him as Lord of our life.

Satan manipulated Judas Iscariot to betray Jesus for thirty pieces of silver. After Satan possessed Judas, he persuaded him to present to the chief priests and the officers of the temple guard a plot to betray Jesus (Luke 22:3-5). Then Satan used Judas' despair over his betrayal of Jesus as a wedge. Seeing Jesus condemned to death, Judas repented of betraying the innocent blood and attempted to return the silver to the chief priests and elders. They disparaged Judas, so he tossed the silver at their feet and hanged himself (Matt. 27:3-5). Unable to put his sin behind him, Judas succumbed to and acted upon feelings of overwhelming hopelessness.

Similarly, self-absorbed, impetuous Peter dismissed Jesus' clear warnings that on the night of His capture His disciples would abandon Him. And He warned Peter unequivocally that, before the cock crowed, he would deny Jesus three times. When Jesus' prediction became a reality, Peter, full of remorse and shame but unlike Judas, repented and received forgiveness. That made all the difference in the world.

Turn to Jesus. Whatever difficulty, setback, evil, or loss you are enduring, seek Jesus. The Lord is a strong tower; the righteous run to Him and are safe. He is a rock and a fortress and a deliverer. Turn to Him!

July 6

God Favors the Lowly

Though the LORD is on high, he looks upon the lowly, but the proud he knows from afar. Ps. 138:6, NIV.

Aurora, a young preteen, walked in silence with her mother on the seaside after a violent thunderstorm. Lying on the sand were hundreds of starfish washed up by the storm and struggling to breathe outside of their watery environment. As she walked, Aurora scooped up many and tossed them back into the sea. As the seashore covered many miles, she had no hope of rescuing all the beached starfish. Soon, her mother broke the silence and discussed the insignificance of starfish and how the few she had thrown back didn't matter. Aurora, holding a starfish in each hand, responded that they mattered to her and to them.[190]

Unlike man, there is no partiality in God; we all matter to Him. Society holds the powerful and rich in high esteem while disrespecting the poor and lowly. But God regards not the rich above the poor or the exalted above the lowly, for He equally loves the work of His hands—all of His children (Job 34:19). Still, He greatly esteems the lowly who are identified by a meek spirit and humble themselves under the mighty hand of God (1 Peter 5:5, 6). The lowly spirit reveals itself when sin is exposed in their lives, for when rebuked they confess, repent, and accept the consequences.

"For thus says the One who is high and lifted up, who inhabits eternity, whose name is Holy: 'I dwell in the high and holy place, and also with him who is of a contrite and lowly spirit, to revive the spirit of the lowly, and to revive the heart of the contrite'" (Isa. 57:15, ESV). The God who is and was and is to come, who spans the present, past, and the future, welcomes the penitent and humble to inhabit eternity with Him. He intends to replace the lost angels, expelled from heaven alongside Lucifer, with purchases of Jesus' blood. The new heavenly tenants must possess a lowly spirit opposite from the proud spirit that condemned Lucifer (Eze. 28:17).

The lowly, of whom Jesus approves and guarantees a place in the kingdom of God, are poor in spirit (Matt. 5:3). A highly regarded cohort of people whom God exalts, they recognize their penchant to sinfulness, their helplessness, their status as the chief of sinners, and that Jesus is their only hope. To them, others are regarded as "higher than I" because after looking daily in the face of Jesus who "made himself of no reputation, and took on him the form of a servant" self is minimized (Phil. 2:7).

Spiritually bankrupt as we all are, the lowly are hypersensitive to the fact that God's grace and mercy are the only barriers standing between them and death and that they can never repay the debt owed to Jesus for bankrolling their salvation with His life. As spiritually destitute as the materially penniless, the lowly fall broken and penitent at the feet of Jesus in full surrender, trusting that He will provide life-giving spiritual nourishment.

July 7

Anger Management

Be angry and do not sin; do not let the sun go down on your anger, and give no opportunity to the devil. Eph. 4:26, 27, ESV.

A father told his ill-tempered son to bang a nail in the fence each time he lost his temper. On the first day, the young man used up a small bag of nails. Each day he banged fewer nails in the fence until finally he checked his anger before it erupted. Then his father suggested he pull a nail out of the fence each day he held his temper. Elated, the son told his father that he removed all the nails. Replied his father, "You've done well, my son, but look at the holes in the fence. The fence will never be the same. When you say things in anger, they leave a scar just like this one."[191]

Anger, a brawny emotion directed at a real or perceived injustice, strides the scale from beneficial to sin. Anger and righteous anger/righteous indignation are not the same. Righteous anger/righteous indignation, a permitted exercise, rises in the face of sin and injustices and signals the necessity of behavior modification on someone's part. Indignant at the selfishness and hypocrisy of the Pharisees who fashioned laws against healing on the Sabbath, Jesus "looked around at them with anger, grieved by their hardness of heart" (Mark 3:5, ESV)

However, anger that rises to destruction and chaos is a sin. "See to it ... that no bitter root grows up to cause trouble and defile many" (Heb. 12:15, NIV). The seeds of unresolved anger become noxious when they produce weeds of bitterness, hate, and unforgiveness that threaten our health, our relationships, and our Christian walk. Anger that is allowed to fester opens the door to Satan's evil influence and invites in his lies and deceptions. Once he steps in, situations escalate in intensity and result. Count the number of times defendants have pled temporary insanity after anger has escalated to murder and mayhem.

Christians who follow Jesus' example have a role similar to a fire retardant. In the face of harsh words or escalating anger, Jesus is pleased when we work to reduce the flammability of the situation or delay the combustion. Wisely, Solomon prescribes a God-ordained way to cool down the flames, "A gentle answer turns away wrath, but a harsh word stirs up anger" (Prov. 15:1, NIV). The carnal nature demands that we respond word for word until we say or do something that we might regret for a lifetime. But the way of Jesus is to exercise self-control and remain humble enough to be right but compliant enough to yield.

"Whoever is slow to anger is better than the mighty and he who rules his spirit than he who takes a city" (Prov. 16:32). Using the biblical method of anger management, Jesus' followers are equipped to stop the vicious cycle of escalating anger to preserve our personal relationships, our health, and our walk with God. Satan promotes the belief that when right stand your ground but, "Anger, if not restrained, is frequently more hurtful to us than the injury that provokes it."[192] Sinful anger lies in the bosom of fools not in the heart of the wise. Be wise!

July 8

Benevolence Not Tyranny

In righteousness you will be established: Tyranny will be far from you; you will have nothing to fear. Terror will be far removed; it will not come near you. Isa. 54:14, NIV.

In sixth century Athens, Peisistratus, with popular support and some intrigue, overthrew the government and became tyrant. Overall, his three-term rule as tyrant was benevolent and productive. In the original Greek, tyrant simply meant a leader who possessed absolute power after a successful coup with the support of the populous of the existing government. The word tyrant comes from the Latin *tyrannus*, meaning "illegitimate ruler" and the Greek word *týrannos*, meaning "sovereign, master." However, tyrant has taken on a negative connotation.

Today, tyranny is the selfish, oppressive rule of an absolute ruler who steps on human rights and spits on human dignity. Earthly dictators like Iraq's Saddam Hussein and Cambodia's Pot Pol had consciences seared so thoroughly as to silence the voice of the Holy Spirit. Bearing their rotten fruit, they swayed as corrupt trees in Satan's shadow. These evil megalomaniacs instilled fear in their populace through illogical massacre, religious persecution, inhumane imprisonment, torture, rape, and other demonic atrocities. When Satan gains authority, rotten fruit is always the result.

Tyranny is Satan's personal mode of rule. An illegitimate ruler, he used deception in the Garden of Eden to wrench authority from its inhabitants to imprison the citizens of earth. His kingdom is based on hate and destruction, and he hates every created being, including his fellow demons (John 10:10). Jesus shut him out of heaven, but Satan vengefully took a third of the angels with him and beguiled Eve, starting a domino effect that left all humans facing a death sentence. But Jesus ransomed us and freed us from Satan's captivity.

One day God will judge the workers of evil ushered into our world through Satan's reign. He will crush tyranny and oppression along with fear under His heavy feet of justice. And the evil that metastases in unregenerate hearts as an aggressive cancer spreading malignant cells will undergo radical surgery by God's own hand. Evil will no longer have space or opportunity to multiply and destroy (Heb. 2:14).

Until then, the kingdom of God within us moves us from darkness to the light of heaven; snatches us from the bondage to sin, offers forgiveness and a place among the faithful (Acts 26:18). This spiritual kingdom makes available to humans here on earth the holiness of God, a holiness unique to heaven. But the day is coming when Jesus will reign benevolently and justly as King of kings in the holy mountain of God, and the redeemed will dwell in a peaceable habitation and in quiet resting places. "Violence shall no more be heard in thy land, wasting nor destruction within thy borders; but thou shalt call thy walls Salvation, and thy gates Praise" (Isa. 60:18).

July 9

Sin Blocks the Blessings

Fear not, neither be dismayed: take all the people of war with you, and arise, go up to Ai: see, I have given into your hand the king of Ai. Joshua 8:1.

The Israelites fled like cowards from the men of Ai who chased them to their tents. They were at the Promised Land and were trusting God to fight their battles against the inhabitants of Canaan. Exuberant in the thrill of victory, they reveled over the previous battle at Jericho where they marched, shouted, and blew trumpets and the walls fell down, allowing them to easily overpower the foe. But the battle at Ai was different. Overconfident and failing to consult their Captain, Joshua sent spies to Ai who reported that the city was easy pickings. They marched proudly into Ai but were humiliated and soundly defeated.

Disgraced and bewildered in the agony of defeat, Joshua now sought guidance from God who pointed out the sin in the camp, which blocked His promised protection. The late Moses had delivered God's requirement throughout their long sojourn—blessings for obedience and cursing for disobedience. "Now, Israel, what does the LORD your God require from you, but to fear the LORD your God, to walk in all His ways" (Deut. 10:12, NASB). "No good thing does he withhold from those who walk uprightly" (Ps. 84:11, ESV).

It took a humiliating defeat for Joshua's continued spiritual growth. "Therefore let anyone who thinks that he stands take heed lest he fall" (1 Cor 10:12, ESV). Joshua learned the valuable lesson that God's people are nearest to a fall after a great victory. "Pride is the most pregnant cause of presumption. In all its various shapes it is the fountain of carnal security."[193] Presumption and pride are used by the enemy as weapons of defeat; thus, our security lies in daily submitting our will to God and not trusting self to single-handedly manage our affairs. Apart from God we can do nothing but fail.

The Israelites could not and did not prevail until they excised sin from the camp (Joshua 7). Sin is like a cancer. Until surgically removed, it consumes and destroys the entire body. One rogue cell invades and corrupts the good cells and grows until it takes complete control; then it overwhelms one or more systems, bringing death. Similarly, greed overpowered Achan and grew, causing his spiritual and physical death.

Thus, God impressed on the minds of His chosen people how egregious sin is to Him; that no sin is slight in His eyes. The enemy lulls many people, like Achan, into complacency regarding sin, the transgression of God's law (1 John 3:4). Some believe that, under grace, they are relieved of obedience to the Word. If that were true, Jesus died in vain, but He died because God's law is settled and unchangeable.

Although God is merciful and forgiving, He will judge the guilty sooner or later. Achan's judgment came sooner. After he was exposed and punished, God forgave Israel and conquered their enemy, thereby, restoring His protection and His other blessings.

July 10

The Long Arms of God

Surely the arm of the LORD is not too short to save, nor his ear too dull to hear. Isa. 59:1, 2, NIV.

In the 1993 movie *The Fugitive* a one-armed man kills Richard Kimble's wife. Kimble discovers the man in his home minutes after the attack, and, while wrestling with the killer, discovers that one of his arms is a prosthesis. The murderer escapes, leaving Kimble as the lone suspect in his wife's murder. Kimble flees after a train accident on his way to the state penitentiary and, in a desperate search for the one-armed man to prove his innocence, returns to his hometown. After much heart-stopping action and intrigue, Kimble locates the one-armed man and is exonerated.

There is an obvious reason why the killer opted for a prosthetic arm rather than operate with one arm. Many of the basic activities successfully completed with two arms would be frustrating and well-nigh impossible for a person missing an arm. Considered disabled, a one-armed person has many limitations and may need assistance to function normally. Combine deafness with the confines of having one arm and the situation is bleak. Thus, the image of God with one short or one amputated arm and a deaf ear conjures up helplessness and restrictions.

But Isaiah's graphic image conveys that God has limitless power and no restrictions. He is an autonomous, self-governing, self-existent, munificent monarch with immeasurable might and in total control of the universe He created. "For the LORD your God is God of gods and Lord of lords, the great God, mighty and awesome" (Deut. 10:17, NIV). He has a mighty arm and a strong and lifted up right hand symbolizing His miraculous deeds, His consummate prowess, and His effortless victories in the battles against both spiritual powers of darkness and foolish human foes (Ps. 89:13). "No one can deliver out of my hand," God declares (Isa. 43:13).

While on the road to the Promised Land, Moses despaired at providing food for six hundred thousand ungrateful families. God countered, "Is the LORD's arm too short? You will now see whether or not what I say will come true for you" (Num. 11:23). He summoned a strong wind that drove quail in from the sea to the camp where they hovered three feet above the ground. Each person easily gathered no less than sixty bushels of quail (Num. 11:31, 32). Moses' despair resulted from looking at how short his arms were—at His own limitations—not at the illimitable power and resources of God.

Thank God His arms are long enough, His heart is compassionate enough, and His ears are attuned to hear the call of the lost. Furthermore, we can rest in the assurance that He is powerful enough to save. The Word made flesh is "God's power working unto salvation [for deliverance from eternal death] to everyone who believes with a personal trust and a confident surrender and firm reliance" (Rom. 1:16, AMP). Look away from the short arms that hang just below your waist and lock your gaze on the limitless assets and might of the Sovereign of heaven, on His long, long arms and superhuman hearing.

July 11

The Fountainhead of Life

Seek Me and live. Amos 5:4, NKJV.

Pursuant to a study of shipwreck victims during World War II, researchers found that the maximum amount of survival time before dehydration caused death amounted to eleven days. However, more current data indicates that death, a slow, torturous death, occurs between ten to fourteen days. Dehydration transpires when the body loses too much fluids without replenishing them since cells and tissues need a "delicate fluid-salt balance" to remain healthy. This loss of fluids may "result from illness; a hot, dry climate; prolonged exposure to sun or high temperatures; not drinking enough water; and overuse of diuretics or other medications that increase urination."[194]

Death by extreme thirst is slow but sure. Dehydration begins with a great thirst for water, and deprived of that water, the victim's mouth becomes dry, tears dry up, and muscle cramps develop. As the level of dehydration increases, nausea and vomiting develop, adding to the loss of fluids and electrolytes. When dehydration reaches a deadly level, kidney function stops, heart rate increases, and all the systems fail.

Inside every created being, God has placed a spiritual thirst satisfied solely by drinking the living water—the Fountainhead. This thirst is a safety mechanism for the soul, and God is the source of "the fountain of living waters" (Jer. 2:13). Sinners have a standing invitation to come to the waters and drink freely without cost since Jesus already paid the price (Isa. 55:1). Drinking from these springs is our guarantee of immortality. Jesus says, "But whosoever drinks of the water ... shall never thirst; but the water ... will become in him a well of water springing up to eternal life" (John 4:14, NASB).

Psalm 119:9 tells us that the only way we can cleanse our ways is "by taking heed thereto according to thy word." Thus, the living water symbolizes the Word of God. Reading the Word is as essential to our spiritual life as drinking literal water is to our physical life. In less than two weeks, we can suffer and die from water deprivation. Just as surely, our spiritual lives will die when we fail to read and study the Word daily. And pursuing a saving relationship with God cannot be retained without quality time spent in His presence.

Dehydration of the soul is equally deliberate and torturous. Those who reject the living water and hold on to their thirst will surely die. Jeremiah cautioned, "All who leave you [God] end up as fools, Deserters with nothing to show for their lives, who walk off from God, fountain of living waters—and wind up dead!" (Jer. 17:13, MSG). But Jesus offers, "If anyone is thirsty, let him come to me and drink" (John 7:37, NIV).

Delight in His law, meditate on it day and night, and thrive like the tree planted by the waters bringing forth abundant fruit (Ps. 1:1-3). We are free to drink the water of no price straight from the Fountainhead where a daily draught will quench our thirst forever.

July 12

Conspiracy Theories and the Kingdom of God

Do not say, 'A conspiracy,' concerning all that this people call a conspiracy, nor be afraid of their threats, nor be troubled. The LORD of hosts, Him you shall hallow; let Him be your fear, and let Him be your dread. Isa. 8:12, 13, NKJV.

In the age of the Internet, the conspiracy theory, disavowed by the scientific and academic communities but embraced by certain fringe elements, explains that several historical, current, or future events are secretly promoted by conspirators. For instance, many people believe that there is a conspiracy aimed at a one-world government controlling the entire world. They posit that the world's richest, most influential banking families with hereditary bloodlines will control the government. And people believe that this group has orchestrated certain current events such as the economic meltdown, 9/11, and our failed foreign policy to dominate the world.

But the Word directs us not to be troubled or afraid of the threat of conspiracy. The truth about a one-world government that will control the world is clearly established in the Word of God. Daniel chapter two gives the history and demise of the four dominating world kingdoms—Babylon, Media-Persia, Greece, and Rome. But Barbarians conquered Rome and divided it into the nations of Europe, save three nations that were eliminated. However, the final world kingdom will be the kingdom of God. "And in the days of these kings the God of heaven will set up a kingdom which shall never be destroyed; and the kingdom shall not be left to other people; it shall break in pieces and consume all these kingdoms, and it shall stand forever" (Dan. 2:44, NKJV).

Daniel saw Jesus receiving His kingdom. "I was watching in the night visions, And behold, One like the Son of Man, Coming with the clouds of heaven! He came to the Ancient of Days, And they brought Him near before Him. Then to Him was given dominion and glory and a kingdom, that all peoples, nations, and languages should serve Him. His dominion *is* an everlasting dominion, which shall not pass away, And His kingdom *the one* which shall not be destroyed" (Daniel 7:13, 14, NKJV).

Jesus receives His literal kingdom before He returns to earth to gather His saints for the return trip to heaven. Then, after the judgment, the kingdom will be given "to the people, the saints of the Most High" (Dan. 7:27, NKJV), those who serve God in "righteousness and peace and joy in the Holy Spirit" (Rom. 14:17, NKJV). Not everyone who calls themselves Christians, who faithfully attend church or who do good deeds, will enter the kingdom of heaven, but only those who do the will of God. What an awful rebuff some will hear, "I never knew you. Away from me, you evildoers!" (Matt. 7:23, NIV).

The day of the final kingdom is fast approaching. Daniel saw a stone, not cut by human hands, shatter the final nations on earth and watched the wind blow them away without a trace. This stone then "became a great mountain and filled the whole earth," symbolizing the ushering in of the glorious one-world government ruled by the King of kings (Dan. 2:35, NKJV).

July 13

Resisting Your Enemy the Devil

Be sober, be vigilant; because your adversary the devil, as a roaring lion, walketh about, seeking whom he may devour. 1 Peter 5:8.

Although a lion's diet typically consists of large animals like antelopes, wildebeest, and zebras, they also devour the flesh of human beings. For instance, two lions in Kenya began a reign of terror on railroad construction workers who were building the Kenya-Uganda Railway Bridge over the Tsavo River in Kenya in the 1800s. Under the cover of darkness, the lions stealthily invaded and dragged the helpless victims from their tents. Legends abound that these huge eight- to nine-foot-long maneless male Tsavo lions killed and ate the flesh of 135 to 140 men.

Lions live in communities of ten to twenty lions called prides. Each lion in a pride can eat seventy-five pounds of meat at a setting; thus, hunger motivates them to travel up to fifteen miles in a day to find a meal. Depending on the prey, they use one of three strategies to catch them. If the prey is swift of foot, they use their thirty-five-mile-per-hour speed to overtake it. For slower moving prey, such as reptiles and rodents, they employ a sneak attack. And at times they apply brute power to steal prey caught by another animal.

Satan is as vicious and destructive as these fearsome lions. But God, in His love for His children, amply warned us of Satan's goal and strategies. His invisibility makes him a very formidable foe, so God warns us that "our struggle is not against flesh and blood, but ... against the powers of this dark world and against the spiritual forces of evil in the heavenly realms" (Eph. 6:12, NIV). For the armorless victims, those who do not appreciate his evil mission and are oblivious to his resolve, he overtakes, pounces on, and devours. These victims have rejected the wise counsel of Scripture, have carelessly tossed aside the whole armor of God and must stand before Satan in their own strength.

The weak in faith, ravaged by discouragement and fear and failing to remain vigilant, allow him to sneak up on them and devour them without strong resistance. To their detriment, they believe Satan's lies and are pressed on all sides by unbelief. Under cover of darkness, these diabolical forces drag the weak victims to their lair while fast asleep in doubt, anxiety, and pain. Gleeful at their weakened condition, the demons go for the jugular.

Wake up! Satan is on the prowl! Shape up in readiness! Daily put on the whole armor of God to counter his attacks. Only a knowledge of the truth permits an "escape from the trap of the devil" (2 Tim. 2:26, NIV), for unless we are aware of and prepared for his schemes, he will surely outwit us every time (2 Cor. 2:11). "Satan studies every indication of the frailty of human nature, he marks the sins which each individual is inclined to commit, and then he" provides opportunities to gratify those evil tendencies.[195]

Resist him and he is compelled to retreat. And resist him standing firm in the faith.

July 14

A Rainbow of Promise

You can depend on God's Word. 1 Cor. 1:9, Clear Word.

A quarrel of self-importance arose between the colors of the world. Green claimed importance as he suggests life and hope, and Blue argued his sky and sea color indicates serenity. But, Yellow dismissed their seriousness, specifying she brings laughter and warmth while Orange contended she had the beautiful color of health and strength. Red exploded that she is supreme since the color of blood signifies bravery, and Purple announced that his royal color commands respect. Lastly, indigo retorted quietly that he is the color of silence and represents reflection and thought. The colors quarreled so shrilly, they awakened Thunder that boomed, loudly signaling Rain to fall. Finally, Rain labeled their pride foolish and enjoined them to clasp hands and form a bow across the sky to signify hope for tomorrow.[196]

The rainbow is a visible sign of a covenant between God and His people. After a global flood destroyed the earth, fulfilling a judgment from God, He covenanted with Noah, thusly: "I have set my rainbow in the clouds, and it will be the sign of the covenant between me and the earth. Whenever I bring clouds over the earth and the rainbow appears in the clouds, I will remember my covenant between me and you and all living creatures.... Never again will the waters become a flood to destroy all life" (Gen. 9:13-15, NIV).

No power in heaven will breach that promise, and no power on earth can for God's Word is faithful and true. The law of God, His Word, is the equivalent of His character, a sacred revelation of His will, and His Son, Jesus, is the Word incarnate. Neither God's character nor His law can change, for the law is His character in human language.[197] While physically on earth, Jesus obeyed the Word and quoted it implicitly. For instance, explaining at the Last Supper that one disciple in His inner circle would betray Him, Jesus stated, "The Son of man goeth *as it is written* of him: but woe unto that man by whom the Son of man is betrayed!" (Matt 26:24).

We are the recipients of very great and precious promises that come directly from the heart of God who cannot lie—all His words are true (Ps. 119:160). To our great benefit, He promises and delivers all we need for life and godliness (2 Peter 1:4). And the greatest promise is the one that put enmity between Satan and mankind. This promise, fulfilled in Jesus, allows us to establish a saving relationship with God.

Through the gift of a Redeemer, promised thousands of years before He arrived, God allows us to partake of His divine nature so we can escape the corruption of our own evil lusts (2 Peter 1:4). To achieve this goal, Jesus disrobed His purity, swathed us in His white robe of righteousness, and then dressed Himself in our filthy, dirty sins. And He wrote the laws in our hearts as a spiritual guide. Should we periodically succumb to the old corrupt nature "the Lord is faithful, and He will strengthen and protect you from the evil one" (2 Thess. 3:3, NASB). His rainbow of promises have held true from the beginning and will endure forever (Ps. 119:160).

July 15

Anxiety Free

Casting all your care upon Him, for He cares for you. 1 Peter 5:7, NKJV.

Useless worrying can make us anxiety-ridden, but we can avoid that if we make two days in every week worry free. "One of these days is Yesterday with all its mistakes and cares, its faults and blunders, its aches and pains. Yesterday has passed forever beyond our control.... We cannot undo a single act we performed; we cannot erase a single word we said.... The other day we should not worry about is Tomorrow with all its possible adversities, its burdens, its large promise and its poor performance; Tomorrow is also beyond our immediate control. Tomorrow's sun will rise, either in splendor or behind a mask of clouds ... Until it does, we have no stake in Tomorrow ... This leaves ... Today. Any person can fight the battle of just one day."[198]

Anxiety, dreading things that have yet to happen, fills its host with fear and uncertainty, and some forty million Americans suffer a range of anxiety disorders from mild to extreme. Fittingly, Jesus chastised Martha for her anxiety and worry. At her home Jesus talked to them about eternal things while Mary sat at His feet listening intently. But Martha scurried around in an attempt to feed and welcome her guests. She implored Jesus to compel Mary to help, but He responded, "Martha, Martha, you are worried and troubled about many things. But one thing is needed, and Mary has chosen that good part" (Luke 10:41, 42, NKJV).

Knowing that anxiety is unsettling and distracting, Jesus also cautioned His disciples. "Therefore I tell you, do not worry about your life, what you will eat; or about your body, what you will wear" (Luke 12:22, NIV). But when layoffs are imminent, how is it possible to stop worrying about job security as it takes money to buy food, clothes, and shelter? How is it possible to stop worrying about our children, our health, our environment, our enemies, and our well-being in a chaotic, violent, and uncertain world?

It requires faith. "The beginning of anxiety is the end of faith; and the beginning of true faith is the end of anxiety."[199] Faith in God and trust in His exact promises are the panacea for worry. As Mary knew and Martha learned, faith is built at the feet of Jesus. Wisely, they chose the righteousness of God and the cultivation of a childlike faith. "I tell you the truth, anyone who doesn't receive the Kingdom of God like a child will never enter it" (Mark 10:15, NLT).

Children are naturally honest, trusting, genuine, and free of anxiety because they trust their parents and their promises. Likewise, we obtain peace after acknowledging our helplessness, surrendering our worries, and yielding to the wisdom of our heavenly Father. "If there be anything that is capable of setting the soul in a large place it is absolute abandonment to God. It diffuses in the soul a peace that flows like a river and the righteousness which is as the waves of the sea."[200] Casting our cares on Him, we find sweet rest for our souls.

July 16

Arising in the First Resurrection

For you, O LORD, have delivered my soul from death, my eyes from tears, my feet from stumbling, that I may walk before the LORD in the land of the living. Ps. 116:8, 9, NIV.

After God separated the sky from the land and created the celestial objects, He fashioned sea creatures, birds, animals, and all nature. Nature is made to glorify Him and testify of His dominion, and within each He instilled obedience to His commands. But when He created Adam from the dry clay, He placed within him a seed of choice despite the possibility that Adam might choose contrarily. Our all-wise God well knew that both bitter and sweet—selfishness and love—accompany the seed of choice. Without the seed of choice the end would be predictable but love would be absent. And the God of love could only create one who loved in return.[201]

Throughout the history of the great controversy between good and evil, humanity has exercised its freedom of choice. When God chose the nation to broadcast His truth throughout the world, He cautioned them to choose wisely. "See, I have set before you today life and good, death and evil, in that I command you today to love the LORD your God, to walk in His ways, and to keep His commandments, His statutes, and His judgments, that you may live … But, if your heart turns away so that you do not hear … and worship other gods and serve them … you shall surely perish" (Deut. 30:15-18, NKJV).

The two choices nestled in our freedom of choice, namely good and life or evil and death, bring about two results at Jesus' return. Both the living and resurrected dead will physically stand before God in judgment. A time is rapidly marching down the halls of time when "all who are in their graves will hear his voice and come out—those who have done good will rise to live, and those who have done evil will rise to be condemned" (John 5:28, 29, NIV). Likewise, "many of them that sleep in the dust of the earth shall awake, some to everlasting life, and some to shame and everlasting contempt" (Dan. 12:2).

How blessed are sanctified believers to participate in the first resurrection! "The second death has no power over them" (Rev. 20:6, ISV). But rebellious sinners who chose poorly will suffer a second death. In vision, John describes the investigative judgment where the books are opened and the resurrected are judged according to their deeds recorded in the book of remembrance and the book of life and sentenced (Phil. 4:3). If anyone's name is not found written in the book of life, he is sentenced to the lake of fire, which is "the second death" (Rev. 20:11-15).

The second death, justice for sinners who spurned a lifetime of offers of mercy, is powerless over those who surrender to the will of God and live righteously. During the history of time on earth, God has sent untold messengers with His ageless message of salvation to beg us to choose life. God is "not wishing that any should perish, but that all should reach repentance" (2 Peter 3:9, ESV). Arising in the first resurrection boils down to our choosing to obey the messages of life.

July 17

Spiritualism Is an Abomination to God

And the king said to her, "Do not be afraid. What did you see?" And the woman said to Saul, "I saw a spirit ascending out of the earth." 1 Sam. 28:13, NKJV.

Sarah Winchester, heir to the Winchester rifle fortune, did a bizarre thing to fend off death. She hired a countless parade of carpenters to build rooms on her house nonstop day and night. After her baby died and then her husband died a short time later, Sarah consulted a medium who told her that the spirits of those killed by the Winchester rifle were haunting her family and had killed her husband and child and would kill her if the sound of hammers ceased. They lied, but for thirty-eight years, until Sarah's death, the sound of banging hammers never ended, increasing the house from 8 rooms to 160 rooms with doors that led to nowhere, stairs that reached the ceiling, windows that opened in the floor, and other oddities.

The untrue but popular belief is that a ghost is the disembodied spirit of a dead person stuck between earth and heaven and can be summoned by a medium. God condemned dabbling in the occult and spiritism, labeling it an abomination and sentencing the offenders to death (Deut. 18:10, 11; Lev. 20:27). But Saul consulted a medium to conjure up the deceased Samuel and inquire what he should do about the gathering Philistine army. The medium said she saw spirits coming out of the earth. "So [Saul] said …, 'What is his form?' And she said, 'An old man is coming up, and he is covered with a mantle.' And Saul *perceived* that it was Samuel" (1 Sam. 28:14, NKJV).

But we do not have to perceive when we have the truth about the dead sent directly from the God of truth through the pen of the wisest man who ever lived. "For the living know that they will die, but the dead know nothing; they have no further reward, and even the memory of them is forgotten. Their love, their hate and their jealousy have long since vanished; *never again will they have a part in anything that happens under the sun*" (Eccl. 9:5, 6, NIV). Since the dead know nothing and are oblivious to everything under the sun, then who talked to Saul during the séance?

Saul queried a familiar spirit. "He did not communicate with Samuel, the prophet of God; but through the sorceress *he held intercourse with Satan* [1 Chron. 10:13, 14]. Satan could not present the real Samuel, but did present a counterfeit, that served his purpose of deception."[202] Satan and his demons, today, still pose as disembodied dead people and have the ability to imitate their walk, their voices, and their mannerism thus thoroughly deceiving those who neglect the Word of God.

Satan is powerful enough to "deceive, if possible, even the elect" with great delusions (Matt. 24:24, NKJV). Paul says "the work of Satan [is] displayed in all kinds of counterfeit miracles, signs and wonders, and in every sort of evil that deceives those who are perishing. They perish because they refused to love the truth and so be saved. For this reason God sends them a powerful delusion so that they will believe the lie" (2 Thess. 2:9-11, NIV). We are safe only if we trust the Word, not what we think, see, or feel when it comes to spiritualism.

July 18

Respect for God

Do not be afraid of the words which you have heard, with which the servants of the king of Assyria have blasphemed Me. 2 Kings 19:6, NKJV.

A 1879 statute in Maryland states, "If any person, by writing or speaking, shall blaspheme or curse God, or shall write or utter any profane words of and concerning our Saviour, Jesus Christ, or of and concerning the Trinity, or any of the persons thereof, he shall, on conviction, be fined not more than one hundred dollars, or imprisoned not more than six months, or both fined and imprisoned as aforesaid, at the discretion of the court."[203] Moreover, Old Testament law deemed blasphemy a capital offense (Lev. 24:16). Today, however, in many industrialized nations it is no longer a crime. In fact, the U.S. Constitution protects blasphemous speech under the First Amendment, and England and Wales purged their books of blasphemy laws in 2008.

Blasphemy in its truest sense is both appropriating the authority of God and showing irreverence and disrespect toward Him which God, Himself, will not tolerate. Although blasphemy is not a crime today in industrialized nations, it is a moral offense to God, for the third commandment, written by His own finger, prohibits taking His name in vain (Deut. 4:13; Ex. 20:7). In *Strong's Hebrew Dictionary*, vain is the English translation for the Hebrew word *shav*, which means empty or false. The Creator of the universe deserves and expects the highest honor and respect, not empty rhetoric and false worship. And those who flippantly denounce His name and character empty Him of His importance and stand condemned under the courts of heaven.

Taking the Lord's name in vain sweeps broader than just swearing. If we deem ourselves Christians, follow the law, brag about our relationship to God, and cannot forgive our enemy, we are taking the name of the Lord in vain. Jesus said, "Love your enemies and pray for those who persecute you" (Matt. 5:44, NASB). If we preach against stealing but are taking what does not belong to us or adding to or padding our tax account, we are using His name falsely by doing wrong in His name. Jesus said, "Let no one seek his own [profit], but each his neighbor's good" (1 Cor. 10:24, ASV).

Are we a guide for the blind, a light for those who are in the dark, an instructor of the foolish, having read in the law about knowledge and truth? If the lessons of morality, humility, unselfishness, peace, and love have not permeated our hearts, we are emptying God of His significance and are taking His name in vain (Rom. 2:17-24). He is the only reason we exist and are sustained. Amazingly, blasphemers blithely and regularly bite the hand that feeds them, both physically and spiritually.

Give God due honor, "For great is the Lord and most worthy of praise; he is to be feared above all gods" (1 Chron. 16:25, NIV). The day is coming when "at the name of Jesus every knee should bow … and every tongue confess that Jesus Christ is Lord," including blasphemers, sinners, and saints alike (Phil 2:10, 11, NIV). Give Him His due by imitating His character, for imitation is the highest compliment.

July 19

Strength to Face Tomorrow

My soul melts from heaviness; strengthen me according to Your word. Ps. 119:28, NKJV.

Imagine a tree living today that was a seedling when Nimrod, the great grandson of Noah, built the Tower of Babel! The bristlecone pine tree is believed to be the oldest living organism on the planet. Methuselah, the nickname of a living bristlecone pine tree located in Eastern California, is more than 4,000 years old. These trees survive in cold climates in rocky, sandy soil and with little precipitation miles above sea level where elements batter them unmercifully. During seasons of drought, they go dormant until the conditions are better. Although gnarled and deformed from the harsh environment, their dense resinous trunks protect them from insects, fungi, and bacteria.

Trees that live in favorable conditions grow quickly and look verdant, but none live for thousands of years like the bristlecone pines. This tree's survival is intimately connected to its adverse living conditions. Likewise, persons who experience hardships are stronger and more resilient than those who are protected from life's pounding. Although God places His elect behind an invisible barrier of protection, He allows the evil prince of this world to penetrate that barrier from time to time for our spiritual growth but always under His strict supervision. Because of His great love for His sin-prone children, He lets Satan's tempests of sorrow and pain batter us.

"We never know how much real faith we have until it is put to the test in some fierce storm; and that is the reason why the Saviour is on board. If you are ever to be strong in the Lord and the power of His might, your strength will be born in some storm."[204] The strength that endures and perseveres while in the tempests comes through the Word. To be strengthened according to the Word points to inner strength, not outer physical strength. And we are strengthened with power in our inner being only through the Spirit of God who fills us with the knowledge of God's will through wisdom and understanding so we may live a life worthy and pleasing to Him. Only then will we acquire the strength that fosters endurance and patience (Col. 1:10, 11).

Without that supernatural strength that embraces patient endurance, we cannot endure the testing circumstances of our Christian journey. Patient endurance pushes back against the adversities of life rather than buckling under in defeat. As Franklin Roosevelt observed, endurance is getting to the end of your rope, tying a knot in it, and holding on. And patient endurance is a necessity for consistent holiness. It took Holy Spirit strength for Noah to stand firm for 120 years on the promises of God and be the butt of jokes and derision by the antediluvian mockers of salvation truth (Gen. 6). But Noah daily drew on this source of strength.

That strength is obtained through prayer and faith. For when we call to Him, He answers without pause and emboldens us with sufficing strength.

July 20

The Temporary Sleep of Death

Consider and answer me, O LORD my God; light up my eyes, lest I sleep the sleep of death. Ps. 13:3, ESV.

A man's daughter became sick, and despite the doctors' best efforts, she died. Sorrow accompanied him, and inconsolable at this great loss, he cried himself to sleep for months. He became bitter and reclusive, but at the thought of his beloved daughter, his tears flowed freely. One night he dreamed he was in heaven and witnessed an endless parade of white robed toddler angels with lit candles except for one little girl. He asked why her candle remained unlit. She replied, "Father, they often relight it, but your tears always put it out."[205]

Typically, the loss of a loved one to death is accompanied by deep sorrow and intense emotional pain. Jesus declares that the dead are asleep, but we still mourn (John 11:11, 12). Since He has an empathetic understanding of the pain when a loved one is snatched away by Death, He is qualified to console us with the promise that mourning, death, and tears will cease forever (Rev. 21:4). In the meantime, we grieve, praying that God will mercifully shorten the raw, agonizing pain so we can reflect on our deceased loved one with fond memories and few tears.

When Jesus compares death to sleep, he dispels its permanence. "'Our friend Lazarus has fallen asleep; but I am going there to wake him up.' His disciples replied, 'Lord, if he sleeps, he will get better'" (John 11:11, 12, NIV) Jesus spoke of his death, but His disciples thought he meant natural sleep. So He told them plainly, "Lazarus is dead" (verse 14). Jesus demonstrated that death is short term, for He "brings death and makes alive" (1 Sam. 2:6, NIV). Using His resurrection power, "Jesus called in a loud voice, 'Lazarus, come out!' The dead man came out" from the grave after his body had lain in a state of decay for four days (John 11:43, 44, NIV).

Sleep is a suitable comparison to death. "Sleep and Death are psycho-physical brothers.... Exactly the same succession of events takes place in death that ensues when we lay ourselves in bed at night and drop off into that wonderland of unconsciousness we call Sleep."[206] As in death, when we fall asleep the lamp of sight is quenched, auditory processes end, and all physical activity ceases. And our sleep environment is usually dark and quiet, like a tomb.

God wants to fellowship with us forever and hear our praise and adoration. But in our present state of corruption, leading toward death, that is only possible for a few short years for "the dead praise not the LORD, neither any that go down into silence" (Ps. 115:17). "Also their love, and their hatred, and their envy, is now perished" (Eccl. 9:6). But those in Christ who are temporarily asleep in their graves will awaken on resurrection morning consumed by love, praise, and adoration and shouting "the LORD is my strength and my song; he has become my salvation" (Ex.15:2).

July 21

Following the Good Way

Stand at the crossroads and look; ask for the ancient paths ... where the good way is, and walk in it, and you will find rest for your souls. Jer. 6:16, NIV.

A shrewd spider kept food in his pantry by keeping his spider web clean of dead fly carcasses, thus unsuspicious flies got caught in his web. One day a fairly intelligent fly flew by and escaped the web for that very reason—no flies were there. But as he looked down, he saw crowds of flies dancing around on a piece of brown sticky paper and decided to join them. As he descended toward the sticky paper, a bee buzzed by and cautioned him not to land on the flypaper. The fairly intelligent fly demurred stating, "There's a big crowd there. Everybody's doing it. That many flies can't be wrong!"[207]

As we choose for our eternal good, God cautions us to stand at the crossroads of life and carefully reason and reflect. We cannot depend on the way forged by the majority, but we must follow Jesus who said, "If you hold to my teaching, you are really my disciples. Then you will know the truth, and the truth will set you free" (John 8:31, 32). But the modern messages offered by many pastors today appear to lift popularity and church growth higher than the pure, unmodified Word of God. Charles Spurgeon wrote, "What have you and I to do with maintaining our influence and position at the expense of truth? It is never right to do a little wrong to obtain the greatest possible good.... Your duty is to do the right: consequences are with God."

The Scriptures direct us to "Remove not the ancient landmark, which thy fathers have set" (Prov. 22:28). These landmarks are the settled Word of God and direct our mind toward holiness (Jer. 31:21). Any interpretations of the Scriptures without the guidance of the Holy Spirit and any traditions or new dogma that contravene the Word of God take us far from the ancient paths and the good ways. For God has not nor will He change (James 1:17). Moreover, His word is eternally established in heaven (Ps. 119:89).

Jesus said, "I am the way and the truth and the life," the only way to the Father (John 14:6). Our advocate, Jesus not only forgives our sins but also pleads with the Father to filter the view of our filthy rags of righteousness through the lens of His perfect righteousness. Furthermore, He is the conduit through whom we receive all our blessings and benefits. For God the Father "has blessed us in the heavenly realms with every spiritual blessing in Christ" (Eph. 1:3, NIV).

According to St. Augustine, "Our hearts are restless until they find their rest in thee." The Bible makes it clear that the wayward will not find rest. "'Their hearts are always going astray, and they have not known my ways.' ... 'They shall never enter my rest'" (Heb. 3:10, 11, NIV). According to the Word, finding rest or peace of mind is a process. First, standing at the crossroads of life and death, at the invitation to serve Jesus, we must choose prudently. Once we choose Him the indwelling Spirit and the Scriptures will show us the good way—the way of life. Next, we walk in obedience as doers of the Word and not just hearers. Only then do we find rest for our souls.

July 22

Jesus—The Suffering Servant

This is my comfort in my affliction, that your promise gives me life. Ps. 119:50, ESV.

"Our suffering is not worthy of the name of suffering. When I consider my crosses, tribulations, and temptations, I shame myself almost to death, thinking what are they in comparison of the sufferings of my blessed Saviour Christ Jesus," wrote Martin Luther. Jesus' physical suffering from Gethsemane to Calvary was excruciating and more than any human should bear. Other humans may have suffered physical agony as intense or longer in duration than He. However, His emotional suffering was immeasurably greater than any human's suffering, far greater than our limited minds can comprehend.

The perfect Son of God became sin for us. Our iniquities became His iniquities and separated Him from God, hiding God's face from Him and closing God's ear to His pleas (Isa. 59:2). Our sins restrained Him in a position of profound psychological separation from God. Undoubtedly, this separation was agonizing for had Jesus sinned in any way by look, word, thought, or deed His separation from God would have become permanent. God's "eyes are too pure to look on evil"; He "cannot tolerate wrong" (Hab. 1:13, NIV). When Jesus became sin for us, He became a lawbreaker and in league with Satan, for whoever sins is of the devil (1 John 3:8-10).

Standing in the gap for sinners, Jesus became a friend of the world and made Himself an enemy of God (James 4:4). Being sin for us, Jesus carried on His back sins of the sexually immoral, idolaters, adulterers, prostitutes, homosexuals, thieves, covetous, drunkards, slanderers, and extortionists. His imputed sins disinherited Him and shut Him out from the fellowship of heaven and the love and admiration of His Father, for God declared that such sinners would never inherit the kingdom (1 Cor. 6:9, 10).

Also, consider the emotionally excruciating disgrace that Jesus endured. Referring to Jesus, the psalmist wrote, "But I am a worm and not a man, scorned by men and despised by the people. All who see me mock me; they hurl insults, shaking their heads" (Ps. 22:6, 7, NIV). It is very difficult for us to comprehend the shame felt by the Commander of the Lords' host to be victimized by His created beings. Moses wrote, "He who is hanged is accursed of God" (Deut. 21:23, NASB). In Jesus' culture, the hanged were so reprehensible that they "deserved permanent removal from the covenantal assembly of God's people." By hanging in public, "the object of that curse was displayed in an atmosphere of humiliation, dishonor, and shame. The body of the offender was subject to the insults and mockery of the bystanders who expressed their revulsion against such a criminal."[208]

From the foundation of the earth, Jesus knew what He would suffer if He became sin for us. He counted the cost and deemed us worth the suffering. The Majesty of heaven became a suffering servant for you and me. Because of this sacrifice, we have a sure promise of eternal life. When affliction strikes, think on that promise!

July 23

Jesus Wept

Refrain your voice from weeping, and your eyes from tears; for your work shall be rewarded. Jer. 31:16, NKJV.

Washington Irving opined, "There is sacredness in tears. They are not the mark of weakness, but of power. They speak more eloquently than ten thousand tongues. They are the messengers of overwhelming grief, of deep contrition, and of unspeakable love." Tears speak of personal anguish and pain and are a sign of deep sorrow. Tears also convey an empathetic understanding of another's heartache.

Jesus, the calm, reflective Son of God shed a torrent of tears for humanity. His great compassion for the condition of the world and the plight of fallen human beings was candidly expressed by His tears. He wept over Jerusalem, over the tenacity of their resolve to disregard sound counsel and to reject Him as Messiah. To the consternation of those who followed Him in jubilation at His triumphant entry into Jerusalem, He audibly wept for His spiritually lost kinsmen and their pending suffering.

Luke used *klaio* to describe Jesus' grief. *Klaio* means to weep with uncontrollable outbursts of audible wailing and crying as one mourning for the dead. Jesus knew that the Jews were headed toward total destruction though their own obstinacy. As he approached Jerusalem and saw the city, he wept (*klaio*) averring, "If you ... had only known on this day what would bring you peace—but now it is hidden from your eyes. The days will come upon you when your enemies will build an embankment against you and encircle you and hem you in on every side. They will dash you to the ground, you and the children within your walls. They will not leave one stone on another, because you did not recognize the time of God's coming to you" (Luke 19: 41-44, NIV).

Even after they were surrounded by the Romans, outnumbered and outmanned, they sent out incursions to kill the Romans troops. The Romans sent a negotiator; the Jews ran him back with an arrow wound. Lamentations provides the grisly details of their existence as the siege continued. "Those killed by the sword are better off than those who die of famine; racked with hunger, they waste away for lack of food.... With their own hands compassionate women have cooked their own children, who became their food" (Lam. 4:9, 10, NIV). Many thousands died from the effects of famine.

Jesus also wept in compassion for the present grief of others. *Dakru*, the Greek word used by John, describes silent weeping where the tears well up and spill down the cheeks. "When Jesus saw her weeping, and the Jews who had come along with her also weeping, he was deeply moved in spirit and troubled.... Jesus wept [*dakru*]. Then the Jews said, 'See how he loved him!'" (John 11:33-36, NIV).

His tears overflow at the many lives wasted because of an addiction to sin and the effects of sin. Compassion so fills Jesus' heart of amazing love for His blood-bought purchases that our suffering greatly moves Him.

July 24

All Our Accomplishments

LORD, you will grant us peace; all we have accomplished is really from you. Isa. 26:12, NLT.

Because of the bloody civil war, Abraham Lincoln proclaimed April 30, 1863, a day of national humiliation, fasting, and prayer. It read in part, "We have been the recipients of the choicest bounties of Heaven; we have been preserved these many years in peace and prosperity; we have grown in numbers, wealth, and power as no other nation has ever grown. But we have forgotten God. We have forgotten the gracious hand which preserved us in peace and multiplied and enriched and strengthened us, and we have vainly imagined, in the deceitfulness of our hearts, that all these blessings were produced by some superior wisdom and virtue of our own."[209]

King Nebuchadnezzar suffered from the same disregard of God's bounties to which the proclamation referred even as God placed Daniel, Shadrach, Meshach, and Abednego in his kingdom to teach him about the living God. He appeared to get it when he saw a fourth man walking in the flames with the three Hebrew boys after they refused to bow to his idol. But his understanding of God's providences soon dissipated. So God sent him a second dream about a huge tree covering the earth that fed and housed birds and animals. But a messenger appeared and told him to cut down the tree (Dan. 4:14).

Daniel explained that his pride and lack of compassion would cause him to lose his kingdom until he acknowledged God's sovereignty and his helplessness. A year later Nebuchadnezzar's arrogance brought the fulfillment of the dream. Walking on the roof of his palace in Babylon, he said, "Is not this the great Babylon I have built as the royal residence, by my mighty power and for the glory of my majesty?" (Dan. 4:30, NIV). Immediately, he lost his sanity and ate grass as cattle. He slept in the open, waking up with a dew-drenched body. His "hair grew like the feathers of an eagle and his nails like the claws of a bird" (verse 33). Seven years later he regained his sanity. Then he honored and praised God, finally learning that sooner or later God humbles those who walk in pride (verses 34-37).

Very importantly, Nebuchadnezzar learned that all that is good and perfect comes from God (James 1:17) who gave the king the power and ability to become wealthy (Deut. 8:18). He also learned not to take anything for granted or to believe that his own personal efforts directly resulted in his accomplishments. God loved him enough to teach him that He gives and sustains "all things by his powerful word" (Heb. 1:3, NIV). Our movement, our breathing, all of our systems—our total human existence—are "in his hands, and he keeps our feet from stumbling" (Ps. 66:9, NLT).

Without the daily renewal of God's infinite mercies, we cannot exist or function in any capacity. As a man hampered by the limitations of humanity, Jesus understood that concept perfectly. He said, "By myself I can do nothing" and neither can we (John 5:30, NIV).

July 25

The Last Laugh

Do not rejoice over me, my enemy; when I fall, I will arise; when I sit in darkness, the LORD will be a light to me. Micah 7:8, NKJV.

He who laughs last, laughs best is an Italian proverb describing a person who wins a skirmish but loses the war. This thought is illustrated in *The Triumph of Mordecai* by Lucas van Leyden, which portrays Mordecai triumphing over his arch enemy, Haman. Haman, an Agagite, served as a high official in King Xerxes' court where noblemen bowed down to him, unlike Mordecai who ignored him. This infuriated Haman who sought revenge not just on Mordecai but on all the Jews in the kingdom. However, Haman's plot backfired and Mordecai and the Jews triumphed (Esther 3).

Leyden's artwork illustrates Mordecai having a proverbial laugh at Haman's expense. By the providence of God, King Xerxes experienced insomnia one night and summoned his staff to fetch the chronicle of his reign. There he read of Mordecai exposing an assassination plot and saving his life. When the king asked Haman's advice on rewarding a person he wanted to honor, Haman presumed himself the honoree and described a dignified way. How humiliated he felt to have to publicly honor the hated Jew, Mordecai, and not himself (Esther 6)!

Mordecai had a louder and last laugh after Haman convinced King Xerxes to pass an edict to exterminate the Jews in all 127 provinces. Through prayer and fasting and Queen Esther's courage, the Jews again triumphed. Officials hanged Haman and his ten sons on the very gallows he built for Mordecai, and the king passed a second edit allowing the Jews to defend themselves. "No one could stand against them, because the people of all the other nationalities were afraid of them" (Esther 9:2, NIV). And all the nobles and other high officials helped the Jews because "fear of Mordecai had seized them" as Mordecai became prominent in the palace (verse 3).

As well, Christians who remain faithful to God's Word will one day have the last laugh. Presently, we experience enemies and enmity for Satan hates all who claim loyalty to Christ. As threats to the building of his kingdom, the redeemed are persecuted, ridiculed, and killed by his demonic agents because a praying, committed Christian erects a roadblock against his plans to destroy them. The powerful, passionate prayer of a righteous person moves the hand of God to reach deep inside Satan's dark kingdom to extract, protect, and guide to heaven those who would otherwise be lost.

"The wicked will perish, the LORD's enemies will be like the beauty of the fields, they will vanish—vanish like smoke" (Ps. 37:20, NIV). Be patient. Though we may fall prey to Satan's hatred now, one glorious day we will rise in victory, our enemies will be eliminated, and the light of God's glory will illuminate our lives forever. Truly the last laugh will belong to the faithful.

July 26

Honor Begets Honor

Those who honor Me I will honor, and those who despise Me shall be lightly esteemed.
1 Sam. 2:30, NKJV.

An aged, feeble father went to live with his son and daughter-in-law. While eating, food and drink dribbled out of his mouth, and he made loud slurping noises that moved them, in disgust, to put his chair in a corner. When he broke his bowl, his daughter-in-law said, "If you are going to eat like a pig and act like a pig, we'll make a trough for you and you can eat out of that. And, they did." Later the son saw his little boy gathering pieces of wood and asked him what he was doing. "'I am making a little trough,' answered the child, 'for father and mother to eat out of when I am big.'"[210]

Says the Lord, "A son honors his father, and a servant his master. If I am a father, where is the honor due me? If I am a master, where is the respect due me?" (Mal. 1:6, NIV). The apathetic attitude of His people toward worship grieved God to the point of making this lament. In a covenant relationship, He required the priests to sacrifice only unblemished animals, animals that symbolized the perfect Son of God. But they accepted from the congregation weak, defective animals and sacrificed them as an offering to God. "When you bring blind animals for sacrifice, is that not wrong? When you sacrifice crippled or diseased animals, is that not wrong? Try offering them to your governor! Would he be pleased with you?... says the LORD Almighty" (verse 8).

Their dishonorable actions indicated the spiritual complacency that characterized the nation, a complacency that separated them from God, allowed compromise, and sanctioned rebellion and disobedience. For a wretched sinner to be honored by God is the highest tribute to which we can aspire. But He will only honor those who honor Him. Therefore, persistent dishonor invites His wrath on those whom He blesses with good and perfect gifts of sustenance, sufficiency and salvation. "Cursed is the cheat who has an acceptable male in his flock and vows to give it, but then sacrifices a blemished animal to the Lord" (verse 14). And to the priests He forecasted, "'If you do not listen, and if you do not set your heart to honor my name,' says the LORD Almighty, 'I will send a curse upon you, and I will curse your blessings'" (Mal. 2:2, NIV).

Disobedience is the highest form of dishonor. "You who brag about the law, do you dishonor God by breaking the law?" (Rom. 2:23, NIV). And down through the ages, God's people have continued to dishonor Him. Jesus regularly chastised the Jewish leaders for dishonoring Him by being applauders and boasters of the law but not appliers of the law. "By boasting of the Law, they proclaimed their conviction that it was from God. By breaking it, they denied it,"[211] prompting Jesus to declare, "These people honor me with their lips, but their hearts are far from me" (Matt. 15:8, NLT). Today, many of us follow suit.

When we give God our whole heart, putting nothing before Him and loving nothing more than He, we honor Him. Jesus said, "If any man serve me, let him follow me; … him will my Father honour" (John 12:26).

July 27

Honoring God's Holy Day of Rest

If you turn away your foot from the Sabbath, From doing your pleasure on My holy day, And call the Sabbath a delight, The holy day of the LORD honorable, And shall honor Him, not doing your own ways ... Then ... I will cause you to ride on the high hills of the earth. Isa. 58:13, 14, NKJV. (See also Eze. 20:12-24).

"That Protestants, who accept the Bible as the only rule of faith and religion, should by all means go back to the observance of the Sabbath.... We Catholics do not accept the Bible as the only rule of faith. We say, this Church, instituted by Christ to teach and guide man through life, has the right to change the ceremonial laws of the Old Testament and hence, we accept her change of the Sabbath to Sunday. We frankly say, yes, the [Catholic] Church made this change, made this law, as she made many other laws."[212]

Contrary to the above assertion, God created the Sabbath at the end of Creation week as a part of His *moral* law for all humanity for all times. "By the seventh day God had finished the work he had been doing; so on the seventh day he rested from all his work. And God blessed the seventh day and made it holy" (Gen. 2:2, 3, NIV). The Sabbath is not simply for the Jews as is the popular sentiment today. The Sabbath "made for man" existed long before the Jews and remains holy.

At Mount Sinai, where God spoke the Ten Commandments, He commanded the Jews to *remember* the Sabbath day (Ex. 20:8-11). The Jews were chosen by God to live godly lives and to spread the truth of salvation throughout the world. Like Christians today, they were chosen to tell about the goodness of God (1 Peter 2:9). Thus, He reminded them at Sinai to proclaim obedience to all His words as "all His commandments are sure" (Ps. 119:86, ESV). "They stand fast for ever and ever" (Ps. 111:8).

"Sunday ... comes branded with the mark of paganism, and christened with the name of the sun god, adopted and sanctioned by the papal apostasy, and bequeathed as a sacred legacy to Protestantism!"[213] The legislative and coercive acts of Constantine, the first Roman Emperor to promote Christianity, changed the observance of Sabbath to Sunday, not God. "The earliest recognition of the observance of Sunday as a legal duty is a constitution of Constantine in A.D. 321, enacting that all courts of justice, inhabitants of towns, and workshops were to be at rest on Sunday, with an exception in favour of those engaged in agricultural labour ... The Council of Laodicea (363) ... forbids Christians from judaizing and resting on the Sabbath day, preferring the Lord's day, and so far as possible resting as Christians."[214]

We offend God by substituting His holy day for the traditions of men as Jesus' followers are not at liberty to select commandments to obey. "If someone obeys all of God's laws except one, that person is guilty of breaking all of them" (James 2:10, GWT). Guided by the Holy Spirit, research this topic; the Bible is its own interpreter. Then follow Jesus' example of worshipping on the seventh day Sabbath. For if you love Him, you will be faithful to walk as He walked and keep all His laws and commands (John 14:15).

July 28

Endurance and Perseverance

God is faithful, who will not allow you to be tempted beyond what you are able, but with the temptation will also make the way of escape, that you may be able to bear it. 1 Cor. 10:13, NKJV.

Sixty-one year old Cliff Young shocked spectators and participants alike at the 543.7-mile Australian endurance race from Sydney to Melbourne. He wore overalls and work boots unlike the other athletes who wore expensive sneakers and outfits in vogue in the 1980s. And the athletes were dismissive of Cliff's weird shuffle. This marathon, among the world's most difficult races, is extremely grueling. The race usually consumes five excruciating days and is only attempted by young under-thirty, well-trained, world-class athletes. Previously, the winners ran eighteen hours and slept six, but Cliff shuffled nonstop to win this taxing race and set a new record. [215]

As well, Jesus won the race to rescue fallen humanity while running the gauntlet marked by violence, mayhem, and rejection. A gauntlet is a type of punishment where the victim is forced to run through lines of men who viciously beat him. Symbolically, Jesus ran the gauntlet of their evil deeds, disrespect and exhaustion, and cold and hunger, but He pressed on. Enduring battering, shame, phlegm-filled spittle in his face, and beard plucking, He pressed on. With His eyes fixed on the prize, He tolerated lies, isolation, rejection, abandonment, and cruel nails in His hands and feet, but He never retreated.

"Keep your eyes on Jesus, who both began and finished this race we're in…. He never lost sight of where he was headed … he could put up with anything along the way: Cross, shame, whatever. And now he's there, in the place of honor, right alongside God. When you find yourselves flagging in your faith, go over that story again, item by item … That will shoot adrenaline into your souls!" (Heb. 12:2, 3, MSG).

Running any race requires discipline, endurance, and perseverance. It is not for the fainthearted or the swift. Likewise, the Christian race is fraught with hardships, setbacks, and suffering for such things produce character and build faith (Rom. 5:3). Be careful to watch for Satan's invisible gauntlet that distracts and discourages us from the prize of eternal life. His rebellion cost him his heritage, and he is relentless to make that our fate as well.

We are not guaranteed an easy course in this race, so do not turn back when you trip over roots and stones. The Bible says, "Here on earth you will have many trials and sorrows. But take heart, because I have overcome the world" (John 16:33, NLT). Endure whatever hardship it takes. Do not surrender to any temptations that will disqualify you and the fellowship of heavenly beings. Lay aside all the snares that delay and detract. "Press on to reach the end of the race and receive the heavenly prize for which God, through Christ Jesus, is calling us" (Phil. 3:14, NLT).

July 29

Dead Men Walking

For we were so utterly burdened beyond our strength that we despaired of life itself. Indeed, we felt that we had received the sentence of death. But that was to make us rely not on ourselves but on God who raises the dead. He delivered us from such a deadly peril, and he will deliver us. 2 Cor. 1:8-10, ESV.

Leon Bass, a young African American soldier walked through the concentration camps at Buchenwald and described what he called the "walking dead." "I saw human beings there that had been beaten and starved and tortured and so mistreated that they were nothing but human skeletons. They were skin and bone and they had those skeletal faces with the deep-set eyes, and their heads had been clean-shaved. And they were standing there holding on to one another, and they were so thin. They had sores on their bodies brought on by malnutrition. And that man held out his hands, and his fingers had webbed together with the scabs that come from malnutrition."[216]

A dead man walking is someone who is in great trouble and facing punishment. Thus, willful sinners who have not accepted Jesus' offer of grace and lukewarm Christians are truly dead men and women walking (John 15:5). Like a fatally wounded deer that runs briefly after it is wounded, they are standing but could lay down in death at any minute. And when Jesus returns fear and regret will consume them, for at His soon coming, rewards will accompany Him (Rev. 22:12).

Lukewarm Christians are detached from Jesus. They look like Jesus' followers, but at heart level it is hard to distinguish them from willful sinners. Any injury or slight causes resentment and bitterness, and unable to forget the injury, they forgive not. The soft word that turns away wrath is not in their vocabulary. However, the raw language they do sometimes emit comes straight from the gutter. Fake Christians and willful sinners alike continue to frequent places that cause their guardian angels to flee in disgust, and they persist in listening to things and viewing things that appeal to the lowest base nature. Self controls the willful sinner and the unconnected Christian as well, thereby stifling the transforming power of the Holy Spirit.

Contrariwise, a Christian connected to the Vine forgives small hurts as well as egregious wrongs as Jesus did. The worldly places, music, and movies they frequented before accepting Jesus as Lord are abandoned; the things they listen to and look at are uplifting and ennobling. Connected to Jesus, His followers strive daily to glorify God by the renewing of the mind (Rom. 12:2). Eventually, their lives exhibit the fruit of the spirit as guided by the Holy Spirit.

The walking dead have the option to die to sin and become alive to God through Christ Jesus who demands that we not let sin reign in our mortal body and not obey its evil desires. We can crucify the old nature and work to overcome through faith and the power of the Holy Spirit. Upon baptism, all are "crucified with Christ." Now claim it, proclaim it, and live it. "Nevertheless I live; yet not I, but Christ liveth in me" (Gal. 2:20).

July 30

Do Not Lose Heart

We are afflicted in every way, but not crushed; perplexed, but not driven to despair; persecuted, but not forsaken; struck down, but not destroyed; always carrying in the body the death of Jesus, so that the life of Jesus may also be manifested in our bodies. 2 Cor. 4:8-10, ESV.

Traveling to heaven, Hopeful and Christian reached the River of Life where the river and the way parted, and the way became difficult to traverse. They took By-Path Meadow thinking it was an easier route. Realizing they made a mistake, they unsuccessfully attempted to turn back. Discouraged and tired, they found a little shelter and went to sleep only to be awakened the next morning by Giant Despair, the landowner. He confined them in his dungeon, withheld food and water for days, and beat them unmercifully. The next morning he returned to persuade them to commit suicide to alleviate their suffering. Christian, losing heart at his colossal suffering, considered it, but Hopeful persuaded him to patiently wait for deliverance.[217]

Losing heart equates to hopelessness and is encouraged by spiritual powers of darkness. Suicide is one way some choose to palliate their despair. One young man's suicide note hangs on the hopelessness that leads to losing heart. "Dear all. I am so very, very sorry. As time has gone on it becomes more and more apparent that my life is pretty much pointless. Having thought of ways to make my life mean anything, I have run out of ideas. I am completely empty."[218] Fortunately, his suicide attempt failed and he rediscovered hope.

But the redeemed have the Word of God to counter the negative emotions that accompany life in perilous times. Paul, an expert on suffering, counsels us to never lose heart. Despite being painful, afflictions are short-lived compared to our glorious unending ending. And the challenges we face slide us up a spectrum from a desire for the pure Word as newborn babies desire milk, to maturing in the righteousness that leads to eternal life. Although our human bodies will wear out, the inner spiritual life is renewed daily by the trials that make us run to Jesus (2 Cor. 4:16-18).

Paul is not perplexed, destroyed, or crushed by stressful and painful circumstances because he is confident that God controls and tempers our struggles. God can do all things; no plan of His can be thwarted (Job 42:2). In love with and in service for Jesus, we will encounter resistance by the powers of darkness determined to make us lose our way, our focus, and our hope. But in the name of Jesus and by His strength, we can withstand the bullets of discouragement and despair.

Accept that the Christian life is fraught with troubles and suffering. Look beyond the present sinful world and all its adversities and focus on the bright future destined for the faithful.

July 31

Extreme Makeovers

This means that anyone who belongs to Christ has become a new person. The old life is gone; a new life has begun! 2 Cor. 5:17, NLT.

A metamorphosis is a marked "change in appearance or character or circumstances." In Franz Kafka's 1915 novella titled *The Metamorphosis*, Gregor Samsa, a dutiful hardworking traveling salesman, wakes up one morning changed into a huge, grotesque insect. His salary is required to provide for the family's needs, but in this state he is unable to work and loses his job. His sister Grete volunteers to take care of Gregor but soon begins to resent him. As times passes, he becomes a dispensable burden to the family, and eventually dies, bringing them a measure of relief.

Unlike Gregor, when we become new creatures in Christ, He begins a welcomed metamorphosis that completely overhauls our character and mindset to His character and mindset. Those who accept the clarion call to surrender to Jesus are destined to be conformed to His likeness (Rom. 8:29). Beholding Him, we become spiritually changed. Our lives gradually become cleaner and brighter and our fruit sweeter as we walk in the footsteps of the soul Purifier. No longer do we have a membership in the world or in the church, but we have a lifetime membership in Jesus.

Our transformation is a gift straight from the hand of God who is unwilling to relinquish us to evil but calls us to Himself through the blood of Jesus. "For God was in Christ, reconciling the world to himself, no longer counting people's sins against them" (2 Cor. 5:19, NLT). When we become reconciled to God through Christ, we reign as Christ's ambassadors through whom God makes His appeal for the salvation of others. As Jesus' converted mouthpieces, we are authorized to evangelize the world.

Transformed into His likeness, Jesus' followers imitate Him in all ways especially in evangelism. His method to reach the unsaved masses involved satisfying their physical and/or emotional needs and demonstrating compassion before sharing the good news of the gospel. Jesus did not attempt to direct soul-saving as a divine being sitting high on a throne in heaven. He became incarnated as a man subject to all our temptations, subject to hunger, homelessness, pain, sin, and fatigue. In essence, He "became flesh and blood, and moved into the neighborhood," establishing loving relationships with the neighbors (John 1:14, MSG).

Becoming a new creature in Jesus equates to an extreme makeover from the inside out. Jesus clothes us with a brand-new nature that is continually being renewed as we learn more and more about Him who created this new nature within us (Col. 3:10). Drug addicts become clean; alcoholics become teetotalers; abusers become kind. Our thoughts change from embracing evil and negativity to focusing on true, honorable, and praiseworthy things. Love and unselfishness replace hate and self-interest. We endure persecution and unfairness without retaliation and kneel in prayer for the persecutor. Oh, the mystery of godliness!

August 1

God Help Me!

I know that nothing good lives in me, that is, in my sinful nature. For I have the desire to do what is good, but I cannot carry it out. For what I do is not the good I want to do; no, the evil I do not want to do—this I keep on doing. Rom 7:18, 19, NIV.

"I am not what I am," said Iago, a sinister antagonist in Shakespeare's play *Othello*. He is a scheming manipulator who destroys several of the characters in the play, chiefly Othello at whom his revenge is directed. Cleverly, Iago built a reputation as honest and just and, therefore, appears trustworthy. But he masks his motives behind this smokescreen of benevolence.[219] His real nature is comparable to the mythical god Janus with two faces looking in opposite directions.

Iago is not who he says he is, and he revels in the power of this deceptive spirit. His deviousness pushes Othello's jealousy buttons until he strangles his innocent wife, Desdemona and kills himself. Evil is second nature to the unregenerate heart; nothing good lives in our sinful natures. Therefore, the conflict between good and evil is nonexistent in evil doers who are controlled by Satan. He holds them captive to do wickedness at his bidding (2 Tim. 2:26). Unless sinful man is born again, he is not free to choose righteousness and can never be subject to God's law.

And, Paul admits he cannot do what he wants to do. Conflict is a constant companion for those who have the Holy Spirit living in their hearts. He wants to do what is right and pleasing in the eyes of God, but does not. Instead, he does the evil that he detests. In desperation he utters the cry that has registered in heaven over the centuries, "O wretched man that I am! who shall deliver me from this body of death?" (Rom. 7:24). Paul represents the spirit that is undeniably willing, but our flesh is weak and fickle, rendering us incapable of changing at the pace we desire (Matt. 26.41).

The struggle to gain mastery over sin will shadow us until Jesus returns and changes our vile bodies into the likeness of His glorious body (Phil. 3: 21). Therefore, we must diligently work for this mastery as long as life lasts. "The warfare against self is the greatest battle that was ever fought. The yielding of self, surrendering all to the will of God, requires a struggle; but the soul must submit to God before it can be renewed in holiness."[220] Crucifying the old nature with Christ and letting Him live in us begins with baptism and the remission of sins. But it takes a lifetime of prayer and self-denial to totally surrender the will and become like Jesus.

Do not let Satan's lies put fear in your heart. We have already been delivered from the body of death based on our faith through Jesus' death by proxy for us (Col. 2:20). Truly, we can do absolutely nothing in our own strength let alone resist the evil hard-wired in our inherited DNA from Adam. But God will help us progress toward perfection as we daily walk in Jesus' footsteps. "As you have therefore received Christ, [even] Jesus the Lord, [so] walk (regulate your lives and conduct yourselves) in union with and conformity to Him" (Col. 2:6, AMP).

August 2

Ask in Faith

If any of you lacks wisdom ... ask of God ... and it will be given to him. But let him ask in faith, with no doubting, for he who doubts is like a wave of the sea driven and tossed by the wind. James 1:5, 6, NKJV.

In the 1991 Perfect Storm, twelve people died and records prove it caused almost one billion dollars in damages. The convergence of three weather fronts created perfect conditions for a maelstrom. A warm weather low-pressure system coming from the east-northeast, cool dry air originating from the southeast, and the remnants of Hurricane Grace bringing moist tropical air fueled the storm. This nor'easter stirred up waves ten stories high and winds at 120 miles per hour. The ill-fated commercial fishing boat, *Andrea Gail,* carrying a crew of six, ended up in the middle of this ferocious once-in-a-century storm and apparently sank.[221]

Strapping winds and bucking waves can break apart the sturdiest sailing vessel. Similarly, a skeptical Christian's faith weakens and may be destroyed by doubt that moves the mind and affections to and fro like agitated sea waves. This wind-whipped mind produces weak, ineffective prayers and actions that are not pleasing to God. And anything that is not pleasing to God comes from an opposite and downward direction. Satan plants seeds of doubt in our minds to counter the plain truth of God's guidance, love, and protection. "Know, recognize, and understand ...the faithful God, Who keeps covenant and steadfast love and mercy with those who love Him and keep His commandments, to a thousand generations" (Deut. 7:9, AMP).

Doubt is an affront to God for "a man of two minds (hesitating, dubious, irresolute), [he is] unstable and unreliable and uncertain about everything" even though there is abundant proof in the Word of God as to His authenticity and faithfulness (James 1:6-8, AMP). The Holy Writ is true from the beginning, and His "righteous judgments endureth for ever" (Ps. 119:160). Doubt leads to unbelief which is never content with the plain truth but insists on ever-increasing evidence. Unbelief pushes us down the slippery slope to losing reverence for the God who holds our present peace and our future hope in His hands. Those who demand an answer to every question have misplaced or lost their faith, and "without faith it is impossible to please [God]" (Heb 11:6).

The person who gains "Wisdom loves his own life; he who keeps understanding shall prosper and find good" (Prov. 19:8, AMP). Similarly, Herbert Lockyer wrote that biblical wisdom is the "ability to judge correctly and to follow the best course of action, based on knowledge and understanding." Wisdom, then, mandates that transferring wise information into action requires industriously following the Word of God no matter the sacrifice or suffering. Those who daily ask God in faith to provide wisdom and to teach them His ways that they may live according to His truth will find the waves of doubt stilled. He is waiting for us to approach the throne of grace boldly, for there lay liberal doses of wisdom that lead to increased faith that lead to perpetual peace.

August 3

As We Forgive Our Debtors

Who is a God like you, who pardons sin and forgives the transgression of the remnant of his inheritance? You do not stay angry forever but delight to show mercy. Micah 7:18, NIV.

An enemy soldier sexually ravaged a young teacher during a war, and the trauma of that horrendous experience left her emotionally debilitated with nightmares and fear. But with God's help, she slowly began to heal. Over a decade later, her boss asked her to host a meeting of teachers in the spirit of reconciliation. As fate would have it, the soldier who assaulted her arrived with the teachers. When she stumbled upon him, a rush of feelings, particularly resentment, anger, and revenge, besieged her. It took nights of fervent prayer and crying out to God for deliverance from the awful, negative feelings that set her free.

"Resentment is like a glass of poison that a man drinks; then he sits down and waits for his enemy to die."[222] How true! After injuring us deeply, the enemy/our debtor slithers away, leaving us full of the poison of bitterness. She moves forward with her life, forgetting the injury while we remain stuck on the flypaper of painful remembrances and seething anger. The more we dwell on the injury, the more negative energy we expend, attracting the enemy. Thus, we enable the devil to establish and strengthen his stronghold, to manipulate our thoughts and to gain control.

Forgiveness is a relinquishment of the resentment, anger, and strong desire for revenge. And it is the antidote for the poison that infiltrates the system after the venom of offense enters our veins, an antidote crucial to our physical health as well as our spiritual and mental health. A study done by the Mayo Clinic concluded that benefits of forgiveness include healthier relationships, greater spiritual and psychological well-being, less stress and hostility, lower blood pressure, fewer symptoms of depression, anxiety and chronic pain, and lower risk of alcohol and substance abuse.[223]

Because of the physical, mental, and spiritual benefits of forgiveness, God requires us to forgive. "Forgive us our debts, as we forgive our debtors" is an integral part of the Lord's Prayer (Matt 6:12). It clearly articulates the message that unless we forgive those who offend us we will not be forgiven when we offend God. Sin is an offense against God and our offenses are nonstop and egregious, but He readily forgives them. Life everlasting is conditioned on both being forgiven and forgiving.

When Jesus died on the cross, He paid the price of our sin debt, wiping clean the ledger listing our sins. Although committed Christians strive to acquire the character of Jesus, we miss some part of the mark requiring daily doses of divine forgiveness. The psalmist says, "If I regard iniquity in my heart, the Lord will not hear me" (Ps. 66:18). But if we repent, forgive, and confess our sins, He will forgive us and cleanse us from all unrighteousness (1 John 1:9).

August 4

Your Heart's Desire

The LORD is near to all who call on him ... in truth. He fulfills the desires of those who fear him; he hears their cry and saves them. Ps. 145:18, 19, NIV.

On her way to work Teressa encountered a man in tattered clothing and bare feet. She greeted the man and wished him a good morning, but the man replied that he had never had a bad morning. She wished him good luck; the man replied that he never had bad luck. Finally, Teressa wished him happiness, but the man replied he was happy. Unable to understand this man's buoyancy, she asked for an explanation. The man explained that whenever he is cold or hungry he praises God and accepts with a grateful heart any deprivation and in total surrender wants what He wants.

This seemingly unfortunate man holds the keys to the realization of one's heartfelt desires. First, note that God is near to all who call on Him *in truth* and promises to answer all who call (Jer. 33:3). As all His commandments are truth, He hears the call of those who worship and obey Him (Ps. 119:151). But the man recognized that although God is vigilant and paternalistic toward those who sincerely call Him Father and submit to His leading, He will not supply every want.

Secondly, He fulfills the desires of those who *fear Him,* an iteration of "to all that call upon him in truth" (Ps. 145:18). The repetition highlights the conditions of obtaining the fulfillment of our desires. David writes, "How great is your goodness, which you have stored up for those who fear you, which you bestow in the sight of men on those who take refuge in you" (Ps. 31:19, NIV). The phrase "fear of God" suggests awe and respect, not fright. It is a belief that His presence, as a lovable, bright silhouette, tags along everywhere we go. Acutely aware of His presence and careful not to offend Him because of His great love and grace, we fine-tune our actions and thoughts to please Him.

When we live in accordance to His Word, the Holy Spirit reveals God's will. The Bible says, "Your ears will hear a voice behind you, saying 'This is the way; walk in it'" (Isa. 30:21, NIV). Carefully listening to His voice and prayerful seeking His guidance in every area of our lives bring our desires in perfect harmony with His will and the desires of our heart are realized. Safe and secure in His perfect will for our lives, we will be loathe to desire relationships or things that are harmful to our physical, emotional, and spiritual health.

The Lord faithfully promises, "I will instruct you and teach you in the way which you shall go: I will guide thee with mine eye" (Ps. 32:8, AKJV). If we commit our ways to Him and trust Him to be the Lord of our life, every heartfelt desire in our inventory and within His will is at our disposal. Furthermore, we have a powerful Best Friend who is a supplier of all our needs, guaranteed deliverance, an imperishable crown, guidance, and protection. What else is there to desire?

August 5

Swim Joyfully Against the Current

If you faint in the day of adversity, your strength is small. Prov. 24:10, ESV.

According to the U.S. Fish and Wildlife Service, Alaskan salmon begin life in small freshwater streams, journey to the ocean, and then return to their original streams beds. Here their life ends after they spawn a new generation. Those which survive predators grow to adolescence, undergo changes that condition them to saltwater, and then swim for years in the salty Bering Sea and the Gulf of Alaska. After becoming mature adults, these Alaskan salmon return to the original freshwater streams to spawn. However, they encounter colossal difficulties from fishermen, hungry bears, whitewater rapids, and vertical waterfalls that impede their upstream swim. Still, they persevere.

Like the Alaskan salmon, Christians have every reason not to allow any obstacle to prevent us from our heaven-bound destination. Life is hard in many ways for Adam's progeny who at times gasp at the painful aspects of the journey. Granted, adversity and hardship are "no crystal stair," but we have to keep on climbing. As we climb the staircase to heaven, there are tacks and splinters and torn up boards that trip us and send us crashing to the hard, bare floor. Sometimes the way is dark and uncertain, but we cannot set down, turn back, or cower in fear at the snares on our journey.

James reminds us not to wallow in misery when trials come but to consider them a joy: "Consider it a sheer gift, friends, when tests and challenges come at you from all sides. You know that under pressure, your faith-life is forced into the open and shows its true colors. So don't try to get out of anything prematurely. Let it do its work so you become mature and well-developed, not deficient in any way" (James 1:2, 3, MSG). Joy is a fruit of the Spirit, a serenity placed in our hearts by the Holy Spirit to brighten our souls. You cannot know how good God is until you come out on the other side of adversity.

Joy in trials proceeds from knowing that God sees something of value in us even while we are encased in mud and filth and wallowing in the pigsty of sin. Joy arises in watching God pave a solid way when no way seems possible, and our escalating faith after enduring adversity brings joy. And the knowledge that God stifles the enemy's destructive blows and permits just enough strikes to hammer and chisel us into the image of Jesus holds joy.

Some of Jesus' followers are similar to toddlers whose fledging independence takes them running down the sidewalk away from the voice of caution. It is not until they fall and skin their knees that they turn toward that reassuring voice for comfort. The lesson that words could not teach spoke volumes in the painful experience of skinned knees. Thus, God uses adversity to fulfill His plan for our lives despite our failings. Joy comes after we accept suffering for a finite period of time to learn the lessons that happiness cannot teach. Soon we will be ushered into the everlasting atmosphere of joy in heaven—therein is the ultimate joy.

August 6

Leaning on Jesus

Trust in the LORD with all your heart, and lean not on your own understanding; in all your ways acknowledge Him, and He shall direct your paths. Prov. 3:5, 6, NKJV.

The Leaning Tower of Pisa, a bell tower for the cathedral located in Pisa, Italy, is a beloved architectural blunder, for the tower is situated on a dense clay mixture too unstable to support the building. Although construction began in 1173, the famous tilt did not begin until they completed the third floor five years later. Meant to be a vertical building, the tower's soft foundation caused it to tilt eleven plus feet from the center. The tower is a source of pride for the citizens who do not want the tilt straightened, so modern architects work to halt its lean.

Time and money is spent to impede the tower's leaning. On the contrary, God urges us to freely lean as far as possible on His broad back. Total dependence on Him requires trust great enough to saturate our mind, crowding out doubt. Faith is a precondition to trust and stems from a settled knowledge of His power, love, and credibility. And that faith stems from the establishment of a solid relationship with Him through reading His Word and through prayer. With intentionality and effort the relationship will grow into a deep intimacy bringing peace. Once we know Him faith must be exercised to believe He will fulfill every promise contained in His Word (John 17:1).

The Pharisees were blessed to have Jesus in their midst, but they continued to trust their own twisted, burdensome beliefs. Dismissing that knowledge, wisdom, and understanding come from "His mouth," they set about to silence Him to the eternal loss of many (Prov. 2:6). Foolishly they leaned on their own understanding, failed to seek Him with all their heart, quenched the Holy Spirit, and, therefore, remained carnal-minded (1 Cor. 2:14). Had they believed and cultivated an ardent trust in God, His Word would have illuminated their minds and changed any negative outcomes.

Who would know better than God, our Creator, what is required to successfully navigate the dangers and temptations that beckon in Satan's dominion? He, who loves us with an abiding love and who knows the future, wants His children to live as peaceably as possible in a sin-polluted world. Thus, He invites us to acknowledge Him, lean on Him, and seek His guidance prior to making decisions or planning. To acknowledge God is to lean almost vertically on Him, thereby, admitting our impotence and His greatness and allowing Him to shield us from our own imprudence.

And He will make our path to righteousness straight. Paul accused Elymas of attempting to make crooked the straight paths of the Lord by preventing unbelievers from hearing the truth of the gospel (Acts 13). Hence, the gospel of Jesus Christ is a spotlight to illuminate our paths, with the Holy Spirit as our guide. He says to our hearts, "This is the way, walk ye in it" (Isa. 30:21). Clearly, the plain, unvarnished truth of the gospel makes our path to heaven direct and certain. Trust Jesus. Lean totally on Him. Lean on those everlasting, secure arms.

August 7

Discouragement-Proof Faith

Do not be afraid; do not be discouraged. Deut. 1:21, NIV.

Muriel's bitterness showed in her attitude when asked to carry chairs to the moving van, having pleaded with her parents to reconsider divorcing, but to no avail. When her uncle cautioned Muriel to lift with her knees and not her back, Muriel's mom used this as a spiritual lesson for her daughter. "I've been lifting my heavy heart to God on my knees in prayer since my husband left. God gives me the strength to carry on. It is not the load that can hurt you; it›s how you carry it. I will not get bitter and discouraged. I will trust God."[224]

In the weakness of humanity, even the most mature Christian cries out to God in despair at times. David, who had his share of disappointments and trials, wrote, "From my distress I called upon the LORD" (Ps. 118:5, NASB). Discouragement, a demonic tool to distract and trap God's people, incites feelings of despair in the face of obstacles. It is a secondary emotion that may stem from back-to-back adversities and/or primary emotions like fear and distrust. Consequently, discouragement destroys our peace if we take our eyes off of God and focus on our circumstances.

"How you look at a situation is very important, for how you think about a problem may defeat you before you ever do anything about it."[225] For instance, ten of the Israelite spies who went to observe the land of Canaan reported that not only were the Canaanites secured in fortified cities but also they were giants. Then, they looked at their own size and apparent helplessness with the eyes of flesh, calling themselves grasshoppers. Because their faith was tiny, they sized up the situation without factoring in the God-equation and became discouraged (Num. 13). "So all the congregation lifted up their voices, and cried; and the people wept that night" (Num. 14:1).

Discouragement also follows a string of troubles. Jeremiah cried, "Woe to me, my mother that you have borne me. As a man of strife and a man of contention to all the land! I have not lent, nor have men lent money to me, yet everyone curses me" (Jer. 15:10, NASB). He sacrificed marriage and family, his health, and his reputation when commissioned as a spokesperson for God to rouse his spiritually comatose brethren to repent and prevent disaster. Years of physical and mental abuse sanctioned by the highest power in the land, concern for his countrymen, and anticipation of the bloodbath when God abandoned them to the Babylonians took its toll.

Unlike the headstrong Israelites who murmured and complained and blamed Moses, Jeremiah took refuge in God. He learned that in times of discouragement, "It is better to take refuge in the LORD than to trust in man" (Ps. 118:8, ESV). He called on God requesting, "Heal me, O LORD, and I shall be healed; Save me, and I shall be saved, For thou art my praise" (Jer. 17:14). "Thou art my hope in the day of evil" (verse 17). When the problems are gigantic or relentless, seek God and trust Him; He is our hope.

August 8

Divine Guidance

Those who love Your law have great peace, and nothing causes them to stumble. Ps. 119:165, NASB.

A national magazine assigned a photographer to take pictures of a forest fire, instructing him that a small plane would be waiting at the airport to fly him over it. An hour before sundown the photographer arrived at the airstrip, jumped into a small Cessna with his equipment, and shouted, "Let's go!" The pilot, a tense-looking man, turned the plane into the wind, and soon they were in the air. " 'Fly over the north side of the fire,' said the photographer, 'and make several low-level passes.' 'Why?' asked the nervous pilot. 'Because I'm going to take pictures,' yelled the photographer.... The pilot replied, "You mean you're not my flight instructor?"[226]

Sadly, many of us chart and navigate our own lives without direction from our Pilot, the Holy Spirit. From the age of reasoning until death, we confront a maze of decisions, many of which will determine our eternal destiny. Relying on our fallible wisdom and our fickle, biased feelings, we are bound to make egregious errors in our decision-making. Since we do not know what will happen from one second to the next, it is wise to relinquish the steering wheel to Him.

God clearly wants to guide us. He said, "I will instruct you and teach you in the way which you should go; I will counsel you with My eye upon you" (Ps. 32:8, NASB). It pleases Him when we trust Him to guide our lives. When Solomon admitted that he was clueless about ruling the nation of Israel upon ascending the throne, God answered his request for wisdom: " 'Since you have asked for ... discernment in administering justice, I will do what you have asked" and gave Solomon an unparalleled wise and discerning heart (1 Kings 3:11, 12, NIV).

The Holy Spirit comforts and protects God's people and guides us in our personal walk with Him. He also works in and through us to fulfill the gospel commission. Jesus said, "I have been given all authority in heaven and earth. Therefore go and make disciples in all the nations, baptizing them into the name of the Father and of the Son and of the Holy Spirit" (Matt. 28:19, 20). Hence, we are empowered to be co-laborers with God to spread His message of love and forgiveness throughout the world.

He yearns for us to seek His guidance on our Christian journey and in our unselfish service to our spiritually lost neighbors. "The Holy Spirit is the breath of spiritual life in the soul. The impartation of the Spirit is the impartation of the life of Christ. It imbues the receiver with the attributes of Christ. Only those who are thus taught of God, those who possess the inward working of the Spirit, and in whose life the Christ-life is manifested, are to stand as representative men, to minister in behalf of the church."[227] We do not have to be eloquent speakers or trained missionaries, Bible workers, or preachers. It is enough to live godly lives and share the love of Jesus and the salvation flowing from His death and resurrection.

August 9

God Is Crazy About Us

And I pray that you, being rooted and established in love, may have power, together with all the saints, to grasp how wide and long and high and deep is the love of Christ. Eph. 3:17, 18, NIV.

The Grand Canyon, carved by the Colorado River, is nearly a mile deep, 277 miles long, and 10 to 15 miles wide. Although very deep, it is arguably not the deepest canyon on earth. The Cotahuasi Canyon in southwestern Peru has been given that distinction. The Rio Cotahuasi River cut the canyon, more than doubling the depth of the Grand Canyon. Others claim that the Yarlung Zangbo Grand Canyon in Tibet, China, is considered the deepest and longest canyon in the world, averaging a depth of 3.10 miles and a length of 308 miles. But, the Guinness Book of Records declares that the Vikos Gorge in Greece is the earth's deepest canyon.

Debates rage over all kinds of things, but there is no question about the depth, width, length, and height of Jesus' love. Deep, yes—so deep, it drew Him to earth to rescue us from this dwelling place of demons. While we live in this polluted sewer of sin and woe, His heart of love reaches down to extricate us from our sinful natures by planting the Holy Spirit in our hearts to empower and guide our deliverance. Jesus' love is deep enough to love sinners in the midst of open warfare with Him reconciling us to God through His death (Rom. 5:10).

Long, definitely—love so long, He waits patiently while we stumble and fall repeatedly into and out of sin as we grow to mature Christians. He is compassionate, gracious, longsuffering, and full of mercy and grace toward His erring children (Ps. 86:15). After Adam's fall and sin became rampant, God decided to destroy man, but He patiently waited 120 years for Noah to preach salvation to the lost while building the ark. "The Lord is not slow in keeping His promise ... He is patient with you, not wanting anyone to perish, but everyone to come to repentance" (2 Peter 3:9, NIV).

Wide, certainly—love so wide, He accepts wretched sinners who are proud and self-sufficient and who arrogantly reject His grace. Still, He counsels us " to buy from me gold refined by fire, so that you may be rich, and white garments so that you may clothe yourself and the shame of your nakedness may not be seen, and salve to anoint your eyes, so that you may see" (Rev. 3:17, 18, ESV). God looks beyond our present wretchedness and sees our future potential. For instance, He loved a ragtag group of uneducated, unconverted fishermen, a zealous tentmaker, and corrupt tax collectors enough to turn them into a force that spread the gospel to the world.

High, indeed—love so high that it attracts us like magnets. "And I, if I be lifted up from the earth, will draw all men unto me," He proclaimed (John 12:32). The utmost attraction for humanity is the love of the crucified and risen Christ. This love, shaped like a cruel cross, bridged the separation between God and man that God might accept us as co-heirs with Jesus. Truly, He is madly in love with us!

August 10

Spiritually Blind

I will bring the blind by a way they did not know; I will lead them in paths they have not known. I will make darkness light before them, and crooked places straight. Isa. 42:16, NKJV.

At the age of nineteen months Helen Keller became gravely ill, moving her doctor to predict her death. However, she survived the illness but emerged a blind-deaf mute. Her parents, desperate to keep their child as normal as possible, hired Anne Sullivan, who was herself visually impaired, to teach Helen. After a month of frustration on both their parts, Helen learned to read and comprehend sign language. The breakthrough came as Anne pumped water over Helen's hand and wrote the word "water" in her palm, thereby revealing the mystery of language to her.[228]

To the blind, Jesus actually restored physical sight during His ministry. And He extensively used the metaphor of blindness to highlight the lack of spiritual sight in the world. When Satan blinds us spiritually, he does a thorough job as he blinds our eyes and deadens our hearts, "so they can neither see with their eyes, nor understand with their hearts" (John 12:40, NIV). Unable to see the truth in God's Word, the spiritually impaired individual tunes out the message of salvation and readily accepts the "hollow and deceptive philosophy, which depends on human tradition and the basic principles of this world rather than on Christ" (Col. 2:8, NIV).

Talking to the multitude, Jesus strongly criticized the Pharisees, repeatedly calling them blind: "Woe to you, blind guides!" (Matt. 23:16, ESV). He said, highlighting their hypocritical leadership. Because He desires the whole heart, He advised His followers to heed the law but not the religious leaders who "draw near with their words and honor Me with their lip service, but they remove their hearts far from Me" (Isa. 29:13, NASB). When told He offended the Pharisees, Jesus replied, "Leave them; they are blind guides. If a blind man leads a blind man, both will fall into a pit" (Matt. 15:14, NIV). This spiritual blindness totally blocks the light of the gospel for unbelievers and strikes sporadic and unconverted Christians with spiritual cataracts that cloud their vision, leading to total blindness (2 Cor. 4:4).

The spiritually blind do extremely foolish things that only appear right to them. For instance, Isaiah describes the man who fells a tree, divides it in half, uses one half to fashion an idol that he falls down to worship while he burns the other half to cook his meals and warm his home. "They know not, nor do they discern, for he [Satan] has shut their eyes, so that they cannot see, and their hearts, so that they cannot understand.... He feeds on ashes; a deluded heart has led him astray, and he cannot deliver himself or say, 'Is there not a lie in my right hand?'" (Isa. 44:18, 20, ESV)

Only God's Spirit supplies and applies the salve, the Word of God, that heals the spiritually blind, spiritually deaf, and those with cataracts. And the Word of God is the only medicine guaranteed to reconnect the severed spiritual optic and auditory nerves and make darkness light.

August 11

Am I My Brother's Keeper?

Verily I say unto you, Inasmuch as ye did it not to one of the least of these, ye did it not to me. Matt. 25:45.

Every day a middle-class gentleman passed by a dirty, unkempt young girl begging for money and wearing ragged clothes and a thin jacket to protect her from the harsh weather. Regularly, he drove by without responding to her pleas for help, proceeding to his comfortable, luxurious home, where he enjoyed a nutritious meal, a hot shower, and a warm bed. His conscience bothered him, but he projected this anger at God, asking Him, "'How can you let this happen? Why don't you help this girl?' Then he heard God in the depths of his being respond, 'I did. I created you!'"[229]

The difference between the heaven-bound and the hell-bound involves love for God and our neighbors. In the parable of the sheep and goats, Jesus separates them when all nations are gathered before His throne for the judgment. He calls these righteous sheep blessed and presents to them their inheritance. The reason? When hungry, thirsty, and a stranger in an alien land, they invited Him into their home and supplied His every need. And while He lay sick or in prison, they ministered to Him. Thus, whatever kindness done for the least of His brothers and sisters, they did for Him (Matt. 25:31-40).

Quite the opposite occurs for the selfish, unrighteous goats placed on His left because their time, talent, and treasure were spent to liberally indulge themselves while they rationalized that their neighbors' needs are their neighbors' problem. Self-centered, their lives revolve around themselves as their own comfort and advantage take precedence over the less fortunate. For them, Jesus' script is already prepared, "Depart from me, you who are cursed, into the eternal fire prepared for the devil and his angels" (Matt. 25:41, NIV).

Love for our neighbors entails forgiveness, compassion, and service. Since Jesus no longer walks the earth ministering and healing, we are commissioned to assume this responsibility. Thus, we are His hands and feet and voice. St. Teresa of Avila captures this moral responsibility pointedly, "Christ has no body now but yours, No hands, no feet, on earth but yours. Yours are the eyes through which he looks compassion on this world. Yours are the feet with which he is to go about doing good. Yours are the hands with which he is to bless men now."

Truly, Jesus and our neighbors would rather see a sermon in action than to hear one. Benevolence toward God's children moves Him to rain bountiful blessings down on the giver. And our lives are transformed in service to others as we receive a heightened sense of satisfaction from knowing our actions made a difference. And binding the wounds of others and focusing on their healing move our trials from center focus and makes them easier to bear. Moreover, the greatest reward comes from our King on the day of judgment.

August 12

The Fight of Our Lives

I have fought a good fight, I have finished my course, I have kept the faith. 2 Tim. 4:7.

"The Fight of the Century" boxing match occurred in Reno, Nevada, in 1910 between Jack Johnson and Jim Jeffries. More than twenty-two thousand spectators gathered to watch Johnson fight Jefferies, hailed as the "Great White Hope." Johnson is distinguished as the first African American to gain the title of boxing world champion. Initially, Jeffries, who retired undefeated as world heavyweight champion, did not want to fight in an interracial bout. But after Johnson beat Sydney Burns, the Canadian world champion, celebrities and the press pressured Jeffries to become the white hope, defeat Johnson, and concretely settle the question of racial superiority.

Jack Johnson fought a good fight in the ring, but his decadent lifestyle and defiance of the rules that prescribed the separation of the races brought him defeat, imprisonment, and exile. Unlike Johnson, Paul's fight was not with human opponents for fleeting fame, monetary rewards, and some respect. His fight of faith, as with all Christians, is with demonic forces. Paul ran the race for perfection with a sure gait and figuratively fought with balled up fists, but he admits that he kept failing at doing the good he wanted to do while doing the evil he hated (Rom. 7:19). Combating our strong hereditary bent toward evil is an uphill struggle requiring prayerful vigilance and Holy Ghost power.

We are admonished to "cleanse ourselves from all filthiness of the flesh and spirit, perfecting holiness in the fear of God" (2 Cor. 7:1). Thus, Paul figuratively pounded his body until it obeyed his commands for fear he would become disqualified for the prize even while preaching to others (1 Cor. 9:26, 27). Bringing our minds and bodies under subjection and keeping them there begins with the indwelling of the Holy Spirit. He is willing and perfectly capable to put to death the misdeeds of the body so we can live a righteous life, but He will not force us to obey His nudging.

If we live according to our sinful nature and disconnect from God, our power source, we will die in our sins, and a dead soul cannot be revived (Rom. 8:13). So we are admonished to "live by the Spirit, and … not gratify the desires of the sinful nature" (Gal. 5:16, 17, NIV). To live by the Spirit necessitates our employment of the triangle of hope comprised of discipline, patience, and prayer. They shield us from our fickle selves in this ferocious and constant battle for supremacy over our will, mind, and body.

Keep your boxing gloves on and your hands in a defensive posture at all times as we battle for our lives. Satan and his demons are experts at battering our resolve to follow God. But every time they knock us down or knock the wind out of us, the Spirit provides supernatural muscle to rebound and fight yet another day. Like Paul, continue to fight the good fight and keep the faith.

August 13

Keep Your Eyes on Jesus

For we have no power to face this vast army that is attacking us. We do not know what to do, but our eyes are upon you. 2 Chron. 20:12, NIV.

Food raining down from heaven and rocks bursting forth with water were miracles offered by God in the sight of and for the Israelites as they traversed the desert and wilderness en route to the Promised Land. "But the people grew impatient … they spoke against God and … Moses, and said, 'Why have you brought us up out of Egypt to die in the desert? There is no bread! There is no water! And we detest this miserable food!'" (Num. 21:4, 5, NIV). Their murmuring and disobedience blocked the blessing of protection from the deadly fiery serpents in the wilderness. After many were bitten and had died, others repented and asked Moses to pray to move God's hand against the serpents (verses 7, 8).

"Let the past sleep, but let it sleep on the bosom of Christ. Leave the irreparable Past in His hands, and step out into the Irresistible Future with Him."[230] Egypt was still in the Israelites systems, just as spiritual Egypt is in ours. Jesus attempted to give them a future and a hope, but they were reluctant to let go of the past and welcome a transformation in outlook and character. Because their eyes looked backward at the past, they could not look up to see Jesus' love and protection. And they also failed to comprehend the great blessing of His guidance through the wilderness of sin into both a physical and spiritual Promised Land.

Moses prayed; God heard and directed him to fashion a serpent of brass, lift it up on a pole, and counsel the people to look up and live. The serpent symbolized Jesus who said, "As Moses lifted up the serpent in the wilderness, even so must the Son of man be lifted up: That whosoever believeth in him should not perish, but have eternal life" (John 3:14, 15). During this crisis, the requirement that the Israelites look heavenward stood as an object lesson in faith. The fiery, deadly serpents crawled all around their feet, but looking down to avoid them meant certain death. Faith impelled them to look up to live.

Although God the Son traveled in their midst, the Israelites did not know Him. Busy looking at their current circumstances and not their blessings, they became weary and discouraged. And we do the same. We take many of our countless daily blessings for granted, forgetting to look to the Grantor of our blessings. Paul admonishes us to look to Jesus who "is the author and finisher of our faith" who endured great hostility from sinners against Himself but did not become discouraged (Heb. 12:2, 3).

All who are confused, anxious, or frustrated keep your eyes upon Jesus. Faith requires us to decrease in self-important independence and to increase in God-assurance and God-dependence. God-assurance comes from a strong, abiding faith in God and His ability to handle all of our crises, troubles, and problems. Look up to Him in faith, and with eyes lifted upon Him, fear packs its bags and leaves room for peace to take up residence.

August 14

God's Sustaining Grace

My grace is sufficient for thee: for My strength is made perfect in weakness. 2 Cor. 12:9.

A wise man saw a scorpion floundering around in the water and stretched out his finger to save it, but the scorpion stung him. Yet again, he tried to get the scorpion out of the water, but again the scorpion stung him. An onlooker advised him to stop the foolish rescue attempt since the scorpion kept stinging him. But the man said, "It is the nature of the scorpion to sting. It is my nature to love. Why should I give up my nature just because it is the nature of the scorpion to sting?"[231]

The wise man's action gives us insight into the grace of God directed at His created beings who sting Him daily. "Grace means God's love in action towards men who merited the opposite of love. Grace means God moving heaven and earth to save sinners who could not lift a finger to save themselves. Grace means God sending His only Son to descend into hell on the cross so that we guilty ones might be reconciled to God and received into heaven."[232] A self-contained, pure gift, grace requires nothing from the recipient. It is undeserved.

The Word clearly defines grace: "But He said to me, My grace (My favor and loving-kindness and mercy) is enough for you [sufficient against any danger and enables you to bear the trouble manfully]; for My strength and power are made perfect (fulfilled and completed) and show themselves most effective in [your] weakness" (2 Cor. 12:9, AMP).

Notwithstanding that grace forgives and saves, *sustaining* grace is a welcomed gift in our troubled and chaotic world. Once we admit defeat and helplessness as the battle rages on all sides, God shows His strength through deliverance, consolation, or both. If He chooses not to deliver us or the deliverance is delayed by our standards, He provides the comfort, peace, and strength we need to fight against the adversity. Like a sustaining wall erected to brace up a building, His sustaining grace sufficiently supports us, transforms us, and provides a crutch of peace even in adverse, unchanging circumstances.

The benefits of sustaining grace are astounding. The Holy Spirit provides resolve to keep marching forward despite difficulties, and He contains our enemies. As well, He wraps us in a zone of supernatural strength as a buffer against suffering and supplies a heightened sense of His presence. When we come through the trials, we recognize the spiritual growth and the bigger faith. Trusting Him, we feel great inner peace even when the war is raging without. God's sustaining grace is bigger than any trial or enemy. Thus, He commands us not to fear our circumstances but allow Him to display His power through our weakness.

August 15

Unload Your Guilt

My guilt has overwhelmed me. Like a heavy load, it is more than I can bear. Ps 38:4 GWT

Pondering the Master's concept of guilt, Alfonso dreamed, "The Master taught that guilt is 'an evil emotion to be avoided like the very devil—all guilt. "But are we not to hate our sins?" a disciple said one day. "When you are guilty, it is not your sins you hate but yourself'"[233] answered the Master. Guilt is a belief that we have trampled on a moral standard and carry the responsibility. King David, the author of Psalm 38, is a poster child for guilt and its negative effects. He committed adultery, impregnating his lover Bathsheba, and frightened of the dishonor and the possibility of her being stoned to death, he murdered her husband, his loyal servant.

When confronted by the prophet Nathan, David's guilt and remorse caused him great agony of spirit. And the guilt paralyzed him and his ability to rule with authority, a man who formerly "executed judgment and justice unto all his people" (2 Sam. 8:15). David "was broken in spirit by the consciousness of his sin and its far-reaching results. He felt humbled in the eyes of his subjects. His influence was weakened.... But now his subjects, having knowledge of his sin, would be led to sin more freely. His authority in his own household, his claim to respect and obedience from his sons, was weakened. A sense of his guilt kept him silent when he should have condemned sin; it made his arm feeble to execute justice in his house."[234]

Psalm 38 offers an image of the guilt-ridden person who carries it like a vast burden that bows the back and incapacitates the holder. Masterfully used by Satan after he tempts us to violate our moral code, guilt moves us to condemn ourselves and engulfs us with discouragement. Sin that causes guilt unleashes a rollercoaster of emotions. Tyrannical in effect, guilt shatters our peace as sin separates us from God and barrages us with fear—"the tax which conscience pays to guilt."[235] Clearly, the conscience God places inside of each of us cannot be violated without enormous cost.

But God freely and graciously forgives any humble, repentant sinner. He said, "Let the wicked forsake his way, and the unrighteous man his thoughts: and let him return unto the LORD, and He will have mercy upon him; and to our God, for he will abundantly pardon" (Isa. 55:7). Once we forsake our sins and ask for forgiveness, He turns His face toward us in love. Moreover, fear and guilt turn into peace, turmoil turns into clarity, and paralysis turns into action.

Visualize our loving Lord leaning over the earth with outstretched hands pleading in a tender voice, "Come to me, all you who are weary and burdened, and I will give you rest" (Matt. 11:28, NIV). Surely it is not His desire that we become riddled with guilt. His rest is there for the asking, freely and abundantly available, and the only thing that stops us from entering is unbelief (Heb. 3:19). Jesus strives to "satisfy the weary ones and refresh everyone who languishes" (Jer. 31:25, NASB). It pays to unload guilt on Him and relieve the conscience and walk in friendship with the Creator.

August 16

Dressed in Wedding White

"Behold, I am coming as a thief. Blessed is he who watches, and keeps his garments, lest he walk naked and they see his shame." Rev. 16:15, NKJV.

When Eve saw that the fruit of the forbidden tree was appetizing and suitable for food, "and desirable for making someone wise. So she took some of the fruit and ate it. She also gave some to her husband … and he ate it. Then their eyes were opened, and they both realized that they were naked. They sewed fig leaves together and made coverings for themselves.… God called to the man and asked him 'Where are you?' He answered, '… I was afraid because I was naked, so I hid" (Gen. 3:6-10, GWT).

Their nakedness symbolizes immorality, impurity, and separation from God. Before the couple transgressed God's law, they were naked but felt no shame (Gen. 2:25). But Satan successfully tempted Eve with a promise of wisdom equal to God's, and she beguiled Adam to join her in disobedience. Their sin ushered in an awareness of good and evil, but it also flooded them with shame and guilt. "The love and peace which had been theirs was gone, and in its place they felt a sense of sin, a dread of the future, a nakedness of soul. The robe of light which had enshrouded them, now disappeared, and to supply its place they endeavored to fashion for themselves a covering; for they could not, while unclothed, meet the eye of God and holy angels."[236]

We are counseled to "clothe yourselves with the Lord Jesus Christ, and do not think about how to gratify the desires of the sinful nature" (Rom. 13:14). Clothing ourselves with Christ, we put on His righteousness ascribed to us by God. Sinful natures will shadow us while we remain in corruptible bodies, but through discipline and Spirit power, we can opt not to gratify that nature else it opens a Pandora's box of woes as it did for our first parents and subsequently all humanity.

God said, "Yet you have a few people … who have not soiled their clothes. They will walk with me, dressed in white, for they are worthy. He who overcomes will, like them, be dressed in white. I will never blot out his name from the book of life …" (Rev 3:4-6, NIV). He is looking for and is pleased with those who stay awake spiritually and keep their clothes unsoiled from sin so the nakedness of souls is clothed in the light of Jesus. Miraculously, Jesus has the only red blood that whitens like crimson bleach. Flowing from His veins, it is a cleansing flood, and whosoever plunges into it becomes "whiter than snow" (Ps. 51:7).

White symbolizes purity, righteousness, and truth. And John saw a countless multitude of people from every corner of the earth standing with Jesus, the Lamb of God, wearing white robes and holding palm branches, the symbol of peace in their hands (Rev. 7:9). We cannot know the precise day of His coming, so it behooves us to remain vigilant about our salvation lest His reappearing surprise us as a thief slipping into an unguarded home.

August 17

You Are My Disciples

Then said Jesus to those Jews which believed on him, if ye continue in my word, then are ye my disciples indeed. John 8:31.

Jean Valjean, an ex-convict character in Victor Hugo's *Les Misérables*, bunks at the home of Bishop Myriel after his release from prison. Unaccustomed to kindness, Valjean steals the bishop's silverware and flees. He is captured by the police, but the bishop protects him by telling the police he gave him the silverware as a gift. Later the bishop tells Valjean, "Forget not, never forget that you have promised me to use this silver to become an honest man.... Jean Valjean, my brother: you belong no longer to evil, but to good. It is your soul that I am buying for you. I withdraw it from dark thoughts and from the spirit of perdition, and I give it to God!"[237] Valjean, changed by love despite a difficult existence, later ministers as a disciple of the Lord.

To be Jesus' disciple is conditioned on our relationship with the Word. Jesus said, "Those who love me will keep my word, and my Father will love them, and we will come to them and make our home with them" (John 14:23, NRSV). But some of Jesus' followers keep the Word wrapped up in perfumed ribbons and placed in a box high up on a shelf to be referred to periodically. That is not what Jesus meant by "keep His Word." The psalmist declared that he hid the Word in his heart so he would not sin against God. Without the wisdom and knowledge contained in the Holy Writ informing us of our fallen state, the controversy between good and evil and the solution to our sin problem, we are putty in the hands of the deceiver, Satan.

The Bible contains no static words as those in a dictionary but is alive, powerful, and sharp enough to cut to the quick. It has the power to awaken not only the physical dead but also the spiritual dead as it will transform the hard-core sinner into a disciple of Christ. Our minds are renewed by the Word, and we are transformed into the image of Jesus. That is the good and perfect will of God (Rom. 12:2). As well, the Word is a teacher and a guide and the light shining in the darkness, thus converting a sinful world.

A true disciple removes the Word from the shelf, dusts it off, and strips off the perfumed ribbon. Through regular Bible study, she earnestly seeks to know her Savior and Redeemer while clinging to His promises of hope, peace, and salvation. Furthermore, disciples are made clean by the Word (John 15:3). Like an effervescent cure, it churns and bubbles to the marrow of our bones, cleansing us from the inside out so one day we can fellowship with the Word made flesh in a heavenly realm.

Moreover, the Word is our inspiration and our song. William Carr wrote, "One of the greatest evidences of the inspiration of Scripture is that it everywhere points to Christ, the living Word. Christ is the very spirit and soul and body of the Scriptures ... He is the 'Yea and Amen' of all the promises of the Word of God."

August 18

Reflecting the Image of the Creator

Do not lie to one another, since you have put off the old man with his deeds, and have put on the new man who is renewed in knowledge according to the image of Him who created him. Col. 3:9, 10, NKJV.

Snakes regularly outgrow their skins and need new ones as babies and toddlers need new clothes. If not discarded, their old skins restrict continued growth. Once the new skin develops beneath the old, the process of shedding begins. Snakes rub against a hard substance to put a rip in the area of the nose and mouth, work to loosen the skin all over the body, then glide free, leaving a dry tunnel of skin behind. The new skin is similar because it has the same patterns and design of the old skin but different as the old skin appears translucent and crumpled.

Figuratively, crucified Christians also put on a new skin. Paul says, "You're done with that old life. It's like a filthy set of ill-fitting clothes you've stripped off and put in the fire. Now you're dressed in a new wardrobe. Every item of the new way of life is custom-made by the Creator, with his label on it. All the old fashions are now obsolete" (Col. 3:9, 10, MSG). He clearly elucidates the sinful behaviors that signify the old life. This roundup includes sins that satisfy our selfishness such as lust, sexual immorality, depravity, and covetousness. And clothed in the old life, we harm our neighbors through gossip, lies, anger, wrath, malice, blasphemy, gestures, and filthy communication.

For continued growth, crucified Christians "dress in the wardrobe God picked out for [us]: compassion, kindness, humility, quiet strength, discipline. Be even-tempered, content with second place, quick to forgive an offense. Forgive as quickly and completely as the Master forgave you. And regardless of what else you put on, wear love. It's your basic, all-purpose garment. Never be without it" (verses 12-14, MSG).

Crucified with Christ, willful sinners die so Christ may live in us. Dying for us, Jesus gives us the option to choose life over the dark, miserable existence in Satan. And to prevent reversion to those old sinful practices, His Spirit stands guard. By His strength, we crucify the old life so the purity of His life becomes ours. Because Satan is still swirling around tempting us to sin, we may fall from grace from time to time, but we are no longer *slaves* to sin. Crucified Christians repent with godly sorrow for transgressions and continue striving to reflect His life of love and service.

Jesus fully paid the price for our brand-new couture wardrobe, leaving us debt free. Now, we are "dressed to kill" the old man as we travel this journey in the stunning attire of godliness. Conversion changes our focus from our own selfish desires to a focus on God's will. And with conversion we grow from a carnal sinner in bondage to Satan, to a saved saint permitting Jesus full authority to rule over our lives, to an obedient child who is the image of the Father in thought, deed, and action. In Him we are a new creation; the old life becomes extinct and the new life roots, blossoms, and flowers.

August 19

Inexhaustible, Inextinguishable, Unfailing Compassion

It is of the LORD's mercies that we are not consumed, because his compassions fail not. They are new every morning: great is thy faithfulness. Lam 3:22, 23.

    The Euonymus alatus, nicknamed burning bush, emerges from the Euonymus species native to Asia. A naturalized shrub, it is a staple for landscaping across parts of the northern United States. Its nickname and popularity stem from the green foliage that turns a startling red in the fall. The original name may stem from the biblical burning bush that captured Moses' attention as he tended his father-in-law's flock. At the base of Mount Horeb, Moses encountered the bush that burned fiercely with orange-red flames, but the bush, oblivious to the flames, was not consumed (Ex. 3:1-3).

    Speaking from the burning bush, God shared with Moses His compassion for the Israelites in bondage to the Egyptians. "The LORD said, 'I have indeed seen the misery of my people in Egypt. I have heard them crying out because of their slave drivers, and I am concerned about their suffering. So I have come down to rescue them from the hand of the Egyptians and to bring them up out of that land into a good and spacious land, a land flowing with milk and honey'" (Ex. 3:7, 8, NIV).

    The compassionate feel great sorrow at another's suffering. Keenly aware of their pain, the compassionate one suffers intensely with the sufferer. She feels a strong sense of pity and, wherever possible, works to alleviate that suffering. And to a degree incomprehensible to our finite minds, the God of love and the Creator of compassion deeply feels His children's pain. His compassion is extraordinarily deep, wide, and broad because it encompasses the entire world. The psalmist declared, "Thou, O Lord, art a God full of compassion" (Ps. 86:15)!

    The Lord empathizes with and responds to those that fear Him as an earthly father relates to his child (Ps. 103:15). One of God's greatest attributes is compassion. Sensing this, the multitudes flocked to Jesus wherever He went, bringing the sick and diseased for healing. One day He looked upon a crowd that followed Him for days without food, and Jesus said to His disciples, "I have compassion on the multitude, because they have now been with me three days, and have nothing to eat: And if I send them away fasting to their own houses, they will faint on the way" (Mark 8:1-3).

    Jesus' loving concern extends also to our spiritual well-being. He directed His disciples, who were tired and hungry after ministering to the multitudes, to a solitary place for relaxation. "But many who saw them leaving … ran … and got there ahead of them. When Jesus … saw a large crowd, he had compassion on them, because they were like sheep without a shepherd," needing spiritual direction (Mark 6:32-34, NIV). Throughout the Bible, we read of God's inextinguishable, inexhaustible, unfailing compassion. His compassions fail not!

August 20

The Price of a Soul

For what shall it profit a man, if he shall gain the whole world, and lose his own soul? Or what shall a man give in exchange for his soul? Mark 8:36, 37.

A brilliant intellectual prompted by excessive pride, Doctor Faustus lamented that he had reached the limits of learning and through magic summoned Mephistophilis, a servant of Lucifer, the prince of demons. The fictional character Mephistophilis reveals to Faustus that he summoned him not by magic but by his rejection of the Scriptures, which gave Lucifer a right to his soul. Faustus makes a pact with Lucifer to live twenty-four years using Mephistophilis to do his bidding. He refuses an opportunity to renege the pact with the devil when the wound needed to seal the pact with blood supernaturally heals and the words "man flee" appears on his arm. Faustus reasons that he has reached the point of no return, and there is nowhere to flee. So he seals the pact to sell his soul to the devil.[238]

A soul is a living, breathing human being. After God formed Adam from the dust, He "breathed into his nostrils the breath of life; and man became a living soul" or living person (Gen 2:7). And souls or humans beings are capable of both physical and spiritual death. According to Ezekiel, the soul that sins will die (Eze. 18:4). Matthew distinguishes the soul from the body, telling us to "fear not them which kill the body, but are not able to kill the soul: but rather fear him which is able to destroy both soul and body" (Matt. 10:28). Here, the soul is the new self that has been changed by submission to the Lordship of Jesus. Human beings can take our physical life and make us miserable, but they are incapable of destroying our inner self or soul that is preserved by God (2 Tim. 1:12).

The only "them" that can take both our physical and spiritual lives is God. Living selfishly and wickedly, we love ourselves to death, for those who love their lives will lose them, while those who hate their earthly, carnal life will receive eternal life (John 12:25). So it is wise to preserve our relationship with God at any physical cost. Loving God more then we love anything, including ourselves, and walking in the light of His Word are perquisites to preserving our soul alive throughout eternity for to "fear God, and keep his commandments" is our whole duty (Eccl. 12:13). There is no middle ground; to transgress God's Word is to accept Satan.

Satan hates and has utter contempt for the human race. And he is convinced by our actions and track record that the majority of us are shallow, weak, and selfish and would denounce God and die rather than relinquish our well-being. Talking to God about Job, he said, "A man will give all he has for his own life. But stretch out your hand and strike his flesh and bones, and he will surely curse you to your face" (Job 2:4, 5, NIV). Amazingly, knowing that Satan is evil, many people trust him with their future rather than our Creator who offers us a future and hope.

Nothing is more precious than each soul. We are so valuable that God gave His innocent Son to pay the wages of *our* sins so we can have a hope and a future. Earthly human life is mist-like; it appears for a short time and then vanishes (James 4:14). But the soul, the born again self, is meant to live forever.

August 21

The Joy of the Lord Is Your Strength

Do not sorrow, for the joy of the LORD is your strength. Neh. 8:10, NKJV.

Great joy bears expressing. And the Jews who lived in the Persian kingdom under King Xerxes were especially expressive because they went from deep sorrow after a national death decree to consuming joy when delivered. The yearly Feast of Purim, marked by dancing, masquerades, feasting, parties, and gift-giving, expressed their joy. It was a time for all Jews to express their joy (Esther 9:22). In addition, the revelers fasted and read the book of Esther in the Temple. "As the scroll is read, the villain, Haman, is vigorously booed at every mention of his name. To blot out his name, noisemakers called groggers are used, sometimes at a deafening volume! By contrast, every mention of the hero, Mordecai, is followed by a thunderous cheer."[239]

Haman climbed the ladder of success to become the king's prime minister, but his success became hollow because Mordecai refused to bow down to him. Thus, he plotted to destroy the entire nation of the Jews, convincing the king that they should not be tolerated. When Mordecai read the decree to kill all the Jews, "he tore his clothes, put on sackcloth and ashes, and went out into the city, wailing loudly and bitterly…. In every province to which the edict and order of the king came, there was great mourning among the Jews, with fasting, weeping and wailing. Many lay in sackcloth and ashes" (Esther 4:1-3, NIV).

Although God's name is absent in the book of Esther, we can trace His hand as He orchestrated events to deliver His people. Not coincidentally, the king chose Mordecai's cousin from the bevy of young virgins in the provinces. And Mordecai overheard a plot to assassinate the king as recorded in the king's chronicles. Before Haman could carry out his secondary plot to hang Mordecai, the king experienced God-induced insomnia and had the chronicles read to him, revealing Mordecai's deed. As well, Esther approached the king, which meant certain death, but received favor and apprised him that Haman's plot included her life being taken.

Several major events pivoted 180-degrees and faced the Jews. Promptly, the king ordered Haman and his ten sons hanged, passed a new decree in favor of the Jews permitting them to kill hundreds of thousands of their enemies, and assigned Haman's estate and his position to Mordecai. Mordecai sent a decree to all the Jews in the provinces "to have them celebrate annually the fourteenth and fifteenth days of the month of Adar as the time when the Jews got relief from their enemies, and as the month when their sorrow was turned into joy and their mourning into a day of celebration" (Esther 9:21, 22, NIV).

The joy of the Lord is our strength! God delights in His obedient children, and from the righteous, He withholds no good thing. "A tower of strength [is] the name of Jehovah, Into it the righteous runneth, and is set on high," for He is a strong tower of strength—a stronghold (Prov. 18:10, YLT). He is our strength and our song of joy and gladness.

August 22

The Greatest Reversal

But many that are first shall be last; and the last shall be first. Matt. 19:30.

The parable of the rich man and Lazarus illustrates the principle of the great reversal. The rich man lived in luxury, dressed regally, and daily ignored Lazarus, a beggar covered in sores who sat at the gate to his mansion. Suffering from a lack of basic needs, Lazarus yearned for food that fell from the rich man's table. Time passed and both the rich man and Lazarus died and met the great reversal. In the parable Lazarus apparently went to his heavenly mansion as the angels carried him to Abraham's side. But the rich man begged Abraham to send Lazarus with water to ease his fiery torment. Abraham refused, reminding him that he received his good things while Lazarus suffered. Now, the last is first (Luke 16:19-25).

When we view life from our limited perspective, we can declare definitively that life is not fair. The humble suffer; the proud thrive. Evil people do evil deeds without check while genuinely good people, recipients of those evil deeds, suffer and die. Christians are expected to pray for their enemies and to forgive them in the midst of this malignant enmity. These enemies are free to follow their true nature, but Christians must struggle to resist the pull of evil inclinations.

God mapped out earth's history before He created the first man and woman, and He has chosen a day when a great reversal will occur. "He who plants and he who waters are one; but each will receive his own reward according to his own labor" (1 Cor. 3:8, NASB). Not one act of injustice escapes His attention, nor will it forever go unpunished. Not one heartfelt prayer of His afflicted saints will be left unanswered. Although it does not seem fair from our standpoint, justice for some will not occur until the day of judgment. But rest assured, God will bring about justice for His chosen ones who cry out to him day and night. He will not keep putting them off (Luke 18:7).

Suffering is a mantle that God's chosen people will wear until the great reversal occurs. After Jesus' suffering, He reaped a glorious heritage, and we, too, will reap thusly. Before we receive our crown, however, we must carry our cross. C.S. Lewis wrote, "The people with very hard problems are understood by God. He knows what wretched machines they are trying to drive. Some day he will fling them away and give those people new ones; then they may astonish everyone, for they learned their driving in a hard school. Some of the last will be first and some of the first will be last."[240]

Beyond the day of that turnabout when the last will be first, the obedient will affirm that "the sufferings of this present time are not worthy to be compared with the glory which shall be revealed in us" (Rom 8:18). Waiting is very difficult as our lives revolve around time and schedules. But this brief affliction is producing for us an "eternal weight of glory" (2 Cor. 4:17). Without a doubt, to be first when the rewards are distributed is worth the wait despite what we endure in these bodies of clay.

August 23

The Land of the Living

I would have despaired unless I had believed that I would see the goodness of the LORD in the land of the living. Ps. 27:13, NASB.

A little boy flew on a plane seated next to Lloyd John Ogilvie who noted his politeness. The boy remained calm at takeoff and as the plane ascended into the sky. Soon, however, they encountered a bad storm with extreme turbulence that shook the plane so badly it felt as though it would rip apart. Still the little boy remained peaceful and unruffled. A woman across the aisle, obviously afraid, asked the little boy if he, too, were frightened. "No, Ma'am," he replied, looking up just briefly from his coloring book. "My dad's the pilot."[241]

Our heavenly Father's Spirit—our Pilot—expertly navigates the redeemed to their heavenly mansions. And if we remain faithful, we will see His goodness in the land of the living. Currently, earth, literally the land of the dead, is sorely littered with the graves of dead men, women, and children as well as dead dreams and hopes. Many the funeral processions and many the caskets we have counted in a lifetime on this dying, decaying earth. Also, earth is a breeding ground for demons that specialize in deception, destruction, and death. Presently, Death is victorious and the Grave has a biting sting sabotaging our peace.

Earth is also a spiritual graveyard for a great multitude of people who nonchalantly reject God's grace. They are dead in Christ and, therefore, cannot comprehend the present joy of the Lord or the future glories of heaven and the earth made new. "No eye has seen, no ear has heard, no mind has conceived what God has prepared for those who love him" (1 Cor. 2:9, NIV). Through Satan's deceptions, many make sport of heaven calling it boring, describe harp-playing angels floating around on clouds all day long, and make jokes about Saint Peter and pearly gates. Do not be deceived, Satan will miss out on an unimaginable delight, and he wants the identical outcome for everyone.

Tomorrow is not promised. Thus, Death, which snatches away every option but the wait for the judgment, may be a second away. Clearly, the rebellious have not counted the cost of their rebellion. The wicked person who never accepts God's grace will die as well as the backslider "because of the unfaithfulness ... and ... the sins he has committed, he will die" (Eze. 18:24, NIV). "Rather, am I not pleased when they turn from their ways and live?" (verse 23).

Without the anticipation of seeing Him face to face in glory, life would have no meaning. It would truly be one long funeral proceeding toward an eternal grave. But God's obedient children have this hope—that we will see God's goodness in the land of the living. And He is faithful to fulfill His promises.

August 24

Accepting Blessings and Adversity

You are talking like a foolish woman. Shall we accept good from God, and not trouble?
Job 2:10, NIV.

The Old Testament book of Job opens with language similar to a fairy tale, "In the land of Uz there lived a man whose name was Job" (Job 1:1, NIV), and like a fairy tale has a happy ending (Job 42:12-17). But cold, hard reality intervenes between the fairy tale beginning and ending. Job wakes up one fine morning and finds his life changed for the worst. His world, framed by agonizing, unexplainable events, spirals downward and out of control while he searches for answers to his suffering. Furthermore, Job's suffering is heightened by insensitive, judgmental friends and a grieving wife.

Most of us can scarcely imagine the agony and shock of losing ten children and all our earthly belongings, our reputation in the community, and our physical well being in a short span of time. After wasting no time in destroying Job's finances, his family, and his health, Satan uses Job's wife as a medium to tempt her husband to abandon God during a time of great need. Looking at him seated on an ash heap scraping pus-filled boils with a potsherd, she spits out, "Do you still hold fast your integrity? Curse God and die!" (Job 2:9, NASB). In her sorrow, she challenges him to forsake God, who claims to be love but who has dumped this unthinkable horror in the middle of Job's life. She counsels Job to give up, give God a good tongue-lashing, and die.

Although God was not disciplining Job, adversity is a form of discipline that God employs to extract us from the curse of death. The Bible says we should not despise or be discouraged by the loving discipline of the Lord, for it trains us to live godly lives (Heb 12:5, 6). In love God limits the adversity and customizes it to fit each person's tolerance level and requirement. As a motivator, it tests our loyalties, shows us our weaknesses and helplessness, and moves us to greater dependency on Him. Adversity can also serve as an attention getter that leads to repentance for those whose backs are turned to God in complete rebellion (Jer. 31:18, 19).

If God could bridge the deep chasm of separation between Himself and His fallen creation by giving us a life chock full of sunshine and joy, He would not hesitate to do so. But He knows our frame; that we are dust (Ps. 103:14). Given a life of ease and comfort, selfishness would move us to feel entitled to His blessings. For considering the "weakness and mortality of our natures, and the frailty of our condition … if he should let loose his hand upon us, we should be irrecoverably destroyed."[242]

Understandably, Job became depressed and wished he had never been born, but he remained righteous. In fact, he labeled his wife's stance as foolish and reminded her that they readily accepted blessings with gratitude and praise, why not adversity. As a lesson for all of us, Job illustrates that we deserve nothing but death, so accept discipline, notwithstanding the pain, because it is a balm for the soul.

August 25

God Requires Obedience

To obey is better than sacrifice, and to hearken than the fat of rams. 1 Sam. 15:22.

Two Christian missionaries approached a Hindu mother at a riverbank looking pensively at the crocodiles. She held a sick baby girl in her arms with a healthy little boy playing nearby. The missionaries counseled her not to sacrifice her child to the crocodiles to appease the gods, but to no avail. Although told about the love of Jesus, she did not renounce her beliefs. The next time the missionaries encountered her the frail little girl accompanied her but not the boy. They knew immediately that she had sacrificed him. Perplexed, the missionaries asked why she had sacrificed her healthy child and not the sick one. She said sternly, "We only give our best to our gods."[243]

This misguided idolater did not hesitate to give the best to her gods. Surely those who serve the Creator of heaven and earth should be compelled by His grace to give Him our best. And the best that we have to offer Him is loving obedience. Solomon concluded, "Let us hear the conclusion of the whole matter: Fear God, and keep his commandments: for this is the whole duty of man" (Eccl. 12:13). Accepting no less, God rejects sacrifices when they substitute for godliness (Ps. 51:16).

Similar to the Hindu mother, we can offer sacrifices without the love of God in our hearts. Love is manifested through obedience. Jesus said, "If you love me, you will obey what I command" (John 14:15, NIV). Understanding our propensity to take the easy route, He declares His preference of obedience over sacrifice. Hordes of people worldwide effortlessly give of their time, finances, and talents to the church and to others but are some of the most mean-spirited hell-raisers you will ever encounter. The Bible says their lips honor Him but their hearts are far from Him (Matt. 15:8). Any sacrifice without a heart change will amount to nothing for the giver but a startling rejection by Jesus at the judgment (Matt. 21:23).

From antiquity God demanded obedience and that demand remains firm. Isaiah, using the images of his era when the animal sacrificial system operated in full swing, wrote, "'The multitude of your sacrifices—what are they to me?' says the LORD. 'I have more than enough of burnt offerings, of rams and the fat of fattened animals; I have no pleasure in the blood of bulls and lambs and goats.... Take your evil deeds out of my sight! Stop doing wrong, learn to do right! Seek justice, encourage the oppressed. Defend the cause of the fatherless, plead the case of the widow" (1:11-17, NIV).

Does God need meaningless sacrifices, including our money, our time, or our talents without the accompanying love to build His kingdom or to ease suffering and quell confusion? Absolutely not! He has billions of angels under His authority who love to fulfill His commands, but He grants humanity this awesome privilege to partner with Him and provides the requisite strength and power. What He requires is obedience.

August 26

Progressing Up the Path of the Righteous

But the path of the righteous is like the light of dawn, which shines brighter and brighter until full day. Prov. 4:18, ESV.

Twilight blinks twice in a twenty-four hour period. At dusk it blinks in sleepiness, and then blinks at dawn to sweep sleep from its eyes. Morning twilight postures between dawn and sunrise, and evening twilight between sunset and dusk. During twilight the earth is not totally dark or totally light, for dawn summons the first light in the morning sky whereas the sun begins its ascension above the horizon at sunrise. Called "nature's alarm clock," sunrise grows from barely light and dressed in vibrant hues of color up the continuum to unmistakably bright.

Likewise, spiritual growth up the scale of godliness marks a Christian's walk with Christ. It is a process of maturing toward perfection. Jesus said, "Be perfect, therefore, as your heavenly Father is perfect" (Matt. 5:48, NIV). Physical growth has a season and then ends, but spiritual growth toward godliness continues throughout our physical existence. C.F.W. Walther wrote, "If a person has become a Christian, a new spiritual being is created in him by faith and the growth of this being never ceases until death. In Christianity, there is no standing still. Whoever does not go forward goes backward. The life of a Christian is not marked by being, but by growing. The goal is so high that he can never say he has reached it and can rest from his efforts."

Godliness, says Jerry Bridges, is the "idea of a personal attitude towards God that results in actions that are pleasing to God." This growth is impossible without godly fear. "The LORD delights in those who fear him, who put their hope in his unfailing love" (Ps.147:11, NIV). God-fearing is a palette arrayed with vibrant colors of God-respect, God-awe, and God-love. We cannot appreciate what it means to fear Him until we comprehend His dominion over the earth's inhabitants, that He is the potter and we are the clay, that our very existence and preservation are in His hands, that we deserve death but for a God-devised plan to give us an inheritance, and that His mercy prevents our being consumed.

Actions pleasing to God are based in the true knowledge of His Word—the Word that counsels us to flee wickedness and "pursue righteousness, godliness, faith, love, steadfastness, gentleness" (1 Tim. 6:11, ESV), beckons us to live in a God-ordained manner, and leads us to His mind and His will. And this growth is not done in solitary confinement. "His divine power has given us everything we need for life and godliness through our knowledge of him ... so that ... you may participate in the divine nature and escape the corruption ... caused by evil desires" (2 Peter 1:3, 4, NIV).

Anything worth having is worth the struggle; hence godliness requires continual work. It necessitates discipline, commitment and effort in Bible study, prayer, and submission to the Holy Spirit's leading. In so doing, our path shines brighter and brighter until the day of His arrival when night will burst into everlasting day.

August 27

You Are Pardoned

Incline your ear, and come unto me: hear, and your soul shall live. Isa. 55:3.

Judicial death by hanging is a gruesome event. The victim is placed over a trap door with a drop long enough to jolt the noose knotted on the left side of the neck under the jaw hard enough to break the neck and sever the spinal cord. Still, George Wilson, convicted of mail robbery and endangering the life of the driver, chose to hang. He received a pardon from the president of the United States but, incredibly, refused to accept the pardon because the other charges were not dropped, leaving him to spend decades in jail. However, the parties involved tried to compel him to accept the pardon.

The case went to the United States Supreme Court where Chief Justice Marshall wrote, "A pardon is an act of grace, proceeding from the power entrusted with the execution of the laws, which exempts the individual on whom it is bestowed from the punishment the law inflicts for a crime he has committed.... A pardon ... is not complete without acceptance. It may then be rejected by the person to whom it is tendered, and if it be rejected, we have discovered no power in a court to force it on him. It may be supposed that no [one] being condemned to death would reject a pardon ... but it is certain that a man may waive the benefit of a pardon."[244]

Life-changing, a pardon forgives a crime and expunges the accompanying penalty; only a supreme authority like a king or president has the power to grant them. The words "pardon" and "forgive" are sometimes used interchangeable in the Scriptures, but pardon contains a legal essence. To clear his name, the law demanded Wilson's pardon because he broke the law and earned a conviction. But the presidential pardon would have cleared his name, absolved him from guilt, and proclaimed him innocent of the crime. Like a magic carpet, the pardon could have transported Wilson from death to life.

Earthly leaders pardon sporadically and selectively, but Jesus, the invisible monarch, pardons abundantly, repeatedly, and impartially (Isa. 56:6, 7). The Christian's pardon is signed in divine, holy blood, and once the pardon is executed, our sins are removed "as far as the east is from the west" (Ps. 103:12). And all are welcome to present their transgressions and petitions for a full and complete pardon. God says, "But you have burdened me with your sins and wearied me with your offenses. I, even I, am he who blots out your transgressions, for my own sake, and remembers your sins no more" (Isa. 43:23, 24, NIV).

Wisdom embraces a pardon, but not the fool who loves sin more than his eternal soul. He despises God and rejects His offers of mercy and " hath said in his heart, There is no God" (Ps. 14:1). But Wisdom fears the Lord and walks carefully as Jesus walked, "not as fools, but as wise" (Eph. 5:15). Fools plunge headlong into destruction while Wisdom queries, "Who is a God like you ... [he will] tread our sins underfoot and hurl all our iniquities into the depths of the sea" (Micah 7:18, 19, NIV). God guarantees that the wise shall live.

August 28

Sow the Wind, Reap the Whirlwind

Give, and it will be given to you. A good measure, pressed down, shaken together and running over, will be poured into your lap. For the measure you use, it will be measured to you. Luke 6:38, NIV.

Scientists have researched for years to discover what God revealed at Creation: "The earth produced vegetation: plants bearing seeds … and trees bearing fruit with seeds, each according to its own type" (Gen. 1:12, GWT). Simpson and Beck wrote, "there is no serious doubt that biogenesis is the rule, that life comes only from other life, that a cell, the unit of life, is always and exclusively the product or offspring of another cell."[245] And in a 1981 *Science Digest*, Martin Moe noted, "A century of sensational discoveries in the biological sciences taught us that life arises only from life, that the nucleus governs the cell through … DNA and that the amount of DNA and its structure determine [both] not only the nature of the species [and] but also the characteristics of individuals."

Biogenesis is the sophisticated scientific word for seeds bearing fruit according to its kind. Sowing and reaping is a simplistic phrase that encapsulates both the agricultural and spiritual connotation of the same law. Agriculturally, it is impossible to plant a tomato seed and produce a green pepper plant. Tomato seeds yield tomatoes, and green pepper seeds yield green peppers. Importantly, one seed yields many plants, indicating that we reap more than we sow. And spiritually, according to the unalterable laws of God, negative and/or positive consequences of past actions will appear one day.

Zedekiah, king of Judah, sowed good sparingly and reaped good sparingly (2 Cor. 9:6). God warned him that Judah's numerous sins offended Him greatly, thus His cup of wrath had filled to overflowing. He counseled Zedekiah to peacefully surrender to the Babylonians and accept the temporary punishment. Although God permitted the king of Babylon to besiege and burn the city, surrender meant Zedekiah would not die by the sword but would die in peace (Jer. 39; 52).

Zedekiah and the Jews "mocked the messengers of God, and despised his words, and misused his prophets" (2 Chron. 36:16). Additionally, Zedekiah broke a solemn oath to Babylon's king who crowned him Judah's puppet king. Rather than obey God, he abused the messenger and hampered and enraged the Babylonians for years before they breached the walls. With an empty pantry, many died from disease and famine. In desperation, they began to eat human flesh to survive (Jer. 52:4-7; Isa. 49:15). Their disobedience unleashed a relentless chain reaction of destruction.

Led by the king, the nation sowed seeds of disobedience, rebellion, vindictiveness, and cruelty, and they reaped the same. Babylon breached the walls, forcing Zedekiah, his sons, and his personal army to flee, but the Babylonians caught and killed his personal army. In horror, Zedekiah watched as the Babylonians killed his sons. Then, they blinded Zedekiah, bound him, and carried him to Babylon with the image of his sons' cruel execution firmly planted in his mind. Zedekiah sowed the wind and reaped the whirlwind.

August 29

The God-shaped Hole in Our Hearts

Be still, and know that I am God. Ps. 46:10.

    A man I call Freddie became silent in a debate with a barber who believed that God did not exist based on the condition of the world. As he left the barbershop, Freddie ran into a man with dirty, long hair and an untrimmed beard. He returned to the barbershop, and said, "Barbers do not exist." The barber laughed. "Well," Freddie replied, "If barbers did exist no one would walk around with long, dirty hair and unkempt beards." The barber retorted haughtily that barbers do exist, but he cannot service people if they refuse to seek his assistance. "That's the point! God, too, does exist! People do evil things and live with unnecessary fear and despair when they overlook God for help."[246]

    If and when we believe and act on the wise counsel of the psalmist to be still and know that He is God, we find peace and rest in a scary, unsafe, uncertain world—a world on a collision course with destruction. "The command to 'be still' comes from the *hiphil* stem of the [Hebrew] verb *rapha* (meaning to be weak, to let go, to release)."[247] In our relationship with God, we are to cause ourselves to let go or to become weak. The key is to admit our helplessness and submit control to God (James 4:7). The Bible reveals He sustained, guided, and protected His people in the past. And He has the requisite wisdom and power to do likewise today, for He changes not.

    With the enemy "is only an arm of flesh, but with us is the LORD our God to help us and to fight our battles" (2 Chron. 32:8). God's Word is absolute, but with our independence and self-will, we bind His arms as surely as if we garb Him in a straitjacket. As a wearer of a straitjacket knows, no matter how much movement is desired, meaningful movement is impossible with sleeves tied to one's back. Submission, however, releases God's almighty arms to fight our battles, to guide us into righteousness, to order our steps, and to plant us in a peaceful place.

    In addition, all of us have a God-shaped hole in our heart that God opens and sutures after He implants His law. From there He courts us into an intimate relationship with Him (Rom. 2:15). Without God as an active, ruling participant in our lives, life is empty. "Meaningless! Meaningless! says the Teacher.... Everything is meaningless" (Eccl. 1:2, NIV). Solomon, the second king of Israel, to whom God gave unreachable wisdom, wealth, and prestige, found fleeting pleasure in women—700 wives and 300 concubines to be exact—and in his wealth and possessions. Even possessing the things that the eyes of flesh covet, he felt empty as he wandered from God through intermarriage with idolatrous women (1 Kings 11:1-3).

    Solomon learned to despise his worldly accomplishments and material acquisitions because they did not satisfy his soul's longing. Life held little meaning until he satisfied his need for God. Hence, after years of emptiness and woe, he filled the hole in his heart with God by establishing a love relationship with Him (Eccl. 12:13).

August 30

In the Image of God

As for me, I will see Your face in righteousness; I shall be satisfied when I awake in Your likeness. Ps. 17:15, NKJV.

In 1839 photography flashed a big grin with the invention of the Daguerreotype, which allowed photographers to create decidedly detailed images on silver-plated sheets of copper. To be effective, the copper sheets had to be cleaned and polished to emulate a mirror and coated in iodine to ensure the surface remained sensitive to light. Louis Daguerre, an expert in camera design, and Joseph Nicéphore Niépce, a photochemist, invented this new phenomenon. Although Daguerreotype photography produced stunningly accurate images, this process had its problems. For instance, the delicate silver-plated copper damaged easily, and chemicals like mercury and chlorine used to produce the images were very toxic.

When God created Adam and Eve in His image, they were perfect physically and spiritually, for the likeness of God equates to righteousness and the holiness of the truth (Matt. 5:48; Eph. 4:24). Made in His image, we reflect His nature and resemble Him in many important ways. For instance, God gave us understanding, wisdom, and intellect to distinguish truth from error and to live righteous lives. Uniquely made, we are intelligent not like "the horse or the mule, which have no understanding but must be controlled by bit and bridle" (Ps. 32:9, NIV).

God also made us coherent beings with reasoning skills to exercise dominion over nature, to use sound judgment, and to make rational decisions. He extols us to "reason together" with Him (Ps. 8:6: Isa. 1:18). He walked beside Adam and Eve in the Garden of Eden to guide them in their moral decision-making and commissioned the Spirit to walk with us and guide us in examining the truths that lead to salvation. He promises, "I will instruct you and teach you in the way you should go; I will counsel you and watch over you" (Ps. 32:8, NIV).

The freedom to make choices is another God-like attribute given to us, so our connection stems from love and respect, not coercion. Adam and Eve were built with the freedom to make morally right as well as morally wrong choices. "And the LORD God commanded the man, 'You are free to eat from any tree in the garden; but you must not eat from the tree of the knowledge of good and evil, for when you eat of it you will surely die'" (Gen. 2:16, 17, NIV). Choosing sin over obedience, they upset God's perfect plan for them and their progeny by introducing rebellion into the world. Thus, their choice marred the image of God in themselves and every following generation.

But through the death of Jesus and His cleansing blood, God is able to reinstate His image in anybody who is willing. To do so, we are guided by His Spirit to slay whatever belongs to our earthly natures and "put on the new man, which is renewed in knowledge after the image of him that created him" (Col. 3:10). Then we can be satisfied that at the resurrection we will awake in His image.

August 31

Standing on High Places

He makes my feet like the feet of a deer; he enables me to stand on the heights. Ps. 18:33, NIV.

In the allegory *Hinds' Feet on High Places*, Much-Afraid leaves the Valley of Humiliation to embark on a very hard journey to the High Places that changes her into a brand-new creation. Terribly insecure, she has crooked feet that cause her to both limp and stumble; and her crooked mouth causes her expression and speech to raise eyebrows. She serves the Chief Shepherd for years and soon asks to leave the valley to go the high places. He readily agreed to take her but cautioned that the way is difficult but worthwhile, for "nothing that is an enemy of Love can make the ascent and invade the kingdom. Nothing blemished or in any way imperfect is allowed there." He promises to make her feet like deer feet and set her upon high places.[248]

The Chief Shepherd assigns Sorrow and Suffering to accompany Much-Afraid on her journey. But instead of taking the direct, easy route to the High Places, Sorrow and Suffering detour down into the desert to Much-Afraid's dismay. She complains to the Shepherd who asks her to trust Him, and she consents to follow them. The Shepherd explains to her the process of battering that grain endures to be turned into fine bread after she consents to follow Sorrow and Suffering wherever they lead.

On the way, they encounter a cliff blocking the route, a fall down a precipice, a forest of danger, and tribulation and a storm. At one point Much-Afraid loses faith when surrounded by a fog that impedes her view. But because the Shepherd had planted a seed of love in her heart at the onset of the journey, she cannot conceive of life without Him and forages ahead. Once she completely surrenders, she rides a suspended chair all the way to the top and awakens from sleep with deer's feet and a new name.

The Christian journey is fraught with obstacles that challenge us. Sometimes events appear cruel and arbitrary. But fear not, "Not 'til the loom is silent, And the shuttle cease to fly, Will God unveil a canvas, And show the reason why, The black threads are as needful, In the weaver's skillful hand, As the threads of gold and silver, In the pattern he has planned," wrote Benjamin Malachi Franklin. God chooses the colors of sorrow and suffering for the tapestry. He sees the whole upper side while we only see a portion of the underside. Only faith and trust will curtail our bewilderment as God uses troubles for our profit.

The hind or deer lives in lofty mountains and easily conquers high, ragged crags and leaps over deep fissures without losing its footing. The deer's feet symbolize that "there are no obstacles which our Savior's love cannot overcome and that to him mountains of difficulty are as easy as an asphalt road."[249] God can move mountainous piles of troubles out of our path in gloriously unthinkable ways or assist us in climbing over them as we ascend to the high places. He is our Rock and a sure foundation who keeps us surefooted and balanced as we journey to meet Him.

September 1

Every Rebellious Sin Forgiven

Do not remember the sins of my youth or my rebellious ways. Remember me, O LORD, in keeping with your mercy and your goodness. Ps. 25:7, GWT.

In a daze the king climbed up to the room over the gateway and bawled. On the way up the steps, in the keenest pain, he wailed, "O my son Absalom! My son, my son Absalom! If only I had died instead of you! O Absalom, my son, my son!" (2 Sam. 18:33, NLT). Although King David's son had plotted to kill him and the rest of his family to ascend the throne, David's anguish and grief are almost intolerable. But the king's rebellion triggered avalanches that descended upon his own head time after time and entrapped him, his family, and the nation in torrents of pain, destruction, and death.

Rebellion is a refusal to follow God's Word, and it leads down a slippery slope to chaos and ruin. It is to deny God the place of authority in our lives. "For rebellion is as the sin of witchcraft, and stubbornness is as iniquity and idolatry" (1 Sam. 15:23). As with idolatry and witchcraft, rebellion nauseates a holy God. While David loved God and had a teachable and contrite spirit, the stunning beauty of Bathsheba stifled his conscience and allowed lust to dictate his actions. The snowball of deception grew into the avalanche of adultery and murder. And this spirit of rebellion transferred to David's son Absalom whose mutiny against his father led to his death.

First, Absalom rebelled against David's inaction to punish his son Amnon for the rape of Absalom's sister. To avenge her endless disgrace in a society that demanded a woman's virginity until marriage, Absalom paid a hit man to kill Amnon. Mustering a modicum of authority, David banned Absalom from the court, but while in exile Absalom gained the hearts of the king's subjects, scheming to oust the current government (2 Sam. 15:6). Thus, Absalom's rebellion extended to the entire nation.

Then, Ahithophel, Bathsheba's grandfather and former loyal counselor to David, advised Absalom in his scheme. Wise and wily, Ahithophel proved invaluable to David before he disgraced his granddaughter. The Bible says, "The advice Ahithophel gave was like that of one who inquires of God" (2 Sam. 16:23, NIV). The consequences of David's initial revolt against God's Word extended to his inner circle, moving Ahithophel to seek revenge. Among other advice, he counseled Absalom to commit incest with the king's concubines in a public place to ensure that David could never reconcile with Absalom and put his own life in jeopardy.[250]

"To the Lord our God belong mercies and forgivenesses, though we have rebelled against him" (Dan. 9:9). Even though the avalanche he unleashed gathered tons of destructive debris and pain and dumped them on his head, David sincerely repented of his sins. He looked to the merciful God to forgive him, and He did (Acts 3:19). "How boundless is that mercy which covers forever the sins and follies of a youth spent without God and without hope! Blessed be the Lord, the blood of the great Sacrifice can wash away every stain."[251]

September 2

When Troubles Multiply

Turn to me and be gracious to me, for I am lonely and afflicted. The troubles of my heart have multiplied; free me from my anguish. Ps. 25:16, 17, NIV.

Rejection, loneliness, and comprehensive abuse shattered Naomi's childhood. Her parents separated when she was nine years old, leaving her Mom as the sole provider. As a result she and her sister were often hungry and homeless. They lived in squalor and poverty in a ghetto where gangs ruled. To alleviate her pain and feelings of worthlessness, Naomi abused illegal drugs, alcohol, and sex and spiraled into a vicious cycle of abusive relationships. In this downward spiral, she endured rape, became depressed, attempted suicide multiple times, suffered mental breakdowns, and lost parental rights to her son.

Lonely and afflicted with multiple troubles, Naomi needed relief. Although doctors prescribe strong painkillers for intense physical pain, sometimes the emotionally afflicted self-medicate with temporary painkillers to soothe their anguish. Naomi, like many others, employed such destructive sedatives. But these measures work temporarily and carry negative side effects that bring long-term results to one's present and future well-being. Still, if the measures work, no matter how temporary or destructive, the desperate continue to seek their relief.

"I was so angry at God. I couldn't understand why he continued to let me live. Yet, through it all, in the darkest times of my life, he remained by my side, even though I rejected him," Naomi stated.[253] It was not until she landed in a place where she could only look up to God for help and submit to His will that she found lasting, beneficial relief. God heard her pleas, saw her need, and freed her from her anguish. Discovering a High Priest who sympathized with her helplessness, Naomi heard Him motion her to boldly approach the throne of grace for mercy to help in her time of need (Heb. 4:15, 16).

No one is immune from multiplying troubles. Even the great luminaries, such as Elijah felt helpless and abandoned at times. His faith turned the heavens to bronze, preventing rain from falling for three years, and caused water to burn like gasoline, yet his multiplying troubles moved him to despair. Running from a threat of death by Queen Jezebel, and depressed and exhausted, he said, "I have been very zealous for the LORD God of hosts ... I alone am left; and they seek to take my life" (1 Kings 19:10, NKJV). And he petitioned God to rid him from this anguish: "I have had enough, LORD ... Take my life" (1 Kings 19:4, NLT). He, too, found grace at the throne of mercy.

As Naomi discovered and Elijah rediscovered, we have a Friend who promises to be with us "always, even to the end of the age" (Matt. 28:20, NASB). He will never abandon His own, and He walks beside us and comforts us in our anguish. "Blessed be ... the Father of mercies and God of all comfort, who comforts us in all our tribulation" (2 Cor. 1:3, 4, NKJV).

September 3

The Righteous March Forward

The righteous keep moving forward, and those with clean hands become stronger and stronger. Job 17:9, NLT.

One day, bored with life in the pond, two frogs journeyed to a neighboring dairy farm where they found a bucket of cream. They hopped in, licked their lips with delight, and momentarily swam around. As cream is much thicker than water, the frogs soon grew tired and decided to return to the lake. The first frog kicked and kicked and kicked but could not get out of the bucket. Soon he gave up, licked his lips, and drowned in the bucket of cream. The second frog determinately kicked nonstop until his kicking made a difference. Eventually the cream turned to butter, and he climbed on the butter, jumped out of the bucket, and returned to the pond.[254]

Similar to the second frog, the righteous, in good standing with God, keep moving forward even when fiery trials and smoke of confusion and doubt obscure the view. Walking forward in faith and not by sight, they cling to the Word as a guide through dense, discouraging smoke and blazing, destructive fires fanned by the enemy. We are directed to press on and never consider defeat an option. The apostle Paul, who walked a fiery and smoke-filled journey, wrote, "But one thing I do: Forgetting what is behind and straining toward what is ahead, I press on toward the goal to win the prize for which God has called me heavenward in Christ Jesus" (Phil. 3:13, 14, NIV).

But it takes clean hands and a pure heart to keep the forward momentum. "Who may go up the LORD's mountain? Who may stand in his holy place? The one who has clean hands and a pure heart" (Ps. 24:3, 4, GWT). Clean hands and a pure heart symbolize our faithfulness to the two great commands to love our God with all our heart and our neighbor as ourselves. "Clean hands will impact our actions; a pure heart will impact our attitudes. Clean hands will be seen by others; a pure heart will be seen by God. Clean hands will do right things; a pure heart will do them for the right reasons. Clean hands are our actions; a pure heart is our motivation. Clean hands are what we do; a pure heart is why we do it. Clean hands express our care; a pure heart expresses our character."[255]

As we march to Zion, a connection to the True Vine is vital. God is looking for a people who avoid the broad path to "become blameless and pure, children of God without fault in a crooked and depraved generation, in which you shine like stars in the universe as you hold out the word of life" (Phil. 2:15, 16, NIV). The righteous cannot be satisfied with stunted growth; therefore, they strive to keep connected to the True Vine for the power to grow from seed to blossom to mature plant.

Thus connected, "the righteous will flourish like the palm tree; he will grow like a cedar in Lebanon. Planted in the house of the LORD, they will flourish in the courts of our God. They will still yield fruit in old age; they shall be full of sap and very green" (Ps. 92:12-14, NASB). The righteous keep moving forward, onward and upward.

September 4

The Double-Minded Christian

Draw near to God and He will draw near to you. Cleanse your hands, you sinners; and purify your hearts, you double-minded. James 4:8, NASB.

Two men in a small village became entangled in an irresolvable dispute that required they individually talk to the town judge. The first man visited the judge's home and explained his version. When he concluded, the judge said, "You're absolutely right." Then the second man told his story. The judge responded, "You're absolutely right." Appalled, the judge's wife scolded him. "Those men told you two different stories, and you told each they were absolutely right. That's impossible—they can't both be absolutely right." Turning to her, the judge replied, "You're absolutely right!"[256]

The judge illustrates double-minded persons unable or unwilling to make a decision as an agonizing game of tug of war is played out in their minds. According to William James, "There is no more miserable human being than one in whom nothing is habitual but indecision." If this vacillating is an attempt to please two opposing factions, it fails because in the end it antagonizes all parties and escalates the matter. Margaret Thatcher wrote, "Standing in the middle of the road is very dangerous; you get knocked down by the traffic from both sides."

Even worse is a double-minded Christian whose indecisiveness is a matter of life and death for remaining steadfast in right-doing is life. Doing otherwise places the Christian in the camp of the enemy and under his rule where the faltering mind is controlled by the most persuasive party. True to his nature, Satan uses every devious trap to coerce a decision (John 10:10). But coercion has no place in a heart of love. God is the perfect gentleman who reaches out in love to receive love. He stands at the door of our hearts, knocks, and waits patiently for our response (Rev. 3:20). And if we choose Him, His Spirit walks over the threshold and settles in our hearts.

A double-minded Christian sways back and forth as a wave tossed by an agitated sea. But the inability to remain faithful usually backfires when we most need the Lord's blessings. "That man should not think he will receive anything from the Lord; he is a double-minded man, unstable in all he does" (James 1:7, 8, NIV). James labels double-minded Jesus followers as spiritual adulterers who profess to love God but walk hand in glove with the world where they become enemies of God (James 4:4).

Similarly, today's double-minded Christians faithfully attend church and hear the Word but are not doers of the Word. Many are selective in the commandments they keep, secure that grace absolves them from obedience. But God clearly said, "If you love me, you will keep my commandments" (John 14:15, ESV). With a single-minded purpose, if we draw near to God in love and surrender, He will draw near to us with spiritual blessings and benefits.

September 5

God Increases Strength

He gives power to the weak, and to those who have no might He increases strength. Isa. 40:29, NKJV.

Popeye the Sailor Man is a fictional character found in comic strips, cartoons, and movies who becomes superhumanly strong after eating spinach. Already strong as indicated by his bulging muscles, Popeye is no match for his giant-sized nemesis, Bluto, who regularly overpowers him. In conflict with Bluto, Popeye endures as long as possible before popping the top of a can of spinach and swallowing it. The jolt of spinach power works instantaneously, and with extraordinary strength, he defeats Bluto.

Popeye garners strength from an external power because he recognizes that he cannot defeat Bluto in his own might. Thus, he seeks a tried and true supply of strength. Wise Christians, too, recognize that there is no power in self or human sources. And they recognize "that your faith might not rest in the wisdom of men but in the power of God" (1 Cor. 2:5, ESV). Thus, to subdue personal and external opponents of good, try God (Phil. 4:13).

The "power to do good is the true and lawful end of aspiring," said Thomas Bacon. But aspiration alone is not sufficient to please God; we must be good. But we are born sinful, and each successive generation from Adam has become weaker in body and resolve. Thus, our ability to build faith and fight the appeal of sinful things is zero without intervention by the ultimate Source of power who points out sin and provides power to resist it (Ps. 68:35). That does not mean sin is defeated, but if we do sin we have an advocate in Jesus (1 John 2:1). Nor does it mean that we will never despair again in the face of trouble and suffering. But "after you have suffered a little while, God ... will himself restore, confirm, strengthen, and establish" us (1 Peter 5:10, ESV).

Moreover, when the winds of strife batter unmercifully, God provides the sustaining strength to stand firmly rooted and grounded in Him. The Spirit settles in our hearts concurrently with our acceptance of Jesus as Lord and empowers us (John 14:17; Acts 1:8). Unlike Popeye, it is pointless to pop a top and swallow vegetables for temporary power, for the Holy Spirit is instantly available, ever vigilant and supernaturally powerful (Eph. 3:20). But if we quench the Holy Spirit or grieve Him through obstinate sin, the power wanes and fades.

God's Spirit empowers us "that [we] might be filled with all the fullness of God" (Eph. 3:19) and strengthens us "with might by his Spirit in the inner man" (verse 16). Our present and eternal good is wrapped up in the fabric of our faith and obedience. Moreover, to live out our years on earth peacefully without fear of the judgment or our enemies or adverse circumstances, we are counseled to "abstain from all appearance of evil" and to persevere (1 Thess. 5:22). Mercifully, God furnishes the power and strength to accomplish just that!

September 6

Conquering Faith

Why are you fearful, O you of little faith? Matt. 8:26, NKJV.

Imagine being in the midst of a tempest at sea at night! The sky turns ominously dark and a menacing wind appears from nowhere. Already furious, the wind heightens in vehemence and intensity as each minute passes. Now vicious and arrogant, the gale-force wind bullies the waves, agitating them with its fury. It draws the helpless waves up and drops them at random on the now unleashed, undulating sea. When the waves rise, they forcible hurl giant buckets of water into the atmosphere, assaulting and engulfing seafaring vehicles and occupants as the drops splatter forcibly down.

A similar storm caught Jesus' disciples unawares as they crossed the Sea of Galilee after a tiring day of accompanying Jesus during His ministry of healing, exorcising, and preaching. The wind whipped the waves enough to put the small boat in danger of capsizing. To their amazement, Jesus peacefully slept through the screeching wind and the rocking boat. They woke Him saying, "Lord, save us! We're going to drown," prompting Jesus to chastise them for such tiny faith (Matt. 8:25, NLT).

What was the difference between Jesus' calm in the midst of the storm and the disciples' fear? A conquering faith! "A living faith means an increase of vigor, a confiding trust, by which the soul becomes a conquering power."[257] The disciples believed Jesus to be the Son of God but did not have the type of faith sufficient to stand firm in the storms of life. Also, they possessed enough faith to call on Jesus in a pinch but conquering faith remained undeveloped.

Jesus' exhibition of conquering faith in the midst of the storm stemmed from an intimate relationship with His heavenly Father. He trusted God to provide whatever He needed to survive the storm as He recognized God's authority over nature, mortals, and evil. He trusted in His abiding presence. "Do not fear, for I am with you; do not anxiously look about you, for I am your God. I will strengthen you, surely I will help you, surely I will uphold you with My righteous right hand" (Isa. 41:10, NASB).

God provides strength to withstand storms that pound against our peace and well-being. Sometimes the storms break down the doors of our lives and vicious waves flood us with suffering. We may lose a beloved child, parent, or spouse; be diagnosed with an incurable disease; or lose all our possessions in a fire or theft. But God has not abandoned us—He never will. Conquering faith will sustain us through the pain and confusion as we cling to Him, trusting that in the darkest hours of our existence He is hovering over us with compassion and our peace is a prayer away.

Conquering faith believes that our Comforter may allow the storms to beset us but carries us through them. He is a safe haven, "a refuge for the oppressed, a refuge in times of trouble" (Ps. 9:9). When the storms come, and they will, climb under His outstretched arms for refuge and wait each one out in peace.

September 7

Forgiving Ourselves

Let's practice real love. This is the only way ... to shut down debilitating self-criticism, even when there is something to it. For God is greater than our worried hearts. 1 John 3:19, 20, MSG.

An episode of the *Tyra Banks Show* titled "Tapeworm Diet" caught viewers' attention even while it disgusted them. Determined to lose weight, two overweight ladies, were not averse to participating in this gross diet that involved swallowing a tapeworm cyst and allowing the larva to grow to mature lengths of up to thirty feet in their intestines. The tapeworm is a parasite with little hooks and suckers used to attach itself to the wall of the host's intestines where it feasts on food eaten by its host. It absorbs nutrients in its own system, keeping it healthy and growing while robbing the host of nourishment. Notwithstanding, treatment is effective upon diagnosis.

Not unlike a voracious tapeworm, self-guilt, the result of not forgiving ourselves, coils inside of us and saps vigor and destroys peace. As the culpable party struggles to bear the weight of her anguish, guilt destroys her mental and physical health and her relationships. Unless we deal with the cause of our guilt and seek forgiveness, guilt will eat us alive. Edmund Burke wrote, "Guilt was never a rational thing; it distorts all the faculties of the human mind, it perverts them, it leaves a man no longer in the free use of his reason, it puts him into confusion."

The inability to forgive ourselves leads to destructive and often fatal actions. After Judas betrayed Jesus for thirty pieces of silver and realized the result of his actions, he became "overwhelmed with anguish, threw the money that he now despised at the feet of those who had hired him, and, in anguish and horror, went and hanged himself."[258] Over the years Judas had learned of Jesus, but loved money and power supremely (John 12:6). Believing that Jesus would establish an earthly kingdom, Judas expected Jesus to work a miracle and escape death, indignities, and cruelty. "But when he saw the infuriated multitude in the judgment hall, thirsting for blood, he deeply felt his guilt; and while many were vehemently accusing Jesus, Judas rushed through the multitude, confessing that he had sinned in betraying innocent blood."[259]

Guilt, a weapon used by Satan to discourage and weaken, is a cruel and relentless tormentor producing mental anguish and unrest. Led in a scheme by his mother, Rebekah, Jacob deceived his father and stole his brother's birthright (Gen. 27). Afraid of the murderous rage of his brother "Jacob fled from his father's home; he was weighed down with a sense of guilt."[260] Guilt at lying to his father and his part in tearing apart the family at such a devastating cost had to be overwhelming. But Jacob forgave himself after he confessed, repented, and accepted responsibility for his deception. Convinced that he received God's forgiveness and in harmony with His will, Jacob's guilt subsided and peace replaced fear (Gen. 32:30). Truly, God is greater than our worried hearts.

September 8

Through Faith Not Works

Good Master, what shall I do to inherit eternal life? Luke 18:18.

Renowned for his David-and-Goliath-type challenge to the corruption and false teachings of the Roman Catholic Church, Martin Luther feared God and yearned for salvation. Early on he believed one earned heaven through works, so he prayed incessantly, fasted until his body wasted away, lived in an unheated cell in the winter, and beat himself bloody. "Verily I was a devout monk, and followed the rules of my order so strictly that I cannot tell you all. If ever a monk entered into heaven by his monkish merits, certainly I should have obtained an entrance there. The doctors and theologians told me to do good works and thus to satisfy divine justice."[261]

After earning his doctoral degree, Martin Luther began to teach biblical studies at the University of Wittenberg. Teaching from the book of Romans, Luther found the peace that had eluded him in his attempt to gain salvation by works. The Holy Spirit convicted him of the power and truth behind Romans 1:17: "The just shall live by faith." In the *Ninety-Five Theses* that he tacked on the chapel door at the university, he criticized the sale of indulgences to atone for sin and pointed out that justification by faith, not works, led to salvation.

Consonant with the unenlightened Martin Luther, the rich young ruler expected to be saved by his works evidenced by a question to Jesus, "What must I *do* to be saved?" But salvation is a gift given to sinners by God's grace. "For the wages of sin is death; but the gift of God is eternal life through Jesus Christ" (Rom. 6:23). A gift is unsolicited and granted freely without cost. "Now to the one who works, his wages are not counted as a gift but as his due. And to the one who does not work but believes in him who justifies the ungodly, his faith is counted as righteousness" (Rom. 4:4, 5, ESV).

Justification means to conform to a certain standard, to be right with God. The justified sinner is deemed right because Jesus paid the penalty of death for all people for all times when He bore our sins on the cross. "By entering through faith into what God has always wanted to do for us—set us right with him, make us fit for him—we have it all together with God because of our Master Jesus.... We find ourselves standing where we always hoped we might stand—out in the wide open spaces of God's grace and glory, standing tall and shouting our praise" (Rom. 5:1, 2, MSG*)*.

Faith and obedience unlock the door of salvation. When asked what was needed to do the works of God, Jesus answered, "The work of God is this: to believe in the one he has sent" (John 6:29, TNIV). We are not saved by our works, for nothing we do in our own strength can justify us in God's eyes. Nevertheless, "faith without works is dead" (James 2:20). Once justified, belief in Jesus carries with it a commitment to love our neighbors and our God by doing good works and producing the fruit of a changed life. We do good works *because* we are saved, not *to be* saved.

September 9

Changing the Person in the Mirror

Anyone who listens to the word but does not do what it says is like a man who looks at his face in a mirror and, after looking at himself, goes away and immediately forgets what he looks like. James 1:23, 24, NIV.

Leo Tolstoy wrote, "Everyone thinks of changing the world, but no one thinks of changing himself." An unknown author pondered changing the world as well. Being young, he wanted to change the world. This proved difficult, so he tried to change his nation. When he couldn't change the nation, he focused on changing his town. Since he couldn't change the town and now older, he tried to change his family. Now a senior, he realizes the only thing he can change is himself. He recognizes that if long ago he had changed himself, he would have impacted his family and impacted his town. Their impact could have changed the nation and he could, indeed, have changed the world.[262]

Undeniably, positive self-change has a domino effect that once set in motion achieves startling results. Changing the world begins small and often unearths vehement detractors who are comfortable with tradition or the current conditions. So do not expect it to be easy. Changing self begins with a painful scrutiny of self, a thorough self-examination using the law as our standard. Seriously accepting the challenge to change ourselves, the grace of God is the divine enabler—"the Law has become our tutor to lead us to Christ" (Gal. 3:24, NASB). Grace, says Joseph Cooke, is "nothing more nor less than the face that love wears when it meets imperfection, weakness, failure, sin."

Sin is universal and all have sinned. And gazing intently at the cross, we see sin in all its repulsiveness—the sin that moved Jesus to become sin and a curse for us. Thus, we are wise to ask the Holy Spirit to search our hearts and reveal those hidden defects that hinder our spiritual growth. We are wise to stay focused on the law, which mirrors our duty to God and to our neighbors. Consider the example of the Jewish leaders. They hung the law around their necks and judged others, but their hearts were unaffected. Though they saw their likeness in the mirror, they lapsed into denial and forgot what they looked like, which placed their spiritual future in jeopardy.

Mahatma Gandhi said, "Be the change you want to see in the world." To effect that personal change, be willing to take the messages echoed throughout the Holy Word and follow them closely. Transformational power at a supernatural level resides in the Word. God says, "It is the same with my word. I send it out, and it always produces fruit. It will accomplish all I want it to, and it will prosper everywhere I send it" (Isa. 55:11, NLT). By the gospel you are saved, if you hold firmly and obediently to it.

Use the Word as a change agent. And keep the mirror of self-examination so sparkling clean that when you look at your face and walk away you remember that you look like a sinner, but one who is striving to overcome by God's grace.

September 10

Penetrating the Darkness

In Him was life, and the life was the light of men. And the light shines in the darkness, and the darkness did not comprehend it. John 1:4, 5, NKJV.

Called the largest in U.S. history, the Northeast Blackout of 2003 occurred in August and plunged upwards of 60 million people in several northeastern states and parts of Canada into darkness. Officials grounded airplanes, public transportation grinded to a halt, people walked miles to return home, and elevators stopped, forcing its occupants to walk down hundreds of stairs to reach the sidewalk. Moreover, electrical necessities like lights and air conditioning and the other conveniences we take for granted became useless.

The blackout points to society's hardships without the power source for light and energy. Franklin D. Roosevelt very profoundly uttered, "Electricity is a modern necessity of life." It is telling that the first words spoken by God recorded in the Bible were, "Let there be light." His first burst of creative power went toward crafting light to illuminate the darkness since "earth was a soup of nothingness, a bottomless emptiness, an inky blackness" (Gen. 1:1-2, MSG). Darkness suggests negativity, death, and fear, and God would loathe to deposit His beloved created beings in a gloomy, foreboding world void of warmth and brightness.

Before the Flood, the human race fell deep into sin, and the darkness of sin settled on the earth. Seeing the great wickedness of man, seeing that every imagination and intention of human thinking remained only evil continually (Gen. 6:5), God destroyed mankind. History repeated itself, and evil again eclipsed the earth. In the fullness of time, however, God sent Light to counter the darkness. For in the counsels of heaven, the Godhead had decided that Jesus would illuminate the world with the brightness of the gospel. He declared, "I am the light of the world; he who comes with me will not be walking in the dark but will have the light of life" (John 8:12, BBE).

Darkness clearly identifies Satan's realm. And through the inky storm clouds of doubt, death, mayhem, and destruction, this prince of shadows spreads gloom and doom over the earth. Not only is he a murderer and a liar, he is the father of lies (John 8:44, 45). Still, many people choose to follow him, preferring his fellowship and choosing to persist in deeds of iniquity rather than conform to righteous living by following the Light. "This is the judgment ... Light has come into the world, and men loved the darkness rather than the Light, for their deeds were evil" (John 3:19, NASB).

Since light is greater than darkness and truth is greater than lies and God rules supreme, Satan cannot extinguish the Light no matter the energy he exerts. Jesus offers the light of truth for salvation, framed by the gospel and the light of His presence glowing though the storms of life. And through Him flow hope, peace, and life without end. "The people walking in darkness have seen a great light; on those living in the land of the shadow of death a light has dawned" (Isa. 9:2, NIV). Follow that Light!

September 11

Blessed Are Those Who Scoff Not

Blessed is the man who walks not in the counsel of the ungodly, nor stands in the path of sinners, nor sits in the seat of the scornful. Ps. 1:1, NKJV.

While the Savior of the world hanged on the cross in shame and searing agony, many of those for whom He died stood at the foot of the cross and mocked and scoffed Him. The Jewish leaders sneered, "He saved others; let Him save Himself, if this is the Christ of God, His Chosen One" (Luke 23:35, NASB). Likewise, the Roman soldiers mocked and snickered, "If You are the King of the Jews, save Yourself!" (verse 37). And they crafted a plaque that said "THIS IS THE KING OF THE JEWS," which was derisively placed above His head (verse 38).

These cruel executioners mocked and derided the Son of God, the incarnation of the Word, the Son who came to bring light and life. Scoffing at the truths in the Holy Bible shows disrespect for the Most High God. In fact, such scoffers are literally calling God a liar and a fraud. "Scoffing should not be confused with jesting. Jesting depicts frivolity, but scoffing is a sin that is deliberate. Scoffing occurs when men show willful contempt for God and His Son"[263] or live as if God does not exist.

Pride and arrogance define the mocker whose own self-estimation is exalted above God and whose wisdom is corrupt and foolish through self-centeredness (Prov. 21:24). Peter said that in the last days scoffers would come "scoffing and following their own evil desires" (2 Peter 3:3, NIV). They disdain the Word in both subtle and not so subtle ways. Either they ridicule it and its Author as did the Jewish leaders and the Roman soldiers, or they invalidate the Word of God by substituting for truth long held traditions handed down from generation to generation (Mark 7:13). Additionally, contempt for truth is shown by disregarding it, adding to it, or subtracting from it (Rev. 22:18).

Today, scoffers present "evidence" that Jesus' remains are still entombed, contending that the resurrection of Jesus, if it occurred, was a spiritual resurrection despite the Word saying His holy one will never see decay (Acts 13:35). "The Lost Tomb of Jesus ... reveals what might be the greatest archaeological find in history. The film presents the latest evidence from experts in Aramaic script, ancient DNA analysis, forensics, archaeology and statistics."[264] Also, these scoffers offer "evidence" that Jesus married and fathered a child. "Among the major discoveries chronicled in the program is new evidence that Jesus and Mary Magdalene … may have had a son named Judah."[265]

Using the most cutting-edge forensic equipment, valid ancient documents, and the greatest scientific minds, theses scoffers deduce that the sacred Word is a lie and that Jesus is a fraud not realizing that they are pawns in the hands of the master deceiver, Satan. His goal is to instill a reasonable doubt about the veracity of the Word in the minds of those whose faith is weak or wavering or in the minds of those who have yet to make a decision for Christ. But the Word says, "Look, you scoffers, wonder and perish, for I am going to do something in your days that you would never believe, even if someone told you" (Acts 13:41, NIV). He *is* coming again!

September 12

The Golden Rule

Whatever you want men to do to you, do also to them, for this is the Law and the Prophets. Matt. 7:12, NKJV.

April 14, 1902, was the beginning of a journey toward service and rewards for the firm of Johnson, Callahan, and Penney who opened the first of their Golden Rule Stores in Kemmerer, Wyoming. Their success rested on their unique governing principles, namely, cash only and treating others as they wanted to be treated. The customers responded to this kindness by buying enough goods to expand that one store to thirty-four stores by 1913. The owners changed the name of the stores to J.C. Penney, but the original Golden Rule Store, still viable, did not change its name.

If the Golden Rule, to do to others as we want them to do to us, had been adhered to, life on earth would be akin to the peace of heaven. If we do nothing because of selfish ambition or conceit, but humbly esteem others better than ourselves and consider not only our own interests but also the interests of others, we are demonstrating the Golden Rule (Phil. 2:3, 4). Imagine a world where thieves, batterers, liars, and bullies do not exist. Imagine also an end to road rage, murders, wars, abuse, divorce, biases, prejudices, and class, race and caste distinctions.

Selfishness is a controlling character trait in human beings because of fallen man's inherited personality flaws. Unless we accept Jesus as Lord of our lives and assume His character, we remain self-centered, not self-sacrificing; self-involved, not other-involved. Selfishness breeds anger, jealousy, hatred, hedonism, entitlement, conceit, and greed. It is looking inward and gratifying our own whims and desires to the detriment of anyone standing in our way. Mother Teresa writes, "One of the greatest diseases is to be nobody to anybody." Truly, selfishness is a viral disease that contaminates the world.

Godly love, which is the sum total of the Word, is the tested antidote for this disease. When a lawyer inquired of the greatest commandment, "Jesus replied: 'Love the Lord your God with all your heart and with all your soul and with all your mind.' This is the first and greatest commandment. And the second is like it: 'Love your neighbor as yourself.' All the Law and the Prophets hang on these two commandments" (Matt. 22:37-40, NIV). And that is the Golden Rule in practice.

Woven throughout the sacred pages of Scripture is the dictate to love your neighbor as much as you love yourself and your God above all others, including self. High is the standard set by God. As Jesus demonstrated, love puts others' needs before one's own. And the Godhead expressed unparalleled love by sending "Christ to die for us while we were still sinners" (Rom. 5:8, NLT). In the language of a child, "God could have said magic words to make the nails fall off the cross, but He didn't. That's love."

September 13

The Race Is Not to the Swift

But he who endures to the end shall be saved. Matt. 24:13, NKJV.

For seventy-six days—two and one half months after his sailboat sank—Steven Callahan drifted 1,800 nautical miles in a life raft on the Atlantic Ocean. He relied on his own ingenuity to survive, fighting against hunger, thirst, and predators. In his book he noted that he leaned to live like an "aquatic caveman," eating raw, bloody fish and birds as well as barnacles. Being resourceful, he devised a solar still to change saltwater to drinking water and maintained a daily schedule including exercise, repairs, and stocking food and water. He suffered both physically and mentally, enduring "a view of heaven from a seat in hell."[266]

Callahan's intense battle to survive required both physical strength and mental stamina. He fought, endured each skirmish in turn, and eventually won the war. Likewise, Christians are required to fight to remain on the right path, to subdue the carnal nature, and to endure the suffering because these things define our earthly experiences. For instance, the apostle Paul worked diligently and, with others, successfully spread the gospel throughout the world. Finally, after enduring extreme hardships, persecution, and ridicule, he wrote, "the time has come for my departure. I have fought the good fight, I have finished the race, I have kept the faith" (2 Tim. 4:6, 7, NIV).

Roger Bannister wrote, "The man who can drive himself further once the effort gets painful is the man who will win." It takes discipline and resolve to endure in this Christian journey. Striving to stay on track spiritually, while buffeted by trials and suffering, requires both self-determination and strength from above. Faith is necessarily tested and tried since untried faith is stunted and, therefore, useless. In fact, we are to not just grin and bear it but also to "greatly rejoice [as we] suffer grief in all kinds of trials. These have come so that your faith—of greater worth than gold ... may be proved genuine and may result in praise, glory and honor" (1 Peter 1:6, 7, NIV).

When we accept Jesus as our Savior and give Him control over our lives, the struggle begins. Satan hates to surrender any of his captives and makes life difficult for those stubborn enough to desert him for Jesus. When trouble strikes and God does not intervene, we can easily become discouraged and doubtful. But filtering Satan's lies through the Word pursuant to diligent Bible study, awareness dawns and we begin to value the heart of God, that these trials promote spiritual growth. Acknowledging His wisdom, accepting the trials, and praying for strength, faith grows. Paul wrote, "May you be strengthened with all power, according to his glorious might, for all endurance and patience with joy" (Col. 1:11, ESV).

The prize is not given to those who accept Jesus and turn back. Only those who endure *to the end*. "Blessed is the man who remains steadfast under trial, for when he has stood the test he will receive the crown of life, which God has promised to those who love him" (James 1:12, ESV). That is my goal, what about you?

September 14

Maintaining Justice

Maintain justice and do what is right, for my salvation is close at hand and my righteousness will soon be revealed. Isa. 56:1, NIV.

"You're out of order! You're out of order! The whole trial's out of order!" explodes Arthur Kirkland, a character in the movie *And Justice for All*. The idealistic and honorable Kirkland is coerced to defend his nemesis Judge Henry Fleming even with evidence that Fleming is guilty of rape and battering. That justice has not been served for two of his clients whose cases were blatant miscarriages of justice fuels his resentment. Kirkland, unable to let Fleming beat the system, shouts uncontrollably in court that Fleming is guilty, an action leading to Kirkland's disbarment.

The Word stands as a sentinel against system-wide injustice or injustices against individuals. "To turn aside the justice *due* a man before the face of the Most High, or subvert a man in his cause—The Lord does not approve" (Lam. 3:35, 36, NKJV). The defenseless, including the fatherless, the widow, and the alien, are protected by God against injustices, and He requires no less of professed Christians (Deut. 10:18; Micah 6:8). Self is enthroned in the hearts of carnal man whose creed is all for me and me alone. Thus, God cautions His saints to maintain justice in dealings with all without regard for class, caste, or origin. We are required to not only be just or work for justice but to maintain justice—to have a heart for justice as He does. "For I, the LORD, love justice; I hate robbery and iniquity" (Isa. 61:8, NIV).

"Power, at its best, is love implementing the demands of justice; justice, at its best, is love correcting everything that stands against love," writes Dr. Martin Luther King Jr. Indeed, injustice stands against love. It is a form of robbery not simply against the individual victim but it extends across society, tainting the peace and security of the nation. It robs the victims of their means and dignity and breeds resentment that stems from unmet needs and the abuse of power. Without resolving the root problem, resentment soon turns to hatred. For example, Esau resented then hated Jacob who cheated him out of the blessing reserved for the firstborn son. He spat out, "The days of mourning for my father are near; then I will kill my brother Jacob" (Gen. 27:41, NIV).

Peace and justice are inextricably bound together (Isa. 32:16-20). Accordingly, H. L. Mencken wrote, "If you want peace, work for justice." This truism is echoed in Psalm 85:10: "Love and faithfulness meet together; righteousness and peace kiss each other" (NIV). The God who created, controls, and maintains the entire universe is a just God who will not forever tolerate injustice (Deut. 32:4). He pleads the cause of the victims of injustice and accordingly will reward perpetrators. But blessed is the man and woman who maintain justice—a demonstration of love for God and humanity—for their salvation is close at hand.

Be careful to remain just for the Lord will one day execute "judgment from his throne. He will judge the world with justice and rule the world with fairness. The LORD is a shelter for the oppressed, a refuge in times of trouble" (Ps. 9:7-9, NLT).

September 15

I Am the Potter; You Are the Clay

Woe to the one who quarrels with his Maker—An earthenware vessel among the vessels of earth! Will the clay say to the potter, 'What are you doing?' Or the thing you are making say, 'He has no hands'? Isa. 45:9, NASB.

One day a couple purchased a beautiful teapot. At home, the little teapot said, "I was not always a beautiful teapot; I began as lump of hard clay. My master slammed and pounded to soften me for shaping on the spinning wheel. I complained and begged for Him to stop, but He said, 'Not yet.' Finally, the pounding and spinning ceased to my relief. But He placed me in a suffocatingly hot oven. Again, I pleaded for mercy. Yet again He said, 'Not yet.' When I thought I could bear no more, he opened the oven and mercifully blew on me to cool me down; then He painted me, but the noxious paint fumes gagged me. Finally, I became this beautiful teapot."[267]

God created us from the dust of the ground, then He shapes and molds us with His right hand (Isa. 64:8). As Creator, He is imminently privileged to do with us as He will. Although sinners rebel against His authority, He still woos us, strengthens the obedient, and then begins the work of remaking us to live an eternal existence. Redesigning is painful for the redesigned, especially since the process continues throughout our human reality, but the process is ultimately less painful than an unshaped life. Therefore, the wise lumps of clay endure the Potter's pounding and shaping in anticipation of the end result promised to be exquisite (Jer. 18:4-6).

Sin has so misshapen the creation God made in His own image we no longer resemble Him. Moved by love and yearning to number us among His treasured possessions, God pounds away with the mallets of suffering and affliction. The obedient remain faithful and submit to this pounding and so become partakers of His holiness. Conversely, the unwise clay is foolish enough to oppose the Potter who holds the power of life and death in His hands. "He shakes his fist at God and vaunts himself against the Almighty, defiantly charging against him with a thick, strong shield" (Job 15:24-26, NIV). His end is the trash heap.

"Yet you, LORD, are our Father. We are the clay, you are the potter; we are all the work of your hand" (Isa. 64:8, NIV). And it is preposterous for mere human beings, motionless and lifeless without His assistance, to set our own agenda and follow our own willful course. We belong to Him, and if our life is to have meaning and peace, the potter needs complete discretion to reshape us as He deems proper.

As He redesigns us to live with Him eternally, trust that God is too wise to make a mistake. Not until we are humbled and broken under His mighty hand do we learn to lean entirely on Him and be exalted to glory in due time. When the crosses we bear are dreadful and our endurance is sorely stretched, God strengthens and sustains us (Ps. 46:1). With our permission and our striving, He can reshape each of us into a flawless masterpiece that looks just like Him.

September 16

The Battle for Purity

Dear friends, now we are children of God, and what we will be has not yet been made known. But we know that when Christ appears, we shall be like him, for we shall see him as he is. Everyone who has this hope in him purifies himself, just as he is pure. 1 John 3:2, 3, NIV.

Noah attempts to ride his new tricycle by pushing down on the pedals simultaneously with both feet. Alas, the tricycle remains stationary. An impatient toddler, he puts both feet on the floor and walks the tricycle across the room. His parents offer him assistance by physically pushing one pedal down separate from the other. To his delight he rides forward, but only momentarily. Until he learns that one pedal must separately dominate the other, he cannot ride his tricycle on his own steam.

Similarly, our flesh and the Holy Spirit cannot move forward or gain supremacy simultaneously; they are at war. Either the flesh overpowers and gains controls or the Spirit overpowers and gains control. Deny the flesh and gain spiritual power or vice versa. Paul writes, "Those who live according to the flesh have their minds set on what the flesh desires; but those who live in accordance with the Spirit have their minds set on what the Spirit desires. The mind governed by the flesh is death, but the mind governed by the Spirit is life and peace. The mind governed by the flesh is hostile to God; it does not submit to God's law, nor can it do so" (Rom. 8:5-7, NIV).

The law of non-contradiction comes into effect when we attempt to satisfy the desires of the flesh while expecting to remain the temple of the Holy Spirit. Aristotle's law of non-contradiction states that something cannot be both true and not true at the same time and in the same sense. No matter how much we justify, deny, add to, or detract from His Word, it remains a sound principle that those who are static in the realm of the flesh cannot please Him. Ultimately, they will perish if they insist on pushing down the two pedals in concert.

Disobedience and wickedness put us in the realm of the flesh. But the flesh can be overcome by the Holy Spirit. John, the disciple distinguished as the one "whom Jesus loved," was not always meek and love-filled. Hot-headed, critical, combative, and newly chosen as a disciple, Jesus labeled him a son of thunder. Also, proud, inclusive, and ruthless for power, he strove to be the greatest in Jesus' kingdom. And revenge filled his spirit, for when the Samaritans rejected Jesus, he wanted fire to rain down and consume them. But looking to Jesus, obeying His teachings, and allowing the Holy Spirit to take control against the natural, evil inclinations of the heart, transformed John into a willing vessel (Luke 9:51-56; Matt 20:20-28; Mark 9:38-40).

Although "the battle against self is the most difficult battle we face, God promises to give us His grace so we can prevail."[268] Putting the flesh to death through prayer and striving, we shall be purified as we wait on that blessed hope and the glorious appearing of God and our Savior Jesus Christ.

September 17

Astonishing Generosity

It is more blessed to give than to receive. Acts 20:35, NKJV.

An old lady whom I call Pauline had few material goods but shared the secret of her joy with her wealthy, but unhappy, employer. Malaria claimed Pauline's husband and not three months later her only child died in a car accident. She lost everything that mattered to her, leaving her sleepless, joyless, and unable to eat. One day a little kitten followed her home, and she welcomed it to protect it against the cold and dark and fed it. After licking the plate clean, the kitten purred and rubbed against Pauline's leg, causing her to smile for the first time in ages. She received so much satisfaction from helping the kitten, she decided to make soup for a sick neighbor. Each day, thereafter, Pauline did something kind for others and rediscovered peace and joy.[269]

What a blessing for Pauline and those she ministered to! She is an example to follow! But we must not stop there. Following the example of the Father and His Son Jesus, we should strive to escalate our level of generosity and "give until it hurts." God gave His one and only beloved Son to keep an ungrateful, sinful mass of people from perishing (John 3:16). "He who did not withhold his own Son, but gave him up for all of us, will he not with him also give us everything else?" (Rom. 8:32, NRSV). Every good and perfect gift that blesses our present and future existence comes from Him (James 1:17). And God generously provides all we need and promises, "Then you will always have everything you need and plenty left over to share with others" (2 Cor. 9:8, NLT).

N. T. Wright coined the phrase "astonishing generosity" when describing the generosity toward this fallen world by the Father and Son. And he follows that the Christian's attitude of giving both to those in need and to those who abuse and misuse us should mimic this astonishing generosity. Jesus said, "Love your enemies, do good to those who hate you, bless those who curse you, pray for those who mistreat you. If someone strikes you on one cheek, turn to him the other also. If someone takes your cloak, do not stop him from taking your tunic. Give to everyone who asks you, and if anyone takes what belongs to you, do not demand it back" (Luke 6:27-30, NIV).

God loves a cheerful giver (2 Cor. 9:7), for cheerful giving is a sign of the effectiveness of the love of Christ in our hearts. Giving to benefit taxes, giving used clothes or things to charity, or giving because we feel guilty when the call to give comes does not reach to the level of astonishing generosity. This smacks of giving reluctantly or under pressure or for our self-interest, not giving cheerfully, but begrudgingly. The Widow of Zarephath exhibited astonishing generosity when, in faith, she gave her last morsel of food to Elijah, leaving her and her son to die of starvation (1Kings 17:10-12).

Eckhart Tolle wrote, "You cannot receive what you don't give. Outflow determines inflow." Surely giving is like a seed. Without planting it, a bounty will never be produced. But planted in the soil of love, it bears fruit with our neighbors and with God from whom all blessings flow.

September 18

Circumcised Ears

Obey my voice, and I will be your God, and ye shall be my people: and walk ye in all the ways that I have commanded you, that it may be well unto you. Jer. 7:23.

During the late 1800s many unemployed deaf people began to peddle wares. Deaf peddling, a variation on panhandling, reaped an income because of the sympathy factor for the hearing disabled. For a time William Rockefeller, father of John D. Rockefeller, posed as a deaf-mute peddling wares in his hamlet. He hung a small slate in a buttonhole at the front of his chest and wrote on it in chalk, "I am a deaf-mute." Under this guise, he sold his product, conversed with people using the slate, and learned secrets that they supposed he could not hear.

Quite the contrary, God has spoken words of life that He wishes all to hear. But there are many people who hear the Word but are resistant to it and the Holy Spirit. They have uncircumcised ears defined by Jeremiah thusly: "To whom can I speak and give warning? Who will listen to me? Their ears are closed so they cannot hear. The Word of the LORD is offensive to them; they find no pleasure in it" (Jer. 6:10).

The owners of these uncircumcised ears do not comprehend the Word, nor do they want to comprehend it. They are, in fact, offended by it. And until we submit our lives to Jesus, we will remain resistant to the Word, for at birth our ears and hearts are uncircumcised. Submitting to Him, we are "circumcised with a circumcision not made with hands, but in a [spiritual] circumcision [performed by] Christ by stripping off the body of the flesh (the whole corrupt, carnal nature with its passions and lusts)" (Col. 2:11, AMP).

Spasmodic obedience, half-hearted worship, and a lukewarm relationship with the Savior on the part of God's people are as much evidence of uncircumcised ears as outright disobedience. "Hear, you deaf! And look, you blind, that you may see! Who is blind but My servant, Or so deaf as My messenger whom I send? Who is so blind as he that is at peace with Me, Or so blind as the servant of the LORD? You have seen many things, but have do not observe them; Your ears are open, but none hears" (Isa. 42:18-20, NASB). But the God who created us also wants to save us and strives to pierce the deafness.

Physically, circumcision is cutting the flesh and removing the foreskin of the male organ. But God uses it in a spiritual sense to plead with His children to cut away sin and attain the righteousness of Jesus by faith. Without a circumcised heart the ears will remain defective. Mercifully, "the LORD your God will circumcise your heart … [to free you] to love the LORD your God with all your heart, and with all your soul, that you may live" (Deut. 30:6, AKJV). Spiritually circumcised, we fall in love with God, and we fully commit our hearts to Him to live by His decrees and obey His commands. Then our ears become unclogged, and after hearing the Word, we become doers and can confidently assert that all is well with our souls.

September 19

Like a Tree Planted By the Water

But blessed is the man who trusts in the LORD, whose confidence is in him. He will be like a tree planted by the water that sends out its roots by the stream. It does not fear when heat comes; its leaves are always green. It has no worries in a year of drought and never fails to bear fruit. Jer. 17:7, 8, NIV.

Cottonwood trees thrive alongside the Rio Grande River in New Mexico. In fact, the world's largest cottonwood forest, called the Rio Grande Bosque, extends 160 miles from the Cochiti Lake to the Elephant Butte Reservoir. Characteristically, cottonwood trees grow near a source of water, giving them the nickname "water tree." The Rio Grande Cottonwood tree welcomed the early settlers as a signpost for water in the 1800s as they traveled through the arid Southwest. Taking advantage of its readily available water source, the cottonwood trees also provide leafy green foliage for shade, an added protection from the harsh desert sun.

The spiritual image of a lush, green vibrant tree planted by the water contrasts diametrically with Jeremiah's image of the bush in the wasteland. "Cursed is the one who trusts in man, who depends on flesh for his strength and whose heart turns away from the LORD. He will be like a bush in the wastelands; he will not see prosperity when it comes. He will dwell in the parched places of the desert, in a salt land where no one lives" (Jer. 17:5, 6). Wholehearted devotion and trust in the Lord highlight the differences in appearance and outcome between the two images.

Trust and commitment to the God of all life compose the root that travels deep enough to drink at the fountain of life for sustenance and peace when the droughts of life materialize. Thus, the wise people may be assailed by trouble and temptation, but he or she stands firm. When the storms of life batter them, they thrust their roots deeper in the Word and hold on tighter to God. And holding onto Him, they are shaped in godliness, transformed into His image, and experience the peace that passes all understanding.

On the other hand, the foolish people place their trust in other finite human beings or things rather than the sovereign God. Resembling the bush in the wasteland, they have no roots and are dead, dry, and helpless—totally at the mercy of the elements. This bush signifies the ungodly who are attached to nothing and thereby lack stability and endurance. Rootless when the inevitable storms approach, the ungodly choose suicide or frivolity or substances to hang onto. Unable to prosper in the things that matter, they live barren lives and die empty.[270]

By God's grace, the empty, barren sinner living in life's wasteland can drink of the Living Water and become transformed into a spiritually lush, vibrant child of God. This miracle emanates from Jesus who is the Source of all life. "All who received him, to those who believed in his name, he gave the right to become children of God" (John 1:12, NIV). Anyone planting their roots deep in Him may claim that right.

September 20

All I Have Belongs to God

Naked I came from my mother's womb, and naked shall I return there. The LORD gave, and the LORD has taken away; Blessed be the name of the LORD. Job 1:21, NKJV.

Unlike many babies in the animal kingdom, human babies are born helpless. Swiss psychologist Jean Piaget published research that reveals four stages of infant development. The first stage is the sensorimotor stage that occurs from birth to two years. During the earliest part of this stage, babies respond primarily through reflexes while their cognitive skills—thinking, talking, reasoning, and learning—develop over a period of time. Infants, then, are born naked, both literally and figuratively.

Likewise, we bring nothing to this life and cannot claim anything we acquire while here because everything belongs to God. "Everything comes from you, and we have given you only what comes from your hand" (1 Chron. 29:14, NIV). The Lord gives life, strength, and the power to acquire wealth (Acts 17:28; Deut. 8:18). As well, He provides jobs we are blessed to have, salaries we are blessed to receive, and the ability and strength to fulfill job requirements.

When death comes and the breath of life returns to God, He receives nothing but what belongs to Him. "I shall be as rich when I die as I was when I was born, and therefore have reason to be contented with my condition, which also is the common lot of all men. Into the lap of our common mother, the earth, the weary child lays its head in its mother's bosom."[271] We depart this life naked and stripped of our earthly goods, clutching only our character developed by God's grace and faith in Jesus.

When the specter of death looms, our perspective changes. My dear friend Edna suffered terminal cancer and time spent with her taught that valuable lesson. With her increased awareness of the finiteness of time, she viewed her life through the lens of essentials. From this perspective, unnecessary, useless, and frivolous things, as well as shallow people, were stripped from the wallpaper of her life. She taught that when our existence becomes fragile, we are wise to draw a line of demarcation separating our before and our now. Before, we majored in minor things; now, our focus locks on the important things in life—lasting things like our salvation, time with family and friends, and making every minute count.

The contentment that ruled her day centered in Jesus who is the doorway to salvation, the calm in the storms of life, and the assurance of eternal life. Edna's example of grace under pressure while enduring unimaginable suffering witnessed to her friends and family of God's grace and the peace that passes understanding. Where most would gripe and complain, she found blessings and remained at ease with her lot. Edna embodied Paul's words. "Now there is great gain in godliness with contentment, for we brought nothing into the world, and we cannot take anything out of the world" (1 Tim. 6:6, 7, ESV). Understanding that, she developed the only thing that will accompany her to her eternal home—a godly character. I am grateful for the lesson.

September 21

Condemned No More

There is therefore now no condemnation to them which are in Christ Jesus ... For the law of the Spirit of life in Christ Jesus hath made me free from the law of sin and death. Rom. 8:1, 2.

San Quentin State Prison in California holds approximately 700 inmates on its death row, making it the largest in the nation. In the United States, death row is the area of a prison where inmates live who are convicted of capital crimes including aggravated murder, felony murder, or contract killing. These inmates received the death penalty pursuant to a trial in a court of law. And unless pardoned by the governor or they win an appeal, these prisoners are condemned to die.

In a broader sense, all humans beings born on earth are condemned to die. Through Adam and Eve's disobedience, the sin virus entered the world, mutated, and lives to infect each child of Adam. Sinful humans "love darkness rather than light, because their deeds are evil" (John 3:19). In a spiritual sense, death is our lot because we are controlled by a sinful nature and sinful passions are at work in our bodies, so we do not bear fruit for God but for death (Rom. 7:5). Thus, the Supreme Judge is obliged, under His unchanging and just law, to find us guilty and sentence us accordingly. But because He loves us so much, He found a way to satisfy the rule of the law while rescuing us from the penalty of the law.

Hence, we are not left without recourse. Jesus said, "I tell you the truth, whoever hears my word and believes him who sent me has eternal life and will not be condemned; he has crossed over from death to life" (John 5:24, NIV). Thus, all who are in Jesus no longer live on death row anticipating execution. He has vindicated us and freed us, allowing God to reconcile "the world to himself in Christ, not counting men's sins against them" (2 Cor. 5:19, NIV). Through Him we are transformed from enemies of God into friends of God.

But the condemnation ends only for those who are in Christ Jesus. A weighty phrase, "in Christ Jesus" takes into account our connection to Him for spiritual revival and survival. Jesus illustrates this connection with the metaphor of a vine and branches. "I am the vine, and you are the branches. If any remain in me and I remain in them, they produce much fruit. But without me they can do nothing" (John 15:5, NCV). Conversely, any who do not remain in Jesus, face an end similar to a branch that is discarded and tossed into the fire (verse 6).

Jesus is the conduit of vital spiritual nutrients for the life and growth of the Christian. This spiritual connection is only viable through continued surrender to God's will, prayer, and Bible study. Although Jesus unshackled us from the bondage of sin and the penalty of sin, we must maintain the connection to Jesus. The power to resist the devil and the power to grow into obedient children flow unrestrained through that connection, a connection that ends the death penalty and makes permanent our salvation.

September 22

The Spirit's Intercession for the Saints

The Spirit helps us in our weakness. We do not know what we ought to pray for, but the Spirit himself intercedes for us with groans that words cannot express. And he who searches our hearts knows the mind of the Spirit, because the Spirit intercedes for the saints in accordance with God's will. Rom. 8:26, 27, NIV.

Communists in the former Soviet Union cruelly imprisoned Pastor Richard Waumbaugh for fourteen years. Describing an attempt to pray he wrote, "In solitary confinement, we could not pray as before. We were unimaginably hungry; we had been drugged until we acted like idiots. We were as weak as skeletons. The Lord's Prayer was much too long for us -- we could not concentrate enough to say it. My only prayer repeated again and again was, 'Jesus, I love You.'"[272]

Prayer is talking to God as to a friend; it is an open, never busy line to the Godhead. And through prayer we receive strength and peace. "Do not be anxious about anything, but in everything, by prayer and petition, with thanksgiving, present your requests to God. And the peace of God, which transcends all understanding, will guard your hearts and your minds in Christ Jesus" (Phil 4:6, 7, NIV). The Bible also counsels us to "pray without ceasing" (1 Thess. 5:17). And we are assured that "the prayer of a righteous man is powerful and effective" (James 5:16, NIV). Sinners can confidently approach a holy and pure God and "if we ask any thing according to his will, he heareth us" (1 John 5:14).

Still there are times when even the most faithful Christian cannot or does not want to pray. When we need Him the most, sometimes words fail us. Overcome by loss or in deep emotional or physical pain or shock, the best we can muster is a groan or a "God help me" as did Pastor Waumbaugh. C. H. Spurgeon wrote, "How can I pray? My mind wanders: I chatter like a crane; I roar like a beast in pain; I moan in the brokenness of my heart, but oh, my God, I know not what it is my inmost spirit needs; or if I know it, I know not how to frame my petition aright before thee."[273]

But the Holy Spirit comes to the rescue. He stoops down and puts His heavenly shoulders squarely under our burdens, lifts them so we can stand up, and carries them together with us. Then He takes the unspoken plea in our hearts that we are too broken to articulate, carries it to the throne of grace, and whispers it directly in the ear of God in language that we cannot comprehend.

Even when we are capable of praying and want to pray, sometimes our prayers totally miss the mark. We pray for things that might harm us or neglect to pray for the things that usher us closer to God and our final destination. Again, the Holy Spirit, who accompanies us everywhere and knows our needs and wants, intercedes on our behalf. He deciphers our incoherent and inaccurate requests, presenting them to God in the most expressive language imaginable. What he presents to God is what we would have presented if we could see the end from the beginning. Mercifully, God's blessings to his weak and sinful, but treasured, possessions never cease.

September 23

More Than Conquerors

Yet in all these things we are more than conquerors through Him who loved us. Rom. 8:37, NKJV.

A descendant of the Vikings who settled in France, William attacked England after the king died without a male heir. He successfully wrenched the kingdom away from the Anglo-Saxons at the battle of Hastings. Now called William the Conqueror, William ascended the throne as king of England. Despite the conquest, William encountered rebellion and uprisings by the natives, but he kept his family and officials safe by constructing castles surrounded by moats. Although he won the war, it took many years to achieve change and acceptance of his rule.

William was a conqueror, but obviously, that was not sufficient. He gained the victory in battle by physically overcoming the English warriors, but he needed to be more than a conqueror to deal with the negative attitudes and actions of those conquered. Paul used the Greek word *hypernikáō* translated "more than a conqueror," which means a super conqueror or an incomparable conqueror or one wholly and perfectly victorious . That is humanely impossible without God on our side, for only a faithful Christian is *more* than a conqueror in spiritual matters.

Obviously, Jesus was more than a conqueror. He faced torture and shame on the cross not for himself but for fallen humanity, thus gaining the victory over Satan. Moreover, when He arose from the grave, He opened many graves of faithful Christians as trophies of His victory over sin and death. Matthew wrote, "And the graves were opened; and many bodies of the saints which slept arose, And came out of the graves after his [Jesus'] resurrection, and went into the holy city, and appeared unto many" (Matt. 27:52, 53).

Jeremiah, too, was more than a conqueror. He spent more than two decades warning the Judeans of the coming Babylonian army. For his efforts, he was beaten, imprisoned in dungeons and in mire, starved, harassed, and reviled, but he never stopped preaching the Word of God. He remained faithful in the midst of the most trying times, and God protected and preserved him from death. When the invasion occurred as he predicted, those who reviled and persecuted him themselves were reviled and persecuted. Incredibly, the enemy freed Jeremiah. King Nebuchadnezzar of Babylon ordered the commander of the imperial guard to, "See that he [Jeremiah] isn't hurt … Look after him well, and give him anything he wants" (Jer. 39:12, NLT).

God promises to make us more than conquerors—super overcomers. "So, what do you think? With God on our side like this, how can we lose? If God didn't hesitate to put everything on the line for us, embracing our condition and exposing himself to the worst by sending his own Son, is there anything else he wouldn't gladly and freely do for us? And who would dare tangle with God by messing with one of God's chosen?" (Rom. 8:31-36, MSG). With Jesus leading, we will become and remain far more exceeding conquerors.

September 24

Fear Oppressors? Never!

I am he who comforts you; who are you that you are afraid of man who dies ... and have forgotten the LORD, your Maker, who stretched out the heavens and laid the foundations of the earth, and you fear continually all the day because of the wrath of the oppressor? Isa. 51:12, 13, ESV.

By his actions King Zedekiah believed the prophecy preached by Jeremiah but remained disobedient. Secretly, he met with Jeremiah and asked for the truth about the coming Babylonian invasion. Jeremiah reiterated that if he surrendered to them, he and his city would be spared and he and his family would live peacefully in captivity. Zedekiah responded, "I am afraid of the Jews who have gone over to the Babylonians, for the Babylonians may hand me over to them and they will mistreat me" (Jer. 38:19, NIV). Then he beseeched Jeremiah to keep the conversation a secret (Jer. 38:17-24). Clearly, his faith languished on life support.

The last king of Judah, Zedekiah reigned in Jerusalem eleven years and "did evil in the eyes of the LORD ... It was because of the LORD's anger that all this happened to Jerusalem and Judah, and in the end he thrust them from his presence" (2 Kings 24:19, 20, NIV). Sin evokes fear, which is one of the greatest detriments to faith and obedience. Unconnected to God, Zedekiah feared his oppressors more than he loved his Creator, not comprehending that "even if you suffer for doing what is right, God will reward you for it. So don't worry or be afraid of ... threats" (1 Peter 3:14, NLT).

On the other hand, Hezekiah, an earlier king of Judah, "did that which was right in the sight of the LORD" (2 Chron. 29:2). He prayed for protection and humbled his heart before God when threatened by a powerful oppressor. In response, God promised that the Assyrians would not enter the city or shoot an arrow in it or build a siege ramp before it. And He promised to defend the city, and He did. Hezekiah and his army did not lift a finger. One angel destroyed the entire army, prompting the boastful king of Assyria to return to Nineveh and remain there in fear of God's power (Isa. 37).

Hezekiah's humbleness, obedience, and strong faith made a difference in outcomes. He leaned solely on God who rescued him from the Assyrians, an oppressor who boasted more in number, more in weaponry, and more in military victories—a world conqueror. The Assyrians were squeezed like putty in the hands of the almighty God while He withdrew His protection from Zedekiah, leaving the cruel Babylonians unrestrained to do barbarous acts to him, his family, and his city.

Why do we fear human oppressors when God is a capable ally? He is all-powerful; He *spoke* things into existence. By His power He created man out of dust and blew the breath of life in his nostrils, giving him a mind and body that is still a marvel to the greatest intellects on earth. He says, "I am the LORD, and there is none else" (Isa. 45:18). What oppressor is a match for God?

September 25

God's Short-Lived Anger

For a brief moment I abandoned you, but with deep compassion I will take you back. In a burst of anger I turned my face away for a little while. But with everlasting love I will have compassion on you. Isa. 54:7, 8, NLT.

The Israelites had a history of rebellion, backsliding, and punishment before fleeing back to God. True to form, "the Israelites did evil in the eyes of the LORD, so the LORD delivered them to the Philistines for forty years." Even as He abandoned them temporarily to the Philistines, He raised up Samson their deliverer. But Samson's indulgence in willful sin separated him from God. After his mistress learned the secret of his strength, she had his locks cut, "Then she called, 'Samson, the Philistines are upon you!' He awoke from his sleep and thought, 'I'll go out as before and shake myself free.' *But he did not know that the LORD had left him"* (Judges 16:20, NIV).

God promises to never leave or forsake us, and His promises are true. But if we forsake Him, He is too much of a gentleman to impose since He honors our desire to exercise the gift of free will. "The lost enjoy forever the horrible freedom they have demanded and are therefore self-enslaved."[274] And many, like Samson, quench the Holy Spirit and do not realize they are renounced. "Why do you disobey the LORD's commands? You will not prosper. Because you have forsaken the LORD, he has forsaken you" (2 Chron. 24:20, NIV).

God gives the impenitent and backsliders "over to the stubbornness of their heart, to walk in their own devices" and suffer the consequences (Ps. 81:12, NASB). His wrath is reserved for sinners and for all ungodliness and unrighteousness—sins separates us from God (Acts 14:18; Isa. 59:2). Hence, when Jesus assumed our sins, He cried out, "My God, My God, why have you forsaken me?" (Matt. 27:46, ESV). Although sinless, Jesus carried all of our sins to the cross as His own and felt the abandonment that lost sinners will feel when God rejects them eternally.

The psalmist iterates and reiterates the anguish when God hides His face from us." My God, my God, why have you abandoned me? Why so far from my call for help, from my cries of anguish? My God, I call by day, but you do not answer; by night, but I have no relief" (Ps. 22:1, 2, NAB). "Do not hide your face from me; do not repel your servant in anger. You are my help; do not cast me off; do not forsake me, God my savior" (Ps. 27:9, NAB).

But He will welcome us back. "Return to me, and I will return to you, says the LORD of hosts" (Mal. 3:7, ESV). As soon as we repent and confess, He again turns His smiling face in our direction—instantly without hesitation. His compassionate mercy is such that He accepts our rejection and uses trials as an attention getter while commissioning the Holy Spirit to continue to court us. God's anger is short-lived toward those who repent and return to the path of righteousness. And if we remain humble and obedient, He will personally escort us through the pearly gates of heaven.

September 26

Unimaginable Glories of Heaven

Eye has not seen, nor ear heard, nor have entered into the heart of man the things which God has prepared for those who love Him. I Cor. 2:9, NKJV.

A tax assessor asked a pastor I call Wendy, who claimed to be rich, to list her assets so he could determine her taxable effects. She told him she had ten invaluable possessions—eternal life, a mansion in heaven, a Substitute who redeemed her, peace beyond understanding, and divine unfailing love. The assessor declared that she only offered five. She added that she has a crown of life, resurrection from death, His eternal presence, joy unspeakable, and a Champion who fights her battles.[275]

An abundant God guarantees to all who love Him priceless treasures. What more can we ask for that really and truly matters while we are waiting for a better world? This is as good as it gets here. But heaven is another glorious story. Our magnificent mansions in the New Jerusalem are waiting to be occupied as soon as Jesus returns to liberate His saints from a sin-polluted earth and deposit us in heaven (John 14:2, 3). Once safely home, Jesus' own scarred hands will set a crown on our heads, a crown of victory. "Henceforth there is laid up for me a crown of righteousness, which the Lord, the righteous judge, shall give me at that day: and not to me only, but unto all them also that love his appearing" (2 Tim. 4:8).

Because we washed our robes in His blood and stood for His truth, Jesus welcomes us to share in the glories of heaven. The New Jerusalem is rife with streets of pure gold, foundations of precious stones, and gates of gigantic pearls. And our very being will sparkle like precious jewels because every reason for tears will vanish as death, grief, worry, and suffering receive a death blow (Rev. 21:1-4). From Adam to the last saint standing, we will gather around a super-elongated welcome table laden with indescribably delicious and specially prepared provisions. "Many will come from the east and the west, and will take their places at the feast with Abraham, Isaac and Jacob in the kingdom of heaven" (Matt. 8:11, NIV).

Jesus is the fountain of youth and vigor, the fountain of wealth and happiness, and the fountain of love and peace. No inhabitant of heaven or, later, the New Jerusalem will have a physical deformity or a mental disability, problems or poverty. The blind will see, the deaf will hear, the mentally disabled will have clear minds, and He will also transform the land (Isa. 35:5, 6; Luke 8:35). We will run and walk and never get tired, for nighttime and beds will not exist (Isa. 40:31).

The most glorious of the glories will be the likeness of our Creator reflected in our minds and body, "and through ceaseless ages to advance in wisdom, in knowledge, and in holiness … ever increasing in capacity to know and to enjoy and to love, and knowing that there is still beyond us joy and love and wisdom infinite."[276]

September 27

God Is Not Through With Me Yet

And I am sure that God who began the good work within you will keep right on helping you grow in his grace until his task within you is finally finished on that day when Jesus Christ returns. Phil. 1:6, TLB.

According to experts, romantic love goes through three distinct phases. First, the couple is strongly attracted to each other as endorphins inundate the brain, causing strong, blissful feelings of excitement and romance, but during the second stage, the ardor cools and power struggles emerge. Coping skills and behavior change must be cultivated to navigate this stage successfully. To survive, they must face their own control issues honestly, confront issues tactfully, and communicate clearly. Finally, if a mature and lasting love relationship is to transpire, the couple must work toward unconditional love and acceptance using outside resources if necessary.[2778]

Likewise, there are three phases to salvation. The first phase is justification where we *are saved* from the *penalty* of sin. Through God's grace we *are saved* through faith, not because of our works but as "a gift of God" (Eph. 2:8). Here we accept Jesus as the Lord of our lives, confess our sins, and are baptized. Our sins are excused and no longer held against us *if we remain faithful to Him*. Because the blood of Jesus justifies us, when God gazes at a forgiven sinner, He sees Jesus' virtue, not our spiritual foulness (Rom. 5:9).

During the second stage, or sanctification, salvation is ongoing—we *shall be saved* from the *power* of sin (Matt. 1:21). Sanctification continues for a lifetime—it is an ongoing process toward spiritual maturity until the Second Coming or death. It requires a daily struggle with self to whip the old sinful nature into a new creature in Christ. With the Holy Spirit living inside of us upon justification, we "*shall be saved* from wrath through Him" (Rom. 5:9). In cooperation with Him, we are transformed by the renewing of the mind, and we are directed and empowered to walk in obedience (Rom. 12:2). And the "God of peace Himself [will] sanctify you entirely; and may your spirit and soul and body be preserved complete, without blame at the coming of our Lord Jesus Christ" (1 Thess. 5:23, NASB). This is spiritual maturity.

Glorification is the final stage of salvation. Glorification *is being saved* from the *presence* of sin and clothed in immortal bodies. "And it shall be said in that day, Lo, this *is* our God; we have waited for him, and he *will save* us" (Isa. 25:9). That is in the future. Now we live in corruptible bodies prone to death and disease, but soon we will possess glorified bodies, for when the trump is sounded and Jesus returns to earth for His people, "we will all be changed ... in the twinkling of an eye, at the last trumpet" into immortal bodies (1 Cor. 15:51, 52, NASB).

With glorified bodies, we enter fully into our eternal inheritance purchased by our Savior, Redeemer, and Friend. "Those whom He called, He also justified ... and those whom He justified, He also glorified [raising them to a heavenly dignity]" (Rom. 8:30, AMP).

September 28

Jesus, the Ultimate Advocate

Though I sit in darkness, the LORD will be my light. Because I have sinned against him, I will bear the LORD's wrath, until he pleads my case and establishes my right. Micah 7:8, 9, NIV.

François Benjamin Courvoisier, a valet for a wealthy Englishman, went on trial for his employer's murder in 1840. Represented by Charles Phillips, the best criminal defense lawyer in England, he initially pleaded not guilty. On day two of the trial, Courvoisier admitted to his lawyer that he, indeed, had committed the murder but wanted Phillips to continue his vigorous defense. This confession placed Phillips in a quandary. Although he desired to withdraw from the case, he persevered. However, word leaked of Courvoisier's confession of guilt, which forever ruined Phillips' career.[278]

Every person born of woman, except Jesus, is guilty *as* sin *of* sin. We are sinners; it is our nature to sin. Even as we grow into spiritual maturity and become new creatures in Christ, we continue to sin. "But if anyone does sin we have an advocate with the Father, Jesus Christ the righteous" (1 John 2:1, NASB). Unlike the standard of "a right to a lawyer" in the American criminal justice system, sinners are not guaranteed a spiritual lawyer until we admit our guilt. But confession and reformation is the satisfactory retainer Jesus needs to intercede and plead His blood on our behalf. "Neither by the blood of goats and calves, but by his own blood he entered in once into the holy place, having obtained eternal redemption for us" (Heb. 9:12).

We dare not hesitate to cry out to him, "Lord, you are my lawyer! Plead my case! For you have redeemed my life" (Lam. 3:58, NLT). As for those who take refuge in Jesus, the penultimate Advocate, He puts on a vigorous defense that consistently wins acquittals. Where we were once lightning rods for God's wrath, we become recipients of His grace, for He is well pleased with Jesus, the "one mediator between God and men" (1 Tim. 2:5). God's eyes are too pure to look on evil, and He cannot tolerate wrong (Hab. 1:13). Thus when we hide in Jesus, God sees only the covering of Jesus' blood. Seeing "the blood He knows all His claims against us have been met at every point and His righteousness has been exalted by the death of Jesus. He no longer has judgment against us. He invites us to draw near to Him."[279]

Job said, "My advocate is on high. My intercessor is my friend" (Job 16:19, 20, NIV). When Satan, the accuser of the brethren, brings his case to the high court of God, pointing out our sins day and night, Jesus rises to our defense as He did for Joshua the high priest. "And the LORD said unto Satan, The LORD rebuke thee, O Satan … is not this a brand plucked out of the fire? Now Joshua was clothed with filthy garments" (Zech. 3:2, 3). Jesus removed Joshua's filthy garments, representing his sin, and dressed him in a white robe of righteousness. Then God wrote pardon beside his name (verses 4, 5).

Case presented, case won, case closed! Truly, if we acknowledge Jesus before men, He will represent us before His Father, for our Advocate is also our best Friend.

September 29

Choose Life in the Love of God

'As I live,' says the Lord GOD, 'I have no pleasure in the death of the wicked, but that the wicked turn from his way and live. Turn, turn from your evil ways! For why should you die? Eze. 33:11, NKJV.

In an early morning accident, two teens died when their vehicle veered off the road and crashed into a tree. Neither of the teens wore seatbelts. The Centers for Disease Control and Prevention report that automobile accidents are the leading cause of death for American teenagers, killing approximately twelve teenagers *each day*. And according to the National Highway Traffic Safety Administration, approximately 60 percent of teens killed in accidents in 2006 were not wearing seatbelts. Most states have laws that require seatbelt use, and they advertise extensively to promote buckling up for safety. In addition, parents/guardians cajole and harass their teens, demanding that they wear their seatbelts. Their unspoken plea is, "Why die?"

God asks His rebellious offspring that same question when He sees them heading for a collision with their chosen destiny—death. "Why will you die?" is the question He poses. "I have set before you life or death, blessing and curse. Therefore choose life, that you and your offspring may live" (Deut 30:19, ESV). Imagine, the eternal, immortal God, the Creator and sustainer of the universe, bending low to beg His disobedient children to obey Him so He can provide the gifts of life and happiness and peace! What love!

"Woe unto them that seek deep to hide their counsel from the LORD, and their works are in the dark" (Isa. 29:15). Those who straddle the fence will be rejected by God because they favor both sides of the issue. Praising God with one side of their mouth and talking like Satan with the other, they speak with the forked tongue of hypocrites. Jesus articulated, "No one can serve two masters" (Matt. 6:24, NLT). If we love God with all our heart, soul, and mind, there is no room to love a substitute god. To be double minded is deceitful, for their "loyalty is divided between God and the world," making them unbalanced in everything they do (James 1:8, NLT).

Then there are those who sit on the fence, failing to decide between the possibilities. They, too, are doomed. There is no neutrality in spiritual things because not to make a choice for God is to choose Satan. The Word says if we are not with God we are against Him (Luke 11:23). Obviously, we cannot expect to hide behind a middle-of-the-road stand in this great controversy where such a fierce battle is raging between good and evil. Keep in mind, "The hottest places in hell are reserved for those who in a period of moral crisis maintain their neutrality."[280]

Even as Joshua challenged the Israelites to choose whom they would serve, he made a wise and decisive choice that led to life. "As for me and my house we will serve the Lord" (Joshua 24:15).

September 30

Compromising With Sin

We have come to share in Christ if we hold firmly till the end the confidence we had at first. Heb. 3:14, NIV.

Screwtape is a fictional senior demon who trains his young demon nephew, Wormwood, the way to tempt and secure the allegiance of a Christian named Patient. He said, "You will say that these are very small sins; and doubtless, like all young tempters, you are anxious to be able to report spectacular wickedness.... It does not matter how small the sins are, provided that their cumulative effect is to edge the man away from the Light and out into the Nothing.... Indeed, the safest road to Hell is the gradual one -- the gentle slope, soft underfoot, without sudden turnings, without milestones, without signposts."[281]

Compromise and expediency are twin pitfalls for God's people. Many have fallen into the clutches of Satan the gradual way, starting with a little compromise with sin comparable to how King Solomon's relationship with God went south. Opening the door to intermarriage with heathen women, he began the slow but sure descent into the abyss of compromise. His 700 wives and 300 concubines led him astray, turning "his heart after other gods" (1 Kings 11:4). Indeed, his marriage to pharaoh's daughter smacked of political expediency and a lack of faith, for he "formed a marriage alliance with Pharaoh king of Egypt" (1 Kings 3:1, NASB). His compromise also showed a sinful disregard for the clear word of God (Deut. 7:4).

Compromise is "a weakening or giving up of our principles or ideals for reasons of expediency. Expediency is doing or considering what is of selfish use or advantage rather than what is right or just."[282] Compromise progresses similar to an apple's destruction by maggots. A newly worm-infested apple looks red and healthy on the outside, but inside it is diseased by maggots who deposit larvae just until the skin. These larvae burrow inward further and further, slowly feeding on the solid parts of the apple. Soon the entire apple turns brown with rot.

Likewise, many Christians are indistinguishable from impenitent sinners on the outside, for it is vogue today to be a Christian, worshipping God with "feel-good" sermons and rousing music and believing that regular church attendance is a high enough standard. Many accept Jesus at head level but do not submit their whole heart to Him, and after conversion they begin to compromise their Christian principles by again acting and thinking as the world. But compromise is an exit onto the road to eternal death for "there is a way that seems right to a man, but its end is the way of death" (Prov. 14:12, ESV).

God's standard is nothing less than obedience—a 180-degree heart change—to love others as we love ourselves, to abolish all selfishness, to forgive offenses, to trust Him explicitly, and to do as Jesus does. Remember, sin is sin no matter our perception of its weight. So hold firmly to Jesus and frustrate Satan's plan to fool you through the deception of compromise.

October 1

Unbelief Shouts God Is a Liar

All who believe in the Son of God know in their hearts that this testimony is true. Those who don't believe this are actually calling God a liar because they don't believe what God has testified about his Son. 1 John 5:10, NLT.

Roger Clemons, a seven time Cy Young Award winner, instrumental in the New York Yankees winning two World Series and considered one of history's greatest pitchers, received an indictment for making false statements to Congress about steroid and human growth hormones use. Under oath, he denied using steroids, but evidence presented contained his DNA on needles and gauze used to administer the drugs. Perjury, or lying under oath, occurs when one "willfully subscribes as true any material matter which he does not believe to be true."[283]

Unbelief in what God presents in His Word and through His Spirit is tantamount to labeling God a lying perjurer. His Word is so faithful that He swore under oath to Himself, for there is no one greater for Him to swear by outside Himself (Heb. 6:13). After Abraham obediently endeavored to sacrifice his beloved son, Isaac, God said, "I swear by myself … that because you have done this and have not withheld your son, your only son, I will surely bless you … and through your offspring all nations on earth will be blessed, because you have obeyed me" (Gen. 22:16-18, NIV). And, faithfully, God sent Jesus to bless sinners by paying our sin debt.

Jesus said, "Yet because I tell the truth, you do not believe me!… If I am telling the truth, why don't you believe me? He who belongs to God hears what God says. The reason you do not hear is that you do not belong to God" (John 8:45-47, NIV). People who hate God turn their backs on His extension of mercy and grace. They pledge to the evil trinity—the world, the flesh, and the devil—and boldly proclaim in actions and allegiance that God is a liar. The world and worldliness embrace the evil that is opposed to God's standards; the flesh allows sin to reign and dictate one's actions; and Satan is the instigator that blinds the eyes of unbelievers and keeps them in bondage to the world and sin (1 John 2:16). Unbelievers, similar to idolaters, do not believe that God is sovereign; atheists do not believe God exists; and other lawbreakers disrespect Him and care not nor believe that there is a penalty for their actions.

Moreover, there are Christians who read and hear the Word but fail to trust God. Thus, they live in fear of their circumstances and evil doers. With the pink slip comes panic, with sickness or tragedy comes despair, and with the actions of evil people destroying reputations or wreaking havoc in their lives comes hopelessness. Throughout His Word, God's faithfulness proclaims, "Trust Me." He is always in control; no power or circumstance can penetrate His protective shield unless He authorizes it. Even so, He monitors the attacks, allowing only enough distress to make us run to Him.

Remember, "God, who has called you into fellowship with his Son, is faithful" and His Word is true for He is Truth (1 Cor. 1:9). Believe it!

October 2

Good Soldiers Endure Hardship

You therefore must endure hardship as a good soldier of Jesus Christ. No one engaged in warfare entangles himself with the affairs of this life, that he may please him who enlisted him as a soldier. 2 Tim. 2:3, 4, NKJV.

As an Army recruit passes from civilian life to that of a soldier, he or she must endure three phases of training—red, white, and blue. In Phase 1 soldiers must pass a rigorous fitness test to measure their physical and mental endurance. The test is administered several more times throughout their enlistment to keep them in tip-top shape. In Phase 2 the recruits must excel in marksmanship, combat training, and rappelling up and down high edifices to bolster their confidence. Finally, in Phase 3 the recruits use their training in practical ways. This training mentally and physically prepares soldiers for the challenges, hardships, and deprivations they will face in actual combat situations.[284]

Soldiers are no longer civilians living as they choose. When they enlisted, they relinquished their own will to follow the will of their commanding officers, who possess the experience and wisdom to march to victory. Likewise, soldiers of the cross must be prepared to endure hardship in the battle between good and evil while following Jesus. Satan, the master deceiver and opposing commanding officer, uses tactics to weary our souls, distracting us from the battlefield. Remaining vigilant, we gain a victory; otherwise we go spiritually AWOL.

The hardships we endure as soldiers of the cross are prerequisites in the warfare for our souls. Knowing our characters, God discerns that happiness will not transform us as will affliction. "Christ desires nothing so much as to redeem His heritage from the dominion of Satan. But before we are delivered from Satan's power without, we must be delivered from his power within. The Lord permits trials in order that we may be cleansed from earthliness, from selfishness, from harsh, unchristlike traits of character.

He suffers the deep waters of affliction to go over our souls that we may know Him and Jesus Christ whom He has sent, that we may have deep heart longings to be cleansed from defilement, and that we may come forth from the trial purer, holier, and happier. Often we enter the furnace of trial with our souls darkened with selfishness; but if patient under the crucial test, we shall come forth reflecting the divine character. When His purpose in the affliction is accomplished, 'He shall bring forth thy righteousness as the light, and thy judgment as the noonday' Psalm 37:6."[285]

Good soldiers of the cross march faithfully toward a singular goal of winning the war. Since God is our Commander of heaven, we are never alone or forsaken. The long days of marching will leave us blistered and fatigued, but we march on. Despite the heavy burdens in our backpacks, we march forward with eyes focused on the prize and ears attuned to God's voice uttering promises that will not fail. And soon the battle is won.

October 3

To Be Content in My Circumstances

For I have learned to be content whatever the circumstances. Phil. 4:11, NIV.

As illustrated by the complaining and murmuring of the Israelites, "Life is 10% what happens to you and 90% how you respond to it."[286] The Israelites groaned while laboring as slaves in Egypt; God heard and sent a deliverer. Freed from bondage, they rejoiced for a minute. But two months later their murmuring kick-started. "If only we had died by the LORD's hand in Egypt!" (Ex. 16:3, NIV). After being miraculously fed, they resumed their incessant complaining about the food, the lack of meat, and the lack of water. They also complained that Moses stayed on the mountain too long, that there were giants in the Promised Land, and that the chosen route was unnecessarily long (Ex. 16).

Unlike Paul, who suffered tremendously as he spread the gospel, many of the Israelites failed to learn the secret of contentment. Their murmuring and complaining revealed their ingratitude and selfishness, which directly indicted God and His providence although physically directed at His representatives. Murmuring is an offense to Him who provides from deep pockets of benevolence. "How long shall I bear with this evil congregation, which murmur against me? I have heard the murmurings of the children of Israel, which they murmur against me" (Num 14:27). Discontentment with their lot produced negativity that stood as a brick wall blocking the view of their favored condition and plentiful blessings.

Covetousness is a stumbling block to contentment. Most of us have enough tangible and intangible basics and necessities. But at times our eyes are lifted from our blessings to see someone else whose blessings differ or are more abundant, and we yearn for their gain and dissatisfaction takes root. "Contentment is not just a 'peaceful, easy feeling' or a way to rationalize laziness. It is a deep, easy-breathing wisdom that knows what can and can't be changed, and more important, knows when to do and when to wait. The contented person watches the world closely, but does not stare it down. She enjoys things, rather than trying to possess them or straighten them out."[287]

Additionally, contentment depends on one's viewpoint and one's belief in God. When Joshua and Caleb saw the giants in the Promised Land, they remained undaunted, reporting, "Let us go up at once, and possess it; for we are well able to overcome it" (Num. 13:30). Trusting in their own strength and assailed with doubts by Satan, who established a stronghold in their minds through their habitual pessimism, the other ten spies saw defeat and cautioned, "We be not able to go up against the people; for they are stronger than we" (verse 31). When we distrust God and habitually complain, our situation will loom above us like an unconquerable giant.

"Godliness with contentment is great gain" (1 Tim. 6:6). Thus, it would behoove us to stroke optimistic—a prelude to contentment—and let our problems be opportunities to witness God's solutions. He is bigger and more powerful than any circumstance we can possibly encounter.

October 4

The Lord Is in Control; Wait on Him

I wait for the LORD, my soul does wait, and in His word do I hope. Ps. 130:5, NASB.

As earthbound, time-controlled human beings, we are at the mercy of our timepieces. The more things we acquire to save time, the less time and patience we have. Vehicles crafted to transport us quickly to our destinations facilitate impatience and rage as we wait in traffic jams. Complaints abound regarding the amount of time it takes to read and respond to *instant* messaging. Obviously our patience quota is compromised by drive-through food, microwaves, airplanes, and mobile telephones.

Impatience brings anxiety and frustration, stressors that may lead to a loss of control where we say or do regrettable and/or life-changing things. On the other hand, patience is a virtue—one of the fruit of the Spirit (Gal. 5:22-23). "Patience is waiting. Not passively waiting. That is laziness. But to keep going when the going is hard and slow—that is patience."[288] As we face affliction and other hardships, patience is an absolute necessity if God is truly the Lord of our life.

When impatience moves us to resolve our own problems, it may take forever to rise up on the other side of the damage. Sarah and Abraham are prime examples of the short-term and far-reaching consequences of self-help. God promised them a son, but after decades of waiting and with bodies no longer youthful or fruitful, they chose Hagar to bear Abraham's son. "Sarai, Abram's wife ... gave her to Abram her husband as a wife. And he went in to Hagar, and she conceived. And when she saw that she had conceived, she looked with contempt on her mistress" (Gen. 16:3, 4, ESV).

In the short term, Hagar became proud, incorrigible, and presumed herself to be Sarah's superior after she gave birth to the tribal chieftain's son. Secondly, after Sarah finally conceived and bore Isaac, Hagar's son, Ishmael, the father of the Arab nation, mocked Isaac. Sarah banished both Hagar and the teenage Ishmael from the camp, which broke Abraham's heart. Fulfilling His covenant with Abraham, God promised to make Ishmael a great nation, but He cautioned, "He will be a wild donkey of a man; his hand will be against everyone and everyone's hand against him, and he will live in hostility toward all his brothers" (Gen. 16:12, NIV). Even today, thousands of years later, the Jews and the Arabs are at enmity, which has impacted the entire world.

E. M. Forster wrote, "We must be willing to let go of the life we have planned, so as to have the life that is waiting for us."[289] That is sound advice. We are finite beings who cannot discern what today will bring let alone tomorrow. Conversely, God is everywhere at once, in the present, past, and future. And He already has a plan for our lives—"plans to prosper you and not to harm you, plans to give you hope and a future" (Jer. 29:11, NIV). Doesn't it make sense to surrender our plans and problems to Him? Isn't it wise to "wait for the LORD; be strong and let your heart take courage" (Ps. 27:14, NASB)? Wait, I say, on the Lord!

October 5

Journey Out of Darkness

Then they cried out to the LORD in their trouble, and He saved them out of their distresses. He brought them out of darkness. Ps. 107:13, 14, NKJV.

Can you imagine darkness so potent that it mimics the power of centrifugal force? The supernatural darkness inflicted on pharaoh raged powerful enough to flatten the Egyptians to their seats and suck the peace out of them. God inflicted this plague on Egypt because of pharaoh's stubborn refusal to release the Israelite captives. "Then the Lord said to Moses, Stretch out your hand toward the heavens, that there may be darkness over the land of Egypt, a *darkness which may be felt*. So Moses stretched out his hand toward the sky, and for three days a thick darkness was all over the land of Egypt. The Egyptians could not see one another, nor did anyone rise from his place for three days" (Ex. 10:21-23, AMP).

This was no ordinary darkness. "Ralbag claims that the Egyptians were literally and physically scared to death because of this plague. The Egyptians feared the thick darkness would enter their body and kill them. Josephus, similarly states: 'darkness so thick that their eyes were blinded by it and their breath choked, and they either met with a miserable end or lived in terror of being swallowed up by the fog.'"[290]

Darkness symbolizes chaos, wickedness, and evil—the characteristics of anyone or anything under Satan's dominion. The darkness of sin is seen and felt not only in our lives and colors our existence but also in nature. Satan covers those who are blinded by his lies and deceptions with the inky black mantle of evil and the land with decay and death. Suicide bombers, thieves, and rapists ravage our existence. Deadly viruses, bacteria, and parasites attack our bodies while drought, floods, earthquakes, and volcanoes wreak havoc on the land.

Rebellion and disobedience usher in the black nights of our existence, and traveling in the realm of darkness, we set in motion problems and calamities from which we cannot extricate ourselves. "Some sat in darkness and the deepest gloom, prisoners suffering in iron chains, for they had rebelled against the words of God and despised the counsel of the Most High" (Ps. 107:10, 11, NIV). Satan is gleeful when we heed his counsel of evil and denounce our Redeemer's counsel of love.

Jesus is the one guaranteed solution to transform the darkness of our existence to the light of harmony and serenity. Through the Son He loves, God peeled back the power of darkness, rescued us, and brought us into the kingdom of Light (Col. 1:13). God counsels us to, "Arise, shine, for your light has come, and the glory of the LORD rises upon you. See, darkness covers the earth and thick darkness is over the peoples, but the LORD rises upon you and his glory appears over you" (Isa. 60:1, 2, NIV).

The wise turn from darkness to light and from the power of Satan to God to establish a solid place among those who are sanctified by faith in Jesus (Acts 26:17, 18).

October 6

You Do Not Own Your Body

Or do you not know that your body is the temple of the Holy Spirit who is in you, whom you have from God, and you are not your own? I Cor. 6:19, NKJV.

Renters have a key and permission to enter, but they do not own the property they pay to inhabit. They are not at liberty to damage or change the infrastructure as their heart desires. However, they are required to treat the property as their own by keeping it undamaged and habitable. To inhabit the property, they sign a covenant that outlines their rights and responsibilities and the penalty for violations. Tenants who fail to pay rent or damage the place break the agreement and face eviction.

Similarly, as born-again Christians, we do not own our bodies. They were bought with blood. "You were bought at a price. Therefore honor God with your body" (1 Cor. 6:20, NIV). We were redeemed with something more precious than silver and gold; not with the blood of lambs or sheep but with the precious, inestimable, and priceless blood of Jesus. Trapped in sin, the enemies of God stood under a sentence of death until Jesus purchased us. To keep guard over our souls, He sent the Holy Spirit to dwell inside of us—God's temple (1 Cor. 3:16).

Since He created us and bought us with a price, God owns us twofold. And He has the authority to prescribe the terms for a healthy and happy temple. "So whether you eat or drink, or whatever you do, do it all for the glory of God" (1 Cor. 10:31, NLT). We cannot eat or drink things that destroy His temple. Certain animals created by God are not fit for human consumption, but they are *good* for the purpose they were made. Pigs, shellfish, and catfish, for instance, are scavengers created to cleanse the earth and waterways of dead carcasses, and *their purpose never changed* (Lev. 11). God is not glorified when we defile His temple by ingesting foods that damage our health.

Those who eat unclean foods that bring disease and death will be banned from heaven. "For, behold, the LORD will come with fire ... and by his sword will the LORD plead with all flesh: and the slain of the LORD shall be many. *They that sanctify themselves, and purify themselves ... eating swine's flesh, and the abomination, and the mouse, shall be consumed together,* saith the LORD" (Isa. 66:15-17). Read the Bible carefully and prayerfully and let the Holy Spirit guide you in this very important matter.

What we eat is very important to God because He wants us to prosper and be healthy as our soul prospers (3 John 1:2). And it is faithfulness in seemingly small things that test our faith and obedience. Satan deceived Eve into eating the forbidden fruit in disobedience to the Word of God. "You will not surely die," the serpent said to the woman. And, when she saw that it *looked appetizing*, she ate it (Gen. 3:4, 6, ESV). But by eating that piece of fruit, which was a seemingly small matter, they sent a train wreck of sin and evil to derail our world. Faithfulness, therefore, allows God to be the "author of eternal salvation unto all them that obey him" (Heb. 5:9).

October 7

Bragging About God

Don't let the wise brag of their wisdom. Don't let heroes brag of their exploits. Don't let the rich brag of their riches. If you brag, brag of this and this only: That you understand and know me. Jer. 9:23, MSG.

Why is so hard to admit when we are wrong? Why do we consider ourselves better or more righteous than others? Pride. "According to Christian teachers, the essential vice, the utmost evil, is Pride. Unchastity, anger, greed, drunkenness, and all that, are mere fleabites in comparison: it was through Pride that the devil became the devil: Pride leads to every other vice: it is the complete anti-God state of mind."[291]

Lucifer, the covering cherub, was perfect until he allowed the sin of pride to consume and deprave him. "Sin originated with him who, next to Christ, had been most honored of God and was highest in power and glory among the inhabitants of heaven. Lucifer, 'son of the morning,' was first of the covering cherubs, holy and undefiled. He stood in the presence of the great Creator."[292] The sin of pride caused his downfall, turned him into Satan, the archenemy of His Creator, and "brought [him] down to the grave, to the depths of the pit" (Isa. 14:15, NIV).

Bragging is a form of self-exaltation that evidences a proud heart. "Self-exaltation is an excessively intensified sense of well-being, power, or importance. At its worst, it is self-tribute, self-praise, self-honoring, self-glorifying, and self-worshipping. It overtly breaks the first three commandments by placing oneself as more important than God, setting oneself up as an idol, and making the name of one's god, 'I' or 'me.'"[293] And as we inherited the sinful nature of Adam and Eve and are the devil's children—sinners from the time we were conceived—each Christian has to battle self-exaltation.

Battling pride is as difficult as keeping a helium-filled balloon from rising because it is the nature of helium to rise. To combat pride, we fight an uphill battle against our natural propensity to be proud and to exalt self. Satan used the desire for self-exaltation as the bait to capture Eve. He said, "For God knows that when you eat of it your eyes will be opened, and you will be like God, knowing good and evil" (Gen. 3:5, NASB). She allowed the desire to be parallel with her Creator to supersede her common sense.

It is the pinnacle of audacity to exalt ourselves when we live and function through God who upholds us. Bragging to the level of sin minimizes our total dependence on Him. He is the Most High God over all the earth responsible for our breathing, our rising and walking, our intelligence, and the myriad other blessings we receive from His hand.

Humbleness—a fruit of the Spirit achieved through prayer and faith—is vital in large doses to counter pride. Heed the Word, "For everyone who exalts himself will be humbled, and he who humbles himself will be exalted" (Luke 14:11, ESV). When we fully realize our gross insufficiencies and fully grasp the far reach of God's grace and mercy to those who deserve nothing but death, self-exaltation will cease.

October 8

The Tempered Rod of God's Discipline

If they do not obey my decrees and fail to keep my commands, then I will punish their sin with the rod, and their disobedience with beating. But I will never stop loving him nor fail to keep my promise to him. Ps. 89:31-33, NLT.

Angry at his mother, Denise's eight-year-old son decided to run away from home. On a cold, snowy Saturday morning before his parents came downstairs, he left home. Denise arose and fixed his favorite breakfast to show her love, but when his dad went to rouse him, he discovered the boy's note. Frantic, his parents called the police and waited. After several hours the police found him. When united, his parents hugged and smothered him in kisses. But between tears, hugs, and kisses, he was met with a stern scolding for breaking the rules.

As well, God will never stop loving His children with a love rich in mercy and grace so much so that He made us alive in Christ when we were dead in sin. "[T]he love of God to his people is an everlasting love; it always continues; it never did, nor never will depart, notwithstanding their fall in Adam, their depraved state by nature, their actual sins and transgressions, their many revoltings and backslidings; though the Lord may hide his face from them, and afflict them, still he loves them; whatever departs from them, his kindness shall not; though riches may flee away from them, friends stand aloof off from them, health may be taken away, and life itself, yet the love of God is always the same."[294]

Disobedience and rejection by His children do not diminish His love. They propel Him into action, prompting a scolding with a rod to curtail our headlong flight into darkness and death. God used the Assyrian rod to discipline Israel, Judah, and Damascus. "O Assyrian, the rod of mine anger, and the staff in their hand is mine indignation. I will send him against an hypocritical nation" (Isa. 10:5, 6). But those who learn their lesson and return to him are greeted with open arms. "The remnant shall return, even the remnant of Jacob, unto the mighty God" (verse 21).

As many of us do, David received the rod of affliction to return him to the straight and narrow path. Recognizing the benefit of suffering, David praised God for His love. "It is *good* for me to be afflicted so that I might learn your decrees" (Ps. 119:71, NIV). In the deepest love for a man after His own heart, God unsparingly used the rod of affliction on David as His desire to save His son from eternal death superseded His desire to make him happy. God counseled, "He who spares the rod hates his son, but he who loves him is careful to discipline him" (Prov. 13:24, NIV).

"Heed the rod and the One who appointed it" (Micah 6:9, NIV). All of His rods are tempered in fairness, kindness, and love, so rest in His assurance that we will be disciplined with the most effective rod. "But", He says, "I will chasten and correct you in *just measure*" (Jer. 46:28, AMP).

October 9

Drinking From My Overflowing Cup

You anoint my head with oil; my cup runs over. Ps. 23:5, NKJV.

Figuratively God gives each of us a huge, deep cup and a high-rimmed saucer to hold our abundant blessings. The cup alone is not sufficient because the blessings are poured nonstop even when we are distracted by Satan or bowed down with trials. When trials close in and linger our faith wears thin. One day, however, the dark clouds will dissolve and allow the sun to peep through again. So, persevere during the dark times and receive the crown of life waiting for those who endure testing (James 1:12). Make your prayer, "So Lord, help me not to gripe about the tough rows that I've hoed. I'm drinking from my saucer 'Cause my cup has overflowed."[295]

Closer than a sister, my friend Edna had ovarian cancer and, battling the fight of her life, accepted with grace and dignity the tough row she hoed. Hooked up to a portable IV of liquid nourishment and a pump that injected painkillers at regular intervals, she summoned energy to celebrate my special birthday. Her love shone through her actions as she overflowed with the love *for* her family and friends. "Haven't got a lot of riches and sometimes the going's tough. But I've got loving ones around me and that makes me rich enough. I thank God for his blessings and the mercies He's bestowed. I'm drinking from my saucer, 'Cause my cup has overflowed."[296]

Rather than look inward at her suffering, she looked outward in love to her family and friends, moving us to respond in kind. Edna personified the concept of the Good Samaritan and was never been too busy to help others. When she underwent hospice care, we visited to encourage and uplift her. Amazingly, she encouraged and uplifted *us*, making us feel comfortable in a place that embraces death. She regaled us with funny stories and anecdotes, keeping us in stitches. That indomitable spirit continues to marvel us. Although her body was weakened, she still managed to plant seeds of compassion and love. "I'm reaping better than I sow. I'm drinking from my saucer 'Cause my cup has overflowed."[297]

Edna's faith deepened through her affliction. She prayed for and received strength and courage as the way grew steeper and tougher. "I'll not ask for other blessings I'm already blessed enough."[298] Blessed with the comfort of God's presence and filled with a living hope, she looked forward with all of us "to possessing the rich blessings that God keeps for his people. He keeps them … in heaven, where they cannot decay or spoil or fade away" (1 Peter 1:4, GNT).

Even in affliction, Edna lived an abundant life. Jesus said, "I am come that they might have life, and that they might have it more abundantly" (John 10:10, AKJV). An abundant life is over and beyond ordinary with immeasurable spiritual blessings folded inside God's grace. Salvation from justification to sanctification is a sampling of God's super abundance of grace. It is my plan to keep drinking from that saucer. "'Cause my cup has overflowed."

October 10

Diligence and Delight in the Law of the Lord

Thy word have I hid in mine heart, that I might not sin against thee. Ps. 119:11.

In an episode of *Mama's Family* titled "Pomp and Circumstance," Mama tried to persuade Bubba to attend his graduation although his parents could not attend by relating a story about her brother, Claude, who wanted a new rifle for a graduation gift. Even though it was expensive, Claude was convinced his father would buy it for him. Instead, his father gave him a new Bible. Disappointed and angry, Claude left home. Upon his father's death, he returned home and found the Bible in the box. Upon opening it, he discovered a $50 bill—the cost of the rifle. Bubba asked, "Why didn't his daddy just tell him?" Mama replied, "Why didn't Claude read the Bible?"

My mother, a Christian in word and deed, believed strongly that reading and studying the Bible are non-negotiable. She found the key to victorious living in the Word. Being deprived of a formal education because of a childhood injury did not stop Mama's resolve to know God's Word. She fearlessly tackled the King James Version because she trusted that "the LORD gives wisdom, and from his mouth come knowledge and understanding" (Prov. 2:6, NIV). I cannot remember a time that she did not have the Bible on her lap reading it or close by to read when she could. Her diligence shouted to us, "Oh, how I love your law! I meditate on it all day long" (Ps. 119:97, NIV).

The Word is God's revealed will aimed at providing His children the best life possible in a fallen world. He describes it as a "lamp" and a "light" to point the way out of the darkness of Satan's realm into His "marvelous light." God promises to instruct us and teach us in the way we should go, to counsel us and watch over us all the way to eternity (Ps. 32:8). Mama assimilated the Word in her life. She spoke softly, but her life was a loud rousing sermon in godliness. Loving God with all her heart, she chose to be a doer of the Word and not just a hearer, so she read it and hid His Word in her heart as an aid against sinning (Ps. 119:11).

Those who hate knowledge—God calls them fools—have chosen an inglorious life and future. "They will call to me but I will not answer; they will look for me but will not find me. Since they hated knowledge and did not choose to fear the LORD, since they would not accept my advice and spurned my rebuke, they will eat the fruit of their ways and be filled with the fruit of their schemes. For the waywardness of the simple will kill them, and the complacency of fools will destroy them; but whoever listens to me will live in safety, and be at ease, without fear of harm" (Prov. 1:28-33, NIV).

Listen to His voice through the hearing and reading of His Word. Learn to love and fear Him, to discover His will and to live godly. My mother possessed a richness of spirit, a majestic meekness, a depth of love, and a quality of faith gleaned from her constant exposure to the inspired Words she read in her well-worn Holy Bible. I aspire to her standard of diligence and delight in the law of God. I pray you will as well.

October 11

Stand Firm Until the End

By this gospel you are saved, if you hold firmly to the word I preached to you. Otherwise, you have believed in vain. 1 Cor. 15:2, NIV.

Ordained by God Himself, Lucifer stood in the presence of God as one of two covering cherubs. Sinless, he could withstand the intense light of God's glory without being consumed. Lucifer modeled perfection, exhibited a fullness of wisdom, and possessed perfect beauty. As well, he remained blameless in his ways from the day God created him until wickedness unearthed itself in him (Eze. 28).

Although saved by God's grace and considered blameless, Lucifer's salvation was not irrevocably sealed. Once his desire to be exalted above God turned him into Satan, an unrepentant sinner, God expelled him from heaven to face eternal death. The Word clearly says, "the soul who sins is the one who will die" (Eze. 18:20, NIV). Satan deceived Adam and Eve who received counsel directly from God. And he is deceiving many people today who want to believe that salvation is guaranteed once they are justified by the blood of Jesus—that by God's grace nothing more is required and they are sealed for eternity.

The doctrine of "once saved always saved" is a ploy by Satan to lull us into a false sense of security and a loss of eternal life. One argument Satan advances for this doctrine is that those who return to sin were not really saved in the first place. But the Word begs to differ, pronouncing that the once righteous can backslide and be lost. "For if we sin willfully after we have received the knowledge of the truth, there no longer remains a sacrifice for sins, but a certain fearful expectation of judgment, and fiery indignation which will devour the adversaries" (Heb. 10:26, 27, NKJV).

Ezekiel tackles the never unsaved issue with a rhetorical question and an emphatic answer. "But if a righteous man turns from his righteousness and commits sin and does the same detestable things the wicked man does, will he live? None of the righteous things he has done will be remembered. Because of the unfaithfulness he is guilty of and because of the sins he has committed, he will die" (Eze. 18:24, NIV).

"Come now, and let us reason together, saith the Lord" (Isa. 1:18). We must couple reasoning with a call to the Holy Spirit whose job is to guide us to the truth. God allowed His only Son to die a cruel and dishonorable death because He could not renege on His Word—unconfessed and unrepentant sin warrants eternal death (Rom. 6:23). Believe Him when He says, "Do you not know that the wicked will not inherit the kingdom of God? Do not be deceived: Neither the sexually immoral nor idolaters nor adulterers nor male prostitutes nor homosexual offenders nor thieves nor the greedy nor drunkards nor slanderers nor swindlers will inherit the kingdom of God" (1 Cor. 6:9, 10, NIV).

Salvation requires faithful obedience. "Whoever says, 'I know him,' but does not keep his commandments is a liar, and the truth is not in him ... whoever says he abides in him ought to walk in the same way in which he walked" (1 John 2:4, 6, ESV).

October 12

Walking in the Law Under Grace

For sin shall not have dominion over you: for ye are not under the law, but under grace. Rom. 6:14.

How chaotic would be our society and lives without laws and rules to govern conduct? In practically every aspect of our lives, we are benefitted by the boundaries they offer. "What would a football field be like if there were no sidelines, no end zones, no yard markers? What if the goalposts were moved in the middle of the game? What would basketball be like if the court had no boundaries and the player dribbling the ball had no limitations? What would keep him from running into the bleacher section?"[299]

We serve a God of decency and order who established physical laws to uphold and sustain nature and the moral code to guide His created beings into righteousness. Without the laws of physics, creation would be in a tailspin. Without God's moral laws, sin would be unchecked and run rampart. Why, then, do so many people believe that the moral code is abolished and they are not under the law but under grace? True, our sins are abolished because of grace; nevertheless, obedience is required.

God did not nor can He condone lawlessness. "Everyone who sins breaks the law; in fact, sin is lawlessness. But you know that he [Jesus] appeared so that he might take away our sins" (1 John 3:4, 5, NIV). Not under the law means we are no longer under the *penalty* of the law; that we are no longer condemned to die and that our confessed sins are forgiven. Christians are expected to obey the law, but in the event we fall short, the blood of Jesus covers our sins by God's grace. Thus, Jesus died so we might live.

Not under the law also means that we are *not saved* by the law but by God's grace. The law cannot save us; it reveals that sin is a violation of the law. Like the rich young ruler, who had zeal for God but not according to knowledge, and the Pharisees, we can abide by the law from childhood, but never have a heart change and be lost eternally. Ignorant of the righteousness of God, and establishing their own righteousness, they spurned the righteousness of God (Rom. 10:2, 3).

Paul made it crystal clear that he did not mean the law is void. "Shall we sin because we are not under law but under grace? By no means!" (Rom. 6:15, NLT). We do not have license to break the law because we are pardoned, nor is the law made void through faith. "Faith is a law; it is a working grace, not an act of obedience or a good work, but forms a bond between Christ and the sinner so that the believer is pardoned and justified. The unbeliever who is not thus united to him remains under condemnation"[300] But those who walk in the law of the LORD are blessed, and have a bright future (Ps. 119:1).

Jesus fulfilled the requirements of the law at the cross, but in so doing, He bound us to Him with cords of obedience. We are not at liberty to sin because He expects us to obey His commandments through yielding to the power of the Spirit who dwells within us. That is grace.

October 13

God Holds All Wisdom and All Power

Praise the name of God ... for he has all wisdom and power. He controls the course of world events ... He gives wisdom to the wise ... He reveals deep and mysterious things and knows what lies hidden in darkness. Dan. 2:20-22, NLT.

A man escaping a tiger ran until he reached the edge of a cliff. With a sigh of relief, he saw a branch growing a few feet below the edge and jumped onto it. But later a rat began to gnaw at the branch. The man began to panic when he saw how far he would fall if the branch broke. He began to pray, "Lord, I will do anything if You will just save me." After he prayed, he was impressed to let go of the branch. He hesitated, then heard an audible voice say, "Let go of the branch." Not content with the response, he responded, "Is there anyone else up there?"[301]

Why do we have difficulty trusting God's Word? Perfectly faithful, God created truth and has unlimited power to back up all His promises. "For the word of the LORD is right and true; he is faithful in all he does" (Ps. 33:4, NIV). Our Lord God Almighty, He reigns over the heavens and the earth with unrivaled and unlimited power (Rev. 19: 6). At His word, diseases are cured and sins are forgiven (Matt 8:3; 9:2). Deformed bodies straighten at His touch, and the dead become alive (Matt. 8:13; Luke 7:14). Demons beg for mercy, and nature bows reverently to Him (Mark 5:12; Luke 4:35).

God is the only Being who predicts the future thousands of years before it is manifested, and only He directs the events of history. He sets up kingdoms and brings them down. "The Most High is sovereign over the kingdoms of men and gives them to anyone he wishes" (Dan. 4:17, NIV) Although we may be stymied at certain events, certain leaders, and deep silence when we sorely need Him, He never ceases to direct, control, and resolve what works best for our good. Why, "everything he does is right and all his ways are just" (Dan. 4:37, NIV).

"[T]he Sovereign LORD does nothing without revealing his plan to his servants the prophets" (Amos 3:7, NIV). He sent Noah to preach salvation to the antediluvian society before the Flood (Gen 6:13). Prior to the plagues in Egypt, Moses warned Pharaoh (Ex. 7-11). John wrote the book of Revelation to reveal last day events. And He gave Daniel the interpretation of the king's dream that foretold the history of the world (Dan. 2). By studying Daniel 2, we discern that we are living in the tip of the toes of the statue in the king's dream. The four world kingdoms rose and fell, and Rome, the fourth and last world kingdom, is divided into today's European nations, destined to never to be united as indicated by the toes of iron and clay.

God "cannot be false in His thoughts, Words, or actions. There is no shadow of a lie upon anything which God thinks, or speaks, or does."[302] God's law is truth—all His commandments are true. And His Word is truth (Ps. 119). His law is an expression of His nature; thus, He is Truth personified. And God is not a man that He can lie. So when He asks of us the seemingly impossible, trusting Him makes sense.

October 14

Our Conquering King

Arise, O LORD! Confront him, cast him down; Deliver my life from the wicked with Your sword. Ps. 17:13, NKJV.

There are conquerors and there are the conquered. The history of battles and wars reveal that sometimes the tables turn and the conqueror becomes the conquered and strives to rise up from defeat. As well, the oppressed seek to rise. Maya Angelou wrote, "Out of the huts of history's shame, I rise. Up from a past that's rooted in pain, I rise. I'm a black ocean, leaping and wide. Welling and swelling I bear in the tide. Leaving behind nights of terror and fear, I rise. Into a daybreak that's wondrously clear I rise. Bringing the gifts that my ancestors gave, I am the dream and the hope of the slave. I rise. I rise. I rise."[303]

The prayer of the oppressed remains "Arise, O LORD; save me, O my God" (Ps. 3:7). Jesus, who relinquished His equality with God, Himself became marginalized. Therefore, He truly identifies with the subjugated (Phil 2:5-7). But one day the faithful who are tempted, marginalized, and vilified by man and Satan will be snatched from their oppressors by the coming King. Those wearing the character of Jesus will arise from the dust in victory, for He returns with authority and great power. No longer is He the helpless Baby Jesus or the maligned Savior walking the streets of Jerusalem. He will come "with ten thousands of his saints, to execute judgment upon all, and to convince all that are ungodly among them of all their ungodly deeds" (Jude 14, 15).

He encourages the righteous who have the law of God in their heart, saying, "Do not fear the reproach of men or be terrified by their insults [or the traps set by Satan]. For the moth will eat them up like a garment; the worm will devour them like wool" (Isa. 51:7, 8, NIV). Once the message of redemption has fully lit up the earth and everyone has an opportunity to choose whom they will serve, Jesus' mediation for the redeemed will end (1 Tim. 2:5). Then, "Michael, the great prince who protects your people, will arise.... Everyone whose name is found written in the book—will be delivered" (Dan. 12:1, NIV).

The conquered will be delivered, lifted up from the dust, and welcomed into the heavenly city by Jesus, the mighty conqueror who will take away the rebuke of His people (John 14:3; Isa. 25:8). "The heirs of God have come from garrets, from hovels, from dungeons, from scaffolds, from mountains, from deserts, from the caves of the earth, from the caverns of the sea. On earth they were 'destitute, afflicted, tormented.' Millions went down to the grave loaded with infamy because they steadfastly refused to yield to the deceptive claims of Satan. By human tribunals they were adjudged the vilest of criminals.... Now the decisions of earth are reversed."[304]

Our goal should be to live godly lives, pray for the courage of our convictions, and be patient. Living thusly or dying in Christ, we will arise in the absolute victory of eternal life guaranteed by the King of kings, the coming King—our conqueror.

October 15

Be Holy as I Am Holy

As obedient children, do not conform to the evil desires you had when you lived in ignorance. But just as he who called you is holy, so be holy in all you do; for it is written: "Be holy, because I am holy." 1 Peter 1:14-16, NIV.

Daily, boulders of difficulties confront us that require a supreme push to move forward. But struggles are unavoidable and necessary to strengthen our mental muscles and our resolve. Frederick Douglas said, "If there is no struggle there is no progress. Those who profess to favor freedom and yet deprecate agitation are men who want crops without plowing up the ground; they want rain without thunder and lightning. They want the ocean without the awful roar of its many waters"[305]

Being holy as Jesus is holy requires a struggle with the natural inclination to satisfy self. The propensity to selfishness is hard wired into our system and is as natural and effortless as breathing. In fact, it is the root sin that caused Satan's expulsion from heaven and Adam and Eve's expulsion from the Garden of Eden. The couple's desire to propel self above God is a genetic trait transmitted through their genes to each living human being. Therefore, to be holy we are cautioned to "prepare your minds for action; be self-controlled; set your hope fully on the grace" of God (1 Peter 1:13, NIV).

Evil desires dominate before we accept the mastery of Jesus over self-mastery. The desire to please self above others and above God is always present and active. Unchecked, selfishness keeps us in bondage to Satan whose reign is marked by sinful deeds and desires. But there is a power greater than self at our disposal—the Spirit of God. He can assist us in emptying our spiritual coffer of self and filling it with the holiness of Jesus who is the standard. He said, "I do nothing of myself" (John 8:28). When we surrender to the power of the Holy Spirit, we are slowly purged of worldly selfishness and begin to assume the divine, holy nature of God.

In heaven the never-ending refrain is, "Holy, holy, holy is the LORD God Almighty, which was, and is, and is to come" (Rev. 4:8). God requires us to be holy as He is holy and sets us apart to be His own (Lev. 20:26). Being set apart means that we act and think differently from the world where Satan reigns. It means we learn to hate the evil from which God wants to deliver us (Gal. 1:4). And with the Spirit in us, we struggle onward toward a heightened level of spiritual maturity and moral excellence.

"Who is like you—majestic in holiness, awesome in glory, working wonders?" (Ex. 15:11, NIV). We have every spiritual tool necessary to be holy as God is holy. Working in tandem with God's Spirit, a person determined to be holy denounces willful sin and prays daily for a closer walk with Jesus. By God's grace we bury that old nature and rise up with a made-up mind to do what is pleasing in His sight. The holy person makes "every effort to live in peace with all men and to be holy; [for] without holiness no one will see the Lord" (Heb. 12:14, NIV).

October 16

When You Pray

You ask and do not receive, because you ask amiss, that you may spend it on your pleasures. James 4:3, NKJV.

Huck Finn could not find merit in prayer. "Miss Watson she took me in the closet and prayed, but nothing come of it. She told me to pray every day, and whatever I asked for I would get it. But it warn't so. I tried it. Once I got a fishline, but no hooks. It warn't any good to me without hooks. I tried for the hooks three or four times, but somehow I couldn't make it work… I set down one time back in the woods, and had a long think about it. I says to myself, if a body can get anything they pray for, why don't Deacon Winn get back the money he lost on pork? Why can't the widow get back her silver snuffbox that was stole?… No, says I to myself, there ain't nothing in it."[306]

Huck's prayer, motivated by selfishness, points to many people's confusion about the purpose of prayer. When the result he desired did not ensue in his time frame, he denounced the practice of praying and, therefore, diminished his power and blessings. This type of grasping prayer, attended by a selfish attitude that dishonors God, nullifies the power of prayer. "Prayer honors God; it dishonors self. It is man's plea of weakness, ignorance, need- a plea that heaven cannot regard. God delights to have us pray."[307]

Prayer provides the initiative for fallen human beings to communicate one-on-one with God. It is the highest privilege of our existence as prayer marshals in supernatural power from the armory of God. "And Jesus answered them, "Truly, I say to you, if you have faith and do not doubt, you will not only do what has been done to the fig tree, but even if you say to this mountain, 'Be taken up and thrown into the sea,' it will happen. And whatever you ask in prayer, you will receive, if you have faith" (Matt. 21:21, 22, ESV). Even if we are faith-filled to the brim, that does not mean that mountain moving will occur anytime we pray. It does mean, however, that God is monumentally capable of moving any literal or figurative mountain, and He does so if it fits His purposes.

Also, prayer marshals in the presence of God who wants intimacy with His children and waits for us to communicate our desires. He said, "I've made myself available to those who haven't bothered to ask. I'm here, ready to be found by those who haven't bothered to look" (Isa. 65:1, 2, MSG). Many times we do not receive because we do not ask (James 4:2). Still, when we ask with the wrong motives or with impatience, petulance and doubt because of a delayed or non-response, our prayers may bounce back rather than ascend to the ear of God.

Moreover, prayer that honors God is a sweet fragrance, a mist on which we float our petitions to His throne. Like sweet incense, they ascend to heaven and are registered in the heart of God never to be forgotten. "The smoke of the incense, together with the prayers of the saints, went up before God from the angel's hand" (Rev. 8:4, NIV). Let our selfless, persistent prayers proceed from a broken and contrite heart to set before God as incense, and let us gladly wait for His response as a sign of our faith in His wisdom.

October 17

Seek the Lord's Strength

Seek the LORD and his strength, seek his face continually. 1 Chron. 16:11.

As a Cub Scout, Gilbert responded to his leader's mandate to craft a derby car. However, his lopsided car looked homemade because he did not have his dad's help as did the other boys. When he entered it in the derby race, he realized no other car looked as pitiful as his. But by the process of elimination, two cars remained—Gilbert's and the sleekest, fastest car there. Gilbert asked and received permission to pray before the final race. His car reached the finish line a fraction of a second before the other car, prompting the Scout Master to say, "So you prayed to win." "No," answered Gilbert, "I just asked Him to make it so I don't cry when I lose."[308]

As young as he was, Gilbert knew intuitively that he needed more than a win. Thus, he did not ask God to make him a winner; he asked for strength to endure the humility of a loss. Mercifully, God rewarded him with *both* a win and strength for the next battle. "Perhaps we spend too much of our prayer time asking God to rig the race, to make us number one, or too much time asking God to remove us from the struggle, when we should be seeking God's strength to get through the struggle."[309]

Look around you. Look at the carnage and bloodshed, the fires and floods, the lying and cheating, the broken homes and broken relationships, and the fear and mistrust. Difficult times have confounded and overwhelmed earth's inhabitants. For selfishness has reached an all-time high because self is the supreme ruler. God warned us that in the last days, "People will be lovers of themselves, lovers of money, boastful, proud, abusive, disobedient to their parents, ungrateful, unholy, without love, unforgiving, slanderous, without self-control, brutal, not lovers of the good, treacherous, rash, conceited, lovers of pleasure rather than lovers of God— having a form of godliness but denying its power" (2 Tim. 3:1-5, NIV).

To endure these perilous times requires intimacy—a close personal relationship with God—and a persistent prayer life. Intimacy means being vulnerable, sharing our deepest thoughts and desires, trusting, and loving. God shared a beautiful intimacy with Adam and Eve. They walked together in the Garden of Eden, talking and sharing before the couple sinned (Gen. 2, 3). Since the Fall, which caused a separation between God and humanity, God has worked tirelessly, involving every agency in heaven and the life of His Son to recapture that intimacy. Paul wrote, "I consider everything a loss compared to the surpassing greatness of knowing Christ Jesus my Lord, for whose sake I have lost all things" (Phil. 3:8, NIV).

Our strength springs from that intimate relationship with God. He is quite attentive to and strengthens those who seek His face—who confess and refrain from willful sin—and those who run to Him for refuge. Through Him and Him alone do the weak become strong (Isa. 40:29)

October 18

Spiritual Lethargy

I know all the things you do, that you are neither hot nor cold. I wish that you were one or the other! But since you are like lukewarm water, neither hot nor cold, I will spit you out of my mouth! Rev. 3:15, 16, NLT.

Indifference, marked by apathy, is a powerful tool in the hands of Satan. Apathetic Christians teeter between heaven and hell courting disaster. They walk onto the battlefield of life without the full armor of God, allowing Satan freedom to tilt them in his direction. Roger Waters wrote, "Not the torturer will scare me, nor the body's final fall, nor the barrels of death's rifles, nor the shadows on the wall, nor the night when to the ground the last dim star of pain, is hurled but … blind indifference …" is fatal.

Spiritual lethargy places one in a state of limbo. Neither passionate nor passionless, the spiritually lethargic occupy a place called "whatever" for their "heart has become calloused; they hardly hear with their ears, and they have closed their eyes. Otherwise they might see with their eyes, hear with their ears, understand with their hearts and turn, and I would heal them" (Matt. 13:15, NIV). They know the truth but do not follow the path of spiritual growth and are now dangerously stagnant.

God is nauseated by spiritual indifference. And those indifferent to Him and His Word, who call themselves by His name, are as disgusting as lukewarm water to the digestive system. It is loathsome enough to turn the stomach and forcibly eject its foul contents. Many Christians have deviated off the narrow path to embrace the soft words and easy religion of today, leaving a very dim line of demarcation between the church and the world. "This is what the LORD says: 'Stand at the crossroads and look; ask for the ancient paths, ask where the good way is, and walk in it …' But you said, 'We will not walk in it'" (Jer. 6:16, NIV).

"Spiritual lethargy means—being lazy in spiritual matters! Prayer, Bible study, fasting, meditation, living and applying God's laws and principles -these are spiritual matters. And the problem with too many in God's Church is that they will not discipline themselves to do these things as they should! Too many lack character, and will not repent and change!"[310] God does not want a sacrifice of church going or tithe paying or clinging to the church of our ancestors. This is superficial Christianity and requires no striving after righteousness. He requires that we put His Word into practice and transform our minds through the power of His Spirit.

Lethargic Christians are Satan's delight because many resolutely believe they are heaven-bound. But God says, "You say, 'I am rich; I have acquired wealth and do not need a thing.' But you do not realize that you are wretched, pitiful, poor, blind and naked" (Rev. 3:17, NIV). This blind indifference translates into spiritual impoverishment that will exclude people from heaven. In love, God counsels us to shake off that lethargy and buy gold from Him to become rich in righteousness, white raiment to cover our shameful nakedness—our sin—and eye salve to become spiritually discerning (verse 18).

October 19

Pulling Down Strongholds

For the weapons of our warfare are not carnal, but mighty through God to the pulling down of strong holds. 2 Cor. 10:4.

A creative judge defined adverse possession in terms of a conquering hero. "The person claiming the property by adverse possession must unfurl his flag on the land and keep it flying so that the owner may see if he wishes, that an enemy has invaded his domain and planted the flag of conquest."[311] Adverse possession, a method of obtaining real property without compensation to the owner, is a legal right under certain conditions. The claimant openly lives on the property, and the owner accepts this occupation. The possession must also be "notorious, exclusive, hostile, under cover of claim or right, and continuous and uninterrupted for the statutory period."

Similar to adverse possession, Satan has a legal right to establish strongholds under certain conditions. A stronghold is an area where the enemy is entrenched because of persistence in wrongdoing, ignorance, or otherwise. Satan, the god of this world, wrenched dominion over every living thing from Adam and Eve after they disobeyed God (Gen 1:28), and he will possess us if we grant him permission. He reminded Jesus when He tempted him in the wilderness that all the treasures of the world "has been given to me, and I can give it to anyone" (Luke 4:6, NIV).

"By consenting to break one precept, men are brought under Satan's power."[312] Although Judas was privileged to be in Jesus' inner circle and had first-hand knowledge of the gospel and Jesus' love, he walked into enemy territory. The lessons that lead to life entered his head but never penetrated his heart. Because he "was a thief; as keeper of the money bag, he used to help himself to what was put into it," he unwittingly beckoned Satan to establish a stronghold and control him (John 12:5).

Strongholds are impossible to control without confession and divine intervention. Judas' stronghold was the unapologetic sin of stealing. He knew it was wrong; yet, he persisted in stealing from Jesus and His disciples. As he grew bolder, he justified his behavior and became a prisoner of Satan, which contributed to the death of our Savior and brought infamy to his name evermore. Likewise, Margaret justified her anger against her cousin for an insult that galled her. Then baited by Satan, who claimed his legal right to control her thoughts, she mulled over the offense again and again until she got angrier and angrier to the point of breaking a familial tie and dividing the family. However, her mother persuaded Margaret to pray for forgiveness, which broke Satan's stronghold.

Unless we deny him permission, Satan will assert his legal right to establish thought control when we persist in wrongdoing. God will protect us from demons if we will allow Him. But Satan breaches that wall of safety *with* God's permission when we batter holes in it with hammers of sin. Honoring God in surrender and morality, our weapons to demolish Satan's stronghold are mighty because of God's power to cast them down and trample them in the dust.

October 20

The Promise of Protection

The LORD himself goes before you and will be with you; he will never leave you nor forsake you. Do not be afraid; do not be discouraged. Deut. 31:8, NIV.

Traveling to Zambia, Innoce and his family were ordered off the bus after waiting hours for its arrival. His mother insisted vigorously that they remain on the bus, even dissolving in tears, but the porter politely stood firm. Other passengers intervened, pleading with the porter, but to no avail. Having no option, they reluctantly got off the bus and waited for the next one. Later, the loudspeaker announced that the bus they were forced to exit had crashed, killing all on board.[313]

God provided cover in front of Innoce and protection from the rear during the battle for his and his family's lives. He says, "for the LORD will go before you … [and] be your rear guard" (Isa. 52:12, NIV). When God chooses, He covers His people like an invisible and impenetrable shield from left to right and from top to bottom, fighting the battle victoriously from every direction. Nobody can pull off a sneak attack and penetrate His defense of those who love Him.

Death is the physical end for everyone. But why did other good people on Innoce's bus die in the crash? Obviously God is capable of providing complete protection for His created beings and has done so for many. But sometimes His wisdom and love require His redeemed to go through the fire that may result in present physical death while He is working out our future spiritual life. Faith requires that we accept His plan and purpose for our lives, for His plan is perfect with perfect timing and a perfect ending.

We are too finite to understand God's thoughts and ways, which are a far cry from ours and are incomparably higher than high (Isa. 55:7). We serve a big God—big in wisdom, love, power, and presence. If we, as frail humans, were identical with Him in any way, particularly in wisdom and power, He would not be God. To understand Him fully, we would need to miniaturize Him to the level of created humans, but then He would be too small to be the God we need, respect, and trust.

God promises that the faithful are always in His presence and under the banner of special protection spiritually, but we may not be protected physically. Many of His saints will suffer and die as did those on the bus, thus leaving us perplexed. But God is good and His mercy endures forever. He loves us dearly; His wisdom is infallible. "Precious in the sight of the LORD is the death of his saints" (Ps. 116:15). Each saint is as valuable in death as in life to Him, for their life and death are a part of His master plan—a plan that will come to fruition on that great and glorious day of the Lord.

And at that time we will understand and our suffering and death will seem insignificant when we have the capacity to compare it to the glory of immortality (2 Cor. 4:17).

October 21

From the Depths of the Pit

But I called on your name, LORD, from deep within the pit. You heard me when I cried ... you came when I called; you told me, "Do not fear." Lam. 3:55-57, NLT.

Joseph, the oldest of Rachel's children was the obvious favorite of the patriarch Jacob. And when Joseph described a dream to his ten older brothers where they bowed down to him, the seething cauldron of anger, resentment, and jealousy reached the surface and erupted. They plotted to kill him and drop him in an empty cistern. Reuben, an older brother, intervened and saved his life, but when Reuben left, the others sold Joseph to slave traders who carried him to Egypt (Gen 37:19-23).

Imagine Joseph's fear when his brothers' murderous rage threatened his future! Imagine the terror at being dropped in the deep, dark pit and his pitiful pleas for help ignored! Many of us have figuratively been dropped or fallen into a pit—the lowest most depressing place of our existence. We land ingloriously at the bottom of pits of illness, financial ruin, heartbreak, loneliness, loss, or guilt. Some of these pits result from willful sin, others from evil people and/or circumstances. Nevertheless, they are very scary black holes chock full of anguish and discouragement.

In the depth of the pit, we have nowhere to go but up and no one to hear our call but God. "Know that the LORD has set apart the godly for himself; the LORD will hear when I call to him" (Ps. 4:3, NIV). Joseph called on God to release Him from the pit, and He did. But further hardship, necessary to fulfill God's purposes for Joseph's spiritual growth and his family's long-term survival, rapidly advanced. On the way to Egyptian slavery, slander, and prison, Joseph surely prayed and cried out in agony to be released and returned to his family. God heard his call and answered, but not in Joseph's time frame. Although it appeared that God did not hear or heed His call, He did. Accordingly, with faultless timing He intently worked out His good and perfect will for Joseph's life.

Too wise to make a mistake and too loving to abandon any of His faithful children, God remained close to Joseph especially in his dark pits. As well, Joseph remained true to God's commands, and God protected him and blessed him materially. "The LORD was with Joseph and he prospered" (Gen. 39:2, NLT). After Potiphar's wife unjustly accused Joseph of rape, he was sent to prison, which sullied his good name. "But while Joseph was there in the prison, the LORD was with him; he showed him kindness and granted him favor in the eyes of the prison warden" (Gen. 39:20, 21, NIV). Joseph's behavior brought glory to God in the midst of idol worshippers even while in the pit.

Finally, God gave Joseph the power to interpret pharaoh's dreams, changing his situation after years of hardship and pain, and pharaoh put him "in charge of the whole land of Egypt" (Gen. 41:41, NLT). Joseph could joyously exclaim, "I waited patiently for the LORD; he turned to me and heard my cry" (Ps. 40:1, NIV). Likewise, our cry is heard from the depth of the pit.

October 22

The Sin Virus Destroyed by Mercy

For as the heavens are high above the earth, so great is His mercy toward those who fear Him. Ps. 103:11, NKJV.

Computer viruses and worms are as lethal to computers as biological viruses and tapeworms are to the human body. A computer virus is a "small piece of software that piggybacks on real programs." This software runs when the original program runs but infects it and wreaks havoc with the computer and its contents. A computer worm, however, is a self-replicating malware computer program that uses computer networks to copy itself. Experts have identified some very malignant computer viruses and worms like the Mydoom worm and the Melissa virus. The Mydoom worm infected almost 250,000 computers in one day while the Melissa virus infected so many computers that e-mails were suspended until the virus was controlled and eradicated.[314]

Similarly, Satan infected the entire world with a lethal sin virus that wreaks havoc with our souls until it is combated and eradicated. A sinner's only hope of a cure for the infection is a transfusion of the blood of Jesus through which flows forgiveness. But those who are infected are powerless to escape the malignancy and powerless to desire the blood transfusion without intervention. So what is a caring God to do? With a basis in mercy, He founded a supernatural remedy—the Holy Spirit.

The Holy Spirit is a grand expression of God's mercy toward sinners. While we are lost in sin and in open hostility toward Him, He gently pursues us and patiently awaits our acceptance of His offer of freedom. He works day and night, almost unnoticeably, softening and subduing hearts to receive the gospel truths that convert the soul. Without the Spirit's influence on our hearts sensitizing us to the Word of God, we could *never* accept the offer of mercy. "Now we have received … the Spirit who is from God, that we might know the things that have been freely given to us by God.… But the natural man does not receive the things of the Spirit of God, for they are foolishness to him; nor can he know them, because they are spiritually discerned" (1 Cor. 2:12-14, NKJV).

God is merciful to both sinner and saint alike. Daily sustaining us, He supplies all our needs, causing "His sun [to] rise on the evil and on the good, and sends rain on the just and the unjust" (Matt. 5:45, NKJV). And His mercy extends to the natural creation for "His tender mercies are over *all* his works" (Ps. 145:9). Without a special expression of His mercy toward sinners by the substitution of Jesus' life for ours, we would have no hope for the future because sin earns us death. But, "Christ hath redeemed us from the curse of the law, being made a curse for us" (Gal. 3:13, 14).

The Lord is good and His *mercy endures forever*, but not to the impenitent. The mercy extended to those who do not fear/reverence Him is temporal and will end in eternal death. Only the God-fearing receive everlasting mercy. To them, His mercy endures through the ceaseless ages of eternity in the myriad blessing given to the redeemed.

October 23

Help Me Overcome My Doubt

Lord, I believe; help my unbelief! Mark 9:24, NKJV.

Mount St. Helens, a mountain in Washington State, blew its top in 1980 after 123 years of dormancy. Seismologists announced an imminent eruption, prompting state officials to warn the nearby residents to evacuate immediately. One elderly man, Harry Truman, who lived at the base of the mountain refused to leave his home and possessions, apparently dismissing the warning and believing that he would be safe. When the eruption occurred, Truman and all his possessions were buried under millions of tons of ash, mud, and trees that were uprooted in droves.

Truman, true to his defective judgment despite scientific proof, rejected the route to safety after experts pointed out the looming eruption. Steadfast in his rejection of sound counsel, he perished. However, a father who wanted Jesus to exorcise demons from his son doubted Jesus' power but halted at absolute unbelief, for he maintained a mustard-seed size faith. Unlike Truman, he was not immovable and cried out to God for help, which changed the outcome. He said to Jesus, "But *if* you can do anything, take pity on us and help us" (Mark 9:22, NIV). His plaintive plea prompted Jesus' assurance that everything is possible with faith. Hearing the father's heartfelt plea that he believed, despite his wavering, Jesus exorcised the demons (Mark 9:21-24).

We all have or will experience doubt in our walk with Jesus. Even the most seasoned Christian who has walked with Him over many decades sometimes struggles with God's silence and/or the horror at difficult circumstances and events beyond understanding. Doubt walks in the door, causing a serious struggle between believing the enemy of faith and the Giver of faith. "I believe; help my unbelief" is a statement of benign double-mindedness, a double-mindedness that is acceptable to God. It points to someone who is fighting to get back on track, fighting to regain their faith footing. And it moves one to reach out to the Author and Finisher of their faith.

There is a sound remedy for the doubt that creeps in at times, and it is instantly available. Call on God who understands our weaknesses. We have instant access to Him through prayer, and may call on Him anywhere and at anytime. When we fall helpless in submission at the foot of the cross, our Savior responds. "Cast your cares on the LORD and he will sustain you; he will never let the righteous fall" (Ps. 55:22, NIV).

Also, when doubts slither into our mind with the goal of undermining our faith in God, we can repel them with the truth of Scripture that stands the test of time. "It is written, Man shall not live by bread alone, but by every word that proceedeth out of the mouth of God." (Matt. 4:4).

The Bible declares that God is in control, but the devil is defeated; that God is love, but the enemy is a murderer and a thief; that God wants to save us, but the enemy wants to destroy us. If we ask Him, He will bolster our faith.

October 24

What God Requires of Us

But let justice run down like water, and righteousness like a mighty stream. Amos 5:24, NKJV.

"Mysterious Flood,--that through the silent sands Hast wandered, century on century, Watering the length of great Egyptian lands, Which were not, but for thee."[315] The Nile River, located in Africa and considered to be the world's longest river, meanders more than 4,000 miles through nine countries. The huge Nile River Delta, or drainage basin, without equal, covers 1,293,000 square miles. Egypt is called the "gift of the Nile" by Herodotus, a Greek historian, because without the life-sustaining waters of the Nile, Egypt would be a barren, lifeless desert.

Bodies of water are symbols used by the prophet Amos to highlight the life-giving aspects of justice and righteousness. A God of mercy expects justice and, therefore, righteousness in return from those created by His hand. "Biblical justice means very practical, down-to-earth actions which take place to ensure that the weak are protected from abuse, that the poor have what they need, the stranger in the land is shown hospitality and that the socially disadvantaged are cared for."[316] And those who claim to be His children will be disappointed on that last day unless righteousness is united with justice in their relational undertakings. God utters, "Maintain justice and do what is right, for my salvation is close at hand and my righteousness will soon be revealed" (Isa. 56:1, NIV).

By using synonymous parallelism or repetition of the same idea as illustrated in Amos 5:24—justice running like water and righteousness like a stream—the interconnection between righteousness and justice is made. "Righteousness *is* justice within the context of a covenant relationship. When a person fulfills the obligation of a relationship that person is said to be righteous."[317] That kind of right justice keeps the way of the Lord and is pleasing in His sight. On the other hand, injustice is not only a travesty but also dampens faith and, hence, is soundly rebuked by God. "You have disheartened the righteous falsely ... and you have encouraged the wicked, that he should not turn from his evil way to save his life" (Eze. 13:22, ESV).

As well, the parallelism emphasizes the importance of our practicing godliness as signified by God's pleas to "Do what is just and right" (Jer. 22:3, NIV). We are the salt of the earth used by God to be effective witnesses of His grace and mercy to benefit the building up of His kingdom, but our failure to do what is right works the opposite effect. To save our own souls and to temper the evil that is bringing the wrath of God upon our society, we should consistently practice these twin virtues for, according to Paul Marshall, "justice [which is righteousness] is: right relationships among all things in the created order of things."

One day justice will flow through the streets like a river and righteousness like a never-ending stream. But only those who practice these virtues will be witnesses to this perfect justice.

October 25

Do You Rob God?

"Will a man rob God? Yet you have robbed Me! But you say, 'In what way have do we rob you?' In tithes and offerings. Mal. 3:8, NKJV.

Lanette Sansoni, an office manager and title clerk at JRS Settlement Services, stole $475,000 from her employer. She received a unique sentence of twenty-one years of house arrest, possibly a record for house arrest in Pennsylvania according to Assistant District Attorney Steven Bunn. "She was basically … living the high life while this company went under," causing six people to lose their jobs, including the employer and his family.[318] "Employee dishonesty and theft costs U.S. business over $50 billion dollars annually. National estimates show that 75% of all employees steal from their employers at least once throughout their careers." And "a majority of employee theft goes undetected by supervisors and management."[319]

Although many employers are unaware of the thievery going on among their employees, God sees and knows everything. "You know when I sit and when I rise; you perceive my thoughts from afar. You discern my going out and my lying down; you are familiar with all my ways" (Ps.139:2, 3, NIV). And His angels faithfully record all our words and deeds. "Behold, *it is written* before Me: I will … repay … your iniquities" (Isa. 65:6, 7, NKJV). If we call ourselves Christians and do not return faithful tithes and offering, we are robbing God, and that fact is registered in heaven.

Tithing is an example of God's love as it heightens our spiritual growth. For instance, tithing is a "recognition of God's Lordship." He owns the universe and all we possess, including our salaries. He reminds us, "The world is mine, and all that is in it" (Ps. 50:12, NIV). And when we return our tithes to Him, we acknowledge His generosity. Tithing is also a "witness to God's power to preserve life," for without His sustaining power, we would collapse like an empty suit. He is "the God who holds in his hand your life and all your ways" (Dan. 5:23, NIV). Indeed, it is the "restoration of human dignity before God" as well. He restores His faith in our ability to be good stewards over His possessions while bringing glory to Himself. Lastly, tithing is "an instrument in character development" where we learn to relinquish selfish self-indulgence for loving self-sacrifice.[320]

Tithes are 10 percent of our gross salary; the offering is at our discretion, but both are required. When there are more bills and debts than income, tithing becomes a measure of faith in God. "'Test me in this,' says the LORD Almighty, 'and see if I will not throw open the floodgates of heaven and pour out so much blessing that you will not have room enough for it'" (Mal. 3:10, NIV). Since God cannot lie and He promises to bless us greatly for faithfulness, we can bank on His Word. I can truly attest to His trustworthiness in tithing as it highlights the principle of reaping and sowing.

The whole nation of Israel labored under a curse for withholding their tithes and offerings—for robbing God (Mal. 3:9). But we can stand solidly under the umbrella of blessings as we return what already belongs to Him.

October 26

God Cannot and Will Not Fail

He never fails. Zeph. 3:5, NKJV.

In 1945 Betty Lou Oliver received injuries while operating an elevator in the Empire State Building when a B-25 bomber crashed into the building. It struck between the 78th and 80th floor, killing fourteen people and causing extensive damage. Her rescuers chose to transport her down to safety by elevator, not realizing that the accident had weakened the cables. After the elevator doors closed, the cables snapped, causing the elevator to plunge 75 stories to the bottom of the shaft. Had the Empire State Building installed a failsafe device such as an elevator brake, the elevator would have stopped safely.

One definition of failsafe is "having no chance of failure: infallibly problem-free." The only Beings who are failsafe and failure proof are God the Father, God the Son, and God the Holy Spirit. Even the people we love the most and trust explicitly will in some fashion disappoint us, fail us, and/or abandon us. Love dries up, vows and promises are broken or death short-circuits the promises. But God is the same yesterday, today, and forever, and His promises are as permanent and consistent as is His character. He says, "I will never fail you. I will never abandon you" (Heb. 13:5, NLT).

God is love. He loves us intensely and is our truest Friend. Everything and everybody else will fail, but not God's love. "Love never fails. But where there are prophecies, they will cease; where there are tongues, they will be stilled; where there is knowledge, it will pass away" (1 Cor. 13:8, NIV). The true love He has for His anointed "always protects, always trusts, always hopes, always perseveres" (verse 7, NIV). We can depend on His protection and faithfulness. We can depend on Him as a fulfiller of our hopes. We can also depend on Him to lead, guide, and direct us through Satan's minefields of difficulties as we journey toward the kingdom.

God's love is unconditional. Not out of pity for us or because of our righteousness, but "he chose us in him before the creation of the world to be holy and blameless in his sight. In love he predestined us to be adopted as his sons through Jesus Christ, in accordance with his pleasure and will" (Eph. 1:4, 5, NIV). His love transcends our sinful actions and our negative thoughts and focuses on our potential to grow in the fertile soil of His love. Even if we fail to grow, He continues to lavish us with His love and weeps at our foolishness. "Though the mountains be shaken and the hills be removed, yet my unfailing love will not be shaken nor my covenant of peace be removed, says the LORD" (Isa. 54:10, NIV).

A sure failsafe is our God! Because He is God and is perfect in power and wisdom, He *cannot* fail. And because His great love for His fallen children glows like a multifaceted diamond, He *will not* fail. The Holy Spirit automatically compensates for our momentary spiritual failures if we heed His voice and direction. In the event of a failure to stay on the narrow path or a spiritual malfunction, He secures us and returns us to a safe place in a stronger condition. He never fails.

October 27

He Revives the Contrite and Lowly in Spirit

I dwell in the high and holy place, with him also that is of a contrite and humble spirit, to revive the spirit of the humble, and to revive the heart of the contrite ones. Isa. 57:15.

Suitably named, snow leopards live high in the frigid snow-capped mountains in Central Asia at altitudes between 9,800 and 18,000 feet above sea level. They are smaller than most wild cats but are uniquely built by God to withstand the environment. Snow leopards have thick fur on their stocky bodies and thick fur and fat on their long bushy tails to keep the snow out of their faces while sleeping. To prevent cold from penetrating their bodies, God gave them tiny ears and placed fur on their undersides. And to breathe the thin cold air at high elevations, they have short muzzles and domed foreheads with very large nasal cavities.[321]

High above the snow leopards' habitat, high above both the first and second heavens, in the third heaven is the habitat of our God. "And I saw a new heaven and a new earth: for the *first heaven* and the first earth were passed away; and there was no more sea" (Rev. 21:1). The first heaven is the sky created when God separated the waters and "called the firmament heaven" (Gen. 1:8). The area of the planets and stars called outer space is the second heaven. When the angel of the Lord blessed Abraham for His obedience, He said, "I will multiply thy seed as *the stars of the heaven*" (Gen. 22:17), while the third heaven or Paradise is the location of God's throne. Paul, apparently in vision, was "caught up to the *third heaven*" (2 Cor. 12:2).

And, "*heaven and the heaven of heavens* belong to the LORD's thy God" (Deut. 10:14). He is countless light years above the earth in a pure and holy atmosphere surrounded by adoring angels. Yet, He is not so high or so lofty that He is not intimately involved with His treasured possessions—the contrite and lowly in spirit. "God opposes the proud, but gives grace to the humble" (James 4:6, ESV). The humble spirit *is* a contrite spirit moldable in the potter's hands. In fact, God prefers a righteous sacrifice—a broken spirit and a contrite heart over any sacrifice (Ps. 51: 17).

To be contrite is to express a heartfelt remorse for the rebellion that separates us from God. King David, a murderer, liar, and adulterer, is a prime example of that spirit. Without excuse or blame, David honestly confessed his wrongdoing, genuinely repented, and reformed his behavior (2 Sam. 11). And He became a "man after his own heart" (1 Sam. 13:14). On the other hand, King Saul proudly indulged, justified, and covered his sin, making the separation from God permanent (1 Sam. 14). Pride and contriteness are poles apart. Thus, unless a sinner humbles himself, he cannot and will not confess, repent, or reform for he answers to no one and has need of no one.

Brokenness in heart and spirit and understanding that we are weak and God is able are the unfolding of a revival in our lives. God dwells with the broken, "the low-spirited, the spirit-crushed," and puts a new Spirit in them (Isa. 57:15, MSG).

October 28

The Testimony of God

This is the testimony: God has given us eternal life, and this life is in his Son. He who has the Son has life; he who does not have the Son of God does not have life. 1 John 5:11, 12, NIV.

In the legal profession, expert witnesses can make or break a case based on the jury's trust in their testimony. An expert witness is a professional witness with education, training, and skills as well as expertise and specialized knowledge in a particular subject that is superior to the average person and is adequate enough that others may rely upon his opinion. And they are only as good as their credibility. In the code of ethics for such witnesses, one requirement is that "an expert shall not knowingly present opinions or testimony that is false or misleading."[322]

Spiritually there is no better witness than God, *the* expert witness for eternal life that is in His Son. God swears by Himself because there is no one above Him. "For men swear by one greater than themselves, and with them an oath given as confirmation is an end of every dispute. In the same way God, desiring even more to show to the heirs of the promise the unchangeableness of His purpose, interposed with an oath, so that by two unchangeable things in which it is impossible for God to lie, we who have taken refuge would have strong encouragement to take hold of the hope set before us" (Heb. 6:16-18, NASB). God swears that those who have the Son have eternal life. Choosing to live for Jesus, committed Christians enter into a lifelong covenant with Him and vow to be faithful and obedient. Similar to the terms in the marriage vows, we promise "to have and to hold from this day forward, for better for worse, for richer for poorer, in sickness and in health, to love and to cherish" after accepting Him as Lord and Savior. Fulfilling the terms of the binding covenant with Jesus guarantees an everlasting inheritance.

To have Jesus is to spend time with Him in prayer. Martin Luther King. Jr. wrote, "To be a Christian without prayer is no more possible than to be alive without breathing." Praying is as necessary to our spiritual life as breathing is to our physical well-being. Also, to have Jesus is to daily read the Bible—in it are the words of life. Read and meditate on the Scriptures day and night "so that you may be careful to do everything written in it. Then you will be prosperous and successful" (Joshua 1:8, NIV). We cannot know the way unless we read the roadmap. All Scripture is God-inspired and "is useful to teach us what is true and to make us realize what is wrong in our lives. It corrects us when we are wrong and teaches us to do what is right" (2 Tim. 3:16, NLT).

Moreover, to have Jesus is to submit to Him by fully surrendering our will to His (James 4:7). As Christians we are no longer free to follow our own selfish inclinations and desires. Once we surrender to His perfect knowledge, to His perfect wisdom, and to His perfect control we gain inner peace now as we transition into eternal joy.

October 29

Sprinkle My Heart, Lord

Let us draw near to God with a sincere heart in full assurance of faith, having our hearts sprinkled to cleanse us from a guilty conscience and having our bodies washed with pure water. Heb. 10:22, NIV.

The jets of gas spewing from the planetary nebulae called Henize 3-1475 continue to perplex astronomers. A group of international scientists believe that the "nebula's S-shape and hypervelocity outflow is created by a central source that ejects streams of gas in opposite directions and processes once every 1500 years. It is similar to an enormous, slowly rotating garden sprinkler." Thus, it is nicknamed the 'Garden-sprinkler' nebula. Unlike the regularity of the water flow from the multiple curved arms of a rotating lawn and garden sprinkler, the flow of gas is not smooth, "but rather episodic with an interval of about 100 years."[323]

Contrariwise, the flow of the shed blood of Jesus is not episodic. His blood symbolizes an infinite fountain constantly emitting jets of life-giving blood that cascade over us in sparkling, light-filled drops. These sprinkles purify our desperately wicked hearts, minds, and consciences. Without the sprinkling and effectiveness of the blood of Jesus, the human mind, which is the most deceitful of all things, is incurable (Jer. 17:9). Satan deposits his lies and deceptions in our mind. And through this medium "come evil thoughts, sexual immorality, theft, murder, adultery, greed, malice, deceit, lewdness, envy, slander, arrogance and folly" (Mark 7:21, NIV).

As the pre-emancipated Jews were directed to sprinkle the blood of sacrificial lambs on the doorpost of their homes to protect them from death, Jesus' blood sprinkled on the doorposts of our hearts provides life-giving protection that converts a perverted heart (Ex.12:22). David prayed for that heart cleansing after his fall into sin, asking God to purge him with hyssop and create in him a clean heart (Ps. 51:10). As hyssop is a symbol of purification, the blood of Jesus purifies us to the point where we are permitted to march boldly to God's throne to seek mercy and answers to prayers.

In addition, His blood provides protection from the wiles of the devil as we watch over our "heart with all diligence" (Prov. 4:23). Satan wants to claim us as his own then destroy us body and soul, but he is no match for the power of the blood. Sprinkled with the blood, we stand obediently under the unfurled banner of God, safe in the ranks of His powerful and vigilant angelic hosts.

He "washed us from our sins in his own blood" (Rev. 1:5). Then, with the sprinkled blood, He cleanses our "conscience from dead works" to faithfully serve the living God (Heb. 9:14). For without the blood sprinkled on the heart, our consciences would remain polluted by sin. Combine the sprinkled blood with the power of God's Spirit and we remain contamination free so that "from it flow the springs of life" (Prov. 4:23, ESV).

October 30

Tomorrow Is Not Promised

And the LORD said, "My Spirit shall not strive with man forever, for he is indeed flesh. Gen. 6:3, NKJV.

An unknown author wrote that God watches us rise every morning, hoping that we will take the time to talk to Him. But we are too busy to spend time with Him. At work, even when we are overwhelmed, we do not turn to God. Busy watching TV or eating our meal, we continue to ignore Him. Finally, we fall into bed exhausted from the day. All the while God patiently waits while we appear unconcerned about our eternal destiny. [324]

Similarly, Richard dreamed that he crucified God the Son anew each time he ignored God's overtures to establish an intimate relationship with him. In the dream, God said that He loves Richard deeply and is patiently waiting for him to acknowledge Him before his probation on earth ends. It pains Him that Richard may wait too late and miss out on eternal life. For only God knows the length of Richard's tomorrows.

God's Spirit has strived with Richard over the years for his acceptance of saving grace. But he passively and consistently resists the gentle overtures. He and many others believe that if they are "good" citizens and "good" people they are fit for heaven although they reject the outstretched hand of God and neglect to build a saving relationship with Him. There is no fence sitting in the spiritual realm—you either belong to God or to Satan. "The master of our heart may be fitly termed the love that reigns in it. We serve that only which we love supremely. A man cannot be in perfect indifference betwixt two objects which are incompatible: he is inclined to despise and hate whatever he does not love supremely."[325]

The striving of the Spirit "is an energy of God, applied to the mind of man, setting truth before his mind, debating, reasoning, convincing, and persuading. The sinner resists God's claims, cavils and argues against them; and then God, by His Spirit, meets the sinner and debates with him, somewhat as two men might debate and argue with each other. You are not, however, to understand that the Holy Ghost does this with an audible voice, to the human ear, but He speaks to the mind and to the heart. The inner ear of the soul can hear its whispers."[326]

Mercifully, God will not execute judgment on sinners without first giving us fair and sufficient warning. He is striving and has strived with every person ever born on earth to rescue us from darkness and bring us into His marvelous light and a glorious future. Jesus said, "Behold, I stand at the door, and knock: if any man hears my voice, and open the door, I will come in to him, and will sup with him, and he with me" (Rev. 3:20). O, the perfect love of God! The sinless and pure Majesty of heaven, who is adored by angels, pleads with us—decaying worm food—to accept Him and to fellowship with Him! He begs repeatedly for us to agree to His offer of mercy and grace and to accept the bounties of heaven!

But the day will come when the Spirit will cease striving with those who continue to rebuff him. So for life's sake, heed the pleading of that small voice before it is too late.

October 31

Peace When Destruction Looms

You shall be hidden from the scourge of the tongue, and you shall not be afraid of destruction when it comes. Job 5:21, NKJV.

On August 6, 1945, the Enola Gay, a B-29 airplane dropped a nuclear bomb named "Little Boy" on Hiroshima, Japan. Reports estimated that 90,000 to 166,000 people died in that bomb drop. Japan failed to surrender after the attack, and on August 9 another B-29 unloaded a plutonium bomb named "Fat Man" on Nagasaki. Six days after "Fat Boy" detonated over Nagasaki, the Japanese surrendered, ending World War II.

Even with that kind of destruction unleashed all around us, God promises peace. And slander, as destructive to the reputation and the mind as a nuclear bomb destroys physically, will not tear us down. Called the scourge of the tongue, slander is deadly. Shakespeare wrote, "No, 'tis slander, Whose edge is sharper than the sword, whose tongue Outvenoms all the worms of Nile, whose breath Rides on the posting winds, and doth belie All corners of the world." There will be many times when events and people cause us anxiety and grief, but trusting God keeps us in a zone of peace. The greater the trust, the less fear we experience and the more peace we realize.

That promised *perfect* peace that *passes understanding* is spiritual peace. "Everything is quiet, for we dwell in our Father's house. Look upward and you will perceive no seat of fiery wrath to shoot devouring flame. Look downward and you discover no hell, for there's no condemnation to those that are in Christ Jesus. Look backward, and sin is blotted out. Look around, and all things work together for good to them that love God. Look beyond, and glory shine[s] through the veil of the future like the sun through a morning mist. Look outward, and the stones of the field, and the beasts of the field are at peace with us. Look inward, and the peace of God which passe[s] all understanding keeps your hearts and minds by Christ Jesus."[327]

Only the godly know this peace for their minds are stayed on God (Isa. 26:3). Before Jesus returned to His Father in heaven, He told His disciples, "Peace I leave with you, my peace I give unto you" (John 14:27). He left them with *His* peace. *His* peace sustained Him when He was ridiculed and slandered. *His* peace buffered Him when others shamed and battered Him. *His* peace carried Him through the disbelief and rejection by His fellow Jews. And *His* peace consoled Him as He finally gave up on the nation He tenderly cultivated that became wild grapes despite showers of blessings.

Jesus' peace comes from the portals of heaven. With that peace safeguarding our minds, we shall not fear when destruction comes in its myriad forms. When fires, cruel words, wars, diseases, and tempests threaten, we have peace in knowing that our Father in heaven has His hand on the pulse of our existence and will never let go.

November 1

Are You Worth Your Salt?

You're here to be salt-seasoning that brings out the God-flavors of this earth. If you lose your saltiness, how will people taste godliness? You've lost your usefulness and will end up in the garbage. Matt. 5:13, MSG.

"Flee for your lives! Don't look back, and don't stop anywhere in the plain! Flee to the mountains or you will be swept away!" (Gen. 19:17, NIV). Lot, afraid the disaster would overcome them before they reached the mountains, asked the accompanying angels if he and his family could find refuge in Zoar instead. "By the time Lot reached Zoar, the sun had risen over the land. Then the LORD rained down burning sulfur on Sodom and Gomorrah—from the LORD out of the heavens. Thus he overthrew those cities and the entire plain, including all those living in the cities—and also the vegetation in the land. *But Lot's wife looked back, and she became a pillar of salt*" (Gen. 19:23-26, NIV).

Although changed into a pillar of salt, Lot's wife apparently lost her saltiness long before her destruction. Living in the midst of a perverted society, she became contaminated with their pagan culture, decadent lifestyle, and lack of values and could not let go even after a personal warning from heavenly messengers. God destroyed Sodom and Gomorrah because "[t]he outcry against Sodom and Gomorrah is so great and their sin so grievous" (Gen. 18:20, NIV). The occupants of these cities lacked salt.

Salt, multi-faceted and multi-purposeful, is timeless, and since the beginning of recorded history, its worth and value are considered legendary. "From the early salt trade comes two opposite expressions of the value of human life: a person can be 'the salt of the earth' (high value, righteous, honest), or 'not worth your salt' (low value, lazy, dishonest)."[328] Trusting Christians to be the salt of the earth, God expects us to cultivate characters and actions that season the world as we spread the gospel of truth to a world awash in sin.

Paul says "Let your conversation be always full of grace, seasoned with salt, so that you may know how to answer everyone" (Col. 4:6, NIV). Sharing the gospel in the spirit of a fear-monger, telling of a fire-and-brimstone God, being critical or self-righteous is a conversation not *full of grace* and not *seasoned* with salt. Such a conversation works the opposite effect and weakens our ability to plant the seeds so the Holy Spirit can water and reap an increase. A conversation seasoned with salt is identified by the message of grace and the love of God.

"Have salt in yourselves, and have peace one with another" (Mark 9:50). Our hearts should be preserved by the salt of righteousness and be "zealous of good works" (Titus 2:14). Jesus peppered His conversation with compassion, and doing likewise we are able to attract the lost to Christ as a deer is attracted to a nutritious salt lick. Jesus expects, no requires, His anointed to be worth our weight in salt. Are you?

November 2

Put Your Neck in Jesus' Yoke

Take My yoke upon you and learn from Me, for I am gentle and lowly in heart, and you will find rest for your souls. For My yoke is easy and My burden is light. Matt. 11:29, 30, NKJV.

Oxen are steers or castrated bulls four years or older that are trained as work animals. Developing countries still use oxen to plow and/or pull wagons. To help them pull together and equally share the load, farmers yoke or join together two or more oxen by a crossbar with two U-shaped pieces that surround their necks. Without the use of a yoke, "one animal will pull the full load every time it takes a step slightly ahead of the other, meaning that each animal experiences the work as a series of tiresome bumps and jerks.... [that] will eventually exhaust the animals and little work gets done."[329]

Jesus wishes us to put our necks in His symbolic yoke and walk in step with Him, thus enabling Him to alleviate our heavy burdens by lifting, lightening, or moving them aside. He pleads with those whose burdens are exhausting to come to Him and find rest (Matt. 11:28). Trying to pull or carry the load of cares in our own strength frustrates and overwhelms us, but foolishly, many of us choose to be frustrated and overwhelmed because of our limited notion of who Jesus is. The inability to relinquish our burdens shows a lack of trust in the lovingkindness of the Savior and a vast trust in our own feeble efforts.

A yoke is restrictive and prevents the oxen from wandering away and getting lost, and it keeps them true to the task at hand. Likewise, Jesus' yoke restricts us, checks any movements toward the pursuit of lustful desires, and steers us back to the narrow path that leads to salvation. And only he "whose walk is blameless and who does what is righteous" will be saved (Ps. 15:2, NIV). When we submit to the will of God and offer Him our childlike faith, His yoke becomes easy and His burden light, for He simply asks us to trust and obey and even provides the power to do so.

Trained to wear a yoke, oxen learn from suffering. While young the trainers place halters on them and jolt them with goads or prods, conditioning them to obey their commands. The Christian, too, learns from jolts and prods "for our light and momentary troubles are achieving for us an eternal glory that far outweighs them all" (2 Cor. 4:17, NIV). Jesus will not remove the painful burdens we bear; He uses them to fulfill His will and to prepare us to walk in His will. Through trials we also learn of His mercy, grace, and faithfulness. And because of His great love, He accepts our accusations of His being uncaring and distant when He fails to remove the source of pain in the manner we choose and in our time. Still His yoke is easy.

It is wise to eliminate futile striving using faulty human reasoning and dodging Jesus' yoke. Wearing it, our load grows lighter and our back stronger as we surrender to His leading and trust His divine purpose for our life.

November 3

Lip Service or Heartfelt Service?

The Lord says: "These people come near to me with their mouth and honor me with their lips, but their hearts are far from me. Their worship of me is made up only of rules taught by men." Isaiah 29:13 NIV

Two men covered from head to toe in black and carrying sub-machine guns surprised a 2,000-member congregation one Sunday morning during service. One of the hooded men proclaimed, "Anyone willing to take a bullet for Christ remain where you are!" Immediately, the choir fled, the deacons fled, and most of the congregation fled. Out of 2,000 members only 20 remained. The spokesman took off his hood, looked at the preacher and said, "Okay Pastor, I got rid of all the hypocrites. Now you may begin your service. Have a nice day!" And they left.[330]

Dramatic? Yes. Funny? Absolutely. But through the drama and the humor, the hooded men made a serious point about our commitment to God. Do we have a relationship with Jesus that puts His will first? Or is it simply a shallow, superficial attachment to Him leading nowhere? How many Christians stand up in protest, no matter the cost, when the Word of God is twisted to fit the traditions of man? How many depend on another's interpretation without reading the Word, as guided by the Spirit, for themselves? How many test spiritual leaders by the Word of God? Or do we accept their spiritual teachings blindly over the Word because of their charisma and knowledge?

The Scriptures "are able to make you wise for salvation through faith in Christ Jesus" (2 Tim. 3:15, ESV). Do you neglect to read the Scriptures daily? Then you offer lip service. Do you talk to God only when an emergency occurs? That, too, is lip service. "And pray in the Spirit on all occasions with all kinds of prayers and requests" (Eph. 6:18, NIV). Do you listen to the Words of life and ignore them as if they were from "one who sings love songs with a beautiful voice and plays an instrument well, for they hear words *but do not put them into practice*" (Eze. 33:32). Again—only lip service.

Getting it right is serious business, serious because the consequences are either life or death. Without a heart change, our hearts are wicked and deceitful. For we are "broken beings, born onto a broken planet, into a universe broken by the rebellion of sin.... When we give our heart to Jesus, we are giving a broken and polluted life back into the hand that was nailed to the cross to heal what was broken and cleanse what we have polluted."[331] There is no place for pride or selfishness or disobedience after we commit our hearts to Jesus. That He wants to spend eternity with us is a marvel and should invoke gratitude from the recipients of His grace, not halfhearted service.

Relationships require work and quality time spent together. Reading the Bible daily, we hear God speaking to us. Praying regularly, God listens as we talk to Him. Obedience to His Word and submission to the leading of His Spirit are practical applications of our intimate relationship with him. My friends, love God with *all* your heart, soul, strength, and mind by doing what He requires and live (Luke 10:27). This is serious!

November 4

Afflictions—Sanctified Promotions

I am not at ease, nor am I quiet; I have no rest, for trouble comes. Job 3:26, NKJV.

Eagles do not fear strong wind currents caused by storms. They use the gusty wind to help gain altitude in preparation for long flights. When the storm winds come, eagles set their wings in a fixed position so the wind lifts them with little effort. Allowing the wind to work for them, they are recharged for the next leg of the journey. Skillfully, the eagle does not avoid the storm winds but uses them to its advantage, for while the storm rages below, the eagle effortlessly soars above it.

Storms are unavoidable. There are periods in our lives when we lament as Job did that there is no peace, no quiet, no rest, only turmoil. These are times of severe and long-term storms of affliction that try our very souls. But through it all, God is working out His plan. Many times these afflictions occur to get our attention, but always they teach us to trust God and to lean on Him for peace. C. H. Spurgeon wrote, "In seasons of severe trial, the Christian has nothing on Earth that he can trust to, and is therefore compelled to cast himself on his God alone. When his vessel is on its beam-ends, and no human deliverance can avail, he must simply and entirely trust himself to the providence and care of God.... O blessed hurricane that drives the soul to God and God alone!"

Affliction prepares us to be the bride of Christ. One day He wants to "present it to himself a glorious *church*, not having spot, or wrinkle, or any such thing; but that it should be holy and without blemish" (Eph. 5:27). To vanquish the deep spots and dark stains of sin, God scrubs us on the washboard of tribulation. "When you use bleach to get rid of stains, it's a harsh process. Getting rid of wrinkles is even more painful: ironing means a combination of heat plus pressure."[332] And some stains take longer, need more detergent and more pressure to remove. Suffering develops holiness in unholy people. But getting there is painful in the laundry room of the Lord.

Every person born in this fallen world can expect to suffer. That's a given (Rom. 8:22). But the suffering should not manhandle us; we are empowered to survive trials no matter how long or how ferocious. Sooner or later they subside. But God's power enables us to soar above the storms even while they are battering us seemingly unmercifully. Listen carefully to His voice, respect and trust His reason for the trials even if they are perplexing. "God whispers to us in our pleasures, speaks in our consciences, but shouts in our pain: it is His megaphone to rouse a deaf world."[333]

Eagles are not alone in soaring above the winds of the storm. "Those who hope in the LORD will renew their strength. They will soar on wings like eagles" (Isa. 40:31, NIV). Every time we ride out a storm in the arms of Jesus, we emerge intact; although battered, our spiritual life greatly benefits. Matthew Henry wrote, "Sanctified afflictions are spiritual promotions." Thus, storms endured promote us to heaven.

November 5

The Greatest Rescue in History

The Son of Man came to seek and save those who are lost. Luke 19:10, NLT.

"The greatest rescue story ever told" is how one National Public Radio newscaster described the Chilean mine rescue. Thirty-three miners trapped 2,300 feet underground for more than two months were rescued one by one. In this record-breaking rescue—having stayed underground longer than any persons in history—each miner emerged from his underground tomb alive and grateful. For sixteen days the rescuers could not locate the miners. However, on the seventeenth day they established contact but were unable to extract them immediately. The rescuers drilled a six-inch-wide hole to the shelter that became a lifeline, delivering communications, supplies, and fresh air to the miners until the escape tunnel was completed.[334]

The whole world's attention was riveted to their ordeal. And we can all agree that this rescue was spectacular and unique. However, I beg to differ about their rescue being the greatest rescue story ever told. That distinction would have to go to Jesus' rescue of the entire human race from extinction after only two people were created. God appointed Him to save the world from sin even before Creation (1 Peter 1:20). His name, based on the Hebrew tradition of names having significance, is noteworthy for sinners. Yeshua, the Hebraic word for Jesus, is translated "to deliver, to rescue, He saves, and salvation." An angel told Joseph, "She will bear a Son; and you shall call His name Jesus, *for He will save His people from their sins*" (Matt. 1:21, NASB).

Despite having to swap the unimaginable splendors of heaven and the adoration and respect of the angels for rejection in a sin-polluted earth, Jesus came to rescue us. "We marvel at the Saviour's sacrifice in exchanging the throne of heaven for the manger, and the companionship of adoring angels for the beasts of the stall.... Yet this was but the beginning of His wonderful condescension. It would have been an almost infinite humiliation for the Son of God to take man's nature, even when Adam stood in his innocence in Eden. But Jesus accepted humanity when the race had been weakened by four thousand years of sin. Like every child of Adam He accepted the results of the working of the great law of heredity.... He came with such a heredity to share our sorrows and temptations, and to give us the example of a sinless life."[335]

In Jesus and Him alone is there salvation free and fully accessible (Acts 4:12). As sheep we went astray, became trapped in sin, and were subject to death, still He came to the rescue and "*gave his life a ransom for many*" (Matt. 20:28), being assigned a grave with the wicked. In so doing, He bears our iniquities, makes intercession for our transgressors, and offers His righteous life as a guilt offering for the guilty. Truly His sacrifice came at a great cost to Himself as His enemies, who are among those whom He came to save, oppressed and severely afflicted Him unto death (Isa. 53:4-12*)*.

Jesus came to earth to seek and save those lost in darkness. Clearly, at an incredible cost, He rescued us—*the greatest rescue in history!*

November 6

Building for Eternity

According to the grace of God which was given to me, as a wise master builder I have laid the foundation, and another builds on it. But let each one take heed how he builds on it. 1 Cor. 3:10, NKJV.

After showing that he was capable of building a house without supervision, a young carpenter's boss put him in charge of the next building project. His boss allowed him to oversee the entire job, including buying all the materials. The young carpenter was very excited about this responsibility, but before long selfishness emerged, and he decided to cut corners. Thus, he bought inferior building materials, reported the purchase of superior materials, and put the difference in his own bank account. Upon a cursory inspection, the contractor, who had trusted this young carpenter, remarked that he had done a superior job and gave him the house as a gift.[336]

Experts contend that poor building materials and lack of building standards contributed to the huge loss of life in the 2010 Haitian earthquake. To save money, builders added lots of water to the concrete and then spread it very thin, leaving the multi-story structures too weak to withstand even normal adverse conditions. Building inspectors note that cracks in the walls are the most revealing sign of substandard construction and may indicate a weak foundation.

Building for eternity requires a sound foundation—the base support for a structure. Spiritually, a person's eternal life rests on this base, namely, our Savior. "For no one can lay any foundation other than the one already laid, which is Jesus Christ" (1 Cor. 3:11, NIV). Obeying His commands and following His example of a prayer-filled and a spirit-filled life, a person builds a spiritual house that withstands the winds of strife. But the foundation is the launching of the spiritual house.

Next, the builder must follow the blueprint to ensure that the rest of the spiritual house is sound. So he pounds the nails of holiness into the wood frame to keep it upright. Holiness is marking off a boundary of righteousness and staying within it. It is setting apart for God's sake, belonging solely to God, and living a life that is uncompromising and morally pure. "Who may stand in his holy place?" The answer is given: "He who has clean hands and a pure heart" (Ps. 24:3, 4, NIV).

Importantly, the builder must be careful that the structure does not contain shoddy materials like selfishness and other sins. "Take particular care in picking out your building materials. Eventually there is going to be an inspection. If you use cheap or inferior materials, you'll be found out. The inspection will be thorough and rigorous. You won't get by with a thing" (1 Cor. 3:12-14, MSG). Check out your spiritual building inventory and be sure to use the finest and most durable materials possible for your house, especially love and faith. Remember, you are building for eternity!

November 7

Regarding God's Discipline

But please stop striking me! I am exhausted by the blows from your hand. Ps. 39:10, NLT.

Sometimes Betty's mother disciplined her children by using switches from young trees that grew nearby. These long, thin green twigs were little but sturdy and stung when they made contact with bare legs. Once, her sister had us in stitches after revealing the drama that occurred at Betty's turn to be punished by the switch. Betty ran around and around the kitchen table holding on to the switch and calling on the Lord at the top of her lungs to save her. Her siblings forgot about their stinging legs and convulsed with laughter at her performance. And their mother cut Betty's punishment short as she exited the room to keep from dissolving into laugher with them.

Betty's mother subscribed to multilevel forms of discipline to teach her children obedience. Her methods ranged from talking to them, withdrawing things they enjoyed, and using the rod when everything else failed. Discipline is as hurtful to the giver as to the receiver but necessary out of love and concern for the receiver's present and future happiness. That accounts for the heavy hand our heavenly Father sometimes lays on us. William Gurnall wrote, "Discipline is painful and God would not rub so hard if it were not to fetch out the dirt that is ingrained in our natures. God loves purity so well He had rather see a hole than a spot in His child's garments."[337]

Love demands discipline and God loves His children dearly. Hebrews chapter twelve gives a dissertation on the merits of God's instructive and corrective discipline. "My son, do not make light of the Lord's discipline, and do not lose heart when he rebukes you, because the Lord disciplines those he loves and he punishes everyone he accepts as a son" (Heb. 12:5, 6, NIV). When discipline is withheld, the results are disturbing.

For instance, "Eli's sons were wicked men; they had no regard for the LORD" (1 Sam. 2:12, NIV). Eli served as high priest with his two sons, Hophni and Phineas, in the sanctuary. That Eli's sons lacked discipline is evident by their wicked actions with far-reaching, negative consequences. They "accepted bribes and perverted justice" (1 Sam. 8:3, NLT). And they defiled the Temple by indulging in illicit sex with the women who served there. Eli's inability to discipline them effectively brought death to all three in the same day. God told Eli, "The time is coming when I will cut short your strength and the strength of your father's house, so that there will not be an old man in your family line and you will see distress in my dwelling" (1 Sam 2:31, 32, NIV).

Be thankful for God's discipline, for it makes us holy. According to John Trapp, "It is better to be pruned to grow than cut up to burn." Pruning is truly painful but spiritually useful. "No discipline seems pleasant at the time, but painful. Later on, however, it produces a harvest of righteousness and peace for those who have been trained by it" (Heb. 12:10, 11, NIV). And righteousness is our passport to heaven.

November 8

You Take the First Step

Draw near to God and He will draw near to you. James 4:8, NKJV.

Extremely hungry, weary, and bogged down with regret and guilt, the prodigal son's mind became cloudy. But soon he regained his senses and said, "How many of my father's hired men have food to spare, and here I am starving to death! I will set out and go back to my father and say to him: Father, I have sinned against heaven and against you. I am no longer worthy to be called your son; make me like one of your hired men. So he got up and went to his father. But while he was still a long way off, his father saw him and was filled with compassion for him; he ran to his son, threw his arms around him and kissed him" (Luke 15:17-20, NIV).

With a broken heart and many tears, the father helplessly watched as his son left the safety, security, and love of their home. As much as he wanted to rescue him from the decadent lifestyle that would be his ruin, he would not force his compliance, intuitively understanding as Sir Walter Raleigh relayed, "a man convinced against his will; is of the same opinion still." Having no other recourse, his father waited for his foolish son's return.

On one level, the parable of the prodigal son brings home to us the deep yearnings God has for the safety and security of His children. And on another level, it highlights that God will not force His will on anyone as painful as it is for Him to watch us self-destruct. Through His Spirit, however, He courts both backsliders and unbelievers almost imperceptibly. And in love He garners our attention through the working out of painful situations. Pursuant to Richard Sibbes, "When we grow careless of keeping our souls, then God recovers our taste of good things again by sharp crosses."

We live in a society where a sense of entitlement is spelled with a capital E. Intruders have no thought about stealthily entering homes or boldly invading homes to bully the occupants. But Jesus says, "Behold, I stand at the door, and knock: if any man hear my voice, and open the door, I will come in to him, and will sup with him, and he with me" (Rev. 3:20). God respectfully approaches the closed door of our hearts to seek admittance. Since He gives us an inalienable right to choose, which is impossible for Him to repeal, He will never intrude on our privacy or against our will. First, we must willingly unbolt the door before He will enter. When or if we allow Him access, He fellowships with us, befriends us, and leads us to His kingdom.

But similar to the prodigal son, sinners, backsliders, and lukewarm Christians are sojourners in a far country, signifying their alienation and distance from God in character and deed. But forgiveness and union, or reunion with God, are possible. "Let the wicked forsake his way, and the unrighteous man his thoughts: and let him return unto the LORD, and he will have mercy upon him; and to our God, for he will abundantly pardon" (Isa. 55:7). Obviously it is foolish to the highest degree to ignore the knock and disregard the voice of the God of heaven. Swing the door open and let the Son in.

November 9

God's Unsearchable Ways

Show me Your ways, O LORD; Teach me Your paths. Ps. 25:4, NKJV.

God's ways are not our ways. His ways and judgments are unsearchable, too profound and too deep for our comprehension. "Imagine yourself as a living house. God comes in to rebuild that house. At first, perhaps, you can understand what He is doing. He is getting the drains right and stopping the leaks in the roof and so on; you knew that those jobs needed doing and so you are not surprised. But presently He starts knocking the house about in a way that hurts abominably and does not seem to make any sense. What on Earth is He up to?"[338]

Clearly God's ways are at times perplexing. "When God wants to drill a man, and thrill a man, and skill a man, when God wants to mold a man to play the noblest part. When He yearns with all His heart to create so great and bold a man that all the world shall be amazed. Watch His methods, watch His ways!"[339] Moses had no idea that his flight to Midian after killing an Egyptian and forty years of tending sheep was preparing him to lead God's enslaved children for forty years through a barren desert (Ex. 3:1-10).

Plus, His ways are unsearchable. "How He ruthlessly perfects whom He royally elects! How He hammers him and hurts him, and with mighty blows converts him into trial shapes of clay which only God understands. While his tortured heart is crying and he lifts beseeching hands!"[340] Jesus labeled John the Baptist the greatest man ever born for his role in preparing the way for Christ, but John became discouraged, which is evidenced by his disciples inquiry into whether Jesus was the Messiah (Matt. 11:1-11).

Only God knows God's ways. "How He bends but never breaks when his good He undertakes. How He uses whom He chooses, and which every purpose fuses him. By every act induces him to try His splendor out- God knows what He's about."[341] God purposed to use Jonah as the prophet to warn Nineveh about their coming doom if they did not repent, but Jonah had other plans. He fled on a ship in the opposite direction from Nineveh. God then sent a vicious storm that was instrumental in Jonah being tossed overboard where he was swallowed by a large fish. Three days later the fish vomited him onto the shore. Imagine Jonah's dark, dank, stinking reality in the fish's digestive system (Jonah 1-2)!

What is God up to? "He is building quite a different house from the one you thought … You thought you were being made into a decent little cottage: but He is building a palace. He intends to come and live in it Himself."[342] Choosing to be a new creature in Christ requires lots of hammering and chiseling by the hand of love to refashion us into the likeness of Jesus. It hurts because God reshapes us using any means necessary for as long as necessary. "For as the heavens are higher than the earth, so are my ways higher than your ways, and my thoughts than your thoughts" (Isa. 55:9). Trust His ways even if mystified by them. He is God!

November 10

Careful to Keep All of God's Law

For the person who keeps all of the laws except one is as guilty as a person who has broken all of God's laws. James 2:10, NLT.

Robin Laird excelled as South Pasadena High School's star pole vaulter, and her spectacular jump won the league championship for her team. However, after the win, the opposing coach noticed that she was wearing a string bracelet and contended that she should be disqualified. Section 3, Article 3 of the National Federation of State High School Associations states, "Jewelry shall not be worn by contestants." For this infraction, "the competitor is disqualified from the event." Robin's team, by far the best pole vaulting team, became disqualified after offending one rule out of many.

Team Jesus is also expected to abide by *all* the rules in the game of life—namely God's laws. What God expects from the kingdom-bound is total compliance, and He provided a way to satisfy the conditions. "The condition of eternal life is now just what it always has been,—just what it was in Paradise before the fall of our first parents,—perfect obedience to the law of God, perfect righteousness. If eternal life were granted on any condition short of this, then the happiness of the whole universe would be imperiled. The way would be open for sin, with all its train of woe and misery, to be immortalized."[343]

Yes, it *is* impossible to keep the whole law of God in our own power. But perfect obedience to the law of God is achievable when we allow the Spirit of God full rein in our lives. Then we can echo Paul, "The life which I now live in the flesh I live by the faith of the Son of God, who loved me, and gave himself for me" (Gal. 2:20). If we abide in Him, He promises to abide in us. And in this two-way abiding, our selfish, carnal natures are exchanged for Jesus' perfect, sinless nature. Still, the process of transformation from carnal-minded to heavenly-minded does not happen overnight. It is a slow, meticulous process of striving to do the will of God *in the power of God*.

Sometimes, we go one step forward and fall two steps backward, but do not despair. That is progress. As we yield to the Holy Spirit's leading, guiding, and directing, we will see a marked and positive transformation in our thinking and actions. "A change will be seen in the character, the habits, the pursuits. The contrast will be clear and decided between what they have been and what they are. *The character is revealed, not by occasional good deeds and occasional misdeeds, but by the tendency of the habitual words and acts.*"[344]

Confronting the unbelievers, Jesus made it clear that His law remained alive, healthy, and immortal. "I am not come to destroy the Law or the prophets, but to fulfill. And whoever breaks one of these commandments, and shall teach men so, he shall be called the least in the kingdom of heaven" (Matt. 5:17-20). God equips us to keep His law; He will put His Spirit in us and move us to follow His decrees and keep His laws (Eze. 36:27).

November 11

Does It Pass the Test?

Test all things; hold fast what is good. Abstain from every form of evil. 1 Thess. 5:21, 22, NKJV.

In their advertising, Coke hyped "the cold crisp taste of Coke," while Pepsi plugged, "the taste that beats the others cold." Although cola tastes good, it can interact adversely with antacids, possibly causing constipation, calcium loss, hypertension, nausea, vomiting, headaches and kidney damage. The bubbles and fizz in soft drinks, caused by the phosphoric acid and carbon dioxide, can burn the inside of the stomach. The phosphorus in the acid upsets the body's calcium-phosphorus ratio and strips calcium out of the bones, resulting in osteoporosis. "Pour cola over an extracted baby tooth or a 10-penny nail and see it totally dissolve in a few days!'"[345]

Not everything that tastes good, sounds good, looks good, smells good, and feels good is good for us. That is why God, out of love and concern over our well-being, demands that we *test everything* concerning our salvation. Test by the Word of God what you eat and drink, what you wear and where you go, who you associate with, and what you read and think on. In three-dimensional human beings there is a connection among the tripod of body, mind, and spirit. One stands on the other, and when one is sick, the others suffer negatively. "Anything that lessens physical strength enfeebles the mind and makes it less capable of discriminating between right and wrong."[346]

Test also the source of your beliefs and to whom you obey if in opposition to the clear Word of God. A man of God prophesized to Judah's King Jeroboam who became so incensed at the prophecy, he attempted to seize him. The hand Jeroboam used to seize him shriveled, and he begged the man of God to restore it. Grateful, Jeroboam invited the man to dinner and offered him a gift, but the man of God refused, remembering that God said, "You must not eat or drink anything while you are there, and do not return … by the same way you came" (1 Kings 13:17, NLT). An old prophet who heard the story, lied and told the man of God that an angel gave him permission to go the prophet's house and eat and drink. The man of God believed him despite God's caution and was fatally punished (1 Kings 13).

"Do not believe every spirit, but test the spirits to see whether they are from God, for many false prophets have gone out into the world" (1 John 4:1, ESV). Basing a belief on one Bible text to the exclusion of many others on the same subject leads us down the slippery slope of deception by Satan. Jesus triumphed over Satan's temptations by the Word of God, and so can we if we live by every word that issues from the mouth of God and no one else (Matt. 4:4).

"The Bible is its own interpreter and its own dictionary. It explains itself."[347] Prayer, the use of a comprehensive concordance to locate all relevant texts, and sound reasoning are the keys to the Bible explaining itself, for the Bible is God-inspired, infallible, and open to accurate interpretation (2 Tim. 3:16). Remaining in error because we do not properly handle God's word is way too costly (Matt. 22:29).

November 12

Submitting to Authority

Honor your father and your mother, so that you may live long in the land the LORD your God is giving you. Ex. 20:12, NIV.

Flipping though television channels, Eiyana saw a photograph of a woman covered with bruises and bite marks. Amazed, Eiyana heard her explain that these injuries were inflicted by her fourteen-year-old daughter whom she feared. This daughter menaced the family. Once she put a knife to her sister's throat and threatened to kill her, and often she called her mother the 'B' word among other epithets. When Dr. Phil asked the mother if she had contributed to the daughter's abusive behavior, she admitted when the daughter grew into the temper-tantrum stage, she pacified her tantrums by submitting to her demands or rewarding her to end the tantrums.

By pacifying her, the mother taught her daughter to disrespect all authority figures. She neglected sound wisdom and the whole family suffered. "Discipline your son, and he will give you peace; he will bring delight to your soul" (Prov. 29:17, NIV). By inference, those children who are not disciplined bring their parents shame and woe. In biblical days because of the ruinous results of contempt for authority, children who disrespected or physically abused their parents were stoned to death (Ex. 21:15, 17).

"In our era of lax parenthood, a death penalty for cursing one's parents seems overly harsh. But there is reason behind this law. A child, who holds his parents in contempt, will hold other forms of authority in contempt as well. If a child believes he can ignore his parents as he pleases, he will assume that he can ignore the laws of society and the laws of God as well."[348]

The child who feels at liberty to strike or curse his parents would be incapable of "living under authority as a citizen, as an employee, as a church member. Learning to live life under authority is preparation for submitting to the ultimate authority who is God in Christ. Without obedience to the 5th commandment, the screaming young toddler quickly becomes the rebellious teenager, who slowly becomes the empty young adult, who finally becomes a bitter and lonely senior...."[349]

The command follows us into adulthood. Respecting and caring for loving parents is easy. But the command does not stop at honoring those who deserve honor; the honoring extends to the abusive parent, the emotionally distant parent, the neglectful parent, and the absentee parent. As Christians we are required to forgive others as Jesus forgives us for "if you do not forgive men their sins, your Father will not forgive your sins" (Matt. 6:15, NIV). The chains of anger, bitterness, and hatred from a painful childhood may still be holding you prisoner, but prayerfully placing this burden on the broad shoulders of God will release the chains and slowly but surely bring healing. He promises to "heal the brokenhearted and bind up their wounds" (Ps. 147:3, ESV).

Honor your parents and other authority figures especially God whether easy or difficult. This is the first commandment with a promise.

November 13

Purity of Thought and Mind

Finally, brothers, whatever is true, whatever is noble, whatever is right, whatever is pure, whatever is lovely, whatever is admirable—if anything is excellent or praiseworthy—think about such things. Phil. 4:8, NIV.

The book *As a Man Thinketh* begins, "Mind is the Master power that moulds and makes, And Man is Mind, and evermore he takes The tool of Thought, and, shaping what he wills, Brings forth a thousand joys, a thousand ills, He thinks in secret, and it comes to pass: Environment is but his looking-glass." James Allen's essay explores the truism that thoughts are very powerful and that a person becomes what he or she thinks. Similarly, Napoleon Hill wrote, "Self-discipline begins with the mastery of your thoughts. If you don't control what you think, you can't control what you do. Simply, self-discipline enables you to think first and act afterward."

Without a Savior man's thoughts control him as unregenerate hearts are under the unchecked influence of Satan. He very effectively blinds the minds of unbelievers so they cannot understand the truths found in the gospel (2 Cor. 4:4). To be more exact, spiritual things are meaningless while Satan's schemes, temptations, and deceptions poured into the vulnerable mind are accepted and acted upon. Without the desire or the power to resist his advances, unbelievers allow Satan to flood the mind with wicked and immoral thoughts as well as tormenting and debilitating ones.

Those who are grounded in Christ, however, have unlimited power through the Spirit to control their thoughts. "The weapons we use in our fight are not made by humans. Rather, they are powerful weapons from God. With them we destroy people's defenses, that is, their arguments and all their intellectual arrogance that oppose the knowledge of God. We take every thought captive so that it is obedient to Christ" (2 Cor. 10:4, 5, GWT). All lies and deceptions deposited into our mind by Satan are torn down and cast aside if we use the Word of God as a test of their sincerity.

Sanctified believers must purify the thoughts to imitate the mind of Christ. To begin, a change or modification of lifestyle is paramount. "For as he thinketh in his heart, so is he" (Prov. 23:7). If carnal-centered rubbish is poured into our minds from the things we read, view, and visit, carnal-centered rubbish will inform our thoughts and actions. "You may think that what you think about is unimportant, but your thoughts are the bricks you use to build your life. Negative thoughts build a prison. Positive thoughts build a comfortable home."[350] Thus, the bricks of a Christian home are tempered with the Word of God and fired in the kiln of the Spirit.

Consistently inundating one's mind with the Word is a bona fide mind transformer and a weapon against the enemy's strategies. If heaven is our goal, then we must train our mind to think on pure things. For, "nothing impure will ever enter [heaven], nor will anyone who does what is shameful or deceitful, but only those whose names are written in the Lamb's book of life" (Rev. 21:27, NIV).

November 14

Watching and Praying

Watch and pray, lest you enter into temptation. The spirit indeed is willing, but the flesh is weak. Mark 14:38, NKJV.

Psychological warfare is a time-worn tactic against one's enemies. Sanballat the Horonite, an upper-class Samaritan, used it against Nehemiah when Nehemiah took the lead to rebuild the broken down walls of Jerusalem. He both envied and resented the restoration of Israel as it showed the changing fortunes of the Jews. When the mind games did not work, Sanballat stirred up the ire of the Arabs, the Ammonites, and the Ashdodites against the Jews and schemed to ambush them while they were preoccupied with building. Also, he challenged the Jews repeatedly to do battle and plotted to ambush Nehemiah in the Temple. But all his schemes failed (Neh. 4).

Why did Peter, James, and John fail in prevailing against the enemy at Gethsemane while Nehemiah triumphed? Jesus asked his three disciples three times to watch and pray. He took them along with him to the Garden of Gethsemane where He became deeply distressed and troubled and asked them to remain close by, observe and pray. Upon returning, He found them sleeping and queried why they could not stay awake and keep watch for *one* hour. Forgetting about His own needs, He cautioned them to "Watch and pray so that you will not fall into temptation" (Mark 14:38, NIV). However, they yielded to sleep and failed to keep watch and pray. Thus, Satan triumphed, causing them such fear they abandoned Jesus in His time of great need and moved Peter to lie and curse to avoid detection.

Nehemiah, however, used potent weapons of prayer, perseverance, and obedience against evil as he accomplished the work *of God*, bolstered by an abiding faith *in God*. Because they depended on God to protect them, and they remained vigilant, all of the plotting and scheming did not bear fruit. Nehemiah and the workers "prayed to our God and posted a guard day and night to meet this threat" (Neh. 4:9, NIV). He used half of the work force to build the walls and the other half held spears, shields, bows, and armor to prevent sneak attacks. Those who delivered materials up and down the walls did so with one hand while holding a weapon in the other hand, and each builder hung his sword at his side while officers stood behind them (verses 16-18).

Satan uses his human agents as well as invisible demons to distract, harass, oppress, and persecute Christ's followers. Fighting both enemies requires the same ammunition—vigilance, faith, and prayer. But as the invisible enemies are in a better position to launch sneak attacks, "We must watch always against spiritual enemies, and not expect that our warfare will be over till our work is ended. The Word of God is the sword of the Spirit, which we ought to have always at hand, and never to have to seek for it, either in our labors, or in our conflicts, as Christians. Every true Christian is both a laborer and a soldier, working with one hand, and fighting with the other."[351]

Take Jesus' wise counsel to heart. Watch to ensure the enemy is not deceiving you, and pray to keep connected to your life-giving, life-saving connection with God.

November 15

In the Circle of God's Protection

"Don't be afraid of anyone, because I am with you to protect you," says the Lord. Jer. 1:7, 8, NCV.

Kingdom of Heaven is a movie that focuses on the crusades between Europe and the Middle East. The plot centers around a blacksmith named Balian whose wife commits suicide, but at her burial his half brother beheads her and steals her crucifix. Furious, Balian kills his brother and later flees to Jerusalem to find redemption for himself and his wife. There he reencounters his father, is knighted, and stays to battle the Muslims. His father, Godfrey de Ibelin, speaks the oath that all knights must uphold: "Be without fear in the face of your enemies. Speak the truth, always, even if it leads to your death. Safeguard the helpless and do no wrong."

Godfrey's oath echoes Jeremiah's mission after God chose him to warn his countrymen of their impending doom. Jeremiah learned that before the miracle of conception in his mother's womb, God had ordained him to prophesy to the Israelites. Even then he balked at the magnitude of this mission (Jer. 1:4-9). God commissioned him to deliver the message of deliverance and judgment and set him over the nation to "root out, and to pull down, and to destroy, and to throw down, to build, and to plant" (verse 10).

Beforehand, God prepared Jeremiah for the difficulty of prophesying hard truths. "Get yourself ready! Stand up and say to them whatever I command you. Do not be terrified by them" (Jer. 1:17, NIV). And He promised him strength and protection to withstand the tide of suffering accompanying this task. He made Jeremiah "a fortified city, an iron pillar and a bronze wall to stand against the whole land—against the kings of Judah, its officials, its priests and the people of the land. They will fight against you but will not overcome you, for I am with you and will rescue you," God declared (verses 18, 19).

The truth is a two edged sword meant to cut deep. It pierces "until it divides soul from spirit, joints from marrow; it is able to judge the thoughts and intentions of the heart" (Heb. 4:12, NRSV). And true to form, it showed the thoughts and intentions of the nation of Israel. Hard hearted and incorrigible, they physically and verbally battered the messenger, steadfastly refusing to heed the truth (Jer. 26:1-24, 37:14-16).

God's promise to protect Jeremiah did not shield him from their cruelty, but God never removed His hand from His servant. As any human being, Jeremiah wanted to have a peaceful existence even in the midst of vast wickedness and lost souls. But God nudged him out of complacency to do a great work for Him. This experience moved Jeremiah from a babe in the faith to a sanctified giant. Initially shrinking from the task, he learned to trust God. He wrote, "I know, O LORD, that a man's life is not his own; it is not for man to direct his steps" (Jer. 10:23, NIV). As Christians we stand under the order of the Great Commission and are commanded to seek and warn lost souls even if we are rejected or put in harm's way. God promises to support and protect us.

November 16

Denying Self to Death

Whoever desires to come after Me, let him deny himself, and take up his cross, and follow Me. Mark 8:34, NKJV.

A young boy felt terribly embarrassed by his mother's empty socket instead of a right eye. He cruelly declared to her that he hated her. Moving away, he became a successful adult and purposely did not contact her. Once she visited; he screamed at her, "I don't know you! How dare you come to my house and scare my daughter! Get out here now!" She quietly answered, "Oh, I'm so sorry. I may have gotten the wrong address," and disappeared. Years later, he returned for a school reunion and discovered his mother had died. Delivered a note by a neighbor, he read, "When you were very little, you got into an accident, and lost your eye.… I couldn't stand watching you … grow up with one eye. So I gave you mine."[352]

Self-sacrifice characterizes true love. The young man's mother willingly sacrificed her joy and bore a physical deformity to give her son a normal life. He, on the other hand, placed his selfish desires on the throne of his life, unwilling to accept her and her perfect love housed in an imperfect body. Echoing Jesus, she denied herself for him, endured the burden that the sacrifice carried, and took the scars on her body and in her heart to the grave. With a gentle and quiet manner, she took whatever came, and put up with her selfish son in love (Eph. 4:2).

Jesus asks us to likewise sacrifice our own selfish desires and bear whatever burden, privation, or suffering necessary to follow Him as He did for us. If we do otherwise, we are not worthy of Him (Matt. 10:38). God's will *must* take precedence over ours. His perfect will is to change us into carbon copies of Jesus in whom unselfishness shines like burnished gold. To effect that transformation, we are obliged to *decrease* and let Jesus *increase*, for barking at the heels of selfishness is sin. "Where you have envy and selfish ambition, there you find disorder and every evil practice" (James 3:16, 17, NIV).

It behooves us to toss those desires and deeds that thwart God's will in the trash bin unless they overrule God's will and lead us into sin. Denying self and dying to self are the death knell to sin because it cannot thrive in self's cold, dark grave. T. Austin Sparks wrote, "The unalterable basis of an open heaven is a grave, and a crisis at which you come to an end of your own self-life. It is the crisis of real experiential identification with Christ in His death." Unselfishness, altruism, and self-sacrifice all live in a heart that, like Christ, suffers in the flesh and rejects self's reign. "For if you have suffered physically for Christ, you have finished with sinning" (1 Peter 4:1, NLT).

Denying self and giving God full reign in our lives is a struggle because it goes contrary to our sinful natures, but it must be a daily reality for those who call themselves Christians. Jesus asks us to willingly give our all to Him, to deny self to death. By His grace and power, we can do it. He did it for us!

November 17

The Rebuke of God

Take a deep breath, GOD; calm down— don't be so hasty with your punishing rod. Your sharp-pointed arrows of rebuke draw blood; my backside smarts from your caning. Ps. 38:1, 2, MSG.

William Gurnall wrote, "God's wounds cure, sin's kisses kill." The Bible is a sort of wounding rebuke that enlightens us and is therapy for sin and sinning. A rebuke is another example of God's grace intended to recoup lost sheep and prevent others from jumping over the fence into pits of evil or wandering away into the wilderness of sin. Defined as an attempt to correct through reasoning by the Word or by painful situations, a rebuke is utilized by God to achieve and preserve morality in His children.

Slow to anger, God reproves those He loves and labors relentlessly to bring all of His children to repentance. However, He will forever punish unconfessed sins sooner or later. For instance, even though the Ninevites practiced idolatry, child sacrifice, and evil cruelty, He sent His prophet to preach the Word as a rebuke (Jonah 1:1). They repented momentarily, and then slid back into wickedness. Much later, God sent Nahum to warn them, "The LORD is good, a refuge in times of trouble. He cares for those who trust in him, *but with an overwhelming flood he will make an end of Nineveh; he will pursue his foes into darkness"* (Nah. 1:7, 8, NIV).

The fear that the scolding brought to the Ninevites moving them to repentance reached their heads but did not reach their hearts. Momentarily they believed and trembled. But after the sting of Jonah's preaching stopped smarting, they resumed life as usual and soon suffered God's wrath through Babylonian captors. Generally God's rebuke is a stern verbal reprimand through the Word, dressing down those who profess to be godly and holding them accountable for wrongdoing. Quite unpleasant, a rebuke is "often hated and despised because it pricks at the soil of the corrupted flesh, and disturbs it. It breaks up the fallow ground and attempts to plant good seeds in good soil that grow into righteousness."[353]

The Ninevites' reaction to Jonah's preaching mimicked the reaction of many Americans to the terrorist attack on the Twin Towers in New York City. In the uncertainty of another attack, churchgoing surged. "Fundamentalist Christian Pat Robertson said that the attack was bringing about one of the greatest spiritual revivals in the history of America ... People are turning to God. The churches are full."[354] However, two months later the percentage of churchgoers lessened to normal. Apparently, by the masses who resumed churchgoing and praying, many people are aware of their need to repent and turn wholeheartedly to Him.

Christians should welcome rebukes with open arms for "It is better to hear the rebuke of the wise, than for a man to hear the song of fools" (Eccl. 7:5). Listen intently and patiently endure His extension of grace for God says, "As many as I love, I rebuke and chasten" (Rev. 3:19).

November 18

The Sustaining Power of God

I laid me down and slept; I awaked; for the LORD sustained me. Ps. 3:5.

Thomas Otway wrote, "Clocks will go as they are set, but man, irregular man is never constant, never certain." The first mechanical clocks, created in medieval Europe, used gears and wheels turned by attached weights. As the force of gravity pulled downward on the weights, the wheels turned in a slow, consistent manner. These timepieces would gain or lose approximately a half hour daily. In the 1400s German scientists invented the spring-powered clock. Inside, coiled springs driven by a main gear motorized them. But like the mechanical clocks, they slowed when the mainspring wound down. Centuries later we have a motley crew of timepieces, but they, too, stop working when the battery or electricity fails.

But God does not wind us up and leave us floundering. Similar to Timex's claim, the power of God to sustain us physically and spiritually *keeps on ticking*—it never fails. At giving us life, God is not finished with His created beings. He also provides daily life support containing all necessities and many wants as well as abiding support whether we are at enmity with him or whether we love Him. Granted we have a limited capacity to understand the mind and power of God and are amazed at the creation of the heavens and the earth—a stupendous act. But comprehending that His creative and sustaining powers are achieved *through speech* is so stupefying that Satan can deceive unbelievers into trusting that the earth and life boomed into existence and evolved over millions of years.

"The Son is the radiance of God's glory and the exact representation of his being, *sustaining all things by his powerful word*" (Heb. 1:3, NIV). Although we take our ability to move, think, and awake each day for granted, without God's consistency in keeping us wound up and powered, we not only would be unable to function in mind or body but also we would cease to exist. The psalmist reminds us, "You take away their breath, and they die and return to dust" (Ps. 104:29, GWT).

Moreover, His creative and sustaining Word still thunders through the universe, and all nature responds accordingly. A present perfect continuous power, His Word commenced at Creation and continues until the present and onward. "By the word of the LORD were the heavens made" (Ps. 33:6). A God of order, He created laws of physics to govern nature, and they operate flawlessly. Incredibly, the planets, moons, and stars hang in space supported only by His Word. "He spreads out the northern skies over empty space; he suspends the earth over nothing" (Job 26:7, NIV).

What unimaginable power is contained in the Word of God! Jesus demonstrated that power while here on earth. He forgave sins, restored sinners, healed the sick, and resurrected the dead through the spoken word. Wrote C. H. Spurgeon, "What a serene and quiet life might you lead if you would leave providing to the God of providence!" God's sustaining power is limitless, and His spoken word is all powerful for it "will accomplish what I desire and achieve the purpose for which I sent it" (Isa. 55:11, NIV).

November 19

Overcome Evil With Good

Love your enemies, do good to those who hate you, bless those who curse you, pray for those who mistreat you. Luke 6:27, 28, NIV.

Labeled one of the dirtiest rivers in the world, the Buriganga River in Bangladesh is being cleaned. More than ten million people live in the capital city of Dhaka, which is built on its banks. The river serves as a fluid dump where citizens toss trash; where Dhaka's sewage waste discharges; and where factories discharge chemical waste. Obviously the Buriganga is highly polluted, destroying fish and other sea life. Cleaning this river, that holds a layer of trash and debris nearly ten feet deep, is a tall order rising to the level of an impossible task because millions of people continue to use the river as a trash can even as the government attempts to clean it.[355]

A tall order is a formidable chore or requirement, a big job, a difficult challenge. Jesus' demand that we love our enemies is also a tall order, rising to the level of impossible without our full surrender to His Spirit. Even when we are in Christ, loving our enemies may sometimes be a tall order but is fully attainable. It is intrinsic to our fallen natures to retaliate against injustice, particularly if we are the victim. When someone purposely injures us, it takes agonizing prayer for relief and God's help to forgive and love the injurer through Him. Then it is possible to rise above the bitterness and "not repay evil with evil or insult with insult, but with blessing" (1 Peter 3:9, NIV).

Asking for God's help to love our enemies is not the stopping point, however. A higher level of godliness moves us to pray for their salvation and well-being even in the midst of the persecution. Loving our enemies by the power of Christ in us and praying for them, we mediate on their behalf through intercessory prayers. Alfred Lord Tennyson wrote, "More things are wrought by prayer than this world dreams of." Indeed, Moses persuaded God not to destroy the ungrateful, defiant Israelites as He led them from Egypt to the Promised Land. Moses pleaded, "Turn from your burning anger and relent from this disaster against your people.... And the Lord relented from the disaster that he had spoken of bringing on his people" (Ex. 32:12, 14, ESV).

Intercessory prayer pursues sinners past the boundary and into the middle of Satan's territory. Our prayers are capable of raiding his prisons and freeing the captives, for some persecutors are caught like flies in a spider's web of evil and sin and cannot extricate themselves. Praying on their behalf, we give the Spirit permission to pursue them and to work at softening the unsown ground of their hearts so the seeds of truth can root and grow. "Do not be overcome by evil, but overcome evil with good" (Rom. 12:21, NIV). This is the love that pleases God for, "Anyone who loves another brother or sister is living in the light and does not cause others to stumble" (1 John 2:10, NLT).

Though it feels good momentarily, "Do not take revenge ... but leave room for God's wrath" against persecutors (Rom. 12:19, NIV). Love your enemies through His power no matter the injury; win the victory over Satan; *and* reap God's blessing. That is truly a win-win situation.

November 20

Nonstop Gratitude

When you have eaten and are full, then you shall bless the LORD your God. Deut. 8:10, NKJV.

Ten lepers accosted Jesus as He traveled to Jerusalem and begged Him to heal them. He did and advised them to go and present themselves to the priests. However, "one of them, when he saw that he was healed, turned back, praising God with a loud voice; and he fell on his face at Jesus' feet, giving him thanks" (Luke 17:15, 16, ESV). Jesus queried rhetorically if there were not ten lepers that He healed. If so, "Was no one found to return and give praise to God except this foreigner?" (Luke 17:18, ESV).

The terms thanksgiving, gratitude, and praise are pregnant with great appreciation for undeserved generosity given to us or done for us at a cost to the giver. And who has given us any greater benefits at such great cost than our Lord and Savior. Charles E. Jefferson observes, "Gratitude is born in hearts that take time to count past mercies." Have you, like the Samaritan leper, ever been so filled with wonder at a glorious gift received that you burst out in thanksgiving to the giver? Consider the psalmist who exclaims, "Oh, that men would give thanks to the LORD for His goodness and for His wonderful works to the children of men! For He satisfies the longing soul, and fills the hungry soul with goodness" (Ps. 107:8, 9, NKJV).

Did you know that failure to express appreciation for God's blessings reaches the level of sin? "Giving thanks to God for both His temporal and spiritual blessings in our lives is not just a nice thing to do - it is the moral will of God. Failure to give Him the thanks due Him is sin."[356] When we fail to thank God for His bountiful blessings and His wondrous works that edify all aspects of our lives, we tread on the path of self-praise or pride. Self-praise reports that all I have and all that I am stems directly from my efforts and good fortune. It tempts us to forget that the very bread we eat, the very clothes we wear, the very breath we take spring from His grace.

"The LORD, He is God; it is He who has made us, and not we ourselves" (Ps. 100:3, NKJV). The key to sustaining gratitude is awareness that we are helpless in every way without Him. "Beware that you do not forget the LORD your God by not keeping His commandments ... lest—*when* you have eaten and are full ... *then you say in your heart, 'My power and the might of my hand have gained me this wealth'*" (Deut. 8:11-17, NKJV). A proud man is very seldom grateful because he is never satisfied with what he has, believes he deserves more and disregards God's generosity. "Pride slays thanksgiving, but a humble mind is the soil of which thanks naturally grow," wrote Henry Ward Beecher.

Not just obedience, but "all morality is gratitude." At every opportunity, publish the wonders of God with the voice of thanksgiving, for according to John Jowett, "Life without thankfulness is devoid of love and passion. Hope without thankfulness is lacking in fine perception. Faith without thankfulness lacks strength and fortitude. Every virtue divorced from thankfulness is maimed and limps along the spiritual road."

November 21

Poking Holes in the Darkness

Let your light so shine before men, that they may see your good works, and glorify your Father which is in heaven. Matt. 5:16.

Robert Louis Stevenson, Scottish poet and writer, inherited his mother's consumptive lungs. Early on he developed respiratory problems that plagued him the rest of his life. The story is told that one night his nurse found him peering intently through a cold windowpane and cautioned him to return to bed for warmth. But Robert stayed put, mesmerized by an "old lamplighter slowly working his way through the black night, lighting each street lamp along his route. Pointing, Robert exclaimed, 'See; look there; there's a man poking holes in the darkness.'"[357]

Literally, darkness is an absence of light. Therefore, depending on the degree of light, whenever light is introduced to darkness, darkness is partially or totally diminished. Even a small candle will illumine the dark. Jesus, who came to rescue us from moral darkness, used the light metaphor to describe Christians who have assumed His character. "Ye are the light of the world," He said (Matt. 5:14). Light bearers and lamplighters walk lockstep in the footsteps of Jesus who glorified His Father. As the light in their corner of the world, their brightness pokes holes in the darkness of ignorance and evil.

With the production of light, God began His creative process on earth. "In the beginning God created the heavens and the earth. The earth was formless and empty, and darkness covered the deep waters" (Gen. 1:1, 2, NLT). And when moral darkness descended like a haze on the earth after the Fall, He raised up prophets, priests, judges, apostles, and disciples—lamplighters—to poke holes in that darkness. Lamplighters are commissioned to jab holes enough to transmit the dazzling light of sanctified lives that light up the earth with the gospel of salvation.

Having brought sinners out of darkness into His marvelous light, God cautions us not to dim or extinguish that light by returning to lawless living. Anyone professing to be a Christian but choosing to live and act like the world brings disrepute to the gospel message and to the Giver of the message. Stumbling blocks for the babes in Christ will be held accountable however. Many people have returned to darkness or never accepted Christ as savior because they held up so-called Christians as a standard rather than Jesus. Let your light shine for "A city on a hill cannot be hidden. Neither do people light a lamp and put it under a bowl. Instead they put it on its stand, and it gives light to everyone in the house. In the same way, let your light shine before men, that they may see your good deeds and praise your Father in heaven" (Matt. 5:14-16, NIV).

Evil thrives in the dark. Hence, God sent Jesus to enlighten and illuminate. Love moves the redeemed to share that light with those who remain in the moral shadows. "For once you were full of darkness, but now you have light from the Lord. So live as people of light! For this light within you produces only what is good and right and true" (Eph. 5:8, 9, NLT). Is *your* light poking holes in the darkness?

November 22

The Boast of Weakness

> *"My grace is sufficient for you, for My strength is made perfect in weakness." Therefore most gladly I will rather boast in my infirmities, that the power of Christ may rest upon me. 2 Cor. 12:9, 10, NKJV.*

"All God's giants have been weak men."[358] In our confused world, those are contradictory terms—weak giants. We value strength and beauty despite being housed in immoral vessels, but weakness and unattractiveness even in God-fearing vessels are devalued. Contrarily, God turns man's wisdom on its head. He chooses and uses the weak who are broken and receptive to His grace and empty of self-importance and self-sufficiency. God can only use a willing, empty vessel.

Martin Luther describes the empty vessel, "It is certain the man must utterly despair of his own ability before he is prepared to receive the grace of Christ." Only after Samson's pride and self-sufficiency were stripped away subsequent to capture by the Philistines who blinded and humiliated him could God use him again. Contrary to the Philistines' and his belief after he wandered into sin, his strength came not from the uncut hair but from God. "There was no virtue in his long hair merely, but it was a token of his loyalty to God; and when the symbol was sacrificed in the indulgence of passion, the blessings of which it was a token were also forfeited."[359] Now an empty, weak vessel, Samson was filled through God's power and destroyed more Philistines in death than during his lifetime.

Likewise, bloodthirsty and committed to ethnic cleansing, Saul vigorously pursued the Christian sect who claimed Jesus as the Messiah. "Saul laid waste the church, entering into every house, and dragging men and women … to prison" (Acts 8:3, ASV). Spreading the net to persecute fleeing Christians, Saul heard a voice from heaven and saw a bright light that blinded him. Trembling and terrified, he fell to the ground (Acts 22: 6-11). This experience humbled the prideful Pharisee, Saul, and transformed him into the obedient apostle Paul. To Paul's advantage, God turned a deaf ear to his prayer to remove a weakness, a "thorn in the flesh," for without total dependence on God for strength, he would "be exalted above measure" (2 Cor. 12:7).

Emptied, then refilled, neither by his might nor by his power but by God's Spirit, Paul boasted in a way pleasing to God. He said, "If I must boast, I will boast of the things that show my weakness" (2 Cor. 11:30, NIV). Hunted as an animal by the governor of Damascus, Paul's friends lowered him "in a basket from a window in the wall and [he] slipped through his hands" (verse 33, NIV). Saul (now Paul), a member of the ruling class specifically "a Pharisee and a son of a Pharisee," wielded control, and the people highly respected him. To flee rather than fight must have been quite humiliating.

But weaknesses that leave us humble and teachable are an attribute in God's eyes because His power is compellingly evident as we depend on Him.

November 23

Believe to the Glory of God

Jesus said to her, "Did I not say to you that if you would believe you would see the glory of God?" John 11:40, NKJV.

Glory in Hebrew means weight or mass or substance. Intrinsic to God, glory portrays His eternal substance, His essence, and His majesty. "Glory is to God what style is to an artist. A painting by Vermeer, a sonnet by Donne, a Mozart aria—each is so rich with the style of the one who made it that to the connoisseur it couldn't have been made by anybody else and the effect is staggering."[360] Glory is the outward expression of God's hand in His handiwork just as holiness is the inward expression.

God is the sum and substance of perfection and love, and His manifested attributes and character point out His glory. His *amazing* love, His *unlimited* grace, His *awesome* power, His *unwavering* truth, His *great* mercy, His *unvarying* forgiveness, and His *solid* justice all speak to His glory. Asked by Moses to show His glory, God replied, "I will cause all my goodness to pass in front of you, and I will proclaim my name, the LORD, in your presence.… There is a place near me where you may stand on a rock. When my glory passes by, I will put you in a cleft in the rock and cover you with my hand until I have passed by" (Ex. 33:19, 21-22, NIV). Passing by the cleft of the rock, God pointed out His characteristics and essence, "The LORD, The LORD God, merciful and gracious, longsuffering, and abundant in goodness and truth … and that will by no means clear the guilty" (Ex. 34:6, 7).

Also, His creative powers, saving grace, and compassion are expressions of His glory. He promises to save, guide, keep, and covenant with His desired ones to spread the gospel and counteract ignorance, to heal and minister, and to alleviate suffering. "Thus says God the LORD, Who created the heavens and stretched them out, Who spreads out the earth and its offspring, Who gives breath to the people on it and spirit to those who walk in it, "I am the LORD, I have called You in righteousness" (Isa. 42:5, 6, NASB). When we go astray or go lukewarm, others replace Him in the center of our affections, denying Him His rightful glory. A jealous God who lays legitimate claim to His redeemed possessions and shares His power and nature with no one states, "I am the LORD; that is my name! I will not yield my glory to another or my praise to idols" (verse 8, AKJV).

Resurrection power, too, reveals His glory. Lazarus died before Jesus returned to Judea, and his distraught sisters chastised Jesus for His delay in responding to their cry for help while Lazarus lived. "Martha said to Jesus, 'Lord, if you had been here, my brother would not have died'" (John 11:21, ESV). When Jesus asked that the stone covering the tomb be removed, "Martha …said to him, 'Lord, by this time there will be an odor, for he has been dead four days.' Jesus said to her, 'Did I not tell you that if you believed you would see the glory of God?'" (verses 39, 40, ESV). Jesus beckoned Lazarus to come forth and come forth he did.

"Stand up and bless the LORD your God Forever and ever! Blessed be Your *glorious* name, which is exalted above all blessing and praise!" (Neh. 9:5, NKJV).

November 24

Self-seekers Are Magnets for God's Wrath

To those who by persistence in doing good seek glory, honor and immortality, he will give eternal life. But for those who are self-seeking and who reject the truth and follow evil, there will be wrath and anger. Rom. 2:7, 8, NIV.

Folklore and legend declare that a Cretan shepherd named Magnes discovered magnets. In fact, the word magnet is allegedly derived from the legendary shepherd's name. Centuries ago, while herding his sheep in a place in Northern Greece near Mt. Ida, he began to climb up the mountain. But his feet stuck to the rock via the nails in his shoes and the tip of his staff. Fascinated, he pulled himself free, dug in the earth to understand this phenomenon, and found lodestones containing magnetite.

Magnetism, produced by iron magnets, remained unique until 1821. Then the French discovered a different type of magnetism, a "force between electric currents: two parallel currents in the same direction *attract,* in opposite directions *repel.*"[361] This type of magnetism defines God's attraction to obedient, penitent sinners and His repulsion to rebellious, impenitent sinners. After accepting God as Master and Lord, the godly person seeking glory, honor, and immortality, who persists in obedience, will receive eternal life. They and God are walking on the same path in the same direction. A crown of righteousness is waiting for these, His special treasures, a crown the Lord will give to all those who love Him on the day He appears (2 Tim. 4:8).

However, those self-seekers who profess to be holy but whose hearts are far from Him, those who openly reject the Word, or those who remain lukewarm are traveling in the opposite direction from the life-giving, life-sustaining Savior. This path is rife with magnets that attract God's wrath and eventually move Him to perform the odd act of giving up His offspring to eternal death. "He will rouse himself as in the Valley of Gibeon—to do his work, his strange work, and perform his task, his alien task" (Isa. 28:21, NIV). God is a God of love who created human beings for His glory and yearns to spend eternity with us. But many stymie His purpose by rebellion and self-seeking.

Self-seekers "live for themselves … [and] refuse to obey the truth and instead live lives of wickedness" (Rom. 2:8, NLT). God loved sinners enough to let His Son die for us, but He hates the sin and has no pleasure in the death of the wicked (Eze. 33:11). But if we insist and persist in being inextricably bound by sin, He has no recourse but to send that sinner into the lake of fire reserved for Satan and his demons, for nothing impure or unclean will enter heaven to corrupt it as earth is corrupted.

Jesus is the lightening rod to conduct God's wrath at the judgment—a wrath that Jesus' ultimate sacrifice already appeased. He "gave himself for us to redeem us from all wickedness and to purify for himself a people that are his very own, eager to do what is good" (Titus 2:14, NIV). God begs us to flee from our self-seeking. Those who are persistent in doing good down to heart level will inherit eternal life.

November 25

The Path to a Reprobate Mind

And just as they did not see fit to acknowledge God any longer, God gave them over to a depraved mind, to do those things which are not proper. Rom. 1:28, NASB.

In our society, animal cruelty toward a vulnerable animal or fowl is met with anger and indignation and loud calls for justice. Imagine the outrage if a representative of the SPCA had seen Balaam striking and kicking his docile donkey! Three times he viciously beat the donkey, using his thick wooden staff the third time. The donkey stopped twice and sank to the ground fearful of an angel who, unbeknownst to Balaam, blocked his path with a drawn sword. The donkey even spoke to Balaam who was hurrying to Moab to curse the Israelites at the request of King Balak, who sweetened the deal by offering him treasures and honor (Num. 22).

God gave His *former* obedient prophet several opportunities to denounce evil and return to Him. But Balaam loved money and self-exaltation more than he loved God. As Balak stroked his ego, Balaam's covetousness and pride led him to disregard God's express command. "Do not go with them. You must not put a curse on those people, because they are blessed" (verse 12, NLT). Balaam, craving riches and honor, asked the messengers twice to spend the night while he made his decision, prompting God to relent but only to bless the Israelites (Num. 22).

Balaam, intent on following his own self-centered, self-sufficient course, ignored the offers of mercy and grace. So God gave him up to a reprobate mind—a depraved, immoral mind. Balaam did not heed God's voice, so He let go and Balaam followed his own desires and walked in his own counsels (Ps. 81:11, 12). Losing his promised treasure at the inability to curse Israel, Balaam recouped by counseling Balak to overpower them in a covert, demonic way. The Moabites invited Israel to offer sacrifices and worship their gods and enticed them to engage in debased, immoral sexual activities with the Moabite women (Num. 31:16).

Balaam's covetousness became the foothold Satan needed to blind his mind to the wise counsel in the Word. "By consenting to break one precept, men are brought under Satan's power."[362] "Every act of transgression, every neglect or rejection of the grace of Christ, is reacting upon yourself; it is hardening the heart, depraving the will, benumbing the understanding, and not only making you less inclined to yield, but less capable of yielding, to the tender pleading of God's Holy Spirit."[363]

When we disregard all of the opportunities to accept and abide by the plain Word of God, when we prefer soft words that require no self-sacrifice, we convey a message to God. "God," we say, "I choose to die for worldly error rather than accept spiritual certainty." So He obliges us and does not temper the consequences. Please, avoid that path!

November 26

Isn't It Ironic?

He saved others; himself he cannot save. Mark 15:31.

Ronnie's voicemail states, "Say what you mean and mean what you say." Irony, on the other hand, shouts, "Say what you *did not* mean and mean what you *did not* say." Irony is a figure of speech whereby the meaning vocalized or intended is the opposite of what is actually stated or "a literal meaning is contrary to its intended effect." The Bible itself is full of irony, especially in the life, work, and death of Jesus.

The Bible announces unequivocally that Jesus as God created the worlds and everything they contain (Gen. 1:1). The gospels echo and reecho that Jesus is God, Creator of all. "Through him all things were made … [and] in him was life, and that life was the light of men" (John 1:3, 4, NIV). Ironically, Jesus created the world and its inhabitants, but the world neither recognized Him nor welcomed Him. He was then and is now rejected by a majority of the people He created and daily sustains (verses 10, 11).

Jesus stooped low to inhabit the earth and reside among those living under the curse of sin. "The Word became flesh and made his dwelling among us. We have seen his glory, the glory of the One and Only, who came from the Father, full of grace and truth" (verse 14, NIV). Quite ironically, the ruling class sentenced Jesus to death for blasphemy "because you, a mere man, claim to be God" (verse 33, NIV). Josephus portrays the Pharisees as a "body of Jews who profess to … explain the laws more precisely." Case in point, Jesus told Nicodemus, a Pharisee, that as Israel's teacher he should understand the Word. They, the ruling class, pored over the law and the prophets, including Isaiah who prophesied about the Messiah's birth, life, and death. These prophecies pointed like a laser at Jesus, but they concluded He was an imposter.

When Jesus was baptized, the Holy Spirit descended on Him in the form of a dove and God spoke His approval of Him. Yet, ironically, when He exorcised demons, the Pharisees said, "It is by the prince of demons that he drives out demons" (Matt. 9:34, NIV). Imagine, they accused Him of being in league with Satan for whom the lake of fire is reserved, Satan who is responsible for Jesus' brutal death, for the horrible condition of the once perfect earth and for the evil nature of His created beings (Matt. 25:41).

Isn't it ironic? Those Jews involved in the crucifixion of Jesus stood at the foot of the cross and taunted Jesus. "He saved others … but he can't save himself," they gloated, not grasping that to save Himself meant abandoning them and all sinners to God's wrath and eternal death (Mark 15:31, NIV). He is the promised Messiah sorely injured in the spiritual battle with Satan but victoriously alive in God (Gen. 3:15).

After the Fall, Adam and Eve sacrificed an unblemished lamb to represent atonement for sin. This prefigured the Lamb of the world, slain to satisfy the unbreakable mandate that the wages of sin is death (Rom. 6:23). Ironically, one day this slain, bloody Lamb will return as the conquering Lion of Judah arrayed in pristine white!

November 27

Faithful at All Costs

Be faithful until death, and I will give you the crown of life. Rev. 2:10, NKJV.

Brownie and Scotty were inseparable. Daily the two dogs played together and explored the nearby woods. One day Brownie failed to return home, moving his master Knox to search diligently but to no avail. Scotty, however, pestered the family, barking and yelping and whining. Soon he became more aggressive than usual, and his actions shouted, "Follow me." Finally Knox followed Scotty deep into the empty lot past the woods. Under heavy brush he found Brownie caught in a trap. Evidence showed that Scotty had stayed with Brownie throughout the ordeal, protecting him from predators, sleeping next to him, and feeding him scrapes from his own bowl.[364]

Scotty willingly gave up his comfort, placed his own well-being in jeopardy, made a determined effort to save Brownie, and remained by his side through rescue or death. That is faithfulness! Faithfulness or trustworthiness denotes a committed devotion to someone or something to which we are attached because of a promise or an obligation. Trust is important to maintain strong relationships, including our relationship with God. "Without trust, words become the hollow sound of a wooden gong. With trust, words become life itself," wrote John Harold.

Faithfulness is an attribute of God that He extends to all generations, and as we grow in godliness, we begin to emulate that attribute (Ps. 119:90). The standard of trustworthiness straddles the continuum all the way from belief to giving the ultimate sacrifice—our lives. Ittai the Hittite expressed that degree of faithfulness to King David as he followed him out of Jerusalem to avoid a battle with Absalom, who was attempting to wrench away the kingdom. Ittai said to David, "As surely as the LORD lives, and as my lord the king lives, wherever my lord the king may be, whether it means life or death, there will your servant be" (2 Sam. 15:21, NIV).

When this life is over and Jesus gathers those who will inherit the kingdom, He will judge them on their trustworthiness. The multitude will be held accountable for all the grace, opportunities, and talents He provided to help strengthen and broaden His kingdom. The faithful unto death will hear, "Well *done*, good and faithful servant. You have been faithful over a little; I will set you over much. Enter into the joy of your master" (Matt. 25:21, ESV). Faithfulness in a few things, no matter how small, points to the tip of the iceberg. Deep under the water is a large heart full of love for God and a commitment to love Him more than our comfort, our desires, or even our lives.

Faithfulness to God is tied up in ribbons of obedience and love, wrapped in colorful paper of steadfastness despite the strong winds of strife, and taped with the fruit of the Spirit. If we faithfully tread over the stones, rocks, boulders, and potholes on the narrow path in His strength, we will receive the gift of eternal life. God will open wide the gates of heaven for us to enter into the eternal Kingdom (2 Peter 1:11).

November 28

And We Are Not Saved?

The harvest is past, the summer has ended, and we are not saved. Jer. 8:20.

"Shine on Harvest Moon" is a popular song written by a vaudeville couple named Nora Bayes and Jack Norworth that debuted at the Ziegfeld Follies in 1908. The harvest moon at the heart of the song is quite different from the garden-variety full moon. This full moon is nearest to the Autumn Equinox and generally occurs annually in September. It rises in the early evening not long after sunset, giving farmers additional needed time to gather their harvest. Exceptionally bright and to the farmer's joy, the light from the harvest moon lasts for a few evenings.

Not long after the harvest moon debuts, the days literally begin to get shorter as winter approaches. Similarly, the days left in preparation for Jesus' return to gather His harvest of souls are shortening as well. Rather than delight in the nearness of time and carefully prepare, many are asleep, oblivious to the encroaching judgment. "The hour has come to wake up from your slumber, because salvation is nearer now than when we first believed. The night is nearly over; the day is almost here" (Rom. 13:11).

We live in the night of earth's existence and the light of day will soon be eclipsed by a time of unprecedented turmoil just before Jesus returns. "And there shall be a time of trouble, such as never was since there was a nation … and at that time thy people shall be delivered, *every one that shall be found written in the book*" (Dan. 12:1). Those whose names are not written in the book of life will beg the mountains and rocks to, "Fall on us, and hide us from the face of him that sitteth on the throne, and from the wrath of the Lamb" (Rev. 6:16). What needless terror and tragedy!

While physical existence lasts, professed Christians and impenitent sinners alike are on probation. Born under a sentence of death after Adam and Eve's sin, we are freed from the prison of sin and death row because Jesus paid the penalty in full. But we are not free to return to a life of rebellion; certain conditions must be met. To end probation and achieve permanent pardon, we are obliged to "put aside the deeds of darkness and put on the armor of light" (Rom. 13:12, NIV). Keep in mind that our probation ends at either the end of *our* days or the end *of* days whichever comes first, for the decision for eternal life or eternal death is made *before* Jesus returns (Rev. 22:11).

Imprisoned under horrible conditions by Emperor Nero, the chief of reprobates, Paul knew when his departure neared. But confident of salvation he stated, "I have fought the good fight, I have finished the race, I have kept the faith. Now there is in store for me the crown of righteousness, which the Lord, the righteous Judge, will award to me on that day—and not only to me, but also to all who have longed for his appearing" (2 Tim 4:7, 8, NIV).

Are you as sure of your salvation as Paul? We, too, can be confident of receiving that crown of righteousness if we fear God and keep His commandments by fulfilling our whole duty to Him (Eccl. 12:13).

November 29

Fasting and Praying

But this kind does not come out except by prayer and fasting. Mark 9:29, ISV.

God created our bodies as engineering marvels with eleven systems working together like a well-oiled machine. And He provided the perfect fuel to efficiently maintain them. Nuts, fruits, and grains were the original diet with clean animals, fowl, and fish added after the Flood. Among these foods are superfoods that surpass basic nutrition and are powerful enough to prevent diseases and lower cholesterol. Superfoods, such as blueberries are anti-inflammatory, contain antioxidants and phytoflavinoids, and are laden with potassium and vitamin C, properties that lower the risk of heart disease and cancer and prevent chronic diseases.

Superfoods and regular nutritious food are to each other as prayer is to fasting.

Prayer is powerful, but when fasting is added to the mix, prayer becomes super powerful. Certain problems, situation and habits are so huge and so overwhelming that they require a one-two-combo punch. As well, some demons of the flesh triumph over our best desires to live godly lives. Evil propensities—demonic gunk—like lying, lust, pride, covetousness, bitterness, and unforgiveness may need more than prayer to dislodge. Such gunk clogs up our character development and necessitates the use of the God—approved gunk remover which is prayer laced with fasting.

Fasting coupled with prayer moves God to greater lengths than would prayer alone because it displaces physical undertakings with a spiritual focus that is God-centered. "For certain things fasting and prayer are recommended and appropriate. In the hand of God they are a means of cleansing the heart and promoting a receptive frame of mind. We obtain answers to our prayers because we humble our souls before God."[365]

Fasting coupled with prayer moved God to intercede on behalf of Jews living in Susa and turned their mourning into gladness as only He could. When the command came down from King Xerxes to kill the Jews, they mourned, wept, and prayed, but they also fasted (Esther 4:1-3). Esther told Mordecai to implore the Jews to "fast for me. Do not eat or drink for three days, night or day" (verse 16, NIV). She wanted to seek God's protection and guidance before she approached the king to beg for mercy.

A spiritual fast also turns our focus on the power of God to make a difference, recognizing our ineffectual efforts to fix things and carry our own burdens. The act of fasting speaks to God, telling Him that we are weak and He is strong, that we respect Him and His awesome power, that our minds are willing but our flesh has its own will, that we choose to hear His voice over the clamor of our lives, that we desire to focus on His will and purpose for our live, and that we are ready to receive the bounties He has already stored up for us. Humbleness and faithfulness of that sort perks up God's ears to hear and moves Him to answer our prayers.

Fasting is an exhibition of faith in a God. Coupled with prayer, fasting greatly assists in gaining the victory over Satan's deceptions and problems. This dynamic duo also evicts the entrenched demons of the flesh.

November 30

No More Excuses

And as he reasoned of righteousness, temperance, and judgment to come, Felix trembled, and answered, Go thy way for this time; when I have a convenient season, I will call for thee. Acts 24:25.

Some societies in days gone by practiced ritual suicide to restore honor when defeat or failures were too shameful to bear. The Japanese practiced hari-kari using a short sword to disembowel themselves. And, the ancient Greeks fell on a sword aimed at the heart. "Finally, he [Brutus] spoke to Volumnius ... and begged him to grasp his sword with him and help him drive home the blow. And when Volumnius refused, and the rest likewise ... grasping with both hands the hilt of his naked sword, he fell upon it and died."[366] Today falling on the sword means to accept responsibility for a failure, mistake, or wrongdoing. However, accepting blame for one's actions in today's world is a rare occurrence; making excuses is far more commonplace.

Making excuses has been a staple since God created humans to inhabit the earth. When God confronted Adam to inquire about his disobedience in eating the fruit of the forbidden tree, he blamed Eve and God. "The man said, 'The woman you put here with me--she gave me some fruit from the tree, and I ate it.'" Likewise, Eve blamed the serpent. "The serpent deceived me, and I ate" (Gen 3:12, 13, NIV). Each determined to vindicate his and her behavior by excusing self and blaming the other, God, and their circumstances. This character flaw is natural to the fallen human race.

Marcus Antonius Felix, an ancient Roman procurator of the Judaea Province and known for his cruelty, corruption, and depravity, heard the truth of salvation, the love of Jesus, and the judgment from Paul. Obviously the Holy Spirit convicted him of these precious truths, which penetrate to the marrow of the bone. It opened his eyes to his vile character and the dark, dastardly deeds of his past. Afraid, he stopped Paul's discourse and dismissed him by telling him to come back at a more convenient time. An old Yiddish proverb captures his response perfectly, "If you don't want to do something, one excuse is as good as another."

We are without an excuse if we are not among the heaven bound when Jesus returns. God promises that the gospel shall be preached to the entire world before the end comes; thereby, ensuring that one and all are given an opportunity to accept Him and claim their inheritance. And He offers the Holy Spirit and His inspired Word to point the way. "For since the creation of the world God's invisible qualities—his eternal power and divine nature—have been clearly seen, being understood from what has been made, so that *men are without excuse*" (Rom 1:20, NIV).

Now is the convenient time to accept Jesus, to exercise righteousness and self-control, to get back on track if you have fallen off. Now is the time to strive for the perfection of character that will open the gates of heaven. For we have no excuse at the judgment if we neglect to do so.

December 1

When God Arises

Let God arise, let His enemies be scattered: let those also who hate Him flee before Him. Ps. 68:1, NKJV.

The righteous rest in excellent hands, for "security is not the absence of danger, but the presence of God, no matter the danger."[367] God's presence has surrounded and protected His people since sin polluted the earth. In a physical manifestation of Jesus' promise to be with us, the pillar of cloud by day and pillar of fire by night directed the Israelites through the Sinai desert (Ex. 13:21). "Lo, I am with you always" is a statement pregnant with a pledge to never abandon us (Matt. 28:20). In addition, His presence is a sure guide for "Whenever the cloud lifted from above the Tent, the Israelites set out; wherever the cloud settled, the Israelites encamped" (Num. 9:17, NIV).

When the cloud lifted, the camp dismantled, packed up, and followed wherever it led. As they proceeded, Moses rallied the Israelites with the battle cry, "Let God arise; let his enemies be scattered: let those also who hate Him flee before Him" (Ps. 68:1, NKJV). And that battle cry reverberates with His people to the present day, for the enemies of His people are God's enemies. When several kings united to destroy the Israelites during Jehoshaphat's reign "the LORD had made them to rejoice over their enemies.... And the fear of God was on all the kingdoms of those countries, when they had heard that the LORD fought against the enemies of Israel" (2 Chron. 20:27-29).

Let God arise, let His enemies be scattered! When the Pharisees, in an attempt to best Jesus, entrapped the woman caught in adultery and brought her to Him, He scattered them. "'He who is without sin among you, let him throw a stone at her first.' And again He stooped down and wrote on the ground. Then those who heard *it,* being convicted by *their* conscience, went out one by one, beginning with the oldest *even* to the last. And Jesus was left alone, and the woman standing in the midst" (John 8:7-9, NKJV).

Let God arise, let His enemies be scattered! Possessed with a legion of demons that rendered him naked, homeless, and insane, a demonic man silently begged Jesus to rescue him. "When he saw Jesus, he fell down before him and shouted at the top of his voice, 'What have you to do with me, Jesus, Son of the Most High God? I beg you, do not torment me' for Jesus had commanded the unclean spirit to come out of the man" (Luke 8:28-35, NRSV). After Jesus had scattered his demonic enemies, the man sat at His feet clothed and sane. Likewise, through prayer, praise, and a desire for righteousness, we authorize Jesus to arise and scatter our enemies and demons, among which are pride, envy, addictions, and other wicked desires of the flesh.

Let God arise, let His enemies be scattered! "Friendship of the world is enmity with God? whosoever therefore will be a friend of the world is the enemy of God" (James 4:4). But through God's grace and mercy, the disobedient, who are His enemies, can rise to the level of friend by putting their all on the altar of sacrifice for Him.

December 2

Love That Won't Let Go

Do not be afraid-I am with you! I am your God-let nothing terrify you! I will make you strong and help you; I will protect you and save you. Isaiah 41:10, GNT.

One day a little boy encountered an alligator in a swimming hole behind his home. His mother saw the alligator approaching and rushed to her son's rescue. Just as she grabbed his arms to pull him out of the water, the alligator grasped him by the legs. A life and death struggle began as his mother held on fiercely while screaming for help. Soon a farmer arrived and shot the alligator. The boy survived but with huge, ragged scars on his legs. When his friends marveled at his scars, the boy responded, "But look at my arms. I have great scars on my arms, too. I have them because my mom wouldn't let go."[368]

Just as his mother clung to him, not considering the cost to herself, God clings to those who trust Him and who look to Him for deliverance. Her fierce love is a miniature example of God's love for us. But we will never fully understand the depth of His love until we have been changed into immortality and know as we are known. "God's love is meteoric, his loyalty astronomic, His purpose titanic, his verdicts oceanic. Yet in his largeness nothing gets lost; Not a man, not a mouse, slips through the cracks" (Ps. 36:5, 6, MSG*)*.

David poses a question after viewing the numberless stars, the radiant sun, the celestial moon, and other wonders of space: "What is man that you are mindful of him, the son of man that you care for him?" (Ps. 8:4, NIV). Compared to the heavens and the works of His hand, we are puny, pitiful globs of protoplasm. Nevertheless, we reign as the crowning act of Creation as we are made in His image. Omniscient, God knew that man would exercise his free will and sin, but He created us nevertheless. After the first couple fell into sin, He provided a way of escape through Jesus for all who are willing.

Similar to a mother's love for her child, God's love is unconditional, not based on what we do or who we are. Most of us love with conditions—you make me happy; you provide my earthly needs; you are attractive. However, provisional love appears shallow and painful when the conditions are not met and the relationship ends. God demonstrated unconditional love for "while we were yet sinners, Christ died for us" (Rom. 5:8). We are all wretched sinners, but many indifferently snub His outstretched hand and His pleading heart. Still He paid the price and continues to plead for His ungrateful created beings to accept His grace.

God's love is everlasting and His appeal is lovingkindness (Jer. 31:3). He will ever protect, comfort, and save us from dangers seen and unseen and from human and spiritual predators although we may emerge with battle scars. If we choose Him and call on Him for deliverance, He will never let go even when the fiercest predators threaten to pull us under. He will never let go!

December 3

Gain Everything; Lose Nothing

Whoever believes in Him should not perish but have everlasting life. John 3:16, NKJV.

"God is, or He is not," wrote Blaise Pascal, a seventeenth century philosopher, scientist, and mathematician who ventured that believing God exists is of more value than believing that He does not exist. Investigate, he implores, as God's existence is not determined by reason and " weigh the gain and loss in wagering that God is.... If you gain, you gain all; if you lose, you lose nothing. Wager then without hesitation that he is."[369] In short, if you believe God is and serve Him, you lose nothing if He does not exist. But if He does exist and you believe He is not, then you lose the infinite value of eternal life.

Although good stewards do not squander money on the lottery, this activity exemplifies a principle in Pascal's wager. Any astute gambler considers at least three things before he places his bet—a consideration of the amount of the prize, the amount of risk, and the probability of winning. Winning the lottery may mean a gain of millions of dollars so the amount of the prize is lofty while the risk is very low because a single lottery ticket is generally one dollar. But the probability of winning the gamble is remote—the odds of winning a Powerball lottery are 80,089,128 to 1.[370]

Believing that God is and acting on that belief presents a far superior prize/reward with absolutely no risk and a 100 percent probability of winning. We are privy to the huge bonanza of eternal life by choosing to fear, love, and serve God. Heaven holds perfect peace and perfect joy, complete fulfillment and lasting intimacy, unmarred beauty, unmatched love, and selfless generosity forever and ever. Words are inadequate to accurately portray the brilliance, beauty, and glories of heaven; thus, we cling to the promise that "no eye has seen, no ear has heard, and no mind has imagined" the height, breadth, and depth of heaven's splendor (1 Cor. 2:9, NLT).

There is no risk in choosing to believe that God is, for He promises the prize/reward to whoever believes. However, belief goes far deeper than just knowing that God exists. Belief means faith in His promises, loyalty in serving Him, obedience to His Word, striving for mastery over sin, and following the promptings of the Holy Spirit. "Without faith it is impossible to please God, because anyone who comes to him must believe that he exists and *that* he rewards those who earnestly seek him" (Heb. 11:6, NIV). And the probability of winning the prize/reward of eternal life in the celestial kingdom is 100 percent guaranteed. *All* who receive Him, who believe in His name, He gives the right to become children of God (John 1:12). *All* who confess that Jesus is Lord and believe that God raised Him from the dead will be saved (Rom. 10: 9).

Wisdom is sweet to the soul, but the fool says in his heart, "There is no God" (Ps. 14:1). Accordingly, fools are the only ones who will walk away from such tremendously weighted odds so squarely in their favor. Thank God, we are wise enough to act on the belief *that* God is and that one day we will be *where* He is.

December 4

The Problem With Tradition

In vain they do worship me, teaching for doctrines the commandments of men. Matt. 15:9.

June watched her mother, Francine, roll out pie dough and asked why she removed the arms from the new rolling pin. Francine explained that her great grandmother, her grandmother, and her mother had rolled dough with armless rolling pins. Thus, it was a family tradition that she continued. Curious, June researched the history of the armless rolling pins. From Great Aunt Alice she learned that Francine's great grandmother had found an affordable armless rolling pin at a salvage sale, used it, and handed it down. Following tradition and without thinking, Francine removed the arms of a new one.

Some traditions are benign, delightful, and treasured. But when tradition supersedes the Word of God without an investigation of its origin and purpose, it may bring ruin to generations of people. Many who cling to tradition despite the express Word of God will trip and topple over it. "Tradition can be very comfortable, as it saves us from taking responsibility to think things through in the light of God's revealed will. It is much easier and 'safer' just to say, 'We've always done it like this.'"[371]

If you preach tradition loud enough, practice it long enough, or repeat it often enough, it becomes fact for many. But that does not change the Word of God. "It is very easy to put a false [or private] interpretation on scripture, placing stress on passages, and assigning to them a meaning, which, at the first investigation, may appear true, but which by further search, will be seen to be false. If *the seeker after truth* will compare scripture with scripture, he will find the key that … gives him a true understanding of the Word of God. Then he will see that his first impressions would not bear investigation and that continuing to believe them would be mixing falsehood with truth."[372]

For instance, throughout much of Christendom, as fueled by tradition, the Lord's Day is heralded as Sunday. However, the single reference to the exact term "Lord's day" is spoken by John, a disciple of Jesus. "I was in the Spirit on the Lord's day" (Rev. 1:10). Jesus clarifies which day is the Lord's day, "For the Son of man is Lord even of the sabbath day" (Matt. 12:8), and points to the day of the week on which the Sabbath day falls: "The seventh day is the sabbath of the LORD thy God" (Ex. 20:10). The Sabbath is also referred to as "my holy day" (Isa. 58:13). God neither sanctified nor set apart Sunday as His day of worship. Mind you, as Creator, *He* established the day chosen as His holy day not vice versa and uses it as a test of obedience.

Breaking with tradition is not easy. It takes prayer, courage, and a commitment to follow God wherever He leads. Otherwise, look for a horrible accounting should we let go of the commands of God and hold on to human traditions "for not the hearers of the law are just before God, but the doers of the law shall be justified" (Rom. 2:13). Bear in mind, the majority is not always right, for *narrow* is the road that leads to life and *only a few* find it.

December 5

Grieve, But Hope in the Resurrection

We do not want you to be ignorant about those who fall asleep, or to grieve like the rest of men, who have no hope. 1 Thess. 4:13, NIV.

"They turned the lights out, NaNa," said two-year-old Noah who had his first experience with daylight savings time and going home in the dark. Before the time change when his grandmother picked him up from the daycare, the sun shone in his eyes, and he could point to the fire trucks, tow trucks, and police cars that excited him. His innocent observation, however, captures the sting of grief at the loss of a loved one. The lights go out in our hearts and in the world around us, shrouding us with pain so deep, so intense, and so overwhelming that it sucks the breath out of our lungs.

But declared Robert Ingersoll, "In the night of death, hope sees a star...." That star is Jesus' radiant promise to resurrect His valuable possessions and take us to heaven. Hence, He counsels us not to grieve inconsolable as if we have no hope, but to keep the hope alive that alleviates grief. If we believe that our loved ones, who died in Christ will live again, we can claim as Thomas Moore wrote, "Earth has no sorrow that Heaven cannot heal."

In faith, the psalmist exclaimed, "Weeping may endure for a night, but joy cometh in the morning," acknowledging that we live and suffer in the night season of sin and corruption (Ps. 30:5). Inevitably tears and grief are dogged companions of this transitory night season, but we can ask for and receive comfort from our Savior who promises to be an ever present help. "Be merciful to me, O LORD, for I am in distress; my eyes grow weak with sorrow, my soul and my body with grief" (Ps. 31:9, NIV). One glorious day the Son will eclipse the night season by capping the wells from which tears spring and effectively wipe every vestige of them from our existence (Rev. 7:17).

With the blessed hope of the Second Coming of Jesus, the morning of our deliverance is the end of our suffering, and that morning will appear as surely as night turns into day at the rising of the sun. "For the Lord himself will come down from heaven, with a loud command, with the voice of the archangel and with the trumpet call of God, and the dead in Christ will rise first. After that, we who are still alive and are left will be caught up together with them in the clouds to meet the Lord in the air. And so we will be with the Lord forever" (1 Thess 4:16, 17, NIV). Just like that, He turns our mourning into dancing, strips us of our mourning garments and clothes us with joy (Ps. 30:11).

To quell doubts, provide comfort, and arrest fears, the psalmist echoes Isaiah. He was anointed "to comfort all who mourn, and provide for those who grieve in Zion—to bestow on them a crown of beauty instead of ashes, the oil of gladness instead of mourning, and a garment of praise instead of a spirit of despair" (Isa. 61:2, 3, NIV). Therefore, we are to be encouraged and to encourage each other with those comforting words (1 Thess. 4:18).

It is advantageous to allow Jesus to enter our space of grief to share it with us while we wait faithfully for Him to end all seasons of mourning.

December 6

Afflictions Are Our Friend

Through many tribulations we must enter the kingdom of God. Acts 14:22, NASB.

Furious, Bennie washed his hands of God after his colon cancer diagnosis. Then, to make matters worse, he lost his job and the bank foreclosed on his home. The stress of this turn of events created friction in his marriage, prompting his wife to file for divorce. Bewildered, he recounted that he had been a committed Christian who faithfully returned tithes and offerings and served his church and community. Thus, he could not understand the tribulations that assaulted him so viciously. He blamed God for not intervening and foolishly walked away from His sufficiency. Noted Abraham Wright, "I am mended by my sickness, enriched by my poverty, and strengthened by my weakness.... What fools are we, then, to frown upon our afflictions! These, how crabbed soever, are our best friends. They are not indeed for our pleasure, they are for our profit."

Although, his statement sounds contradictory and trite, Wright has a valid point—afflictions *are* our best friends. Similar to the value in tribulation, true friendships have value that is missing in associations and acquaintances. Some best friends are akin to a mirror that candidly reflects our weaknesses and shortcomings and, in love, supports us and nudges us toward overcoming, reaching maturity, and gaining wisdom. And because they put our best interests front and center, we endure the painful honesty, sometimes combatively and sometimes at a snail's pace, but we endure nevertheless. And, as we measure the spiritual growth, our appreciation outweighs the sting.

If we live a godly life, we are red meat to Satan who will persecute us, but we are always under the watchful eye of our best Friend, Jesus (2 Tim. 3:12). Anyone who suffers through tribulations and continues to walk hand in hand with Jesus can testify to the spiritual growth and expanding love for Him. Trials *are* painful and only masochists welcome pain. But once peace is restored in our lives, gratitude fills the heart for His abiding presence and for tempering the fire, for the invaluable lessons learned and for the growth. C.S. Lewis observes, "God, who foresaw your tribulation, has specially armed you to go through it, not without pain but without stain."

Each trial builds our faith and nudges us up the ladder toward the perfection that outfits us for heaven. Like a Father, God uses prickly ways to assist our growth, such as adversity, which allows Him to fulfill His will in our lives and fine-tune our characters to readjust us to live in His coming kingdom. God is concerned with the product of the suffering not with how much and how long He must test us to achieve that refined character.

Unlike Bennie, we loathe not walk away from our Sufficiency, particularly when the fire threatens to consume us. Let God have His way, for He cherishes us and yearns to bring us home. When the fires of persecution return and again burn up the fragile house of peace, be confident that He will comfort, maintain, and restore our smile, for according to Thomas Watson, "God sweetens outward pain with inward peace."

December 7

Living the Word

Oh, how I love thy law! It is my meditation all the day. Ps. 119:97.

Bill, a shabbily dressed, long-haired, hippy-type, marched to his own drumbeat. He became a Christian while in college and found a church across the street from campus. He walked into the church, but it was full, moving Bill to set cross-legged on the carpet directly in front of the pulpit. In a very traditional church, the members were astonished and outraged at this unorthodox intruder. However, one elderly, well-dressed deacon walked slowly to the front, sat on the floor beside Bill, and worshipped there. Emotional, the pastor choked, "What I'm about to preach, you will never remember. What you have just seen, you will never forget. Be careful how you live. You may be the only 'Bible' some people will ever read."[373]

Concisely, the Bible is a must read and a must study because what it offers, free of charge, is of inestimable value. It testifies about the existence and essence of Jesus (John 5:39). Knowing its value and its transformative powers, the Christian's delight is in the law of the Lord on which we mediate day and night (Ps. 1:2). The Scriptures are the bread of life and ought not to be devoured in haste but divided into small bites, chewed and relished. Also, they are the living water that we dare not gulp down quickly, but sip slowly, roll over the tongue and savor.

Kenneth Boa said, "To own a Bible is a tremendous responsibility—to whom much has been given, much is required (Luke 12:48). The Scriptures must not merely be owned, but known; not merely known, but believed; and not merely believed, but obeyed." In obeying the Word, we become living breathing sermons, glorifying God and guaranteeing the title deed to our inheritance. One person, whose life is the Word in action, is more effective in soul-winning and glorifying God than a dozen preachers as couched in Edgar A. Guest's poem: "The best of all the preachers are the men who live their creeds, for to see good put in action is what everybody needs."

Conversely, point to a shallow caricature of a Christian, one whose words and deeds arrest the work of soul-winning and who brings contempt to the name of Christ, and you will find someone who neglects to read, live, and breathe the Word. God warned His chosen people that a neglect of the Word of God brings spiritual starvation. Without the wisdom gleaned from the pages of Holy Writ and without knowledge of God, we perish. Without that knowledge there is no faithfulness or kindness, but plenty of swearing, lying, killing, stealing, and committing adultery—all moral boundaries are crossed (Hos. 4:1-6).

God-inspired, the Scriptures offer wisdom, instruction in right doing, and thorough preparation to stand firm against the deceptions of the devil and cunningly devised fables of false prophets designed to lead us astray. By meditating habitually and prayerfully on the Word, we attain spiritual maturity and become effective ambassadors for Jesus.

December 8

Fear and the Hidden Dark Side

For with You is the fountain of life; in Your light we see light. Ps. 36:9, NKJV.

In *The Strange Case of Dr. Jekyll and My Hyde*, Robert Louis Stevenson explores man's dark, hidden side through an experiment by the respected and honorable Dr. Jekyll. Dr. Jekyll theorized that man has a dual nature of good and evil and successfully separated his own two natures. Mr. Hyde, a cruel, inhuman murderer, personified that dark side and possessed a "moral insensibility and insensate readiness to evil." Finally, Dr. Jekyll, unable to obtain the drug that controlled this dark side and, slowly becoming integrated with Hyde, killed himself.[374]

Dr. Jekyll, "learned to recognize the thorough and primitive duality of man;... if I could rightly be said to be either, it was only because I was radically both."[375] No matter how much we deny, minimize, ignore, or sanitize it; no matter how far we have traveled on our Christian journey; no matter how long and how wide we preach to others, we possess a dual nature, a dark side, and will do so until Jesus eradicates sin, temptation, and Satan. In some of us that dark tendency to evil causes pain but is hidden so deep in our psyche as to be undetectable without fervent prayer for God to shine a spotlight on it. In others, the dark side is simmering below the surface, ready to erupt in times of crisis, stress, frustration, and anger. Peace demands we cry, "Search me, O God, and know my heart: try me, and know my thoughts" (Ps. 139:23).

Those wounded from childhood have dark places deep inside covered with fragile, painful scabs that certain triggers can break and push the wounded psyche to ooze, throb, and ache. Then we become addicted or depressed or lose control or lash out, blaming others for our pain without recognizing it as a scam by Satan to destroy us. To make it worse, we become fearful and ashamed of our reality. Therefore, we cover the pain with a mask that shouts "I am OK" to hide our true, authentic selves from each other and from the only Physician who can heal the wounds and bring peace out of the chaos churning inside of us. He promises, "For I will restore health to you, and your wounds I will heal" (Jer. 30:17, ESV).

The dark side moves us to become "the pot that called the kettle black" or "the camel that cannot see his own crooked neck," accusing others of the same sins and wrongdoing that we commit. Case in point: after Senator Henry Hyde led the impeachment charge against Bill Clinton based on his affair with Monica Lewinsky, reporters uncovered Mr. Hyde's seven-year affair with a married woman. The louder we condemn others, the better we quiet that inner voice of conscience within us. But Jesus recognizes our dark sides and asks, "Why do you see the speck that is in your brother's eye, but do not notice the log that is in your own eye?" (Matt 7:3, ESV).

Darkness is an option not a certainty for the redeemed since Jesus is "the light of the world" (Matt. 5:14) and, whoever follows him *"will never walk in darkness* but will have the light of life" (John 8:12, NIV). Allow Him to search and destroy those dark places with the healing laser of love.

December 9

Walk Not in Circles

Let your eyes look directly ahead and let your gaze be fixed straight in front of you. Watch the path of your feet and all your ways will be established. Prov. 4:25, 26, NASB.

Did you know that people who get lost while hiking or walking tend to walk around in circles if they have nothing on which to focus? Based on a study of six participants who walked in a flat, forested region or in the Sahara Desert and, despite their efforts, four traveled in circles without realizing they crossed their own paths. These four walked in overcast conditions and at night after the moon had set. However, the two who could see the sun or the moon were able to walk in straighter paths.[376]

The gist of the experiment is that people cannot walk in a straight line, no matter their intentions or efforts, unless guided by a visual point of reference. That same principle holds true in our Christian walk. The old man in us, the former unconverted person we were before beholding Jesus, walked in the circle of sin going nowhere spiritually. Hopelessly lost, we were directionless without the light of the Son to guide us though the mire of immorality onto the firm ground of righteousness.

To reach that firm ground takes dogged determination and supernatural assistance. Therefore, we are wise to pray for the victory and to fix our gaze straight ahead toward Jesus, our point of reference. As we embark on that rocky road to heaven and if we desire to make continuous progress toward that goal, our focus must remain singularly on Him who is the Way to truth and life. Obviously it is quite difficult to look straight ahead *and* watch the path at our feet. But trusting Jesus, we follow Him onto the firm path of righteousness straight to heaven.

Viktor Frankl wrote, "Those who have a 'why' to live, can bear with almost any 'how.'" The why of the Christian's existence is Jesus. Be warned that the firm path at times will be buffeted by storms and gale-force winds and by fire and flood, but keep that gaze fixed straight ahead and vicariously watch the path of His feet as you follow the perfect Guide. Jesus, who is walking both ahead of us and beside us, will calm the storms. He will not allow the rivers to sweep us away or the flames to consume us (Isa. 43:2).

Jesus does not lead us in circles; He leads "in the way of righteousness, in the midst of the paths of judgment" (Prov. 8:20). By precept and example, through His Spirit and through the Holy Bible, by His grace and His faithful watchmen, our Lord leads us. Follow, "Christ, in whom are all the treasures of wisdom and knowledge; it is Christ in the Word, and Christ in the heart; not only Christ revealed to us, but Christ revealed in us."[377] Following Jesus wherever He leads despite the difficulties culminates in rest in God's presence where He will commend us with, "well done."

December 10

Our Neighbors' Keeper

But if the watchman sees the sword coming and does not blow the trumpet, and the people are not warned, and the sword comes and takes any person from among them, he is taken away in his iniquity; but his blood I will require at the watchman's hand. Eze. 33:6, NKJV.

The Feast of Trumpets reigned as the second most solemn day of the year for the Israelites. Its solemnity surpassed only by the Day of Atonement that occurred ten days later. Heralded by trumpets or the shofar, this feast called the people to repentance and reformation prior to standing before God in judgment on the Day of Atonement. As the Israelites wandered farther and farther away from God, He called His prophets to be watchmen to warn them of their need to repent and tasked them to warn sinners of their transgressions and urge them to return to God.

God appointed Ezekiel as "a watchman for the house of Israel; therefore you shall hear a word from My mouth and warn them for Me" (Eze. 33:7, NKJV). Being the same God yesterday, today, and forever, He gives us the same responsibility after we "put on the new self, which is created in God's likeness and reveals itself in the true life that is upright and holy" (Eph. 4:24, GNT). When we are transformed into His image, we receive the mind of Christ whose premier goal remains soul-winning.

Although, the "old man" was crucified with Christ, Satan still tempts us by hook or crook. If we dig in our heels and keep away from willful sin, he lulls us into complacency at the very time we should look up for our salvation and warn others. When we let down our vigilance, he deceives us into being self-satisfied and pleased with ourselves. And self-satisfied Christians are smug, no longer hungering after righteous and have shelved that burden for lost souls. Deluded, they believe they are already Spirit-filled, fully satiated with godliness and ready for translation (1 Cor. 4:8).

Complacent Christians become an unwitting tool of Satan by accepting and perpetrating a lowering of biblical standards and with folded hands watch others teeter on the brink of destruction. We begin to concede to small societal pressures until we have stepped on our Bible-based principles. In an attempt to be politically correct, we go along to get along, motivated by a fear of offending church members, family, or friends who are living below the biblical standard set by Jesus. Additionally, we fear being labeled judgmental, legalistic, or holier-than-thou.

Really, the trumpet also needs to be blown in *our* lives, summoning *us* to danger and to look at Jesus. He was a radical whose radical teachings offended many, but He never deviated even unto death. Today, the church and the world need more benign radicals similar to Jesus who shun political correctness and strive for the salvation of lost souls not people pleasing. He stations us as watchmen in His stead to warn people of the approaching danger and the coming judgment. If we fail to do so, their blood is on our hands, but if they disregard the warning, our hands are clean.

December 11

Supernatural Circumcision

And the LORD your God will circumcise your heart and the heart of your descendants, to love the LORD your God with all your heart and with all your soul, that you may live. Deut. 30:6, NKJV.

An ambulance transported Marion to the emergency room because she was experiencing extreme fatigue, dizziness, and shortness of breath. Doctors put her through a battery of tests and diagnosed her condition as bradycardia, meaning her heart beat too slowly. They implanted a pacemaker in her chest cavity to regulate the sluggish heartbeat, discerning a defective sinus node function. The sinus node, a natural pacemaker, regulates the heart by spreading electrical charges throughout to regulate its beat.

In reality, every person born of woman has a defective heart. Matthew describes us as having callused hearts that are hard and thick from the continual friction of sin in our lives (Matt. 13:15). Jeremiah adds that our hearts are deceitful and desperately wicked (Jer. 17:9). And Mark declares evil thoughts, sexual immorality, murder, adultery, and other transgressions percolate in and overflow from these defective hearts (Mark 7:21). Sadly, sin distorted God's plan for a perfect heart in humanity. When God made Adam and Eve, He looked upon His creation and announced that it "was very good." But sin changed our hearts from very good to wicked in the time it took to bite a piece of fruit.

Thank God He has a remedy for our defective hearts—a "supernatural circumcision." But He cannot do the surgery unless we put our life and well-being in His hands and sign the extended consent form. Then and only then can He remove the stony hearts, the callused hearts, the desperately wicked hearts, and replace them with hearts of flesh, hearts that beat in tandem with His heart of love and righteousness. Undergoing supernatural circumcision is God cutting out the world and the carnal body of self and implanting His Spirit. Afterward, we heal spiritually to love Him with all our heart in all its newness.

Baptism, generally following that circumcision made without hands, is a symbolic "burial of your old life; coming up out of it was a resurrection, God raising you from the dead as he did Christ. When you were stuck in your old sin-dead life, you were incapable of responding to God. God brought you alive—right along with Christ! Think of it! All sins forgiven, the slate wiped clean, that old arrest warrant canceled and nailed to Christ's cross. He stripped all the spiritual tyrants in the universe of their sham authority at the Cross and marched them naked through the streets" (Col. 2:12, 13, MSG).

When God circumcises the heart, He cuts deep to remove the heart defects and bathes it in antiseptics to cleanse it thoroughly. David pleaded for that deep heart cleansing. "Create in me a clean heart, O God; and renew a right spirit within me. Cast me not away from thy presence; and take not thy holy spirit from me. Restore unto me the joy of thy salvation; and uphold me with thy free spirit" (Ps. 51:10-12). Truly, heart circumcision is a spiritual lifesaver.

December 12

As the Twig Is Bent

Behold, I was shapen in iniquity; and in sin did my mother conceive me. Ps. 51:5.

Virgil penned a powerful truism, "As the twig is bent the tree inclines." Alexander Pope expanded the quote with, "'Tis education forms the common mind; just as the twig is bent the tree's inclined." This observation has been used extensively in the field of education to establish that the adults we become is shaped by the early education we receive. In fact, a book titled *As the Twig Is Bent: Lasting Effects of Preschool Programs* explores the connection between early childhood education and the long-term, scholastic performance of children from low-income families.

Like wind-blown twigs, we are bent toward evil from the time we are conceived in our mother's womb as we inherited a sin nature (Rom. 5:12). Even babies know instinctively how to bite, hit, and throw tantrums and must be taught to be social beings. Teaching them to be well-adjusted beings and nudging them to grow spiritually straight is at times very frustrating and requires diligence and a patience borne from above. Knowing our tendencies and our bent toward evil, God required the Israelites to teach His commandments to their offspring not haphazardly but in a concerted, systematic way. "Teach them to your children, and talk about them when you sit at home and walk along the road, when you lie down and when you get up" (Deut. 6:7, NCV).

As any loving parent, God desires the best for His children. Hence, He has set down between the pages of Holy Writ wisdom for our joy, peace, health, and spiritual growth. "That our sons may be as plants grown up in their youth; that our daughters may be as corner stones, polished after the similitude of a palace" requires our cooperation (Ps. 144:12). Children are great imitators, and during those first few formative years, they learn best by modeling their parents' behavior. Therefore, *we* need to be staked to the True Vine to prevent our leaning and bending toward sin. He straightens us, establishes our roots, and points us heavenward through His Word and the Holy Spirit. But unless we model Him, these spiritual tools are useless.

Being doers of the Word, we must live the life we profess. Model for your children or babes in the faith a commitment to tools like daily Bible reading, devotions, and prayer. Commitment to this tested and verified triangle of spiritual preparation will bring to us a circle of eternity with the Holy Trinity. Living intimately with this triumphant triangle brings peace where there is discord, comfort where there is distress and pain, and wisdom to counter foolishness. They are also a roadmap to heaven, a training ground for our children, and they launch an intimate relationship with our Lord and Savior.

Although the twig is bent toward evil, it will grow strong and straight to unbelievable heights if painstakingly nurtured and trained. So neglect not nor minimize the importance of the triumphant triangle along with the guidance of the Holy Spirit.

December 13

From the Power of Satan to the Power of God

To open their eyes, in order to turn them from darkness to light, and from the power of Satan to God, that they may receive forgiveness of sins and an inheritance among those who are sanctified by faith in Me. Acts 26:18, NKJV.

Murder, mayhem, mystery, and malevolent characters dot the landscape of the same Bible that leads to eternal life. Arguably Jezebel reigned as one of the most infamous female purveyors of evil in the Bible. Daughter of a pagan king and an idol worshipper, she wielded a powerful, but negative, influence over her weak husband, Ahab, king of Israel. He built an altar to Baal and became an idol worshipper himself. Selfish with a sense of entitlement, she "judicially" murdered Naboth who refused to sell his ancestral land to Ahab. She fraudulently accused him of blasphemy, prompting townsmen to stone him to death. Even worse, she killed the prophets of the Lord (1 Kings 16-21).

Jezebel reigned brazenly in the power and kingdom of Satan; she never repented of her evil and never sought forgiveness. Ahab, on the other hand, "tore his clothes and put sackcloth on his body, and fasted and lay in sackcloth, and went about mourning" after Elijah spelled out God's judgment over him and his family for his evil (1 Kings 21:27). But, perhaps, Ahab experienced only partial and fleeting repentance, being moved by fear of the consequences, not fear of the Lord. Later, his character is revealed as he mouths his hatred of the prophet Micaiah (1 Kings 22:8).

Evil cannot control us unless we extend a welcoming hand through insistent, willful sin. To protect His faithful ones from the swarm of demons who roam around the earth under Satan's command, God erects a wall of protection that never fails unless we commit a breach. Apparently, Mary Magdalene beckoned them to fellowship with her, for she is described as a woman "who had been healed of evil spirits and infirmities—Mary called Magdalene, out of whom had come seven demons" (Luke 8:2). But when she chose to break the power of Satan and walk in the power of God, He forgave her sins and promised her a heavenly inheritance pursuant to her faithfulness.

Similarly, the woman caught in adultery and the woman at the well both broke the seventh commandment. For many years and for various reasons, Satan held them in bondage, but both wisely changed their power source. The Samaritan woman bumped into Jesus at a well where He offered her living water; she accepted, and Jesus washed away her sins. The accusers of the woman caught in adultery dragged her to Jesus after an entrapment, condemned her, and planned to execute her at His word. But Jesus, condemning *them* for hypocrisy and inhumanity, offered *her* mercy, not condemnation, and she, too, readily accepted (John 8:4).

Matthew Henry wrote, "If a pretending partial penitent shall go to his house reprieved [as with Ahab], doubtless a sincere penitent shall go to his house justified." By God's grace these women made a 180-degree turn from the power of evil to the power of God, which justified them and insured their inheritance among those sanctified by faith.

December 14

The Right Perspective

A person who isn't spiritual doesn't accept the teachings of God's Spirit. He thinks they're nonsense. He can't understand them because a person must be spiritual to evaluate them. 1 Cor. 2:14, GWT.

"What is the matter with him? Why doesn't he stop those children from running up and down the aisles disturbing everybody on the train? Conductor, do something!" The passengers were outraged at George's detachment and his children's unruliness on an Amtrak train from Philadelphia to Atlanta. The conductor became as outraged as the passengers until George explained they were returning from burying his wife, the young children's mother. When the passengers heard this, their sympathy took precedence over their comfort, allowing them to accept the family's unseemly behavior.

Perspective is defined as "the appearance of things relative to one another as determined by their distance from the viewer." Initially, from where the passengers sat, they saw only unruly children and an indulgent parent. But when allowed inside the circumstances that dictated the family's actions, their perspective changed. The conductor's involvement allowed them to rise above the obvious and discern what sat at the heart of the matter.

The conductor's role echoes that of the Holy Spirit who is the only One who can facilitate our grasp of spiritual matters. Carnal man and woman can never value teachings of the Spirit; if so, no one would be spiritually lost. "Every impenitent man is deceived and blinded. He is deceived about his own character; … about his prospects for eternity; about death, about judgment; heaven, hell. On none of these points has he any right apprehension; and on none is it possible for any human power to break the deep delusion, and to penetrate the darkness of his mind."[378]

For instance, as Paul was defending himself against the charges leveled by unbelieving Jews, he discussed Jesus' life and death, resurrection and salvation. "At this point Festus interrupted Paul's defense. 'You are out of your mind, Paul!" he shouted. "Your great learning is driving you insane'" (Acts 25:24, NIV). Festus succeeded Felix as the Roman procurator or governor of Judea and neither had a concept of the gospel nor a relationship with the Holy Spirit as evidenced by his outburst.

Christians, too, need to rely on the Holy Spirit since the Bible contains many things that *appear* illogical, indiscernible, contradictory, and/or open to varying interpretations. These things should not cause the Christian confusion or eternal death. Jesus clearly said that when the Spirit of truth, comes, "He will guide you into *all truth*" (John 16:13, NKJV). Sometimes when we hold erroneous beliefs about the interpretation of Bible verses, God will send a messenger to espouse the truth. But many dismiss the messenger and continue to hold onto their belief without the benefit of the Spirit's interpretation. But why, since He *is only a prayer away*. Remember, there is a difference between seeking support for our beliefs and searching for the truth.

December 15

Prisoners of Hope

Turn you to the strong hold, ye prisoners of hope. Zech. 9:12.

What seemed more hopeless than the events of Good Friday culminating with Jesus, the Messiah and giver of life, hanging lifeless on a Roman cross? The hope of forgiveness, the hope of freedom from sin, and the hope of life eternal seemed unattainable. Throughout the long hours of the Sabbath while He lay in the tomb, hope fizzled and died for His inner circle and the larger circle of converts. But hope rekindled and burst into flames on Resurrection Sunday when Jesus broke the fetters of death, sin, and the grave. South African Archbishop Desmond Tutu remarks that this turn of events makes us "prisoners of hope."

The term "prisoners of hope" appears to be an oxymoron—a contradiction in terms. To the contrary, a Christian prisoner of hope is gladly handcuffed to Jesus who gives us every good and perfect gift (James 1:17). When we were without Christ, we "were excluded from citizenship in Israel, and the pledges God made in his promise were foreign to you. You had no hope and were in the world without God" (Eph. 2:12, GWT). In that state of darkness and condemnation, sin separated us from God, and we cared not about a pledge of pardon or hope of eternal life.

Prisoners of hope taste the good Word of God and place hope in the promise of the world to come. "God has given both his promise and his oath. These two things are unchangeable because it is impossible for God to lie. Therefore, we who have fled to him for refuge can have great confidence as we hold to the hope that lies before us" (Heb. 6:18, NLT). A lying God is a moral impossibility and a classic oxymoron. And since His Word personifies His character, it will never fail. "Those who know Your name will … trust in You; for You, LORD, have not forsaken those who seek You" (Ps. 9:10, NKJV).

He is a certain, steadfast anchor for our souls in a world adrift. Similar to the rooster whose coop blew apart by a fierce storm and had to dig itself out of the rubble, keep hope alive. He shook off the rain that matted his feathers, disregarded the cuts, bruises, and the rubble where his home once stood. And instinctively knowing the sun shone above the clouds, he crowed with all his heart. Look to Jesus, the Light of the world, when your world disintegrates in the storms of life, when there are no answers in sight, and when all you desire is to lie down in defeat. If you really know Jesus, you know the hope that springs eternal in Him.

Aurelia McCarthy offers, "Allow hope to take you over. Allow hope to reign." Nestle in Jesus, the blessed hope; trust that the hope of the afflicted will not be forgotten; rest on the hope of eternal life. To bolster the hope that is within you, forget not His awesome deeds and keep His commands. Moreover, be prepared to "give the reason for the hope that you have" to everyone who asks (1 Peter 3:15, NIV). Truly, God, our only hope, is a refuge, a stronghold, and a supplier of peace and comfort. He is a reservoir of hope.

December 16

Grasping Hands in Love and Support

Above all, continue to love each other deeply, because love covers a multitude of sins. 1 Peter 4:8, ISV.

"Tall Tree" in Redwood National Park is the name of the tallest California redwood tree on earth, soaring 367.8 feet in height with a base measuring 44 feet in circumference. Not only are they the tallest living things on earth, redwoods typically live 500 to1,000 years, and even up to 2,000 years. Amazingly, their roots are very shallow, growing a scarce six feet deep but may branch out underground more than 120 feet. These shallow roots make them susceptible to toppling by wind or floodwaters. However, because their roots grasp each other's hands, they are able to withstand storms and floods. Growing close together, the roots of neighboring trees interconnect with their fellow redwoods and sustain each other.

God placed roots deep inside of us that require an interconnection with other human beings to benefit our emotional well-being. He made Eve for Adam, stating "it is not good for the man to be alone" (Gen. 2:18, NIV). Thus, at Creation He endowed the human race with a basic need for a nurturing, sustaining, and secure relationship. "The quality of our personal connections has a great impact on our emotional and physical health. Research has shown that having supportive relationships has a greater impact on health than diet, exercise, stress, smoking, drugs, and even genetics."[379]

Love deep enough to bury self defines such interconnection. For example, Rachel's relationship with a terminally ill friend testifies to a loving interconnection that echoes the relationship that God wants to establish with His children. In excess of two years, she faithfully and cheerfully accompanied her friend on the train for many chemotherapy sessions, holding her up when she was too weak to stand. She helped her bathe and dress, cooked for her, planned her memorial service with her, and led daily morning devotions as well as other gracious assists. Rachel abandoned herself and her needs to provide a welcomed, sustained, and supportive relationship for her friend. She tightly clasped her friend's hand and would not let go, enduring with her to the end and providing peace and comfort.

God desires an intimate relationship, an interconnection, with the children He created, sustains, and supports. That connection obliges love, "This is My commandment, that you love one another, just as I have loved you" (John 15:12, NASB); self-sacrifice, "Greater love has no one than this, than one lay down his life for his friends" (verse 13); obedience, "You are My friends if you do what I command you" (verse 14); and communication, "No longer do I call you slaves ... I have called you friends, for all things that I have heard from My Father I have made known to you" (verse 15) .

Moreover, He will sustain us when the way gets rocky and clouds obscure our view. His strong right hand is extended to anyone who will grasp it. "For I the LORD thy God will hold thy right hand, saying ... Fear not; I will help thee" (Isa. 41:13). He promises to "uphold thee with the right hand of my righteousness" (Isa. 41:10).

December 17

Whose Child Are You?

This is how we know who the children of God are and who the children of the devil are: Anyone who does not do what is right is not a child of God; nor is anyone who does not love his brother. 1 John 3:10, NIV.

"Take the sword and cut the baby in half and give half to the mother and the other half to the other woman." King Solomon's verdict probably stunned the spectators as he presided over a dispute between two women. One of the babies had died soon after his birth, and his mother had tiptoed into the other woman's room and stole her living baby while she slept. Thus, both women claimed to be the baby's mother. As he entered the verdict, the first women begged, "Give her the child; do not kill him," while the other woman coldly agreed with the verdict. Solomon said, "Don't kill the baby." Then he pointed to the first woman, "She is his real mother. Give the baby to her" (1 Kings 3:16-30).

Today, parental testing, using such modern methods as genetic fingerprinting, renders a sound verdict in such cases. When testing DNA, the current cutting edge technology, the probability of paternity is generally more than 99.9 percent when the parent is biologically related. Likewise, the results of the test of worldliness prove conclusively that those who indulge are Satan's children. Choosing not to be made alive in Christ, they are strolling cadavers dead in trespasses and sin. To their father the devil, they pledge allegiance and behave as sons and daughters who mimic him by indulging the appetites of the flesh and following its desires and thoughts (Eph. 2:1-3).

"Adultery, sexual immorality, uncleanness, lustfulness, idolatry, sorcery, hatred, strife, jealousies, outbursts of anger, rivalries, divisions, heresies, envyings, murders, drunkenness, orgies" partially catalog the desires of the flesh (Gal. 5:19-21, WEB). Slaves of sin, impenitent sinners are free to disregard the Words of life and indulge such evil passions, but in so doing they will attract God's wrath (John 8:44).

The test *for* a child of the King, however, is actualized by progressive righteousness produced through obedience as we are led by the Spirit of God (Rom. 8:17). "It shall be our righteousness, if we observe to do all these commandments before the LORD our God, as he hath commanded us (Deut. 6:25). Moreover, the test *of* love for our Father is expressed by Jesus: "If you love me, you will obey what I command" (John 14:15, NIV). Failing the tests, we can expect a rejection note or a pink slip from Him.

The righteous do what is morally true as prescribed by "every word that comes from the mouth of God" (Matt. 4:4, NIV). And by His Word, we shall be evaluated. "He who rejects Me, and does not receive My words, has that which judges him—the word that I have spoken will judge him in the last day" (John 12:48, NKJV). Embrace the Bible as the standard for righteous living, for as D.L. Moody wrote, "its doctrines are holy. Its precepts are binding; its histories are true and its decisions immutable." When God scrutinizes our deeds, thoughts, and motives, will He claim us as His children? I pray so!

December 18

The LORD is My Inheritance

"The LORD is my inheritance; therefore, I will hope in him!" The LORD is good to those who depend on him, to those who search for him. So it is good to wait quietly for salvation from the LORD. Lam. 3:24-26, NLT.

Most people with assets and capital, particularly the very wealthy, have an estate plan including a will far in advance of their death. Leona Helmsley, the billionaire hotelier who became infamously known as the "queen of mean" along with her husband made a fortune in the hotel business. Reporters quoted Helmsley as saying that only the little people pay taxes. She died in 2007 and left an estate estimated at more than four billion dollars with the bulk of the estate going to a charitable trust; twelve million dollars to her dog Trouble; and a total of ten million dollars each to two grandchildren if they visited their father's gravesite once a year. However, Helmsley disinherited two other grandchildren.

Those who inherit wealth will one day die and leave it to another or squander it while alive. But a will allows the owner of the wealth to stipulate conditions and control the dispersion of the estate even in death. Nevertheless, "the form of this world is passing away," making way for an eternal kingdom (1 Cor. 7:31, ISV). Then life will reverse and the poor in the eyes of the world who are rich in faith will gain an everlasting inheritance secured through the blood of Jesus (James 2:5). As adopted children of God, we receive full rights to share this inheritance with His only begotten Son (Gal. 4:1-7).

As heirs of God we are joint heirs with Jesus. And the indwelling of the Holy Spirit guarantees the inheritance of the redeemed who are the sons and daughters of God. However, not unlike two of the Helmsley grandchildren, we are susceptible to being disinherited. The guarantee of an everlasting inheritance is conditioned on our remaining humble, patient, loving, and obedient even when evil people and their evil deeds tempt us to evil (Rom. 8:16; 1 Peter 3:9).

Reserved in heaven for us, this inheritance is incorruptible, undefiled, and permanent (1 Peter 1:3-4). It is both a present spiritual kingdom and a future literal kingdom prepared for the holy children of God since the foundation of the world (Matt. 25:34). And it is a place of unimaginable light and beauty: "No eye has seen, no ear has heard, and no mind has imagined what God has prepared for those who love him" (1 Cor. 2:9, NLT). John uses the simile of a bride adorned for her wedding to describe the New Jerusalem (Rev. 21:2). Typically, at a wedding no expenses are spared to create an atmosphere as elegant as possible to impress and welcome the honored guests. Likewise, God will spare nothing to create our new bodies and a pure, stable atmosphere in our heavenly home, which is our inheritance.

It pays to be God's child. Those of us who conquer willful sin stand to gain all good and perfect gifts as His adopted sons and daughters, and we will never be disinherited. His heirs will eat from the tree of life, which guarantees life everlasting in an inconceivably perfect place (Rev. 2:7).

December 19

By Their Fruit

"Why do you call me 'Lord, Lord,' and do not do what I say?" Luke 6:46, NIV.

Two officers pulled over a driver, demanded she exit the car, and searched for weapons. They checked her license plate, driver's license, and registration card. Satisfied they were mistaken, they told her they assumed she was driving a stolen car because her bumper sticker read "Honk if you love Jesus," a Jesus fish was attached to her car, and the license plate displayed a Bible text. But after trailing her for several blocks, the officers saw her weave in and out of traffic, pull in front of a car almost causing an accident, and tailgate a driver to force him out of her way while incessantly honking the horn. When anyone protested, she made obscene gestures with her middle finger. Seeing her actions, they suspected her car was stolen.

The driver remains an avid churchgoer, tithes regularly, and is a committed ministry leader, but her actions illustrate that Jesus does not live in her heart. "Yes, just as you can identify a tree by its fruit, so you can identify people by their actions" (Matt. 7:20, NLT). Wearing a cross is not bearing a cross; carrying a Bible is not living the Bible; and attaching a Jesus fish to your car is not Jesus living in the heart. Jesus wants to be the center of our lives not hauled out and put on display once a week. He iterated and reiterated that, "Not everyone who says to me, 'Lord, Lord,' will enter the kingdom of heaven, but only he who does the will of my Father who is in heaven" (Matt 7:21, NIV).

Christians who have the right to call Him "Lord, Lord" are true disciples. About them He said, "When you produce much fruit, you are my true disciples. This brings great glory to my Father" (John 15:8, NLT). True disciples are self-sacrificing lovers of God who live to please Him as doers of His Word, not simply hearers. The seeds sown on good ground represent His true disciples—"those who hear the word, accept it, and bear fruit: some thirtyfold, some sixty, and some a hundred" (Mark 4:20, NKJV). Their striving coupled with the power of the indwelling Spirit of God brings the flesh under control and their mindset shifts from self-centered to God-centered. At the core, disciples of Christ love Him more than they love themselves.

If the only way we can be identified as a Christian is to say so or by wearing a breast pin shouting JESUS or the cross hanging around our neck, then we are not producing the fruit that pleases God. True disciples, "Bring forth fruit that is consistent with repentance [let your lives prove your change of heart]" (Matt. 3:8, AMP). God is not mocked. We may deceive ourselves and others sometimes, but we cannot deceive God anytime. "I the LORD search the heart and examine the mind, to reward a man according to his conduct, according to what his deeds deserve" (Jer. 17:10, NIV).

An unknown author wrote, "O Lord, how many read the Word, and yet from vice are not deterred." If we so choose, the limitless power of the Word will change us. Hence, God's disciples are changed by the Word and reach God's standard of growth from carnal to godliness measured by the production of good fruit.

December 20

Finding Perfect Peace

Thou wilt keep him in perfect peace, whose mind is stayed on thee: because he trusteth in thee. Isa. 26:3.

God made sea creatures that live at the ocean depths such as jellyfish whose bodies are filled with water and are unaffected by underwater pressure. Some fish, including the Atlantic herring or carp, have swim bladders filled with gases that adjust as they swim closer to the surface or near the very bottom of the ocean. On the other hand, to withstand the outside water pressure in the depths of the ocean, submarines have pressure hulls made of thick high-strength steel, but the tough outer shells may warp, buckle, or crack.

The fish, however, have a Creator-endowed super strength that allows them to withstand tons of pressure without effort or mishap. Similar to the sea creatures, if we crave that illusive "perfect peace," we must be strengthened from the inside out. The weight of the external pressure on every Christian's life is great at times, and many are crushed because of tiny inner strength. They have not found the key to unlock the door of perfect peace as promised in the Word.

Perfect peace does not just materialize once we become Christians, for there are important conditions to be met. First, our minds must be stayed on God. "Stayed" means to stop moving or skid to a halt and to endure or persist. With a mind skidding to a halt at Jesus' feet and remaining there, the enemy cannot bombard it with doubt and fear. "Let the word of Christ richly dwell within you, with all wisdom teaching and admonishing one another with psalms *and* hymns *and* spiritual songs, singing with thankfulness in your hearts to God" (Col. 3:16, NASB).

Second, perfect peace comes from trust in God and His Word. Thus, falling in love with God's law and believing that He will do what He says He will do produces an untroubled mind. "And those who know Your name will put their trust in You; For You, LORD, have not forsaken those who seek You" (Ps. 9:10, NKJV). But we cannot know Him unless we spend quality time with Him through reading the Word and abiding in His presence through prayer and meditation. Knowing God, we deposit our concerns with Him while retaining a childlike trust that He will handle them. And, He does.

That promised *perfect* peace, that promised peace that *passes understanding* is God-induced peace. "Everything is quiet, for we dwell in our Father's house. Look upward and you will perceive no seat of fiery wrath to shoot devouring flame. Look downward and you discover no hell, for there's no condemnation to those that are in Christ Jesus. Look backward, and sin is blotted out. Look around, and all things work together for good to them that love God. Look beyond, and glory shine[s] through the veil of the future like the sun through a morning mist. Look outward, and the stones of the field, and the beasts of the field are at peace with us. Look inward, and the peace of God which passeth all understanding keeps your hearts and minds by Christ Jesus."[380]

December 21

Pushed to the Limit?

No temptation has overtaken you except such as is common to man; but God is faithful, who will not allow you to be tempted beyond what you are able, but with the temptation will also make the way of escape. 1 Cor. 10:13, NKJV.

Aristotle wrote, "I count him braver who overcomes his desires than him who conquers his enemies; for the hardest victory is the victory over self." Evil desires are temptations that spring from Satan's evil heart to our minds as suggestions to act contrary to the Word of God. Temptations are not sin, but when we flirt with, embrace, coddle, and submit to temptation, we give birth to sin, which upon maturity spawns death. Sin occurs after we allow these evil desires to take root in our minds—the center of our decision making—and move us to action. Scripture admonishes us to "Keep thy heart with all diligence: for out of it are the issues of life" (Prov. 4:23). Life or death is determined by the diligence we exert to guard the door to temptation.

Gehazi, the servant of Elisha, a great prophet of God, lost the battle with self and succumbed to the temptation that led him down the slippery slope to destruction. Obviously, he regularly heard the voice of God, if only through his master, but he chose to listen to the voice of the enemy who allured him with riches. After God empowered Elisha to cure Naaman of leprosy, Naaman gratefully offered Elisha "ten talents of silver, six thousand shekels of gold, and ten changes of clothing" which he refused (2 Kings 5:5, NKJV). But Gehazi took the second step toward yielding to temptation by rationalizing his covetousness. He convinced himself that his master was too easy on the idolatrous foreigner "by not accepting from him what he brought" (verse 20, NIV). Then he turned the thoughts into action. "As surely as the LORD lives, I will run after him and get something from him" (verse 20).

One sin opens the door to a closet jammed full of wrongdoing. When Gehazi caught up with Naaman, he lied about a need to assist two young prophets and led Naaman to believe that the request for a talent of silver and two sets of clothing came from Elisha. Then he covered the first lie with a second after Elisha confronted him about his whereabouts. Yielding to temptation, Gehazi condemned himself and his descendants to be plagued forever with Naaman's leprosy (2 Kings 5:22, 27).

A made-up mind to serve God at any cost and knowledge of the Word will jam the trap of temptation that ensnared Gehazi. God promises that any temptations we encounter are common to all Christians and can be successfully resisted. When the temptations are greater than our ability to resist, submit them to Jesus and trust Him to help. He, too, was tempted in all points as we are and offers both empathy and deliverance. Remember His example. Jesus resisted temptations by complete submission to His Father and to the Word.

Is there anything too hard for God? Of course not! Then call on Him when tempted and trust He will provide an escape and render each temptation resistible. He will not allow the enemy to push us beyond our limits.

December 22

The Mighty Big "If"

If you confess with your mouth that Jesus is Lord and believe in your heart that God raised him from the dead, you will be saved. Rom. 10:9, ESV.

A British expatriate born in Mumbai, India, Rudyard Kipling authored "If," to be considered one of the twentieth century's greatest poems. The shortest title of most literary works, it is big on advice to his son, which if followed, will make him an honorable, well-adjusted, productive citizen of earth and a potential candidate for heaven. Also, "if" is a small coordinating conjunction that provides a connection between thoughts and is weighty with conditions.

John prefaced a string of Bible verses in 1 John 1 with this conjunction to highlight some important truths about salvation and sin. Notably he asserts that God is light and punctuates that truth by affirming that there is absolutely no darkness in Him since darkness is the absence of light. That God is light means He is holy and embodies love and truth, realities that inform His fundamental nature. His light radiates throughout this earth to disperse the shadows and gloom of ignorance and sin. Thus, "*If* we claim to have fellowship with him yet walk in the darkness, we lie and do not live by the truth" (1 John 1:6, NIV). But *if* we walk in the light, He purifies and saves us.

And *if* we claim to be sinless, we are liars deceiving ourselves since the Word declares all have sinned (verse 8). "*If* we claim we have not sinned, we make him out to be a liar and his word has no place in our lives" (verse 10, NIV). Those in this category have a tendency to whitewash their actions or deny the existence of or ignore God. But "*If* the righteous are barely saved, what will happen to godless sinners?" (1 Peter 4:18, NLT). Some deliberately sin while disguised as Christians and follow their own way with the expectation that when Jesus returns a quick prayer will acquire His forgiveness. On the contrary, He says, "Behold, I come quickly; *and my reward is with me*, to give every man according as his work shall be" (Rev. 22:12).

"*If* we confess our sins, he is faithful and just to forgive us our sins, and to cleanse us from all unrighteousness" (1 John 1:9). After conversion, consistently confessing our sins and yielding to the Spirit of God are requisites for Christians since the "old man" shadows us everywhere. Like an ominous dark cloud, the old man hovers over us and at times blocks the light, seeking to plunge us into darkness because we have not yet achieved perfection but are striving to that end. Augustine writes, "If thou shalt confess thyself a sinner, the truth is in thee; for the truth is itself light. Not yet has thy life become perfectly light, as sins are still in thee, but yet thou hast already begun to be illuminated, because there is in thee confession of sins."

God did not destine us for wrath. He yearns for us to obtain salvation through Jesus Christ, who died for us so we might spend eternity with Him *if* we are obedient.

December 23

Strangers and Pilgrims on Earth

These all died in faith, not having received the promises, but having seen them afar off, and were persuaded of them, and embraced them, and confessed that they were strangers and pilgrims on the earth. Heb. 11:13.

Generally pilgrims are folks who embark on a journey for religious purposes. Those who cherish freedom of religion are grateful to a specific group of Pilgrims who sailed on the Mayflower from England to Plymouth, Massachusetts, in 1620. They set sail across a vast ocean toward a strange, unknown environment where they faced daily hardships to escape religious persecution and to worship God according to their own consciences. Although they came from afar as strangers and pilgrims to a new home, they planned to settle here permanently.

However, Christians are pilgrims and strangers sojourning *temporarily* in this world. The pilgrim's journey is long and fraught with hardship and toil as Jesus said, "In the world ye shall have tribulation" (John 16:33). There are mountains of difficulties to climb, rivers of inherited and cultivated inclinations to navigate, a wilderness of trials to negotiate, and valleys of sin to ascend all with an expected earthly end of death. But the faithful pilgrims who have stored up treasures in heaven will awaken to an end of a long weary night and rest with endless days of peace and joy.

We checked in to this earthly inn but dare not stay forever. Even though the inn may at times be inviting, it is foolish to become so attached to possessions and people that it is difficult to continue the journey. God's apostle beseeches us "as strangers and pilgrims, abstain from fleshly lusts, which war against the soul" (1 Peter 2:11). These lusts keep us earthly minded and fickle, not heavenly minded and faithful. "So, do not let sin control your life here on earth … offer yourselves to God as people who have died and now live" (Rom. 6:12, 13, NCV).

The inn has a noble purpose; it is a stopping point for this night of life where pilgrims are prepared and energized for the eagerly-awaited journey to the final destination. That energy comes directly from the Spirit of God, for we will not succeed on own strength or by our own power but by God's Spirit (Zech. 4:6). Preparation for the journey requires the daily use of two power cords—the Bible and fervent prayer. Without those connections, the journey will never be completed.

Says Amy Carmichael, "We profess to be strangers and pilgrims, seeking after a country of our own, yet we settle down in the most un-stranger-like fashion, exactly as if we were quite at home and meant to stay as long as we could."[382] It is impossible to be absorbed in worldly cares and remain in a waiting, watching position. To secure the heavenly treasure, we must sacrifice the earthly, for we cannot have both worlds.[383]

Be mindful of how brief our life on earth really is. Our days are numbered, and earth is not our true country. Soon earth and its contents will exist no more.

December 24

Christmas Givers

They hurried to the village and found Mary and Joseph. And there was the baby, lying in the manger. Luke 2:16, 17, NLT.

A wealthy man's only son died a hero in a war. One of the men whom the son rescued in the battle that took his life delivered a handmade portrait of the son to the father. Grateful, the father stipulated in his will that this portrait must sell first when his art collection went up for bid. However, no one bid on the son's portrait except a neighbor who only had ten dollars to spend, which prompted cheers, for now the buyers could bid on the "real treasures." But the auctioneer stunned the crowd by declaring that the bidding had ended. Someone said, "What about the valuable paintings worth millions of dollars!" The auctioneer replied, "It's very simple. According to the will of the father, whoever takes the son … gets it all."[381]

So that we could get it all, Jesus gave His all, a gift of salvation and life eternal. But before Jesus gave His all, before He spread the gospel to hungry and thirsty souls, before He was baptized and began His ministry of healing and exorcising demons, before His glorious birth was celebrated, His earthly mother and father gave selflessly to teach and model a godly life to spiritually and physically sustain Jesus.

Mary obediently surrendered her body to carry the embryo destined to become our Savior. Obviously, being chosen to bear Him in her womb was a singular blessing, prompting Elisabeth to exclaim, "God has blessed you above all women, and your child is blessed" (Luke 1:42, ESV). Even so, it required a great sacrifice. Unmarried and pregnant, she sacrificed her reputation and put her life in jeopardy. In her culture sex outside of marriage was a capital offense and such an "evil" woman "must be brought to the door of her father's house. Then the men of the town must put her to death by throwing stones at her" (Deut. 22:21, NCV).

In addition, her gift carried an unshakable stigma even if she avoided the death sentence. According to the law of Moses, an adulterer "has done a disgraceful thing in Israel by having sexual relations before she was married. You must get rid of the evil among you" (Deut. 22:21, NCV). Even her betrothed doubted the Immaculate Conception. "Joseph, being a righteous man and unwilling to disgrace her, decided to divorce her secretly" (Matt 1:19, GWT). For the doubters, Jesus birth was a source of gossip, and the family surely heard the whispering and felt the slights and insults.

Joseph, too, gave sacrificially. Obedient and godly, he willingly provided the gift of marriage to repress the stigma and gossip, and Jesus became known as the carpenter's son (Mark 6:3). He protected Mary and Jesus from the murderous intent of Herod who meant to eliminate a perceived rival. Three separate times he was commanded to "arise and take the young child and his mother" and go. Without hesitation or debate, Joseph promptly gave up home, friends, and job and followed God's leading (Matt. 2:13, ASV). Raising the Son of God was an awesome responsibility that eventually pierced Mary's soul, but Mary and Joseph freely gave to give us the greatest Christmas gift imaginable—a Savior of the world.

December 25

What Child Is This?

Fear not: for, behold, I bring you good tidings of great joy ... For unto you is born this day ... a Saviour, which is Christ the Lord. Luke 2:10, 11.

That "all children have the right to a legally registered name, and nationality" is a right mandated by Article 7 of the United Nations Convention on the Rights of Children. The recording of birth records for military and tax purposes had a long history dating back to the ancient civilizations. In ancient Israel priests registered Jesus' name at the Temple after Mary's days of purification had ended. There His parents paid the required redemption price for Israel's firstborn sons and an additional offering of two turtle doves. Although he should have been acutely aware, the officiating priest comprehended not what Child this was.

What Child is this? The Lamb of God, this Child was born to die to redeem and to save. The Author of eternal life, He sacrificed once to take away the sins of many people and will appear a second time to bring deliverance to those who are eagerly waiting for Him. Now grown up and ascended to heaven, He is our Advocate who pleads His blood to cover our sins. Uniquely perfect, our Defense Attorney never loses a case despite the satanic plaintiff's accusations and temptations against His anointed. As the Horn of Salvation, He became a mighty Savior raised up in the family of David and became the one Mediator between God and man reconciling us to God.

What Child is this? He is our Shield and a Stronghold; a Banner over us and a Rock of Refuge that is higher than I, providing protection from our enemies when the arrows of evil fly hot and heavy and strength when we are burdened beyond measure. He is our Blessed Hope who keeps us anchored in troublous time while we wait for His glorious appearing. He is the Lion of the tribe of Judah, roaring in from heaven to rescue His treasured possessions from the evil one, and our Deliverer from Zion who changes godlessness into glory.

What Child is this? He is the Root and Offspring of David and the Bright and Morning Star who is the Great Source of life and light. Through His powerful Word, He disperses the darkness of ignorance and bondage and brings clarity to cloudy minds. He is the Fairest of Ten Thousand, the Rose of Sharon, the Lily of the Valley, and a Pearl of Great Price. The most precious possession we could ever expect, Jesus is a Sanctuary of love and hope and the Giver of every good and precious gift. The Good Shepherd, He leads us safely through the valley of the shadow of death and delivers us intact to our heavenly mansions.

What Child is this? He is Immanuel who is always with us, the King of kings and Lord of lords, a Potentate with power and authority who will reign over us in the glories of life everlasting and provide perfect peace and safety. His birth was truly a happy birthday and ushered in glad tidings for the world.

December 26

Every Which Way

We faced conflict from every direction, with battles on the outside and fear on the inside.
2 Cor. 7:5, NLT.

Describing a fictional account of the Norwegian Lofoten Maelstrom, Edgar Allan Poe described how the choppy ocean rapidly changed into an eastward current and spread ferociously. "In five minutes the whole sea, as far as Vurrgh, was lashed into ungovernable fury; but it was between Moskoe and the coast that the main uproar held its sway. Here the vast bed of the waters, seamed and scarred into a thousand conflicting channels, burst suddenly into frenzied convulsion --heaving, boiling, hissing --gyrating in gigantic and innumerable vortices, and all whirling and plunging on to the eastward with a rapidity which water never elsewhere assumes except in precipitous descents."[384]

Made famous by the fiction of Jules Vern and Poe, a maelstrom "in English designates a large, fatal whirlpool, engulfing vessels and men, or a figurative application of the idea." In a figurative sense, a maelstrom is a violent or turbulent situation or a violently confused or dangerous state of mind, emotions, or affairs. For instance, baby Moses, blissfully unaware, was sucked into a maelstrom of a battle on the outside and fear and trembling in the hearts of his parents and neighbors.

After Joseph died, a new pharaoh determined that the Hebrew slaves were multiplying rapidly and may prove to be a military threat; thus, he issued a death warrant for all male newborn babies of Hebrew parentage (Ex. 1:9, 22). Moses' mother gave birth at the time of pharaoh's edict, and fearing for her baby's life, she hid him for three months. Imagine the scurrying and worrying attached to keeping a newborn quietly hidden. Who knew when the secret would unravel or when the baby might cry at a most inopportune moment? The time came when keeping him at home no longer seemed practical, so Jochebed made a basket, sealed it with tar and pitch, put her precious baby inside, and deposited him and her heart on the riverbank of the Nile where crocodiles nest.

Outside their home carnage and raw anguish emerged as the death squads carried out the pharaoh's cruel edict. Obviously, Jochebed felt her neighbors' pain, but her strong faith, courage, and resilience kept her sane and functional. "By faith Moses' parents hid him for three months … because they saw he was no ordinary child, and they were not afraid of the king's edict" (Heb. 11:23, NIV). She took God at His Word and trusted Him to provide cover for Moses after exhausting all human options. Knowing God intimately, no doubt, she fervently called out to Him day and night until the wee hours of the night to keep watch over her helpless son. And He did (Ex. 2:5-10).

The psalmist wrote, "And they that know thy name will put their trust in thee: for thou, LORD, hast not forsaken them that seek thee" (Ps. 9:10). Comparable to a maelstrom, conflict may come from every direction, but our God is bigger than any conflict, battle, or fear.

December 27

Fear God and Give Glory to Him

Fear God, and give glory to him; for the hour of his judgment is come: and worship him that made heaven, and earth, and the sea, and the fountains of waters. Rev. 14:7.

Because he glorified himself, he died. Thus was the downfall of King Herod Agrippa who murdered the apostle James, arrested Peter because it pleased the Jews, executed the soldiers who guarded Peter, and harassed the fledgling early church among other atrocities. But after he set a day to publicly glorify himself, he filled God's cup of wrath to overflowing. "Herod, arrayed in royal apparel, sat upon his throne, and made an oration unto them. And the people gave a shout, saying, It is the voice of a god, and not of a man. And immediately the angel ... smote him, because he gave not God the glory: and he was eaten of worms" and died (Acts 12:21-23).

Death is the end for anyone who fails to give glory to God. Our sufficiency, He shed His blood at Calvary, pleads for our devotion through spokespersons and His Word and patiently endures our dalliances with Satan. Moreover, He offers every spiritual help through the Holy Spirit and provides for our physical needs in every way. What more can He do? If we choose to ignore Him and cling to sin, we are doomed to be eaten by worms. Even if we rebel against or ignore or are indifferent to the Maker and Ruler of heaven and earth, we "can no more diminish God's glory by refusing to worship Him than a lunatic can put out the sun by scribbling the Word, 'darkness' on the walls of his cell."[385]

Give God the glory. Doesn't He warrant it? Giving Him glory is reverence, "fear the name of the LORD from the west, and his glory from the rising of the sun" (Isa. 59:19). Glorify Him in His holiness "Who is like you—majestic in holiness, awesome in glory, working wonders?" (Ex. 15:11, NIV); in our worship "let us worship and bow down: let us kneel before the LORD, our maker" (Ps. 95:6); and in our praise and thanksgiving, "Oh give thanks to the LORD; call upon his name; make known his deeds among the peoples! Sing to him, sing praises to him; tell of all his wondrous works!" (Ps. 105:1, 2, ESV).

Giving glory to God is manifest also in our righteousness: "Being filled with the fruits of righteousness, which are by Jesus Christ, unto the glory and praise of God" (Phil. 1:11). It is also manifest in humility: "But let him that glorieth glory in this, that he understandeth and knoweth me, that I am the LORD which exercise lovingkindness, judgment, and righteousness, in the earth: for in these things I delight" (Jer. 9:24).

The admonition to give God glory is a part of the "everlasting gospel" to be preached throughout the world just before Jesus returns for His faithful few. John shows the urgency, importance, and truth of the message by the use of a symbolic angel who flies "in the midst of heaven, having the everlasting gospel to preach to those who dwell on the earth" (Rev. 14:6, NKJV). Glorify God! By glorifying Him with our worship, with our praise, and with our obedience, we will be counted among those to be fitted with a crown of life and a white robe of righteousness (Rev. 14:6).

December 28

Babylon Is Fallen

Babylon the great is fallen, is fallen, and is become the habitation of devils ... For all nations have drunk of the wine of the wrath of her fornication ... Come out of her, my people, that ye be not partakers of her sins. Rev. 18:2-4.

When a disembodied hand appeared suddenly and wrote on the wall, King Belshazzar turned pale with shock. He was so frightened that his legs buckled and his knees knocked together. Thus ended the large party he threw for decadent Babylonians like himself who used the sacred vessels from the Temple of Jerusalem to drink alcoholic beverages while praising gods of precious metals, wood, and stone. Daniel, summoned to interpret the words on the wall, explained that the kingdom and the king's life were to be taken that very night. And so it was (Dan. 5).

Literal Babylon fell after those seated in authority showed contempt for sacred things and rebelled against the God who made heaven and earth. Nimrod, great grandson of Noah whose pride and self-sufficiency led him to build "a city, with a tower that reaches to the heavens, so that we may make a name for ourselves," founded Babylon (Gen. 11:4, NIV). Thus, the Babylon of Revelation 14 symbolizes a spirit of rebellion, pride, and disobedience toward the Word of God and its Author. "It is self glory, a narcissistic elevation of one's own worth. It is a spirit of enslavement. The spirit of Babylon is a desire to afflict others with the same corrupt practices and thoughts as has afflicted one's own self. Not content to be corrupt alone, this spirit seeks to entice and enslave others who willingly submit to its seduction."[386]

God brought an end to Nimrod's city, echoing the fate of literal Babylon, but this time by confusing the language so they could not communicate. Thus, "its name is called Babel, because there the LORD confused the language of all the earth" (Gen. 11:9, NKJV). Looking down the centuries in vision to today, John saw spiritual Babylon exhibiting that spirit of rebellion, pride, and disobedience through establishing and spreading false systems of worship based on "private interpretation" (2 Peter 1:20). These private interpretations replace the Bible truth, creating confusion for the sincere children of God. This John describes as drinking the "wine of the wrath of her fornication" which "all nations have drunk" (Rev. 18:3).

Being drunk with the wrath of the wine of spiritual fornication is betraying God, forsaking Him, worshipping idols, and substituting the Word of God for the word of man (Eze 16:26; Hos. 1:2). Hundreds of denominations with differing doctrines dot the landscape today. But there is only "one Lord, *one faith*, one baptism" (Eph. 4:5). And God is earnestly calling the sheep who know His voice to come out of spiritual Babylon into that one faith of His remnant church.

How do we find that one faith that is not about traditions or feelings but about Scripture? Guided by the Holy Spirit, look to the Word that declares His remnant church keeps the commandments of God (Rev. 12:17).

December 29

The Mark of the Beast

And the third angel followed them, saying with a loud voice, If any man worship the beast and his image, and receive his mark in his forehead, or in his hand, the same shall drink of the wine of the wrath of God. Rev. 14:9, 10.

For seven years, beginning in 1984, Resurreccion "Sony" Florendo battled the Japanese-based giant corporation Sony in court pursuant to a $2.9 million trademark lawsuit against her. She owned restaurants in metropolitan Baltimore named Sony, her nickname. However, in 1992, pursuant to an agreement with Sony, she removed her name from her businesses.[387] According to federal law, "A trademark is a word, symbol, or phrase, used to identify a particular manufacturer or seller's products and distinguish them from the products of another."

Also, a trademark, synonymous with mark, sign, or seal, is an identifier. Biblically, it identifies whose we are based on *whom* we worship and serve for "To whom ye yield yourselves servants to obey, his servants ye are to whom ye obey" (Rom. 6:16). Succinctly, "whosoever shall trample upon God's law to obey a human enactment receives the mark of the beast; he accepts the sign of allegiance to the power which he chooses to obey instead of God."[388] Countless numbers today worship Satan, showing their allegiance to him through defiance of the inspired Word of God and therefore to God Himself. In addition, many "nullify the word of God for the sake of … tradition" (Matt. 15:6, NIV) or through one's uninspired interpretation of His Word.

Throughout the ages, Satan has been bent on being like the Most High who solely deserves worship. His litany of victims include our first parents, the Israelites, and the Jews whom he tempted to serve false gods and reject the true God, and God-fearing Christians who were persecuted in the first centuries. And through the power of the papal system, Satan prohibited the circulation of the Bible to keep people in ignorance of the Word and changed the fourth commandment day of worship from Saturday to Sunday. Today, he sends false prophets, charismatic and entertaining, who lull us into a false sense of security, preaching peace and safety when all hell is about to be unleashed on this sin-infected world according to the prophecies of Daniel and Revelation.

Thus, the great controversy between God and Satan began and ends on the theme of worship, which envelopes service and obedience. The three angels seen flying through heaven with a loud voice command us to fear God and worship Him; to run from those faiths that promote error; and to issue a warning regarding the penalty for worshipping the beast power who "will speak against the Most High and oppress his saints and try to change the set times and the laws" (Dan. 7:25, NIV).

Heed God's urgent warning. Although patient, loving, and merciful, He does not take lightly this usurpation of His powers and our willful disobedience. The penalty, His wrath unmingled with mercy and the full fierceness of his anger, is great. Choose this day whom you will serve; and serve Him!

December 30

Nearing the End

When you hear of wars and revolutions, don't be terrified! These things must happen first, but the end will not come immediately. Luke 21:9, GWT.

Labor pains and childbirth are typical companions. Short, regular contractions of the uterus or labor pains change the condition of the uterus. These pains cause the uterus, which lengthens and thickens during pregnancy, to soften, shorten and dilate the cervix, the outer narrow end of the uterus through which the baby enters the birth canal. Labor pains are a fluctuating cycle of pain, coming in waves, that peak and subside alternately. The frequency of this cycle increases as delivery is imminent.[389]

The analogy of childbirth very fittingly describes the beginning of the end of human history. The earth is experiencing birth pangs and the contractions are now stronger and closer together. Since Adam sinned and through him sin entered the world, the earth has experienced fluctuating cycles of pain. The Flood; the crucifixion of Jesus; the persecution of Christians; two world wars; atomic bombs disintegrating thousands of innocent people; huge, devastating earthquakes like the Great Lisbon Earthquake; massacres of millions of people; suicide bombers; and other terrorists' acts resemble strong, undulating, painful contractions.

Truly, the earth is in travail. These cycles of pain and suffering caused by the devil and his agents over the centuries have propelled the earth to the brink of that blessed hope—Jesus' Second Coming (Titus 2:13). Although the earth has always endured disasters and evil people, the evil and calamities in the earth today are more frequent and occur with greater intensity. But scoffers dismiss the signs of Jesus' coming by rationalizing that history is riff with such events. Paul counters, "For when they shall say, Peace and safety; then sudden destruction cometh upon them, as travail upon a woman with child; and they shall not escape" (1 Thess. 5:3).

When asked, Jesus gave His disciples signs to signal His return to this earth—false prophets would come in His name; wars and rumors of wars; famines and pestilences; winds and seas roaring in the form of hurricanes and tsunamis; great signs in the heavens; violence; and the fulfillment of the Great Commission. And now His Word is present in almost every nook and cranny of the world. Radio, television, Internet, and print media all attest to the fact that these signs have escalated in intensity, duration, and frequency in this century. We are now experiencing the "beginning of sorrows" or hard labor pains—the period immediately prior to Jesus' breaking through the clouds of heaven (Matt. 24).

Earth is fully dilated and in the second stages of labor as the frequency and painfulness of the beginning of sorrows are escalating. The push through the birth canal is almost finished, resulting in the "crowning" moment when Jesus returns and ushers in a new heaven and a new earth. Are you ready for Jesus to come?

December 31

Special Delivery to Heaven

The Lord will rescue me from every evil attack and will bring me safely to his heavenly kingdom. 2 Tim. 4:18, NIV.

Special delivery mail, now replaced by priority and express mail, went the way of the high top shoe and the cassette tape in 1997. Still, it had an auspicious tenure. The earliest special delivery mail included letters without envelopes or stamps simply marked "immediately." One Confederate cover, obviously from a soldier, was marked "Double Quick." In 1847, the first paid special delivery letter was marked "WILL THE PENNY POSTMAN DELIVER THIS LETTER IMMEDIATELY."[390] Organized and more reliable special delivery service finally became a reality in 1885 at limited locations pursuant to an act of Congress. A special delivery stamp on a letter meant it would be delivered the same day it arrived at the post office. It was not until 1886 that special delivery became available in post offices throughout the U.S.

No stamp is required when Jesus specially delivers His remnant people to our heavenly mansions. Heaven is a real place built by God who dwells there. "Wherefore God is not ashamed to be called their God: for he hath prepared for them a city" (Heb. 11:16; see also 1 Kings 8:28-30). The heavenly city is a square; each side is 375 miles long and every street is paved with transparent gold. The walls of the city, called the New Jerusalem, have twelve foundations made of various kinds of precious jewels sparkling with the colors of a rainbow. Situated in the heart of the city in the middle of the street and flanking the river of life that originates from the throne of God is the tree of life that bears twelve different kinds of fruit every month (Rev. 21:14- 21, 22:2).

Like any king, King Jesus' second coming will be gloriously visible and unmistakably audible. When He ascended to heaven after His resurrection, an angel told His followers, "Jesus ... will so come in like manner as you saw Him go into heaven" (Acts 1:9-11, NKJV). Jesus reiterated the visibility of His second coming when He said, "So if anyone tells you, 'There he is, out in the desert,' do not go out; or 'Here he is, in the inner rooms,' do not believe it. For as lightning that comes from the east is visible even in the west, so will be the coming of the Son of Man" (Matt. 24:26, 27, NIV). And His arrival will be announced with a great sound of the trumpet played by a retinue of angels as He comes in the clouds with "power and great glory" (verse 30, NIV). These angels "will gather his elect ... from one end of heavens to the other" (verse 31, NIV).

Jesus' second coming will usher in the respite from sin and the lasting peace for which we yearn— the glorious morning after a night of suffering. It will fulfill His promise that, "Weeping may endure for a night, but joy cometh in the morning" (Ps. 30:5). The dark night of our existence in a world polluted by sin will become a morning flooded with light never to know darkness again! The gates of the heavenly city will never be shut at all by day "for there shall be no night there" (Rev. 21:25). We will forever dwell in the presence of God who "is light, and in him is no darkness at all" after Jesus, Himself, specially delivers us to His heavenly kingdom (1 John 1:5).

Endnotes

1. Ellen G. White, *The Great Controversy* (Nampa, ID: Pacific Press Publishing Association, 1939), p. 531.
2. Adrian Dieleman, "Sermon on Isaiah 7:14," Trinity United Reformed Church, http://www.trinityurcvisalia.com/sermons/is07v14.html (accessed December 25, 2001).
3. Charles Swindoll, "The Finishing Touch," *Christianity Today*, vol. 40, no. 14.
4. Roland Bainton, *Here I Stand* (New York: Penguin Books, 1977), p. 266.
5. Author Unknown, "Refining Silver," Bulletin Fodder, http://www.vscoc.org/Bulletinfdr/refining_silver.htm (accessed May 5, 2011).
6. Christine Ammer, *Dictionary of Cliches*, 2nd ed. (New York: Facts on File), p. 478.
7. The Physics Classroom, "The Law of Momentum Conservation," http://www.physicsclassroom.com/Class/momentum/U4L2a.cfm (accessed January 4, 2010).
8. Contend for the Faith, "Original Sin," http://contendforthefaith2.com/orig2.html (accessed May 7, 2011).
9. Robert Longman Jr., "Faith and Trust," Spirit Home, http://www.spirithome.com/definif.html (accessed May 7, 2011).
10. Marelisa Fábrega, "Six Things to Do When Life Throws you a Curveball, Abundance Blog at Marelisa Online, http://abundance-blog.marelisa-online.com/2009/06/25/six-things-to-do-when-life-throws-you-a-curveball/ (accessed May 7, 2011).
11. John F. Kennedy, *Profiles in Courage,* (New York: Harper & Brothers, 1956).
12. Robert Browning Hamilton, "Along the Road," WorldofQuotes.com, http://www.worldofquotes.com/author/Robert-Browning-Hamilton/1/index.html (accessed February 2, 2010).
13. Mohandas Gandhi, BrainyQuote, http://www.brainyquote.com/quotes/quotes/m/mohandasga164549.html (accessed January 18, 2011).
14. Lucius Annaeus Seneca, BrainyQuote, http://www.brainyquote.com/quotes/quotes/l/luciusanna106288.html (accessed March 18, 2010).
15. E. M. Bounds, *Satan, His Personality, Power and Overthrow* (London: Fleming H. Revell Company, 1933), p. 140.
16. Thomas Garnett, *Observations on a Tour through the Highlands and part of the Western Isles of Scotland, particularly Staff and Icolmkill* (London: Richard Taylor and Co., 1811), pp. 69, 70.
17. Herbert E. Douglass, *Love Makes a Way: Walking with God from Eden to Eternity* (Nampa, ID: Pacific Press Publishing Association), p. 32.
18. Charles Spurgeon, *The Treasury of David,* vol. 1 (Wheaton, IL: Crossway Book, 1993).
19. Scot McKnight, "The Problem for Prosperity Gospel," Beliefnet, http://www.beliefnet.com (accessed May 10, 2011).
20. Edmund Francis Burton, *Reminiscences of Sport in India* (London: W. H. Allen and Company, 1885), p. 123.
21. Joshua Harris, "Affluenza: The Disease of Greed," Christianity Today International, http://PreachingTodaySermons.com (accessed May 10, 2011).
22. Author Unknown, "Materialism, Greed, Avarice Quotes," Tentmaker Ministries, http://www.tentmaker.org/Quotes/greedquotes.htm (accessed May 10, 2011).
23. John Warrenner, "Why God Doesn't Seem to Answer Prayer," The World is My Parish, http://ucmpage.org/jwarrene/Default.htm (accessed May 10, 2011).
24. Pat Alger, Larry Bastian, and Garth Brooks, *Unanswered Prayers,* Risa Song Lyrics Archive, http://www.risa.co.uk/sla/song.php?songid=15384 (accessed May 10, 2011).
25. Jerry Sittser, "The Gift of Unanswered Prayer," *Today's Christian,* July/August 2004.

26. Arthur W. Pink, "Conclusion," http://www.freegrace.net/library/pink/sovereignty/pink_sov_con.html (accessed May 10, 2011).
27. Marsha Walton, "Scientists: Sumatra quake longest ever recorded," CNN, May 20, 2005.
28. National Geographic News, "Tsunami Facts: How They Form, Warning Signs, and Safety Tips," http://news.nationalgeographic.com/news/2007/04/070402-tsunami.html (accessed May 10, 2011).
29. Peter Russell, "What is Wisdom?" Spirit of Now, http://www.peterrussell.com/SP/Wisdom.php (accessed May 10, 2011).
30. Andy Stanley, Creative Results Management, http://www.creativeresultsmanagement.com/coaching/index.htm (accessed May 10, 2011).
31. Ellen G. White, *Patriarchs and Prophets* (Nampa, ID: Pacific Press Publishing Association, 1958), p. 99.
32. Daniel Blake, "Death Threats for Ethiopian Islamic Convert After Dreaming of Jesus," Christian Today, http://www.christiantoday.com/article/death.threats.for.ethiopian.islamic.convert.after.dreaming.of.jesus/12316.htm (accessed May 10, 2011).
33. "Citizenship in a Republic," speech given at the Sorbonne, Paris, April 23, 1910.
34. Gary Priour "A Story of Perseverance," Corral Newsletter, http://www.youth-ranch.org/newsletter/perseverance.htm (accessed May 10, 2011).
35. Rushe Dominic, "Nouriel Roubini: I fear the worst is yet to come," *The Sunday Times,* October 26, 2008
36. Jim Pavia, "The Loneliness of the Long Term Advisor," *Investment News*, March 29, 2009.
37. Islam QA, http://www.islam-qa.com/en/ref/82120 (accessed May 11, 2011).
38. StasoSphere, "Lesson I. The Story of How Silk Is Produced," http://chestofbooks.com/crafts/needlework/Clothing-And-Health/Lesson-I-The-Story-Of-How-Silk-Is-Produced.html (accessed May 11, 2011).
39. Present Truth Magazine, "The Theology of Ellen G. White," http://www.presenttruthmag.com/7dayadventist/EGWhite_theology/10.html (accessed June 2, 2011).
40. Ellen G. White, *The Great Controversy* (Nampa, ID: Pacific Press Publishing Association, 1939), p. 640.
41. Ellen G. White, *The Great Controversy* (Nampa, ID: Pacific Press Publishing Association, 1939), pp. 641, 642.
42. Beulah Cornwall, "The Chosen Vessel," God's Work Ministry, http://www.godswork.org/enpoem42.htm (accessed May 11, 2011).
43. Christian Classics Ethereal Library, "The Voyage to England," *Journal of John Wesley*, http://www.ccel.org/ccel/wesley/journal.vi.ii.vii.html (accessed May 11, 2011).
44. Lord Tennyson Alfred, "The Higher Pantheism," Poets' Corner, http://theotherpages.org/poems/tenny16.html (accessed May 11, 2011).
45. John Steinbeck, *The Grapes of Wrath* (New York: Viking Press, 1939).
46. Herbert Lockyer, *All the Apostles of the Bible* (Grand Rapids, MI: Zondervan Publishing House, 1972), pp. 63, 64.
47. Charles Spurgeon, "Intercessory Prayer," delivered Sunday, August 11, 1861, at the Metropolitan Tabernacle, Newington, England.
48. Charles Spurgeon "The Power of the Holy Spirit," Bible Bulletin Board, http://www.biblebb.com/files/spurgeon/0030.htm (accessed May 11, 2011).
49. W. E. Vine, Merrill F. Unger, and William White Jr., *Vine's Complete Expository Dictionary of Old and New Testament Words* (Asheville: Thomas Nelson, Inc., 1996).
50. Errol T. Stoddart (sermon, Miracle Temple SDA Church, Baltimore, MD, November 28, 2009).

51. Adland, "MasterCard – Supermarket Icons," http://adland.tv/commercials/mastercard-supermarket-icons-2005-030-usa (accessed May 14, 2011).
52. Pete Lowman, "Identity after God," UCCF: The Christian Unions, http://www.bethinking.org (accessed May 14, 2011).
53. John Milton, *Paradise Lost*, Book I, pp. 678-690, *The Literature Network,* http://www.online-literature.com/milton/paradiselost/1/ (accessed August 8, 2011).
54. John Fox, "The Trial of John Huss," *Fox's Book of Martyrs*: *The Acts and Monuments of the Church* (London: George Virtue, 1751), p. 843.
55. Believer's Web, "John Huss, 1369-1415, Bohemian Reformer," http://www.believersweb.org/view.cfm?ID=109 (accessed May 14, 2011).
56. YouTube, "Amazing Grace commercial," http://www.youtube.com/watch?v=90cfMSqAj0o (accessed May 14, 2011).
57. D.M. Scholer, "Women," *Dictionary of Jesus and the Gospels,* eds. Joel B. Green, Scot McKnight. et al (Illinois: Inter Varsity Press, 1992), p. 880.
58. Ellen G. White, *The Desire of Ages* (Nampa, ID: Pacific Press Publishing Association, 1940), p. 772
59. Ellen G. White, *Education* (Nampa, ID: Pacific Press Publishing Association, 2002), p.169.
60. James McCullen, "Biblical Prayer Request," Cross & Crown Sermons, http://preachhim.org/COL1-4.htm (accessed May 14, 2011).
61. Susan Castillo, adapted, "God's Stubborn Warrior," *Sabbath School Quarterly*, May 1, 2009.
62. Ellen G. White, *The Ministry of Healing* (Nampa, ID: Pacific Press Publishing Association), p. 143.
63. Ellen G. White, *Maranatha* (Hagerstown, MD: Review and Herald Publishing Association, 2004), p. 29.
64. Author Unknown, "Did God Create Evil?" Lutheranism.
65. Ellen G. White, *Testimonies for the Church,* vol. 5 (Nampa, ID: Pacific Press Publishing Association, 2007), p. 69.
66. Franklin Delano Roosevelt, "The Only Thing We Have to Fear is Fear itself: FDR's First Inaugural Address," History Matters, http://historymatters.gmu.edu/d/5057/ (accessed May 14, 2011).
67. Franklin Delano Roosevelt, "The Only Thing We Have to Fear is Fear itself: FDR's First Inaugural Address," History Matters, http://historymatters.gmu.edu/d/5057/ (accessed May 14, 2011).
68. *Catechism of the Catholic Church*, sec. 1, chap. II, p. 213.
69. Awareness of God, "Names of God," http://www.parentcompany.com/awareness_of_god/nog6.htm (accessed May 14, 2011).
70. Awareness of God, "Names of God," http://www.parentcompany.com/awareness_of_god/nog6.htm (accessed May 14, 2011).
71. Got Questions Ministries, "What is the Davidic covenant?" http://www.gotquestions.org/Davidic-covenant.html (accessed June 2, 2011).
72. Ellen G. White, *The Great Controversy* (Nampa, ID: Pacific Press Publishing Association, 1939), p. 641.
73. David Hall, "Philosophical Contemplations: The Universe," Dave's Cave Contemplations, http://www.davehall.force9/co.uk (accessed May 17, 2011).
74. Market Ticker Forums, http://www.tickerforum.org/cgi-ticker/akcs-www?post=75227 (accessed May 17, 2011).
75. Author Unknown, "Carl's Garden," Motivating Moments LLC, http://www.motivateus.com/stories/carls.htm (accessed May 18, 2011).
76. DM Fitness, http://dmfitness.net/index.php?option=com_content&task=view&id=50&Itemid=1 (accessed May 18, 2011).

77. Dick Ham, "Thinking About Precious Children," The Richmond Register, http://richmondregister.com/lifestylescommunity/x775919193/Thinking-about-precious-children (accessed August 15, 2011).
78. Author Unknown, adapted, "The Moth and the Cocoon," Life Enterprises Unlimited, http://www.trosch.org/lif/moth.html (accessed May 18, 2011).
79. J.H. Robinson, ed., *Readings in European History*, vol. 2 (Boston: Ginn, 1906), pp. 179-183.
80. J.H. Robinson, ed., *Readings in European History*, vol. 2 (Boston: Ginn, 1906), pp. 179-183.
81. Dietrich Bonheoffer, *The Cost of Discipleship* (Touchstone Books: 1995), p. 91.
82. CBS Interactive, "Charles IX of France," http://search.com/reference/Charles_IX_of_france#_note-0 (accessed June 2, 2011).
83. Irma Bombeck, *Forever Erma: Best loved Writing from America's Favorite Humorist* (New Jersey: Andrews McNeel Publishing, 1967), p. 61.
84. James Underwood, *Being Human, Being Hopeful* (Abington Press, 1987), pp. 12, 13).
85. The Motivational Speakers Hall of Fame, "Leo Buscaglia," http://www.getmotivation.com/leo-buscaglia-hof.html (accessed May 18, 2011).
86. Michael McCullough, *Beyond Revenge: The Forgiveness Instinct* (San Francisco, CA: Jossey-Bass, 2008).
87. Emotional Competency, "Revenge," http://www.emotionalcompetency.com/revenge.htm (accessed May 18, 2011).
88. Author Unknown, "Pray, Aim High, And Stay Focused," Talk Jesus, http://www.talkjesus.com/daily-devotionals/28729-pray-aim-high-stay-focused.html (accessed May 18, 2011).
89. Author Unknown, adapted, http://www.empoweredwealth.com/forms_pdfs/rules.pdf (accessed May 18, 2011).
90. Eye Witness to History, "The Black Death, 1348," http://www.eyewitnesstohistory.com (accessed May 18, 2011).
91. *The Messenger,* "Elm or Evergreen?" http://www.cocsy.org/media/bulletin/2006/2006-12-24.pdf (accessed May 18, 2011).
92. Clifford Notarius and Howard Markman, *We Can Work It Out* (New York: The Berkley Publishing Group, 1993).
93. Elizabeth Loftus, *Memory: Surprising New Insights into How We Remember and Why We Forget* (Reading, MA: Addison-Wesley Publishing, 1980).
94. Author Unknown, "Frozen in Sin," Semons.org, http://www.sermons.org/consequences.html (accessed May 18, 2011).
95. Joseph Parker, *The Ark of God: The Transient Symbol of an Eternal Truth with Various Pulpit Matters*, vol. 1 (London: S.W. Partridge & Co., 1877), p. 8.
96. Kristy LeAnn Morgan, "The Effects of Alcohol on Society," *Associated Content-Society*, September 19, 2008.
97. MADD, "Statistics," http://www.madd.org/statistics/ (accessed May 18, 2011).
98. Thomas Watson, Quotationpark.com, http://www.quotationpark.com/topics/obedience.html (accessed May 18, 2011).
99. Henry Morris, Ph.D., "The Law for Today," Institute for Creation Research, http://www.icr.org/article/4451/ (accessed May 19, 2011).
100. "Harold 'Pee Wee' Reese - Playing With Jackie Robinson," http://sports.jrank.org/pages/3814/Reese-Harold-Pee-Wee-Playing-with-Jackie-Robinson.html (accessed May 19, 2011).
101. Phillip Weiss, "Truth Be Told They Lied," Outside magazine, http://outside.away.com/outside/magazine/0597/9705biglie.html (accessed May 19, 2011).
102. R. Cody Smith, "Confess Sins To One Another," Walk This Way, http://www.walk-this-way.com/confession.htm (accessed June 2, 2011).

103. Harry Conn, *Four Trojan Horses of Humanism* (Michigan: Mott Media, 1982), pp. 80, 81.
104. Enchanted Learning, "The Brain," http://www.enchantedlearning.com/subjects/anatomy/brain/ (accessed May 22, 2011).
105. Michael McCoy, "I AM Sent Me to You," Redeemer Lutheran Church, http://www.scholia.net/ (accessed March 5, 2000).
106. Richard Strauss, "A Jealous God," bible.org, http://bible.org http://bible.org/seriespage/jealous-god (accessed May 22, 2011).
107. Paul Tillich, *The New Being* (Lincoln, NE: Bison Books, 2005), p. 50.
108. Ellen G. White, *The Desire of Ages* (Nampa, ID: Pacific Press Publishing Association, 1940), pp. 122, 123.
109. Azzan Yadin, "Goliath's Armor and Israelite Collective Memory," *Vetus Testamentum*, LIV, 3 (2004): p. 379.
110. Ellen G. White, *The Desire of Ages* (Nampa, ID: Pacific Press Publishing Association, 1940), p. 761.
111. John Charles Ryle. *The Christian Leaders of the Last Century* (Edinburgh and New York: Nelson & Sons, 1869), p. 383.
112. Ellen G. White, *Early Writings* (Hagerstown, MD: Review and Herald Publishing Association, 1994), p. 179.
113. Soren Kierkegaard, Howard Vincent Hong, and Edna H. Hong, *Soren Kierkegaard's Journals and Papers: Autobiographical, 1829-1848* (Indiana: Indiana University Press, 1978), p. 412.
114. Oswald Chambers, *The Shadow of an Agony* (Basingstoke, Hants, England: Marshall, Logan & Scott Publishers, 1934).
115. Author Unknown, "You're Not Home Yet," Hidden Treasures, http://hiddentreasures.wordpress.com/2006/03/29/your-not-home-yet/ (accessed June 3, 2011).
116. Ellen G. White, *Testimonies for the Church*, vol. 2 (Nampa, ID: Pacific Press Publishing Association, 2007), p. 194.
117. Buzzle.com, "The Pumpkin," http://www.buzzle.com/articles/the-pumpkin.html (accessed May 22, 2011).
118. Ellen G. White, *The Great Controversy* (Nampa, ID: Pacific Press Publishing Association, 1939), p. 643.
119. Author Unknown, "Unseen Gifts," Positive Energy, http://positive-energy-team.blogspot.com/2010/12/unseen-gifts-poem-untitled-and-author.html (accessed May 22, 2011).
120. Ellen G. White, *The Great Controversy* (Nampa, ID: Pacific Press Publishing Association, 1939), pp. 649, 650.
121. Yellowstone National Park Geysers, http://www.yellowstoneparknet.com/geothermal_features/geysers.php (accessed May 22, 2011).
122. Corrie Ten Boom, John and Elizabeth Sherrill, *The Hiding Place* (New Jersey: Fleming H. Revel Publishers, 1971).
123. Author Unknown, "Thank God for an Open Bible," The Wicket Gate Magazine, http://www.wicketgate.co.uk/e44_4.html.(accessed May 24, 2011).
124. Ellen G. White, *Patriarchs and Prophets* (Nampa, ID: Pacific Press Publishing Association, 1958), p. 115.
125. David Erik Jones, *My Struggle, Your Struggle: Breaking Free from Habitual Sins* (Florida: Xulon Press, 2007).
126. C.S. Lewis. *The Chronicles of Narnia* (New York: Harper-Collins, 1954).
127. Henry Clay Trumbull, *The Blood Covenant: A Primitive Rite and its Bearings on Scripture* (Philadelphia, PA: John D. Wattles Publishers, 1893).
128. Quality Club International, http://www.customerdelight.com (accessed May 24, 2011).

129. Frances Hitching, *The Neck of the Giraffe* (New York, NY: Signet Books, 1983), p. 86.
130. Charles Darwin, *The Origin of Species* (New York: The New American Library, 1958), p. 146).
131. Lawrence O Richards, *It Couldn't Just Happen* (Nashville, TN: Thomas Nelson, Inc., 1989), pp. 139, 140.
132. E.M. Bounds, *The Necessity of Prayer* (Ada, MI: Baker Publishing Group, 1976).
133. Ellen G. White, *Christ's Object Lessons* (Silver Spring, MD: Better Living Publications, 1990), p. 63.
134. Vince's Worthwhile Website, "World's Deadliest Snake," http://www.vincelewis.net/snake.html (accessed May 24, 2011).
135. Max Lucado, *Grace for the Moment* (Nashville, TN: Thomas Nelson, Inc, 2007), p. 679.
136. Dr. S.M. Lockeridge (sermon, Detroit, MI, May 27, 1976).
137. Augustine, "On the Nature of Good," New Advent, http://www.newadvent.org/fathers/1407.htm (accessed May 24, 2011).
138. Providence Baptist Ministries, "The Goodness of God," http://www.pbministries.org/books/pink/Attributes/attrib_11.htm (accessed May 24, 2011).
139. James Orr, M.A., D.D. "Entry for 'LOVINGKINDNESS'," *International Standard Bible Encyclopedia*, 1915.
140. Author Unknown, "Silver Linings," Life With Confidence, http://www.life-with-confidence.com/true-meaning-of-life-reflections.html (accessed May 24, 2011).
141. Ellen G. White, *The Desire of Ages* (Nampa, ID: Pacific Press Publishing Association, 1940), p. 772.
142. Ellen G. White, *Testimonies for the Church,* vol. 9 (Nampa, ID: Pacific Press Publishing Association, 2007), pp. 285, 286.
143. bible.org, "Wonderful Burden," http://bible.org/illustration/wonderful-burden (accessed May 24, 2011).
144. Charles Spurgeon, "Daily Blessings for God's People" (sermon, Metropolitan Temple, Newington, England, September 21, 1871).
145. David Limmer, "Loads of Benefits," Restoration Church, http://www.wyrchurch.com/index.php?option=com_myblog&show=Loads-of-Benefits.html&Itemid=1 (accessed May 24, 2011).
146. Charles Swindoll, *Laugh Again* (Nashville, TN: W. Publishing Group, 1992).
147. Ellen G. White, *Counsels to Parents, Teachers, and Students* (Nampa, ID: Pacific Press Publishing Association), p. 467.
148. Ralph Waldo Emerson, QuotationsBook, http://quotationsbook.com/quote/9680/#axzz1NIfwSnlH (accessed May 24, 2011).
149. Grantley Morris, "Christian Help and Inspiration When Gripped by Fear," http://net-burst.net/help/fear.htm (accessed May 24, 2011).
150. Ron Clarke, "And the Devil Will Flee," http://www.sermonillustrator.org/illustrator/sermon7/devil_will_flee.htm (accessed May 24, 2011).
151. Life Gate Ministries, "Specks and Planks and Pigs and Dogs," http://www.lifegatechurch.com/sermons/a26.%20Specks%20and%20Planks%20and%20Dogs%20and%20Pigs.htm (accessed May 24, 2011).
152. Cate Doty, "The Neediest Cases; Mother Abandoned as a Child Reclaims Her Own Children," *New York Times*, November 30, 2004.
153. Dr. Randy Wysong, "Mother Love," Ezine @rticles, http://ezinearticles.com/?Mother-Love&id=84242# (accessed May 24, 2011).
154. Jess Blumberg, "A Brief History of the St. Bernard Rescue Dog: The canine's evolution from hospice hound to household companion," http://Smithsonian.com (accessed January 1, 2008).
155. Joseph Philpot, "Light Affliction and Eternal Glory" (sermon, North Street Chapel, November 5, 1857).

156. Ellen G. White, *Patriarchs and Prophet* (Nampa, ID: Pacific Press Publishing Association, 1958), p. 516.
157. National Eating Disorders Association Fact Sheet, May 2008.
158. Catherine Kaputa, "The Beauty Premium: Why Attractive People Get Paid More and What You can Do About It," SelfBRAND, http://www.selfbrand.com/artbeauty.shtml (accessed May 24, 2011).
159. Paul Bunyan, *The Pilgrim's Progress* (New York: Pocket Books, 1976).
160. "Could you tell me, what causes doubt, and unbelief, and how do I combat it?" ask Gramps, http://www.askgramps.org/could-you-tell-me-what-causes-doubt-and-unbelief-and-how/ (accessed July 10, 2011).
161. Lord Acton written in a letter to Bishop Mandell Creighton in 1887.
162. "Dark Night of the Soul," Mystic World Fellowship, http://www.themystic.org/print/dark-night.htm (accessed July 11, 2011).
163. James F. Miller (sermon, First Presbyterian Church, Charlotte, NC, March 9, 2008).
164. Tom Kovach, "Tear Toxins," *Omni*, December 1982.
165. Philip Keller, *A Shepherd Looks at Ps. 23* (Grand Rapids, MI. Zondervan Pub. Company, 1997).
166. Philip Keller, *A Shepherd Looks at Ps. 23* (Grand Rapids, MI. Zondervan Pub. Company, 1997).
167. Author Unknown, "Two Wolves," Rosenbloom Things, http://www.rosenbloomthings.com/twowolves.htm (accessed May 25, 2011).
168. Spurgeon's Sermons with Charles Spurgeon, devotionals by Spurgeon's Sermons, January 11, 2010, http://www.OnePlace.com (accessed June 3, 2011).
169. Ellen G. White, *Patriarchs and Prophets* (Nampa, ID: Pacific Press Publishing Association, 1958), p. 631.
170. Francis S. Collins, *The Language of Go* (New York: Free Press, 2006), p. 1.
171. Douglas Quan, "THE USERS: One recovering addict's struggle to stay clean illustrates the challenges," *The Press-Enterprise*, Friday, May 16, 2008.
172. Paulo Coelho's Blog, "20 SEC READING The kingdom of this world," http://paulocoelhoblog.com/?s=i+have+the+music (accessed May 26, 2011).
173. Author Unknown, "Unselfish Giving," Kids Sunday School Place, http://www.kidssundayschool.com/Gradeschool/Stories/inspirations1.php (accessed May 26, 2011).
174. Author Unknown, "The Wise Woman's Stone," Inspiration Peak, http://www.inspirationpeak.com/kindness.html (accessed May 26, 2011).
175. Preceptaustin, "Galatians 5:23 Commentary," http://www.preceptaustin.org/galatians_523.htm (accessed May 26, 2011).
176. Christian Resource Centre Bermuda, "Chap. 1 – Our Enemy, The World," http://www.crcbermuda.com/satans-attacks/creeping-compromise/1017-our-enemy-the-world (accessed May 26, 2011).
177. Ellen G. White, *Testimonies for the Church*, vol. 6 (Nampa, ID: Pacific Press Publishing Association, 2007), p. 146.
178. Cliff Pickover, "The Scales of Good and Evil," http://sprott.physics.wisc.edu/pickover/good.html (accessed June 3, 2011).
179. Jodi Kozan, "Grace for Regrets," Power to Change, http://www.powertochange.ie/changed/jodi_regrets.html (accessed May 26, 2011).
180. William Edwy Vine, Merrill F. Unger, and William White, *Vine's Expository Dictionary of Biblical Words* (Nashville, TN: Thomas Nelson, Inc., 1985).
181. Barna Group, "The Bible," http://www.barna.org (this information is based 1993 figures).
182. Alec Gallup and Wendy W. Simmons, "Six in Ten Americans Read Bible at Least Occasionally," The Gallup Organization, http://www.gallup.com (accessed October 20, 2000).
183. Author Unknown, "Faith Can Move Mountains," The Inspirational Nook, http://www.inspirationalnook.com/ (accessed June 3, 2011).

184. Liz Hayes, "Team Hoyt," *Sixty Minutes*, http://sixtyminutes.ninemsn.com.au/stories/lizhayes/269257/team-hoyt (accessed May 26, 2011).
185. Anonymous, "Pile of Troubles," Motivating Moments, http://www.motivateus.com/stories/troubles.htm (accessed May 26, 2011).
186. Straight Path Program, "Armageddon When and How," http://www.rofe.net/www/armageddon.htm (accessed May 26, 2011).
187. Author Unknown, "Thankful for the Thorns," Luvdalot Graphics & Design, http://www.heavensinspirations.com/thankful-for-thorns.html (accessed June 3, 2011).
188. PHPKB Knowledge Base Software, "Miracle happened in One Dollar & Eleven Cents" http://www.knowledgebase-script.com/demo/article-438.html (accessed May 26, 2011).
189. Sir John Powell, FamousQuotesAbout.com, http://www.famousquotesabout.com/quote/Human-beings-like-plants/298781 (accessed January 14, 2010).
190. Loren Eiseley, "A Single Starfish," All Creatures Animal Stories, http://www.all-creatures.org/stories/starfish.html (accessed May 26, 2011).
191. Author Unknown, "The Nails in the Fence," A Gift of Inspiration, http://www.agiftofinspiration.com.au/stories/attitude/nails.shtml (accessed May 26, 2011).
192. Seneca, Roman philosopher, Thinkexist.com, http://thinkexist.com/quotation/anger-if_not_restrained-is_frequently_more/167369.html (accessed May 26, 2011).
193. Charles Spurgeon, "A Caution to the Presumptuous," http://www.spurgeon.org/sermons/0022.htm. (accessed May 26, 2011).
194. Healthline, "Dehydration," http://www.healthline.com/galecontent/dehydration-1?print=true, (accessed May 26, 2011).
195. Ellen G. White, *The Great Controversy* (Nampa, ID: Pacific Press Publishing Association, 1939), p. 555.
196. Author Unknown, "Rainbow Story," http://rainbowpetsitting.com/story.htm (accessed May 26, 2011).
197. *Amazing Facts*, "Written in Stone," Study Guide #6.
198. Author Unknown, "Two Days We Should Not Worry," Afterhours Inspirational Stories, http://www.inspirationalstories.com/4/476.html (accessed July 12, 2011).
199. George E. Mueller, QuotationsBook, http://quotationsbook.com/quote/14000/ (accessed May 26, 2011).
200. Francois Fenelon, Daily Christian Quote, http://dailychristianquote.com/dcqsubmission.html (accessed May 26, 2011).
201. Author Unknown, "The Seed," SkyWriting.net, http://www.skywriting.net/inspirational/stories/the_choice.html (accessed May 26, 2011).
202. Ellen G. White, *Patriarchs and Prophets* (Nampa, ID: Pacific Press Publishing Association, 1958), p. 684.
203. MD Code Public General Laws, 1904. 782. Crimes and Punishment, Art. 27, sec.189.
204. Anonymous, Daily Christian Quote, http://dailychristianquote.com/dcqfaith5.html (accessed May 27, 2011).
205. Gillian Strickland, "The Dark Candle," Home & Holidays, http://homeandholidays.com/dark-candle-the/ (accessed May 27, 2011).
206. G. de Purucker, *Questions We All Ask,* Series II, No. 19., "Mysteries of Sleep and Death," lecture delivered November 23, 1930.
207. Charles Swindoll, *Living Above the Level of Mediocrity* (Nashville, TN: Thomas Nelson, Inc., 1989).
208. Amy Miller, "Old Testament Prophecies of the Messiah, Cursed the Cross," ShareFaith, http://www.http://faithclpiart.com/guide/ChristianHolidays/ (accessed May 28, 2011).
209. Roy P. Basler, ed., *The Collected Works of Abraham Lincoln*, vol. 6 (New Brunswick, NJ: Rutgers University Press, 1953), p. 156.

210. Brothers Grimm and Josef Scharl, "The Old Man and His Grandson," *The Complete Grimm's Fairy Tales* (New York: Random House, 1972).
211. Albert Barnes, "Notes on the Bible," Sacred Texts, http://www.sacred-texts.com/bib/cmt/barnes/index.htm (accessed August 15, 2011).
212. Peter R. Kraemer, *Catholic Church Extension Society,* 1975.
213. William Owen Carver, *The Lord's Day in Our Day* (Nashville, TN: Broadman, 1940), p. 49.
214. *Encyclopedia Britannica*, 1899 edition, vol. XXIII, p. 654.
215. Shane, "The Legend of Cliff Young: The 61 Year Old Farmer Who Won the World's Toughest Race" *Elite Feet for Runners*, December 30, 2007.
216. Leon Bass and Pam Sporn, "I Saw The Walking Dead: A Black Sergeant Remembers Buchenwald," History Matters, http://historymatters.gmu.edu/d/142/ (accessed May 29, 2011).
217. John Bunyan, *Pilgrim's Progress* (Oxford: Oxford University Press, 1882), pt. 1, The Seventh Stage.
218. Jude Redmond, "My Suicide Attempt," NHS Choices Information, http://www.nhs.uk/Livewell/Suicide/Pages/JudeRedmond.aspx (accessed May 29, 2011).
219. William Shakespeare, *Othello* (Philadelphia: J.B. Lippincott, 1882), act 1, scene i.
220. Ellen G. White, *Steps to Christ* (Hagerstown, MD: Review and Herald Publishing Association, 1983), p. 43.
221. NOAA Satellite and Information Service, "The Perfect Storm," http://www.ncdc.noaa.gov/oa/satellite/satelliteseye/cyclones/pfctstorm91/pfctstorm.html (accessed June 3, 2011).
222. Author Unknown, "Forgiveness Quotes," Tentmaker Ministries, http://www.tentmaker.org/Quotes/forgivenessquotes.htm (accessed May 29, 2011).
223. Mayo Clinic Staff, "Forgiveness: Letting Go of Grudges and Bitterness," Mayo Clinic, http://www.mayoclinic.com/health/forgiveness/MH00131 (accessed May 29, 2011).
224. Josh Dowell, "Bend Your Knees," *The One Book of Family Devotions* (Illinois: Tyndale House Publishing, Inc., 2000), p. 13.
225. Franco Harris, QuotationsBook, http://quotationsbook.com/quote/38914/#axzz1NoHV1S9v (accessed May 29, 2011).
226. Author Unknown, "Photographer/Instructor," FlightHumor.com, http://www.flighthumor.com/view.php?joke=796 (accessed May 30, 2011).
227. Ellen G. White, *The Desire of Ages* (Nampa, ID: Pacific Press Publishing Association, 1940), p. 805.
228. RNIB, "Helen Keller," http://www.rnib.org.uk/aboutus/aboutsightloss/famous/pages/helenkeller.aspx (accessed May 30, 2011).
229. Brian Cavanaugh, "I Created You!" Afterhours Inspirational Stories, http://www.inspirationalstories.com/1/147.html (accessed May 30, 2011).
230. Oswald Chambers, *My Utmost for His Highest* (Uhrichsville, OH: Barbour and Co., 1999), p. 366.
231. Author Unknown, "A Scorpion Moment," Afterhours Inspirational Stories, http://www.inspirationalstories.com/9/926.html (accessed May 30, 2011).
232. I. Packer, *Knowing God* (Downers Grove, IL: Inter-Varsity Press, 1973), p. 226.
233. Anthony de Mello, "Violence," Afterhours Inspirational Stories, http://www.inspirationalstories.com/1/100.html (accessed August 15, 2011).
234. Ellen G. White, *Patriarchs and Prophets* (Nampa, ID: Pacific Press Publishing Association, 1958), p. 723.
235. T.S. Eliot, Search Quotes, http://www.searchquotes.com/quotation/Fear_is_the_tax_which_conscience_pays_to_guilt/31808/ (accessed May 30, 2011).
236. Ellen G. White, *Patriarchs and Prophets* (Nampa, ID: Pacific Press Publishing Association, 1958), p. 57.
237. Wikipedia, Bishop Myriel, http://en.wikipedia.org/wiki/Bishop_Myriel (accessed May 30, 2011).

238. Christopher Marlowe, *The Tragical History of Doctor Faustus* (Canberra: Australian National University Press, 1982).
239. Marji Hughes, "The Feast of Purim - Part Two," Foundations Ministries, http://www.foundationsmin.org/studies/purim_2.htm (accessed May 30, 2011).
240. C.S. Lewis, *Mere Christianity* (New York: Simon & Schuster, Inc., 1996).
241. Lloyd John Ogilvie, *In Silent Strength for My Life* (Oregon: Harvest House Publishers, 1990).
242. Christ Notes, "John Wesley's Explanatory Notes on Psalm 103," http://www.christnotes.org/commentary.php?b=19&c=103&com=wes (accessed May 30, 2011).
243. Adrian Dieleman, "Sermon on Psalm 116:12-14" (sermon, Trinity United Reform Church, Visalia, CA, November 25, 1999).
244. United States v. Wilson, Peters 7 Report Sections 150-163.
245. George Gaylord Simpson and William S. Beck, *Life: An Introduction to Biology* (New York: Harcourt, Brace & World, Inc, 1965). p. 144.
246. Author Unknown, "The Barber and God," Holy Trinity Lutheran Church, http://www.holytrinitynewrochelle.org/yourti88545.html (accessed May 30, 2011).
247. John J. Parsons, "God's Irrepressible Care of the World," Hebrew for Christians, http://www.hebrew4christians.net/Meditations/Be_Still/be_still.html (accessed May 30, 2011).
248. Hannah Hurnard, *Hinds Feet on High Places* (Ohio: Tyndale House), p.19.
249. Hannah Hurnard, *Hinds Feet on High Places* (Ohio: Tyndale House).
250. Ellen G. White, *Patriarchs and Prophets* (Nampa, ID: Pacific Press Publishing Association, 1958), p. 739.
251. *Matthew Henry's Concise Commentary on the Whole Bible* (Nashville: Thomas Nelson, 2000).
252. Naomi, "Naomi's Darkest Times: Child Abuse and Neglect Christian Testimony," About.com, http://christianity.about.com/od/physicalandsexualabuse/a/naomitestimony.htm (accessed May 30, 2011).
253. Naomi, "Naomi's Darkest Times: Child Abuse and Neglect Christian Testimony," About.com, http://christianity.about.com/od/physicalandsexualabuse/a/naomitestimony.htm (accessed May 30, 2011).
254. Author Unknown, "Kick On," Inspirational Christian Stories and Poems Archive, http://www.inspirationalarchive.com/texts/topics/perseverance/kickon.shtml (accessed May 30, 2011).
255. Roy Lessin, "Meet Me in the Meadow," DaySpring, http://roy.dayspring.com/2010/05/clean-hands-and-a-pure-heart-part-2.html (accessed June 3, 2011).
256. Sermon Illustrations, "My Mind's Made Up," http://www.sermonillustrations.com (accessed June 3, 2011).
257. Ellen G. White, *The Desire of Ages* (Nampa, ID: Pacific Press Publishing Association, 1940), p 347.
258. Ellen G. White, *Early Writings* (Hagerstown, MD: Review and Herald Publishing Association, 1994), p. 172.
259. Ellen G. White, *Early Writings* (Hagerstown, MD: Review and Herald Publishing Association, 1994), pp. 171, 172.
260. Ellen G. White, *Steps to Christ* (Hagerstown, MD: Review and Herald Publishing Association, 1983), pp 19, 20.
261. Ian RK Paisley, "Unholy Prayers, Unholy Stairs And The Transformation of Martin Luther's Soul," (sermon, Martyrs Memorial Free Presbyterian Church, Belfast, Ireland, October 2001).
262. Author Unknown, The Quote Garden, http://www.quotegarden.com/helping.html (accessed May 31, 2011).
263. Simon J. Kistemaker, *Peter and Jude* (Grand Rapids: Baker Book House, 1987), p. 325.
264. Science Daily, "Lost Tomb Of Jesus' Reveals New Scientific Evidence Supporting Possible Find Of Jesus Family Tomb," http://www.sciencedaily.com/releases/2007/02/070226212800.htm (accessed May 30, 2011).

265. Science Daily, "Lost Tomb Of Jesus' Reveals New Scientific Evidence Supporting Possible Find Of Jesus Family Tomb," http://www.sciencedaily.com/releases/2007/02/070226212800.htm (accessed May 30, 2011).
266. Steven Callahan, *Adrift: 76 Days Lost at Sea* (Boston: Houghton Mifflin Company, 1986).
267. Author Unknown, "The Little Tea Cup," Safe Am I.com, http://www.kimberlypardue.com/TheLittleTeaCup.html (accessed May 31, 2011).
268. Herbert Edgar Douglass, *Love Makes a Way: Walking with Jesus From Eden to Eternity* (Nampa, ID: Pacific Press Publishing Association, 2007), p. 334.
269. Author Unknown, "Happiness Comes From Giving," Afterhours Inspirational Stories, http://www.inspirationalstories.com/9/920.html (accessed May 31, 2011).
270. Ellen G. White, *SDA Bible Commentary,* vol. 3 (Hagerstown, MD: Review and Herald Publishing Association, 2000), pp. 630-632.
271. Christ Notes, "John Wesley's Explanatory Notes on Job 1," http://www.christnotes.org/commentary.php?com=wes&b=18&c=1 (accessed May 30, 2011).
272. Richard Wumbrand, *Tortured for Christ* (Living Sacrifice Book Company, 1998).
273. Daniel Partner, ed, *The Essential Works of Charles Spurgeon* (Uhrichsville, OH: Barbour Publishing, Inc., 2009).
274. C.S. Lewis, *The Problem of Pain,* (New York: Harper Collins, 1940).
275. Author Unknown, "Tax Assessment," Inspirational Moments, http://living4jesus.net/dynamic/in.txassesment.htm (accessed July 12, 2011).
276. Ellen G. White, *In Heavenly Places* (Hagerstown, MD: Review & Herald Publishing Association, 2004), p. 367.
277. Suzanne Harrill, ed, "The Three Stages of Love," *The Innerwords Newsletter*, http://www.InnerworksPublishing.com (accessed June 3, 2011).
278. *Southern California Interdisciplinary Law Journal*, vol. 18:229, "When the Lawyer Knows the Client is Guilty" (2009), pp 230, 231.
279. Wil Pounds, "God's Throne of Grace-His Mercy Seat," Abide in Christ. http://www.abideinchrist.com/messages/ex25v22.html (accessed June 3, 2011).
280. Dante Alighieri, Famous Quotes and Authors.com, http://www.famousquotesandauthors.com/authors/dante_alighieri_quotes.html (accessed May 31, 2011).
281. C.S. Lewis, *The Screwtape Letters* (New York: Macmillan, 1961), p. 560).
282. Martin G. Collins, "Expediency," Bible Tools, http://www.bibletools.org/index.cfm/fuseaction/Topical.show/RTD/cgg/ID/1354/Expediency.htm (accessed May 31, 2011).
283. 18 U.S.C. § 1505.
284. U.S. Army, "Soldier Life: Basic Combat Training," http://www.goarmy.com/soldier-life/becoming-a-soldier/basic-combat-training.html (accessed May 31, 2011).
285. Ellen G. White, *Christ's Object Lessons* (Silver Spring, MD: Better Living Publications, 1990), pp. 174, 175.
286. Robin Meyers, *The Virtue in the Vice, Finding Seven Lively Virtues in the Seven Deadly Sins* (Deerfield, FL: Health Communications, 1952).
287. Robin Meyers, *The Virtue in the Vice: Finding Seven Lively Virtues in the Seven Deadly Sins* (Deerfield, FL: Health Communications, 1952).
288. Unknown Source, Proverbia.net, http://en.proverbia.net/citastema.asp?tematica=873 (accessed May 31, 2011).
289. E.M. Forster, BrainyQuote, http://www.brainyquote.com/quotes/quotes/e/emforste100809.html (accessed May 31, 2011).

290. Mordy Friedman, "What's so Bad about the Plague of Darkness?" http://www.tzemachdovid.org/Vsamachta/Pesach01/darkness.shtml (accessed May 31, 2011).
291. C.S. Lewis, "The Great Sin," *Mere Christianity* (New York: Simon & Schuster, Inc., 1996).
292. Ellen G. White, *Patriarchs and Prophets*, (Nampa, ID: Pacific Press Publishing Association, 1958), p. 35.
293. Martin G. Collins, " Self-Exaltation," Bible Tools, http://www.bibletools.org/index.cfm/fuseaction/Topical.show/RTD/cgg/ID/406/Self-Exaltation.htm (accessed May 31, 2011).
294. BibleStudyTools.com, *John Gill's Exposition of the Bible, Isaiah 54*, http://www.biblestudytools.com/commentaries/gills-exposition-of-the-bible/isaiah-54-10.html (accessed May 31, 2011).
295. John Paul Moore, "Drinking From My Saucer," Webtree, http://www.webtree.ca/inspiration/drinking_from_my_saucer.html (accessed May 31, 2011).
296. John Paul Moore, "Drinking From My Saucer," Webtree, http://www.webtree.ca/inspiration/drinking_from_my_saucer.html (accessed May 31, 2011).
297. John Paul Moore, "Drinking From My Saucer," Webtree, http://www.webtree.ca/inspiration/drinking_from_my_saucer.html (accessed May 31, 2011).
298. John Paul Moore, "Drinking From My Saucer," Webtree, http://www.webtree.ca/inspiration/drinking_from_my_saucer.html (accessed May 31, 2011).
299. Jeff Kemp, "Rules to Live by On and Off the Playing Field," *Imprimis* (speech, Hillsdale College, Hillsdale, MI, July 1998).
300. *Matthew Henry's Concise Commentary on the Whole Bible* (Nashville: Thomas Nelson, 2000).
301. Author Unknown, "The Tiger, the Man and God," SermonCentral.com, http://www.sermoncentral.com/illustrations/humorous-illustrations-about-cliff.asp (accessed August 8, 2011).
302. Charles Spurgeon, "What God Cannot Do!" (sermon, Metropolitan Tabernacle Pulpit, Newington, England, May 8, 1864).
303. Maya Angelou, "Still I Rise," *And Still I Rise* (New York: Random House, Inc., 1978).
304. White. Ellen G. *The Great Controversy* (Nampa, ID: Pacific Press Publishing Association, 1939), p 650.
305. "West India Emancipation," (speech, Canandaigua, New York, August 3, 1857).
306. Mark Twain, *The Adventures of Huckleberry Finn* (London: CRW Publishers, 2004).
307. E.M. Bounds, *On Prayer* (New Kensington, PA: Whitaker House, 1997), p. 37.
308. Peggy Porter, "Gilbert and the Pinewood Derby," U.S. Scouting Service Project, http://usscouts.org/usscouts/pinewood/gilbert.asp (accessed May 31, 2011).
309. Peggy Porter, "Gilbert and the Pinewood Derby," U.S. Scouting Service Project, http://usscouts.org/usscouts/pinewood/gilbert.asp (accessed May 31, 2011).
310. Dennis G. Luker, "Enemy Number One! Spiritual Lethargy in God's Church," *Good News Magazine*, July 1969, http://www.friendsofsabbath.org/ABC/Miscellaneous/Lethargy_D%20Luker.pdf (accessed May 31, 2011).
311. Peoples Savings Bank v. Bufford, 90 Wash at 206 (quoting 1.R.C.L at 693)
312. Ellen G. White, *The Desire of Ages* (Nampa, ID: Pacific Press Publishing Association, 1940), p. 763.
313. Innoce Chapamba, "The Persistent Porter," *Adult Sabbath Quarterly Bible Study Guide*, 2009.
314. Marshall Brain, "How Computer Viruses Work," HowStuffWorks, Inc., http://computer.howstuffworks.com/virus.htm (accessed May 31, 2011).
315. Bayard Taylor, "To the Nile," GIGA Quotes, http://www.giga-usa.com/gigaweb1/quotes2/qutopnileriverx001.htm (accessed May 31, 2011).
316. Brian Edgar, "Biblical justice," Brian's Public Theology, http://brian-edgar.com/theeology/ministry-and-mission/biblical-justice/ (accessed June 1, 2011).
317. Jeffrey Bromiley, "Righteous," *International Standard Bible Dictionary*, vol. Q-Z (1995).

318. Fox News, "Philly-area woman in $475,000 theft gets 221 years house arrest so she can work, repay employer," August 12, 2010, http://www.foxnews.com/us/2010/08/12/philly-area-woman-theft-gets-years-house-arrest-work-repay-employer/ (accessed June 1, 2011).
319. Justin A. Walsh, "Employee Theft," International Foundation for Protection Officers, http://www.ifpo.org/articlebank/employee_theft.html (accessed June 1, 2011).
320. Angel Manuel Rodridguez, "Tithing in the Writings of Ellen G. White," Biblical Research Institute, http://www.adventistbiblicalresearch.org/documents/Tithe-Theology-EGW.htm (accessed June 1, 2011).
321. Mei Sunquist, *Wild Cats of the World* (Chicago: University of Chicago Press, 2000), pp. 377-394.
322. Robert Ambrogi, ed., "Proposed: Expert Witness Code of Ethics," *BullsEye Newsletter*: February 2009, http://www.ims-expertservices.com/newsletters/feb/expert-witness-code-of-ethics.asp (accessed June 1, 2011).
323. Hubble Space Telescope, "The Mysterious 'Garden-sprinkler' nebula," http://www.spacetelescope.org/news/heic0308/ (accessed June 1, 2011).
324. Kara, "Pretty Deep," BulterWebs, http://www.butlerwebs.com/inspiration/religious.htm (accessed June 1, 2011).
325. "Adam Clarke's Commentary on Matthew 6:24," PreteristArchive.com, http://www.preteristarchive.com/Books/1810_clarke_commentary.html (accessed August 15, 2011).
326. C. G. Finney, "The Spirit Not Striving Always," Gospel Truth Ministries, http://www.gospeltruth.net/1848OE/481011_spirit_striving.htm (accessed June 1, 2011).
327. Charles Spurgeon, "The Song of a City, and the Pearl of Peace," The Spurgeon Archive, http://www.spurgeon.org/sermons/1818.htm (accessed June 1, 2011).
328. WordFixx, "Salary -- worth your salt?" http://Wordfixx.blogspot.com/2009/03/salary-worth-your-salt.html (accessed June 1, 2011).
329. Church of the East, "The Yoga of Jesus," http://churchoftheeast.ca/yoga_of_jesus_%281%29.htm (accessed June 1, 2011).
330. Author Unknown, "Food for Thought," St. Louis Inspirational Christian Connection, http://www.gatewaytojesus.com/inspiringstoriespage3.html (accessed June 1, 2011).
331. Larry Kirkpatrick, "I Want to Give My Heart to Jesus # 1," (sermon, Mentone Church of Seventh-day Adventists, Mentone, CA, July 14, 2001).
332. Sue Bohlin, "The Value of Suffering," Surf-in-the-Spirit, http://www.surfinthespirit.com/healthy-living/value.html (accessed June 1, 2011).
333. C.S. Lewis, *The Problem of Pain* (New York: Harper Collins, 2002), p. 91.
334. CNN, "Chile Mine Rescue," http://www.cnn.com/SPECIALS/2010/chile.miners/ (accessed June 1, 2011).
335. Ellen G. White, *Desire of Ages* (Nampa, ID: Pacific Press Publishing Association, 1940), pp. 48, 49.
336. Author Unknown, Jewel Diamond Taylor's motivational web site, http://www.donotgiveup.net/stories2.htm (accessed June 1, 2011).
337. William Gurnall, "Christian Quotes," Christian Resources Today, http://www.christian-resources-today.com/christian-quotes.html (accessed August 8, 2011).
338. C.S. Lewis, *Mere Christianity* (New York: Simon & Schuster, Inc., 1996).
339. Author Unknown, Sermon Illustrator, http://www.sermonillustrator.org/illustrator/sermon5/when_god_wants_to_drill_a_man.htm (accessed June 1, 2011).
340. Author Unknown, Sermon Illustrator, http://www.sermonillustrator.org/illustrator/sermon5/when_god_wants_to_drill_a_man.htm
341. Author Unknown, Sermon Illustrator, http://www.sermonillustrator.org/illustrator/sermon5/when_god_wants_to_drill_a_man.htm

342. C.S. Lewis, *Mere Christianity* (New York: Simon & Schuster, Inc., 1996).
343. Ellen G. White, *Steps to Christ* (Hagerstown, MD: Review and Herald Publishing Association, 1983), p. 61).
344. Ellen G. White, *Steps to Christ* (Hagerstown, MD: Review and Herald Publishing Association, 1983), pp. 57, 58, italics added.
345. William Frazier, "Soft Drink Warning," Why I Don't Drink Soft Drinks (And Wish You Didn't), http://www.themuslimwoman.com/hertongue/SoftDrink.htm (accessed June 1, 2011).
346. Ellen G. White, *Christ's Object Lessons* (Silver Spring, MD: Better Living Publications, 1990), p. 346.
347. "The Bible Explains the Bible," http://www.whatdoesthebiblesay.com/the_bible_explains_itself.html (accessed June 1, 2011).
348. La Vista Church of Christ, "Honor Your Father and Mother," http://lavistachurchofchrist.org/LVstudies/TenCommandments/05HonorYourFatherAndMother.htm (accessed June 1, 2011).
349. Tony Kummer, "Father's Day Ideas," *Christian Parenting*, June 19, 2007.
350. *Matthew Henry's Concise Commentary on the Whole Bible* (Nashville, TN: Thomas Nelson, 2000).
351. *Matthew Henry's Concise Commentary on the Whole Bible* (Nashville, TN: Thomas Nelson, 2000).
352. Some Musing! Blog, "Story of a Mother with one eye," http://abhask.blogspot.com/2006/02/story-of-mother-with-one-eye.html (accessed June 1, 2011).
353. A Puritan's Mind, "The Rebuke," http://www.apuritansmind.com/christianwalk/McMahonRebuke.htm (accessed June 1, 2011).
354. Laurie Goodstein, "As Attacks' Impact Recedes, a Return to Religion as Usual," *New York Times*, November 26, 2001, http://www.nytimes.com/.
355. The France 24 Observers, "The impossible task of cleaning the Buriganga river," http://observers.france24.com/en/content/20100203-impossible-task-cleaning-buriganga-river-dhaka-bangladesh-pollution-environment (accessed June 1, 2011).
356. Jerry Bridges, *Respectable Sins: Confronting the Sins We Tolerate* (Colorado Springs, CO: Nav Press, 2001).
357. My Sacred Obsession Blog, "Poking Hole in the Darkness," http://mysacredobsession.wordpress.com/tag/matthew-5/ (accessed June 1, 2011).
358. Hudson J. Taylor, Goodreads, http://www.goodreads.com/quotes/show/266309 (accessed June 1, 2011).
359. Ellen G. White, *Patriarchs and Prophets* (Nampa, ID: Pacific Press Publishing Association, 1958), p. 566.
360. Frederick Buechner, "Spelling Out the Truth," *Third Way*, June 1994, vol. 17, no. 5.
361. The Encyclopedia of Science, "Magnetism," http://www.daviddarling.info/encyclopedia/M/magnetism.html (accessed June 1, 2011).
362. Ellen G. White, *Desire of Ages* (Nampa, ID: Pacific Press Publishing Association, 1940), p.763.
363. Ellen G. White, *Steps to Christ* (Hagerstown, MD: Review and Herald Publishing Association, 1983), p. 33.
364. Author Unknown, "Faithful Friends," PetHumor e-mail.
365. Ellen G. White, *Medical Ministry* (Nampa, ID: Pacific Press Publishing Association, 1963), p. 283.
366. Plutarch, *Shakespeare's Plutarch,* The Online Library of Liberty, http://oll.libertyfund.org/title/1842/144265 (accessed August 8, 2011).
367. Author Unknown, Thinkexist.com, http://thinkexist.com/quotation/security_is_not_the_absence_of_danger-but_the/251265.html (accessed August 8, 2011).
368. Author Unknown, "He Never Let's Go," God Is Always Faithful Blog, http://godisalwaysfaithful.wordpress.com/2009/08/27/he-never-lets-go (accessed June 1, 2011).

369. Religious Tolerance.org, "Pascal's Wager: Is it safer to believe in God even if there is no proof that one exists?" http://www.religioustolerance.org/pascal_w.htm (accessed June 1, 2011).
370. Adapted from a sermon by David Asscherick, November 15, 2010, Three Angels Broadcasting Network.
371. Clifford Goldstein, ed., "Background Characters in the OT, Oct-Dec," *Adult Sabbath School Bible Study Guides*.
372. Ellen G. White, Manuscript Releases, vol. 4, p. 56.
373. Rise Up Country with John Ritter, "A Guy Named Bill," http://www.rise-up.com/guy-named-bill-rebecca-manley-pippert-chicken-soup-christian-family-soul (accessed June 2, 2011).
374. Robert Louis Stevenson, *The Strange Case of Dr. Jekyll and My Hyde* (New York: W. W. Norton & Company, 2002).
375. Robert Louis Stevenson, *The Strange Case of Dr. Jekyll and My Hyde* (New York: W. W. Norton & Company, 2002).
376. Jan Souman, *Current Biology*, vol. 19, September 29, 2009, pp. 1-5.
377. *Matthew Henry Commentary on the Whole Bible* (Nashville: Thomas Nelson, 2000).
378. Albert Barnes, ed., *Barnes' Notes on the New Testament* (Grand Rapids, MI: Kregel Publications, 1976).
379. Northwestern Health Sciences University, "The Importance of Healthy Relationships," http://www.nwhealth.edu/media/healthnews/healthypeople.html (accessed June 5, 2011).
380. Charles Spurgeon, "The Song of a City, and the Pearl of Peace," The Spurgeon Archive, http://www.spurgeon.org/sermons/1818.htm (accessed June 2, 2011).
381. Author Unknown, "Whoever Takes the Son Gets it All," Tony Cooke Ministries, http://www.tonycooke.org/free_resources/stories_illustrations/son_getsitall.html (accessed June 2, 2011).
382. Amy Carmichael, Goodreads, http://www.goodreads.com/quotes/show/7595 (accessed June 2, 2011).
383. Ellen G. White, *Testimonies for the Church*, vol. 2, (Nampa, ID: Pacific Press Publishing Association, 1948), p. 193.
384. Edgar Allan Poe, "A Descent into the Maelstrom," http://classiclit.about.com/library/bl-etexts/eapoe/bl-eapoe-descent.htm (accessed June 2, 2011).
385. C.S. Lewis, *The Problem of Pain* (New York: Harper Collins, 1940).
386. J.R. Davis, "The Spirit of Nimrod," http://www.apostolic.edu/biblestudy/files/nimrod.htm (accessed June 5, 2011).
387. Todd J. Gillman, "Sony Corp. v. Sony's Restaurant; Baltimore Restauranteur Loses Battle Over Name to Electronics Giant," HighBeam Research, http://www.highbeam.com/doc/1P2-1331412.html (accessed August 15, 2011).
388. Ellen G. White, *The Great Controversy* (Nampa, ID: Pacific Press Publishing Association, 1939), p. 604.
389. Herbs2000.com, "Labor Pains," http://www.herbs2000.com/disorders/labor_pains.htm (accessed May 25, 2011).
390. U.S. Special Delivery.com, "U.S. 10¢ Special Delivery Rate 1885-1917," http://www.usspecialdelivery.com/library_sd/garfield.html (accessed May 29, 2011).

www.ingramcontent.com/pod-product-compliance
Lightning Source LLC
Chambersburg PA
CBHW081143230426
43664CB00018B/2787